PRAISE FOR *GAZA*

"This is the voice I listen for, when I want to learn the deepest reality about Jews, Zionists, Israelis, and Palestinians. Norman Finkelstein is surely one of the forty honest humans the Scripture alludes to who can save 'Sodom' (our Earth) by pointing out, again and again, the sometimes soul-shriveling but unavoidable Truth. There is no one like him today, but in my bones I know this incredible warrior for Humanity and Justice is an archetype that has always been. And will always be. Small comfort in these dark times, perhaps, but a comfort I am deeply grateful for."
   —Alice Walker, winner of the Pulitzer Prize and National Book Award for *The Color Purple*

"As a modern-day Sisyphus, rolling the heavy boulder up the hill of disinformation, Norman Finkelstein does not waver in his determination to take it to the crest. Although a non-lawyer, he masters the legal issues, the Geneva Conventions, ICJ advisory opinions, UN resolutions, and commission reports, weaving them into a compelling narrative, an articulate appeal for justice, a protest against the moral cop-out of the international community. Finkelstein refutes the Big Lie and many arcane little lies about Gaza and Palestine. A scholarly manual for every politician and every person concerned with human rights."
   —Alfred de Zayas, Professor of Law, Geneva School of Diplomacy, and UN Independent Expert on the Promotion of a Democratic and Equitable International Order

"Norman Finkelstein, probably the most serious scholar on the conflict in the Middle East, has written an excellent book on Israel's invasions of Gaza. Its comprehensive examination of both the facts and the law of these assaults provides the most authoritative account of this brutal history."
   —John Dugard, Emeritus Professor of Public International Law, Leiden University, and former Special Rapporteur to the UN Human Rights Council on Human Rights in the Occupied Palestinian Territory, 2001–2008

T0310953

Gaza

Gaza

AN INQUEST INTO ITS MARTYRDOM

Norman G. Finkelstein

UNIVERSITY OF CALIFORNIA PRESS

University of California Press, one of the most distinguished university presses in the United States, enriches lives around the world by advancing scholarship in the humanities, social sciences, and natural sciences. Its activities are supported by the UC Press Foundation and by philanthropic contributions from individuals and institutions. For more information, visit www.ucpress.edu.

University of California Press
Oakland, California

First Paperback Printing 2021
Library of Congress Cataloging-in-Publication Data
Names: Finkelstein, Norman G., author.
Title: Gaza : an inquest into its martyrdom / Norman G. Finkelstein.
Description: Oakland, California : University of California Press, [2018] | Includes bibliographical references and index. |
Identifiers: LCCN 2017015719 (print) | LCCN 2017028116 (ebook) | ISBN 9780520968387 (ebook) | ISBN 9780520318335 (pbk) Subjects:
LCSH: Human rights—Gaza Strip. | Palestinian Arabs—Crimes against—Gaza Strip. | Arab-Israeli conflict—1993– | Gaza Strip—History—21st century.
Classification: LCC JC599.G26 (ebook) | LCC JC599.G26 F55 2018 (print) | DDC 953/.1—dc23
LC record available at https://lccn.loc.gov/2017015719

27   26   25   24   23   22   21
10   9   8   7   6   5   4   3   2

To Gaza,
The Truth

The massacre of innocent people is a serious matter. It is not a thing to be easily forgotten. It is our duty to cherish their memory.

MAHATMA GANDHI

CONTENTS

PREFACE

This book is not about Gaza. It is about what has been *done* to Gaza. It is
fashionable nowadays to speak of a victim's agency. But one must be realistic
about the constraints imposed on such agency by objective circumstance.
Frederick Douglass could reclaim his manhood by striking back at a slave
master who viciously abused him. Nelson Mandela could retain his dignity
in jail despite conditions calibrated to humiliate and degrade him. Still, these
were exceptional individuals and exceptional circumstances, and anyhow,
even if he acquits himself with honor, the elemental decisions affecting the
daily life of a man held in bondage and the power to effect these decisions
remain outside his control. Gaza, as former British prime minister David
Cameron observed, is an "open-air prison."[1] The Israeli warden is in charge.
In the popular imagination confected by state propaganda, and dutifully
echoed by everyone else in authority, Israel is almost always reacting to or
retaliating against "terrorism." But neither the inhuman and illegal blockade
Israel imposed on Gaza nor the periodic murderous "operations" Israel has
unleashed against it trace back to Hamas rocket fire. These were Israeli political decisions springing from Israeli political calculations, in which Hamas
military actions figured as a null factor. In fact, Israel more often than not
reacted to Hamas *in*action: the Islamic movement refused to provide the
"terrorist" pretext Israel sought in order to launch an operation, the predicate
of which was political, not military (self-defense). Of course, if Gaza "would
just sink into the sea" (Nobel Peace Prize laureate Yitzhak Rabin),[2] or if it
unilaterally surrendered its destiny to Israeli caprice, Israel wouldn't brutalize

1. "David Cameron Describes Blockaded Gaza as a 'Prison,'" *BBC* (27 July 2010).
2. Amira Hass, *Drinking the Sea at Gaza: Days and nights in a land under siege* (New
York: 1999), p. 9.

it. But short of these options, Gaza could only exercise as much, that is, as little, agency as is allocated to any people held in bondage. The notion that enhanced fireworks emanating from an anthill could, in and of themselves, inflect state policy of one of the world's most formidable military powers is laughable—or would be, were it not for that power's formidable disinformation apparatus.

The focus of this book is the politics of Gaza's martyrdom. Its economic dimension has already been exhaustively and competently dissected.[3] An observer cannot but be struck by the reams of paper that have been expended on analyses of, and prescriptions for, Gaza's economy, even though its economy is more notional than real. The World Bank reported in 2015–16 that Gaza "is now dependent for about 90 per cent of its GDP on expenditures by the Palestinian Government, the United Nations and other external remittances and donor projects."[4] No doubt, those who compiled these economic reports were spurred by a desire to do good, although in the end most of them capitulated to Israeli diktat.[5] But if Gaza survives, it's because of foreign subventions delivered in synchrony with the occasional loosening—to sycophantic international fanfare—of an Israeli screw. Indeed, the paradox is that as each new economic report is churned out, the day of Gaza's complete "de-development" draws nearer. It is also hard to resist the thought that Gaza would have benefited more if the time, energy, and expense invested in these meticulous reports replete with mind-numbing minutiae had simply been channeled into an open-air swimming pool, inside the open-air prison, for Gaza's bereft children. Still, they constitute an ineffaceable record of and testament to the horror that has been inflicted on Gaza. They are an eternal monument to the martyrs and an eternal accusation against their tormenters. The human rights reportage on Gaza, which forms the primary subject matter of this book, mirrors the content and has suffered the fate of these economic reports. The sheer number of human rights reports could by now fill a medium-sized library; they have generally upheld exacting standards of accuracy, and they record a ghastly tale of suffering and misery, on the one hand, and criminal excess and heartlessness, on the other. But they have been largely ignored outside a narrow cadre of specialists, and in the end the

3. Sara Roy, *The Gaza Strip: The political economy of de-development,* expanded third edition (Washington, DC: 2016).

4. United Nations General Assembly, "Situation of Human Rights in the Palestinian Territories Occupied since 1967" (19 October 2016), para. 46.

5. See the Conclusion.

human rights community itself succumbed to the Israeli juggernaut. All the same, the reports constitute the essential resource for those who care about truth and for whom truth is precious, while even if mostly underutilized, they are the most potent weapon in the arsenal of those who hope against hope to mobilize public opinion so as to salvage a modicum of justice.

What has befallen Gaza is a human-made human disaster. In its protractedness and in its starkness, in its unfolding not in the fog of war or in the obscurity of remoteness but in broad daylight and in full sight, in the complicity of so many, not just via acts of commission but also, and especially, of omission, it is moreover a distinctively evil crime. Readers will be able to judge for themselves whether this depiction is naïve or whether the documentary record bears it out; whether this writer is partisan to Gaza or whether the facts are partisan to it; whether Gaza poses the challenge of competing "narratives," or whether it poses the challenge of disengaging its innocence from the skein of lies concealing it. It might be politically prudent to expatiate on the complexity of Gaza. But it would also be a moral cop-out. For Gaza is about a Big Lie composed of a thousand, often seemingly abstruse and arcane, little lies. The objective of this book is to refute that Big Lie by exposing each of the little lies. It has not been a labor of love. On the contrary, it has been a painstaking, fastidious undertaking born of a visceral detestation of falsehood, in particular when it is put in the service of power and human life hangs in the balance. If the evil is in the detail, it can only be confronted and disposed of in methodical parsing of logic and evidence. The reader's forbearance must in advance be begged, as perusing this book will require infinite patience.

Norman G. Finkelstein
31 December 2016
New York City

ACKNOWLEDGMENTS

I wish to thank for their assistance and cooperation Usama Antar, Rudolph Baldeo, Kayvan Beklik, Alex Davis-Lawrence, John Dugard, Marilyn Garson, Jason Gordon, Maren Hackmann-Mahajan, Jens Ole Bach Hansen, Siham Faidoli Hansen, Abdalla Hassan, Ria Julien, Sana Kassem, Yarden Katz, Philip Luther, Deborah Maccoby, Sanjeev Mahajan, Alex Nunns, Mouin Rabbani, Sara Roy, Rana Shubair, Jamie Stern-Weiner, Desmond Travers, and Jeff Wyneken. I wish also to acknowledge a UN spokesperson who prefers to remain anonymous. Earlier drafts of parts of this manuscript have appeared in prior publications of mine.

This book has richly benefited from the absence of support from any institution or foundation. If he who pays the piper calls the tune, then no one paid this piper, so he was free to call his own tune.

FIGURE 1. White phosphorus attack. © UNRWA 2009.

PART ONE

———

Operation Cast Lead

ONE

Self-Defense

ON 29 NOVEMBER 1947, THE UN GENERAL ASSEMBLY approved a resolution partitioning British-mandated Palestine into a Jewish state incorporating 56 percent of Palestine, and an Arab state incorporating the remaining 44 percent.[1] In the war that ensued after passage of the resolution, the newly born State of Israel expanded its borders to incorporate nearly 80 percent of Palestine. The only areas of Palestine not conquered comprised the West Bank, which the Kingdom of Jordan subsequently annexed, and the Gaza Strip, which came under Egypt's administrative control.

The panhandle of the Sinai Peninsula, Gaza is bordered by Israel on the north and east, Egypt on the south, and the Mediterranean Sea on the west. Approximately 250,000 Palestinians driven out of their homes during the 1948 war fled to Gaza and overwhelmed the indigenous population of some 80,000. Today, more than 70 percent of Gaza's inhabitants consist of expellees from the 1948 war and their descendants, and more than half of this overwhelmingly refugee population is under 18 years of age; Gaza has the "second-highest share of people aged 0 to 14 worldwide." Its current 1.8 million inhabitants are squeezed into a sliver of land 25 miles long and 5 miles wide; it is among the most densely populated areas in the world, more crowded than even Tokyo. Between 1967, when the Israeli occupation began, and 2005, when Prime Minister Ariel Sharon redeployed Israeli troops from inside Gaza to its perimeter, Israel imposed on Gaza a uniquely exploitive regime of "de-development." In the words of Harvard political economist Sara Roy, it deprived "the native population of its most important economic

---

1. Less than one percent of Palestine was set aside for an international zone (*Corpus separatum*) incorporating Jerusalem.

resources—land, water, and labor—as well as the internal capacity and potential for developing those resources."[2]

The road to modern Gaza's desperate plight is strewn with multiple atrocities, most long forgotten or unknown outside Palestine. After the cessation of battlefield hostilities in 1949, Egypt kept a tight rein on the activity of *Fedayeen* (Palestinian guerrillas) in Gaza. But in early 1955, Israeli leaders plotted to lure Egypt into war in order to topple President Gamal Abdel Nasser. They launched a bloody cross-border raid into Gaza killing 40 Egyptian soldiers. The Gaza raid proved a near-perfect provocation, as armed border clashes escalated. In October 1956, Israel (in collusion with Great Britain and France) invaded the Egyptian Sinai and occupied Gaza, which it had long coveted. The prominent Israeli historian Benny Morris described what happened next:

> Many *Fedayeen* and an estimated 4,000 Egyptian and Palestinian regulars were trapped in the Strip, identified, and rounded up by the IDF [Israel Defense Forces], GSS [General Security Service], and police. Dozens of these *Fedayeen* appear to have been summarily executed, without trial. Some were probably killed during two massacres by the IDF troops soon after the occupation of the Strip. On 3 November, the day Khan Yunis was conquered, IDF troops shot dead hundreds of Palestinian refugees and local inhabitants in the town. One UN report speaks of "some 135 local residents" and "140 refugees" killed as IDF troops moved through the town and its refugee camp "searching for people in possession of arms."
>
> In Rafah, which fell to the IDF on 1–2 November, Israeli troops killed between forty-eight and one hundred refugees and several local residents, and wounded another sixty-one during a massive screening operation on 12 November, in which they sought to identify former Egyptian and Palestinian soldiers and *Fedayeen* hiding among the local population. . . .
>
> Another sixty-six Palestinians, probably *Fedayeen,* were executed in a number of other incidents during screening operations in the Gaza Strip between 2 and 20 November. . . .
>
> The United Nations estimated that, all told, Israeli troops killed between 447 and 550 Arab civilians in the first three weeks of the occupation of the Strip.[3]

2. Sara Roy, *The Gaza Strip: The political economy of de-development,* expanded third edition (Washington, DC: 2016), pp. xxxii, 3–5; for the distinctiveness of Israel's economic policy in Gaza, see ibid., pp. 117–34. United Nations Country Team in the Occupied Palestinian Territory, "Gaza in 2020: A liveable place?" (2012) ("second-highest share").

3. Benny Morris, *Israel's Border Wars, 1949–1956* (Oxford: 1993), pp. 407–9. Morris documents that until the 1955 Israeli raid on Gaza, the "overriding concern" of Egypt "in its relations with Israel was to avoid sparking IDF attacks"; "Egypt generally sought tranquility

In March 1957, Israel was forced to withdraw from Gaza after US president Dwight Eisenhower exerted heavy diplomatic pressure and threatened economic sanctions. By the operation's end, more than a thousand Gazans had been killed. "The human cost of the four-month Israeli occupation of the Gaza Strip was alarmingly high," a historian recently observed. "If the figures for those wounded, imprisoned and tortured are added to the number who lost their lives, it would seem that one inhabitant in 100 had been physically harmed by the violence of the invaders."[4]

The etiology of Gaza's current afflictions traces back to the Israeli conquest. In the course of the 1967 war, Israel reoccupied the Gaza Strip (along with the West Bank) and has remained the occupying power ever since. As Morris narrated the story, "the overwhelming majority of West Bank and Gaza Arabs from the first hated the occupation"; "Israel intended to stay . . . and its rule would not be overthrown or ended through civil disobedience and civil resistance, which were easily crushed. The only real option was armed struggle"; "like all occupations, Israel's was founded on brute force, repression and fear, collaboration and treachery, beatings and torture chambers, and daily intimidation, humiliation, and manipulation"; the occupation "was always a brutal and mortifying experience for the occupied."[5]

From the start, Palestinians fought back against the Israeli occupation. Gazans put up particularly stiff unarmed and armed resistance, while Israeli repression proved equally unremitting. In 1969, Ariel Sharon became chief of the IDF Southern Command and not long after embarked on a campaign to crush the resistance in Gaza. A leading American academic specialist on Gaza recalled how Sharon

---

along its border with Israel." However, "from some point in 1954," IDF chief of staff Moshe Dayan "wanted war, and periodically, he hoped that a given retaliatory strike would embarrass or provoke the Arab state attacked into itself retaliating, giving Israel cause to escalate the shooting until war resulted." The "policy of trapping Nasser into war was hammered out between [David] Ben-Gurion and Dayan." The predicate of their indirect strategy of provocation was that "because Israel could not afford to be branded an aggressor, war would have to be reached by a process of gradual escalation, to be achieved through periodic, large-scale Israeli retaliatory attacks in response to Egyptian infractions of the armistice." When "Egypt refused to fall into the successive traps set by Dayan," Israel colluded with Great Britain and France to attack Egypt outright (ibid., pp. 85, 178–79, 229–30, 271–72, 279–80, 427, 428).

4. Jean-Pierre Filiu, *Gaza: A history* (New York: 2014), p. 105.

5. Benny Morris, *Righteous Victims: A history of the Zionist-Arab conflict, 1881–2001* (New York: 2001), pp. 340–43, 568. See also Zeev Schiff and Ehud Ya'ari, *Intifada: The Palestinian uprising—Israel's third front* (New York: 1990).

placed refugee camps under twenty-four-hour curfews, during which troops conducted house-to-house searches and mustered all the men in the central square for questioning. Many men were forced to stand waist-deep in the Mediterranean Sea for hours during the searches. In addition, some twelve thousand members of families of suspected guerrillas were deported to detention camps . . . in Sinai. Within a few weeks, the Israeli press began to criticize the soldiers and border police for beating people, shooting into crowds, smashing belongings in houses, and imposing extreme restrictions during curfews. . . .

In July 1971, Sharon added the tactic of "thinning out" the refugee camps. The military uprooted more than thirteen thousand residents by the end of August. The army bulldozed wide roads through the camps and through some citrus groves, thus making it easier for mechanized units to operate and for the infantry to control the camps. . . . The army crackdown broke the back of the resistance.[6]

In December 1987, a traffic accident on the Gaza-Israel border that left four Palestinians dead triggered a mass rebellion, or intifada, against Israeli rule throughout the occupied territories. "It was not an armed rebellion," Morris recalled, "but a massive, persistent campaign of civil resistance, with strikes and commercial shutdowns, accompanied by violent (though unarmed) demonstrations against the occupying forces. The stone and, occasionally, the Molotov cocktail and knife were its symbols and weapons, not guns and bombs." It cannot be said, however, that Israel reacted in kind. Morris continued: "Almost everything was tried: shooting to kill, shooting to injure, beatings, mass arrests, torture, trials, administrative detention, and economic sanctions"; "A large proportion of the Palestinian dead were not shot in life-threatening situations, and a great many of these were children"; "Only a small minority of [IDF] malefactors were brought to book by the army's legal machinery—and were almost always let off with ludicrously light sentences."[7]

By the early 1990s, Israel had successfully repressed the first intifada. It subsequently entered into an agreement secretly negotiated in Oslo, Norway, with the Palestine Liberation Organization (PLO) and ratified in September 1993 on the White House lawn. Israel intended via the Oslo Accord to streamline the occupation by removing its troops from direct contact with Palestinians and supplanting them with Palestinian subcontractors. "One of

6. Ann Mosely Lesch, "Gaza: History and politics," in Ann Mosely Lesch and Mark Tessler, *Israel, Egypt, and the Palestinians: From Camp David to intifada* (Bloomington: 1989), pp. 230–32.

7. Morris, *Righteous Victims,* pp. 561, 580, 587, 591, 599.

the meanings of Oslo," former Israeli foreign minister Shlomo Ben-Ami observed, "was that the PLO was . . . Israel's collaborator in the task of stifling the intifada and cutting short . . . an authentically democratic struggle for Palestinian independence."[8] In particular, Israel contrived to reassign to Palestinian surrogates the sordid tasks of occupation. "The idea of Oslo," former Israeli minister Natan Sharansky acknowledged, "was to find a strong dictator to . . . keep the Palestinians under control."[9] "The Palestinians will be better at establishing internal security than we were," Israeli prime minister Yitzhak Rabin told skeptics in his ranks, "because they will not allow appeals to the Supreme Court and will prevent the Association for Civil Rights in Israel from criticizing the conditions there. . . . They will rule by their own methods, freeing, and this is most important, the Israeli soldiers from having to do what they will do."[10]

In July 2000, PLO head Yasser Arafat and Israeli prime minister Ehud Barak joined US president Bill Clinton at Camp David to negotiate a final settlement of the conflict. The summit collapsed in mutual recrimination. But which side bore primary culpability for the aborted talks? "If I were a Palestinian," Ben-Ami, one of Israel's chief negotiators at Camp David, later commented, "I would have rejected Camp David as well," while Israeli strategic analyst Zeev Maoz concluded that the "substantial concessions" Israel demanded of Palestinians at Camp David "were not acceptable and could not be acceptable."[11] Subsequent negotiations also failed to achieve a breakthrough. In December 2000, President Clinton unfurled his "parameters" for resolving the conflict; both sides accepted them with reservations.[12] In January 2001, parleys resumed in Taba, Egypt. Although both parties

8. Shlomo Ben-Ami, *Scars of War, Wounds of Peace: The Israeli-Arab tragedy* (New York: 2006), pp. 191, 211.

9. Andy Levy-Ajzenkopf, "Sharansky on Tour Promoting Identity, Freedom," *Canadian Jewish News* (1 July 2008). Sharansky held several ministerial positions between 1996 and 2005.

10. Graham Usher, "The Politics of Internal Security: The PA's new intelligence services," *Journal of Palestine Studies* (Winter 1996), p. 28; *The B'Tselem Human Rights Report* (Spring 1994).

11. Shlomo Ben-Ami, interview on *Democracy Now!* (14 February 2006); Zeev Maoz, *Defending the Holy Land: A critical analysis of Israel's security and foreign policy* (Ann Arbor: 2006), p. 476 (see also p. 493).

12. Yossi Beilin, *The Path to Geneva: The quest for a permanent agreement, 1996–2004* (New York: 2004), pp. 52–53, 219–26; Clayton E. Swisher, *The Truth about Camp David* (New York: 2004), p. 402. For detailed analysis of the various phases in the 2000–2001 negotiations, see Norman G. Finkelstein, *Knowing Too Much: Why the American Jewish romance with Israel is coming to an end* (New York: 2012), pp. 229–48.

affirmed that "significant progress had been made" and they had "never been closer to agreement," Prime Minister Barak unilaterally "called a halt" to these negotiations, and as a result "the Israeli-Palestinian peace process had ground to an indefinite halt."[13]

In September 2000, amid the diplomatic stalemate and after Israeli provocation, Palestinians in the occupied territories once again entered into open revolt. Like its 1987 precursor, this second intifada was at its inception overwhelmingly nonviolent. However, in Ben-Ami's words, "Israel's disproportionate response to what had started as a popular uprising, with young, unarmed men confronting Israeli soldiers armed with lethal weapons, fueled the [second] intifada beyond control and turned it into an all-out war."[14] It is forgotten that the first deadly Hamas suicide bombing of the second intifada did not occur until five months into Israel's relentless bloodletting. Israeli forces had fired one million rounds of ammunition in just the first few days of the uprising, while the ratio of Palestinians to Israelis killed during the first weeks was 20:1.[15] In the course of the spiraling violence triggered by its "disproportionate response," Israel struck Gaza with special vengeance. In a cruel reworking of Ecclesiastes, each turn of season presaged yet another Israeli attack on Gaza that left scores dead and fragile infrastructure destroyed: "Operation Rainbow" (2004), "Operation Days of Penitence" (2004), "Operation Summer Rains" (2006), "Operation Autumn Clouds" (2006), "Operation Hot Winter" (2008).[16] In the warped memory of Israeli president and Nobel Peace Prize laureate Shimon Peres, however, this period was "another mistake—we restrained ourselves for eight years and allowed [Gazans] to shoot thousands of rockets at us ... restraint was a mistake."[17]

13. Morris, *Righteous Victims*, p. 671.

14. Ben-Ami, *Scars of War*, p. 267; see also Idith Zertal and Akiva Eldar, *Lords of the Land: The war over Israel's settlements in the occupied territories, 1967–2007* (New York: 2007), pp. 412–15.

15. Norman G. Finkelstein, *Beyond Chutzpah: On the misuse of anti-Semitism and the abuse of history,* expanded paperback edition (Berkeley: 2008), ch. 4. The first suicide attack during the second intifada occurred in March 2001.

16. More than 400 Palestinians (including 85 children) were killed, while five Israeli soldiers were killed, during "Summer Rains" and "Autumn Clouds." Fully 33 Palestinian children were killed, while one Israeli civilian was killed, in just five days during "Hot Winter." Al Mezan Center for Human Rights, *Bearing the Brunt Again: Child rights violations during Operation Cast Lead* (September 2009), pp. 8, 18–19.

17. Benny Morris, "Israeli President Shimon Peres Reflects on His Mentor, His Peace Partner, and Whether the State of Israel Will Survive," *Tablet* (26 July 2010).

Despite continual Israeli assaults, Gaza continued to roil. Already at the time of the Oslo Accord its intractability caused Israel to sour on the Strip. "If only it would just sink into the sea," Rabin despaired.[18] In April 2004, Prime Minister Sharon announced that Israel would "disengage" from Gaza, and by September 2005 both Israeli troops and Jewish settlers had been pulled out. Dov Weisglass, a key advisor to Sharon, laid out the rationale behind the disengagement: it would relieve international (in particular American) pressure on Israel, in turn "freezing . . . the political process. And when you freeze that process you prevent the establishment of a Palestinian state."[19] Israel subsequently purported that it was no longer the occupying power in Gaza. However, human rights organizations and international institutions rejected this contention; the fact was, in myriad ways Israel still preserved near-total dominance of the Strip. "Whether the Israeli army is inside Gaza or redeployed around its periphery," Human Rights Watch concluded, "it remains in control."[20] Israel's own leading authority on international law, Yoram Dinstein, aligned himself with the "prevalent opinion" that the Israeli occupation of Gaza was not over.[21]

The received wisdom is that the process initiated at Oslo must be reckoned a failure because it did not yield a lasting peace. But such a verdict misconstrues

18. Amira Hass, *Drinking the Sea at Gaza: Days and nights in a land under siege* (New York: 1996), p. 9.

19. Sara Roy, *Failing Peace: Gaza and the Palestinian-Israeli conflict* (London: 2007), pp. 327–28. See also Roy, *Gaza Strip*, pp. xxiii–xxv; and Galia Golan, *Israel and Palestine: Peace plans from Oslo to disengagement* (Princeton: 2007).

20. Human Rights Watch, "'Disengagement' Will Not End Gaza Occupation" (29 October 2004). HRW's *World Report 2006* reiterated this position:

In August and September 2005, Israel unilaterally withdrew approximately eight thousand settlers, along with military personnel and installations, from the Gaza Strip and four small settlements in the northern West Bank near Jenin. While Israel has since declared the Gaza Strip a "foreign territory" and the crossings between Gaza and Israel "international borders," under international humanitarian law (IHL), Gaza remains occupied, and Israel retains its responsibilities for the welfare of Gaza residents. Israel maintains effective control over Gaza by regulating movement in and out of the Strip as well as the airspace, sea space, public utilities and population registry. In addition, Israel declared the right to re-enter Gaza militarily at any time in its "Disengagement Plan." Since the withdrawal, Israel has carried out aerial bombardments, including targeted killings, and has fired artillery into the northeastern corner of Gaza.

For detailed legal analysis, see Gisha (Legal Center for Freedom of Movement), *Disengaged Occupiers: The legal status of Gaza* (Tel Aviv: January 2007).

21. Yoram Dinstein, *The International Law of Belligerent Occupation* (Cambridge: 2009), p. 277.

its actual objective. If Israel's goal was, as Ben-Ami pointed out, to groom a class of Palestinian collaborators, then Oslo was a stunning success for Israelis. Indeed, not just for them. A look at the Oslo II Accord, signed in September 1995 and spelling out in detail the mutual rights and duties of the contracting parties to the 1993 agreement, suggests what loomed largest in the minds of Palestinian negotiators: whereas four full pages are devoted to "Passage of [Palestinian] VIPs" (the section is subdivided into "Category 1 VIPs," "Category 2 VIPs," "Category 3 VIPs," and "Secondary VIPs"), less than one page—the very last—is devoted to "Release of Palestinian Prisoners and Detainees," who numbered in the many thousands.[22]

In a telling anomaly, the Oslo Accord stipulated a five-year interim period for so-called confidence building between the former foes. Contrariwise, when and where Israel genuinely sought peace, the reconciliation process unfolded at a rapid clip. Thus, for decades Egypt was Israel's chief nemesis in the Arab world, and it was Egypt that launched a surprise attack in 1973, in the course of which thousands of Israeli soldiers perished. Nevertheless, only a half year separated the 1978 Camp David summit convened by US president Jimmy Carter, which produced the Israeli-Egyptian "Framework for Peace," and the 1979 "Treaty of Peace," which formally terminated hostilities; and only three more years elapsed before Israel evacuated (in 1982) the whole of the Egyptian Sinai.[23] A half decade of confidence building did not insert itself in the Israeli-Egyptian negotiations.

The barely disguised purpose of Oslo's protracted interim period was not confidence building to facilitate an Israeli-Palestinian peace but collaboration building to facilitate a burden-free Israeli occupation. The operative premise was that after growing accustomed to the emoluments of power and privilege, the stratum of Palestinian beneficiaries would be averse to parting with them; however reluctantly, they would do the bidding of the power that meted out the largesse and "afforded them significant perquisites."[24] The transition period also enabled Israel to gauge the dependability of these Palestinian sub-

22. *Israeli-Palestinian Interim Agreement on the West Bank and the Gaza Strip* (Washington, DC: 1995), pp. 92–96, 314. For analysis of Oslo II, see Norman G. Finkelstein, *Image and Reality of the Israel-Palestine Conflict,* expanded second paperback edition (New York: 2003), pp. 172–83.

23. A border dispute over a tiny triangle of land was resolved later in Egypt's favor by international arbitration.

24. International Crisis Group, *Tipping Point? Palestinians and the search for a new strategy* (April 2010), p. 2.

contractors, as crises periodically erupted that tested their loyalty. By the end of the Oslo "peace process," Israel could count among its many blessings that the number of Israeli troops serving in the occupied Palestinian territories was at the lowest level since the start of the first intifada.[25] The only holdout in the Palestinian leadership was its chairman. Notwithstanding his legendary opportunism, Arafat carried in him a residue of his nationalist past and would not settle for presiding over a South Africa–like Bantustan. Once he passed from the scene in 2004, however, all the pieces were in place for the "Palestinian Authority" implanted in the occupied territories to reach a modus vivendi with Israel. Except that it was too late.

In 2006, disgusted by years of official corruption and fruitless negotiations, Palestinians voted into office the Islamic movement Hamas, in an election that was widely heralded as "completely honest and fair" (Jimmy Carter).[26] Privately, Senator Hillary Clinton rued that the United States didn't rig the outcome: "we should have made sure that we did something to determine who was going to win."[27] Since its establishment in 1988, Hamas had formally rejected the internationally endorsed terms for resolving the Israel-Palestine conflict. However, its participation in the electoral contest signaled the possibility that the Islamic movement "was evolving and could evolve still more."[28] But Israel immediately tightened its siege, and "economic activity in Gaza came to a standstill, moving into survival mode."[29] The United States and European Union followed suit, as they inflicted "devastating" financial sanctions.[30] If the

25. "Israel Army's West Bank Presence 'Lowest in 20 Years,'" *Agence France-Presse* (28 November 2010).

26. "Opening Remarks by Former US President Jimmy Carter to the 2006 Human Rights Defenders Policy Forum" (23 May 2006). See also Pamela Scholey, "Palestine: Hamas's unfinished transformation," in Jeroen de Zeeuw, ed., *From Soldiers to Politicians: Transforming rebel movements after civil war* (Boulder, CO: 2008), which describes the election as a "model of democratic reform" (p. 138).

27. Ken Kurson, "2006 Audio Emerges of Hillary Clinton Proposing Rigging Palestine Election," *Observer* (28 October 2016).

28. Álvaro de Soto, *End of Mission Report* (2007), para. 44. De Soto was "United Nations Special Coordinator for the Middle East Peace Process and Personal Representative of the Secretary-General to the Palestine Liberation Organization and the Palestinian Authority Envoy to the Quartet" between 2005 and 2007. His report is the single most authoritative and revealing document on the period running from Israel's redeployment in Gaza to Hamas's electoral victory and its aftermath. On Hamas's political trajectory prior to the 2006 elections toward acceptance of the State of Israel, see International Crisis Group, *Enter Hamas: The challenges of political integration* (January 2006), pp. 2, 19–22.

29. De Soto, *End of Mission Report,* paras. 25, 52.

30. Ibid., para. 51.

noose was tightened around Hamas alongside the people of Gaza, it was because they did as told: they participated in democratic elections. The unstated subtext, ignorance of which cost Gaza dearly, was that Hamas was obliged to lose. The UN special rapporteur on human rights in the occupied Palestinian territories noted other anomalies of this punitive response:

> In effect, the Palestinian people have been subjected to economic sanctions— the first time an occupied people have been so treated. This is difficult to understand. Israel is in violation of major Security Council and General Assembly resolutions dealing with unlawful territorial change and the violation of human rights and has failed to implement the 2004 advisory opinion of the International Court of Justice, yet it escapes the imposition of sanctions. Instead the Palestinian people ... have been subjected to possibly the most rigorous form of international sanctions imposed in modern times.[31]

The impetus behind this ruthless economic warfare targeting "a freely elected government of a people under occupation" was to ensure Hamas's failure so as to discredit it as a governing body.[32] The Islamic movement was called upon simultaneously by Washington and Brussels to renounce violence, and recognize Israel as well as prior Israeli-Palestinian agreements.[33] These preconditions for international engagement were unilateral: Israel wasn't compelled to renounce violence; Israel wasn't compelled to recognize the reciprocal Palestinian right to statehood along the 1967 border; and whereas Hamas was compelled to recognize prior agreements, such as the Oslo Accord, which legitimated the occupation and enabled Israel to vastly increase its illegal settlements, Israel was free to eviscerate prior agreements, such as the Bush administration's 2003 *Road Map*.[34] In effect, Western powers were "setting unattainable preconditions for dialogue" with the Islamic

---

31. John Dugard, *Report of the Special Rapporteur on the Situation of Human Rights in the Palestinian Territories Occupied since 1967* (A/HRC/2/5) (5 September 2006). The special rapporteur continued: "It is interesting to recall that the Western States refused to impose meaningful economic sanctions on South Africa to compel it to abandon apartheid on the grounds that this would harm the black people of South Africa. No such sympathy is extended to the Palestinian people or their human rights."

32. De Soto, *End of Mission Report,* paras. 50, 53.

33. Although many of the hostile initiatives against Hamas formally emanated from the Middle East Quartet—US, EU, Russia, UN secretary-general—in reality, this grouping was the plaything of the United States, often in concert with the European Union (ibid., paras. 63, 69, 78–79).

34. Jimmy Carter, *Palestine Peace Not Apartheid* (New York: 2006), pp. 159–60; Golan, *Israel and Palestine,* p. 90; de Soto, *End of Mission Report,* paras. 30, 81n6, 131.

movement.[35] "Hamas's success in the Palestinian elections of January 2006," a 2014 study concludes, could have augured a peaceful political evolution, "but only if the active interference of the United States and the passivity of the European Union had not sabotaged this experiment in government."[36]

In 2007, Hamas consolidated its control of Gaza after foiling a coup attempt orchestrated by Washington in league with Israel and elements of the Palestinian old guard.[37] "When Hamas preempts [a putsch]," a senior Israeli intelligence figure later scoffed, "everyone cries foul, claiming it's a military putsch by Hamas—but who did the putsch?"[38] Although reviling Hamas as "cruel, disgusting and hate-filled," an editor of Israel's largest circulation newspaper echoed this heterodox take on what had transpired: "Hamas did not 'seize control' of Gaza. It took the action needed to enforce its authority, disarming and destroying a militia that refused to bow to its authority."[39] The United States and Israel reacted promptly to Hamas's rejection of this "democracy promotion" bid (i.e., the coup attempt) by further tightening the screws on Gaza.[40] In June 2008, Hamas and Israel entered into a cease-fire brokered by Egypt, but in November of that year Israel violated the cease-fire. It carried out a lethal border raid on Gaza reminiscent of its 1955 cross-border attack. Then and now, the objective was to provoke retaliation and thus provide the pretext for a massive assault.

Indeed, the border raid proved to be the preamble to a bloody invasion. On 27 December 2008, Israel launched "Operation Cast Lead."[41] It began with an aerial blitz that was followed by a combined aerial and ground assault. Piloting the most advanced combat aircraft in the world, the Israeli air force flew nearly three thousand sorties over Gaza and dropped one thousand tons of explosives, while the Israeli army deployed several brigades equipped with

35. De Soto, *End of Mission Report*, para. 50.

36. Filiu, *Gaza*, p. 306; see also de Soto, *End of Mission Report*, paras. 50, 52.

37. David Rose, "The Gaza Bombshell," *Vanity Fair* (April 2008); International Institute for Strategic Studies, "Hamas Coup in Gaza" (2007); Björn Brenner, *Gaza under Hamas: From Islamic democracy to Islamist governance* (London: 2017), pp. 35–40. The preemptive strike was launched by Hamas's military wing, and subsequently endorsed by Hamas political leaders. For Washington's machinations to foment a civil war in Gaza prior to the coup attempt, and the complicity of senior officials in the Palestinian Authority, see de Soto, *End of Mission Report*, paras. 55–57, 123, 127.

38. Paul McGeough, *Kill Khalid: The failed Mossad assassination of Khalid Mishal and the rise of Hamas* (New York: 2009), p. 377.

39. Ed O'Loughlin, "Hopeless in Gaza," *Sydney Morning Herald* (23 June 2007).

40. The ballyhooed centerpiece of Bush's foreign policy was "democracy promotion."

41. "Cast Lead" referred to a line in a Hanukkah song.

sophisticated intelligence-gathering systems, and weaponry such as robotic and TV-aided remote-controlled guns. On the other side, Hamas[42] launched several hundred rudimentary rockets and mortar shells into Israel. On 18 January 2009, Israel declared a unilateral cease-fire, "apparently at the behest of Barack Obama, whose presidential investiture was to take place two days later."[43] However, the siege of Gaza persisted. The Bush administration and the US Congress lent Israel unqualified support during the attack. A resolution laying full culpability on Hamas for the ensuing death and destruction passed unanimously in the Senate and 390 to 5 in the House.[44] But overwhelmingly, international public opinion (including wide swaths of Jewish public opinion) recoiled at Israel's assault on a defenseless civilian population.[45] In 2009, a United Nations Human Rights Council Fact-Finding Mission, chaired by the respected South African jurist Richard Goldstone, released a voluminous report documenting Israel's commission of massive war crimes and possible crimes against humanity. The report accused Hamas of committing cognate crimes but on a scale that paled by comparison. It was clear that, in the words of Israeli columnist Gideon Levy, "this time we went too far."[46]

Israel officially justified Operation Cast Lead on the grounds of self-defense against Hamas rocket attacks.[47] Such a rationale did not, however, withstand even superficial scrutiny. If Israel wanted to avert Hamas rocket attacks, it would not have triggered them by breaching the 2008 cease-fire.[48] It could also have opted for renewing—and for a change, honoring—the cease-fire. In fact, as a former Israeli intelligence officer told the Crisis Group, "The cease-fire options on the table after the war were in place there before it."[49] If the goal of Cast Lead was to destroy the "infrastructure of terrorism,"

42. When referring to Palestinian military actions and capabilities, *Hamas* is used as shorthand for all Palestinian armed groups operating in Gaza.

43. Filiu, *Gaza*, p. 316.

44. Stephen Zunes, "Virtually the Entire Dem-Controlled Congress Supports Israel's War Crimes in Gaza," *Alternet* (13 January 2009).

45. Norman G. Finkelstein, *"This Time We Went Too Far": Truth and consequences of the Gaza invasion,* expanded paperback edition (New York: 2011), pp. 107–29.

46. Gideon Levy, "Goldstone's Gaza Probe Did Israel a Favor," *Haaretz* (2 October 2009).

47. Mouin Rabbani, "Birth Pangs of a New Palestine," *Middle East Report Online* (7 January 2009).

48. See Chapter 2.

49. International Crisis Group, *Gaza's Unfinished Business* (April 2009), p. 21; see ibid., pp. 27–28, for the postinvasion cease-fire terms. See also "Israeli Leaders 'To Topple Hamas,'" *BBC News* (22 December 2008); Zvi Bar'el, "Delusions of Victory in Gaza," *Haaretz* (28 December 2008).

then Israel's alibi of self-defense appeared even less credible after the invasion. Overwhelmingly, Israel targeted not Hamas strongholds but "decidedly 'non-terrorist,' non-Hamas" sites.[50]

The human rights context further undermined Israel's claim of self-defense. The 2008 annual report of B'Tselem (Israeli Information Center for Human Rights in the Occupied Territories) documented that between 1 January and 26 December 2008, Israeli security forces killed 455 Palestinians, of whom at least 175 were civilians, while Palestinians killed 31 Israelis, of whom 21 were civilians. Hence, on the eve of Israel's so-called war of self-defense, the ratio of total Palestinians to Israelis killed stood at almost 15:1, while the ratio of Palestinian civilians to Israeli civilians killed was at least 8:1. In Gaza alone, Israel killed at least 158 noncombatants in 2008, while Hamas rocket attacks killed 7 Israeli civilians, a ratio of more than 22:1. Israel deplored the detention by Hamas of one Israeli combatant captured in 2006, yet Israel detained some 8,000 Palestinian "political prisoners," including 60 women and 390 children, of whom 548 were held in administrative detention without charge or trial (42 of them for more than two years).[51] Its ever-tightening noose around Gaza compounded Israel's disproportionate breach of Palestinian human rights. The blockade amounted to "collective punishment, a serious violation of international humanitarian law."[52] In September 2008, the World Bank described Gaza as "starkly transform[ed] from a potential trade route to a walled hub of humanitarian donations."[53] In mid-December, the United Nations Office for the Coordination of Humanitarian Affairs (OCHA) reported that Israel's "18-month-long blockade has created a profound human dignity crisis, leading to a widespread erosion of livelihoods and a significant deterioration in infrastructure and essential

50. *Report of the Independent Fact-Finding Committee on Gaza: No safe place.* Presented to the League of Arab States (2009), para. 411(3). The committee was chaired by eminent South African jurist John Dugard. On a related note, the committee observed:

> Had the IDF wanted to completely destroy the tunnels [under the southern border of Gaza] this would have been relatively easy to achieve. They are easily discernible and given the IDF's aerial surveillance capability, they must have been aware of the exact location of the tunnels. However, it was clear to the Committee they had not all been destroyed during the conflict. In the Committee's view this raises questions about the Israeli claim that it acted in self-defense against the smuggling of weapons through the tunnels. (ibid., para. 394)

51. B'Tselem (Israeli Information Center for Human Rights in the Occupied Territories), *Human Rights in the Occupied Territories: 2008 annual report* (Jerusalem: 2009).

52. Human Rights Watch, "Donors Should Press Israel to End Blockade" (1 March 2009).

53. Roy, *Gaza Strip*, p. xxxi.

services."[54] If Gazans lacked electricity for as many as 16 hours each day; if Gazans received water only once a week for a few hours, and 80 percent of the water was unfit for human consumption; if one of every two Gazans was unemployed and "food insecure"; if 20 percent of "essential drugs" in Gaza were "at zero level" and more than 20 percent of patients suffering from cancer, heart disease, and other severe conditions were unable to get permits for medical care abroad—if Gazans clung to life by the thinnest of threads, it traced back, ultimately, to the Israeli siege. The people of Gaza, OCHA concluded, felt "a growing sense of being trapped, physically, intellectually and emotionally." To judge by the human rights balance sheet at the end of 2008, and setting aside that the cease-fire was broken by Israel, didn't Palestinians have a much stronger case than Israel for resorting to armed self-defense?

54. United Nations Office for the Coordination of Humanitarian Affairs (OCHA), *Gaza Humanitarian Situation Report—The Impact of the Blockade on the Gaza Strip: A human dignity crisis* (15 December 2008).

TWO

Deterring Arabs, Deterring Peace

"OPERATION CAST LEAD" PROVED TO BE a public relations debacle for Israel. However much they might have preferred otherwise, Western media, pundits, and diplomats could not ignore the massive death and destruction in Gaza. If it wasn't self-defense, what then impelled Israel to prosecute a campaign against a civilian population that was bound to elicit stinging rebukes abroad? Early speculation focused on the jockeying for votes in the upcoming 2009 election. Polls during the invasion showed that 80–90 percent of Israeli Jews supported it. "In the context of almost unanimous support of the operation by the Israeli public," the Association for Civil Rights in Israel subsequently noted, "tolerance of any dissent was minimal."[1] But as veteran Israeli journalist Gideon Levy pointed out, "Israel went through a very similar war . . . two-and-a-half years ago [in Lebanon], when there were no elections."[2] In fact, Israeli leaders recoil at jeopardizing critical state interests, such as by launching a war, simply for electoral gain. Even in recent decades, when the Israeli political scene has become more squalid, one would be hard-pressed to name a major military campaign set in motion for partisan political ends.[3] The principal motives behind the Gaza invasion traced back

1. Ethan Bronner, "In Israel, a Consensus That Gaza War Is a Just One," *New York Times* (13 January 2009). Association for Civil Rights in Israel, *The State of Human Rights in Israel and the Occupied Territories: 2009 report* (Jerusalem: December 2009), p. 6.

2. Gideon Levy, *Democracy Now!* (29 December 2008), democracynow.org/2008/12/29/israeli_attacks_kill_over_310_in.

3. Whereas it is arguable that Prime Minister Menachem Begin's decision to bomb the Iraqi OSIRAK reactor in 1981 was an electoral ploy, the facile operation didn't jeopardize state interests. Indeed, the alleged existential threat posed to Israel by Saddam Hussein was unfounded; he hadn't embarked on a nuclear weapons program prior to the bombing. Richard Wilson, "Incomplete or Inaccurate Information Can Lead to Tragically Incorrect

not to the election cycle but to the dual necessity of restoring Israel's "deterrence capacity," and scotching the threat posed by a new Palestinian "peace offensive."

Israel's "larger concern" in Cast Lead, *New York Times* Middle East correspondent Ethan Bronner reported, quoting Israeli sources, was to "reestablish Israeli deterrence," because "its enemies are less afraid of it than they once were, or should be."[4] Preserving its deterrence capacity looms large in Israeli strategic doctrine. Indeed, this consideration was a major impetus behind Israel's first strike against Egypt in June 1967, which resulted in Israel's occupation of Gaza and the West Bank. To justify Cast Lead, Israeli historian Benny Morris recalled that "many Israelis feel that the walls ... are closing in ... much as they felt in early June 1967."[5] But although ordinary Israelis were filled with foreboding before the June war, Israel did not face an existential threat at the time (as Morris knows[6]) and Israeli leaders did not doubt they would emerge victorious in the event of war. After Israel threatened, and then laid plans, to attack Syria in May 1967,[7] Egyptian president Gamal Abdel Nasser deployed Egyptian troops in the Sinai and announced that the Straits of Tiran would be closed to Israeli shipping. (Egypt had entered into a military pact with Syria a few months earlier.) Israeli foreign minister Abba Eban emotively declared that because of the blockade, Israel could only "breathe with a single lung." But except for the passage of oil, of which it then had ample stocks, Israel made practically no use of the straits. Besides, Nasser did not enforce the blockade: vessels were passing freely through the straits within days of his announcement. What then of the military threat posed by Egypt?

Decisions to Preempt: The example of OSIRAK," paper presented at Erice, Sicily (18 May 2007, updated 9 February 2008), users.physics.harvard.edu/~wilson/publications/pp896 .html; Richard Wilson, "A Visit to the Bombed Nuclear Reactor at Tuwaitha, Iraq," *Nature* (31 March 1983); Wayne White, Former Deputy Director, Near East and South Asia Office, State Department, in "Fifty-Third in the Capitol Hill Conference Series on US Middle East Policy" (20 June 2008).

4. Ethan Bronner, "Israel Reminds Foes That It Has Teeth," *New York Times* (29 December 2008).

5. Benny Morris, "Why Israel Feels Threatened," *New York Times* (30 December 2008). Gideon Levy mocked Israel's incessant fearmongering as "the devil's refuge" that "explains and justifies everything." "Waiting for the All Clear," *Haaretz* (30 April 2009).

6. Benny Morris, *Righteous Victims: A history of the Zionist-Arab conflict, 1881–2001* (New York: 2001), p. 686.

7. Ami Gluska, *The Israeli Military and the Origins of the 1967 War: Government, armed forces and defence policy 1963–1967* (New York: 2007), pp. 74–76, 80, 94–100, 103–6, 114–18.

Multiple US intelligence agencies had concluded that Egypt did not intend to attack Israel and that in the improbable case that it did, alone or in concert with other Arab countries, Israel would—in President Lyndon Johnson's words—"whip the hell out of them."[8] Meanwhile, the head of the Mossad told senior American officials on 1 June 1967 that there were "no differences between the US and the Israelis on the military intelligence picture or its interpretation."[9] So, Israel itself must have been aware that Nasser did not intend to attack and that the Egyptian army would be trounced if he did. The real predicament facing Israel was the growing perception in the Arab world, spurred by Nasser's radical nationalism and climaxing in his defiant gestures in May 1967, that it no longer needed to fear the Jewish state. Divisional Commander Ariel Sharon admonished cabinet members hesitating to launch a first strike that Israel was losing its "deterrence capability ... our main weapon—*the fear of us.*"[10] In effect, *deterrence capacity* denoted, not warding off an imminent existential threat, but putting rivals on notice that any future challenge to Israeli power would be met with decisive force. The Israeli army command "was not too worried about an Egyptian surprise attack," Israeli strategic analyst Zeev Maoz concluded. "Rather, the key question was how to restore the credibility of Israeli deterrence."[11]

The ejection of the Israeli occupying army from Lebanon in 2000 by Hezbollah posed a new challenge to Israel's deterrence capacity. The fact that it suffered a humiliating defeat, and that Hezbollah's victory was celebrated throughout the Arab world, made another war well-nigh inevitable. Israel immediately began planning for the next round.[12] It found a plausible pretext in 2006 when Hezbollah killed several Israeli soldiers and captured two, and then demanded in exchange the release of Lebanese prisoners held in Israeli jails. Although it unleashed the full fury of its air force and geared up for a

8. Norman G. Finkelstein, *Image and Reality of the Israel-Palestine Conflict,* expanded second paperback edition (New York: 2003), pp. 134–40 (Johnson quote at p. 135, Eban quote at p. 139).

9. "Memorandum for the Record" (1 June 1967), *Foreign Relations of the United States, 1964–1968,* vol. 19, *Arab-Israeli Crisis and War, 1967* (Washington, DC: 2004).

10. Tom Segev, *1967: Israel, the war, and the year that transformed the Middle East* (New York: 2007), p. 293, emphasis added.

11. Zeev Maoz, *Defending the Holy Land: A critical analysis of Israel's security and foreign policy* (Ann Arbor: 2006), p. 89.

12. Benjamin S. Lambeth, *Air Operations in Israel's War against Hezbollah: Learning from Lebanon and getting it right in Gaza* (Arlington, VA: 2011), p. 97; Matthew Kalman, "Israel Set War Plan More than a Year Ago," *San Francisco Chronicle* (21 July 2006).

ground invasion, Israel suffered a second ignominious defeat in the summer 2006 war. "The IAF [Israeli Air Force], the arm of the Israeli military that had once destroyed whole air forces in a few days," a respected US military analyst concluded, "not only proved unable to stop Hezbollah rocket strikes, but even to do enough damage to prevent Hezbollah's rapid recovery," while "Israeli ground forces were badly shaken and bogged down by a well-equipped and capable foe."[13] The juxtaposition of several figures highlights the magnitude of the Israeli setback. Israel deployed 30,000 troops against 2,000 regular Hezbollah fighters and 4,000 irregular Hezbollah and non-Hezbollah fighters; Israel delivered and fired 162,000 weapons whereas Hezbollah fired 5,000 weapons (4,000 rockets and projectiles at Israel and 1,000 antitank missiles inside Lebanon).[14] What's more, "the vast majority of the fighters" Israeli troops did battle with "were not ... regular Hezbollah fighters and in some cases were not even members of Hezbollah," and "many of Hezbollah's best and most skilled fighters never saw action, lying in wait along the Litani River with the expectation that the IDF [Israel Defense Forces] assault would be much deeper and arrive much faster than it did."[15] On the political front, it was indicative of Israel's reversal of fortune that for the first time, it fought not in defiance of a UN cease-fire resolution but, instead, in the hope that such a resolution would rescue it from a quagmire. "Frustration with the conduct and outcome of the Second [2006] Lebanon War," an influential Israeli think tank later reported, led Israel to "initiate a thorough internal examination ... on the order of 63 different commissions of inquiry."[16]

After the 2006 war, Israel was itching to reengage Hezbollah but wasn't yet confident it would emerge triumphant from the battlefield. In mid-2008, Israel sought to conscript the United States for a joint attack on Iran, which perforce would also decapitate Hezbollah (Iran's junior partner), and consequently neuter the principal rivals to its regional hegemony. Israel and its quasi emissaries, such as Benny Morris, warned that if the United States did not go along, "then nonconventional weaponry will have to be used," and

13. William Arkin, *Divining Victory: Airpower in the 2006 Israel-Hezbollah war* (Maxwell Air Force Base, AL: 2007), pp. xxv–xxvi, 54, 135, 147–48.

14. Ibid., pp. xxi, 25, 64.

15. Andrew Exum, *Hizballah at War: A military assessment* (Washington, DC: 2006), pp. 9, 11–12.

16. Reut Institute, *Building a Political Firewall against Israel's Delegitimization* (Tel Aviv: 2010), para. 35.

"many innocent Iranians will die."[17] To Israel's chagrin and mortification, Washington vetoed an attack and Iran went its merry way. The credibility of Israel's capacity to terrorize had slipped another notch. The time had come to find a different target. Tiny Gaza, poorly defended but proudly defiant, fitted the bill. Although feebly armed, Hamas had resisted Israeli diktat. It even crowed that it had forced Israel to "withdraw" from Gaza in 2005 and had compelled Israel to acquiesce in a cease-fire in 2008. If Gaza was *where* Israel would restore its deterrence capacity, one theater of the 2006 war hinted at *how* it might be done. In the course of its attack, Israel flattened the southern suburb of Beirut known as the Dahiya, which was home to Hezbollah's poor Shiite constituents. After the war, Israeli military officers gestured to the "Dahiya doctrine" as they formulated contingency plans:

> We will wield disproportionate power against every village from which shots are fired on Israel, and cause immense damage and destruction. This isn't a suggestion. This is a plan that has already been authorized. (Head of IDF Northern Command Gadi Eisenkot)

> The next war ... will lead to the elimination of the Lebanese military, the destruction of the national infrastructure, and intense suffering among the population. Serious damage to the Republic of Lebanon, the destruction of homes and infrastructure, and the suffering of hundreds of thousands of people are consequences that can influence Hezbollah's behavior more than anything else. (Head of Israeli National Security Council Giora Eiland)

> With an outbreak of hostilities, Israel will need to act immediately, decisively, and with force that is disproportionate.... Such a response aims at inflicting damage and meting out punishment to an extent that will demand long and expensive reconstruction processes. (Reserve Colonel Gabriel Siboni)[18]

17. Benny Morris, "A Second Holocaust? The Threat to Israel" (2 May 2008), mideast freedomforum.org/de/node/66. When Israel again threatened to attack Iran in late 2009 and early 2010, Morris did reprises of his signature 2008 performance by conjuring apocalyptic scenarios if the United States did not back an Israeli attack. Benny Morris, "Obama's Nuclear Spring," *Guardian* (24 November 2009); Benny Morris, "When Armageddon Lives Next Door," *Los Angeles Times* (16 April 2010).

18. Yaron London, "The Dahiya Strategy," *ynetnews.com* (6 October 2008); Giora Eiland, "The Third Lebanon War: Target Lebanon," *Strategic Assessment* (November 2008); Gabriel Siboni, "Disproportionate Force: Israel's concept of response in light of the Second Lebanon War," *Institute for National Security Studies* (2 October 2008); Amos Harel, "Analysis: IDF plans to use disproportionate force in next war," *Haaretz* (5 October 2007); Joseph Nasr, "Israel Warns Hezbollah War Would Invite Destruction," *Reuters* (2 October 2008); Jean-Loup Samaan, "The Dahya Concept and Israeli Military Posture vis-à-vis Hezbollah since 2006," *Comparative Strategy* (2013).

The use of disproportionate force and targeting civilian infrastructure constitute war crimes under international law. Although the Dahiya doctrine was formulated with all of Israel's rivals in mind, Gaza was singled out as the prime target. "Too bad it did not take hold immediately after the [2005] 'disengagement' from Gaza and the first rocket barrages," a respected Israeli pundit lamented in October 2008. "Had we immediately adopted the Dahiya strategy, we would have likely spared ourselves much trouble." If and when Palestinians launched another rocket attack, Israeli interior minister Meir Sheetrit exhorted a month before, "the IDF should ... decide on a neighborhood in Gaza and level it."[19] The operative plan for Cast Lead could be gleaned from authoritative Israeli statements as the assault got under way: "What we have to do is act systematically, with the aim of punishing all the organizations that are firing the rockets and mortars, as well as the civilians who are enabling them to fire and hide" (Reserve Major-General Amiram Levin); "After this operation, there will not be one Hamas building left standing in Gaza" (Deputy IDF Chief of Staff Dan Harel); "Anything affiliated with Hamas is a legitimate target" (IDF Spokesperson Major Avital Leibowitz). For sheer brazenness and brutality, however, it would be hard to beat Deputy Prime Minister Eli Yishai: "It [should be] possible to destroy Gaza, so that they will understand not to mess with us.... It is a great opportunity to demolish thousands of houses of all the terrorists, so they will think twice before they launch rockets.... I hope the operation will come to an end with ... the complete destruction of terrorism and Hamas.... [T]hey should be razed to the ground, so thousands of houses, tunnels and industries will be demolished." The military correspondent for Israel's Channel 10 News observed that Israel "isn't trying to hide the fact that it reacts disproportionately."[20]

19. London, "Dahiya Strategy"; Attila Somfalvi, "Sheetrit: We should level Gaza neighborhoods," *ynetnews.com* (2 October 2008).

20. "Israeli General Says Hamas Must Not Be the Only Target in Gaza," IDF Radio, Tel Aviv (26 December 2008; BBC Monitoring Middle East); Tova Dadon, "Deputy Chief of Staff: Worst still ahead," *ynetnews.com* (29 December 2008); "B'Tselem to Attorney General Mazuz: Concern over Israel targeting civilian objects in the Gaza Strip" (31 December 2008); *Report of the United Nations Fact-Finding Mission on the Gaza Conflict* (25 September 2009), para. 1204; hereafter: Goldstone Report. See also Public Committee against Torture in Israel (PCATI), *No Second Thoughts: The changes in the Israeli Defense Forces' combat doctrine in light of "Operation Cast Lead"* (Jerusalem: 2009), pp. 20–28.

Israeli media exulted at the "shock and awe" (*Maariv*) of the opening air campaign that was designed to "engender a sense of dread."[21] No doubt, it was mission accomplished. Whereas Israel killed 55 Lebanese during the first two days of the 2006 war, it killed as many as 300 Gazans in just four minutes on the first day of Cast Lead. The majority of targets were located in "densely populated residential areas," while the bombardments began "at around 11:30 a.m., . . . when the streets were full of civilians, including school children leaving classes at the end of the morning shift and those going to school for the second shift."[22] A respected Israeli strategic analyst observed several days into the slaughter, "The IDF, which planned to attack buildings and sites populated by hundreds of people, did not warn them in advance to leave, but intended to kill a great many of them, and succeeded."[23] In the meantime, Benny Morris praised "Israel's highly efficient air assault on Hamas," and a US military analyst marveled at the "masterful precision" of the attack.[24] But veteran Israeli columnist B. Michael was less impressed by the dispatch of helicopter gunships and jet planes "over a giant prison and firing at its people."[25] On just the first day, Israeli aerial strikes killed or fatally injured at least 16 children, while an Israeli drone-launched precision missile killed nine college students (two of them young women) "who were waiting for a UN bus" to take them home. Human Rights Watch (HRW) found that "no Palestinian fighters were active on the street or in the immediate area just prior to or at the time of the attack" on the collegians.[26] As Cast Lead proceeded apace, prominent Israelis dropped all pretense that its purpose was to stop Hamas rocket fire. "Remember, [Israeli defense minister Ehud] Barak's real foe is not Hamas," a former Israeli minister told the Crisis Group. "It is the memory of 2006."[27] Others gloated that "Gaza is to Lebanon as the

21. Seumas Milne, "Israel's Onslaught on Gaza Is a Crime That Cannot Succeed," *Guardian* (30 December 2008); Shay Fogelman, "Shock and Awe," *Haaretz* (31 December 2010).

22. Amnesty International, *Operation "Cast Lead": 22 Days of death and destruction* (London: 2009), p. 47.

23. Reuven Pedatzur, "The Mistakes of Cast Lead," *Haaretz* (8 January 2009).

24. Morris, "Why Israel Feels Threatened"; Matt M. Matthews, "The Israeli Defense Forces Response to the 2006 War with Hezbollah," *Military Review* (July–August 2009), p. 45.

25. B. Michael, "Déjà vu in Gaza," *ynetnews.com* (29 December 2008).

26. Al Mezan Center for Human Rights, *Bearing the Brunt Again: Child rights violations during Operation Cast Lead* (2009), p. 28; Human Rights Watch, *Precisely Wrong: Gaza civilians killed by Israeli drone-launched missiles* (2009), pp. 14–17.

27. International Crisis Group, *Ending the War in Gaza* (2009), p. 18. Defending Cast Lead while willfully oblivious to its actual objective, Israeli philosopher Asa Kasher opined that "a democratic state . . . cannot use human beings as mere tools to create deterrence"

second sitting for an exam is to the first—a second chance to get it right," and that Israel had "hurled back" Gaza not just 20 years (as in Lebanon), but "into the 1940s"; that if "Israel regained its deterrence capabilities," it was because "the war in Gaza has compensated for the shortcomings of the ... Lebanon War"; that "there is no doubt that Hezbollah leader Hassan Nasrallah is upset these days. . . . There will no longer be anyone in the Arab world who can claim that Israel is weak." Looking back a year later, an Israeli military correspondent recalled that the Israeli assault "was considered to be an effective remedy to the failures of the 2006 Second Lebanon War."[28]

Thomas Friedman, *New York Times* foreign affairs expert, joined in the chorus of hallelujahs during Cast Lead. Israel actually won the 2006 Lebanon war, according to Friedman, because it had administered an "education" to Hezbollah by inflicting "substantial property damage and collateral casualties on Lebanon." Fearing the Lebanese people's wrath, Hezbollah would "think three times next time" before defying Israel. He also expressed hope that Israel would "'educate' Hamas by inflicting a heavy death toll on Hamas militants and heavy pain on the Gaza population." To justify its targeting of Lebanon's civilian population during the 2006 war, Friedman alleged that Israel had no choice: "Hezbollah created a very 'flat' military network ... deeply embedded in the local towns and villages," and insofar as "Hezbollah nested among civilians, the only long-term source of deterrence was to exact enough pain on the civilians ... to restrain Hezbollah in the future."[29] If, for argument's sake, Friedman's hollow coinage is set aside (what does "flat" mean?), and if it is also set aside that he not only alleged that killing of civilians was unavoidable but also *advocated targeting civilians* as a deterrence strategy —still, the question remains, Was Hezbollah "embedded in," "nested among," and "intertwined" with the civilian population? An exhaustive investigation

because "human beings are not tools to be used," and "killing for the sake of deterrence is something akin to terrorism." Asa Kasher, "Operation Cast Lead and Just War Theory," *Azure* (Summer 2009), p. 51; Asa Kasher, "A Moral Evaluation of the Gaza War," *Jerusalem Post* (7 February 2010).

28. Amos Harel and Avi Issacharoff, "Israel and Hamas Are Both Paying a Steep Price in Gaza," *Haaretz* (10 January 2009); Ari Shavit, "Israel's Victories in Gaza Make Up for Its Failures in Lebanon," *Haaretz* (12 January 2009); Guy Bechor, "A Dangerous Victory," *ynetnews.com* (12 January 2009); Amos Harel, "Israel Stuck in the Mud on Internal Gaza Probe," *Haaretz* (30 January 2010).

29. Thomas L. Friedman, "Israel's Goals in Gaza?," *New York Times* (14 January 2009). See also Thomas L. Friedman, "War, Timeout, War, Time . . . ," *New York Times* (26 June 2010).

by HRW concluded that, overwhelmingly, it was not: "We found strong evidence that Hezbollah stored most of its rockets in bunkers and weapon storage facilities located in uninhabited fields and valleys, that in the vast majority of cases Hezbollah fighters left populated civilian areas as soon as the fighting started, and that Hezbollah fired the vast majority of its rockets from pre-prepared positions outside villages"; "In all but a few of the cases of civilian deaths we investigated, Hezbollah fighters had not mixed with the civilian population or taken other actions to contribute to the targeting of a particular home or vehicle by Israeli forces"; "Israel's own firing patterns in Lebanon support the conclusion that Hezbollah fired large numbers of its rockets from tobacco fields, banana, olive and citrus groves, and more remote, unpopulated valleys."[30] A US Army War College study, based largely on interviews with Israeli soldiers who fought in the 2006 Lebanon war, echoed HRW's conclusions: "The key battlefields in the land campaign south of the Litani River were mostly devoid of civilians, and IDF participants consistently report little or no meaningful intermingling of Hezbollah fighters and noncombatants. Nor is there any systematic reporting of Hezbollah using civilians in the combat zone as shields."[31] "Rather than confronting Israel's army head-on," Friedman went on to assert, Hezbollah targeted Israel's civilian population so as to provoke Israeli retaliatory strikes that would unavoidably kill Lebanese civilians and "inflame the Arab-Muslim street." But numerous studies have shown,[32] and Israeli officials themselves have conceded,[33] that during the guerrilla war it waged against the Israeli occupying army, Hezbollah targeted Israeli civilians only after Israel targeted Lebanese civilians. In the 2006 war, Hezbollah again targeted Israeli civilian concentrations after Israel inflicted heavy casualties on Lebanese civilians, and Hezbollah leader Sayyed Hassan Nasrallah avowed that it would target

30. Human Rights Watch, *Why They Died: Civilian casualties in Lebanon during the 2006 war* (New York: 2007), pp. 5, 14, 40–41, 45–46, 48, 51, 53.

31. Stephen Biddle and Jeffrey A. Friedman, *The 2006 Lebanon Campaign and the Future of Warfare: Implications for army and defense policy* (Carlisle, PA: 2008), pp. 43–45. On a related note, the study found that "the great majority of Hezbollah's fighters wore uniforms. In fact, their equipment and clothing were remarkably similar to many state militaries'—desert or green fatigues, helmets, web vests, body armor, dog tags, and rank insignia."

32. Human Rights Watch, *Civilian Pawns: Laws of war violations and the use of weapons on the Israel-Lebanon border* (New York: 1996); Maoz, *Defending the Holy Land,* pp. 213–14, 224–25, 252; Augustus Richard Norton, *Hezbollah: A short history* (Princeton: 2007), pp. 77, 86.

33. Judith Palmer Harik, *Hezbollah: The changing face of terrorism* (London: 2004), pp. 167–68.

Israeli civilians only "as long as the enemy undertakes its aggression without limits or red lines."[34]

If Israel targeted the Lebanese civilian population during the 2006 war, it was not because another option didn't present itself, and not because Hezbollah had provoked it. Rather, it was because terrorizing Lebanese civilians appeared to be a low-cost method of "education." Such a strategy was clearly preferable to tangling with a determined foe and enduring heavy combatant casualties. It didn't work out quite as planned, however. Hezbollah's unexpectedly fierce resistance prevented Israel from claiming victory. Still, Israel did successfully educate the Lebanese people. Hezbollah was accordingly chastened not to provide Israel a casus belli two years later during Cast Lead.[35] Israel's pedagogy scored a yet more smashing success in Gaza. "It was hard to convince Gazans whose homes were demolished and family and friends killed and injured," the Crisis Group observed after Cast Lead, "that this amounted to 'victory,'" as Hamas boasted.[36] In the case of Gaza, Israel could also lay claim to a military victory, but only because—in the words of Gideon Levy—"a large, broad army is fighting against a helpless population and a weak, ragged organization that has fled the conflict zones and is barely putting up a fight."[37]

The rationale for Cast Lead advanced by Friedman in the pages of the *New York Times* amounted to apologetics for state terrorism.[38] Indeed, Israel's evolving modus operandi for restoring its deterrence capacity described a curve steadily regressing into barbarism. Israel won its victory in 1967 primarily on the battlefield—albeit in a "turkey shoot"[39]—while in subsequent armed hostilities it endeavored both to achieve a battlefield victory and to bombard the civilian population into abjection. But Israel

34. Human Rights Watch, *Civilians under Assault: Hezbollah's rocket attacks on Israel in the 2006 war* (New York: 2007), p. 100. HRW asserts that Hezbollah rocket attacks on Israeli civilians were not retaliatory, but it adduces no supporting evidence.

35. Yair Evron, "Deterrence: The campaign against Hamas," *Strategic Assessment* (February 2009), p. 81; International Crisis Group, *Gaza's Unfinished Business* (2009), p. 19n198.

36. International Crisis Group, *Gaza's Unfinished Business*, pp. 7–8.

37. Gideon Levy, "The IDF Has No Mercy for the Children in Gaza Nursery Schools," *Haaretz* (15 January 2009).

38. Glenn Greenwald, "Tom Friedman Offers a Perfect Definition of 'Terrorism,'" *Salon.com* (14 January 2009).

39. "Memorandum for the Record" (17 November 1968), n. 13, *Foreign Relations of the United States, 1964–1968*. The quoted phrase is from W. W. Rostow, a senior advisor to President Johnson.

targeted Gaza to restore its deterrence capacity because it eschewed *any* of the risks of a conventional war. It targeted Gaza *because* it was largely defenseless. Its resort to unalloyed terror in turn revealed the IDF's relative decline as a fighting force, while the celebration of Israel's military prowess during and after Cast Lead by the likes of Benny Morris registered the growing detachment of Israeli intellectuals, and a good share of the public as well, from reality.[40] A supplementary benefit of the high-tech, cost-free deterrence strategy targeting civilians was that it restored Israel's domestic morale. A 2009 internal UN document found that "one significant achievement" of Cast Lead was that it dispelled doubts among Israelis about "their ability and the power of the IDF to issue a blow to its enemies.... The use of 'excessive force' ... proves Israel is the landlord.... The pictures of destruction were intended more for Israeli eyes than those of Israel's enemies, eyes starved of revenge and national pride."[41]

Beyond restoring its deterrence capacity, Israel's principal objective in Operation Cast Lead was to fend off the latest threat posed by Palestinian pragmatism. The Palestinian leadership was aligning itself too closely with global opinion for Israel's comfort. The international community has consistently supported a settlement of the Israel-Palestine conflict that calls for two states based on a full Israeli withdrawal to its pre-June 1967 borders, and a "just resolution" of the refugee question based on the right of return and compensation.[42] The two notable exceptions to this broad consensus have been Israel and the United States. Consider the annual UN General Assembly (UNGA) vote on the resolution titled "Peaceful Settlement of the Question of Palestine." The resolution incorporates these tenets for achieving a "two-State solution of Israel and Palestine": (1) "Affirming the principle of the inadmissibility of the acquisition of territory by war"; (2) "Reaffirming the illegality of the Israeli settlements in the Palestinian territory occupied since 1967, including East Jerusalem"; (3) "Stresses the need for: (a) The withdrawal of Israel from the Palestinian territory occupied since 1967, including

40. Amir Kulick, "'Lebanon Lite': Lessons from the Operation in Gaza and the Next Round against Hizbollah," *Military and Strategic Affairs* (April 2009), pp. 57, 59.

41. International Crisis Group, *Gaza's Unfinished Business*, p. 19.

42. Noam Chomsky, *The Fateful Triangle: The United States, Israel and the Palestinians* (Boston: 1983), ch. 3; Norman G. Finkelstein, *Knowing Too Much: Why the American Jewish romance with Israel is coming to an end* (New York: 2012), pp. 203–21.

TABLE 1 UNGA Vote on "Peaceful Settlement of the Question of Palestine" Resolution

Year	Vote [yes-no-abstained]	Negative votes cast by...
1997	155-2-3	Israel, United States
1998	154-2-3	Israel, United States
1999	149-3-2	Israel, United States, Marshall Islands
2000	149-2-3	Israel, United States
2001	131-6-20	Israel, United States, Marshall Islands, Micronesia, Nauru, Tuvalu
2002	160-4-3	Israel, United States, Marshall Islands, Micronesia
2003	160-6-5	Israel, United States, Marshall Islands, Micronesia, Palau, Uganda
2004	161-7-10	Israel, United States, Australia, Grenada, Marshall Islands, Micronesia, Palau
2005	156-6-9	Israel, United States, Australia, Marshall Islands, Micronesia, Palau
2006	157-7-10	Israel, United States, Australia, Marshall Islands, Micronesia, Nauru, Palau
2007	161-7-5	Israel, United States, Australia, Marshall Islands, Micronesia, Nauru, Palau
2008	164-7-3	Israel, United States, Australia, Marshall Islands, Micronesia, Nauru, Palau

East Jerusalem; (b) The realization of the inalienable rights of the Palestinian people, primarily the right to self-determination and the right to their independent State"; and (4) "Also stresses the need for justly resolving the problem of Palestine refugees in conformity with its resolution 194 (III) of 11 December 1948."[43] Table 1 records the vote on this resolution in the years preceding Cast Lead.

At the regional level, a 2002 Arab League summit in Beirut unanimously put forth a peace initiative echoing the UN consensus, while all 57 members of the Organization of the Islamic Conference (OIC), including the Islamic Republic of Iran, "adopted the Arab peace initiative to resolve the issue of Palestine and the Middle East . . . and decided to use all possible means in order to explain and clarify the full implications of this initiative and win

43. The wording of this section of the resolution varies slightly from year to year.

international support for its implementation."[44] The Arab League initiative commits it not just to recognize Israel but also to "establish normal relations" once Israel implements the consensus terms for a comprehensive peace.

Israel began construction in 2002 of a physical barrier that encroached deeply into the West Bank and took a sinuous path incorporating the large settlement blocs. The UN General Assembly requested that the International Court of Justice (ICJ) clarify the "legal consequences arising from the construction of the wall being built by Israel." In 2004, the Court rendered its landmark advisory opinion.[45] In the process of ruling that the wall was illegal, the ICJ also reiterated key elements of the juridical framework for resolving the Israel-Palestine conflict.[46] It inventoried these "rules and principles of international law which are relevant in assessing the legality of the measures taken by Israel": (1) "No territorial acquisition resulting from the threat or use of force shall be recognized as legal"; and (2) "the policy and practices of Israel in establishing settlements in the Palestinian and other Arab territories occupied since 1967" have "no legal validity." In its subsequent deliberations on "whether the construction of the wall has breached these rules and principles," the ICJ found that

> [B]oth the General Assembly and the Security Council have referred, with regard to Palestine, to the customary rule of "the inadmissibility of the acquisition of territory by war." ... It is on this same basis that the [Security] Council has several times condemned the measures taken by Israel to change the status of Jerusalem ...
>
> As regards the principle of the right of peoples to self-determination, ... the existence of a "Palestinian people" is no longer in issue. ... [Its] rights include the right to self-determination. ...
>
> ... The Court concludes that the Israeli settlements in the Occupied Palestinian Territory (including East Jerusalem) have been established in breach of international law.

44. *Final Communiqué of the Twenty-Ninth Session of the Islamic Conference of Foreign Ministers (Session of Solidarity and Dialogue),* Khartoum, Republic of the Sudan (25–27 June 2002). In the hands of Israel's propagandists, this fact got transmuted into "all 57 members of the OIC are virulently hostile to Israel." Robin Shepherd, *A State beyond the Pale: Europe's problem with Israel* (London: 2009), p. 205. The OIC was subsequently renamed the Organization of Islamic Cooperation. Iran also consistently voted with the UNGA majority on the "Peaceful Settlement" resolution.

45. International Court of Justice, Advisory Opinion, *Legal Consequences of the Construction of a Wall in the Occupied Palestinian Territory* (9 July 2004).

46. For detailed analysis, see Finkelstein, *Knowing Too Much,* pp. 307–53.

Not one of the 15 judges sitting on the ICJ registered dissent from these basic principles and findings. It can scarcely be argued, however, that they evinced prejudice against Israel, or that it was a "kangaroo court," as Harvard law professor Alan Dershowitz alleged.[47] Several of the judges, although voting with the majority, expressed profound sympathy for Israel's plight in their respective separate opinions. If the judges were nearly of one mind in their final determination, this consensus sprang not from collective prejudice but from the factual situation: the uncontroversial nature of the legal principles at stake and Israel's unambiguous violation of them. Even the one judge who voted against the 14-person majority condemning Israel's construction of the wall, Thomas Buergenthal (from the US), was at pains to stress that there was "much" in the advisory opinion "with which I agree." On the critical question of Israeli settlements, he stated: "Paragraph 6 of Article 49 of the Fourth Geneva Convention . . . does not admit for exception on grounds of military or security exigencies. It provides that 'the Occupying Power shall not deport or transfer parts of its own civilian population in the territory it occupies.' I agree that this provision applies to the Israeli settlements in the West Bank and that their existence violates Article 49, paragraph 6."

A broad international consensus has also crystallized upholding the Palestinian "right of return." The annual UN resolution, supported overwhelmingly by member states, calls for a settlement of the refugee question on the basis of UNGA resolution 194. This latter resolution "resolves that the refugees wishing to return to their homes and live at peace with their neighbors should be permitted to do so at the earliest practicable date, and that compensation should be paid for property of those choosing not to return." In addition, respected human rights organizations "urge Israel to recognize the right to return for those Palestinians, and their descendants, who fled from territory that is now within the State of Israel, and who have maintained appropriate links with that territory" (HRW), and "call for Palestinians who fled or were expelled from Israel, the West Bank or Gaza Strip, along with those of their descendants who have maintained genuine links with the area, to be able to exercise their right to return" (Amnesty International).[48] The upshot is that a broad consensus has long existed on the

47. Andrew C. Esensten, "Dershowitz Advises Israel on Wall Dispute," *Harvard Crimson* (24 February 2004).

48. "Human Rights Watch Urges Attention to Future of Palestinian Refugees" (21 December 2000), hrw.org/en/news/2000/12/21/human-rights-watch-urges-attention-future-palestinian-refugees; "Israel, Palestinian Leaders Should Guarantee Right of Return as Part

full spectrum of purportedly vexed final status issues—borders, settlements, East Jerusalem, refugees—while Israel's stance on each of these issues has been overwhelmingly rejected by the most representative political body in the international community, as well as by the most authoritative judicial body and human rights organizations in the world.

The Palestinian Authority not only acquiesced in the terms of the global consensus before Cast Lead, but also made significant concessions going beyond it.[49] But what about the Hamas authorities in Gaza? A 2009 study by a US government agency concluded that Hamas had "been carefully and consciously adjusting its political program for years" and had "sent repeated signals that it is ready to begin a process of coexisting with Israel."[50] Just a few months before Cast Lead, Khalid Mishal, the head of Hamas's politburo, stated in an interview that "most Palestinian forces, including Hamas, accept a state on the 1967 borders."[51] Even right after the devastation wreaked by the invasion, Mishal reiterated that "the objective remains the constitution of a Palestinian state with East Jerusalem as its capital, the return of the Israelis to the pre-67 borders and the right of return of our refugees."[52] In a complementary formula, Mishal told former US president Jimmy Carter in 2006 that "Hamas agreed to accept any peace agreement negotiated between the leaders of the PLO [Palestine Liberation Organization] and Israel, provided it is subsequently approved by Palestinians in a referendum or by a democratically

of Comprehensive Refugee Solution" (21 December 2000), hrw.org/en/news/2000/12/21 /israel-palestinian-leaders-should-guarantee-right-return-part-comprehensive-refugee-; Amnesty International, *The Right to Return: The Case of the Palestinians. Policy Statement* (London: 29 March 2001).

49. Finkelstein, *Knowing Too Much*, pp. 229–48.

50. Paul Scham and Osama Abu-Irshaid, *Hamas: Ideological rigidity and political flexibility*, United States Institute of Peace Special Report (Washington, DC: 2009), pp. 2–4. See also Khaled Hroub, "A 'New Hamas' through Its New Documents," *Journal of Palestine Studies* (Summer 2006); and Jeroen Gunning, *Hamas in Politics: Democracy, religion, violence* (New York: 2008), pp. 205–6, 236–37. Hamas's political evolution retraced the PLO's, in which the call for a state in the whole of Palestine was superseded, first by a strategy of "phased" liberation starting with a state in the West Bank and Gaza, and then by acquiescence in a two-state settlement. Shaul Mishal and Avraham Sela, *The Palestinian Hamas: Vision, violence, and coexistence* (New York: 2006), pp. 108–10.

51. Mouin Rabbani, "A Hamas Perspective on the Movement's Evolving Role: An interview with Khalid Mishal, Part II," *Journal of Palestine Studies* (Summer 2008).

52. Gianni Perrelli, "Con Israele non sarà mai pace" (Interview with Khalid Mishal), *L'espresso* (26 February 2009).

elected government."[53] But what about Hamas's notoriously anti-Semitic charter? In fact, from the mid-1990s onward, Hamas "rarely, if at all" invoked its charter, to the point that it "no longer cites or refers" to it.[54] Israeli officials knew full well before they launched Cast Lead that a diplomatic settlement could have been reached with Hamas despite the charter. "The Hamas leadership has recognized that its ideological goal is not attainable and will not be in the foreseeable future," former Mossad head Ephraim Levy observed in 2008. "They are ready and willing to see the establishment of a Palestinian state in the temporary borders of 1967. . . . They know that the moment a Palestinian state is established with their cooperation, . . . [t]hey will have to adopt a path that could lead them far from their original ideological goals."[55]

The flagrant pragmatism of Palestinian leaders figured as a critical factor in Israel's decision to attack. After rejecting Hamas's cease-fire proposals for months, Israel finally agreed to them in June 2008.[56] It's instructive to recall what happened next. Hamas was "careful to maintain the cease-fire," a semiofficial Israeli publication conceded, despite the fact that Israel reneged on the crucial quid pro quo to substantially relax the siege of Gaza. "The lull was sporadically violated by rocket and mortar shell fire, carried out by rogue terrorist organizations," the Israeli source continued. "At the same time, the [Hamas] movement tried to enforce the terms of the arrangement on the other terrorist organizations and to prevent them from violating it."[57] The

53. Jimmy Carter, *We Can Have Peace in the Holy Land: A plan that will work* (New York: 2009), pp. 137, 177. See also Nidal al-Mughrabi, "Hamas Would Honor Referendum on Peace with Israel," *Reuters* (1 December 2010).

54. Khaled Hroub, *Hamas: Political thought and practice* (Washington, DC: 2000), p. 44 (see also p. 254); Sherifa Zuhur, *Hamas and Israel: Conflicting strategies of group-based politics* (Carlisle, PA: 2008), pp. 29–31 (this study was published by the Strategic Studies Institute of the US Army War College). See also Gunning, *Hamas in Politics,* pp. 19–20.

55. "What Hamas Wants," *Mideast Mirror* (22 December 2008).

56. Zuhur, *Hamas and Israel,* pp. ix, 14.

57. Intelligence and Terrorism Information Center at the Israel Intelligence Heritage and Commemoration Center, *The Six Months of the Lull Arrangement* (December 2008), pp. 2, 6, 7; see also point (3) of "Defense Minister Barak's Discussions . . . " (29 August 2008), *WikiLeaks*. According to Egyptians who brokered the 2008 cease-fire, it provided for an immediate cessation of armed hostilities; a gradual lifting of the economic blockade that after ten days would allow for the passage of all products, except materials used in the manufacture of projectiles and explosives; and negotiations after three weeks for a prisoner exchange and the opening of Rafah crossing. International Crisis Group, *Ending the War in Gaza,* p. 3; Carter, *We Can Have Peace,* pp. 137–38. After the abortive coup attempt in 2007, which led to Hamas's consolidation of power in Gaza (see Chapter 1), Israel severely restricted entry of goods "not considered essential for the basic subsistence of the population."

Islamic movement had on this occasion honored its word and consequently made itself a credible negotiating partner. Hamas's acceptance of the two-state settlement, on the one hand, and the cease-fire, on the other, put Israel on the diplomatic defensive. It could no longer justify shunning Hamas, and it was only a matter of time before Europeans renewed dialogue and relations with the Islamic movement. The prospect of an incoming US administration negotiating with Iran and Hamas, and inching closer to the international consensus for settling the Israel-Palestine conflict—which some centrist US policy makers now advocated[58]—threatened to cast a yet more piercing light on Israeli intransigence. In its 2008 annual assessment, the Jewish People Policy Planning Institute, headquartered in Jerusalem and chaired by the redoubtable Dennis Ross, cautioned: "The advent of the new administration in the US could be accompanied by an overall political reassessment . . . the Iran issue could come to be viewed as the key to the stabilization of the Middle East, and . . . a strategy seeking a comprehensive 'regional deal' may be devised, which would include a relatively aggressive effort to resolve the Israeli-Arab conflict."[59] In an alternate scenario, speculated on later by Hezbollah's Nasrallah, the incoming US administration planned to convene an international peace conference of "Americans, Israelis, Europeans and so-called Arab moderates" to impose a settlement. The one obstacle was "Palestinian resistance and the Hamas government in Gaza"; "getting rid of this stumbling block is . . . the true goal" of Cast Lead.[60] In either case, Israel needed to provoke Hamas into resuming its attacks. If Hamas rose to the bait and armed hostilities ensued, it would be disqualified as a legitimate negotiating partner,

It permitted passage of only a "humanitarian minimum"—a benchmark that was arbitrarily determined, not sanctioned by international law, and in fact fell below Gaza's minimal humanitarian needs. When the 2008 cease-fire went into effect, Israel allowed only a "slightly increased" movement of supplies into Gaza. Gisha (Legal Center for Freedom of Movement), *Red Lines Crossed: Destruction of Gaza's infrastructure* (2009), pp. 11, 13, 41–42, 45–46, 50; see also Oxfam et al., *The Middle East Quartet: A progress report* (25 September 2008), pp. 14–15; UNICEF, *Humanitarian Action Update* (23 October 2008); Amnesty International, "Gaza Ceasefire at Risk" (5 November 2008); Gisha, "Israel Reveals Documents Related to the Gaza Closure Policy" (21 October 2010).

58. Richard N. Haass and Martin Indyk, "Beyond Iraq: A new US strategy for the Middle East"; and Walter Russell Mead, "Change They Can Believe In: To make Israel safe, give Palestinians their due," in *Foreign Affairs* (January–February 2009).

59. The Jewish People Policy Planning Institute, *Annual Assessment 2008* (Jerusalem: 2008), p. 27. Ross has been a chief architect of US policy in the Israel-Palestine conflict.

60. Hezbollah Secretary General Sayyed Hassan Nasrallah's Speech Delivered at the Central Ashura Council, 31 December 2008.

as intransigents got the upper hand in internal struggles, or it would be physically wiped out so as to make way for a settlement on Israel's terms.

This was not the first time Israel had confronted such a triple threat—Arab League peace initiative, Palestinian acquiescence in a two-state settlement, Palestinian acceptance of a cease-fire—and it was also not the first time Israel had embarked on provocation and war to nip it in the bud. "By the late 1970s," a pair of Israeli scholars recalled, "the two-state solution had won the support of the Palestinian leadership in the occupied territories as well as that of most Arab states and other members of the international community."[61] In addition, PLO leaders headquartered in Lebanon had strictly adhered to a cease-fire with Israel negotiated in 1981,[62] while Saudi Arabia unveiled in 1981, and the Arab League subsequently approved, a peace plan based on the two-state settlement.[63] Mindful of these ominous developments, Israel stepped up preparations in late 1981 to destroy the PLO.[64] In his analysis of the buildup to Israel's 1982 invasion of Lebanon, Israeli strategic analyst Avner Yaniv reported that PLO leader Yasser Arafat was contemplating a historic compromise with the "Zionist state," whereas "all Israeli cabinets since 1967" as well as "leading mainstream doves" opposed a Palestinian state. Fearing diplomatic pressure, Israel maneuvered to sabotage the two-state settlement by eliminating the PLO as a potential negotiating partner. It conducted punitive military raids "deliberately out of proportion" that targeted "Palestinian and Lebanese civilians," in order to weaken "PLO moderates," strengthen the hand of Arafat's "radical rivals," and guarantee the PLO's "inflexibility." Ultimately, however, Israel had to choose between two stark options: "a political move leading to a historic compromise with the PLO, or preemptive military action against it." To fend off Arafat's "peace offensive"—Yaniv's telling phrase—Israel embarked on military action in June 1982. The Israeli invasion "had been preceded by more than a year of effective cease-fire with the PLO." But after murderous Israeli provocations, the last of which left as many as 200 civilians dead (including 60 occupants of a Palestinian children's hospital), the PLO finally retaliated, causing a single Israeli casualty. Although Israel exploited the PLO's resumption of rocket attacks on northern Israel to justify its invasion ("Operation Peace in

61. Mishal and Sela, *Palestinian Hamas,* p. 14.

62. Chomsky, *Fateful Triangle,* chs. 3, 5.

63. Yehuda Lukacs, ed., *The Israeli-Palestinian Conflict: A documentary record, 1967–1990* (Cambridge: 1992), pp. 477–79.

64. Yehoshaphat Harkabi, *Israel's Fateful Hour* (New York: 1988), p. 101.

the Galilee"), Yaniv concluded that the *"raison d'être* of the entire operation" was "destroying the PLO as a political force capable of claiming a Palestinian state on the West Bank."[65]

Fast-forward to the eve of Cast Lead. In early December 2008, Israeli foreign minister Tzipi Livni posited that although Israel could benefit from a temporary period of calm with Hamas, an extended truce "harms the Israeli strategic goal, empowers Hamas, and gives the impression that Israel recognizes the movement."[66] Translation: a protracted cease-fire that spotlighted Hamas's pragmatism in word and deed, and that consequently increased public pressure on Israel to lift the siege and negotiate a diplomatic settlement, would undercut Israel's strategic goal of entrenching the occupation. In fact, Israel had already resolved to attack Hamas as far back as early 2007 and only acquiesced in the 2008 truce because "the Israeli army needed time to prepare."[67] Once the pieces were in place, Israel still required a pretext to abort the pestiferous cease-fire. On 4 November 2008, while Americans were riveted to the historic election-day returns (Barack Obama was elected president), Israel broke the cease-fire with Hamas[68] by killing Palestinian

65. Avner Yaniv, *Dilemmas of Security: Politics, strategy and the Israeli experience in Lebanon* (Oxford: 1987), pp. 20–23, 50–54, 67–70, 87–89, 100–101, 105–6, 113, 143, 294n46; Robert Fisk, *Pity the Nation: The abduction of Lebanon* (New York: 1990), pp. 197, 232. In his history of the "peace process," Martin Indyk, former US ambassador to Israel, contrived this capsule summary of the sequence of events just narrated: "In 1982, Arafat's terrorist activities eventually provoked the Israeli government of Menachem Begin and Ariel Sharon into a full-scale invasion of Lebanon." Martin Indyk, *Innocent Abroad: An intimate account of American peace diplomacy in the Middle East* (New York: 2009), p. 75.

66. Saed Bannoura, "Livni Calls for a Large Scale Military Offensive in Gaza," IMEMC (8 December 2008); "Livni 'Ashamed' of State of Gaza Truce," *Jerusalem Post* (9 December 2008).

67. Uri Blau, "IDF Sources: Conditions not yet optimal for Gaza exit," *Haaretz* (8 January 2009); Barak Ravid, "Disinformation, Secrecy, and Lies: How the Gaza offensive came about," *Haaretz* (28 December 2008).

68. A careful study covering the period 2000–2008 demonstrated that "overwhelmingly" it was "Israel that kills first after a pause in the conflict." Nancy Kanwisher, Johannes Haushofer, and Anat Biletzki, "Reigniting Violence: How do ceasefires end?," *Huffington Post* (6 January 2009); see also Johannes Haushofer, Anat Biletzki, and Nancy Kanwisher, "Both Sides Retaliate in the Israeli-Palestinian Conflict," *Proceedings of the National Academy of Sciences of the United States* (4 October 2010), which found that Palestinian violence—far from being random and senseless—"reveals a pattern of retaliation." On a related point, it was Israel, not Hamas, that broke the de facto truce after the Gaza redeployment in late 2005. Fully 30 Palestinians were killed in the three months following the redeployment without the death of a single Israeli. Israel also persisted in its illegal practice of "targeted assassinations" despite Hamas's unilateral cease-fire after winning the 2006

militants on the spurious pretext of preempting a Hamas raid.[69] It hoped that the murderous breach would provoke Hamas, and the prayers were answered. "A cease-fire agreed in June between Israel and Palestinian armed groups in Gaza held for four-and-a-half months," Amnesty observed in its annual report, "but broke down after Israeli forces killed six Palestinian militants in air strikes and other attacks on 4 November."[70]

The Israeli attack predictably triggered a resumption of Hamas rocket attacks "in retaliation" (the quoted phrase is from the semiofficial Israeli publication).[71] Still, Hamas was "interested in renewing the relative calm with Israel," according to Israeli internal security chief Yuval Diskin, and it was prepared to accept a "bargain" in which it "would halt the fire in exchange for easing of . . . Israeli policies [that] have kept a choke hold on the economy of the Strip," according to former IDF Gaza commander Shmuel Zakai.[72]

---

election and its concurrent diplomatic démarche to achieve a "peace in stages" with Israel. Jerome Slater, "A Perfect Moral Catastrophe: Just War philosophy and the Israeli attack on Gaza," *Tikkun*, March–April 2009; Jean-Pierre Filiu, *Gaza: A history* (New York: 2014), pp. 288–91. To demonstrate that Hamas is driven not by pragmatism and "legitimate grievance" but instead by murderous ideology, a pair of veteran Israel-apologists pointed to its rocket attacks after Israel's 2005 Gaza redeployment:

> During Hamas's rise to power (January 2006 to April 2008), more than 2,500 rockets were launched from Gaza, landing in Israeli cities and villages. Israel no longer occupies Gaza, but the rockets have largely continued—under Hamas's control. Some say that the rockets are a response to Israeli retaliation. But it is easy to disprove this. If there were no rockets, the odds are very high that Israel would have no reason to retaliate. Even during periods without retaliation, the rocket fire has continued. (Dennis Ross and David Makovsky, *Myths, Illusions and Peace: Finding a new direction for America in the Middle East* [New York: 2009], p. 255 [see also ibid., pp. 138–39, 243, 252])

Once the factual record is restored, it's child's play to disprove their so-called proof: leaving aside that Israel continued to occupy Gaza and then imposed an illegal blockade, it was Israel, not Hamas, that "overwhelmingly" broke the cease-fires.

69. Zvi Bar'el, "Crushing the Tahadiyeh," *Haaretz* (16 November 2008); Uri Avnery, "The Calculations behind Israel's Slaughter of Palestinians in Gaza," *redress.cc* (2 January 2009).

70. *Amnesty International Report 2009: The State of the World's Human Rights* (2009), entry for "Israel and the Occupied Palestinian Territories," pp. 182–83; see also Human Rights Watch, *Rockets from Gaza: Harm to civilians from Palestinian armed groups' rocket attacks* (New York: 2009), p. 2.

71. Intelligence and Terrorism Information Center, *Six Months*, p. 3.

72. "Hamas Wants Better Terms for Truce," *Jerusalem Post* (21 December 2008); Bradley Burston, "Can the First Gaza War Be Stopped before It Starts?," *Haaretz* (22 December 2008). Diskin told the Israeli cabinet that Hamas would renew the truce if Israel lifted the siege of Gaza, stopped military attacks, and extended the truce to the West Bank. Robert Pastor, senior Middle East advisor with the Carter Center, testified that in December

But Israel tightened the suffocating blockade another notch while demanding a unilateral and unconditional cease-fire by Hamas. Even before Israel intensified the blockade, former UN high commissioner for human rights Mary Robinson decried its effects: Gaza's "whole civilization has been destroyed, I'm not exaggerating."[73] By late 2008, Israel had brought Gaza's infrastructure "to the brink of collapse," according to an Israeli human rights organization.[74] "Food, medicine, fuel, parts for water and sanitation systems, fertilizer, plastic sheeting, phones, paper, glue, shoes and even teacups are no longer getting through in sufficient quantities or at all," Harvard political economist Sara Roy reported. "The breakdown of an entire society is happening in front of us, but there is little international response beyond UN warnings which are ignored."[75]

If Hamas had not reacted after the 4 November killings, Israel would almost certainly have ratcheted up its provocations—just as it did in the lead-up to the 1982 Lebanon war—until restraint became politically untenable for Hamas. In any event, faced with the prospect of an asphyxiating Israeli blockade even if it ceased firing rockets, forced to choose between "starvation and fighting,"[76] Hamas opted for resistance, albeit largely symbolic. "You cannot just land blows, leave the Palestinians in Gaza in the economic distress they're in, and expect that Hamas will just sit around and do nothing," the former Israeli commander in Gaza observed.[77] "Our modest, home-made rockets," Hamas leader Khalid Mishal wrote in an open letter during the invasion, "are our cry of protest to the world."[78] But Israel could now enter a

---

2008 he personally presented the Israeli government with an offer from Khalid Mishal to renew the June 2008 cease-fire if Israel ended the blockade, as stipulated in the June cease-fire agreement. Israel balked. "The conclusion," Pastor reported, "seems inescapable": "Israel had the option to open the crossings, and if it had done so, the rockets would have stopped." Robert Pastor, "Memorandum to the UN Fact-Finding Mission on the Gaza Conflict: Operation 'Cast Lead' and the right of self-defense" (6 December 2009); Robert Pastor, "Email: Israeli invasion of Gaza, December 2008" (8 December 2013). Copies on file with this writer.

73. "Gaza Residents 'Terribly Trapped,'" *BBC News* (4 November 2008).

74. Gisha, *Red Lines,* pp. 5, 26, 33.

75. Sara Roy, "If Gaza Falls . . . ," *London Review of Books* (1 January 2009). For a comprehensive description of the blockade in its various phases and crippling long-term impact, see Sara Roy, *The Gaza Strip: The political economy of de-development,* expanded third edition (Washington, DC: 2016), pp. xxx–lxix.

76. International Crisis Group, *Ending the War in Gaza,* pp. 3, 10–11.

77. Burston, "Can the First Gaza War."

78. Khalid Mishal, "This Brutality Will Never Break Our Will to Be Free," *Guardian* (6 January 2009).

plea of self-defense to its willfully gullible Western patrons as it embarked on yet another brutal invasion to foil yet another Palestinian peace offensive. Apart from minor adaptations in the script—the bogey was not "PLO terrorism" but "Hamas terrorism"; the pretext was not shelling in the north but rocket fire in the south—the 2008 reprise stayed remarkably faithful to the 1982 original, as it derailed a functioning cease-fire and preempted a diplomatic settlement of the conflict.[79]

79. It was, incidentally, not the first time Israel sought to provoke Hamas after it mooted a modus vivendi. In September 1997, just days before an abortive Israeli assassination attempt on Khalid Mishal, "Jordan's King Hussein delivered a message from the Hamas leadership to Israel's Prime Minister Benjamin Netanyahu. In it Hamas suggested opening an indirect dialogue with the Israeli government, to be mediated by the king, toward achieving a cessation of violence, as well as a 'discussion of all matters.' But the message was ignored or missed and, in any case, became irrelevant following the attempt" on the Hamas leader's life. Mishal and Sela, *Palestinian Hamas*, p. 72; see also Paul McGeough, *Kill Khalid: The failed Mossad assassination of Khalid Mishal and the rise of Hamas* (New York: 2009), esp. pp. 141, 146, 226.

THREE

Spin Control

DISTRESSED BY THE IMAGES OF CARNAGE coming out of Gaza and flooding the international media, Israel and its supporters set out to restore the Jewish state's tarnished reputation. Shortly after Operation Cast Lead ended on 18 January 2009, Anthony Cordesman published a report titled *The "Gaza War": A strategic analysis.*[1] It warrants close scrutiny both because Cordesman has been an influential military analyst,[2] and because the report neatly synthesized and systematized Israel's makeshift rebuttals as criticism of the invasion mounted.

Cordesman's report overwhelmingly exculpated Israel of wrongdoing, and he explicitly concluded that "Israel did not violate the laws of war."[3] However, Cordesman also entered the "key caveat" that he was not passing a "legal or moral" judgment on Israel's conduct and that "analysts without training in the complex laws of war" should not render such judgments. His full-blooded exoneration, on the one hand, and cautious caveat, on the other, did not easily hang together. He asserted that neither the "laws of war" nor "historical precedents" barred "Israel's use of massive amounts of force," while he also and at the same time refrained from venturing a "legal or moral" judgment

---

1. Anthony H. Cordesman, *The "Gaza War": A strategic analysis* (2009).

2. At the time, Cordesman held the Arleigh A. Burke Chair in Strategy at the Center for Strategic and International Studies and was a national security analyst for ABC News.

3. He allowed only that Israel might have unjustifiably hit "some" civilian targets "like an UNRWA school where 42 Palestinians died." These atrocities rated a two-sentence mention in his 92-page report. "There is no evidence that any abuses of the other narrow limits imposed by laws of war occurred," he continued, "aside from a few limited cases," and the "only significant incident that had as yet emerged was the possible misuse of 20 phosphorus shells in built-up areas in Beit Lahiya." Cordesman, *"Gaza War,"* pp. ii, 1–3, 63–64.

on the "issue of proportionality."[4] In essence, he categorically absolved Israel of criminal guilt even as he went on to plead agnosticism. He also alleged that the laws of war were "often difficult or impossible to apply."[5] If that's the case, whence his conclusion that "Israel did not violate the laws of war"? He additionally purported that the laws of war were biased against Israel because they "do not bind or restrain non-state actors like Hamas."[6] As a practical matter, it is not immediately apparent that the laws of war have bound or restrained Israel either. That said, "the laws of war," according to Harvard law professor Duncan Kennedy, actually "favor conventional over unconventional forces in asymmetric warfare."[7]

The analysis presented by Cordesman was based entirely on "briefings in Israel . . . made possible by a visit sponsored by Project Interchange, and using day-to-day reporting issued by the Israeli Defense Spokesman."[8] Shouldn't he have mentioned that Project Interchange is an affiliate of the reflexively apologetic American Jewish Committee? In the course of his junket, Cordesman put full faith in the pronouncements of Israeli officialdom. Contrariwise, respected Israeli commentators have grown skeptical of Israeli government sources. "The state authorities, including the defense establishment and its branches," Uzi Benziman observed in *Haaretz,* "have acquired for themselves a shady reputation when it comes to their credibility." The "official communiqués published by the IDF [Israel Defense Forces] have progressively liberated themselves from the constraints of truth," B. Michael wrote in *Yediot Ahronot,* and the "heart of the power structure"—that is, the police, army, and intelligence—has been infected by a "culture of lying."[9] During Cast Lead, Israel was repeatedly caught misrepresenting, among many other things, its deployment of white phosphorus.[10] As the invasion got under way, an IDF spokesman informed CNN, "I can tell you with certainty that white phosphorus is absolutely not being used," while IDF chief of staff Gabi Ashkenazi told the Knesset Foreign Affairs and Defense Committee, "The IDF acts only in

4. Ibid., pp. 1, 10.

5. Ibid., p. 2.

6. Ibid.

7. Duncan Kennedy, "A Context for Gaza," *Harvard Crimson* (2 February 2009).

8. Cordesman, *"Gaza War,"* p. ii.

9. Uzi Benziman, "Until Proved Otherwise," *Haaretz* (18 June 2006); B. Michael, "Of Liars and Hunters," *Yediot Ahronot* (3 September 2005); B. Michael, "Stop the Lying!," *Yediot Ahronot* (5 September 2008). See also Gideon Levy, "Israel: Where the media will blindly buy what the ruling authorities dictate," *Haaretz* (27 August 2016).

10. Kenneth Roth, "The Incendiary IDF," *Human Rights Watch* (22 January 2009).

accordance with what is permitted by international law and does not use white phosphorus."[11] Even after numerous human rights organizations conclusively documented Israel's illegal use of white phosphorus, an Israeli "military inquiry" persisted in these prevarications.[12] A former senior Pentagon analyst and senior military analyst with Human Rights Watch (HRW), recalling Israel's train of lies during both the 2006 Lebanon war and Cast Lead, rhetorically asked, "How can anyone trust the Israeli military?"[13]

A chunk of Cordesman's "strategic analysis" consisted of reproducing verbatim the daily press releases of the Israeli air force and army spokespersons. He obligingly dubbed them "chronologies" of the war, alleged that they offer "considerable insight" into what happened,[14] and recycled them multiple times. For example, he repeatedly peppered his text with each of these statements or versions thereof: "The IDF will continue operating against terror operatives and anyone involved, including those sponsoring and hosting terrorists, in addition to those that send innocent women and children to be used as human shields"; "The IDF will not hesitate to strike those involved both directly and indirectly in attacks against the citizens of the State of Israel"; "The IDF will continue to operate against Hamas terror infrastructure in the Gaza Strip according to plans in order to reduce the rocket fire on the south of Israel"; "IDF Infantry Corps, Armored Corps, Engineering Corps, Artillery Corps and Intelligence Corps forces continued to operate during the night against Hamas terrorist infrastructure throughout the Gaza Strip."[15] Much of Cordesman's report, in other words, simply reiterated ad nauseam the Israeli military's generic PR materials. Meanwhile, on a specific point of contention, he reproduced an Israeli press release claiming that Israel hit "a vehicle transporting a stockpile of Grad missiles."[16] But an investigation by B'Tselem (Israeli Information Center for Human Rights in the Occupied Territories) at the time found, and the IDF eventually conceded,

11. Ben Wedeman, "Group Accuses Israel of Firing White Phosphorus into Gaza," *CNN* (12 January 2009); Robert Marquand and Nicholas Blanford, "Gaza: Israel under fire for alleged white phosphorus use," *Christian Science Monitor* (14 January 2009).

12. B'Tselem (Israeli Information Center for Human Rights in the Occupied Territories), "Military Rejects Horrific Results of Use of White Phosphorus in Operation Cast Lead" (21 May 2009); see also Dinah PoKempner, "Valuing the Goldstone Report," *Global Governance* 16 (2010), p. 149.

13. Amira Hass, "In the Rockets' Red Glare," *Haaretz* (15 January 2009).

14. Cordesman, *"Gaza War,"* pp. 20, 27.

15. Ibid., pp. 20–27 passim, 42–57 passim.

16. Ibid., p. 22.

that they were almost certainly oxygen canisters.[17] The vehicle was targeted in a precision drone-missile attack that left eight civilians dead, although according to HRW, "the drone's advanced imaging equipment should have enabled the drone operator to determine the nature of the objects under surveillance."[18] It would appear that the Israeli drone operator premeditatedly targeted a civilian vehicle carrying noncombatants. Cordesman also alleged that official Israeli data were "far more credible" than non-Israeli data, such as from UN sources. He based this conclusion on, among other things, the fact that "many Israelis feel that such UN sources are strongly biased in favor of the Palestinians."[19] Should the Israeli figure that Hamas fighters comprised two-thirds of the casualties in Gaza be credited,[20] even as it was belied by every reputable independent source?[21] Cordesman trumpeted, in particular, the exceptional care that Israel took during Cast Lead to limit civilian casualties and damage to civilian infrastructure. He alleged that "every aspect" of the Israeli air force's targeting plan "was based on a detailed target analysis that explicitly evaluated the risk to civilians and the location of sensitive sites like schools, hospitals, mosques, churches, and other holy sites"; that Israel used the "smallest possible weapon" coupled with precision intelligence and guidance systems to "deconflict military targeting from damage to civilian facilities"; that "Israel did plan its air and air-land campaigns in ways that clearly discriminated between military and civilian targets and that were intended to limit civilian casualties and collateral

17. B'Tselem (Israeli Information Center for Human Rights in the Occupied Territories), "Suspicion: Bombed truck carried oxygen tanks and not Grad rockets" (31 December 2008); Israel Ministry of Foreign Affairs, "Conclusions of Investigations into Central Claims and Issues in Operation Cast Lead—Part 2" (22 April 2009).

18. Human Rights Watch, *Precisely Wrong: Gaza civilians killed by Israeli drone-launched missiles* (2009), pp. 17–21.

19. Cordesman, *"Gaza War,"* pp. 58, 62.

20. Ibid., p. 58; Amos Harel, "Israel: Two-thirds of Palestinians killed in Gaza fighting were terrorists," *Haaretz* (13 February 2009); Yaakov Katz, "IDF: World duped by Hamas's false civilian death toll figures," *Jerusalem Post* (15 February 2009).

21. Israel's inflationary tally of enemy combatant deaths during Cast Lead fit a familiar pattern. Whereas it alleged after the 2006 war that 60 percent of Lebanese casualties were Hezbollah fighters, all independent sources put the figure at closer to 20 percent. William Arkin, *Divining Victory: Airpower in the 2006 Israel-Hezbollah war* (Maxwell Air Force Base, AL: 2007), p. 74; Human Rights Watch, *Why They Died: Civilian casualties in Lebanon during the 2006 war* (2007), pp. 76, 79; Mitchell Prothero, "Hizbollah Builds Up Covert Army for a New Assault against Israel," *Observer* (27 April 2008); Alastair Crooke and Mark Perry, "How Hezbollah Defeated Israel; Part 2, Winning the Ground War," *Asia Times* (13 October 2006).

damage."[22] If he confidently attested to these precautions, that's because his Israeli interlocutors and Israeli press releases repeatedly attested to them.

Israel had to cope not only with adverse media coverage during Cast Lead but also with an avalanche of postwar human rights reports condemning its prosecution of the invasion. Because of the sheer number of them, the broad array of reputable organizations issuing them, and the uniformity of their principal conclusions, these reports could not easily be dismissed as anti-Israel propaganda.[23] Although the reports made extensive use of Palestinian eyewitnesses, these testimonies also could not easily be dismissed as Hamas-inspired or tainted by Hamas intimidation. "Delegates who visited Gaza during and after Operation 'Cast Lead,'" Amnesty International observed, "were able to carry out their investigations unhindered and people often voiced criticisms of Hamas's conduct, including rocket attacks."[24]

The widespread censure by human rights professionals compelled Israel in 2009 to issue a "factual and legal" brief in its defense, *The Operation in Gaza*.[25] It alleged that these critical human rights reports "too often" amounted to a "rush to judgment," inasmuch as they were published "within a matter of hours,

---

22. Cordesman, *"Gaza War,"* pp. 16–17, 63.

23. The ensuing exposition focuses on violations of international humanitarian and human rights law resulting directly from Cast Lead. Some human rights reports also documented indirect violations, such as Hamas repression of Fatah members in Gaza and reciprocal Palestinian Authority repression of Hamas members in the West Bank, as well as Israel's repression of dissent in Israel and the West Bank, and its failure to provide air-raid shelters for Bedouins in southern Israel.

24. Amnesty International, *Operation "Cast Lead": 22 Days of death and destruction* (2009), p. 4. The Goldstone Report noted that it was "faced with a certain reluctance by the persons it interviewed in Gaza to discuss the activities of the armed groups." It nonetheless found that Palestinian testimonies could be vetted for accuracy:

> Taking into account the demeanor of witnesses, the plausibility of their accounts and the consistency of these accounts with the circumstances observed by it and with other testimonies, the Mission was able to determine the credibility and reliability of those people it heard.... The final conclusions on the reliability of the information received were made taking all of these matters into consideration, cross-referencing the relevant material and information, and assessing whether, in all the circumstances, there was sufficient information of a credible and reliable nature for the Mission to make a finding in fact." (*Report of the United Nations Fact-Finding Mission on the Gaza Conflict* [25 September 2009], paras. 35, 170–71, 440; hereafter: Goldstone Report)

The somewhat discrepant experiences of Amnesty and the Goldstone Mission might be accounted for by the higher profile of the Mission, which prompted greater intrusion by Hamas and, concomitantly, greater circumspection by the population.

25. The State of Israel, *The Operation in Gaza, 27 December 2008–18 January 2009: Factual and legal aspects* (2009).

days or weeks" after Cast Lead.[26] In fact, most of the reports came out months later. The critical evidence adduced in the Israeli brief consisted largely of testimonies extracted from Palestinian detainees during "interrogation." The circumstances surrounding these alleged confessions cast doubt on their evidentiary value. The Goldstone Report found that Palestinian detainees rounded up during Cast Lead were "subjected ... to cruel, inhuman and degrading treatment throughout their ordeal in order to terrorize, intimidate and humiliate them. The men were made to strip, sometimes naked, at different stages of their detention. All the men were handcuffed in a most painful manner and blindfolded, increasing their sense of fear and helplessness"; "Men, women and children were held close to artillery and tank positions, where constant shelling and firing was taking place, thus not only exposing them to danger, but increasing their fear and terror"; Palestinian detainees were "subjected to beatings and other physical abuse that amounts to torture," were "used as human shields," and were subjected to "methods of interrogation [that] amounted not only to torture ... but also to physical and moral coercion of civilians to obtain information."[27] It would appear then that the "confessions" of these Palestinian detainees should be taken with a boulder of salt.

Parrying the censorious thrust of these human rights reports, Israel's brief declared that it "took extensive measures to comply with its obligations under international law," and that the IDF's "mode of operation reflected the extensive training of IDF soldiers to respect the obligations imposed under international law."[28] In particular, it alleged that Israeli forces fired only on legitimate targets and exercised maximum feasible caution. The IDF directed attacks "solely against military objectives," and endeavored to ensure that "civilians and civilian objects would not be harmed"; "where incidental damage to civilians or civilian property could not be avoided, the IDF made extraordinary efforts to ensure that it would not be excessive"; the IDF "used the least destructive munitions possible to achieve legitimate military objectives," as well as "sophisticated precision weapons to minimize the harm to civilians"; the IDF "carefully checked and cross-checked targets ... to make sure they were being used for combat or terrorist activities, and not instead solely for civilian use."[29]

26. Ibid., para. 34. To be sure, Israel was not wholly dismissive of these human rights reports. It did affirmatively cite one that condemned Hamas suicide bombings (ibid., p. 52n139).

27. Goldstone Report, paras. 1107–64 passim.

28. State of Israel, *Operation in Gaza,* paras. 22, 25.

29. Ibid., paras. 6, 8, 84, 115, 222–23.

Based on what journalists and human rights organizations found, and what Israeli soldiers in the field later testified, however, a radically different picture of Cast Lead comes into relief. "We're going to war," a company commander told his soldiers before the attack. "I want aggressiveness—if there's someone suspicious on the upper floor of a house, we'll shell it. If we have suspicions about a house, we'll take it down. . . . There will be no hesitation."[30] A combatant remembered a meeting with his brigade commander and others where the "rules of engagement" were "essentially" conveyed as, "if you see any signs of movement at all you shoot."[31] Other soldiers recalled, "If the deputy battalion commander thought a house looked suspect, we'd blow it away. If the infantrymen didn't like the looks of that house—we'd shoot" (unidentified soldier); "If you face an area that is hidden by a building—you take down the building. Questions such as 'who lives in that building[?]' are not asked" (soldier recalling his brigade commander's order); "As for rules of engagement, the army's working assumption was that the whole area would be devoid of civilians. . . . Anyone there, as far as the army was concerned, was to be killed" (unidentified soldier); "We were told: 'any sign of danger, open up with massive fire'" (member of a reconnaissance company); "We shot at anything that moved" (Golani Brigade fighter); "Despite the fact that no one fired on us, the firing and demolitions continued incessantly" (gunner in a tank crew).[32] "Essentially, a person only need[ed] to be in a 'problematic' location," a *Haaretz* reporter found, "in circumstances that can broadly be seen as suspicious, for him to be 'incriminated' and in effect sentenced to death."[33]

Although the Israeli brief purported that "the protection of IDF troops did not override all other factors,"[34] both journalistic investigations and the

30. Amos Harel, "Testimonies on IDF Misconduct in Gaza Keep Rolling In," *Haaretz* (22 March 2009).

31. Donald Macintyre, "Israeli Commander: 'We rewrote the rules of war for Gaza,'" *Independent* (3 February 2010).

32. Anshel Pfeffer, "Gaza Soldiers Speak Out," *Jewish Chronicle* (5 March 2009); Breaking the Silence, *Soldiers' Testimonies from Operation Cast Lead, Gaza 2009* (Jerusalem: 2009), pp. 24 (Testimony 9), 29 (Testimony 10), 62 (Testimony 26). The Goldstone Report disputed the IDF's premise that Palestinian civilians would already have fled areas under Israeli attack (para. 522); on this point, see also Public Committee against Torture in Israel (PCATI), *No Second Thoughts: The changes in the Israeli Defense Forces' combat doctrine in light of "Operation Cast Lead"* (2009), pp. 18–19.

33. Amos Harel, "What Did the IDF Think Would Happen in Gaza?," *Haaretz* (27 March 2009).

34. State of Israel, *Operation in Gaza,* para. 232.

testimonies of Israeli combatants suggested otherwise. "Israelis would have trouble accepting heavy Israel Defense Forces losses," *Haaretz* reported in its reconstruction of the invasion's planning stage, so the army resorted to "overwhelming firepower. . . . The lives of our soldiers take precedence, the commanders were told in briefings." (The IDF General Staff anticipated before the onslaught that "600–800 Palestinian civilians" would be killed.[35]) It was an "atmosphere," one IDF soldier remembered, in which "the lives of Palestinians, let's say, is something very, very less important than the lives of our soldiers." Another combatant recalled the order of his battalion commander, "Not a hair will fall off a soldier of mine, and I am not willing to allow a soldier of mine to risk himself by hesitating. If you are not sure—shoot," while a squad commander recollected how the IDF "used a huge amount of firepower and killed a huge number of people along the way, so that we wouldn't get hurt and they wouldn't fire on us."[36] "When we suspect that a Palestinian fighter is hiding in a house, we shoot it with a missile and then with two tank shells, and then a bulldozer hits the wall," a senior IDF officer told *Haaretz*. "It causes damage but it prevents the loss of life among soldiers."[37] An officer who served at a brigade headquarters recalled a year after the invasion that IDF policy amounted to ensuring "literally zero risk to the soldiers."[38]

Still, didn't Israel try to protect civilians by forewarning them of imminent attacks? "Israel distributed hundreds of thousands of leaflets," Cordesman touted, "and used its intelligence on cell phone networks in Gaza to issue warnings to civilians."[39] The Israeli brief pointed up its "extraordinary steps to avoid harming civilians in its Gaza Operation" and "significant efforts to minimize harm to civilians," such as dropping "leaflets warning occupants to stay away from Hamas strongholds and leave buildings that Hamas was using to launch attacks," and contacting "occupants by telephone, to warn of impending attacks on particular buildings."[40] But the leaflets and phone calls "failed to give details of the areas to be targeted," according to

35. Harel, "What Did the IDF Think."

36. Breaking the Silence, *Soldiers' Testimonies,* p. 20 (Testimony 7); Amos Harel, "IDF in Gaza: Killing civilians, vandalism, and lax rules of engagement," *Haaretz* (18 March 2009); Amos Harel, "Shooting and Crying," *Haaretz* (19 March 2009).

37. Amos Harel, "IDF Officer: 'It will take many years to restore' bombwracked Gaza," *Haaretz* (7 January 2009).

38. Macintyre, "Israeli Commander."

39. Cordesman, *"Gaza War,"* p. 17.

40. State of Israel, *Operation in Gaza,* paras. 8, 17, 24, 138, 141, 154, 262–65.

human rights reports, "and conversely which areas were safe." Moreover, because the entirety of Gaza came under attack, on the one hand, and its borders with Israel and Egypt were sealed, on the other, there was "nowhere for the civilian population to have gone." The inevitable and foreseeable consequence of these so-called warnings, amid the indiscriminate and sustained bombing and shelling of this tightly sealed territory, was, according to a fact-finding committee led by South African jurist John Dugard, "a state of terror, confusion, and panic among the local population."[41] Indeed, Israeli interior minister Meir Sheetrit alleged that "the army called [sic] 250,000 telephone calls to the people to leave their houses." Nonplussed, Amnesty rejoined: "There are barely 250,000 households in Gaza. If indeed the Israeli army called that many families to tell them to leave their homes, this would mean that virtually every family was told to do so."[42] How could pandemonium and mayhem *not* have ensued? Nonetheless, deeply impressed by the quantity of Israeli warnings, an American legal scholar contended in a novel interpretative twist that these warnings should be credited even as Palestinians could not heed them: "the law contains no requirement that the civilian population be able to act on the warnings in order to find them effective."[43] Is it "effec-

---

41. *Report of the Independent Fact-Finding Committee on Gaza: No safe place,* presented to the League of Arab States (30 April 2009), para. 13 of Executive Summary; paras. 283–99, 467–68, 483, 490; hereafter: Dugard Report. On a related note, the report observed:

> In order to provide a meaningful warning by telephone, the IDF would have to be aware not only of the telephone numbers of the residents of Gaza, but more importantly of the numbers of the residents in a particular building or area. The Committee is not aware of how the IDF managed to obtain and confirm this information when the majority of telephones in Gaza are mobile or cell phones and are not associated with a particular address or location, and when the utility of advising someone to vacate on their mobile phone requires knowledge of their actual location. (Ibid., para. 293 [see also ibid., para. 467])

For a "clearly documented and large-scale case, reported in real time, that the IDF only paid lip service regarding the warnings to civilians to minimize damage," see PCATI, *No Second Thoughts,* pp. 17–18. See also Human Rights Watch, *White Flag Deaths: Killings of Palestinian civilians during Operation Cast Lead* (New York: August 2009), p. 5; Goldstone Report, paras. 37, 501–2, 511, 515, 531–42 (the Report allowed that warnings might have been effective in "some" instances); and PoKempner, "Valuing the Goldstone Report," p. 152.

42. Jeremy Bowen, "Gaza Stories: Israeli minister," interview with Meir Sheetrit, *BBC News* (9 February 2009); Amnesty International, *Operation "Cast Lead,"* pp. 3, 50–51. The Israeli brief reported "more than 165,000 phone calls warning civilians to distance themselves from military targets," while the IDF's senior legal advisor alleged that "more than 250,000" calls were made. State of Israel, *Operation in Gaza,* paras. 8, 264; Yaakov Katz, "Security and Defense: Waging war on the legal front," *Jerusalem Post* (18 September 2009).

43. Laurie R. Blank, "The Application of IHL in the Goldstone Report: A critical commentary," *Yearbook of International Law* 12 (2009), pp. 47–48.

tive" to post signs warning, *In case of fire, use emergency exit*, if the building doesn't have an emergency exit?

Israel's brief not only foregrounded its prior warnings during Cast Lead but also played up its relief efforts. It alleged that Israel "sought to provide and facilitate humanitarian assistance," and implemented a "far-reaching effort to ensure that the humanitarian needs of the civilian population in Gaza were met."[44] If this solicitude occasioned skepticism, Cordesman laid it to rest. He brandished Israeli press releases as well as "Israeli Ministry of Defense claims" affirming it, and even cited no lesser a personage than Defense Minister Ehud Barak: "We are well aware of the humanitarian concerns; we are doing and will continue to do everything possible to provide all humanitarian needs to the residents of Gaza."[45] The facts on the ground looked rather different, however. "UN agencies and humanitarian NGOs continued to carry out operations despite extreme insecurity," the United Nations Office for the Coordination of Humanitarian Affairs (OCHA) observed. "In the course of the three weeks of hostilities, five UNRWA [United Nations Relief and Works Agency] staff and three of its contractors were killed while on duty, and another 11 staff and four contractors were injured; four incidents of aid convoys being shot at have been reported; at least 53 United Nations buildings sustained damage."[46] Foreign Minister Tzipi Livni audaciously declared in the midst of Cast Lead that "no humanitarian crisis" existed in Gaza. But UNRWA's director of operations fired back: "We have a catastrophe unfolding in Gaza for the civilian population. ... They're trapped, they're traumatized, they're terrorized."[47] Although entering some generic caveats acknowledging Israel's "delays and mistakes" in its relief efforts, and although citing countless Israeli press releases, Cordesman could not find the space to quote this or numerous other critical statements by relief organizations and UN officials.[48] The Goldstone Report concluded that Israel "violated its obligation to allow free passage of all consignments of medical and hospital objects, food and clothing"; that "the

44. State of Israel, *Operation in Gaza*, paras. 86, 266.

45. Cordesman, *"Gaza War,"* pp. 37, 64.

46. United Nations Office for the Coordination of Humanitarian Affairs (OCHA), *Humanitarian Monitor* (January 2009); see also Amnesty International, *Operation "Cast Lead,"* pp. 51–53.

47. Hazem Balousha and Chris McGreal, "Tanks, Rockets, Death and Terror: A civilian catastrophe unfolding," *Guardian* (5 January 2009).

48. Cordesman, *"Gaza War,"* p. 64.

amounts and types of food, medical and hospital items and clothing [allowed in] were wholly insufficient to meet the humanitarian needs of the population"; and that from its tightening of the blockade in 2007 to the end of the invasion, Israel impeded passage of sufficient goods "to meet the needs of the population."[49] Even after the January 2009 cease-fire went into effect, Israel persisted in blocking humanitarian assistance, including shipments of chickpeas, dates, tea, macaroni, sweets, jam, biscuits, tomato paste, children's puzzles, and plastic bags to distribute food.[50] "Little of the extensive damage [Israel] caused to homes, civilian infrastructure, public services, farms and businesses has been repaired," 16 respected humanitarian and human rights organizations reported in a comprehensive study released one year after the invasion. "This is not an accident; it is a matter of policy. The Israeli government's blockade ... not only forbids most Gazans from leaving or exporting anything to the outside world, but also only permits the import of a narrowly restricted number of basic humanitarian goods." The study found that as a direct result of the continuing Israeli blockade, "all kinds of construction materials—cement, gravel, wood, pipes, glass, steel bars, aluminum, tar—and spare parts are in desperately short supply or completely unavailable"; "90 percent of the people of Gaza continue to suffer power cuts of four to eight hours a day—while the rest still have no power at all"; thousands were left "to an existence without piped water"; and there were "long delays in or denial of entry of basic educational supplies such as textbooks and paper," while "children, already traumatized by the military offensive, cannot learn and develop in these unsafe and unsanitary conditions."[51]

Israel's interference with humanitarian relief efforts during Cast Lead was of a piece with its broader assault on UN agencies and Gazan medical facilities. After Israel fired white phosphorus shells at an UNRWA installation, setting it ablaze, UN secretary-general Ban Ki-moon gave public vent to his anger: "I am just appalled ... it is an outrageous and totally unacceptable attack against the United Nations."[52] A UN-commissioned Board of Inquiry

49. Goldstone Report, paras. 72, 317, 1297, 1315; see also para. 1299 for Israeli misrepresentation of the amounts and types of humanitarian provisions it allowed into Gaza.

50. Human Rights Watch, "Choking Gaza Harms Civilians" (18 February 2009); OCHA, "Field Update on Gaza from the Humanitarian Coordinator" (10–16 March 2009); see also Amira Hass, "Israel Bans Books, Music, and Clothes from Entering Gaza," *Haaretz* (17 May 2009).

51. Amnesty International et al., *Failing Gaza: No rebuilding, no recovery, no more excuses* (2009), pp. 3, 6, 10, 12.

52. UN News Center, "Opening Remarks at Press Conference" (20 January 2009).

that investigated assaults on multiple UN sites during Cast Lead found Israel culpable inter alia for a "direct and intentional strike" that killed three young men at an UNRWA school sheltering some four hundred civilians; firing a "series of mortar shells" that struck the immediate vicinity of an UNRWA school, killing and injuring scores of civilians; a "grossly negligent" white phosphorus attack amounting to "recklessness" on the "hub and nerve center for all UNRWA operations in Gaza"; and a "highly negligent" white phosphorus attack amounting to "reckless disregard" on an UNRWA school sheltering some 2,000 civilians, killing 2 children and injuring 13. (It also found that in one incident a UN warehouse was damaged by a Qassam-type rocket that "had most likely been fired from inside Gaza by Hamas or another Palestinian faction.") The Board of Inquiry concluded that "no military activity was carried out from within United Nations premises in any of the incidents"; that Israel "must have expected" that Palestinians would respond to the "ongoing attacks by seeking refuge within UNRWA premises"; and that Israel "continued" to make false allegations that Hamas militants had been firing from UN premises even "after it ought to have been known that they were untrue."[53] Still, denigrating the UN report as "unfair and one-sided," Israeli president Shimon Peres declared, "We will never accept it. It's outrageous." The Defense Ministry alleged that an internal IDF investigation "irrefutably" belied the board's findings, yet again demonstrating—if further vindication were still needed—that "we have the most moral army in the world."[54]

The humanitarian crisis was exacerbated as Israel's assault targeted and took a heavy toll on Gaza's medical facilities. Already before Cast Lead, Israel had deprived ailing Gazans of access to medical care abroad and held them

---

53. UN General Assembly, *Letter dated 4 May 2009 from the Secretary-General addressed to the President of the Security Council: Summary by the Secretary-General of the report of the United Nations Headquarters Board of Inquiry into certain incidents in the Gaza Strip between 27 December 2008 and 19 January 2009* (2009), A/63/855-S/2009/250, paras. 10–28, 46–67, 77–84, 97, 100, 107. Opting (or pressured) to shield the report from public scrutiny, Ban Ki-moon released only a summary of it. He was arm-twisted by the Obama administration to reject in his cover letter to the report the Board of Inquiry's recommendation that the incidents be further investigated. See Jamie Stern-Weiner, "Ban Ki-moon Stars in Live Puppet Show" (22 June 2015), jamiesternweiner.wordpress.com/2015/06/22/ban-ki-moon-stars-in-live-puppet-show/.

54. Barak Ravid, "Peres Tells Ban: Israel will never accept UN Gaza probe," *Haaretz* (7 May 2009); Barak Ravid, "Barak: IDF did not mean to shoot at UN facilities in Gaza," *Haaretz* (5 May 2009).

hostage to collaborating with Israeli intelligence in exchange for an exit permit.[55] The Israeli brief crowed that during the invasion it facilitated the transfer abroad of many Gazan patients requiring treatment.[56] But human rights organizations reported that Israel created nearly insuperable obstacles preventing injured Gazans from accessing such treatment.[57] The medical disaster caused by Israel's denial of access abroad was complemented and compounded by Israel's assault on medical facilities inside Gaza. In the course of Cast Lead, direct or indirect Israeli attacks damaged or destroyed 29 ambulances and almost half of Gaza's 122 health facilities, including 15 hospitals. Fully 16 medical personnel were killed and a further 25 injured while on duty.[58] Cordesman faithfully echoed Israel's claim that it "coordinated the movement" of ambulances, and the Israeli brief spotlighted "a special medical coordination center" set up by it to handle the "evacuation of the wounded and dead from areas of hostilities."[59] But according to B'Tselem, "even where coordination was arranged, soldiers reportedly fired at ambulances."[60] A Physicians for Human Rights–Israel report documented Israeli attacks on medical crews and ambulances, as well as "countless" Israeli obstacles blocking the path of "rescue teams in the field that attempted to evacuate trapped and injured persons."[61] A supplementary

55. Physicians for Human Rights–Israel, *Holding Health to Ransom: GSS interrogation and extortion of Palestinian patients at Erez crossing* (2008).

56. State of Israel, *Operation in Gaza*, para. 274.

57. Between 2006 and the end of Cast Lead, nearly 300 Gazans seeking health care abroad died because of the border closure. Al Mezan Center for Human Rights, "Yet Another Child Casualty Due to Israel's Closure Policies" (2009). On a related note, Cordesman credited the Israeli accusation that Hamas "prevent[ed] medical evacuation of Palestinians to Israel," although in fact Hamas had no control over such medical referrals. After the cease-fire came into effect on 18 January, Israel opened a "humanitarian clinic" at the Erez crossing, but by this time the medical emergency had passed and Palestinian officials ignored it. The facility was widely perceived (including by Physicians for Human Rights–Israel) as an Israeli public relations stunt. On 28 January, Israel announced the closure of the clinic due to the absence of patients. Cordesman, *"Gaza War,"* p. 66; Physicians for Human Rights–Israel, *"Ill Morals": Grave violations of the right to health during the Israeli assault on Gaza* (2009), pp. 18–20, 23, 51.

58. Jan McGirk, "Gaza's Health and Humanitarian Situation Remains Fragile," *Lancet* (4 February 2009); Amnesty International et al., *Failing Gaza*, p. 11.

59. Cordesman, *"Gaza War,"* p. 64; State of Israel, *Operation in Gaza*, para. 274.

60. B'Tselem (Israeli Information Center for Human Rights in the Occupied Territories), *Guidelines for Israel's Investigation into Operation Cast Lead, 27 December 2008–18 January 2009* (Jerusalem: 2009), p. 14.

61. Physicians for Human Rights–Israel, *"Ill Morals,"* p. 35.

report by an independent team of medical experts commissioned by Physicians for Human Rights–Israel and the Palestinian Medical Relief Society found that Israel "prohibited" wounded Gazans "from being evacuated by ambulances," and that it "targeted" ambulances and their crews. It concluded that the "underlying meaning of the attack on the Gaza Strip appears to be one of creating terror without mercy to anyone."[62] The normally discreet International Committee of the Red Cross issued a public rebuke of Israel after a "shocking incident" in which Israeli soldiers turned back a Red Cross rescue team dispatched to aid injured civilians, leaving them to die.[63] The Al Mezan Center for Human Rights tallied that Israel's systematic obstruction of medical access during the invasion caused the deaths of at least 258 Gazans.[64]

But didn't Hamas commandeer and make nefarious use of ambulances? Cordesman alleged that Hamas used "ambulances to mobilize terrorists," but he adduced no evidence.[65] The Israeli brief contended that Hamas made "extensive use of ambulances bearing the protective emblems of the Red Cross and Red Crescent to transport operatives and weaponry" and "use of ambulances to 'evacuate' terrorists from the battlefield." The only independent proof it could muster, however, didn't exactly overwhelm: a fabulating Italian "reporter," on the one hand, and a Gazan ambulance driver who recounted how Hamas militants sought, unsuccessfully, to commandeer his vehicle, on the other.[66] The Israeli brief goes so far as to allege that "the IDF refrained from attacking medical vehicles *even* in cases where Hamas and

62. Sebastian Van As et al., *Final Report: Independent fact-finding mission into violations of human rights in the Gaza Strip during the period 27.12.2008–18.01.2009* (Brussels: 2009), p. 77.

63. "Gaza: ICRC demands urgent access to wounded as Israeli army fails to assist wounded Palestinians," press release (8 January 2009).

64. Al Mezan Center for Human Rights, *Bearing the Brunt Again: Child rights violations during Operation Cast Lead* (2009), p. 32.

65. Cordesman, "*Gaza War,*" p. 65.

66. State of Israel, *Operation in Gaza,* paras. 7, 23, 141, 171, 174, 176, 177–79, 371–72, 377–80; see also Intelligence and Terrorism Information Center, *Hamas and the Terrorist Threat from the Gaza Strip: The main findings of the Goldstone Report versus the factual findings* (2010), pp. V, 173–77 (this document also cited evidence gleaned from a "Fatah-affiliated website"). The Israeli brief is dotted with references to the dubious reportage of Italian journalist Lorenzo Cremonesi. It prudently did not, however, cite Cremonesi's sensational finding that altogether "not more than 500–600" Gazans perished during Cast Lead. If that figure were accurate, then not only did human rights organizations exaggerate the Palestinian death toll, but Israel itself also inflated it. Lorenzo Cremonesi, "Così i ragazzini di Hamas ci hanno utilizzato come bersagli," *Corriere della Sera* (21 January 2009); "Palestinians Confirm Hamas War Crimes, Refute Gaza Death Toll," *Israel Today* (22 January 2009).

other terrorist organizations were using them for military purposes."[67] But if the IDF didn't target ambulances commandeered by Hamas for military purposes, and if "there is absolutely no doubt" that the IDF "targeted a large number of ambulances,"[68] then the ambulances it targeted must *not* have been used for military purposes. "The argument that Palestinians abused ambulances has been raised numerous times by Israeli officials," B'Tselem recalled, "although Israel has almost never presented evidence to prove it."[69] Indeed, Israel had targeted clearly marked Lebanese ambulances with missile fire during the 2006 war, even though, according to HRW, there was "no basis for concluding that Hezbollah was making use of the ambulances for a military purpose."[70] But what about Cast Lead? The Goldstone Report "did not find any evidence to support the allegations that . . . ambulances were used to transport combatants or for other military purposes." If doubts lingered on this score, they were squelched by Magen David Adom, Israel's national emergency medical, disaster, ambulance, and blood bank service. It unequivocally attested that "there was no use of PRCS [Palestinian Red Crescent Society] ambulances for the transport of weapons or ammunition."[71] Still, didn't Hamas militants fire from and take refuge in hospitals? "Vast amounts of . . . information, from both intelligence sources and reports from IDF forces on the ground," Israel contended, "show that Hamas did in fact make extensive military use of hospitals and other medical facilities."[72] But according to Amnesty, Israeli officials did not provide "evidence for even one such case." Amnesty itself "found no evidence during its on-the-ground investigation that such practices, if they did occur, were widespread"; Physicians for Human Rights–Israel did not find "any evidence supporting Israel's official claim that hospitals were used to conceal political or military personnel"; the Goldstone Report "did not find any evidence to support the allegations that hospital facilities were used by the Gaza authorities or by

67. State of Israel, *Operation in Gaza,* para. 371, emphasis in original.

68. Sebastian Van As et al., *Final Report,* p. 77.

69. B'Tselem, *Guidelines,* p. 16. See also Norman G. Finkelstein, *Beyond Chutzpah: On the misuse of anti-Semitism and the abuse of history,* expanded paperback edition (Berkeley: 2008), pp. 128–30, and Ed O'Loughlin, "Israel Withdraws Disputed Footage," *Age* (8 October 2004).

70. Human Rights Watch, *Why They Died,* p. 160.

71. Goldstone Report, paras. 36, 468–73 (Magen David Adom testimony at para. 473), 485.

72. Intelligence and Terrorism Information Center, *Hamas and the Terrorist Threat,* p. 164; see also State of Israel, *Operation in Gaza,* paras. 7, 23, 141, 171–72, 175.

Palestinian armed groups to shield military activities."[73] The Israeli brief further contended that the IDF "refrained from attacking Shifa Hospital in Gaza City, despite Hamas's use of an entire ground floor wing as its head-quarters . . . , out of concern for the inevitable harm to civilians also present in the hospital." Toeing the party line, Israeli historian Benny Morris also declared, "Hamas leaders sat out the campaign in the basement of Gaza's Shifa Hospital, gambling—correctly—that Israel would not bomb or storm a hospital." Except for the ubiquitous Italian reporter, who hopped from one journalistic coup to another, the sole source in the Israeli brief was the confession of a Palestinian detainee "during his interrogation."[74] If Israel didn't target this hospital, where Hamas's senior leadership was allegedly ensconced, then it is cause for wonder why it did target many other Palestinian hospitals. The two top floors of al-Quds Hospital, along with its adjacent administrative building and warehouse, were completely destroyed; al-Wafa Hospital sustained direct hits from eight tank shells, two missiles, and thousands of bullets; the European Hospital of Khan Yunis sustained artillery damage to its walls, water mains, and electricity; the emergency room of al-Dorah Hospital was hit twice; al-Awda Hospital sustained damage from two artillery shells that landed near the emergency room.[75] It might be argued that the IDF was returning enemy fire when these hospitals were hit, except that Israel also proclaimed it did not target "terrorists" who launched attacks "in the vicinity of a hospital."[76]

Israel did not just attack Gaza's civilian population and its humanitarian support system. It also systematically targeted Gaza's civilian infrastructure. In the course of Cast Lead, Israel destroyed or damaged 58,000 homes (6,300 were completely destroyed or sustained severe damage), 280 schools and kindergartens (18 schools were completely destroyed and 6 university buildings

73. Amnesty International, *Operation "Cast Lead,"* p. 43 (see also *Amnesty International Report 2010: The State of the World's Human Rights* [2010], entry for "Israel and the Occupied Palestinian Territories," p. 183); Physicians for Human Rights–Israel, *"Ill Morals,"* p. 41; Goldstone Report, paras. 36, 466–67, 485.

74. State of Israel, *Operation in Gaza,* paras. 172, 175; see also Intelligence and Terrorism Information Center, *Hamas and the Terrorist Threat,* pp. V, 163–77. Benny Morris, "Derisionist History," *New Republic* (28 November 2009).

75. United Nations Development Program, *Gaza, Early Recovery and Reconstruction Needs Assessment—One Year After* (2010), p. 20.

76. State of Israel, *Gaza Operation Investigations: Second update* (2010), para. 69.

were razed to the ground), 1,500 factories and workshops (including 22 of Gaza's 29 ready-mix concrete factories), several buildings housing Palestinian and foreign media (two journalists were killed while working; four others were also killed), electrical, water, and sewage installations (more than one million Gazans were left without power during the invasion and a half million were cut off from running water), 190 greenhouse complexes, 80 percent of agricultural crops, and nearly one-fifth of cultivated land.[77] The Israeli brief nonetheless contended that Israel took every precaution not to damage civilian objects. Indeed, who can doubt that the IDF "carefully checked and cross-checked targets ... to make sure they were being used for combat or terrorist activities" when, according to the Goldstone Report, it launched an "intentional and precise" attack destroying the "only one of Gaza's three flour mills still operating"? The Report concluded that the "only purpose" of this attack "was to put an end to the production of flour in the Gaza Strip" and "destroy the local capacity to produce flour."[78] Who can doubt that the IDF "clearly discriminated between military and civilian targets" (Cordesman) when it "systematically and deliberately" "flattened" a large chicken farm that supplied 10 percent of the Gaza egg market? The Goldstone Report con-

77. Margaret Coker, "Gaza's Isolation Slows Rebuilding Efforts," *Wall Street Journal* (5 February 2009); OCHA, *The Humanitarian Monitor;* Ethan Bronner, "Amid the Destruction, a Return to Life in Gaza," *New York Times* (25 January 2009); United Nations Office for the Coordination of Humanitarian Affairs (OCHA), "Tough Times for University Students in Gaza" (26 March 2009); Reporters without Borders, *Operation "Cast Lead": News control as military objective* (2009); Al Mezan, *Bearing the Brunt,* pp. 10, 62, 81; Amnesty International et al., *Failing Gaza,* p. 9; United Nations Institute for Training and Research, *Satellite Image Analysis in Support to the United Nations Fact-Finding Mission on the Gaza Conflict* (2009), p. ii; Gisha (Legal Center for Freedom of Movement), *Red Lines Crossed: Destruction of Gaza's infrastructure* (2009), pp. 5–6, 19, 27. Between the destruction inflicted during Cast Lead and Israel's expansion of its "buffer zone" in Gaza after the invasion, nearly half of Gaza's agricultural land was out of production a year later. For the most comprehensive analysis of the destruction wreaked by the Israeli attack and its enduring consequences, see United Nations Development Program, *Gaza, Early Recovery.*

78. Goldstone Report, paras. 50, 913–41. The flour mill produced "the most basic staple ingredient of the local diet." Israel subsequently sought to defend its attack on the flour mill (State of Israel, *Gaza Operation Investigations: An update* [January 2010], pp. 41–44), but compelling evidence belied the Israeli version of what had transpired (Anshel Pfeffer, "UN Insists Israel Bombed Flour Mill during Cast Lead," *Haaretz* [4 February 2010]; Human Rights Watch, *"I Lost Everything": Israel's unlawful destruction of property during Operation Cast Lead* [New York: January 2010], pp. 5, 83–86). Still, Israel stuck to its original story. *Gaza Operation Investigations: Second update* (July 2010), paras. 141–45. One year after the invasion, Israel continued to block cement deliveries to rebuild the flour mill (Amnesty International et al., *Failing Gaza,* p. 6).

cluded that "this constituted a deliberate act of wanton destruction not justified by any military necessity."[79] The United Nations Development Program reported that "over 4,000 cattle, sheep and goats and more than one million birds and chickens (broilers and egg layers) were killed during Operation Cast Lead, with evidence of livestock being the direct target of Israeli machine guns."[80] If the death and destruction appeared to be indefensible, Israel alleged after the invasion, it was only because of the "limit to the amount of intelligence it can share with commissions of inquiry without compromising operational capabilities and intelligence sources."[81] If the world only knew what was in those chickens. . . .[82] The total direct cost of the damage to Gaza's civilian infrastructure during Cast Lead was estimated at $660–900 million, while total losses from the destruction and disruption of economic life were put at $3–3.5 billion.[83] Some 600,000 tons of rubble were left behind after Israel's "mega display of military might" (IDF General Staff officer).[84] Eager for "round two," a member of Israel's regional council adjoining Gaza exhorted the military that next time they should "flatten Gaza into a parking lot, destroy them."[85] A juxtaposition of the destruction inflicted *by* Israel and *on* Israel in and of itself tells a story. Hamas rocket attacks on Israel damaged "several civilian homes and other structures . . . , one was almost completely destroyed,"[86] while total Israeli damages came to just $15 million.[87]

79. As a result of this single Israeli strike, "65,000 chickens were crushed to death or buried alive." Amnesty International, *Operation "Cast Lead,"* p. 62; Goldstone Report, paras. 51, 942–61.

80. United Nations Development Program, *Gaza, Early Recovery,* p. 67.

81. Amir Mizroch, "Analysis: Grappling with Goldstone," *Jerusalem Post* (18 September 2009); see also Israel Ministry of Foreign Affairs, "Israel Gaza FAQ: Goldstone Mission" (n.d.).

82. In a report issued a year and a half after Cast Lead, Israel alleged, predictably, that the chicken coops were destroyed "for reasons of military necessity." *Gaza Operation Investigations: Second update,* paras. 122–29.

83. Amnesty International et al., *Failing Gaza,* p. 7; United Nations Conference on Trade and Development, "Report on UNCTAD Assistance to the Palestinian People: Developments in the economy of the occupied Palestinian territory" (August 2009), para. 20.

84. Amnesty International et al., *Failing Gaza,* p. 7; Barbara Opall-Rome, "Israel's New Hard Line on Hizbollah," *DefenseNews* (31 May 2010).

85. International Crisis Group, *Gaza's Unfinished Business* (2009), p. 21.

86. Amnesty International, *Operation "Cast Lead,"* p. 66; see also Human Rights Watch, *Rockets from Gaza: Harm to civilians from Palestinian armed groups' rocket attacks* (2009), pp. 2, 20 (reporting damage to a synagogue, school, and kindergarten); and Goldstone Report, paras. 1659–61.

87. State of Israel, *Operation in Gaza,* p. 17n27.

In postinvasion testimonies, IDF soldiers recalled the macabre scenes of destruction in Gaza: "We didn't see a single house that remained intact.... Nothing much was left in our designated area. It looked awful, like in those World War II films where nothing remained. A totally destroyed city"; "We demolished a lot. There were people who had been in Gaza for two days constantly demolishing one house after the other, and we're talking about a whole battalion"; "One night they saw a terrorist and he disappeared so they decided he'd gone into a tunnel, so they brought a D-9 [bulldozer] and razed the whole orchard"; "The amount of destruction there was incredible. You drive around those neighborhoods, and can't identify a thing. Not one stone left standing over another. You see plenty of fields, hothouses, orchards, everything devastated. Totally ruined. It's terrible. It's surreal"; "There was a point where D-9s were razing areas. It was amazing. At first you go in and see lots of houses. A week later, after the razing, you see the horizon further away, almost to the sea."[88] One veteran of the invasion designed a T-shirt depicting a King Kong–like soldier clenching a mosque while glowering over a city under attack, the shirt bearing the slogan "If you believe it can be fixed, then believe it can be destroyed!" "I was in Gaza," he told *Haaretz,* "and they kept emphasizing that the object of the operation was to wreak destruction on the infrastructure."[89] The only reported penalty Israel imposed for unlawful property destruction during Cast Lead was an unknown disciplinary measure taken against one soldier.[90]

The Israeli brief alleged that its "overall use of force against Hamas during the Gaza Operation was ... proportional to the threat posed by Hamas."[91] The postinvasion testimonies of Israeli soldiers vividly depicted what such "proportional" use of force *felt* like: "This was firepower such as I had never known ... there were blasts all the time ... the earth was constantly shaking"; "On the ground you hear these thunderous blasts all day long. I mean, not just tank shelling, which was a tune we'd long gotten used to, but blasts that actually rock the outpost, to the extent that some of us were ordered out of the house we were quartered in for fear it would collapse."[92] Indeed, one

88. Breaking the Silence, *Soldiers' Testimonies,* pp. 26 (Testimony 10), 59 (Testimony 24), 60 (Testimony 25), 85 (Testimony 38), 101 (Testimony 47).

89. Uri Blau, "Dead Palestinian Babies and Bombed Mosques—IDF Fashion 2009," *Haaretz* (20 March 2009).

90. Human Rights Watch, *"I Lost Everything,"* p. 7.

91. State of Israel, *Operation in Gaza,* para. 71.

92. Breaking the Silence, *Soldiers' Testimonies,* pp. 69 (Testimony 29), 83 (Testimony 37).

soldier after another after another testified that Israel deployed "insane" amounts of firepower during the invasion: "We are hitting innocents and our artillery fire there was insane"; "Fire power was insane"; "He said we were going to exercise insane firepower with artillery and [the] air force"; "This was the general attitude in the army: go in with insane firepower because this is our only advantage over them."[93] The Israeli brief also alleged that "IDF orders and directions ... stressed that all demolition operations should be carried out in a manner that would minimize to the greatest extent possible the damage caused to any property not used by Hamas and other terrorist organizations in the fighting."[94] But human rights organizations painted an altogether different picture. Amnesty found that "much of the destruction" of civilian buildings and infrastructure "was wanton and resulted from deliberate and unnecessary demolition of property, direct attacks on civilian objects and indiscriminate attacks that failed to distinguish between legitimate military targets and civilian objects."[95] The timing, location, and pace of the devastation buttressed Amnesty's finding and undercut official Israeli claims. As much as 90 percent of the destruction of civilian buildings and infrastructure—including juice, ice cream, biscuit, and Pepsi-Cola factories—took place in the last days of Cast Lead, according to the Dugard Report, in areas fully pacified by the IDF, and much of this destruction was wreaked by Israeli troops as they withdrew.[96] An HRW study found that "virtually every home, factory and orchard had been destroyed within certain areas, apparently indicating that a plan of systematic destruction was carried out in these locations." Using satellite imagery "taken at intervals during the conflict," HRW documented numerous cases "in which Israeli forces caused extensive destruction of homes, factories, farms and greenhouses in areas under IDF control without any evident military purpose. These cases occurred when there was no fighting in these areas; in many cases, the destruction was carried out during the final days of the campaign when an Israeli withdrawal was imminent." In the Izbt Abd Rabbo neighborhood, for

93. Breaking the Silence, *Soldiers' Testimonies*, pp. 18 (Testimony 6), 20 (Testimony 7), 46 (Testimony 18), 60 (Testimony 25), 85 (Testimony 38); see also ibid., pp. 47—"massive fire" (Testimony 19), 48—"fired like crazy" (Testimony 20), 67—"I never knew such firepower. They were using every weapon I know" (Testimony 29), 76—"In general, everything that could fire, did" (Testimony 33).

94. State of Israel, *Operation in Gaza*, para. 445.

95. Amnesty International, *Operation "Cast Lead,"* p. 55.

96. Dugard Report, paras. 300, 372–87; see also Goldstone Report, paras. 53, 351, 1004, 1207, 1319.

example, the "vast majority" of the "wholesale destruction of entire blocks of buildings" took place "after the IDF exercised control."[97] An expanse in eastern Gaza embracing farms, factories, and homes was "virtually flattened," according to the Crisis Group, while Israel's "deliberate and systematic" destruction of that sector through a combination of bulldozers and antitank mines, according to a military expert, "took at least two days of hard labor."[98] It might be contended that if Israel targeted so many homes, it was because "Hamas is booby-trapping every home that is abandoned by its residents" (IDF spokesman, quoted by Cordesman).[99] But this prima facie implausible argument was fatally undermined after the invasion when the IDF itself conceded that the "scale of destruction" was legally indefensible.[100] Still, an Israeli security official beamed with pride that by "flattening buildings

97. Human Rights Watch, *"I Lost Everything,"* pp. 1, 4, 41, 44.

98. International Crisis Group, *Gaza's Unfinished Business,* p. 2. Apparently referring to this same zone, Amnesty reported that it "looked as if it had been wrecked by an earthquake." *Operation "Cast Lead,"* p. 61.

99. Cordesman, *"Gaza War,"* p. 49.

100. Amos Harel, "IDF Probe: Cannot defend destruction of Gaza homes," *Haaretz* (15 February 2009). Apropos the razing of Palestinian homes, Amnesty observed:

Many of the houses destroyed during Operation "Cast Lead" had been raided or temporarily taken over by Israeli soldiers during incursions in recent years. It is unlikely that Hamas or other Palestinian groups would have located their command centers, rocket manufacturing workshops or weapons stores in the areas most accessible [to] and most easily overrun by Israeli troops. . . .

The fact that the soldiers used [antitank mines]—which required them to leave their tanks, walk between buildings and enter houses in order to place the explosive charges inside the houses along the supporting walls—indicates that they felt extremely confident that there were no Palestinian gunmen inside or around the houses. It also indicates their confidence that there were no tunnels under the houses which gunmen could use to capture them, and that the houses were not booby-trapped. (*Operation "Cast Lead,"* p. 56)

The Goldstone Report subdivided the house destruction into chronologically discrete phases: "a first phase of extensive destruction of housing for the 'operational necessity' of the advancing Israeli forces in these areas was followed by a period of relative idleness on the part of the Israeli bulldozers and explosives engineers. But during the last three days, aware of their imminent withdrawal, the Israeli armed forces engaged in another wave of systematic destruction of civilian buildings" (paras. 990–1004, 1323). The Al Mezan Center for Human Rights reported that "at least 1,732 shelters" were destroyed "after the end of hostilities when they had come under Israel's effective control, [which] indicates that they could no longer be military objectives or near any other legitimate military targets, and should therefore have been respected as civilian objects." Al Mezan, *Bearing the Brunt,* pp. 80–94. On a related point, HRW noted the absence of any evidence that "explosive booby-traps planted by Palestinian armed groups or secondary explosions caused by weapons stored by these armed groups were responsible for any significant amount of the damage seen in Gaza." Human Rights Watch, *"I Lost Everything,"* p. 18.

believed to be booby-trapped," Israel had broken "the DNA of urban guerrilla fighting," while Deputy Prime Minister Eli Yishai declared after the cease-fire had come into effect, "Even if the [Hamas] rockets fall in an open air [*sic*] or to the sea, we should hit their infrastructure, and destroy 100 homes for every rocket fired."[101] It appears that the ratio of 6,300 Gazan homes destroyed to one Israeli home "almost completely destroyed" did not yet quench his thirst for destruction.

Israel targeted not only civilian buildings and infrastructure but also Gaza's cultural inheritance. Fully 30 mosques were destroyed and 15 more damaged during the Israeli assault. If Cordesman concluded that "IDF forces almost certainly were correct in reporting that Hamas used mosques and other sensitive sites in combat," that's because his "chronologies" based on IDF press releases purported this.[102] Initially, Israel alleged that secondary explosions ensued after mosques had been struck, thus confirming that weapons had been stored in them. But it subsequently dropped this defense altogether, even as it continued to target mosques.[103] The Goldstone Report documented an "intentional" Israeli missile attack on a mosque that killed at least 15 people attending prayers. It found "no evidence that this mosque was used for the storage of weapons or any military activity by Palestinian armed groups."[104] Israel did not even attempt to refute this particular finding of the Goldstone Report[105] until it came under withering criticism. It then

101. International Crisis Group, *Gaza's Unfinished Business*, p. 19; Goldstone Report, para. 1201.

102. Cordesman, *"Gaza War,"* pp. 18, 24, 26.

103. Both the Israeli press releases cited by Cordesman, *"Gaza War,"* pp. 24, 26, and State of Israel, *Operation in Gaza*, p. 61n161, para. 234, alleged secondary explosions only in the cases of two mosques targeted respectively on 31 December 2008 and 1 January 2009. In a rebuttal issued long after the Gaza assault ended, Israel conjured a secondary explosion in a mosque attacked on 13 January 2009. Intelligence and Terrorism Information Center, *Hamas and the Terrorist Threat*, p. 157.

104. The Goldstone Report cautiously concluded, "Although the situations investigated by the Mission did not establish the use of mosques for military purposes or to shield military activities, the Mission cannot exclude that this might have occurred in other cases" (paras. 36, 464–65, 486, 497, 822–43, 1953). In a pair of newspaper articles, B'Tselem executive director Jessica Montell alleged that the Goldstone Report was insufficiently critical of Hamas because it "ignored" evidence contradicting this tentative conclusion. However, despite repeated requests by this writer, Montell was unable to substantiate her allegation that Hamas had misused mosques. Jessica Montell, "A Time for Soul-Searching," *Jerusalem Post* (30 September 2009); Jessica Montell, "The Goldstone Report on Gaza," *Huffington Post* (1 October 2009).

105. Intelligence and Terrorism Information Center, *Hamas and the Terrorist Threat*, pp. 143–44.

belatedly discovered that—who could have guessed?—the missile was "directed at two terrorist operatives standing near the entrance to the mosque."[106] In general, the case Israel mounted to justify its targeting of mosques did not persuade. It alleged that Hamas used mosques to stash weapons. But as the Goldstone Report's military expert observed, with "abundant hideaways in the labyrinthine alleyways of Gaza," Hamas would have been foolhardy to "store anything in an open building like a mosque, which had been pre-targeted and pre-registered by Israeli intelligence."[107] Israel also alleged that Hamas stored weapons in mosques as Hamas "assumed" on the basis of past experience "that the IDF would not attack them." But to the contrary, Israel had damaged or destroyed fully 55 mosques in Gaza between 2001 and 2008.[108] Going one step further, Harvard law professor Alan Dershowitz alleged that "Hamas leaders boast of" having stored weapons in mosques.[109] But per usual, he adduced no evidence, and apparently none exists. Israel's various explanations also could not account for its systematic targeting of minarets, which being too narrow for snipers to ascend, possessed no apparent military value. The Dugard Report concluded that "mosques, and more particularly the minarets, had been deliberately targeted on the grounds that they symbolized Islam."[110] Postinvasion IDF testimony confirmed the indiscriminate targeting of mosques.[111] Israel justified its targeting of educational institutions by claiming that Hamas "did in fact make use" of them.[112] However, when challenged in a specific instance to provide proof of its allegations, Israel conceded that its photographic evidence was

106. State of Israel, *Gaza Operation Investigations: Second update,* para. 69.

107. Hanan Chehata, "Exclusive MEMO Interview with Colonel Desmond Travers," *Middle East Monitor* (23 January 2010). In addition, since the targeted mosques were "frequented" by senior Hamas officials (Intelligence and Terrorism Information Center, *Hamas and the Terrorist Threat,* pp. 147–48), they were likely under Israeli surveillance.

108. Intelligence and Terrorism Information Center, *Hamas and the Terrorist Threat,* p. 146; Al Mezan Center for Human Rights database. It might also be hypothesized that Hamas stored weapons in mosques because Hamas wanted to demonize Israel by luring it to target them, but such speculation would be hard to square with the fact that Hamas was also said to have *hidden* the weapons in mosques. Intelligence and Terrorism Information Center, *Hamas and the Terrorist Threat,* pp. 147, 152, 158.

109. Alan Dershowitz, *The Case against the Goldstone Report: A study in evidentiary bias* (www.alandershowitz.com/goldstone.pdf), pp. 4, 39–41.

110. Dugard Report, paras. 349–53, 498, 502; see also Amnesty International, *Operation "Cast Lead,"* p. 15.

111. Breaking the Silence, *Soldiers' Testimonies,* p. 70.

112. Intelligence and Terrorism Information Center, *Hamas and the Terrorist Threat,* p. 179.

from 2007.[113] To extenuate its attack on the Islamic University in Gaza, Israel alleged that it was the nerve center of Hamas's "weapons research and development" and "military terrorist activities." One searched in vain, however, for evidence to corroborate this claim.[114] If Israel targeted the Islamic University because it was a terrorist hub, it might nonetheless be wondered why "virtually all universities sustained damages."[115] The Goldstone Report "did not find any information" confirming the use of educational institutions "as a military facility or their contribution to a military effort."[116] The Israeli brief alleged that after his arrest, a Palestinian detainee "admitted" under interrogation that "Hamas operatives frequently carried out rocket fire from schools ... precisely because they knew that Israeli jets would not fire on schools."[117] But why would he make such a confession if, over and over again, that's precisely what Israel did?

The havoc wrought by Cast Lead might have been wanton, but a method incontestably informed this madness. If Israel possessed fine "grid maps" of Gaza and an "intelligence gathering capacity" that "remained extremely effective"; and if it made extensive use of state-of-the-art precision weaponry; and if "99 percent of the firing that was carried out [by the air force] hit targets accurately"; and if it only once targeted a building erroneously—indeed, if Israel itself provided most of the data just cited, then, as the Goldstone Report logically concluded, the massive destruction Israel inflicted on Gaza's civilian infrastructure must have been premeditated. It "resulted from deliberate planning and policy decisions throughout the chain of command, down to the standard operating procedures and instructions given to the troops on the ground."[118] In other words, if Israel was able to pinpoint its targets and if, by its own acknowledgment, it could and did hit these designated targets with pinpoint accuracy, then it cannot be contended that the criminal wreckage resulted from mishap or a break in the chain of command. What happened in Gaza was *intended* to happen, by everyone from the soldiers who executed the orders to the officers who issued them to the politi-

113. Dugard Report, para. 347.

114. Intelligence and Terrorism Information Center, *Hamas and the Terrorist Threat*, pp. V, 193–94.

115. United Nations Development Program, *Gaza, Early Recovery*, p. 26.

116. Goldstone Report, para. 1273.

117. State of Israel, *Operation in Gaza*, para. 158; see also Intelligence and Terrorism Information Center, *Hamas and the Terrorist Threat*, p. 185.

118. Goldstone Report, paras. 54, 61, 1180, 1182, 1185–91, 1891; Cordesman, *"Gaza War,"* p. 18.

cians who approved them. "The wholesale destruction was to a large extent deliberate," Amnesty concluded, "and an integral part of a strategy at different levels of the command chain, from high-ranking officials to soldiers in the field."[119]

To justify the magnitude of the devastation it wreaked, Israel endeavored to depict the Gaza invasion as a genuine military contest. Cordesman delineated in ominous detail, enhanced by tables, graphs, and figures, the vast arsenal of rockets, mortars, and other weapons that Hamas allegedly manufactured and smuggled in through tunnels (including "Iranian-made rockets" that could "strike at much of Southern Israel" and "hit key infrastructure"), as well as the "spider web of prepared strong points, underground and hidden shelters, and ambush points" Hamas allegedly constructed.[120] He reported that according to "Israeli senior officials," Hamas mustered 6,000–10,000 "core fighters."[121] He juxtaposed the "Gaza war" with the 1967 war, the 1973 war, and the 2006 war, as if they belonged on the same plane.[122] He expatiated on Israel's complex war plans and preparations, and he purported that Israel's victory was partly owing to its "high levels of secrecy," as if the outcome would have been different had Israel not benefited from the element of surprise.[123] The Israeli brief alleged that Hamas had "amassed an extensive armed force of more than 20,000 armed operatives in Gaza," "obtained military supplies through a vast network of tunnels and clandestine arms shipments from Iran and Syria," and "acquired advanced weaponry, developed weapons of their own, and increased the range and lethality of their rockets."[124]

Nonetheless, even Cordesman was forced to acknowledge, if obliquely, that what Israel fought was scarcely a war. He conceded that Hamas was a "weak non-state actor," whereas Israel possessed a massive armory of state-of-the-art weaponry; that the Israeli air force "faced limited threats from Hamas's primitive land-based air defense"; that "sustained ground fighting was limited"; that the Israeli army avoided engagements where it "would be

---

119. Amnesty International, *Operation "Cast Lead,"* p. 55.
120. Cordesman, *"Gaza War,"* pp. 8–9.
121. Ibid., p. 27.
122. Ibid., pp. ii, 1, 15–16, 18, 19, 28, 38, 40, 57.
123. Ibid., pp. 15ff.
124. State of Israel, *Operation in Gaza,* paras. 4, 59, 73–82. See also Intelligence and Terrorism Information Center, *Hamas and the Terrorist Threat,* pp. 6–7, 45–55, 76–78.

likely to suffer" significant casualties; and that "the IDF used night warfare for most combat operations because Hamas did not have the technology or training to fight at night."[125] However, overwhelmingly, Cordesman persisted in his dubious depiction of Cast Lead. Israel had demonstrated that it could fight "an air campaign successfully in crowded urban areas," according to him, as well as "an extended land battle against a non-state actor."[126] In fact, its air campaign was not a "fight" any more than shooting fish in a barrel is a fight. As if (however unwittingly) to bring home this analogy, Cordesman quoted a senior Israeli air force officer who boasted, "The IAF had flown some 3,000 successful sorties over a small dense area during three weeks of fighting without a single accident or loss." But how could it be otherwise if "the planes operated in an environment free of air defenses, enjoying complete aerial superiority"?[127] Depicting Cast Lead as a protracted land war was no less detached from reality. Hamas was barely equipped, barely present in the conflict zones, and barely engaged by Israeli forces except when it could not fight back.

Not all Israelis celebrated their country's triumph in this non-war. "It is very dangerous for the Israel Defense Forces to believe it won the war when there was no war," a respected Israeli strategic analyst warned. "In reality, not a single battle was fought during the 22 days of fighting."[128] The Crisis Group reported that Hamas "for the most part avoided direct confrontations with Israeli troops," and "consequently, only a limited number of fighters were killed." A former Israeli foreign ministry official scoffed, "There was no war. Hamas sat in its bunkers and came out when it was all over," while an Israeli officer derisively noted, "Not even light firearms were directed at us. One doesn't see [Hamas] that much, they mostly hide."[129] The postinvasion testimonies of IDF soldiers repeatedly confirmed the near absence of an enemy in the field: "There was nothing there. Ghost towns. Except for some livestock, nothing moved"; "Most of the time it was boring. There were not really too many events"; "Some explosives are found in a house, weapons, significant stuff like that, but no real resistance"; "I did not see one single Arab the whole time we were there, that whole week"; "Everyone was disappointed about not

125. Cordesman, *"Gaza War,"* pp. 10, 16, 28, 39, 42.

126. Ibid., pp. 27, 57.

127. Ibid., p. 41; Reuven Pedatzur, "The War That Wasn't," *Haaretz* (25 January 2009).

128. Pedatzur, "War That Wasn't."

129. International Crisis Group, *Gaza's Unfinished Business,* pp. 2, 21 (see also ibid., pp. 8n82, 19); Amnesty International, *Operation "Cast Lead,"* p. 56.

engaging anyone"; "Usually we did not see a living soul. Except for our soldiers of course. Not a soul"; "Go ahead and ask soldiers how often they
encountered combatants in Gaza—nothing. . . . There was supposed to be a
tiny resistance force upon entry, but there just wasn't"; "Nearly no one ran
into the enemy. I know of two encounters during the whole operation. The
soldiers, too, were disappointed for not having had any encounters with
terrorists."[130] The Goldstone Report noted that it had "received relatively few
reports of actual crossfire between the Israeli armed forces and Palestinian
armed groups."[131] Hamas did not even manage to fully disable a single Israeli
tank.[132] In his defense of IDF conduct and the ensuing civilian deaths, a
Hebrew University philosopher pointed up the challenge facing an Israeli
soldier: he had to "decide whether the individual standing before him in
jeans and sneakers is a combatant or not," and he found himself fighting on
an "extremely densely populated" terrain.[133] Still, judging by all the available
evidence, the truly daunting challenge in Gaza was not differentiating
between civilians and militants but, on the contrary, encountering *any* militant; no battles occurred in densely populated or, for that matter, sparsely
populated areas. Simply put, there was no heat of battle, no fog of war.

The death and destruction wreaked by Cast Lead clearly went beyond
Israel's declared mission of eliminating "terrorists" and "terrorist infrastructure" or even collective punishment of Palestinian civilians. The systematic
destruction of homes and schools, factories and farms, hospitals and mosques,
the purpose of which seemed to be to make Gaza literally unlivable, ineluctably posed the question, *What was Israel really trying to accomplish?* In fact,
the murder and mayhem were both critical and integral to the success of the
operation. Its purpose, according to Cordesman—and here the evidence, for
a change, supported him—was to "restore Israeli deterrence, and show the
Hezbollah, Iran, and Syria that it was too dangerous to challenge Israel."[134]

130. Breaking the Silence, *Soldiers' Testimonies,* pp. 25 (Testimony 9), 36 (Testimony 13),
47 (Testimony 19), 54 (Testimony 23), 60 (Testimony 25), 68 (Testimony 29), 77 and 80
(Testimony 34), 90 (Testimony 41).
131. Goldstone Report, para. 459.
132. Dugard Report, para. 214. In light of this operational failure, Israel's allegation that
Hamas had amassed "thousands" of "advanced . . . anti-tank rockets" appears far-fetched.
Intelligence and Terrorism Information Center, *Hamas and the Terrorist Threat,* pp. 7, 52,
104.
133. Moshe Halbertal, "The Goldstone Illusion: What the UN report gets wrong about
Gaza—and war," *New Republic* (6 November 2009).
134. Cordesman, *"Gaza War,"* p. 11.

But if Israel sought to restore its deterrence capacity, it couldn't attain this end by inflicting a military defeat, because Hamas was manifestly not a military power. It "is not clear," Cordesman observed, "that any opponent of Israel felt Hamas was really strong enough to be a serious test of Israeli ground forces."[135] Consequently, Israel could reinstate the region's fear of it only by demonstrating the amount of sheer devastation it was prepared to inflict. It "had [to] make its enemies feel it was 'crazy'" (Israeli official) and was ready to cause wreckage on a "scale [that] is unpredictable" and heedless of "world opinion" (Cordesman).[136] In other words, and contradicting Israel's official pretense that the use of force in Gaza was "proportional" and "discriminate," the IDF deliberately escalated the level of destruction to a degree that was disproportional and indiscriminate, even insane. In less guarded moments, Israeli officials acknowledged the real objective of Cast Lead. As the invasion wound down, Foreign Minister Livni declared that it had "restored Israel's deterrence. . . . Hamas now understands that when you fire on [Israel's] citizens it responds by going wild—and this is a good thing." The day after the cease-fire went into effect, she bragged that "Israel demonstrated real hooliganism during the course of the recent operation, which I demanded."[137] Later, Livni declared that she was "proud" of her decisions during the Gaza invasion and would "repeat" every one of them because they were "meant to restore Israel's deterrence and did restore Israel's deterrence."[138] A former Israeli defense official told the Crisis Group that "Israel decided to play the role of a mad dog for the sake of future deterrence," while a former senior Israeli security official gloated to the Crisis Group that Israel had regained its deterrence because it "has shown Hamas, Iran and the region that it can be as lunatic as any of them."[139] "The Goldstone Report, which claimed that Israel goes crazy when it is being attacked, caused us some damage," a prominent Israeli pundit observed, "yet it was a blessing in our region.

135. Ibid., p. 68.

136. Ibid., pp. 11, 32.

137. Kim Sengupta and Donald Macintyre, "Israeli Cabinet Divided over Fresh Gaza Surge," *Independent* (13 January 2009); PCATI, *No Second Thoughts*, p. 28.

138. Adrian Blomfield, "Israeli Opposition Leader Tzipi Livni 'Cancels London Visit over Prosecution Fears,'" *Daily Telegraph* (14 December 2009); Herb Keinon, "Miliband 'Shocked' at Livni's Warrant," *Jerusalem Post* (15 December 2009); Daniel Edelson, "Livni: We must do what's right for us," *ynetnews.com* (15 December 2009).

139. International Crisis Group, *Ending the War in Gaza* (2009), p. 19; International Crisis Group, *Gaza's Unfinished Business*, p. 19.

If Israel goes crazy and destroys everything in its way when it's being attacked, one should be careful. No need to mess with crazy people."[140]

After the invasion, Israeli and American Jewish philosophers engaged the subtle moral quandaries of Israel's conduct. Hawkish Philosopher A posited that Israel "should favor the lives of its own soldiers over the lives of the neighbors of a terrorist," while dovish Philosophers B and C rejoined that it did not suffice that Israel was "not intending" to kill civilians in the war against "terrorism"; the IDF must "*intend not* to kill civilians."[141] It appears that both sides in this learned disputation on the morally correct balance between preserving the life of a soldier, on the one hand, and the life of an enemy civilian, on the other, somehow missed the crux of what happened during Cast Lead: upon entering Gaza, the IDF blasted everyone and everything in sight. Basing itself not on the gaseous lucubrations of a philosophy seminar but on the actual facts, the Goldstone Report found that a nuanced analysis of whether or not Israel properly calibrated the principle of "proportionality" was beside the point: "deeds by the Israeli armed forces and words of military and political leaders prior to and during the operations indicate that, as a whole, they were premised on a deliberate policy of disproportionate force aimed not at the enemy but at the ... civilian population." It also concluded that subtle parsing of whether or not Israel properly applied the principle of "distinction" (between combatants and civilians) was beside the point: "the effective rules of engagement, standard operating procedures and instructions to the troops on the ground appear to have been framed in order to create an environment in which due regard for civilian lives and basic human dignity was replaced with disregard for basic international humanitarian law and human rights norms."[142] While the erudite philosophers debated the correct interpretation of the laws of war and both sides tacitly imputed to Israel the elevated motive of wanting to obey them, the actual premise of Cast Lead and the essential precondition for its success was the wholesale breach of these laws.

---

140. Guy Bechor, "Israel Is Back," *ynetnews.com* (19 February 2010). In postinvasion testimony, an IDF soldier mused that "there was no need for such intense fire, no need to use mortars, phosphorus ammunition.... The army was looking for the opportunity to hold a spectacular maneuver in order to show its muscle." Breaking the Silence, *Soldiers' Testimonies,* pp. 68–69 (Testimony 29).

141. Asa Kasher, "Operation Cast Lead and Just War Theory," *Azure* (Summer 2009), pp. 64–67; Avishai Margalit and Michael Walzer, "Israel: Civilians & combatants," *New York Review of Books* (14 May 2009), emphasis in original.

142. Goldstone Report, paras. 1886–87.

FOUR

Human Shields

SOME 1,400 PALESTINIANS WERE KILLED during Operation Cast Lead, of whom up to four-fifths were civilians and 350 children.[1] On the other side, total Israeli casualties amounted to ten combatants (four killed by

---

1. Palestinian Center for Human Rights, "Confirmed Figures Reveal the True Extent of the Destruction Inflicted upon the Gaza Strip" (12 March 2009); Al Mezan Center for Human Rights, "Cast Lead Offensive in Numbers" (2 August 2009); "B'Tselem's Investigation of Fatalities in Operation Cast Lead" (9 September 2009); B'Tselem (Israeli Information Center for Human Rights in the Occupied Territories), *Human Rights Review, 1 January 2009–30 April 2010* (Jerusalem: 2010), p. 5; Al Mezan Center for Human Rights, *Bearing the Brunt Again: Child rights violations during Operation Cast Lead* (2009), p. 16; Amnesty International et al., *Failing Gaza: No rebuilding, no recovery, no more excuses* (2009), p. 7; United Nations Office for the Coordination of Humanitarian Affairs (OCHA), "Field Update on Gaza from the Humanitarian Coordinator" (3–5 February 2009). Israeli officials alleged that total Palestinian deaths came to 1,166, of whom at least 60 percent were "terrorists." The discrepancy in the ratio of Palestinian combatant to civilian deaths partly resulted from disagreement on the proper classification of Gazan police. See Shay Fogelman, "Shock and Awe," *Haaretz* (31 December 2010). The broad consensus among human rights organizations was that these police should overwhelmingly be classified as civilians because they did not take a direct part in hostilities and were not members of Palestinian armed groups. The veracity of Israeli figures could be tested by scrutinizing the "under 16" subclassification. Whereas Israel alleged that 89 Palestinians under age 16 were killed, B'Tselem reported that 252 Palestinians under 16 were killed and that it had "copies of birth certificates and death certificates along with other documents regarding the vast majority of the minors who were killed." For critical analysis of Israeli casualty figures, see Public Committee against Torture in Israel (PCATI), *No Second Thoughts: The changes in the Israeli Defense Forces' combat doctrine in light of "Operation Cast Lead"* (2009), pp. 9–11. This study showed that Israel abruptly altered the figures it tabulated for Palestinian deaths, and concluded that "the casualty estimates provided by other sources (around 1,400 killed) are more credible than those provided by the IDF Spokesperson." Even the largely apologetic US Department of State *2009 Human Rights Report* put the number of dead "at close to 1,400

friendly fire) and three civilians.[2] The ratio of total Palestinians to Israelis killed was more than 100:1, and of Palestinian to Israeli civilians killed as high as 400:1.[3] When a BBC reporter confronted Interior Minister Meir Sheetrit with the fact that Israel "imposed 100 times more casualties on Gaza in three weeks than they did on you," he shot back: "That's the idea of the operation, what do you think?"[4] A poll taken shortly after the invasion ended found that two-thirds of Israeli Jews believed that Cast Lead should have gone on until Hamas surrendered.[5] If Israelis rued that the invasion didn't achieve its objectives, the subtext, according to *Haaretz* journalist Gideon Levy, was that "we didn't kill enough."[6]

To deflect its culpability for the loss of life, Israel alleged that if many Gazan civilians were killed, it was because Hamas used them as "human shields." Hamas "chose to base its operations in civilian areas not in spite of, but *because of,* the likelihood of substantial harm to civilians," an Israeli "factual and legal" brief purported, and "Hamas operatives took pride in endan-

---

Palestinians, including more than 1,000 civilians." Hamas originally alleged that only 48 of its fighters had been killed during Cast Lead but then upped the figure to several hundred, in the face of accusations that the people of Gaza "had paid the price" of its reckless decisions. Prime Minister Benjamin Netanyahu seized on Hamas's politically inflated death toll as vindication of the Israeli allegation that a high percentage of Gazan casualties were "Hamas terrorists." "Hamas Confirms Losses in Cast Lead for First Time," *Jerusalem Post* (1 November 2010); Israel Ministry of Foreign Affairs, "PM Netanyahu Addresses the General Assembly of the Jewish Federation of North America" (8 November 2010).

2. Human Rights Watch, *Rockets from Gaza: Harm to civilians from Palestinian armed groups' rocket attacks* (2009).

3. Israel alleged that were it not for its sophisticated warning and shelter system, "the human casualties from Hamas's bombardment undoubtedly would have been substantially greater." State of Israel, *The Operation in Gaza: 27 December 2008–18 January 2009: Factual and legal aspects* (2009), paras. 42–46. But were it not for the heroism of UNRWA employees, Palestinian casualties would also have been much higher. Hundreds of Palestinians taking shelter in the UNRWA Headquarters Compound would almost certainly have perished if employees had not prevented the white phosphorus that Israel dropped on it from reaching the fuel tanks. *Report of the United Nations Fact-Finding Mission on the Gaza Conflict* (25 September 2009), para. 545; hereafter: Goldstone Report. For UNRWA spokesperson Chris Gunness's gripping theatrical reenactment of this incident, see "Building Understanding: Epitaph for a warehouse" (28 October 2014), unrwa.org/newsroom/videos/building-understanding-epitaph-warehouse; for the background to and fate of this production, see "UN Makes a Drama out of Gaza Crisis," *Independent* (25 October 2009).

4. Jeremy Bowen, "Gaza Stories: Israeli minister," interview with Meir Sheetrit, *BBC News* (9 February 2009).

5. Tami Steinmetz Center for Peace Research, "War and Peace Index—February 2009."

6. Gideon Levy, "Everyone Agrees: War in Gaza was a failure," *Haaretz* (12 March 2009).

gering the lives of civilians." But these charges were not borne out by human rights investigations. In one of the most extensive postinvasion human rights reports, Amnesty International did find that Hamas breached certain laws of war. It "launched rockets and located military equipment and positions near civilian homes, endangering the lives of the inhabitants by exposing them to the risk of Israeli attacks. They also used empty homes and properties as combat positions during armed confrontations with Israeli forces, exposing the inhabitants of nearby houses to the danger of attacks or of being caught in the crossfire." The Amnesty report proceeded, however, to enter critical caveats: there was "no evidence that rockets were launched from residential houses or buildings while civilians were in these buildings"; "Palestinian militants often used empty houses but . . . did not forcibly take over inhabited houses"; Hamas "mixed with the civilian population, although this would be difficult to avoid in the small and overcrowded Gaza Strip"; "Palestinian fighters, like Israeli soldiers, engaged in armed confrontations around residential homes where civilians were present, endangering them. The locations of these confrontations were mostly determined by Israeli forces, who entered Gaza with tanks and armored personnel carriers and took positions deep inside residential neighborhoods." On the most explosive charge, Amnesty categorically exonerated Hamas:

> Contrary to repeated allegations by Israeli officials of the use of "human shields," Amnesty International found no evidence that Hamas or other Palestinian fighters directed the movement of civilians to shield military objectives from attacks. It found no evidence that Hamas or other armed groups forced residents to stay in or around buildings used by fighters, nor that fighters prevented residents from leaving buildings or areas which had been commandeered by militants. . . .
>
> Amnesty International delegates interviewed many Palestinians who complained about Hamas's conduct, and especially about Hamas's repression and attacks against their opponents, including killings, torture and arbitrary detentions, but did not receive any accounts of Hamas fighters having used them as "human shields." In the cases investigated by Amnesty International of civilians killed in Israeli attacks, the deaths could not be explained as resulting from the presence of fighters shielding among civilians, as the Israeli army generally contends. In all of the cases investigated by Amnesty International of families killed when their homes were bombed from the air by Israeli forces, for example, none of the houses struck was being used by armed groups for military activities. Similarly, in the cases of precision missiles or tank shells which killed civilians in their homes, no fighters were present in the houses that were struck and Amnesty International delegates

found no indication that there had been any armed confrontations or other military activity in the immediate vicinity at the time of the attack.

If it found no evidence that Hamas used human shields, Amnesty did, however, find ample evidence that *Israel* used them. The Israeli brief avowed that the rules of engagement of the Israel Defense Forces (IDF) strictly forbade the "use of civilians as human shields," and that "the IDF took a variety of measures to teach and instill awareness of these rules of engagement in commanders and soldiers." But in fact, Israeli soldiers "used civilians, including children, as 'human shields,' endangering their lives by forcing them to remain in or near houses which they took over and used as military positions. Some were forced to carry out dangerous tasks such as inspecting properties or objects suspected of being booby-trapped. Soldiers also took position and launched attacks from and around inhabited houses, exposing local residents to the danger of attacks or of being caught in the crossfire." Other human rights investigations (in particular, the graphic accounts in the Goldstone Report) and the postinvasion testimony of Israeli soldiers corroborated the IDF's use of human shields.[7]

Still, it was axiomatic for philosophers Avishai Margalit and Michael Walzer that whereas Israel's enemies "intentionally put civilians at risk by using them as cover," Israel "condemns those practices."[8] In a book that

7. State of Israel, *Operation in Gaza,* paras. 23, 119, 154 (emphasis in original), 170, 186–89, 223–28; Anthony H. Cordesman, *The "Gaza War": A strategic analysis* (Washington, DC: 2009), pp. 10, 18–23 passim, 36, 42, 44, 63–66 passim; Intelligence and Terrorism Information Center, *Hamas and the Terrorist Threat,* pp. 110–42, 195–261; Amnesty International, *Operation "Cast Lead": 22 Days of death and destruction* (London: 2009), pp. 3–4, 47–50, 64, 74–77. For human rights investigations echoing Amnesty's finding that some Hamas militants fought in built-up areas but did not use Palestinian civilians as human shields, see Human Rights Watch, "Letter to EU Foreign Ministers to Address Violations between Israel and Hamas" (16 March 2009); Human Rights Watch, *Rockets from Gaza,* pp. 22, 24; Goldstone Report, paras. 35, 452, 475, 482–88, 494, 1953. For human rights organizations and IDF testimony corroborating Israel's use of human shields, see National Lawyers Guild, *Onslaught: Israel's attack on Gaza & the rule of law* (2009), pp. 14–15; Human Rights Watch, *White Flag Deaths: Killings of Palestinian civilians during Operation Cast Lead* (2009), pp. 11–12; Breaking the Silence, *Soldiers' Testimonies from Operation Cast Lead, Gaza 2009* (2009), pp. 7–8 (Testimony 1), 107 (Testimony 51); Goldstone Report, paras. 55, 1032–1106; Al Mezan, *Bearing the Brunt,* pp. 52–59. In a pair of newspaper articles, B'Tselem executive director Jessica Montell alleged that Hamas did engage in human shielding, but she was unable to provide any corroborative evidence despite repeated requests by this writer. Jessica Montell, "A Time for Soul-Searching," *Jerusalem Post* (30 September 2009); Jessica Montell, "The Goldstone Report on Gaza," *Huffington Post* (1 October 2009).

8. Avishai Margalit and Michael Walzer, "Israel: Civilians & combatants," *New York Review of Books* (14 May 2009).

"explores the myths and illusions" about the Middle East, senior US diplomat Dennis Ross inveighed against Hamas because it used "the civilian population as human shields" and made "extensive use of human shields."[9] British colonel Richard Kemp, who was commander of British forces in Afghanistan, variously alleged that Hamas "deliberately positioned [itself] behind the human shield of the civilian population"; "ordered, forced when necessary, men, women and children from their own population to stay put in places they knew were about to be attacked by the IDF"; "deliberately" lured Israel "into killing their own innocent civilians"; and "of course" deployed "women and children" as suicide bombers. The nexus of these allegations with terrestrial reality was as tenuous as his peroration, ubiquitously quoted by Israel's apologists, that "During Operation Cast Lead the IDF did more to safeguard the rights of civilians in a combat zone than any other Army in the history of warfare."[10] Implausible as this assertion is, it does evoke pity for the civilian population caught in Kemp's theater of operations.

The circumstances surrounding the deaths of many Palestinians underscored the frailty of Israel's "human shields" alibi. "The attacks that caused the greatest number of fatalities and injuries," Amnesty found,

> were carried out with long-range high-precision munitions fired from combat aircraft, helicopters and drones, or from tanks stationed up to several kilometers away—often against pre-selected targets, a process that would normally require approval from up the chain of command. The victims of these attacks were not caught in the crossfire of battles between Palestinian militants and Israeli forces, nor were they shielding militants or other legitimate targets. Many were killed when their homes were bombed while they slept. Others were going about their daily activities in their homes, sitting in their yard, hanging the laundry on the roof when they were targeted in air strikes or tank shelling. Children were studying or playing in their bedrooms or on the roof, or outside their homes, when they were struck by missiles or tank shells.[11]

9. Ross also reported in his "reality-based assessment" that Hamas "rejects the very idea of a two-state solution" (excising Hamas's diplomatic initiatives in recent years); that Hamas "chose to end" the June 2008 cease-fire (excising Israel's deadly 4 November 2008 border raid); and that "an uneasy quiet was restored only after the IDF had destroyed nearly all Hamas military targets" (excising Israel's wholesale assault on Gaza's civilian population). Dennis Ross and David Makovsky, *Myths, Illusions and Peace: Finding a new direction for America in the Middle East* (New York: 2009), pp. 7, 128, 137, 153–54, 244, 247, 252.

10. Colonel Richard Kemp CBE, "International Law and Military Operations in Practice," *Jerusalem Center for Public Affairs* (18 June 2009).

11. Amnesty International, *Operation "Cast Lead,"* p. 7; for details, see ibid., pp. 11ff; see also Goldstone Report, paras. 459, 653–703.

Palestinian civilians, "including women and children, were shot at short range when posing no threat to the lives of the Israeli soldiers," Amnesty further found, and "there was no fighting going on in their vicinity when they were shot."[12] A Human Rights Watch (HRW) study documented Israel's killing of Palestinian civilians who "were trying to convey their noncombatant status by waving a white flag"; "Israeli forces had control of the areas in question, no fighting was taking place there at the time, and Palestinian fighters were not hiding among the civilians who were shot." In a typical incident, "two women and three children from the Abd Rabbo family were standing for a few minutes outside their home—at least three of them holding pieces of white cloth—when an Israeli soldier opened fire, killing two girls, aged two and seven, and wounding the grandmother and third girl."[13] The Goldstone Report concluded that "the Israeli armed forces repeatedly opened fire on civilians who were not taking part in the hostilities and who posed no threat to them," and that "Israeli armed forces had carried out direct intentional strikes against civilians," absent "any grounds which could have reasonably induced the Israeli armed forces to assume that the civilians attacked were in fact taking a direct part in the hostilities."[14] Postinvasion IDF testimonies corroborated the wanton killing of Palestinian civilians: "You see people more or less running their life routine, taking a walk, stuff like that. Definitely not terrorists. I hear from other crews that they fired at people there. Tried to kill them"; "People didn't seem to be too upset about taking human lives"; "Everyone there is considered a terrorist"; "We were allowed to do anything we wanted. Who's to tell us not to?"; "I understood that conduct there had been somewhat savage. 'If you sight it, shoot it'"; "You are allowed to do anything you want . . . for no reason other than it's cool," even firing white phosphorus "because it's fun. Cool."[15]

The absurdly lopsided Palestinian-Israeli casualty ratio attested that Cast Lead was, in reality, not a war but a massacre. It was "typical of a particular kind of 'police action,'" Harvard law professor Duncan Kennedy observed,

12. Amnesty International, *Operation "Cast Lead,"* pp. 1, 24; for details, see ibid., esp. pp. 24–27. See also Goldstone Report, paras. 704–885.

13. Human Rights Watch, *White Flag Deaths,* pp. 2, 4, 10–15.

14. Goldstone Report, paras. 802, 810–11.

15. Amos Harel, "Shooting and Crying," *Haaretz* (19 March 2009); Amos Harel, "Testimonies on IDF Misconduct in Gaza Keep Rolling In," *Haaretz* (22 March 2009); Breaking the Silence, *Soldiers' Testimonies,* pp. 21–23 (Testimony 8), 75 (Testimony 32), 88 (Testimony 39), 89 (Testimony 40).

"that Western colonial powers ... have historically undertaken to convince resisting native populations that unless they stop resisting they will suffer unbearable death and deprivation."[16] Indeed, the specter of a massacre kept creeping into postinvasion IDF testimonies. One soldier recollected how Cast Lead was largely conducted by remote control. "It feels like hunting season has begun," he mused. "Sometimes it reminds me of a PlayStation [video] game." "You feel like a child playing around with a magnifying glass," another soldier remembered, "burning up ants."[17] "Most casualties were inflicted on Palestinians by air strikes, artillery fire, and snipers from afar," a pair of soldiers recalled a year after the invasion. "Combat victory? Shooting fish in a barrel is more like it."[18] To invoke the phrase "pulverization of Gazans," *New Republic* literary editor Leon Wieseltier nonetheless protested, was "calculatedly indifferent to the wrenching moral and strategic perplexities that are contained in the awful reality of asymmetrical war."[19] Indeed, shouldn't we pity the poor Israelis as they wrestled with the perplexities of incinerating ants and shooting fish in a barrel? In the meantime, Israeli philosopher Asa Kasher declared, "I am deeply impressed with the courage displayed by each and every one of the soldiers who participated in Operation Cast Lead and their commanders."[20] Eight Israeli soldiers received medals for "heroism."[21]

The modus operandi of Cast Lead pointed up the appositeness of the soldiers' imagery. An HRW study of Israel's "unlawful" use of white phosphorus fleshed out the burning ants metaphor. Causing "horrific burns," sometimes to the bone, white phosphorus reaches a temperature of 1,500 degrees Fahrenheit (816 degrees Celsius).[22] HRW reported that Israel "repeatedly

16. Duncan Kennedy, "A Context for Gaza," *Harvard Crimson* (2 February 2009).
17. Harel, "What Did the IDF Think"; Breaking the Silence, *Soldiers' Testimonies*, p. 88 (Testimony 40).
18. Arik Diamant and David Zonsheine, "Talk to Hamas," *Guardian* (15 February 2010).
19. Leon Wieseltier, "Something Much Darker," *New Republic* (8 February 2010). The offending phrase "pulverization ..." came from former *New Republic* editor Andrew Sullivan, in his denunciation of Cast Lead.
20. Asa Kasher, "Operation Cast Lead and Just War Theory," *Azure* (Summer 2009), p. 70.
21. "8 Cast Lead IDF Heroes Get Decorated," *Jerusalem Post* (16 December 2009).
22. White phosphorus ignites and burns on contact with oxygen, generating a dense white smoke. It is used primarily to camouflage military operations on the ground. In the instant case, however, HRW found that if Israel wanted an obscurant for its troops, it could have used smoke shells (manufactured by an Israeli company), and that its persistent firing of white phosphorus where no Israeli forces were present on the ground indicated that it did in fact serve as an incendiary weapon.

exploded white phosphorus munitions in the air over populated areas, killing and injuring civilians, and damaging civilian structures, including a school, a market, a humanitarian aid warehouse and a hospital." The IDF fired white phosphorus at the UNRWA headquarters in Gaza City "despite repeated warnings from UN personnel about the danger to civilians"; at the UN school in Beit Lahiya even as "the UN had provided the IDF with the GPS coordinates of the school prior to military operations"; and at al-Quds Hospital although it was "clearly marked and there does not appear to have been fighting in that immediate area." HRW also noted that "all of the white phosphorus shells" recovered by it in Gaza were manufactured in the United States.[23] The PlayStation-like nature of Cast Lead was underscored in another HRW study that documented Israel's high-tech assaults on Gaza's population. "Israel's drone-launched missiles are incredibly precise," it reported. "In addition to the high-resolution cameras and other sensors on the drones themselves, the missile fired from a drone has its own cameras that allow the operator to observe the target from the moment of firing.... If a last-second doubt arises about a target, the drone operator can use the missile's remote guidance system to divert the fired missile, steering the missile away from the target with a joystick." HRW investigated six drone attacks that killed 29 civilians (8 of them children). It found that no Palestinian fighters were "present in the immediate area of the attack at the time," and that five of the six attacks "took place during the day, when civilians were shopping, returning from school, or engaged in other ordinary activities, which they most likely would not have done had Palestinian fighters been in the area at the time."[24]

Unabashed and undeterred, the Israeli brief still sang paeans to the IDF's unique respect for the "paramount values of 'Human Life' and 'Purity of Arms,'" as it did "not use ... weapons and force to harm human beings who [were] not combatants or prisoners of war."[25] Kasher lauded the "impeccable" values of the IDF, among them, "protecting the human dignity of every human being, even the most vile terrorist," and the "uniquely Israeli value ...

23. Human Rights Watch, *Rain of Fire: Israel's unlawful use of white phosphorus in Gaza* (2009), pp. 1–6, 39, 60. See also Al Mezan, *Bearing the Brunt,* pp. 42–45.

24. Human Rights Watch, *Precisely Wrong: Gaza civilians killed by Israeli drone-launched missiles* (2009), pp. 4, 6, 12. Israeli drones killed at least 513 persons, including 116 children. Al Mezan, *Bearing the Brunt,* pp. 37–42.

25. State of Israel, *Operation in Gaza,* para. 213.

Palestinians are often taken to task for not embracing a Gandhian strategy that repudiates violent resistance. "If the Palestinians would adopt the ways of Gandhi," US Deputy Secretary of Defense Paul Wolfowitz told a Georgetown University audience in 2003, "I think they could in fact make enormous change very, very quickly."* He might well be right but still, "the ways of Gandhi" do not oblige Palestinians to set down their makeshift weapons. Gandhi classified forceful resistance in the face of impossible odds—a woman fending off a rapist with slaps and scratches, an unarmed man physically resisting torture by a gang, or Polish armed self-defense to the Nazi aggression—as "almost nonviolence." It was in essence symbolic, less violence than a fillip to the spirit to overcome fear and allow for a dignified death; it registered "a refusal to bend before overwhelming might in the full knowledge that it means certain death."† In the face of Israel's infernal, high-tech slaughter in Gaza, didn't the desultory Hamas projectiles fall into the category of token violence that Gandhi was loath to condemn? Even if the projectile attacks did constitute full-fledged violence, it's still not certain that Gandhi would have disapproved. "Fight violence with nonviolence if you can," he exhorted, "and if you can't do that, fight violence by any means, even if it means your utter extinction. But in no case should you leave your hearths and homes to be looted and burnt."‡ Isn't this what Hamas did as it resolved to "fight violence by any means," even if it meant "utter extinction," after Israel broke the cease-fire and refused to lift the illegal siege that was destroying Gaza's "whole civilization" (Mary Robinson) and causing "the breakdown of an entire society" (Sara Roy)?§

* "Hungry Like the Wolfowitz," *Georgetown Voice* (6 November 2003).

† "What Women Should Do in a Difficult Situation" (4 September 1932), in *The Collected Works of Mahatma Gandhi* (Ahmedabad), vol. 51, pp. 18–19; "Discussion with Mahadev Desai" (4 September 1932), in ibid., vol. 51, pp. 24–25; "Discussion with B.G. Kher and Others" (15 August 1940), in ibid., vol. 72, p. 388; "Discussion with Bharatanand" (2 September 1940), in ibid., vol. 72, p. 434; "Message to States' People" (1 October 1941), in ibid., vol. 74, p. 368; "Speech at Prayer Meeting" (5 November 1947), in ibid., vol. 89, p. 481.

‡ "Speech at Goalundo" (6 November 1946), in ibid., vol. 86, p. 86.

§ See Chapter 2.

of the sanctity of human life."[26] Harvard law professor Alan Dershowitz averred that "Israel went to great lengths to protect civilians," while Human Rights Watch founder Robert Bernstein proposed that "the press might consider praising" Israel for its "successful attempts to minimize civilian casualties."[27] In a *New Yorker* cover story on "what really happened," journalist Lawrence Wright reported that "the Israeli military adopted painstaking efforts to spare civilian lives in Gaza."[28] Which should trouble more: that they did or didn't believe these fantasies?

Israel's "human shields" alibi was symptomatic of its endeavors to obfuscate what actually happened during the invasion. In fact, Israel began its *hasbara* (propaganda) preparations six months before Cast Lead was launched, and a centralized body in the prime minister's office, the National Information Directorate, was specifically tasked with coordinating the PR campaign.[29] Still, after world public opinion turned against Israel, Anthony Cordesman blamed its isolation on a failure to invest in the "war of perceptions." Israel "did little to explain the steps it was taking to minimize civilian casualties and collateral damage on the world stage"; it "certainly could—and should—have done far more to show its level of military restraint and make it credible."[30] In the opinion of *Haaretz.com* senior editor Bradley Burston, the problem was that Israelis "are execrable at public relations," while according to Israeli political scientist Shlomo Avineri, if the world took a dim view of Cast Lead, it was because of "the name given to the operation, which greatly

26. Asa Kasher, "A Moral Evaluation of the Gaza War," *Jerusalem Post* (7 February 2010).

27. Alan Dershowitz, *The Case against the Goldstone Report: A study in evidentiary bias* (www.alandershowitz.com/goldstone.pdf), pp. 7, 11, 21, 22; Robert L. Bernstein, "Human Rights in the Middle East," *UN Watch* (10 November 2010).

28. Lawrence Wright, "Captives: A report on the Israeli attacks," *New Yorker* (9 November 2009). During his sojourn in Gaza, Wright divined that the local population felt a special affinity with an Israeli soldier captured by Hamas: "[Gilad] Shalit's pale features and meek expression haunt the imagination of Gazans. Though it may seem perverse, a powerful sense of identification has arisen between the shy soldier and the people whose government holds him hostage. Gazans see themselves as like Shalit: confined, mistreated, and despairing." This resolved the mystery as to why one Gazan family after another had christened their newborn Gilad...

29. Anshel Pfeffer, "Israel Claims Success in the PR War," *Jewish Chronicle* (31 December 2008); Hirsh Goodman, "The Effective Public Diplomacy Ended with Operation Cast Lead," *Jerusalem Post* (5 February 2009).

30. Cordesman, *"Gaza War,"* pp. 31–32, 68.

affects the way in which it will be perceived."[31] But if the micromanaged *hasbara* blitz ultimately did not convince, the explanation lay neither in Israel's failure to convey its humanitarian ethos nor in the world's misapprehension of what happened. Rather, the scope of the massacre was so appalling that ultimately no amount of propaganda could disguise it. It did take time, however, before the true picture emerged. Israel had imposed "the most draconian press controls in the history of modern warfare."[32] The Foreign Press Association denounced the media clampdown as putting "the state of Israel in the company of a handful of regimes around the world which regularly keep journalists from doing their jobs," while Reporters without Borders protested that it was "outrageous and should be condemned by the international community."[33] But the challenge of filtering images coming out of Gaza proved more intractable after the cease-fire went into effect. Israel could no longer bar foreign journalists on the specious pretexts it had concocted during the assault. Still, more than a half year after Cast Lead ended, Israel obstructed the passage into Gaza of human rights organizations such as Amnesty, HRW, and B'Tselem (Israeli Information Center for Human Rights in the Occupied Territories). "If Israel has nothing to hide," HRW asked rhetorically, "why is it refusing to allow us in?"[34]

Israel's *hasbara* campaign suffered a major setback when several Israeli media outlets circulated the postinvasion testimonies of combat pilots and infantry soldiers who either committed war crimes or witnessed them in Gaza. The Israeli organization Breaking the Silence then published a large compilation of damning IDF testimonies. The Israeli brief reassured readers that "Israel is an open and democratic society which fully respects the freedom of speech. . . . Information on possible misconduct of soldiers reaches the IDF authorities in various ways."[35] But after publication of the damning

31. Bradley Burston, "Why Does the World Media Love to Hate Israel?," *Haaretz* (23 March 2009); Shlomo Avineri, "What Was the Computer Thinking?," *Haaretz* (18 March 2009). Heeding such counsel, Israel in its official brief avoided mentioning Operation Cast Lead except for a parenthetical reference to "the 'Gaza Operation,' also known as 'Operation Cast Lead.'" *Operation in Gaza*, para. 16.

32. Dominic Waghorn, "They Kept Us Out and Israeli Officials Spun the War," *Independent* (25 January 2009); Lisa Goldman, "Eyeless in Gaza," *Forward* (16 January 2009).

33. Ethan Bronner, "Israel Puts Media Clamp on Gaza," *New York Times* (6 January 2009); Reporters without Borders, *Operation "Cast Lead": News control as military objective* (2009).

34. Human Rights Watch, "Israel: End ban on human rights monitors" (22 February 2009); Human Rights Watch, *White Flag Deaths*, p. 7.

35. State of Israel, *Operation in Gaza*, para. 288.

IDF testimonies, the Israeli foreign ministry pressed European governments that funded Breaking the Silence to cease their subsidies.[36] The official refutations of these damning IDF testimonies carried little credibility. After all, what possible motive could have induced the combatants to lie?[37] The other responses oscillated between feigned disbelief and "rotten apple" minimization.[38] Like the film character Captain Louis Renault, who was "shocked, shocked!" to discover that people were gambling in Casablanca, some officials expressed grief-stricken incredulity that Israeli soldiers could have engaged in criminal conduct. But such behavior was "the natural continuation of the last nine years, when soldiers killed nearly 5,000 Palestinians, at least half of them innocent civilians, nearly 1,000 of them children and teenagers," Gideon Levy retorted, mocking the sham consternation. "Everything the soldiers described from Gaza, everything, occurred during these blood-soaked years as if they were routine events."[39] Israeli officials also sought to downplay these confessions by alleging that it was much ado about a few rotten apples. Or as Alan Dershowitz spun it, "rogue soldiers are a fact of war."[40] But the criminal behavior of individual soldiers was the ineluctable outcome of Cast Lead's overarching criminal objective: to restore Israel's deterrence capacity by inflicting massive lethal violence on a civilian population. "These are not instances of 'errant fire,'" Levy continued, "but of deliberate fire resulting from an order."[41] "The stories of this publication prove that we are not dealing with the failures of individual soldiers, and attest instead to failures ... primarily on a systemic level," Breaking the Silence editorialized.[42] "Hundreds of civilians were not killed 'by mistake' or by a handful of 'rotten apples,'" the Public Committee against Torture in Israel

36. Barak Ravid, "Group That Exposed 'IDF Crimes' in Gaza Slams Israel Bid to Choke Off Its Funds," *Haaretz* (26 July 2009); Barak Ravid, "Israel Targets UK Funding of Group That Exposed 'IDF Crimes' in Gaza," *Haaretz* (29 July 2009); Barak Ravid, "Israel Asks Spain to Stop Funding Group That Reported 'IDF Crimes' in Gaza," *Haaretz* (2 August 2009).

37. Amos Harel, "Can Israel Dismiss Its Own Troops' Stories from Gaza?," *Haaretz* (19 March 2009).

38. Amira Hass, "Time to Believe Gaza War Crimes Allegations," *Haaretz* (24 March 2009).

39. Gideon Levy, "IDF Ceased Long Ago Being 'Most Moral Army in the World,'" *Haaretz* (22 March 2009).

40. Dershowitz, *The Case,* p. 27.

41. Levy, "IDF Ceased."

42. Breaking the Silence, *Soldiers' Testimonies,* p. 5.

found after an extensive investigation.[43] "Declarations made by officials together with accumulating data," the Association for Civil Rights in Israel noted in its annual report, "reveal that the strikes on civilians and civilian structures were generally not the result of a spontaneous, low-level decision, but rather of decisions and directives made by senior echelons in the government and the IDF."[44] Basing itself in part on the IDF testimonies, the Goldstone Report concluded that "the repeated failure to distinguish between combatants and civilians appears . . . to have been the result of deliberate guidance issued to soldiers . . . and not the result of occasional lapses."[45]

No doubt, some IDF soldiers exploited the occasion of the unfolding massacre to sate their sadistic impulses, while others were brutalized by the mayhem that was unleashed. IDF testimonies recalled "the hatred and the joy," and "fun" and "delight" of killing Gazans, the wreaking of destruction "for kicks" and to "make [oneself] happy." Other testimonies captured degenerate soldier banter, such as "I killed a terrorist, whoa. . . . We blew his head off"; "Fortunately the hospitals are full to capacity already, so people are dying more quickly"; "He just couldn't finish this operation without killing someone."[46] Still, it was the barbaric essence of Cast Lead that enabled these "excesses." Homing in on IDF sadism, or for that matter rowdy and uncouth behavior, eclipsed the fundamental truth that the most egregious crimes during Cast Lead were executed in a disciplined, routine fashion. One interlocutor of the confessing Israeli soldiers expressed disgust that they did not restore order and cleanliness in the Gazan homes they had occupied: "That's simply behaving like animals. . . . You are describing an army with very low value norms, that's the truth."[47] But he evinced much less unease over the 6,300 homes methodically razed to the ground by the IDF. In a bid to direct culpability for Cast Lead away from the heartland of Israeli society and toward its Jewish-fundamentalist excrescence, the *hasbara* campaign harped on the bigoted expressions and incendiary exhortations of IDF rabbis and recruits from religious schools. The criminality was the handiwork of

43. PCATI, *No Second Thoughts*, p. 29.

44. Association for Civil Rights in Israel, *The State of Human Rights in Israel and the Occupied Territories: 2009 report* (Jerusalem: 2009), p. 52; see also ibid., p. 50, "Israel intentionally and deliberately bombed government buildings and civilian institutions in Gaza."

45. Goldstone Report, para. 1889.

46. Breaking the Silence, *Soldiers' Testimonies*, pp. 16 (Testimony 5), 55 (Testimony 23), 56–57 (Testimony 24), 73 (Testimony 31), 86 (Testimony 38), 92 (Testimony 41), 93 (Testimony 43).

47. Harel, "Shooting and Crying."

"religious nationalists," the *New York Times*'s Ethan Bronner suggested. They "have moved into more and more positions of military responsibility" and displaced the "secular, Western and educated" kibbutzniks who in Israel's glory days commanded and staffed the IDF.[48] But such an explanation conveniently overlooked, on the one hand, that Cast Lead was the brainchild of an eminently secular triumvirate—Prime Minister Ehud Olmert, Defense Minister Ehud Barak, and Foreign Minister Tzipi Livni—and, on the other hand, that the IDF had committed many brutal excesses long before religious zealots infiltrated its ranks.[49]

After the first round of soldier testimonies, the IDF promised an investigation, but it abruptly closed its probe some ten days later when it concluded that these accounts of wanton killing and destruction were just "rumors."[50] A subsequent IDF "internal investigation" found that "no civilians were purposefully harmed by IDF troops during Operation Cast Lead." Barak lauded the probe, as it "once again proves that the IDF is one of the most moral armies in the world." The Israeli brief purported that "Israel's legal and judicial apparatus is fully equipped and motivated to address alleged violations of national or international law by its commanders and soldiers." But the results of the IDF's internal investigation caused human rights groups to conclude otherwise: "the Israeli military will not objectively monitor itself" (HRW); "the army's claims appear to be more an attempt to shirk its responsibilities than a genuine process to establish the truth" (Amnesty); "there are serious doubts about the willingness of Israel to carry out genuine investigations in an impartial, independent, prompt and effective way" (Goldstone Report).[51] The docket on Cast Lead appeared to vindicate this skepticism. Only four Israelis were convicted of wrongdoing; only three of them were expected to serve jail time. The severest sentence meted out was seven and a half months, for the theft of a Gazan's credit card. Two soldiers convicted of

48. Ethan Bronner, "A Religious War in Israel's Army," *New York Times* (22 March 2009).

49. Norman G. Finkelstein, *Beyond Chutzpah: On the misuse of anti-Semitism and the abuse of history,* expanded paperback edition (Berkeley: 2008), pp. 316–19.

50. Anshel Pfeffer and Amos Harel, "IDF Ends Gaza Probe, Says Misconduct Claims Are 'Rumors,'" *Haaretz* (30 March 2009).

51. Anshel Pfeffer, "Barak: Gaza probe shows IDF among world's most moral armies," *Haaretz* (23 April 2009); State of Israel, *Operation in Gaza,* para. 284; Human Rights Watch, "Israeli Military Investigation Not Credible" (23 April 2009); Amnesty International, "Israeli Army Probe Lacks Credibility and Is No Substitute for Independent Investigation" (23 April 2009); Goldstone Report, paras. 1832, 1961.

using a nine-year-old child as a human shield received three-month suspended sentences.[52] In a touching gesture of atonement, Israeli information minister Yuli Edelstein declared, "I am ashamed of the soldier who stole some credit cards."[53]

The proliferation of human rights reports condemning Cast Lead suggested that Israel had not managed to spin public perceptions; indeed, its *hasbara* campaign had backfired. The brutality of the Israeli attack, on the one hand, and the brazenness of its denials, on the other, jolted the human rights community into action. Consider the Amnesty report, *Fueling Conflict: Foreign arms supplies to Israel/Gaza,*[54] which recommended a comprehensive arms embargo: "Amnesty International is calling on the UN, notably the Security Council, to impose an immediate, comprehensive arms embargo on all parties to the conflict, and on all states to take action individually to impose national embargoes on any arms or weapons transfers to the parties to the conflict until there is no longer a substantial risk that such arms or weapons could be used to commit serious violations of international law." It went on to inventory foreign-made weapons deployed by Israel during Cast Lead, such as US-manufactured white phosphorus shells, tank ammunition, and guided missiles. Putting Israel's chief enabler on the spot, Amnesty reported that "the USA has been by far the major supplier of conventional arms to Israel"; that "the USA has provided large funding each year for Israel to procure arms despite US legislation that restricts such aid to consistently gross human rights violators"; and that "Israel's military intervention in the Gaza Strip has been equipped to a large extent by US-supplied weapons, munitions and military equipment paid for with US taxpayers' money." The report also briefly inventoried the supply of foreign-made weapons to Palestinian armed groups, "on a very small scale compared to . . . Israel."

Amnesty's call for a comprehensive arms embargo on Israel and Palestinian armed groups marked a milestone in the conflict. Human rights organizations had in the past pressed Washington to restrict both military

52. B'Tselem (Israeli Information Center for Human Rights in the Occupied Territories), "Israeli Authorities Have Proven They Cannot Investigate Suspected Violations of International Humanitarian Law by Israel in the Gaza Strip" (5 September 2014); Human Rights Watch, "Israel: Soldiers' Punishment for Using Boy as 'Human Shield' Inadequate" (26 November 2010).

53. "UK Officer Slams 'Pavlovian' Criticism of IDF after Gaza War," *Haaretz* (22 February 2010).

54. Amnesty International, *Fueling Conflict: Foreign arms supplies to Israel/Gaza* (2009).

assistance to Israel and Israel's use of specific weapons so long as it systematically violated the law.[55] But no prominent human rights group had ever published such a precise tabulation of foreign weapons' suppliers to Israel, or called so aggressively for a comprehensive arms embargo by these suppliers. Predictably, the US administration rejected Amnesty's call,[56] and Amnesty itself came under withering attack from the likes of the Anti-Defamation League for its "pernicious and biased report" that "is doing nothing short of denying Israel the right to self-defense."[57] The biggest blow to Israeli *hasbara* was not delivered, however, by established human rights organizations. It came from a direction that caught Israel off guard and ill prepared. The UN Human Rights Council had mandated an investigation of human rights violations during Cast Lead, to be led by Richard Goldstone. When the Goldstone Mission published its devastating findings, Israel erupted in shock and rage, not least because on top of being a distinguished jurist, Goldstone was also a committed Zionist.

55. Amnesty International, *Broken Lives: A year of intifada* (London: 2001); Human Rights Watch, *Razing Rafah: Mass home demolitions in the Gaza Strip* (2004).

56. Stephen Zunes, "Obama and Israel's Military: Still arm-in-arm," *Foreign Policy in Focus* (4 March 2009). As Obama's term of office wound down in 2016, Amnesty, noting that US military assistance to Israel has "been used to commit violations of international human rights and humanitarian law," renewed its call on him to "cancel . . . the recently announced $33 billion in military aid via foreign military financing for Israel that was included in the new 10 year agreement with the Government of Israel." Amnesty International, *Letter to President Barack Obama* (12 October 2016).

57. Anti-Defamation League, "Amnesty International Report on Gaza Conflict 'Pernicious and Biased'" (23 February 2009).

FIGURE 2. Richard Goldstone. © UN Photo / Jean-Marc Ferré.

PART TWO

The Goldstone Report

FIVE

A Zionist Bears Witness

IN APRIL 2009, THE PRESIDENT of the UN Human Rights Council appointed a "Fact-Finding Mission" to "investigate all violations of international human rights law and international humanitarian law" during Operation Cast Lead.[1] Richard Goldstone, ex-judge of the Constitutional Court of South Africa and ex-prosecutor of the International Criminal Tribunals for the former Yugoslavia and Rwanda, was named head of the Mission. Its original mandate was to scrutinize only Israeli violations of human rights during Cast Lead, but Goldstone conditioned his acceptance of the job on broadening the mandate to include violations on all sides. The council president invited Goldstone to write the mandate himself, which he proceeded to do, and which the president then accepted. "It was very difficult to refuse . . . a mandate that I'd written for myself," Goldstone later observed. Still, Israel refused to cooperate with the Mission on the grounds that it was biased.[2] In September 2009, the long-awaited report of the Goldstone Mission was released.[3] It proved to be a searing indictment not just of Cast Lead but also of the ongoing Israeli occupation.

1. *Report of the United Nations Fact-Finding Mission on the Gaza Conflict* (25 September 2009), paras. 1, 151; hereafter: Goldstone Report. For a chilling retrospective on the Goldstone Report, written by a member of the Mission five years after the Israeli assault, see Desmond Travers's unpublished manuscript, "Gaza: '. . . for the day after . . .'" (2014).

2. Goldstone Report, paras. 144, 162; Bill Moyers, *Journal* (23 October 2009), pbs.org/moyers/journal/10232009/transcript1.html. For the extended correspondence between Goldstone and the Government of Israel, see Goldstone Report, annex II, pp. 434–50.

3. For a critical but ultimately favorable assessment of the Goldstone Report by "recognized experts" in the relevant bodies of international law, see *Report of an Expert Meeting Which Assessed Procedural Criticisms Made of the UN Fact-Finding Mission on the Gaza Conflict (The Goldstone Report)* (2009). The experts concluded that the Goldstone Report

The Goldstone Report found that much of the devastation Israel inflicted during Cast Lead was premeditated. It also found that the operation was anchored in a military doctrine that "views disproportionate destruction and creating maximum disruption in the lives of many people as a legitimate means to achieve military and political goals," and that it was "designed to have inevitably dire consequences for the non-combatants in Gaza."[4] The "disproportionate destruction and violence against civilians" sprang from a "deliberate policy," as did the "humiliation and dehumanization of the Palestinian population."[5] Although Israel justified the attack on grounds of self-defense against Hamas[6] rocket attacks, the Report pointed to a different motive. The "primary purpose" of the Israeli blockade was to "bring about a situation in which the civilian population would find life so intolerable that they would leave (if that were possible) or turn Hamas out of office, as well as to collectively punish the civilian population," while Cast Lead itself was "aimed at punishing the Gaza population for its resilience and for its apparent support for Hamas, and possibly with the intent of forcing a change in such support."[7] The Report concluded that the Israeli assault constituted "a deliberately disproportionate attack designed to punish, humiliate and terrorize a civilian population, radically diminish its local economic capacity both to work and to provide for itself, and to force upon it an ever increasing sense of dependency and vulnerability."[8] It also paid tribute to "the resilience and dignity" of the Gazan people "in the face of dire circumstances."[9]

In its legal determinations, the Goldstone Report found that Israel had committed numerous violations of customary and conventional international law. It also ticked off a considerable list of war crimes committed by Israel, including "willful killing, torture or inhuman treatment," "willfully

---

"was very far from being invalidated by the criticisms [directed at it]. The Report raised extremely serious issues which had to be addressed. It contained compelling evidence on some incidents."

4. Goldstone Report, paras. 63, 1213–14.

5. Ibid., paras. 1215, 1892.

6. Here as elsewhere in the book, *Hamas* will be used to denote all Palestinian armed factions in Gaza.

7. Goldstone Report, paras. 1208, 1884.

8. Ibid., para. 1893.

9. Ibid., para. 1898. Goldstone afterward recalled that although initially chary of journeying to Gaza ("I had nightmares about being kidnapped. You know, it was very difficult, especially for a Jew, to go into an area controlled by Hamas"), he was "struck by the warmth of the people that we met and who we dealt with in Gaza" (Moyers, *Journal*).

causing great suffering or serious injury to body or health," "extensive destruction of property, not justified by military necessity and carried out unlawfully and wantonly," and "use of human shields."[10] It further determined that Israeli actions that "deprive Palestinians in the Gaza Strip of their means of sustenance, employment, housing and water, that deny their freedom of movement and their right to leave and enter their own country, that limit their access to courts of law and effective remedies . . . might justify a competent court finding that crimes against humanity have been committed."[11] The Report pinned primary culpability for these criminal offenses on Israel's political and military elites: "The systematic and deliberate nature of the activities . . . leaves the Mission in no doubt that responsibility lies in the first place with those who designed, planned, ordered and oversaw the operations."[12] The Report also determined that the fatalities, property damage, and "psychological trauma" resulting from Hamas's "indiscriminate" and "deliberate" rocket attacks on Israel's civilian population constituted "war crimes and may amount to crimes against humanity."[13] A charge of bias was leveled against the Report because only a small fraction of

10. Goldstone Report, paras. 46, 50, 60, 937, 961, 987, 1006, 1171–75, 1935.

11. Ibid., paras. 75, 1334–35, 1936. A fact-finding committee chaired by Goldstone's distinguished South African colleague, John Dugard, went somewhat further in its legal conclusions. It determined that in the course of a "heinous and inhuman" attack, Israel had committed war crimes, such as "indiscriminate and disproportionate attacks on civilians," "killing, wounding and terrorizing civilians," "wanton destruction of property," and the bombing and shelling of hospitals and ambulances and obstructing the evacuation of the wounded. It further determined that Israel was guilty of crimes against humanity, including the intentional and "reckless" killing of civilians, "mass killings—'extermination'—in certain cases," and "persecution." It did not, however, hold Israel culpable for the crime of genocide: "the main reason for the operation was not to destroy a group, as required for the crime of genocide, but to engage in a vicious exercise of collective punishment designed either to compel the population to reject Hamas as the governing authority of Gaza or to subdue the population into a state of submission." Still, it determined that "individual soldiers may well have had such an intent and might therefore be prosecuted for this crime." *Report of the Independent Fact-Finding Committee on Gaza: No safe place.* Presented to the League of Arab States (30 April 2009), paras. 20, 22–23, 25–30 of Executive Summary; paras. 405, 485–91, 496–98, 500–504, 506–10, 519–20, 526–29, 540–47, 554–58, 572–73; hereafter: Dugard Report.

12. Goldstone Report, para. 1895.

13. Ibid., paras. 108, 1691, 1953. The Dugard Committee held Hamas culpable for war crimes, such as "indiscriminate and disproportionate attacks on civilians" and "killing, wounding and terrorizing civilians." However, it entered the caveat that "a number of factors . . . reduce their moral blameworthiness but not their criminal responsibility," among them, "Palestinians have been denied their right to self-determination by Israel and have long been subjected to a cruel siege by Israel"; "the scale of Israel's action"; and "the great difference in

it was devoted to Hamas rocket attacks. The accusation of bias was valid, but the bias ran in the reverse direction. If the ratio of Palestinian to Israeli deaths stood at more than 100:1, and of homes destroyed at more than 6,000:1, then the proportion of the Report devoted to Hamas's crimes was *much greater* than the objective data warranted.[14] When it was subsequently put to Goldstone that the Report disproportionately focused on Israeli breaches of international law, he replied, "It's difficult to deal equally with a state party, with a sophisticated army, . . . with an air force, and a navy, and the most sophisticated weapons that are not only in the arsenal of Israel, but manufactured and exported by Israel, on the one hand, with Hamas using really improvised, imprecise armaments."[15]

The Goldstone Report did not limit itself strictly to Cast Lead. It broadened out into a comprehensive, full-blown indictment of Israel's treatment of Palestinians during the long years of occupation. The Report condemned Israel's fragmentation of the Palestinian people,[16] and its restrictions on Palestinian freedom of movement;[17] its "institutionalized discrimination" against Palestinians both in the occupied Palestinian territories and in Israel;[18] its violent repression of Palestinian (as well as Israeli) demonstrators opposing the occupation, and the violent attacks on Palestinian civilians in the West Bank by Israeli soldiers and Jewish settlers enjoying legal impunity;[19] its wholesale detention, torture, and ill-treatment of Palestinians (including

---

both the weapons capability of the opposing sides and the use of their respective weaponry." Dugard Report, paras. 21, 24, 35 of Executive Summary; paras. 457, 484, 495, 499, 575–77.

14. Dinah PoKempner, general counsel of Human Rights Watch, additionally noted that it was "hardly surprising" that the space given over to Hamas was "fairly brief because there is little factual dispute about whether the Gaza authorities tolerated firing of rockets onto Israel's civilian areas, and no legal ambiguity to discuss." "Valuing the Goldstone Report," *Global Governance* 16 (2010), p. 153.

15. Moyers, *Journal.*

16. "Israel has bureaucratically and logistically effectively split and separated not only Palestinians in the occupied territories and their families in Israel, but also Palestinian residents of Jerusalem and those in the rest of the territory and between Gazans and West Bankers/Jerusalemites." Goldstone Report, para. 205.

17. The Report makes passing reference in this context to "the right of return for refugees" (ibid., paras. 92, 1509).

18. Ibid., paras. 206–7.

19. "In the opinion of the Mission, a line has been crossed, what is fallaciously considered acceptable 'wartime behavior' has become the norm. Public support for a more hard-line attitude towards Palestinians generally, lack of public censure and lack of accountability all combine to increase the already critical level of violence against the protected population" (ibid., para. 1440).

hundreds of children), and the lack of due process;[20] its "silent transfer" of Palestinians in East Jerusalem in order to ethnically cleanse it;[21] its "de facto annexation" of 10 percent of the West Bank on the "Israeli side" of the wall, which "amount[s] to the acquisition of territory by force, contrary to the Charter of the United Nations";[22] and its settlement expansion, land expropriation, and demolition of Palestinian homes and villages.[23] The Report determined that certain of these policies constituted war crimes,[24] and also violated the Palestinians' fundamental (*jus cogens*) right to self-determination.[25] Although it didn't draw a bright-line distinction between the perpetrators and victims of a brutal occupation, the Report did eschew "equating the position of Israel as the Occupying Power with that of the occupied Palestinian population or entities representing it. The differences with regard to the power and capacity to inflict harm or to protect, including by securing justice when violations occur, are obvious."[26]

The Goldstone Report proposed several remedies to hold Israel and Hamas accountable for their respective breaches of international law. Individual states in the international community were exhorted to "start criminal investigations in national courts, using universal jurisdiction, where

20. "The Mission notes the very high number of Palestinians who have been detained since the beginning of the occupation (amounting to 40 percent of the adult male population ...) according to a practice that appears to aim at exercising control, humiliating, instilling fear, deterring political activity and serving political interests" (ibid., para. 1503); "The Mission is ... concerned by the reports of coercion and torture during interrogations, trials based on coerced confessions or secret evidence, and the reportedly systematic and institutionalized ill-treatment in prisons. The Mission is particularly alarmed at the arrest and detention of hundreds of young children, and the rise in child detention during and following the Israeli military operations in Gaza. The ill-treatment of children and adults described to the Mission is disturbing in its seemingly deliberate cruelty" (ibid., paras. 1504–5).

21. Ibid., paras. 1535–37. The Mission explicitly stated that it "considers East Jerusalem part of the Occupied Palestinian Territories" (ibid., p. 369n1062).

22. Ibid., para. 1546.

23. Ibid.

24. "The extensive destruction and appropriation of property, including land confiscation and house demolitions in the West Bank, including East Jerusalem, not justified by military necessity and carried out unlawfully and wantonly, amounts to a grave breach ... of the Fourth Geneva Convention" (ibid., para. 1946).

25. "Insofar as movement and access restrictions, the settlements and their infrastructure, demographic policies vis-à-vis Jerusalem and 'Area C' of the West Bank, as well as the separation of Gaza from the West Bank, prevent a viable, contiguous and sovereign Palestinian State from arising, they are in violation of the *jus cogens* right to self-determination" (ibid., para. 1947).

26. Ibid., para. 1876.

there is sufficient evidence of the commission of grave breaches of the Geneva Conventions of 1949. Where so warranted following investigation, alleged perpetrators should be arrested and prosecuted in accordance with internationally recognized standards of justice."[27] It also called on the UN Security Council to monitor the readiness of Israel and Hamas to "launch appropriate investigations that are independent and in conformity with international standards into the serious violations of international humanitarian and international human rights law." Should either party fail to undertake "good-faith investigations," the Report urged that the Security Council "refer the situation in Gaza to the Prosecutor of the International Criminal Court."[28] It also recommended that Israel pay compensation for damages through a UN General Assembly escrow fund.[29] More broadly, the Report recommended that the High Contracting Parties to the Fourth Geneva Convention "enforce the Convention" and "ensure its respect" in the occupied Palestinian territories. It also called on Israel to "immediately" terminate its blockade of Gaza and strangulation of Gaza's economy, its violence against Palestinian civilians, its "destruction and affronts on human dignity," its impingement on Palestinian political life and repression of political dissent, and its restrictions on freedom of movement. The Report reciprocally called on Hamas to "renounc[e] attacks on Israeli civilians and civilian objects," release the Israeli soldier (Gilad Shalit) held in captivity, release political detainees, and respect human rights.[30]

The Israeli reaction to the Goldstone Report came fast and furious. Apart from a few honorable (if predictable) exceptions, it was subjected for months to a torrent of abuse across the Israeli political spectrum and at all levels of society.[31] Indeed, it was almost impossible to locate the actual Report on the

27. Ibid., paras. 127, 1857, 1975.

28. Ibid., para. 1969.

29. Ibid., paras. 128, 1873, 1971(b).

30. Ibid., paras. 1971–74. The Report also explicitly called on Israel to "release Palestinians who are detained in Israeli prisons in connection with the occupation."

31. The exceptions included Amira Hass, "The One Thing Worse than Denying the Gaza Report," *Haaretz* (17 September 2009); Gideon Levy, "Disgrace in the Hague," *Haaretz* (17 September 2009); Gideon Levy, "Goldstone's Gaza Probe Did Israel a Favor," *Haaretz* (1 October 2009); Yitzhak Laor, "The National Choir," *Haaretz* (22 September 2009); Yitzhak Laor, "Turning Off the Lights," *Haaretz* (7 October 2009); Zeev Sternhell, "A Permanent Moral Stain," *Haaretz* (25 September 2009); Larry Derfner, "A Wake-Up Call from Judge Goldstone," *Jerusalem Post* (16 September 2009); Larry Derfner, "Our Exclusive Right to Self-Defense," *Jerusalem Post* (7 October 2009); Larry Derfner, "Some Victims We Are," *Jerusalem Post* (28 October 2009). The leader of the dovish Meretz party and *Haaretz*

Web amid the avalanche of vicious attacks. After dismissing the Report as a "mockery of history" and Goldstone himself as a "small man, devoid of any sense of justice, a technocrat with no real understanding of jurisprudence," Israeli president Shimon Peres proceeded to set the record straight: "IDF [Israel Defense Forces] operations enabled economic prosperity in the West Bank, relieved southern Lebanese citizens from the terror of Hezbollah, and have enabled Gazans to have normal lives again."[32] Prime Minister Benjamin Netanyahu purported that the Report was "a kangaroo court against Israel,"[33] while Defense Minister Ehud Barak inveighed that it was "a lie, distorted, biased and supports terror."[34] Netanyahu subsequently proposed an initiative to "amend the rules of war" in order to facilitate the "battle against terrorists" in the future. "What is it that Israel wants?" Israeli historian Zeev Sternhell shot back. "Permission to fearlessly attack defenseless population centers with planes, tanks and artillery?"[35] Knesset Speaker Reuven Rivlin warned that the Report's "new and crooked morality will usher in a new era in Western civilization, similar to the one that we remember from the [1938] Munich agreement."[36] Before the hate fest was over, almost every prominent political figure in and out of office had chimed in. Former foreign minister

---

editorials called on the Israeli government to set up a commission of inquiry. Gil Hoffman and Haviv Rettig Gur, "Oron Calls for Israeli Cast Lead Probe," *Jerusalem Post* (18 September 2009); "A Committee of Inquiry Is Needed," *Haaretz* (18 September 2009); "Only an External Probe Will Do," *Haaretz* (3 October 2009); "Israel's Whitewash," *Haaretz* (28 January 2010).

32. "Statement by President Shimon Peres: 'Goldstone Mission report is a mockery of history'" (16 September 2009), mfa.gov.il/mfa/pressroom/2009/pages/president-peres-reply-to-the-goldstone-commission-report-16-sep-2009.aspx; Shuki Sadeh, "Peres: Goldstone is a small man out to hurt Israel," *Haaretz* (12 November 2009).

33. Barak Ravid and Natasha Mozgovaya, "Netanyahu Calls UN Gaza Probe a 'Kangaroo Court' against Israel," *Haaretz* (16 September 2009).

34. "Rights Council to Debate Gaza War," *Al Jazeera* (15 October 2009), aljazeera.com/news/europe/2009/10/2009101521222102631.html; Barak Ravid, "Israel Slams Goldstone 'Misrepresentations' of Internal Probes into Gaza War," *Haaretz* (7 February 2010).

35. Barak Ravid, "Israel Prepares to Fight War Crimes Trials after Goldstone Gaza Report," *Haaretz* (20 October 2009); Barak Ravid, "Israel to Set Up Team to Review Gaza War Probe," *Haaretz* (26 October 2009); Zeev Sternhell, "With a Conscience That Is Always Clear," *Haaretz* (30 October 2009). Apropos Netanyahu's proposal, Goldstone observed, "It seems to me to contain an implicit acceptance that they broke the law that now is, and that's why it needs to be changed." Moyers, *Journal*.

36. Rebecca Anna Stoil and Tovah Lazaroff, "EU to Debate Goldstone Report," *Jerusalem Post* (24 February 2010).

Tzipi Livni declared that the Goldstone Report was "born in sin,"[37] Foreign Minister Avigdor Lieberman declared that it had "no legal, factual or moral value," and Deputy Foreign Minister Danny Ayalon warned that it "provides legitimacy to terrorism" and risks "turning international law into a circus."[38] Dan Gillerman, former Israeli ambassador to the United Nations, ripped the Report for "blatant, one-sided, anti-Israel lies," and Dore Gold, former Israeli ambassador to the United Nations, derided it as "one of the most potent weapons in the arsenal of international terrorist organizations," while Gabriela Shalev, Israeli ambassador to the United Nations, castigated it as "biased, one-sided and political."[39] Michael Oren, Israeli ambassador to the United States, won the Triple Crown for venomous spewings. He alleged in an address to the American Jewish Committee that Hezbollah was one of the Report's principal beneficiaries; intoned in the *Boston Globe* that the Report "must be rebuffed by all those who care about peace"; and reckoned in the *New Republic* that the Report was even worse than "[Iranian president Mahmoud] Ahmadinejad and the Holocaust deniers."[40] IDF chief of staff Gabi Ashkenazi ridiculed the Report as "biased and unbalanced," while IDF senior legal advisor Avichai Mendelblit mocked it as "biased, astonishingly extreme, lack[ing] any basis in reality."[41]

Nongovernmental institutions and public figures also weighed in. The *Jerusalem Post* editorialized that the Report was "a feat of cynical superficiality," and was "born in bias and matured into a full-fledged miscarriage of

37. "Dershowitz: Goldstone is a traitor," *Jerusalem Post* (31 January 2010).

38. Hoffman and Gur, "Oron Calls"; Donald Macintyre, "Israelis Hit Back at UN Report Alleging War Crimes in Gaza," *Independent* (17 September 2009); Ravid and Mozgovaya, "Netanyahu Calls."

39. Shalhevet Zohar, "Peres: Goldstone report mocks history," *Jerusalem Post* (16 September 2009); Dore Gold, "The Dangerous Bias of the United Nations Goldstone Report," *US News & World Report* (24 March 2010).

40. Michael Oren, "UN Report a Victory for Terror," *Boston Globe* (24 September 2009); Michael Oren, "Address to AJC" (28 April 2010), ajc.org/site/apps/nlnet/content2.aspx?c=ijITI2PHKoG&b=5970663&ct=8222031; Michael B. Oren, "Deep Denial: Why the Holocaust still matters," *New Republic* (6 October 2009). Journalist Gideon Levy dubbed Oren "the ambassador-propagandist." Gideon Levy, "Israel's Attacks Will Lead to Its Isolation," *Haaretz* (22 October 2009). For critical analysis of Oren's scholarship, see Norman G. Finkelstein, *Knowing Too Much: Why the American Jewish romance with Israel is coming to an end* (New York: 2012), pp. 221–48.

41. "We'll Defend Ourselves by Any Means," *Jerusalem Post* (21 September 2009); Yaakov Katz, "Security and Defense: Waging war on the legal front," *Jerusalem Post* (18 September 2009); Amos Harel, "IDF: UN Gaza report biased, radical and groundless," *Haaretz* (20 September 2009).

justice." Former *Haaretz* editor in chief David Landau lamented that the Report's "fundamental premise, that the Israelis went after civilians," eliminated any possibility of "honest debate."[42] (Far from its premise, that was the Report's conclusion after scrutinizing mountains of evidence.) Israel Harel, a leader of the settler movement, scoffed at the Report as "destructive, toxic," even worse than the *Protocols of the Elders of Zion,* and misdirected "against precisely that country which protects human and military ethics more than the world has ever seen." Residents of an Israeli town abutting Gaza picketed UN offices in Jerusalem with placards declaring, "Goldstone apologize" and "We're sick of anti-Semites."[43] A Tel Aviv University center for the study of "anti-Semitism and racism" purported that the Report was responsible for a global surge in "hate crimes against Jews" and "the equation of the war in Gaza with the Holocaust."[44] Alleging that Goldstone's accusations against Israel echoed those leveled against Alfred Dreyfus, Professor Gerald Steinberg of Bar Ilan University declared that "Israel had the moral right to flatten all of Gaza."[45] (Steinberg founded the university's program on conflict resolution and management.) Fully 94 percent of those Israeli Jews familiar with the Report held it to be biased against Israel, and 79 percent rejected its accusation that the IDF committed war crimes.[46] Even after Cast Lead and the ensuing lies and cover-ups by the military, fully 90 percent of Israeli Jews ranked the IDF as the state institution they most trusted.[47] Inasmuch as the Report's findings were beyond the pale, the only issue deemed worthy of public deliberation in Israel was whether or not Israel should have cooperated with the Goldstone Mission.[48] But as veteran peace

42. "Goldstoned," *Jerusalem Post* (16 September 2009); "The 'Goldstoning' of Israel," *Jerusalem Post* (2 February 2010); David Landau, "The Gaza Report's Wasted Opportunity," *New York Times* (20 September 2009).

43. Israel Harel, "Venom and Destruction," *Haaretz* (18 September 2009); Israel Harel, "Don't Establish an Investigative Panel," *Haaretz* (1 October 2009); Jack Khoury, "Goldstone Tells Obama: Show me flaws in Gaza report," *Haaretz* (22 October 2009).

44. Stephen Roth Institute for the Study of Contemporary Antisemitism and Racism, *Antisemitism Worldwide 2009* (2010), www.tau.ac.il/Anti-Semitism/, pp. 29, 37, 39.

45. Gerald Steinberg, "From Dreyfus to Goldstone," *Canadian Jewish News* (19 November 2009).

46. "Israel's Jewish Public: Goldstone report biased against IDF," *ynetnews.com* (18 October 2009).

47. Asher Arian et al., *Auditing Israeli Democracy: Democratic values in practice* (Jerusalem: 2010), pp. 88, 133, 173.

48. Yehezkel Dror, "Why Israel Should Have Cooperated with Goldstone on Gaza," *Haaretz* (21 September 2009).

activist Uri Avnery pointed out, the "real answer" why Israel chose not to cooperate "is quite simple: they knew full well that the mission, any mission, would have to reach the conclusions it did reach."[49] In a telling departure from past histrionics, Israelis dispensed after Cast Lead with those emotive outpourings of angst—"shooting and crying"—that cheerleaders abroad used to tout as proof of the uniquely sensitive Jewish soul. Brutalized and calloused, Israelis no longer even bothered to feign remorse. Although calling for a cease-fire after the initial air assault, the icons of Israel's "peace camp"— Amos Oz, A. B. Yehoshua, and David Grossman—still alleged that Hamas was "responsible" for the unfolding horror, and that the Israeli ground-and-air attack was "necessary" because Hamas leaders "refused every Israeli and Egyptian attempt to reach a compromise to prevent this latest flare-up."[50]

In a secondary blast of hot air, the usual suspects in the United States rose (or sunk) to the occasion by lambasting the message and slandering the messenger. Max Boot dismissed the Goldstone Report on *Commentary*'s website as a "risible series of findings," while John Bolton, former US ambassador to the United Nations, opined in the *Wall Street Journal* that "the logical response to this debacle is to withdraw from and defund" the Human Rights Council.[51] Elie Wiesel condemned the Report not only as "a crime against the Jewish people," but also as being "unnecessary": "I can't believe that Israeli soldiers murdered people or shot children. It just can't be."[52] Heading up the domestic witch hunt, Harvard Law School's Alan Dershowitz alleged that the Report "is so filled with lies, distortions and blood libels that it could have been drafted by Hamas extremists"; that it echoed the *Protocols of the Elders of Zion* and was "biased and bigoted"; that "every serious student of human rights should be appalled at this anti-human rights and highly politicized report"; that it made "findings of fact (nearly all wrong)," stated "conclusions of law (nearly all questionable)," and made "specific recommendations (nearly all one-sided)"; that Goldstone himself was "a traitor to the

49. Uri Avnery, "UM-Shmum, UM-Boom," Gush Shalom (19 September 2009), zope .gush-shalom.org/home/en/channels/avnery/1253361627/.

50. Maya Sela, "Amos Oz: Hamas responsible for outbreak of Gaza violence," *Haaretz* (30 December 2008); David Grossman, "Is Israel Too Imprisoned in the Familiar Ceremony of War?," *Haaretz* (30 December 2008).

51. Max Boot, "The Goldstone Report," *Commentary* blog ("Contentions") (16 September 2009); John Bolton, "Israel, the US and the Goldstone Report," *Wall Street Journal* (20 October 2009).

52. "Wiesel: If Ahmadinejad were assassinated, I wouldn't shed a tear," *Haaretz* (9 February 2010); "I Wouldn't Cry If He Was Killed," *Jerusalem Post* (9 February 2010).

Jewish people," an "evil, evil man," and—he proclaimed on Israeli television—on a par with Auschwitz "Angel of Death" Josef Mengele.[53] The
"essence" and "central conclusion" of the Report, according to Dershowitz,
was that Israel had a "carefully planned and executed policy of deliberately
targeting innocent civilians for mass murder"; Israel's "real purpose" was "to
target innocent Palestinian civilians—children, women and the elderly—for
death." He repeated this characterization of the Report on nearly every
page—often multiple times on a single page—of his lengthy "study in evidentiary bias," and then proceeded to handily refute the accusation.[54] But
Dershowitz conjured a straw man: the Report never stated or suggested that
the principal objective of Cast Lead was to murder Palestinians. Otherwise,
it would have had to charge Israel with genocide. It is a commonplace that
the more frequently a lie is repeated the more credible it becomes. The novelty
of Dershowitz's "study" was that it kept repeating a falsehood the more easily
to discredit its alleged purveyor. Goldstone-bashers in the United States also
claimed that Hamas had coached and intimidated Palestinian witnesses,
disguised its militants as witnesses, and fed Goldstone uncorroborated information.[55] However, none of these detractors adduced a shred of evidence,
while Goldstone himself rejoined by offering "every assurance that it didn't
happen."[56] Communal Jewish organizations predictably joined in the gang-
up. The American Israel Public Affairs Committee (AIPAC) called the
Goldstone Mission "rigged" and the Report "deeply flawed";[57] the American

53. Alan M. Dershowitz, "Goldstone Investigation Undercuts Human Rights," *Jerusalem Post* blog ("Double Standard Watch") (17 September 2009); Alan Dershowitz, "Goldstone Criticizes UN Council on Human Rights," *Huffington Post* (22 October 2009); Alan M. Dershowitz, "Goldstone Backs Away from Report: The two faces of an international poseur," *Jerusalem Post* blog ("Double Standard Watch") (15 October 2009); "Dershowitz: Goldstone is a traitor," *Jerusalem Post;* Josh Nathan-Kazis, "Dershowitz Explains Critical Goldstone Remark," *Forward* (3 February 2010); Tehiya Barak, "Judge Goldstone's Dark Past," *ynetnews.com* (6 May 2010).

54. Alan Dershowitz, *The Case against the Goldstone Report: A study in evidentiary bias,* www.alandershowitz.com/goldstone.pdf.

55. Jeffrey Goldberg, "J Street, Down the Rabbit Hole," *Atlantic* blog (30 September 2010); Joshua Muravchik, "Goldstone: An exegesis," *World Affairs* (May/June 2010). Muravchik also conjured the astonishing claim that Goldstone never asked Gazan witnesses to Israeli attacks "whether a Palestinian gunman was nearby." See also Bernard-Henri Lévy, "It's Time to Stop Demonizing Israel," *Haaretz* (8 June 2010).

56. Moyers, *Journal.*

57. Eric Fingerhut, "AIPAC Condemns Goldstone Report," *Jewish Telegraphic Agency* (17 September 2009).

Jewish Committee deplored it as a "deeply distorted document";[58] Abraham Foxman of the Anti-Defamation League was "shocked and distressed that the United States would not unilaterally dismiss it."[59]

The Obama administration quickly fell into lockstep with the Israel lobby. However, it probably did not need much prodding. One of Israel's talking points in Washington was that the Goldstone Report's recommendation to prosecute soldiers for war crimes "should worry every country fighting terror."[60] State Department spokesman Ian Kelly alleged that whereas the Report "makes overly sweeping conclusions of fact and law with respect to Israel, its conclusions regarding Hamas's deplorable conduct ... are more general"; Assistant US Secretary of State for Democracy Michael Posner condemned it as "deeply flawed"; and Deputy US Ambassador to the United Nations Alejandro Wolff faulted its "unbalanced focus on Israel."[61] In its 47-page entry for "Israel and the occupied territories," the US State Department's *2009 Human Rights Report* devoted all of three sentences to Cast Lead, then touched on the Report's findings and disparagingly concluded: "The Goldstone report was widely criticized for methodological failings, legal and factual errors, falsehoods, and for devoting insufficient attention to the asymmetrical nature of the conflict and the fact that Hamas and other Palestinian militants were deliberately operating in heavily populated urban areas of Gaza."[62] Congressman Gary Ackerman, chair of the House Subcommittee on the Middle East and South Asia, mocked Goldstone as inhabiting a "self-righteous fantasyland" and the Report as a "pompous, tendentious, one-sided political diatribe."[63] The probability that any of these critics actually read the Report approaches zero. After mutely absorbing this relentless barrage of attacks, Goldstone finally dared the Obama administra-

58. American Jewish Committee, "Letter to Secretary Clinton Urges Condemnation of Goldstone Report" (23 September 2009).

59. "Rice: 'Serious concerns' about the Goldstone Report," *Jewish Telegraphic Agency* (17 September 2009).

60. Nathan Guttman, "Israel, US Working to Limit Damage of Goldstone Report," *Haaretz* (27 September 2009).

61. Laura Rozen, "State on Goldstone Report: 'Deeply concerned,'" *Politico* (18 September 2009); Barak Ravid and Shlomo Shamir, "PA Pushing for UN to Act on Goldstone 'War Crime' Findings," *Haaretz* (1 October 2009); Shlomo Shamir, "UN Human Rights Chief Endorses Goldstone Gaza Report," *Haaretz* (23 October 2009).

62. US Department of State, *2009 Human Rights Report*.

63. House Subcommittee on the Middle East and South Asia, "Ackerman Blasts Goldstone Report as 'Pompous, Tendentious, One-Sided Political Diatribe'" (16 September 2009).

tion to substantively justify its criticisms.[64] Meanwhile, Human Rights Watch (HRW) took to task the US government for "calling the report 'unbalanced' and 'deeply flawed,' but providing no real facts to support those assertions."[65] The US House of Representatives passed by a vote of 344 to 36 a nonbinding resolution that condemned the Report as "irredeemably biased and unworthy of further consideration or legitimacy."[66] Before the vote was taken, Goldstone submitted a point-by-point rebuttal demonstrating that the House resolution was vitiated by "serious factual inaccuracies and instances where information and statements are taken grossly out of context."[67]

The Obama administration worked behind the scenes in concert with Israel to foreclose consideration of the Report in international forums, and privately gloated at the successes it had scored.[68] Hillary Clinton later bragged that while secretary of state in the Obama administration, she had "defended Israel from isolation and attacks at the United Nations and other international settings, including opposing the biased Goldstone report."[69]

64. Khoury, "Goldstone Tells Obama"; "Goldstone Dares US on Gaza Report," *Al Jazeera* (22 October 2009).

65. Human Rights Watch, "UN, US, EU Undermine Justice for Gaza Conflict" (1 October 2009).

66. "H. RES. 867, 111th Congress" (23 October 2009); Natasha Mozgovaya and Barak Ravid, "US House Backs Resolution to Condemn Goldstone Gaza Report," *Haaretz* (5 November 2009); Nima Shirazi, "Goldstonewalled! US Congress endorses Israeli war crimes," *MRzine* (12 November 2009).

67. "Goldstone Sends Letter to Berman, Ros-Lehtinen Correcting Factual Errors in HR 867, Which Opposes UN Fact Finding Report on Gaza," *uruknet.info* (29 October 2009). After Goldstone submitted his rebuttal, one of the resolution's sponsors entered some cosmetic revisions in it. Spencer Ackerman, "Berman Puts New Language into Anti-Goldstone Resolution," *washingtonindependent.com* (3 November 2009). The liberal Jewish lobby group J Street called for a "better, balanced resolution" than the House draft, but one that would still "urge the United States to make clear that it will use its veto to prevent any referral of this matter to the International Criminal Court." "J Street Position on H.Res. 867" (30 October 2009).

68. An administration official initially stated off the record that the United States would block UN action on the Report, but the White House subsequently repudiated the statement. "US Pledges to Quash Goldstone Recommendations," *Jewish Telegraphic Agency* (22 September 2009); "White House: Official 'misspoke' on Goldstone report," *Jewish Telegraphic Agency* (23 September 2009). However, it later came out that Washington had been quietly applying pressure to contain the Report's fallout. Jared Flanery and Ben Norton, "Deferring Justice: Clinton emails show how State Dept. undermined UN action on Israeli war crimes," *Salon* (19 November 2015).

69. Hillary Clinton, "How I Would Reaffirm Unbreakable Bond with Israel—and Benjamin Netanyahu," *Forward* (4 November 2015).

Pressure was also exerted on the Palestinian Authority (PA) to drop its support of the Report's recommendations. "The PA has reached the point where it has to decide," a senior Israeli defense official declared, "whether it is working with us or against us."[70] The answer was not long in coming. Acting at the behest of President Mahmoud Abbas, the PA representative on the UN Human Rights Council effectively acquiesced in killing consideration of the Report. His decision provoked such outrage among Palestinians, however, that the PA had to reverse itself, and the council convened to deliberate on the Report.[71] It approved a resolution "condemning all targeting of civilians and stressing the urgent need to ensure accountability for all violations" of international law, endorsed the Report's recommendations, and urged the United Nations to act on them.[72] In November 2009, the UN General Assembly passed by a vote of 114 to 18 (44 abstentions) a resolution "condemning all targeting of civilians and civilian infrastructure," and calling on both Israel and Hamas to "undertake investigations that are independent, credible and in conformity with international standards into the serious violations of international . . . law reported by the Fact-Finding Mission."[73] Denouncing the resolution as "completely detached from realities" and a "mockery of reality," Israel proclaimed that the vote "proves that Israel is succeeding in getting across the message that the report is one-sided and not serious," and that the "democratic 'premier league' states voted in line with Israel's position"—among them, the Marshall Islands, Micronesia, and Palau.[74] In February 2010, UN secretary-general Ban Ki-moon reported back

70. Amos Harel and Avi Issacharoff, "Israel Demands PA Drop War Crimes Suit at The Hague," *Haaretz* (27 September 2009).

71. Howard Schneider and Colum Mynch, "UN Panel Defers Vote on Gaza Report," *Washington Post* (3 October 2009); Amira Hass, "PA Move to Thwart Goldstone Gaza Report Shocks Palestinian Public," *Haaretz* (4 October 2009).

72. "The Human Rights Situation in the Occupied Palestinian Territory, Including East Jerusalem" (A/HRC/RES/S-12/1) (16 October 2009). It was gleefully reported by Goldstone's critics that he opposed the council's resolution. The rumor was a half-baked truth and a full-blown lie. Goldstone disapproved of the first draft version, but it was modified after he expressed reservations, and he approved of the final version that was put to a vote. Moyers, *Journal*.

73. United Nations General Assembly, "Follow-Up to the Report of the United Nations Fact-Finding Mission on the Gaza Conflict" (A/64/L.11) (2 November 2009); Shlomo Shamir, "UN General Assembly Adopts Goldstone Report," *Haaretz* (6 November 2009).

74. Shlomo Shamir, "Israel: UN 'detached from reality' for adopting Goldstone report," *Haaretz* (6 November 2009); "FM: UNGA vote shows Israel has moral majority," *Jerusalem Post* (6 November 2009).

to the General Assembly that still "no determination can be made on the implementation" of its November 2009 resolution calling for credible investigations.[75] Later that month, the General Assembly passed another resolution by a vote of 98 to 7 (31 abstentions) reiterating its call on Israel and Hamas to "conduct investigations that are independent, credible and in conformity with international standards," and requesting that the secretary-general report back within five months on the implementation of the resolution.[76] Despite intensive lobbying by European Jewish groups, in March 2010 the European Parliament passed (335 to 287) a resolution "demanding" implementation of the Report's recommendations and "accountability for all violations of international law, including alleged war crimes." The spokesman for the Israeli mission to the European Union deplored the resolution as "flawed and counterproductive."[77]

In January and July 2010, Israel released "updates" on its own investigations.[78] Although the pair of updates indicated that scores of investigations had been conducted, the results overwhelmingly exonerated Israelis of wrongdoing. A handful of soldiers suffered disciplinary sanctions, such as an officer who was "severely reprimanded." The harshest sentence meted out was a seven-and-a-half-month prison term to a soldier who had stolen a credit card.[79] Still, even these token punishments caused the IDF to inveigh against the shackles allegedly being placed on it.[80] The Israeli investigations could not, however, be faulted for lack of creativity. One soldier who killed a woman carrying a white flag was exonerated on the grounds that the bullet

75. United Nations General Assembly, *Follow-Up to the Report of the United Nations Fact-Finding Mission on the Gaza Conflict: Report of the Secretary-General* (A/64/651) (4 February 2010).

76. United Nations General Assembly, "Follow-Up to the Report of the United Nations Fact-Finding Mission on the Gaza Conflict (II)" (A/64/L.48) (23 February 2010). The low vote count was probably due to a massive snowstorm that day.

77. "European Parliament Resolution of 10 March 2010 on Implementation of the Goldstone Recommendations on Israel/Palestine" (P7_TAPROV(2010)0054); Leigh Phillips, "Despite Heavy Lobbying, EU Parliament Endorses Goldstone Report," *euobserver .com* (10 March 2010), euobserver.com/9/29650; "EU Parliament Backs Goldstone Report," *Jerusalem Post* (10 March 2010).

78. State of Israel, *Gaza Operation Investigations: An update* (January 2010); State of Israel, *Gaza Operation Investigations: Second update* (July 2010).

79. State of Israel, *Gaza Operation Investigations: An update,* paras. 100, 108, 137; State of Israel, *Gaza Operation Investigations: Second update,* paras. 10, 11, 37, 46, 60, 73, 74, 94, 102.

80. Amos Harel, "MESS Report: Gaza war probes are changing Israel's defiant ways," *Haaretz* (22 July 2010).

was actually a "warning shot" that "ricocheted"—off a cloud?[81] Despite its vindication by these "investigations," Israel magnanimously "adopted important new written procedures and doctrine designed to enhance the protection of civilians . . . and to limit unnecessary damage to civilian property and infrastructure" in future conflicts.[82] The tacit conceit was that if Israel bore a small measure of responsibility for the death and destruction in Gaza, it had resulted from operational deficits, and not—as the Goldstone Report concluded—from an assault "designed to punish, humiliate and terrorize a civilian population." After the first update, *Haaretz* editorialized that the Israeli investigations were "not persuasive that enough has been done to reach the truth." But in a subsequent editorial, it validated the second round of investigations and implied that it was time to close the book on the Report.[83] Both Amnesty and HRW wholly dismissed the first round of Israeli investigations, while HRW stated after the second update that although "some results" had been achieved, the Israeli investigations still "fall far short of addressing the widespread and serious allegations of unlawful conduct during the fighting."[84] The UN high commissioner for human rights announced in June 2010 the formation of an independent committee to "ensure accountability for all violations of international humanitarian and international human rights laws during the Gaza conflict."[85] The committee's report, issued in September 2010,[86] found that whereas "certain positive steps . . . have resulted from Israel's investigations," the bottom line was that "the military investigations thus far appear to have produced very little."[87] Indeed, while "the Committee cannot conclude that credible and genuine investiga-

81. State of Israel, *Gaza Operation Investigations: Second update,* para. 105.

82. Ibid., paras. 150–56.

83. "Israel Is Being Evasive Again," *Haaretz* (1 February 2010); "Thanks to the Critics," *Haaretz* (27 July 2010).

84. Amnesty International, "Latest Israeli Response to Gaza Investigations Totally Inadequate" (2 February 2010); Human Rights Watch, "Military Investigations Fail Gaza War Victims" (7 February 2010); Human Rights Watch, "Wartime Inquiries Fall Short" (10 August 2010).

85. UN News Service, "UN Rights Chief Unveils Members of Independent Probe into Gaza Conflict" (14 June 2010).

86. *Report of the Committee of Independent Experts in International Humanitarian and Human Rights Laws to Monitor and Assess Any Domestic, Legal or Other Proceedings Undertaken by Both the Government of Israel and the Palestinian Side, in the Light of General Assembly Resolution 64/254, Including the Independence, Effectiveness, Genuineness of These Investigations and Their Conformity with International Standards* (21 September 2010).

87. *Report of the Committee,* paras. 42, 55.

tions have been carried out by the de facto authorities in the Gaza Strip,"[88] at the time of the report's issuance, Hamas had apparently convicted and sentenced to prison time more individuals than Israel.[89] After release of the committee's report, Amnesty urged the UN Human Rights Council to "recognize the failure of the investigations conducted by Israel and the Hamas de facto administration," and to "call on the ICC [International Criminal Court] Prosecutor urgently to seek a determination . . . whether the ICC has jurisdiction over the Gaza conflict."[90]

In March 2010, the semiofficial Israeli Intelligence and Terrorism Information Center (ITIC) released a voluminous response to the Goldstone Report.[91] It was based largely on "interrogations of terrorist operatives," "reports from IDF forces," "Israeli intelligence information," and unverifiable and indecipherable photographic evidence. Ignoring copious evidence amassed by human rights organizations, the ITIC publication denied that Gaza was facing a humanitarian crisis before Cast Lead (it blamed Hamas for the shortages that did arise);[92] it denied that Israel's 4 November 2008 raid on Gaza caused the breakdown of the cease-fire with Hamas;[93] and it denied that Israel used Gazans as human shields.[94] In addition, it falsely alleged that the Goldstone Report made "almost no mention of the brutal means of repression used by Hamas against its opponents";[95] it falsely alleged that the Report devoted "just three paragraphs" to Hamas's "rocket and mortar fire during

---

88. Ibid., para. 101.

89. Ibid., paras. 40, 83. The committee reported that Israel had convicted one soldier for the crime of looting, while a Hamas submission gave "examples of criminal proceedings . . . , including a case where a number of defendants were convicted and imprisoned."

90. Amnesty International, "Time for International Justice Solution for Gaza Conflict Victims" (23 September 2010).

91. Intelligence and Terrorism Information Center, *Hamas and the Terrorist Threat from the Gaza Strip: The main findings of the Goldstone Report versus the factual findings* (2010).

92. Ibid., p. 69.

93. Ibid., pp. IV, 8, 73, 80. Whereas a prior ITIC publication had reported that Hamas was "careful to maintain the cease-fire" and sought to "enforce the terms of the arrangement on the other terrorist organizations" (see Chapter 2), this new publication alleged that the cease-fire was "systematically and repeatedly violated by Hamas," and Hamas "made no effective effort to impose the lull" on the other "terrorist organizations." Still, the new publication's own graphs showed that just one rocket and one mortar shell were fired at Israel in October 2008, and it conceded that "the first five months of the lull were relatively quiet" (ibid., pp. 74, 79).

94. Ibid., p. IV.

95. Ibid., pp. 3, 35 (but see Goldstone Report, paras. 1345–72).

Operation Cast Lead," and downplayed Israeli civilian deaths;[96] it falsely alleged that the Report "absolved" Hamas "of all responsibility for war crimes";[97] it falsely alleged that the Report gave "superficial" treatment to "the terrorist organizations' use of civilians as human shields";[98] and it falsely alleged that the Report depended on "the unreliable casualty statistics provided by Hamas."[99] On more than one occasion the ITIC publication tested the limits of chutzpah and credulity. It rebuked not Israel but Hamas for "unwillingness to cooperate with the [Goldstone] Mission,"[100] and it purported that "Hamas operatives would position innocent civilians near IDF tanks to prevent IDF soldiers from shooting at them."[101] In other words, Hamas dragged Palestinian civilians to Israeli tank positions, ordered them to stay put, and then beat a swift retreat. It is not revealed whether the civilians did stay put.

It might be cause for perplexity why the Goldstone Report provoked so much vituperation in Israel and set in motion a "diplomatic blitz" to contain the fallout.[102] It was, after all, just one of hundreds of human rights reports condemning Cast Lead; its findings did not measurably differ from the others; and Israel had never paid heed to UN bodies.[103] The answer, however, was

96. Ibid., pp. 95, 97 (but see Goldstone Report, paras. 1604–6, 1610–36, 1647–74, 1682–91; the Report stated that "the impact on [Israeli] communities is greater than the numbers of fatalities and injuries actually sustained").

97. Ibid., pp. VIII, 57 (but see Goldstone Report, paras. 1687–91). The ITIC publication also faulted the Report for referring to "Palestinian armed groups" instead of explicitly implicating Hamas, but the Report reciprocally referred to "Israeli armed forces."

98. Ibid., p. 120 (but see Goldstone Report, paras. 475–98).

99. Ibid., pp. 315, 321–22 (but see Goldstone Report, paras. 352–63). The ITIC publication also indulged the baseless speculation that Palestinian families seeking "financial compensation" might have reported deaths from "natural causes" as invasion-related (ibid., p. 322).

100. Ibid., p. 318 (but see Goldstone Report, para. 144: whereas Israel refused to cooperate with the Goldstone Mission, "senior members of the Gaza authorities . . . extended their full cooperation and support to the Mission").

101. Ibid., p. 196.

102. Hoffman and Gur, "Oron Calls"; Eitan Haber, "In Wake of Goldstone Report, Israel Must Launch Battle for Its Image," *ynetnews.com* (17 September 2009).

103. Richard Falk, "The Goldstone Report: Ordinary text, extraordinary event," *Global Governance* 16 (2010), p. 173. A member of the Goldstone Mission tallied "some 300" human rights investigations of Cast Lead, which were "remarkable in the unanimity of their findings against the IDF actions." Desmond Travers, "Operation Cast Lead: Legal and doctrinal asymmetries in a military operation," Irish Defense Forces, *An Cosantóir* (2010), p. 10. Some critics alleged that the Report was more "vicious" than the others. Ethan Bronner, "Israel Poised

not hard to find. Goldstone was not only Jewish but also a self-declared Zionist, who "worked for Israel all of my adult life," "fully support[s] Israel's right to exist," and was a "firm believer in the absolute right of the Jewish people to have their home there." He headed up a Jewish organization that managed vocational schools in Israel, and he sat on the board of governors of the Hebrew University in Jerusalem, from which he had received an honorary doctorate. His mother was an activist in the women's branch of the Zionist movement, while his daughter had emigrated to Israel and was an ardent Zionist.[104] Goldstone had also singled out the Nazi holocaust as the seminal inspiration for the international law and human rights agenda of which he was a leading exponent.[105] In light of his Jewish/Zionist bona fides, Israel could not credibly play its usual cards—"anti-Semite," "self-hating Jew," "Holocaust denier"—against Goldstone. In effect, his persona neutralized the ideological weapons Israel had honed over many decades to ward off criticism. "This time," in Gideon Levy's telling phrase, "the messenger is propaganda-proof."[106] To be sure, some desperadoes did try to discredit Goldstone as an "anti-Semite" (Israeli finance minister Yuval Steinitz), and the Report as "partially motivated by anti-Semitic views of Israel" (philosophy professor Asa Kasher) and the "type of anti-Semitism" that led to the Holocaust (Israeli information minister Yuli Edelstein).[107] A Google search for the words *Goldstone anti-Semite Gaza* one week after the Report's publication brought up over 75,000 websites. Still, the slanders collapsed under the weight of their

---

to Challenge a UN Report on Gaza," *New York Times* (23 January 2010). But the contention did not withstand scrutiny. In critical respects, the Report was actually among the more cautious and conservative. Whereas HRW explicitly denoted Israel's use of white phosphorus in civilian areas a "war crime," the Report did not; whereas the Dugard Report concluded that "individual soldiers" might have been guilty of genocide, the Report did not; and whereas Amnesty recommended a comprehensive arms embargo on Israel (and Hamas), the Report did not.

104. Moyers, *Journal;* The Forward and Claudia Braude, "Will Goldstone's Gaza Report Prove Him Just a Naïve Idealist?," *Haaretz* (23 September 2009); "'My Father Is a Zionist, Loves Israel,'" *Jerusalem Post* (16 September 2009); "Goldstone's Daughter: My father's participation softened UN Gaza report," *Haaretz* (16 September 2009); "Tikkun Interview with Judge Richard Goldstone" (2 October 2009).

105. Anshel Pfeffer, "Goldstone: Holocaust shaped view on war crimes," *Haaretz* (18 September 2009).

106. Levy, "Disgrace."

107. Guttman, "Israel, US Working"; Yaakov Katz, "Mandelblit: Israel right not to cooperate with Goldstone," *Jerusalem Post* (16 September 2009); Herb Keinon and Tovah Lazaroff, "'UNHRC Vote May Affect Moscow Parley,'" *Jerusalem Post* (19 October 2009); Roni Sofer, "Minister Edelstein: Goldstone report anti-Semitic," *ynetnews.com* (25 January 2010); "UK Officer Slams 'Pavlovian' Criticism of IDF after Gaza War," *Haaretz* (22 February 2010).

manifest absurdity. Goldstone's detractors then speculated that the Report was a product of Goldstone's overweening ambition. He was said to be angling for a Nobel Peace Prize or to head the United Nations. But Goldstone's impeccable reputation easily withstood these imputations of opportunism.[108] However, in interviews and statements after the Report was published, and as a harbinger of things to come, Goldstone did appear to backpedal from its more damning conclusions and to downplay the extent of Israeli crimes.[109] It was then alleged that Goldstone had been "suckered into lending his good name to a half-baked report."[110] But the chief prosecutor in multiple international war crimes tribunals was plainly nobody's dupe.

If Goldstone was not an anti-Semite, a self-hating Jew, or a Holocaust denier; if he had never evinced animus toward Israel but, on the contrary, had manifested an abiding affection for it; if he was reputed to be a man of integrity, who put truth and justice above self-aggrandizement and partisanship; if he was neither an incompetent nor a fool—if Goldstone could credibly claim all this and more, then the only plausible explanation for the devastating content of the document he chiefly authored was that it faithfully recorded the damning facts as they unfolded during Cast Lead. "The only thing they can be afraid of," Goldstone later observed of his detractors, "is the truth. And I think this is why they're attacking the messenger and not the message."[111] Compelled to face the facts and their consequences, disarmed and exposed, Israel went into panic mode. Israeli pundits expressed alarm that the Report might impede Israel's ability to launch military attacks in the future,[112] while Prime Minister Netanyahu ranked the "Goldstone

108. Amir Mizroch, "Grappling with Goldstone," *Jerusalem Post* (18 September 2009); Amir Mizroch, "What South African Jews Think of Richard Goldstone," *Jerusalem Post* (1 October 2009); R. W. Johnson, "Who Is Richard Goldstone?," *Radio Free Europe/Radio Liberty* (20 October 2009); Ashley Rindsberg, "UN's Goldstone Sent 13-Year-Old Boy to Prison for Protesting Apartheid," *Huffington Post* (19 November 2009); Dershowitz, "Goldstone Investigation."

109. Richard Goldstone, "Justice in Gaza," *New York Times* (17 September 2009); Richard Goldstone, "Who's Being Unfair?," *Jerusalem Post* (21 September 2009); Gal Beckerman, "Goldstone: 'If this was a court of law, there would have been nothing proven,'" *Forward* (16 October 2009); "Tikkun Interview with Judge Richard Goldstone."

110. Harold Evans, "A Moral Atrocity," *Guardian* (20 October 2009).

111. Moyers, *Journal*.

112. Aluf Benn, "In Wake of UN Gaza Probe, How Can Israel Go to War Again?," *Haaretz* (16 September 2009); Ari Shavit, "Watch Out for the Goldstoners," *Haaretz* (8 October 2009). See also Gideon Levy, "Peres, Not Goldstone, Is the Small Man," *Haaretz* (15

threat" one of the major strategic challenges confronting Israel.[113] In the meantime, Israeli officials fretted that prosecutors might hound Israelis traveling abroad.[114] Indeed, shortly after the Report was published, the ICC announced that it was contemplating an investigation of an Israeli officer implicated in war crimes during Cast Lead.[115] Then, in December 2009, Tzipi Livni was forced to cancel a trip to London after a British court issued an arrest warrant for her role in the commission of war crimes while serving as foreign minister during Cast Lead; and in June 2010, two Belgian lawyers representing a group of Palestinians charged 14 Israeli politicians (including Livni and Ehud Barak) with committing crimes against humanity and war crimes during the attack.[116] Unable to exorcise his ghost, Goldstone's assailants escalated the meanness of their ad hominem attacks. South African communal Jewish leaders plotted to bar Goldstone from attending his grandson's bar mitzvah, but after a wave of embarrassing publicity abroad they reversed themselves.[117] Goldstone's judicial tenure under apartheid rule in South Africa was then dredged up by Israel and dutifully disseminated in the American media by hack journalists, such as Jeffrey Goldberg (in *Atlantic*

November 2009); and Reut Institute, *Building a Political Firewall against Israel's Delegitimization* (Tel Aviv: 2010), paras. 40, 106.

113. "PM: Israel faces the 'Goldstone threat,'" *Jerusalem Post* (23 December 2009).

114. Barak Ravid and Anshel Pfeffer, "Israel Seeks Obama Backing on Gaza Probe," *Haaretz* (26 September 2009).

115. Yotam Feldman, "ICC May Try IDF Officer in Wake of Goldstone Gaza Report," *Haaretz* (24 September 2009); Raphael Ahren, "Israeli Soldiers from South Africa Feel Heat of Prosecution Drive in Old Country," *Haaretz* (22 November 2009).

116. "Livni Reportedly Cancels UK Visit, Fearing Arrest," *Haaretz* (16 December 2009); Danna Harman, "Belgian Lawyers to Charge Barak and Livni for War Crimes," *Haaretz* (23 June 2010). For a belated echo of these episodes, see Barak Ravid, "In Unprecedented Move, British Police Summoned Tzipi Livni over Suspected Gaza War Crimes," *Haaretz* (3 July 2016); and Yonah Jeremy Bob, "Scotland Yard Summons Livni for Cast Lead War Crimes Questioning," *Jerusalem Post* (3 July 2016).

117. Larry Derfner, "Yasher Koah, Judge Goldstone," *Jerusalem Post* (22 April 2010). To justify this abortive attempt at ostracizing him, the chairman of the South African Zionist Federation chastised Goldstone for failing "to demand of Hamas the unconditional release of Gilad Shalit" or at least "to demand that they recognize his status as a prisoner of war." But the Report did "recommend that Palestinian armed groups who hold Israeli soldier Gilad Shalit in detention should release him on humanitarian grounds. Pending such release they should recognize his status as prisoner of war, treat him as such, and allow him ICRC visits." Ironically, Israel *criticized* the Report's recommendation that Shalit be classified a POW. "Opening Statement by Avrom Krengel, Chairman of the SAfr Zionist Fed, delivered at meeting with Judge Richard Goldstone" (4 May 2010); Goldstone Report, para. 1973(b); Intelligence and Terrorism Information Center, *Hamas and the Terrorist Threat*, p. 66n49.

magazine) and Jonathan Chait (in the *New Republic*).[118] Goldstone was tagged a "hanging judge" for his blemished record of service with an "entirely illegitimate and barbaric regime" (Dershowitz).[119] But as Sasha Polakow-Suransky, a senior editor at *Foreign Affairs* magazine and the author of *The Unspoken Alliance: Israel's secret relationship with apartheid South Africa*, pointed out, "By serving as South Africa's primary and most reliable arms supplier during a period of violent internal repression and external aggression, Israel's government did far more to aid the apartheid regime than Goldstone ever did."[120] Indeed, just as South African repression of the black majority peaked, Defense Minister Shimon Peres confided to its leadership that Israeli cooperation with the apartheid regime was "based not only on common interests, but also on the unshakeable foundations of our common hatred of injustice," and Prime Minister Yitzhak Rabin toasted "the ideals shared by Israel and South Africa: the hopes for justice and peaceful coexistence." While sanctimoniously denouncing apartheid in public, Peres had forged and then nurtured at critical junctures the Israeli alliance with South Africa, and both he and Rabin supported this collaboration right through the last years of the apartheid regime.[121] In last desperate gambits to crucify Goldstone, the Hebrew University's board of governors ousted him,[122] and former AIPAC executive director Neal Sher "urged American officials to bar former judge Richard Goldstone from entering the country over his rulings during South Africa's apartheid regime." The moral case Sher mounted was somewhat tainted, however, by the fact that he himself had been disbarred after squandering Holocaust compensation monies on his vacation sprees.[123]

118. Tom Gross, "Goldstone's Death Sentences for Blacks: Just following orders," *Mideast Dispatch Archive* (10 May 2010); M. J. Rosenberg, "The 'Get Goldstone' Campaign," *MEDIAMATTERS Action Network* (10 May 2010).

119. Alan Dershowitz, "Legitimating Bigotry: The legacy of Richard Goldstone," *Hudson New York* (7 May 2010); see also Ilan Evyatar and David Horowitz, "'We Are Not Done with Goldstone,'" *Jerusalem Post* (21 May 2010), where Dershowitz labeled him an "opportunist" reminiscent of "Nazi war criminals. . . . Many of them served as judges."

120. Sasha Polakow-Suransky, "Gold Stones, Glass Houses," *Foreign Policy* (10 May 2010).

121. Sasha Polakow-Suransky, *The Unspoken Alliance: Israel's secret relationship with apartheid South Africa* (New York: 2010), pp. 80, 92.

122. Abe Selig, "Goldstone Stripped of Honorary Hebrew U Governorship," *Jerusalem Post* (5 June 2010).

123. E. B. Solomont, "Attorney Seeks to Bar Goldstone from US," *Jerusalem Post* (14 May 2010); Nacha Cattan, "Restitution Leader Disbarred by Court after Investigation of Job Misconduct," *Forward* (5 September 2003).

The symbolism, indeed pathos, of Goldstone's charge sheet against Israel was hard to miss. A lover of Zion was now calling for Zion to be hauled before the ICC for an array of war crimes and possible crimes against humanity. In effect, Goldstone's entry on the stage of the Israel-Palestine conflict signaled the implosion of that unstable alloy—some would say oxymoron—called liberal Zionism. On the one hand, he was the quintessential liberal Jew, a revered defender of the rule of law and human rights; on the other hand, he had nurtured a profound bond with Israel. Goldstone was now compelled by the circumstance of his appointment to make a choice. Even if disposed by family and faith to do so, he still could not defend Cast Lead. His judicial temperament, public reputation, and personal pride stood in his way. He was constrained by the parameters of the law, which if consulted in good conscience could not be stretched beyond certain limits. He functioned within a human rights milieu that had already rendered a devastating verdict on Cast Lead; he could not ignore it and still preserve his credibility in that community. The fact was, he had a choice in theory only. If Goldstone had elected to defend Israel against the indefensible, he would have committed professional suicide and irrevocably soiled his personal reputation. *That* far in his defense of Israel Goldstone was not prepared to go.

In the meanwhile, as Israel struggled to retain the allegiance of the Jewish diaspora, the Report's publication threw a new spanner in the works. It had become increasingly difficult for self-described liberal Jews in the diaspora to defend Israel's ever more brazen crimes.[124] Cast Lead marked the nadir of Israel's incremental descent into barbarism—or as the Report euphemistically put it, the operation signaled "a qualitative shift" by Israel "from relatively focused operations to massive and deliberate destruction."[125] If even a Jew, Zionist, and liberal with Goldstone's immaculate credentials confirmed this "shift," how could it be ignored? Jews broadly of Goldstone's temper—which was to say, the overwhelming majority of American Jews, who "identify their long-term interests with liberal policies"[126]—would hereafter find it well nigh impossible to brush aside even the harshest criticism of Israel,

---

124. Finkelstein, *Knowing Too Much*, pp. 5–89.

125. Goldstone Report, para. 1193. An accompanying footnote entered the caveat: "The reference to relatively focused operations here should not be misunderstood as an indication that all such actions were acceptable in terms of distinction and proportionality. It is merely a comparative reference."

126. Jewish People Policy Planning Institute, *Annual Assessment 2008* (Jerusalem: 2008), p. 33.

while Israel's defenders would have a harder time deflecting such criticism. "Those groups who unquestioningly attack the report's veracity," a British "friend and supporter of Israel" wrote in the *Guardian*, "find themselves further alienated from significant swaths of Jewish opinion, especially among the younger generation."[127] The reaction in the bastions of American Jewish liberalism to the Report was as notable for what was not said as for what was said. If newspaper editorials and liberal commentary did not come out in Goldstone's defense, they also did not defend Israel against him.[128] The Report appeared to herald the end of one era and the emergence of another: the end of an apologetic Jewish liberalism that denied or extenuated Israel's crimes, and the emergence of a Jewish liberalism that returned to its inspirational heyday, when—if only as an ideal imperfectly realized—all malefactors, non-Jews as well as Jews, would be held accountable as they strayed from the path of justice. "The vicious personal attacks on Judge Goldstone . . . are profoundly disturbing," Rabbi Brant Rosen observed. "What is perhaps more interesting, however, is the fact that so many in the American Jewish community are refusing to join the chorus. . . . American Jews . . . are working to hold Israel to a set of Jewish values that are more important than any political ideology."[129] Even if tempted, diaspora Jews could not bury the Goldstone Report because it had resonated most in the milieus where they worked and socialized. "Western governments may ignore this damning report," an Israeli commentator prophesied, "but it will now serve as a basis of criticism against Israel in public opinion, the media, on campuses and in think tanks, places where UN documents are still taken seriously."[130] An Israeli reserve officer who did double duty as an emissary for Israel on US college campuses lamented that protesting students "quote the Goldstone report. . . . It's become their bible."[131] Among Jews professing to be enlightened, it could hardly be a close call choosing between the credibility of Israel's

127. Daniel Levy, "Israel Must Now Heal Itself," *Guardian* (18 September 2009).

128. Roane Carey, "The Goldstone Report on Gaza," *Nation* blog ("The Notion") (25 September 2009). An occasional word both critical of Israel and supportive of Goldstone could be found. See James Carroll, "A Time of Reckoning," *Boston Globe* (21 September 2009). Although not Jewish himself, Carroll often wrote on Jewish themes from a philo-Semitic perspective.

129. Rabbi Brant Rosen, "Alan Dershowitz and the Politics of Desperation," *Huffington Post* (28 May 2010).

130. Benn, "In Wake of UN Gaza Probe."

131. Amos Harel, "IDF vs. Goldstone: PR 'commando' explains war against Hamas to Americans," *Haaretz* (13 November 2009).

cheerleaders and the likes of Goldstone. "Does it then come down to a matter of whose reputation you trust?" Antony Lerman rhetorically asked. "If so, would it be critics of human rights agencies like Alan Dershowitz, the prominent American lawyer who thinks torture could be legalized, or Melanie Phillips, a columnist who calls Jewish critics of Israel 'Jews for Genocide'...? Or Richard Goldstone, former chief prosecutor of the International Criminal Tribunals for the former Yugoslavia and Rwanda, who is putting his considerable reputation on the line in taking the UNHRC [UN Human Rights Council] assignment? Frankly, I don't think there is a contest."[132]

The Goldstone Report also heralded the dawn of a new era in which the human rights dimension of the Israel-Palestine conflict moved center stage alongside—and even temporarily displacing—the fatuous "peace process." During the first decades of Israel's occupation, advocates of Palestinian human rights perforce leaned on the research and testimony of a handful of courageous but politically marginal Israelis.[133] Take the case of torture. In recent times, respected human rights organizations and Israeli historians have acknowledged that Israel routinely tortured Palestinian detainees from the onset of the occupation.[134] However, until the 1990s and despite a wealth of corroborative evidence, progressive opinion treated reports of Israeli torture gingerly and prudently steered clear of the locution *torture* when referencing these reports.[135] A sea change set in during the first intifada (1987–93) when Palestinians engaged in mass nonviolent civil resistance. On the one hand, torture of Palestinian detainees reached epidemic proportions, and on the other, the newly minted Israeli human rights organization B'Tselem (Israeli Information Center for Human Rights in the Occupied Territories) irrefutably documented Israel's

132. Antony Lerman, "Judge Goldstone and the Pollution of Argument," *Guardian* (15 September 2009). Lerman was former director of the London-based Institute for Jewish Policy Research.

133. Among others, left-wing Israeli lawyers Felicia Langer and Lea Tsemel and Hebrew University chemistry professor Israel Shahak.

134. Amnesty International, *Combating Torture* (London: 2003), section 2.2. Benny Morris, *Righteous Victims: A history of the Zionist-Arab conflict, 1881–2001* (New York: 2001), pp. 341–43, 568, 587, 600–601; Tom Segev, *1967: Israel, the war, and the year that transformed the Middle East* (New York: 2007), pp. 475, 517.

135. In its 1979 "Report and Recommendations... to the Government of the State of Israel" (1980), Amnesty merely stated that "there is sufficient *prima facie* evidence of ill-treatment of security suspects in the Occupied Territories ... to warrant the establishment of a public inquiry," while in its influential study *Torture in the Eighties* (London: 1984), Amnesty cautiously noted that it "continued to receive reports of ill-treatment" in Israeli prisons of "some Palestinians from the Occupied Territories arrested for security reasons" (pp. 233–34).

pervasive use of torture. No longer able to turn a blind eye, but also morally and politically shielded by the escutcheon of reputable Israeli groups, the human rights community in the West began to systematically document Israel's egregious practice of torture and its many other human rights abuses.[136] However, most of these publications just collected dust, as the establishment media scrupulously ignored them and instead feigned despair at ferreting out the truth between Palestinian accusation and Israeli denial. The novelty of the Goldstone Report was that in one stroke it catapulted Israel's human rights record squarely into the court of public opinion, closed the gap between Jewish and Palestinian "narratives" on Israel's human rights record, and charged with political consequence the damning findings of human rights organizations.

The potential political costs having escalated, hysteria over the Goldstone Report unsurprisingly coincided with a vicious campaign in Israel and the United States to discredit human rights organizations. "We are going to dedicate time and manpower to combating these groups," the director of policy planning in the Israeli prime minister's office declared.[137] "For the first time," the director of HRW's Middle East division rued, "the Israeli government is taking an active role in the smearing of human rights groups."[138] These groups and one of their benefactors (New Israel Fund) came under virulent attack in Israel for allegedly providing the data used by the Report to blacken Israel's name. A Knesset subcommittee was established to "examine the sources of funding" of Israel-based human rights groups,[139] and a succession of Knesset bills proposed, respectively, to outlaw NGOs that provided legally incriminating information to foreign bodies, and to compel members of Israeli NGOs to declare their foreign funders at all public functions.[140] An Israel Democracy Institute poll found that "half the general

---

136. Norman G. Finkelstein, *Beyond Chutzpah: On the misuse of anti-Semitism and the abuse of history,* expanded paperback edition (Berkeley: 2008), part II.

137. Chris McGreal, "Israel 'Personally Attacking Human Rights Group' after Gaza War Criticism," *Guardian* (13 November 2009).

138. Adam Horowitz and Philip Weiss, "Israel vs. Human Rights," *Nation* (30 September 2009).

139. NGO Monitor/Institute for Zionist Strategies, *Trojan Horse: The impact of European government funding for Israeli NGOs* (2009).

140. Joshua Mitnick, "Rights Groups under Fire for Scrutiny of Israel's Conduct of Gaza War," *Christian Science Monitor* (3 February 2010); Dan Izenberg, "Cabinet Backs Bill to Register NGOs Funded by Foreign States," *Jerusalem Post* (15 February 2010); Donald Macintyre, "The New McCarthyism Sweeping Israel," *Independent* (13 February 2010); Abe Selig, "'Goldstone Report Was Our Smoking Gun,'" *Jerusalem Post* (18 February 2010).

public agree with the statement that 'Human and civil rights organizations, like the Association for Civil Rights in Israel and B'Tselem, cause harm to the state,'" while a Tel Aviv University poll found that nearly 60 percent of respondents agreed that human rights organizations exposing immoral conduct by Israel should not be "allowed to operate freely."[141] Faced with these unsettling headwinds, Israeli human rights groups noticeably trimmed their sails. In its annual report, B'Tselem devoted more lines to Palestinian than Israeli breaches of international law during Cast Lead; devoted twice as much space to Hamas's "grave breach" (or "war crime") of taking Israeli soldier Gilad Shalit "hostage" as to all Israeli breaches (none of which it denoted as "grave" or a "war crime") during Cast Lead; and disputed key findings of the Goldstone Report but adduced no counterevidence.[142] In a parallel line of attack, the US-based Israel lobby mobilized against what it dubbed "lawfare."[143] The term denoted "isolating Israel through the language of human rights."[144] In other words, lawfare signaled the outrageous notion that Israel should be held legally accountable for its crimes. Under the auspices of major law schools and professional organizations, pseudoacademic symposia convened on topics such as "The Goldstone Report: Lawfare and the threat to Israeli and American national security in the age of terrorism" (Fordham University School of Law),[145] and "Lawfare: The use of the law as a weapon of war" (New York County Lawyers Association).[146] Incensed by the "scandal of the Goldstone report," one learned opponent of "lawfare" thusly corrected for its bias: "No armies in the history of warfare have devoted greater attention or energy than those of Israel and the United States to distinguishing and protecting civilians in warfare and ensuring that the force they use in armed conflict is proportional to the threat faced."[147] Of course,

141. Asher Arian et al., *Auditing Israeli Democracy: Democratic values in practice* (Jerusalem: 2010), p. 128; Nathan Jeffrey, "Kadima Bill: NGOs that assist in war crime accusations should be illegal," *Forward* (12 May 2010).

142. B'Tselem (Israeli Information Center for Human Rights in the Occupied Territories), *Human Rights Review* (1 January 2009–30 April 2010), pp. 5–7, 11–12.

143. Barbara Plett, "Legal Row over Gaza Report Intensifies," *BBC News* (6 November 2009).

144. Gerald Steinberg, "Isolating Israel through Language of Human Rights," *Jerusalem Post* (30 August 2009).

145. 27 April 2010, jewishlawyers.org/comment.asp?x_id=134#top.

146. 11 March 2010, anti-democracy-agenda.blogspot.com/2010/02/lawfare-use-of-law-as-weapon-of-war.html.

147. Peter Berkowitz, "The Goldstone Report and International Law," *Policy Review* (August/September 2010).

this rather large claim was presented evidence-free; as in religion, you were either a believer or you weren't. Simultaneously, perennial apologists for the Holy State, such as Alan Dershowitz and Elie Wiesel, orchestrated a witch hunt against HRW.[148] "I really hesitate to use words like conspiracy, but there is a feeling that there is an organized campaign," HRW's program director observed. "We have been under enormous pressure and tremendous attacks, some of them very personal."[149] HRW founder Robert Bernstein, who had for years muzzled HRW's criticism of Israel from inside the organization, jumped ship and leapt into the fray. After release of the Report and in a highly public defection, Bernstein published an op-ed in the *New York Times* denouncing HRW's allegedly biased reporting on Israel. Alas, the only testimony he could summon forth in Israel's defense was the ubiquitous Colonel Richard Kemp, who lauded Israel for its unparalleled devotion to humanitarian law during Cast Lead.[150] Bernstein's broadside was followed a half year later by a gossipy *New Republic* exposé of discontent within HRW over the group's supposedly anti-Israel tilt.[151] The piece failed to explore the only substantive question prompted by its content: Why did pro-Israel wealthy Jewish donors with no expertise in either human rights or the Middle East—a "legendary Hollywood mogul," a "48-year-old who formerly worked on Wall Street," a "former stockbroker"—exercise power and influence over HRW's Middle East division? Regrettably, HRW proved unable to weather the storm of vilification fully intact. Its 2010 *World Report* stated, for instance, that "reports by news media and a nongovernmental organization indicate that in some cases, Palestinian armed groups intentionally hid behind civilians to unlawfully use them as shields to deter Israeli counter-attacks."[152] It neglected to mention that neither the fact-finding missions nor human rights

148. "NGO Monitor's International Advisory Board Calls for Review of HRW," *ngomonitor.org* (14 October 2009); "Wiesel, Dershowitz: Human Rights Watch Reform Needed," *ynetnews.com* (29 September 2009); NGO Monitor, *Experts or Ideologues? A systematic analysis of Human Rights Watch's focus on Israel* (2009).

149. McGreal, "Israel 'Personally Attacking.'"

150. Robert L. Bernstein, "Rights Watchdog, Lost in the Mideast," *New York Times* (20 October 2009). For Human Rights Watch's reply, see Kenneth Roth, "Human Rights Watch Applies Same Standards to Israel, Hamas," *Haaretz* (27 October 2009); see also Scott MacLeod, "Bashing Human Rights Watch," *Los Angeles Times* (30 October 2009). For Kemp, see Chapter 4.

151. Benjamin Birnbaum, "Human Rights Watch Fights a Civil War over Israel," *New Republic* (27 April 2010).

152. Human Rights Watch, *World Report 2010* (2010), p. 511.

organizations—*not even HRW itself*—found evidence that Palestinian armed groups engaged in human shielding during Cast Lead. Then, in a transparently desperate gesture to placate the Israel lobby, and while Israel persisted in its inhuman and illegal siege of Gaza's 1.5 million residents, HRW reduced itself to publicly condemning a Jordanian restaurant owner who refused to serve two Israelis a meal.[153]

The backpedaling by HRW was symptomatic of the fact that Israel's coordinated and relentless attack on the Goldstone Report had taken its toll. A year after its publication, the Report was not yet dead in the water, but some of the wind had been taken out of its sails. After denying any wrongdoing and lashing out at the Report, and after the targets of its vilification had been softened, Israel deftly changed tack. It administered a handful of token punishments and, promising to mend its ways, professed that in future wars it would heed the Report's lessons.[154] Anxious to rejoin the Israeli consensus, Goldstone's original supporters, such as *Haaretz,* then claimed vindication and praised Israel's capacity (albeit belated) for self-criticism.[155] Defense Minister Barak confidently predicted that he was in the process of dispatching the "remnants of the Goldstone report."[156] Taking his cues from Washington, UN secretary-general Ban Ki-moon praised Israel's "significant progress investigating allegations of misconduct by the IDF," even though these so-called investigations had yielded derisory results.[157] Indeed, its "significant progress" and substantive reply to the Goldstone Report were showcased in late 2010, when the commander of Cast Lead was promoted to IDF chief of staff.[158] The UN Human Rights Council continued to defer action on Goldstone's findings as the PA and the Arab League, preferring that the Report quietly expire, let it languish in the UN bureaucracy. A September 2010 Human Rights Council resolution, which passed by a vote of 27 in favor, 1 against (United States), and 19 abstentions, called on its Committee of Independent Experts to submit yet another progress report for the coun-

153. Human Rights Watch, "Jordan: Restaurant owner ousts Israelis" (7 December 2010).

154. State of Israel, *Gaza Operation Investigations: Second update,* paras. 146–57.

155. "Thanks to the Critics," *Haaretz* (27 July 2010).

156. "Q&A with Israeli Defense Minister Ehud Barak," *Washington Post* (26 July 2010).

157. United Nations General Assembly, *Second Follow-Up to the Report of the United Nations Fact-Finding Mission on the Gaza Conflict: Report of the Secretary-General* (A/64/890) (11 August 2010).

158. Charly Wegman, "Israel Picks Gaza War Commander as New Military Chief," *Agence France-Presse* (5 September 2010).

cil's sixteenth session (in March 2011).[159] The PA and Arab states jointly sponsored this contemptible stalling tactic, while the United States voted against it on the grounds that "because Israel had the ability to conduct credible investigations and serious self-scrutiny, further follow-up of the Goldstone report by United Nations bodies was unnecessary and unwarranted."[160] Palestinian human rights groups denounced the PA for "extending impunity to Israeli military and political leaders"; an Amnesty statement criticized the council's "seriously flawed resolution" that "fails to establish a clear process for justice" and "amounts to a betrayal of the victims," and called on the council to refer the matter to the International Criminal Court for consideration; a representative of Human Rights Watch deemed the resolution a "step backward" and "the start of a slow death" of the Report.[161]

In order to discredit or at least undercut the Goldstone Report, Israel had plunged into the utter depths of its state and society, harnessing and concentrating their full forces, and had simultaneously mobilized the Jewish state's faithful apparatchiks abroad. But although it had managed to take some sting out of the Report, Israel was still left dangerously exposed. The devastating accumulation of evidence endured as a standing indictment of its criminal behavior. The Report's international resonance still hampered Israel's ability to launch another full-scale attack. The human rights community still needed to be put on notice not to pull another such stunt. Even months after it was published, an Israeli columnist rued, "the Goldstone Report still holds the top spot in the bestseller list of Israel's headaches."[162]

---

159. A/HRC/15/L.34.

160. "Human Rights Council Takes Up Human Rights Situation in Palestine and Other Occupied Arab Territories," press release (27 September 2010).

161. Jared Malsin, "Whither Goldstone? Did the PA kill the UN's Goldstone report?," *Foreign Policy* (27 October 2010); Amnesty International, "Human Rights Council Fails Victims of Gaza Conflict" (30 September 2010).

162. Assaf Gefen, "Are We Hiding Something?," *ynetnews.com* (8 February 2010).

SIX

The Star Witness Recants

ON 1 APRIL 2011, ISRAEL'S BIGGEST HEADACHE went away. Dropping a bombshell on the op-ed page of the *Washington Post*,[1] Richard Goldstone effectively disowned the devastating UN report of Israeli crimes carrying his name.[2] Israel waxed euphoric. "Everything that we said proved to be true," Prime Minister Benjamin Netanyahu gloated. "We always said that the IDF [Israel Defense Forces] is a moral army that acted according to international law," Defense Minister Ehud Barak declared. "We had no doubt that the truth would come out eventually," Foreign Minister Avigdor Lieberman proclaimed.[3] The Obama administration used the occasion of Goldstone's recantation to reiterate that Israel had not "engaged in any war crimes" during Operation Cast Lead, while the US Senate unanimously called on the United Nations to "rescind" the Goldstone Report.[4] In short, Goldstone's recantation was a black day for human rights and a red-letter day for their transgressors. Might had yet again brought right to its knees. Those in search of a silver lining in the cloud parsed Goldstone's words to prove that he did not actually recant.[5] While it

1. Richard Goldstone, "Reconsidering the Goldstone Report on Israel and War Crimes," *Washington Post* (1 April 2011).
2. *Report of the United Nations Fact-Finding Mission on the Gaza Conflict* (25 September 2009); hereafter: Goldstone Report.
3. Barak Ravid, "Netanyahu to UN: Retract Gaza war report in wake of Goldstone's comments," *Haaretz* (2 April 2011); "Lieberman Praises Goldstone for 'Vindicating' Israel," *Jerusalem Post* (2 April 2011).
4. "US Agrees: Israel did not commit Cast Lead war crimes," *Jerusalem Post* (5 April 2011); Natasha Mozgovaya, "US Senate Urges UN to Rescind Goldstone's Gaza Report," *Haaretz* (15 April 2011).
5. Jerry Haber, "Judge Goldstone's *Washington Post* Op-ed," *jeremiahhaber.com* (2 April 2011).

might technically be true, such a rhetorical strategy did not wash. Goldstone was a distinguished jurist. He knew how to craft precise language. If he did not want to repudiate the Report, this wordsmith could simply have written, "I am not recanting my original report by which I still stand." He did not say this, or anything like it. He was surely aware exactly how his intervention would be spun, and it was this predictable fallout, not his parsed words, that would be his legacy. The inescapable fact was that he killed the Report, and simultaneously lowered the curtain on his own career.

In one fell swoop, Goldstone inflicted irreparable damage on the cause of truth and justice and the rule of law. Despite the passage of time, his dashing of hope still rankles as these lines are written. He poisoned Jewish-Palestinian relations, undermined the courageous work of Israeli dissenters, "and—most unforgivably—increased the risk of another merciless IDF assault."[6] It did not take long before Israel gave proof to this prediction. There was much speculation on why Goldstone recanted. Was he blackmailed? Did he finally succumb to the relentless hate campaign targeting him? Did he decide to put his tribe ahead of truth? These questions remain open to this day. What can, however, be asserted with certainty is that *his stated rationales cannot account for his decision to reverse himself.* The gist of Goldstone's recantation was that Israel did not commit war crimes during Cast Lead, and that it was fully capable on its own of investigating violations of international law that did occur. The critical passage read:

> Our Report found evidence of potential war crimes and "possibly crimes against humanity" by both Israel and Hamas. . . . The allegations of intentionality by Israel were based on the deaths of and injuries to civilians in situations where our fact-finding mission had no evidence on which to draw any other reasonable conclusion. . . . [T]he investigations published by the Israeli military . . . indicate that civilians were not intentionally targeted as a matter of policy.

It was unclear how to interpret this mea culpa. If he was saying that Israel didn't *systematically target Gaza's civilian population for murder,* his recantation was gratuitous. The Report never entertained, let alone leveled, such a charge, which would have been tantamount to accusing Israel of genocide. Basing itself on voluminous evidence, the Report did accuse Israel of deliberately deploying disproportionate and indiscriminate force in order to "pun-

6. Norman G. Finkelstein, *Goldstone Recants: Richard Goldstone renews Israel's license to kill* (New York: 2011), p. 8.

ish, humiliate and terrorize a civilian population."[7] In his recantation, Goldstone did not take exception to the Report's evidence substantiating this charge. Indeed, how could he? Senior Israeli officials, informed analysts, and combatants didn't themselves shy away from acknowledging—in fact, more often than not they *bragged*—that the IDF unleashed "insane" amounts of firepower, went "wild," demonstrated "real hooliganism," carried on like a "mad dog," acted "lunatic" and "crazy," and "destroyed everything in its way" during Cast Lead.[8] The bottom line was, Goldstone either disavowed what he didn't avow in the first place, or disavowed a pivotal conclusion of the Report but did not, and could not, dispute the mass of evidence on the basis of which that conclusion was reached.

Still, if as Goldstone alleged, Israel's deliberate resort to disproportionate and indiscriminate firepower did not "intentionally" target civilians, did it, as he further suggested, qualitatively differ from a deliberate attack on civilians and not rise to a war crime? It is a tenet of law that "the doer of an act must be taken to have *intended* its natural and foreseeable consequences."[9] If an indiscriminate, disproportionate attack inevitably and predictably results in the injury and death of civilians, then it is legally indistinguishable from a deliberate attack on them. "There is no genuine difference between a premeditated attack against civilians ... and a reckless disregard of the principle of distinction,"[10] according to Yoram Dinstein, Israel's leading authority on international law; "they are equally forbidden."[11] If Goldstone was contending that Israel's "insane" firepower during Cast Lead did not constitute a war crime because it did not intentionally target civilians, and that it was not criminal behavior for an invading army to go "wild," demonstrate "real hooliganism," carry on like a "mad dog," act "lunatic" and "crazy," and "destroy

---

7. Goldstone Report, para. 1893.

8. See Chapter 3.

9. International Court of Justice, Advisory Opinion, *Legality of the Threat or Use of Nuclear Weapons* (8 July 1996), "Dissenting Opinion of Judge Weeramantry," ch. III, "Humanitarian Law," sec. 10, "Specific rules of the humanitarian law of war," (a) "The prohibition against causing unnecessary suffering"; emphasis in original.

10. The principle of distinction requires: "The parties to the conflict must at all times distinguish between civilians and combatants. Attacks may only be directed against combatants. Attacks must not be directed against civilians." Indiscriminate and disproportionate attacks breach this principle. International Committee of the Red Cross, *Customary International Humanitarian Law, Volume I: Rules* (Cambridge: 2005), part I.

11. Yoram Dinstein, *Conduct of Hostilities under the Law of International Armed Conflict* (Cambridge: 2004), p. 117.

TABLE 2 The Al-Samouni Incident: Goldstone v. Goldstone, Amnesty, and UN Experts

Recantation (April 2011)	Goldstone at Stanford (January 2011)	Amnesty (March 2011)	UN Experts (March 2011)
[T]he most serious attack the Goldstone Report focused on was the killing of some 29 members of the al-Simouni [sic] family in their home. The shelling of the home was apparently the consequence of an Israeli commander's erroneous interpretation of a drone image.	[T]he single most serious incident reported in the [Goldstone] Report—[was] the bombing of the home of the al-Samouni family. . . . On January 4, 2009, members of the Givati Brigade of the IDF decided to take over the house of Saleh al-Samouni as part of the IDF ground operation; they ordered its occupants to relocate to the home of Wa'el al-Samouni. It was located about 35 yards away and within sight of the Israeli soldiers. . . . In the result there were over 100 members of the family gathered in the single story home of Wa'el al-Samouni. Early on the cold wintry morning of 5 January, several male members of the al-Samouni family went outside to gather firewood. They were in clear sight of the Israeli troops. As the men returned with the firewood, projectiles fired from helicopter gunships killed or injured them. Immediately after that further projectiles hit the house. Twenty-one members of the family were killed, some of them young children and women. Nineteen were injured. Of those injured, another eight subsequently died from their injuries. . . . [This evidence] led the Fact-Finding Mission to conclude that, as a probability, the attack on the al-Samouni family constituted a deliberate attack on	One prominent case that was examined by the [Goldstone Mission] and various human rights groups and is the subject of an ongoing Israeli criminal investigation is the killing of some 21 members of the al-Samouni family, who were sheltering in the home of Wa'el al-Sammouni when it was struck by missiles or shells on 5 January 2009. The Israeli military announced that an MPCID [Military Police Criminal Investigations Division] investigation had been opened into this incident on 6 July 2010. On 21 October 2010, Colonel Ilan Malka, who was commander of the Givati Brigade . . . and was allegedly involved in approving the air strike which killed 21 members of the al-Sammouni family, was questioned under caution by military police. According to media reports, he claimed that he was unaware of the presence of civilians in the building when he approved the strike. The decision to approve the air strike was	The Committee does not have sufficient information to establish the current status of the ongoing criminal investigations into the killings of Ateya and Ahmad Samouni, the attack on the Wa'el al-Samouni house and the shooting of Iyad Samouni. This is of considerable concern: reportedly 24 civilians were killed and 19 were injured in the related incidents on 4 and 5 January 2009. Furthermore, the events may relate both to the actions and decisions of soldiers on the ground and of senior officers located in a war room, as well as to broader issues implicating the rules of engagement and the use of drones. . . . Media reports further inform that a senior officer, who was questioned "under caution" and had his promotion put on hold, told investigators that he was not warned that civilians were at the location. However, some of those civilians had been ordered there by IDF soldiers from that same officer's unit and air force officers reportedly informed him of the possible presence of civilians. Despite

civilians. The crucial consideration was that the men, women and children were known by the Israeli troops to be civilians and were ordered by them to relocate to a house that was in the vicinity of their command post. Members of the al-Samouni family had regarded the presence of the IDF as a guarantee of their safety.... [A]t the end of October 2010 (almost 22 months after the incident), to the credit of the Israeli Military Police, they announced that they were investigating whether the air strike against the al-Samouni home was authorized by a senior Givati brigade commander who had been warned of the danger to civilians. At about the same time there were reports that the attack followed upon the receipt of photographs by the Israeli military from a drone showing what was incorrectly interpreted to be a group of men carrying rocket launchers towards a house. The order was given to bomb the men and the building. According to these reports, the photograph received from the drone was not of high quality and in fact showed the men carrying firewood to the al-Samouni home. The results of this military police investigation are as yet unknown.

reportedly based on drone photographs of men from the al-Samouni family breaking apart boards for firewood; the photographs were interpreted in the war room as Palestinians armed with rocket-propelled grenades. But at the time the photographs were received, the family had already been confined to the building and surrounded and observed by soldiers from the Givati Brigade in at least six different nearby outposts for more than 24 hours; at least some soldiers in these outposts would have known that the family were civilians since they themselves had ordered the family to gather in Wa'el al-Samouni's home. Some of these officers reportedly testified to the military investigators that they had warned Colonel Malka that there could be civilians in the area.

allegedly being made aware of this information, the officer apparently approved air strikes that killed 21 people and injured 19 gathered in the al-Samouni house. Media sources also report that the incident has been described as a legitimate interpretation of drone photographs portrayed on a screen and that the special command investigation, initiated ten months after the incidents, did not conclude that there had been anything out of the ordinary in the strike.

everything in its way"—if he truly believed this, then he needed to brush up on the law; in fact, he had no business practicing law. An indiscriminate, disproportionate attack on civilian areas is in and of itself a war crime, and no less criminal than a deliberately targeted attack.

To absolve Israel of criminal culpability, Goldstone revisited the single most notorious incident during Cast Lead, in which at least 21 members of the al-Samouni family perished. The Goldstone Report found that Israel had launched a "deliberate attack on civilians."[12] In his recantation, however, Goldstone credited media stories of an Israeli "investigation" that attributed the deaths to a misread drone image. It happened that Goldstone had also commented on this Israeli "investigation" just a couple of months earlier at Stanford University.[13] In addition, Amnesty International[14] and a UN committee that Goldstone himself cited approvingly[15] also presented updated findings on the incident. Table 2 juxtaposes these various testimonies; Goldstone's critical omissions in his recantation are boldfaced. In his recantation, Goldstone excised all the evidence casting doubt on the new Israeli alibi. Whereas at Stanford he judiciously laid out the arguments on both sides and suspended judgment, just two months later he pinned all his faith on secondhand reports of an Israeli "investigation" that hadn't even been completed. What is more, both Amnesty and the UN committee contested the plausibility of the new Israeli alibi. Goldstone's tendentious depiction of the facts in his recantation might have been appropriate if he were Israel's defense attorney, but it hardly befitted the head of a mission that was mandated to ferret out the truth.

Goldstone justified his volte-face on the grounds that "we know a lot more today." It was indeed true that new information on Cast Lead entered the public record after the release of his Report. But the vast preponderance of it sustained and even extended the Report's findings. Consider these examples. A new clutch of Israeli soldiers refuting official propaganda stepped forward. An officer who served at a brigade headquarters recalled that IDF policy amounted to ensuring "literally zero risk to the soldiers," while a combatant

12. Goldstone Report, paras. 706–35.

13. "Judge Goldstone's Notes for the Panel on Civilians in War Zones," paras. 29–35 (maurice-ostroff.tripod.com/id315.html).

14. Amnesty International, *Amnesty International's Updated Assessment of Israeli and Palestinian Investigations into the Gaza Conflict* (18 March 2011).

15. *Report of the Committee of Independent Experts in International Humanitarian and Human Rights Law Established Pursuant to Council Resolution 13/9* (18 March 2011).

remembered a meeting with his brigade commander where it was conveyed, "if you see any signs of movement at all you shoot. This is essentially the rules of engagement."[16] Although Goldstone could have cited these new testimonies to buttress his Report, he opted instead to ignore them. In 2010, Human Rights Watch published a study based on satellite imagery documenting numerous cases "in which Israeli forces caused extensive destruction of homes, factories, farms and greenhouses in areas under IDF control without any evident military purpose. These cases occurred when there was no fighting in these areas; in many cases, the destruction was carried out during the final days of the campaign when an Israeli withdrawal was imminent."[17] Although Goldstone could have cited this new study to buttress his Report, he elected instead to ignore it. If he scrupulously ignored all new evidence confirming the Report's findings, it was hard to avoid the conclusion that Goldstone's recitation of "a lot more" information was tainted by partisanship. It was also telling that as new evidence came to light confirming the Goldstone Report's findings, Israel's renewed attempts to refute these findings repeatedly fell flat. After publication of the Report, Israel responded with a barrage of denials. The most voluminous of these was a 350-page compilation, *Hamas and the Terrorist Threat from the Gaza Strip*, by the Israeli Intelligence and Terrorism Information Center. But on inspection, it turned out to be a mélange of dubious interpretations, flagrant misrepresentations, and outright falsehoods.[18] If Israel's most ambitious refutation of the Report itself wholly lacked in substance, how did Goldstone manage to unearth "a lot more" new information that fatally undercut the Report? How did he manage to invalidate a document critical of Israel that, try as it may, Israel itself could not invalidate?

In fact, the additional information that Goldstone touted did not exactly overwhelm. He gestured to the findings of Israeli military investigations. But what did "we know . . . today" about these in camera hearings shrouded in secrecy except what Israel revealed about them? Israel supplied almost no information on which to independently assess the evidence presented or the proceedings' fairness. It was not known how many were complete and how

16. Donald Macintyre, "Israeli Commander: 'We rewrote the rules of war for Gaza,'" *Independent* (3 February 2010); Anshel Pfeffer, "IDF Officer: Gaza civilians risked to protect Israel troops during war," *Haaretz* (3 February 2010).

17. Human Rights Watch, *"I Lost Everything": Israel's unlawful destruction of property during Operation Cast Lead* (2010). See Chapter 3 for extensive citations from this study.

18. See Chapter 5.

many still ongoing.[19] Even when they resulted in criminal indictments, the investigations were often inaccessible to the public (apart from the indicted soldiers' supporters) and full transcripts were not subsequently made available.[20] The centerpiece of Goldstone's revelatory new information was the drone image in the al-Samouni case. The misreading of it, Israel alleged (and Goldstone tentatively concurred), caused an officer to erroneously target an extended family of civilians. If, as humanitarian and human rights organizations declared right after the attack, it was among the "gravest" and "most shocking" incidents during Cast Lead,[21] and if, as Goldstone himself stated, the attack was "the single most serious incident" documented in his Report, then why didn't Israel hasten to restore its bruised reputation but instead let elapse *22 months* before coming forth with so simple an explanation? In order to defend itself against Goldstone's findings, Israel disseminated numerous aerial photographs taken during Cast Lead. Why didn't Israel make publicly available this drone image that allegedly exonerated it of criminal culpability in the most egregious incident haunting it? It was also cause for perplexity why Goldstone credited this Israeli "evidence" sight unseen yet ignored other pertinent and highly credible new evidence. After his Report's publication, journalist Amira Hass revealed in the pages of *Haaretz* that "a Givati force set up outposts and bases in at least six houses in the Samouni compound" before the attack.[22] Didn't the Givati commander who ordered the aerial assault check with his soldiers on the ground before unleashing the deadly fire, to ascertain that they were out of harm's way? Didn't he ask them to confirm the blurry drone image of men seemingly carrying rocket launchers, and didn't they set him straight? Israel might have been able to provide plausible answers. But Goldstone did not even bother to pose these obvious questions because "we know . . . today" that it was just a simple mistake. After release of the Goldstone Report, Israeli authorities had a ready-made, if evidence-free, explanation for many of the other documented war crimes as well. They alleged that the al-Bader flour mill was destroyed

19. Amnesty International, *Amnesty International's Updated Assessment;* B'Tselem (Israeli Information Center for Human Rights in the Occupied Territories), "Goldstone Then and Now" (5 April 2011).

20. Amnesty International, *Amnesty International's Updated Assessment.*

21. UN Office for the Coordination of Humanitarian Affairs, *Protection of Civilians Weekly Report* (1–8 January 2009); Amnesty International, *Operation "Cast Lead": 22 Days of death and destruction* (2009), p. 20.

22. Amira Hass, "What Led to IDF Bombing House Full of Civilians during Gaza War?," *Haaretz* (24 October 2010).

"in order to neutralize immediate threats to IDF forces";[23] that the Sawafeary chicken farm had been destroyed "for reasons of military necessity";[24] and that the al-Maqadmah mosque was targeted because "two terrorist operatives [were] standing near the entrance."[25] Was the staggering evidence of criminality assembled in the Report, supplemented by thousands of pages of other human rights reports, all false if Israel said so? When Israel was accused of firing white phosphorus into civilian areas during Cast Lead did we also "know" it didn't happen because Israel emphatically denied it?

The only other scrap of novel evidence Goldstone adduced in his recantation was a casualty figure belatedly reckoned by a Hamas official. On the basis of this revised death toll, Goldstone observed, the number of Hamas combatants killed during Cast Lead "turned out to be similar" to the official Israeli figure. The upshot was that Hamas's number appeared to confirm Israel's contention that combatants, not civilians, comprised the majority of Gazans killed. But then Goldstone parenthetically noted that Hamas "may have reason to inflate" its figure. Indeed, firm grounds did exist for doubting the new figure's authenticity. To prove that it defeated Israel on the battle-field, Hamas originally alleged that only 48 of its fighters had been killed. But as the full breadth of Israel's destruction came into relief after its with-drawal, Hamas's boasts of a battlefield victory rang hollow. In the face of accusations that the people of Gaza had shouldered the cost of its reckless decisions,[26] Hamas abruptly upped the figure by several hundred in order to demonstrate that it, too, had suffered major losses.[27] As Goldstone himself put it at Stanford just two months before his recantation, the new Hamas figure "was intended to bolster the reputation of Hamas with the people of Gaza."[28] Whereas Goldstone deferred in his recantation to this politically inflated Hamas figure, his Report had relied on numbers provided by respected Israeli and Palestinian human rights organizations, each of which independently and meticulously investigated the aggregate and

23. State of Israel, *Gaza Operation Investigations: An update* (January 2010), pp. 41–44. Although critical evidence belied the Israeli version of what happened, Israel stuck to its original story. See Chapter 3 for references.

24. State of Israel, *Gaza Operation Investigations: Second update,* para. 123.

25. Ibid., para. 68.

26. Jean-Pierre Filiu, *Gaza: A history* (New York: 2014), p. 318.

27. "Hamas Confirms Losses in Cast Lead for First Time," *Jerusalem Post* (1 November 2010).

28. "Judge Goldstone's Notes," para. 24.

civilian/combatant breakdown of Gazan deaths. Belying the Israeli claim that only 300 civilians were killed, these human rights organizations put the figure at some 800–1,200,[29] and also convincingly demonstrated that official Israeli figures couldn't be trusted. Even the largely apologetic *2009 Human Rights Report* by the US State Department put the number of dead "at close to 1,400 Palestinians, including more than 1,000 civilians."[30] But because a politically manipulated Israeli figure chimed with a politically manipulated Hamas figure, Goldstone discarded the much larger figure for Palestinian civilian deaths documented by human rights organizations and validated by the US State Department.

His hope that Hamas would investigate itself after Cast Lead, Goldstone rued in his recantation, had been "unrealistic." Israel in contrast, he went on to assert, had already carried out investigations "transparently and in good faith . . . to a significant degree," and he was "confident" these inquiries would eventually bring all lawbreakers to justice. One wonders on what basis he could have formed this optimistic prognosis;[31] none of the available evidence, old or new, vindicated it. Consider, first, Israel's judicial track record prior to Cast Lead. Some 1,300 Palestinians were killed in the decade following the outbreak of the first intifada (1987–97), yet only 19 Israeli soldiers were convicted of homicide, and not one served prison time. Some 2,300 Palestinian civilians were killed during the second intifada (2000–2003), yet only 5 Israeli soldiers were held criminally liable for these civilian deaths and not one was convicted on a murder or manslaughter charge. Between 2006 and 2009, a soldier who killed a Palestinian not taking part in hostilities was, according to B'Tselem (Israeli Information Center for Human Rights in the Occupied Territories), "almost never brought to justice for his act." (Jewish settlers who committed acts of violence against Palestinians enjoyed comparable impunity.) Throughout these decades, human rights organizations repeatedly condemned Israel's use of disproportionate, indiscriminate, and targeted firepower against Palestinian civilians, as well as Israel's failure to

---

29. Palestinian Center for Human Rights, "Confirmed Figures Reveal the True Extent of the Destruction Inflicted upon the Gaza Strip" (12 March 2009); Al Mezan Center for Human Rights, "Cast Lead Offensive in Numbers" (2 August 2009); "B'Tselem's Investigation of Fatalities in Operation Cast Lead" (9 September 2009).

30. See Chapter 4 for full references.

31. Although he referenced the UN Committee of Independent Experts (chaired by Mary McGowan Davis), it ultimately concluded that "the military investigations thus far appear to have produced very little" (see Chapter 5).

prosecute the perpetrators of these crimes.[32] If Goldstone's expectation that Hamas would investigate itself after Cast Lead was "unrealistic," how much more realistic was the hope that Israel would carry out bona fide investigations after Cast Lead? In fact, Israel's ensuing performance was exactly what one might have predicted. In the course of Cast Lead, Israel had damaged or destroyed "everything in its way," and not in its way, including 58,000 homes, 1,500 factories and workshops, 280 schools and kindergartens, electrical, water, and sewage installations, 190 greenhouse complexes, 80 percent of agricultural crops, and nearly one-fifth of cultivated land. Whole neighborhoods were laid waste. It also damaged or destroyed 29 ambulances, almost half of Gaza's 122 health facilities (including 15 hospitals), and 45 mosques. By the time it withdrew, the IDF had left behind fully 600,000 tons of rubble and 1,400 corpses, 350 of them children. Fact-finding missions as well as respected international, Israeli, and Palestinian human rights organizations all concluded that much of this destruction and death resulted from Israel's commission of war crimes. But the only penalty Israel imposed for unlawful property destruction during Cast Lead was a disciplinary measure punishing one soldier. At the time of Goldstone's recantation, the only Israeli soldier who had done jail time served seven and a half months for credit card theft. After his recantation, one other soldier was ordered to serve a 45-day sentence after killing two women waving a white flag (he was convicted of "illegal use of weapons").[33] The pitiful results of these judicial proceedings perfectly aligned with Israel's track record. Nonetheless, according to Goldstone, Israel had carried out investigations "transparently and in good faith . . . to a significant degree," and had demonstrated resolve to achieve justice in the few outstanding cases. The fact was, Goldstone was speaking in tongues, or with a forked tongue.

Whereas he could barely contain his praise for Israel, Goldstone could barely contain his contempt for Hamas. Its criminal intent "goes without saying—its rockets were purposefully and indiscriminately aimed at civilian

32. Martin Van Creveld, *The Sword and the Olive: A critical history of the Israeli Defense Force* (New York: 1998), p. 349; Norman G. Finkelstein, *Beyond Chutzpah: On the misuse of anti-Semitism and the abuse of history,* expanded paperback edition (Berkeley: 2008), pp. 96–130; Yesh Din, *A Semblance of Law: Law enforcement upon Israeli civilians in the West Bank* (2006), pp. 6, 26, 91–93; Yesh Din, *Exceptions: Prosecution of IDF soldiers during and after the second intifada* (2008), pp. 19–20; B'Tselem, *Void of Responsibility: Israel military policy not to investigate killings of Palestinians by soldiers* (2010), pp. 7–8, 53.

33. See Chapter 3 and Chapter 4 for full references, and Gili Cohen, "IDF Soldier Sentenced to 45 Days for Death of Mother, Daughter in Gaza War," *Haaretz* (12 August 2012).

targets." The Goldstone Report had based this finding on a couple of public statements by Hamas leaders, on the one hand, and on Hamas's targeting of civilian areas with its projectiles, on the other. But Israeli officials issued comparably incriminating public statements, while its incomparably more lethal firepower was also "purposefully and indiscriminately aimed at civilian targets." Why then did Goldstone indict Hamas for criminal intent in his recantation but absolve Israel of it? In fact, judging by his Report's relevant findings, none of which Goldstone repudiated, the case against Israel was far more compelling. Its bluster notwithstanding, Hamas couldn't more than wishfully target civilian areas with its arsenal of rudimentary projectiles. Only a single Israeli home was partially damaged during Cast Lead. But if Israel possessed fine "grid maps" of Gaza and an "extremely effective" intelligence-gathering capacity; if it made extensive use of state-of-the-art precision weaponry, and if 99 percent of the Israeli air force's combat missions hit targets accurately; and if it only once targeted a building erroneously—indeed, if Israel itself attested to these facts, then as the Goldstone Report logically concluded, the massive death and destruction Israel inflicted on Gaza must have "resulted from deliberate planning and policy decisions throughout the chain of command."[34] Hamas had "done nothing," Goldstone recalled in disgust, to investigate the criminal conduct of Gazans during Cast Lead. How could he not be outraged? Hamas killed three Israeli civilians and rendered one Israeli home unlivable, whereas Israel killed as many as 1,200 Gazan civilians and rendered more than 6,000 Gazan homes unlivable. But Hamas had "done nothing" to prosecute wrongdoers, whereas Israel locked up a soldier for stealing a credit card. Wasn't it blazingly obvious how much more evil Hamas was?

He had agreed to chair the fact-finding mission, Goldstone professed, in order to inaugurate a "new era of evenhandedness" in forums adjudicating the Israel-Palestine conflict. However noble this objective, its realization was prejudiced by the shameless and shameful double standards riddling his recantation. He also claimed credit for "numerous lessons learned" by Israel and concomitant "policy changes, including the adoption of new Israel Defense Forces procedures for protecting civilians in cases of urban warfare."[35] Israel delivered a full-court press of these lessons learned and procedural changes

---

34. See Chapter 3 for full references.

35. Goldstone also took full credit for "limiting the use" by Israel of "white phosphorus in civilian areas." Israel did cease firing white phosphorus in civilian areas after Cast Lead. But Israel's use of it had evoked universal outrage, while the decision was probably taken in Washington, which supplied Israel with the white phosphorus shells.

just a few years later during Operation Protective Edge (2014): instead of killing 350 children, it killed 550 children; instead of destroying 6,300 homes, it destroyed 18,000 homes.[36] The one lesson Israel truly learned from the Goldstone Report was that it was never too late to rupture the spine of human rights advocates and resume its killing spree. Indeed, the singular distinction of Goldstone's recantation was that it renewed Israel's license to kill.

Richard Goldstone plainly did not recant because "we know a lot more today." What he presented as new information consisted *entirely* of unverifiable assertions by parties with vested interests. The fact that he couldn't cite any genuinely new evidence to justify his volte-face was the most telling proof that none existed. What, then, happened? Ever since publication of his Report, Goldstone had been the object of a relentless smear campaign.[37] He was not, however, the only one who came under attack. The UN Human Rights Council appointed eminent international jurist Christian Tomuschat as chair of a follow-up committee mandated to determine whether Israel and Hamas were conscientiously investigating the Report's allegations. Deciding that Tomuschat was insufficiently pliant, Israel's lobby hounded and defamed him until he had no choice but to step down.[38] (He was replaced by New York State judge Mary McGowan Davis, who would later head the UN Human Rights Council fact-finding mission on Operation Protective Edge.[39]) In order to neutralize the Report's impact, Israel was clearly prepared to pull out all the stops.

Many facets of Goldstone's recantation perplexed.

Goldstone was reputed to be highly ambitious.[40] Since Israel had already ostracized itself in public opinion by the time Goldstone agreed to head the fact-finding mission, he no doubt felt secure in the knowledge that the

36. See Chapter 11 for full references.

37. See Chapter 5.

38. "Dershowitz: Goldstone follow-up commission head a 'bigot,'" *Jerusalem Post* (2 November 2010); Benjamin Weinthal, "Tomuschat, Head of Goldstone Follow-Up Committee, Resigns," *Jerusalem Post* (3 December 2010).

39. Although her follow-up report on Cast Lead wasn't a whitewash, McGowan Davis still bent over backward to appease Israel. She even gave guarded praise to the preposterous Turkel Report, which exonerated Israel of any wrongdoing in its assault on the Gaza Freedom Flotilla. *Report of the Committee of Independent Experts,* para. 39. For detailed analysis of the Turkel Report, see Chapter 8.

40. Ethan Bronner and Jennifer Medina, "Past Holds Clue to Goldstone's Shift on the Gaza War," *New York Times* (19 April 2011).

assignment would not mar his career, and might even prove to be a boon, as he upheld the rule of law despite the personal cost. Although Goldstone nonetheless came under savage waves of attack right after publication of his Report, the tide did eventually begin to turn in his favor. *Haaretz* editorialized that it was "time to thank the critics for forcing the IDF to examine itself and amend its procedures. Even if not all of Richard Goldstone's 32 charges were solid and valid, some of them certainly were."[41] The American Jewish magazine *Tikkun* honored Goldstone at a gala 25th anniversary celebration. In South Africa, distinguished personalities, such as Judge Dennis Davis, formerly of the Jewish Board of Deputies, publicly denounced a visit by Harvard law professor Alan Dershowitz because, among other things, he had "grossly misrepresented the judicial record of Judge Richard Goldstone."[42] It was puzzling, then, why an ambitious jurist at the peak of a long and distinguished career would court professional suicide by an erratic public recantation, alienating his colleagues in the human rights community and throwing doubt on his judicial temperament, just as his star was, after a brief waning, on the rise again.

Throughout his professional career, Goldstone functioned in bureaucracies and perforce internalized their norms. But in a shocking break with bureaucratic protocol, he dropped his bombshell without first notifying his three colleagues on the fact-finding mission or anyone at the United Nations. If Goldstone did not confide in them beforehand, wasn't it because he couldn't credibly defend, but didn't want to be shaken from, his resolve to recant? If he was apprehensive that his colleagues wouldn't back him, his intuition proved sound. Shortly after publication of his recantation, the three other members of the Goldstone Mission—Christine Chinkin, Hina Jilani, and Desmond Travers—issued a joint statement unequivocally affirming the Report's original findings: "We concur in our view that there is no justification for any demand or expectation for reconsideration of the report as nothing of substance has appeared that would in any way change the context, findings or conclusions of that report."[43]

Goldstone alleged that it was new evidence apropos Israel's deadly assault on the al-Samouni family, and the revised Hamas casualty figure, that induced him to reverse himself. But just two months earlier at Stanford

41. "Thanks to the Critics," *Haaretz* (27 July 2010).
42. "Dershowitz is Not Welcome Here!," *Cape Times* (24 March 2011).
43. Hina Jilani, Christine Chinkin, and Desmond Travers, "Goldstone Report: Statement issued by members of UN mission on Gaza war," *Guardian* (14 April 2011).

University, he had matter-of-factly addressed these very same points without drawing dramatic new conclusions. No other evidence surfaced in the interim. Goldstone also referenced a UN document so that he could issue Israel a clean bill of health on its internal investigations. But this document was much more critical of Israeli investigations than he let on.[44] It was as if Goldstone was desperately clutching at any shred of evidence, however problematic, to justify his predetermined decision to recant. Indeed, he rushed to acquit Israel of criminal culpability in the al-Samouni deaths even before the Israeli military had completed its investigation.

A few days before submitting his recantation to the *Washington Post,* Goldstone had submitted another version of it to the *New York Times.*[45] The *Times* rejected the submission, apparently because it did *not* repudiate the Report. It was as if Goldstone was being pressed against his will to publicly recant. To avoid tarnishing his reputation and because his heart was not in it, Goldstone initially submitted a wishy-washy recantation to the *Times.* After the *Times* rejected it as not newsworthy, and in a race against the clock, he hurriedly slipped in wording that could be construed as a full-blown repudiation, to ensure that the *Post* would run what was now a bombshell. The exertion of outside pressure on Goldstone would explain the slapdash composition, opaque formulations, and overarching murkiness, in which he seemed to be simultaneously recanting and not recanting the Report. It would also explain his embarrassing inclusion of irrelevances such as his call on the Human Rights Council to condemn the slaughter of an Israeli settler family—two years after Cast Lead in an incident unrelated to the Gaza Strip—by unknown perpetrators.

The eminent South African jurist John Dugard was a colleague of Goldstone's. He had headed a cognate fact-finding mission that investigated Cast Lead. The findings of his report—which contained a finer legal analysis, while the Goldstone Report was broader in scope—largely overlapped with Goldstone's. It concluded that "the purpose of Israel's action was to punish the people of Gaza," and that Israel was "responsible for the commission of internationally wrongful acts by reason of the commission of war crimes and

44. Roger Cohen, "The Goldstone Chronicles," *New York Times* (7 April 2011); Akiva Eldar, "What Exactly Did Goldstone 'Retract' from His Report on Gaza?," *Haaretz* (12 April 2011).

45. "NY Times: We turned down a different version of Goldstone retraction," *Haaretz* (5 April 2011).

crimes against humanity."[46] In a devastating dissection of Goldstone's recantation, Dugard adjudged: "There are no new facts that exonerate Israel and that could possibly have led Goldstone to change his mind. What made him change his mind therefore remains a closely guarded secret."[47] Although Goldstone's secret will perhaps never be revealed and his recantation has caused irreparable damage, it is still possible by patient reconstruction of the factual record to know the truth about what happened in Gaza. Out of respect for the memory of those who perished during Operation Cast Lead, this truth must be preserved and protected from its assassins.

46. *Report of the Independent Fact-Finding Committee on Gaza: No safe place,* presented to the League of Arab States (30 April 2009), paras. 556, 573.

47. John Dugard, "Where Now for the Goldstone Report?," *New Statesman* (6 April 2011).

FIGURE 3. *Mavi Marmara* (on right). © MENAHEM KAHANA/AFP/Getty Images.

PART THREE

———

The Mavi Marmara

SEVEN

Murder on the High Seas

THE DEVASTATION INFLICTED ON GAZA during Operation Cast Lead (2008–9) was designed to exacerbate the effects of the ongoing illegal blockade. "I fully expected to see serious damage, but I have to say I was really shocked when I saw the extent and precision of the destruction," the World Food Program director for the Strip observed after the assault. "It was precisely the strategic economic areas that Gaza depends on to relieve its dependency on aid that were wiped out."[1] The Israel Defense Forces (IDF) destroyed critical civilian infrastructure, such as the only operative flour mill and nearly all of the cement factories, in the hope and expectation that after a cease-fire went into effect, Gazans would be reduced to abject dependency and couldn't rebuild their lives unless and until they bowed to Israeli diktat.[2]

A year and a half after Cast Lead, major humanitarian and human rights organizations uniformly attested that Gaza continued to suffer a humanitarian crisis on account of the siege: "Contrary to what the Israeli government states, the humanitarian aid allowed into Gaza is only a fraction of what is needed to answer the enormous needs of an exhausted people" (Oxfam); "The blockade... has severely damaged the economy, leaving 70 to 80 percent of Gazans in poverty" (Human Rights Watch); "Israel is blocking vital medical supplies from entering the Gaza Strip" (World Health Organization); "The closure is having a devastating impact on the 1.5 million people living in Gaza" (International

---

1. "The Rubble That Was Gaza," *World Food Program News* (25 January 2009). See also European Commission, *Damage Assessment and Needs Identification in the Gaza Strip, Final Report* (2009), pp. xv, 93.

2. Desmond Travers, "Operation Cast Lead: Legal and doctrinal asymmetries in a military operation," Irish Defense Forces, *An Cosantóir* (2010), pp. 10–12.

Committee of the Red Cross).[3] Still, Israeli prime minister Benjamin Netanyahu proclaimed that there was "no humanitarian crisis" and "no lack of medicines or other essential items" in Gaza.[4] "We mustn't tire of reminding others," Parisian media philosopher Bernard-Henri Lévy chimed in, that "the blockade concerns only arms and the material needed to manufacture them."[5] Mocking the reports of a humanitarian crisis, Deputy Foreign Minister Danny Ayalon gestured to Gaza's "sparkling new shopping mall ... new Olympic-sized swimming pool ... five-star hotels and restaurants."[6] To assuage public opinion, Israel disseminated photographs of these lavish scenes on the Internet.[7] Tiny pockets of Gaza did in fact prosper. Harvard political economist Sara Roy noted the emergence of a thin economic stratum that had "grown extremely wealthy from the black-market economy," and the "almost perverse consumerism in restaurants and shops that are the domain of the wealthy."[8] However appalling, such a juxtaposition should scarcely come as a shock, at any rate to students of Jewish history. "The sword of the Nazi extermination policy hung over all Jews equally," a survivor of the Warsaw Ghetto recalled.

> But a social differentiation arose in the ghetto, setting apart substantial groups who had the means even under those infernal conditions to lead a comparatively full, well-fed life and enjoy some kinds of pleasures. On the same streets where daily you could see scenes of horror, amid the swarms of tubercular children dying like flies ... , you would come upon stores full of fine foods, restaurants and cafés, which served the most expensive dishes and drinks.... The clientele of these places consisted principally of Jewish Gestapo agents, Jewish police officials, rich merchants who did business with the Germans, smugglers, dealers in foreign exchange and similar kinds of people.

3. Oxfam, "Gaza Weekly Update" (30 May–5 June 2010); Human Rights Watch, "Israel: Full, impartial investigation of flotilla killings essential" (31 May 2010); World Health Organization, "Medical Supplies Blocked from Entering Gaza" (1 June 2010); International Committee of the Red Cross, "Gaza Closure: Not another year!" (14 June 2010).

4. Israel Ministry of Foreign Affairs, "Statement by Prime Minister Netanyahu: 'No love boat'" (2 June 2010); Israel Ministry of Foreign Affairs, "PM Netanyahu's Statement before the Turkel Commission" (9 August 2010).

5. Bernard-Henri Lévy, "It's Time to Stop Demonizing Israel," *Haaretz* (8 June 2010). See also Gideon Levy, "In Response to Bernard-Henri Lévy," *Haaretz* (10 June 2010).

6. Danny Ayalon, "The Flotilla Farce," *Wall Street Journal* (29 July 2010).

7. Tom Gross, "A Nice New Shopping Mall Opened Today in Gaza: Will the media report on it?," *Mideast Dispatch Archive* (17 July 2010).

8. Sara Roy, "Gaza: Treading on shards," *Nation* (1 March 2010); see also Sara Roy, *The Gaza Strip: The political economy of de-development,* expanded third edition (Washington, DC: 2016), pp. xliii–xlv.

He went on to note, "the Nazis made moving pictures of such festive orgies to show the 'world' how well the Jews lived in the ghetto."[9]

The consensus among human rights and humanitarian organizations was that the Israeli blockade of Gaza constituted a form of collective punishment in flagrant violation of international law.[10] A misplaced controversy unfolded between Israel's critics and supporters, as to whether the blockade had put Gazans on a "starvation" (critics) or "starvation plus" (supporters) regimen. The terms of this debate diverted attention from and obscured the fundamental point: What right did Israel have to put the people of Gaza on *any* diet? Even critics of the siege seconded Israel's right to prevent weapons from entering Gaza. But if Palestinians acquiesced in the legally mandated terms for resolving the conflict,[11] *did* international law in fact debar them from

9. Bernard Goldstein, *Five Years in the Warsaw Ghetto* (Edinburgh: 2005), pp. 77–78.

10. The most authoritative legal analysis was crafted by a UN Human Rights Council fact-finding mission, chaired by a retired judge of the International Criminal Court and including the former chief prosecutor of the UN-backed Special Court for Sierra Leone. It found that (1) "the blockade was inflicting disproportionate damage upon the civilian population in the Gaza Strip and as such the interception [by Israel] could not be justified and therefore has to be considered illegal," and (2) "one of the principal motives behind the imposition of the blockade was a desire to punish the people of the Gaza Strip for having elected Hamas. The combination of this motive and the effect of the restrictions on the Gaza Strip leave no doubt that Israel's actions and policies amount to collective punishment as defined by international law." UN Human Rights Council, *Report of the International Fact-Finding Mission to Investigate Violations of International Law, Including International Humanitarian and Human Rights Law, Resulting from the Israeli Attacks on the Flotilla of Ships Carrying Humanitarian Assistance* (27 September 2010), paras. 53, 54; hereafter: *Report of the Fact-Finding Mission*. One of the Report's central conclusions is suggestive of its balance, judiciousness, and humanity:

> The Mission is not alone in finding that a deplorable situation exists in Gaza. It has been characterized as "unsustainable." This is totally intolerable and unacceptable in the 21st century. It is amazing that anyone could characterize the condition of the people there as satisfying the most basic of acceptable standards. The parties and the international community are urged to find the solution that will address all legitimate security concern[s] of both Israel and the people of Palestine both of whom are equally entitled to "their place under the heavens." The apparent dichotomy in this case between the competing right of security and the right to a decent living can only be resolved if old antagonisms are subordinated to a sense of justice and fair play. One has to find the strength to pluck from the memory rooted sorrows and to move on. (para. 275)

The UN Human Rights Council voted to "endorse the conclusions" contained in the Report by 30 in favor, 1 against, and 15 abstentions (A/HRC/15/L.33) (29 September 2010). Although the United States cast the sole negative vote, in its oral explanation the American representative did not dispute the Report's findings.

11. See Chapter 2.

using armed force or acquiring weapons to end the occupation? The salient points of law were these. *First,* in a 2004 advisory opinion, the International Court of Justice stated that "as regards the principle of the right of peoples to self-determination, the Court observes that the existence of a 'Palestinian people' is no longer in issue"; that the Palestinian people's "rights include the right to self-determination"; and that "Israel is bound to comply with its obligation to respect the right of the Palestinian people to self-determination."[12] *Second,* the territorial unit within which this Palestinian right of self-determination was to be exercised "clearly includes the West Bank, East Jerusalem and Gaza."[13] *Third,* international law prohibited use of military force "by an administering power to suppress widespread popular insurrection in a self-determination unit," while "the use of force by a non-State entity in exercise of a right of self-determination is legally neutral, that is, not regulated by international law at all," and "assistance by States to local insurgents in a self-determination unit may be permissible."[14] *Fourth,* it might be contended that the legal situation in the occupied Palestinian territories was regulated not by the right of self-determination but, instead, by the law of belligerent occupation;[15] that "belligerent occupation is not designed to win the hearts and minds of the local inhabitants: it has military—or security—objectives and its foundation is the 'power of the

---

12. International Court of Justice, Advisory Opinion, *Legal Consequences of the Construction of a Wall in the Occupied Palestinian Territory* (9 July 2004), paras. 118, 149.

13. John Dugard, *Report of the Special Rapporteur on the Situation of Human Rights in the Palestinian Territories Occupied since 1967* (A/HRC/7/17) (21 January 2008), para. 49.

14. James Crawford, *The Creation of States in International Law,* second edition (Oxford: 2006), pp. 135–37, 147. See also Heather A. Wilson, *International Law and the Use of Force by National Liberation Movements* (Oxford: 1988), pp. 135–36 ("[the law] is still not agreed upon" as to the right of national liberation movements to use force, although "the trend ... since 1960 ... has been toward the extension of the authority to use force to national liberation movements," while "the use of force to deny the free exercise of a people's right to self-determination is contrary to the principles of international law"); A. Rigo Sureda, *The Evolution of the Right to Self-Determination: A study of United Nations practice* (Leiden: 1973), pp. 331, 343–44, 354 ("since 1965, the General Assembly has ... started to call upon states to help dependent peoples to achieve self-determination with moral and material assistance," and "The fact that the Security Council has never expressly condemned the guerrilla activities of the Palestinians can be interpreted as an implied recognition of their right to recover at least the territories from which they were displaced in the June 1967 hostilities, and to do so by the use of force if necessary").

15. *Belligerent occupation* referred to the fact that Israel came to occupy the West Bank (including East Jerusalem) and the Gaza Strip in the course of a war.

bayonet'";[16] that, consequently, the civilian population in an occupied territory did not have the right to forcibly resist an occupying power. However, even if Israel did legally qualify as a belligerent occupier, the Israel-Palestine conflict would nonetheless be one of those "situations in which belligerent occupation and wars of national liberation overlap,"[17] and the right of national liberation/self-determination is a peremptory norm of international law from which no derogation is permissible.[18] This peremptory right would thus limit the ambit of the law of belligerent occupation—in particular, its strictures on use of force—in hybrid or overlapping situations. The upshot was that the Palestinian right to self-determination trumped whatever rights Israel might have accrued as a belligerent occupier. *Fifth*, in fact, however, by refusing to negotiate in good faith an end to the conflict, Israel had forfeited any rights it might have invoked under the law of belligerent occupation. It could then legally lay claim to one and only one "right"—to withdraw—while no law debarred Palestinians from using force or acquiring weapons from friendly states to effect that withdrawal.[19] It was a measure of how degraded international law had become that rights and obligations were inverted: the tacit premise of public discourse was that Israel had a right to use armed force, while Palestinians had an obligation to disarm. Even if, for argument's sake, international law did prohibit the Palestinian people from resort to armed resistance, the fact still remained that, as Amnesty International urged (if on different grounds), an arms embargo should have been imposed on both Hamas *and Israel*.[20] It would be a curious conception of justice that denied the victims the wherewithal to resist even as they supported the legally mandated norms for achieving peace, but enabled the perpetrators to replenish their arsenal of repression even as they rejected these norms and rode roughshod over them.

On 31 May 2010, a humanitarian flotilla en route to Gaza and carrying seven hundred passengers came under attack in international waters by Israeli commandos. The flotilla's six vessels were delivering ten thousand tons of badly needed supplies to Gaza's beleaguered population. By the end of the

16. Yoram Dinstein, *The International Law of Belligerent Occupation* (Cambridge: 2009), paras. 80, 218.

17. Wilson, *International Law*, p. 20.

18. Crawford, *Creation*, pp. 99–102; Sureda, *Evolution*, p. 353; see also International Court of Justice, *Legal Consequences of the Construction of a Wall*, paras. 88, 156.

19. See Chapter 11 and Appendix.

20. See Chapter 4.

Israeli assault in the middle of the night, nine passengers aboard the flagship *Mavi Marmara* had been shot to death.[21] "If Cast Lead was a turning point in the attitude of the world towards us," *Haaretz* columnist Gideon Levy rued, "this operation is the second horror film of the apparently ongoing series."[22] Still, ever the public relations maestro, Israel managed to spin the commandos as the *victims* of the attack.[23] In a solipsistic paroxysm of indignation, and with nary a peep of dissent, Israeli officials and media across the political spectrum proclaimed that the commandos were initially armed only with "paintball rifles" and resorted to aggressive tactics "as a last resort" in "self-defense"; they had been "provoked," "ambushed," "duped," "lynched," and "lured" into a "trap" set by a phalanx of "radical anti-Western," "machete-wielding," "bloodthirsty" "jihadists" and "mercenaries" linked with "Al-Qaeda" and other "terrorist" organizations. Israeli vilification zeroed in on *Mavi Marmara* passengers belonging to İnsani Yardım Vakfı (IHH), the Turkish group that sponsored the vessel. IHH was branded a terrorist (or terrorist-affiliated) organization.[24] But in an Israeli information packet distributed just before the commando raid, IHH had been benignly depicted as "a Turkish pro-Palestinian human rights organization with a strong Muslim orientation . . . , which provides humanitarian relief into areas of war and conflict."[25] "The soldiers were beaten," Nobel Peace Prize laureate and Israeli president Shimon Peres solemnly intoned, "just because they did not want to kill anyone." "You fought morally, and showed valor in your acts," he then told the commandos. "I salute you and admire your courage and restraint even in the face of danger to your own lives."[26] Israel's ambassador to Spain likened the *Mavi Marmara* passengers to Islamic terrorists who had killed scores of commuters on Madrid trains in 2004, while bracketing the nine civilians killed aboard the vessel with the "twenty-three Spaniards [who]

21. One passenger fell into a coma as a result of the injuries he sustained, and died four years later.

22. Gideon Levy, "Operation Mini Cast Lead," *Haaretz* (1 June 2010).

23. Arun Gupta, "How the US Corporate Media Got the Israel Flotilla Catastrophe So Wrong," *AlterNet* (16 June 2010).

24. Intelligence and Terrorism Information Center, *Conspicuous among the Passengers and Organizations aboard the* Mavi Marmara *Were Turkish and Arab Islamic Extremists Led by IHH* (26 September 2010), paras. 2, 9, 11.

25. Military Strategic Information Section, International Military Cooperation Department, Strategic Division, Israel Defense Forces, "Free Gaza Flotilla" (27 May 2010).

26. Ahiya Raved, "Peres: Soldiers were beaten for being humane," *ynetnews.com* (1 June 2010); Ronen Medzini, "Peres: World always against us," *ynetnews.com* (3 June 2010).

died on the roads this weekend."[27] Some 90 percent of Israeli Jews supported the decision to stop the flotilla and believed that Israel used the right amount or not enough force, while only 16 percent supported lifting the siege of Gaza.[28] One of the commandos responsible for killing multiple passengers was reportedly in line for a medal of valor, while Deputy Prime Minister Eli Yishai exhorted Defense Minister Ehud Barak to award medals to all the commandos: "The warrior's [sic] courage is exemplary, and they deserve a citation."[29]

The exact sequence of events on that fateful night will probably never be known for certain.[30] But even if it were, it wouldn't materially affect the assignation of blame. If Israel sought to justify its attack on the *Mavi Marmara* on the grounds of self-defense, it came up against the tenet of law that no legal benefit or right could be derived from an illegal act (*ex injuria non oritur jus*). In the instant case, Israel couldn't claim a right of self-defense if its resort to violent force was triggered by its enforcement of the illegal blockade. The passengers aboard a convoy in international waters carrying humanitarian relief to a desperate population did, however, have every right to use force in self-defense against a pirate-like raid.[31] What's more, when Israel attacked the flotilla, it did not harbor a fear that illegal contraband was on board. The flotilla leadership offered to let a neutral body, such as the International Red Cross, verify beforehand the humanitarian nature of the cargo (it appears that the contents had already been rigorously inspected at departure), while Israeli officials neither evinced interest in searching the

27. Giles Tremlett, "Gaza Flotilla Attack: Israeli ambassador to Madrid tries to play down deaths," *Guardian* (4 June 2010).

28. Maayana Miskin, "Poll: Israelis support flotilla raid, Gaza blockade, PM and IDF," *Arutz Sheva* (11 June 2010). See also the articles by Amira Hass, Neve Gordon, and Ilan Pappé in Moustafa Bayoumi, ed., *Midnight on the Mavi Marmara: The attack on the Gaza freedom flotilla and how it changed the course of the Israel/Palestine conflict* (New York: 2010).

29. Hana Levi Julian, "Medal for Israeli Commando for Valor on *Mavi Marmara*?," *Arutz Sheva* (6 June 2010).

30. The most comprehensive collection and analysis of media accounts is Richard Lightbown's unpublished manuscript, *The Israeli Raid of the Freedom Flotilla 31 May 2010: A review of media sources* (31 August 2010). For a Turkish reconstruction of the incident, see İnsani Yardım Vakfı (IHH), *Palestine Our Route, Humanitarian Aid Our Load: Flotilla campaign summary report* (n.d.). See also Friends of Charities Association, *Timeline & Inconsistencies Report Relating to the Gaza-Bound Freedom Flotilla Attack May 31, 2010* (Washington, DC: 2010).

31. The passengers initially used water hoses to repel the Israeli assault, which the International Maritime Organization has "recommended as a means to prevent an attempted boarding by pirates and armed robbers" (*Report of the Fact-Finding Mission*, p. 25n68).

flotilla's cargo nor even pretended that the ships were transporting weapons to Gaza.[32] "A provocation took place off the coast of Gaza, but the provocateurs were not the peace activists," veteran Israeli dissident Uri Avnery declared. "The provocation was carried out by navy ships and commandos... blocking the way of the aid boats and using deadly force." If Israeli officials proclaimed after Cast Lead that they had "acted" lunatic in order to deter their enemies, then it was cause for concern after the commando raid whether they had in fact *become* lunatic. "Only a crazy government that has lost all restraint and all connection to reality," Avnery went on to say, "could do something like that—consider ships carrying humanitarian aid and peace activists from around the world as an enemy and send massive military force to international waters to attack them, shoot and kill."[33]

Even as some points of contention remained murky, insofar as the facts could be ascertained, the vast preponderance of Israeli allegations did not hold up to scrutiny.[34] The attacking force did not initially use only paintball guns; on the contrary, Israeli combatants in Zodiacs abutting the *Mavi Marmara* opened fire with tear gas, smoke and stun grenades, and maybe plastic bullets, and then helicopters hovering above the vessel opened fire with live ammunition before any commando had rappelled on deck.[35] The passengers did not belong to terrorist organizations,[36] nor did they lay a lethal

32. International Crisis Group, *Turkey's Crises over Israel and Iran* (2010), p. 6; Ron Friedman, "IDF: Flotilla supplies unnecessary," *Jerusalem Post* (2 June 2010); *Report of the Fact-Finding Mission,* paras. 55–58, 88–89, 109.

33. Uri Avnery, "A Crime Perpetrated by Order of the Government of Israel and the IDF Command," Gush Shalom (31 May 2010). See also David Grossman, "The Gaza Flotilla Attack Shows How Far Israel Has Declined," *Guardian* (1 June 2010).

34. The evidence adduced by Israel in its internal investigation will be parsed in Chapter 8.

35. *Report of the Fact-Finding Mission,* paras. 112–14. A semiofficial Israeli publication did not contest that "gas, stun, and smoke grenades were fired from the [Israeli] boats" immediately as they approached the *Mavi Marmara,* while a largely apologetic *New York Times* reconstruction conceded that "the crack of an Israeli sound grenade and a hail of rubber bullets from above were supposed to disperse activists" *before* the commandos hit the deck of the *Mavi Marmara.* Intelligence and Terrorism Information Center, *Preparations Made by IHH for Confrontation with the IDF and the Violence Exercised by That Organization's Operatives* (15 September 2010), para. 11; Sabrina Tavernise and Ethan Bronner, "Days of Planning Led to Flotilla's Hour of Chaos," *New York Times* (4 June 2010).

36. One passenger on the *Mavi Marmara* had apparently in the past been convicted and served prison time for his involvement in the 1996 hijacking of a Russian ferryboat. (The hijackers were demanding the release of Chechen prisoners.)

trap; on the contrary, they did not even prepare for injuries,[37] did not possess firearms or discharge captured ones,[38] and did not carry on them monies paid to murder Israelis.[39] The Israeli commandos held by passengers did not endure a lynching; on the contrary, they were provided medical care and then escorted for release.[40] The Israeli commandos did not fire with restraint and only in self-defense; on the contrary, they killed the nine passengers by shooting all but one of them multiple times—five were shot in the head, and at least six of the nine were killed in a manner consistent with an extralegal, arbitrary, and summary execution.[41] "The conduct of the Israeli military and other personnel towards the flotilla passengers was not only disproportionate to the occasion," a prestigious UN fact-finding mission concluded, "but demonstrated levels of totally unnecessary and incredible violence. It betrayed an unacceptable level of brutality."[42] Shortly after release of the UN report, however, Prime Minister Netanyahu praised the "crucial, essential, important and legal" assault and "saluted" the Israeli commandos, who acted "courageously, morally and with restraint" against "those who came to kill you, and tried to kill you"; "There is no one better than you."[43] To be sure, Israeli officials did acknowledge room for operational improvement: "when the next flotilla . . . is boarded by the navy . . . , attack dogs will be the first to board the decks, to prevent harm to soldiers . . . they are strong and merciless."[44] It was unclear whether contingency plans had been put in place should passengers "dupe" and "lynch" the canines. Meanwhile, the semiofficial Israeli

37. Hugh Pope, "Erdogan Is Not the Bogeyman," *Haaretz* (18 June 2010); International Crisis Group, *Turkey's Crises*, p. 7; *Report of the Fact-Finding Mission*, para. 129. The passengers had to break into medical supplies earmarked for Gaza in order to treat the wounded.

38. *Report of the Fact-Finding Mission*, paras. 101, 116, 165. Israel did not produce any evidence substantiating its claim that passengers fired live ammunition at the commandos, while its public statements on this point were riddled with contradictions (ibid., p. 26n70).

39. "Is it really conceivable," Henry Siegman rhetorically queried in *Haaretz*, "that Turkish activists who were supposedly paid ten thousand dollars each would bring that money with them on board the ship knowing they would be taken into custody by Israeli authorities?" "Israel's Greatest Loss: Its moral imagination," *Haaretz* (11 June 2010).

40. *Report of the Fact-Finding Mission*, paras. 125–26.

41. Ibid., paras. 118, 120, 170; Robert Booth, "Gaza Flotilla Activists Were Shot in Head at Close Range," *Guardian* (4 June 2010). About fifty passengers suffered injuries, while Israel reported nine commandos injured, three seriously.

42. *Report of the Fact-Finding Mission*, paras. 264–65 (see also paras. 167–72).

43. "Netanyahu 'Salutes' Commandos Who Raided Gaza Flotilla," *Haaretz* (26 October 2010).

44. Hanan Greenberg, "Dogs to Be Used in Next Flotilla Raid," *ynetnews.com* (7 October 2010).

Intelligence and Terrorism Information Center noted in apparent extenuation of the killings that as many as seven of the nine dead passengers might have sought martyrdom; the last diary entry of one of them, for example, expressed a willingness to die "for a noble cause."[45] Before being hung by the British in 1775, American revolutionary Nathan Hale famously regretted having "but one life to lose for my country." Gandhi exhorted his followers to actively court martyrdom: "It would exhilarate me to hear that a co-worker ... was shot dead or that another co-worker ... had had his skull broken."[46] Does a man's preparedness to make the ultimate sacrifice for a greater good justify killing him?

If so many Westerners initially swallowed the topsy-turvy Israeli story line, it was because the *hasbara* (propaganda) campaign had been so carefully rehearsed and adeptly executed,[47] while the Western media lapped up the Israeli spin. "In an operation reminiscent of the first week or so" of Operation Cast Lead, Antony Lerman observed in the British *Guardian*, "the Israeli PR machine succeeded in getting the major news outlets to focus on its version of events and to use the Israeli authorities' discourse for a crucial 48 hours."[48] The only witnesses able to contest the official Israeli account had been imprisoned and their photographic evidence confiscated. But the Israeli propaganda offensive eventually began to unravel, and international opinion (including wide swaths of Jewish opinion) swung sharply in the reverse direction.[49] Israel then contended that if some people saw things differently, it traced back to "the eternal war against the Jewish people,"[50] and the fact that Israeli officialdom had dropped the ball on the PR front.[51] The international

45. Intelligence and Terrorism Information Center, *According to Well-Documented Information, Seven of the Nine Turks Killed in the Violent Confrontation aboard the* Mavi Marmara *Had Previously Declared Their Desire to Become Martyr[s] (Shaheeds)* (13 July 2010).

46. "Speech at Bulsar" (29 April 1930), in *The Collected Works of Mahatma Gandhi* (Ahmedabad), vol. 43, pp. 327–28.

47. Danny Ayalon, "Public Relations Battle Is a Marathon, Not a Sprint," *Jerusalem Post* (8 June 2010).

48. Antony Lerman, "Israeli PR Machine Won Gaza Flotilla Media Battle," *Guardian* (4 June 2010).

49. Norman G. Finkelstein, *"This Time We Went Too Far": Truth and consequences of the Gaza invasion,* expanded paperback edition (New York: 2011), pp. 168–80.

50. Caroline Glick, "Ending Israel's Losing Streak," *Jerusalem Post* (1 June 2010).

51. Zvi Mazel, "Peace Activists? More Like 'Peace' Militants," *Jerusalem Post* (1 June 2010); Hirsh Goodman, "The Source of Failure: Israel's public diplomacy and the intelligence community," *Institute for National Security Studies* (9 June 2010); Alex Fishman, "Israel Losing the War," *ynetnews.com* (20 June 2010).

community turned hostile, according to the influential Reut Institute, because of "successful efforts to brand [Israel] as an occupying and aggressive entity that ignores and undermines human rights and international law," whereas "the flotillas were branded in the context of resistance to 'occupation' and 'oppression,' the promotion of peace and human rights, a moral response to Gaza's 'humanitarian crisis,' and in the spirit of international law."[52] In other words, if Israel's image had suffered yet another blow, its cause was not the sordid underlying reality but, instead, the distorted "branding" of it.

Despite the groundswell of public outrage, the United States lent Israel blind support throughout its latest diplomatic imbroglio. President Barack Obama merely expressed "deep regret" at the loss of life,[53] while his administration shielded Israel from accountability at international forums. Vice President Joseph Biden defended the commando raid on the grounds that, if the flotilla had just unloaded the cargo at an Israeli port, Israel would have been ready, willing, and able to transfer it to Gaza. In a bizarre sequence of non sequiturs, Biden alternately asserted that Israel was blocking passage of supplies such as building materials, and that the flotilla could have "easily brought" them in.[54] Meanwhile, the US representative at an Emergency Session of the UN Security Council shamelessly denied that Israel had prevented vital goods from reaching Gaza: "mechanisms exist for the transfer of humanitarian assistance to Gaza by member states and groups that want to do so."[55] Eighty-seven of the US Senate's one hundred members signed a letter to Obama declaring that they "fully support Israel's right of self-defense" after the Israeli commandos "arrived" on the *Mavi Marmara* and "were brutally attacked." The US House of Representatives followed suit, as 338 of its 435 members signed a letter expressing "strong support for Israel's right to defend itself" after "passengers on the ship attacked Israeli soldiers with

52. Reut Institute, *The Gaza Flotilla: A collapse of Israel's political firewall* (August 2010), para. 27.

53. "Obama Supports UN Call for Investigation of Flotilla Incident," *America.gov* (1 June 2010).

54. Natasha Mozgovaya, "Biden: Israel right to stop Gaza flotilla from breaking blockade," *Haaretz* (2 June 2010); Richard Adams, "Gaza Flotilla Raid: Joe Biden asks 'So what's the big deal here?,'" *Guardian* blog (2 June 2010).

55. United States Mission to the United Nations, "Remarks by Ambassador Alejandro Wolff, Deputy Permanent US Representative to the United Nations, at an Emergency Session of the Security Council" (31 May 2010).

clubs, metal rods, and iron bars."[56] Congressional leaders, acting at the behest of "Jewish groups," moved to officially designate not the perpetrators but the victims of the attack as terrorists, and the sponsors of the humanitarian mission as a terrorist organization. They also sought to bar survivors of the bloodbath entry into the United States on the grounds that they "should not be allowed to come ... and spill their propaganda and hatred and terrorist rhetoric."[57] "Since the Palestinians in Gaza elected Hamas," New York senator Chuck Schumer told a meeting of Orthodox Jews after the attack, it made sense "to strangle them economically until they see that's not the way to go."[58] On the other hand, US secretary of state Hillary Clinton and other Western officials, alongside the UN Security Council as a whole, experienced an epiphany: on the morning after the flotilla horror, they proclaimed that Israel's siege of Gaza was "unsustainable" and had to be lifted.[59] Still, as the Crisis Group pointedly observed, "International condemnation and calls for an inquiry will come easily, but many who will issue them must acknowledge their own role in the deplorable treatment of Gaza that formed the backdrop" to the Israeli raid.[60] Fully three-quarters of the damage and destruction Israel wreaked during Cast Lead had not yet been repaired or rebuilt when the flotilla embarked on its humanitarian mission.[61] Although Israel prom-

56. "Bipartisan Group of 87 Senators, Led by Reid and McConnell, Send Letter to President Obama in Support of Israel's Right to Self-Defense," *Democrats.senate.gov* (23 June 2010); Congress of the United States, House of Representatives, "Dear Mr. President" (29 June 2010). See also "Congress Shows Israel Support," *Jerusalem Post* (9 June 2010).

57. Nathan Guttman, "Push to Sanction Backers of Gaza Flotilla Gains Steam in US," *Forward* (16 June 2010).

58. "Chuck Schumer: 'Strangle' them economically," *Huffington Post* (11 June 2010). See also Juan Cole, "Schumer's *Sippenhaftung*," *Informed Comment* blog (12 June 2010).

59. Jonathan Ferziger and Calev Ben-David, "Gaza Situation 'Unsustainable,' Clinton Says as Ship Approaches," *Bloomberg Businessweek* (1 June 2010); United Nations Department of Public Information, "Security Council Condemns Acts Resulting in Civilian Deaths during Israeli Operation against Gaza-Bound Aid Convoy, Calls for Investigation, in Presidential Statement" (31 May 2010). See also Bernard Kouchner, Franco Frattini, and Miguel Angel Moratinos, "Averting Another Gaza," *New York Times* (10 June 2010); "EU Strongly Condemns Gaza Flotilla Attack," *EurActiv.com* (2 June 2010); Yossi Lempkowicz, "Gaza Flotilla: EU Parliament calls for international inquiry and end to blockade," *European Jewish Press* (17 June 2010).

60. International Crisis Group, "Flotilla Attack the Deadly Symptom of a Failed Policy" (31 May 2010).

61. Robert H. Serry (UN Special Coordinator for the Middle East Peace Process), "Briefing to the Security Council on the Situation in the Middle East" (15 June 2010), citing a United Nations Development Program survey.

ised after the flotilla carnage and attendant international outcry to "ease" restrictions on some goods bound for Gaza, it still banned items necessary to restore Gaza's manufacturing sector, and put onerous conditions on the entry of critical building materials.[62] The "burdens on the entrance of construction materials," an Israeli human rights organization warned, could "turn the promise of allowing reconstruction into a dead letter."[63] UN officials estimated that under Israeli restrictions still in place, it would take "75 years" to rebuild Gaza.[64] In late 2010, nearly a half year after Israel's publicized commitment to relax the siege, a consortium of more than 20 respected human rights and humanitarian organizations operating in Gaza grimly reported that "there are few signs of real improvement on the ground as the 'ease' has left foundations of the illegal blockade policy intact"; "Gaza requires 670,000 truckloads of construction material, while only an average of 715 of these truckloads have been received per month"; "the private sector is excluded from the possibility to import construction materials including concrete, steel and gravel, hampering efforts of people in Gaza to rebuild their homes, businesses and other property"; "exports remain banned and except for the humanitarian activity of exporting a small amount of strawberries, not a single truck has left Gaza since the easing"; "many humanitarian items, including vital water equipment, that are not on the Israeli restricted list continue to receive no permits"; "ordinary Gaza residents are still denied access to their friends and family, and to educational opportunities in the West Bank, East Jerusalem and abroad"; "access to around 35 percent of Gaza's farmland and 85 percent of maritime areas for fishing remains restricted by the Israeli 'buffer zone,' with devastating impact on the economy and people's rights and livelihoods"; "39 percent of Gaza residents remain unemployed," while "80 percent of the population [remain] dependent upon international aid." "There cannot be a just and durable resolution of the Israeli-Palestinian conflict," the authoritative report concluded, "with-

---

62. State of Israel, *The Civilian Policy towards the Gaza Strip* (June 2010), appendix B; State of Israel, "Briefing: Israel's new policy towards Gaza" (5 July 2010).

63. Gisha (Legal Center for Freedom of Movement), "Unraveling the Closure of Gaza" (7 July 2010).

64. United Nations Office for the Coordination of Humanitarian Affairs (OCHA), *The Humanitarian Monitor* (July 2010), p. 8. For a contemporary report on the history, impact, and legal ramifications of Israel's closure policy in Gaza, see Palestinian Center for Human Rights, *The Illegal Closure of the Gaza Strip: Collective punishment of the civilian population* (2010).

out an end to the isolation and punishment of people in Gaza."[65] Israel curtly dismissed the report as "biased and distorted."[66]

Even if, for argument's sake, Israel's right to block the passage of the flotilla were credited, it still wouldn't explain "why, on a supposedly peaceful interception, its commandos chose to board the ship by rappelling from a military helicopter, in the dark, in international waters."[67] Indeed, Israel elected a modus operandi practically guaranteed to induce panic and mayhem. It could easily have chosen (as Israeli officials conceded) from an array of relatively benign options, such as disabling the propeller, rudder, or engine of the vessel and towing it to the Israeli port at Ashdod, or physically blocking the vessel's passage.[68] (Passengers aboard the flotilla anticipated that "if we fail to stop, they will probably knock out our propellers or rudders, then tow us somewhere for repair."[69]) To go by Israel's own official alibi, a commando raid was a bizarre choice. It purported after the bloodletting that it hadn't foreseen violent resistance; it was "expecting mild violence and mostly curses, shoves and spitting in the face," "a sit-down, a linking of arms," "passive resistance, perhaps verbal resistance," or "to engage with the passengers in conversation."[70] But if Israel didn't expect a violent reception, why didn't it intercept the *Mavi Marmara* in broad daylight, with a full complement of journalists in tow, to

65. Amnesty International et al., *Dashed Hopes: Continuation of the Gaza blockade* (30 November 2010). See also Gisha (Legal Center for Freedom of Movement), "Facts behind MFA Report on 'Easing' of Gaza Closure" (2010). Gisha reported in late December 2010 that apart from "narrow exceptions," Israel "continued to ban the entrance of steel, gravel and cement to Gaza," while "small limited export has begun in the past weeks." "Reconstructing the Closure" (December 2010).

66. Dan Izenberg, "Int'l Groups Say Israel Not Living Up to Gaza Promises," *Jerusalem Post* (30 November 2010).

67. Ben Knight, "Claim and Counterclaim after Deadly Flotilla Raid," *ABC News* (1 June 2010).

68. Nahum Barnea, "The Test of the Result," *Yediot Ahronot* (1 June 2010); Ben Kaspit, "It's Not Enough to Be Right," *Maariv* (1 June 2010); Amos Harel, "Straight into the Trap," *Haaretz* (1 June 2010); Mordechai Kedar, "A War for World's Future," *ynetnews.com* (31 May 2010); Mickey Bergman, "The IDF Soldiers Were Sent on a Mission That Defies Logic," *Huffington Post* (1 June 2010); Yaakov Katz, "Duped," *Jerusalem Post* (4 June 2010).

69. Henning Mankell, "Flotilla Raid Diary," in Bayoumi, *Midnight*, p. 22.

70. Katz, "Duped"; Ahiya Raved, "20 People Threw Me from Deck," *ynetnews.com* (1 June 2010); "Israel Navy's Gaza Flotilla Probe 'Finds Planning, Intel Flaws,'" *Haaretz* (20 June 2010); "Army Inquiry Slams Flotilla Raid's Planning," *ynetnews.com* (8 July 2010); Tavernise and Bronner, "Days of Planning."

show the world its peaceful intentions; why did it disable the vessel's communications beforehand, preventing transmissions to the outside world; why did it initiate contact by using tear gas, smoke and stun grenades, and possibly plastic bullets? If it anticipated chitchatting with passengers, why did it deploy a commando unit trained to kill and not a police unit accustomed to handling civil resisters? To judge by its preplanning, the reasonable inference is that Israel sought a bloody confrontation, although probably not on the scale that ensued. (It couldn't foresee that the commandos would panic at the passengers' determined resistance and then exact several more vengeful murders.) "What did the commandos expect pro-Palestinian activists to do once they boarded the ships," the British *Guardian* editorialized, "invite them aboard for a cup of tea with the captain on the bridge?"[71]

Still, the mystery remains, why did Israel launch a violent assault? In fact, multiple factors converged to make a commando raid the optimal operational plan. Prior to the flotilla attack, Israel had conducted a succession of bungled operations. It suffered a major military setback in 2006 when it invaded Lebanon and tangled with Hezbollah. It undertook to restore its "deterrence capacity" in 2008–9 when it invaded Gaza, yet the attack evoked not awe at Israel's martial prowess but outrage at its lethal cowardice.[72] It dispatched in 2010 a commando team to assassinate a Hamas leader in Dubai, but even as it accomplished its mission, the unit ended up seeding a diplomatic storm on account of its amateurish execution. Israel was desperate to restore the IDF's derring-do image of bygone years. What better way than an Entebbe-like commando raid?[73] The decision to launch the assault on the *Mavi Marmara* was taken jointly by Prime Minister Netanyahu and Defense Minister Barak. Both had belonged to a commando unit in their youth; Barak was Netanyahu's commander and mentor in the unit.[74] A commando raid in 1973 made Barak's reputation,[75] while Netanyahu basked in the reflected glory of his brother Jonathan, who was the only Israeli casualty on the Entebbe raid. Their intersecting personal histories primed Barak and Netanyahu to opt for

71. "Gaza: From blockade to bloodshed," *Guardian* (1 June 2010).

72. See Chapter 2 and Chapter 4.

73. The Entebbe raid was a hostage-rescue operation carried out by elite Israeli commandos at Entebbe airport in Uganda on 4 July 1976.

74. Uzi Mahnaimi and Gareth Jenkins, "Operation Calamity," *Sunday Times* (6 June 2010). The two reportedly still communicated with each other in the coded language of their commando stint.

75. He led an assassination team that killed three senior PLO leaders based in Lebanon.

a violent commando assault, in order to burnish the IDF's—and, not inciden-tally, their own—reputation. The both of them were "dyed-in-the-wool crea-tures of military operations," a *Haaretz* columnist noted after the flotilla raid, "steeped in the instant-heroism mentality and the commando spirit, ... in which a military force shows up at the height of a crisis like a *deus ex machina* and in a single stroke slices through the Gordian knot." And couldn't a com-mando operation redeem the ever-elusive promise of political salvation? "Although decades have passed since the moral high [of such operations] was injected into our veins, our leaders have never stopped trying to recreate it to atone for their ineffectiveness as statesmen. The greater the number of succes-sive failed missions, the greater the longing for the next redemptive mission that will heal the trauma and the bad trip of its predecessor.... They are the responses of addicts who are repeatedly denied their fix: the perfect IDF operation, or the decisive war, which will untangle all complexities and will put to rest all doubts (and any need for statesmanship)."[76]

Unsurprisingly, of the six ships in the flotilla, Israel targeted the *Mavi Marmara* for "special" treatment. Some two-thirds of its six hundred pas-sengers were Turkish citizens. The vessel's core group was alleged to be "a front for a radical Islamist organization, probably with links to the ruling party in Turkey," which made it a yet more tempting target.[77] In recent times, Turkish prime minister Recep Tayyip Erdoğan had become increasingly determined to carve out an independent foreign policy and had been outspo-ken in his criticism of Israel. A diplomatic tit-for-tat ensued. Erdoğan publicly dressed down President Peres at the World Economic Forum right after Cast Lead: "When it comes to killing, you know well how to kill."[78] Deputy Foreign Minister Ayalon publicly humiliated the Turkish ambassador in early 2010 by refusing to shake his hand in front of Israeli television cameras, and seating him in a sofa over which the Israeli minister towered.[79] Erdoğan then seized the initiative (in concert with Brazil) to resolve diplomatically the impasse with Iran over its nuclear program.[80] Israel bridled at the Turkish

76. Doron Rosenblum, "Israel's Commando Complex," *Haaretz* (4 June 2010).
77. Scott Wilson, "Israel Says Free Gaza Movement Poses Threat to Jewish State," *Washington Post* (1 June 2010), quoting Itamar Rabinovich, former Israeli ambassador to the United States; "Eiland: Flotilla was preventable," *Jerusalem Post* (23 July 2010).
78. Katrin Bennhold, "Leaders of Turkey and Israel Clash at Davos Panel," *New York Times* (29 January 2009).
79. "Israel Snubs Turkish Ambassador in Public," *BBC* (12 January 2010).
80. Alexei Barrionuevo, "Brazil and Turkey Near Nuclear Deal with Iran," *New York Times* (16 May 2010).

démarche, as it was hell-bent on a military solution. Just days before the flotilla attack, Netanyahu would later recall, Turkey had "strengthened its identification and cooperation with Iran." When Ankara ignored Tel Aviv's counsel to preempt the *Mavi Marmara,* it was the last straw. (The Turkish government did, however, actively discourage IHH from undertaking the mission.)[81] It was long past time to cut the Turkish upstart down to size, and a sleek (if sanguinary) commando raid was just the reminder Erdoğan needed of who was in charge in that corner of the world. If Israel eschewed less-violent options to halt the flotilla, an Israeli strategic analyst elucidated, it was because it needed "to tell the Islamizing Turkey . . . —no more. The forces of the Ottoman Empire, who aspire to again rule the Middle East as they did almost 500 years ago, will be stopped at Gaza's shores."[82] The rift that opened up with Israel's historic ally appeared to belie such speculation: Why would it risk such a steep diplomatic price? But Israel had grown accustomed to Arab-Muslim leaders meekly absorbing its humiliating blows. If Israeli commandos had killed nine Egyptians on a humanitarian convoy, Egyptian president Hosni Mubarak would almost certainly have turned a blind eye. Even Syrian president Bashar al-Assad stayed mute after an Israeli air assault in 2007 destroyed an alleged Syrian nuclear reactor. "I am certain the Turkish reaction took the Zionist leaders by surprise," Hezbollah secretary-general Sayyed Hassan Nasrallah shrewdly observed.[83]

The commando raid was additionally designed to stem the rising tide of humanitarian vessels destined for Gaza. Israel initially allowed ships carrying supplies to quietly pass through the blockade, hoping that the spirits of the organizers would peter out as public interest flagged. When the organizers

81. "PM Netanyahu's Statement"; International Crisis Group, *Turkey's Crises,* p. 6.
82. Kedar, "A War."
83. "Speech of Secretary-General Nasrallah on Freedom Flotilla Attack" (4 June 2010). But the breadth of Turkey's ensuing rift with Israel was also overblown. It didn't affect the extensive commercial ties between them. (Turkey was Israel's biggest commercial partner in the region.) Israeli trade with Turkey in fact increased by almost one third during the first seven months of 2010. The diplomatic crisis also did not deter Ankara from purchasing Israeli drones. By late 2010, senior Turkish officials expressed a "commitment to preserving warm relations with Israel." James Melik, "Gaza Flotilla: Israeli-Turkish trade 'unaffected,'" *BBC News* (2 June 2010); David Wainer and Ben Holland, "Turks in Tel Aviv Show Business Binds Israel to Muslim Ally in Gaza Crisis," *Bloomberg News* (14 July 2010); Dan Bilefsky, "Turkey and Israel Do a Brisk Business," *New York Times* (4 August 2010); "Israel Exports to Turkey Up 32 Pct Despite Tensions," *Agence France-Presse* (19 August 2010); "Turkish Officials: We're committed to preserving friendly Israel ties," *Haaretz* (26 August 2010).

persisted, the Israeli navy rammed and intercepted vessels en route to Gaza.[84] But more ships kept coming. After Israel blocked a humanitarian vessel from reaching Gaza in 2009, a British-led delegation "worried" out loud to US embassy officials in Beirut "that the Israeli government would not be as 'lenient' in the future should similar incidents occur."[85] If the assault on the flotilla couldn't have shocked those inside the diplomatic loop, it didn't shock seasoned observers of the Israeli scene either. The "violent interception of civilian vessels carrying humanitarian aid," Israeli novelist Amos Oz reflected, was the "rank product" of the Israeli "mantra that what can't be done by force can be done with even greater force."[86] To fortify its claim that the commandos' violence was spontaneous, Israel gestured to the fact that it had merely expected "resistance like we encounter in Bil'in."[87] But Israel had often resorted to deliberate lethal force in order to suppress such civil resistance. What happened aboard the *Mavi Marmara*, a *Haaretz* columnist observed, was "very similar to what Israel has been doing every week for the past four years in Bil'in—injuring and killing unarmed civilian protesters who are demanding their basic rights."[88]

The assault on the *Mavi Marmara* turned into yet another bungled operation, as the once vaunted IDF seemed increasingly to resemble "the gang that cannot shoot straight."[89] The mishandling of this latest military operation could not be swept under the rug. Although Israeli *hasbara* desperately spun the raid as an "operational success,"[90] and the commandos as untarnished heroes, few were taken in. The pundit class deplored this "disgraceful fiasco"

84. *Report of the Fact-Finding Mission,* paras. 76–77.

85. 09Beirut177 Date13/02/2009 05:56 Origin Embassy Beirut Classification SECRET//NOFORM (*WikiLeaks*).

86. Amos Oz, "Israeli Force, Adrift on the Sea," *New York Times* (1 June 2010).

87. That is, during the demonstrations against the wall Israel has been building in the West Bank. "Israel Navy's Gaza Flotilla Probe"; Ron Ben-Yishai, "A Brutal Ambush at Sea," *ynetnews.com* (31 May 2010).

88. Merav Michaeli, "Nothing to Investigate: Everyone knows what was wrong about the flotilla attack," *Haaretz* (3 June 2010). For Israel's use of armed force elsewhere in the West Bank, "even when no violence on the part of the demonstrators preceded the IDF actions," see Association for Civil Rights in Israel, *The State of Human Rights in Israel and the Occupied Territories: 2009 report* (Jerusalem: 2009), p. 13. Between 2002 and 2010, fully 27 Palestinian protesters had been killed by Israeli security forces; no member of the security forces had been killed. International Crisis Group, *Tipping Point? Palestinians and the search for a new strategy* (2010), p. 28n226.

89. John J. Mearsheimer, "Sinking Ship," *American Conservative* (1 August 2010).

90. Katz, "Duped."

and "national humiliation" in which "deterrence took a bad blow."[91] "The magic evaporated long ago, the most moral army in the world, that was once the best army in the world, failed again," Gideon Levy ironically observed. "More and more there is the impression that nearly everything it touches causes harm to Israel."[92] Indeed, the Naval Commandos constituted Israel's "best fighting unit,"[93] and had rehearsed the attack for weeks, even constructing a model of the *Mavi Marmara*.[94] Nonetheless, when 30 of these commandos faced off against an equal number of civilian passengers[95] with only makeshift weapons in hand, three of them allowed themselves to be captured, and photographs of them being *nursed* circulated throughout cyberspace. Israeli soldiers, let alone elite commandos, were not supposed to be taken alive; the last thing Israel needed was a Gilad Shalit redux.[96] "The claim made by the IDF spokesman that the soldiers' lives were in danger and they feared a lynching," a respected military analyst understatedly opined, "is hardly complimentary to the men of the elite naval units."[97] The images of a cowering and inept fighting force could not have comforted the domestic population either. Would it grow jittery about the IDF's ability after so many fiascos to fend off a seemingly endless list of ever more potent enemies? "It's one thing for people to think you're crazy," an Israeli general rued, "but it's bad when they think you're incompetent and crazy, and that's the way we look."[98] A 2010 poll of the Arab world, which showed that only 12 percent of the Arab public believed Israel was "very powerful" while fully 44 percent believed it was "weaker than it looks," couldn't have allayed Israeli anxieties.[99] Each disastrous mission upped the stakes of the next throw of the dice. It appeared as if Israel would sooner rather than later have to launch a yet more

91. Kaspit, "It's Not Enough"; David Horowitz, "The Flotilla Fiasco," *Jerusalem Post* (1 June 2010); Harel, "Straight into the Trap"; Charles Levinson and Jay Solomon, "Israel's Isolation Deepens," *Wall Street Journal* (3 June 2010).

92. Levy, "Operation Mini."

93. Kaspit, "It's Not Enough."

94. Mahnaimi and Jenkins, "Operation Calamity."

95. Barnea, "Test of the Result."

96. Noam Sheizaf, "Flotilla: New *Mavi Marmara* pictures raise more questions regarding IDF attack," *Promised Land* (6 June 2010).

97. Reuven Pedatzur, "A Failure Any Way You Slice It," *Haaretz* (1 June 2010).

98. Jeffrey Goldberg, "Says One Israeli General: 'Everybody thinks we're bananas,'" theatlantic.com (1 June 2010).

99. University of Maryland, in conjunction with Zogby International, *2010 Arab Public Opinion Poll*. Forty-one percent responded that Israel's power "has its strengths and weaknesses."

spectacular mission to compensate for the long string of failures. An Israeli general declared after Cast Lead that the IDF would "continue to apply" the so-called Dahiya doctrine of directing massive force against civilian infrastructure "in the future."[100] The essence of Israeli strategic doctrine, the IDF deputy chief of staff elaborated, was that "each new round" of fighting "brings worse results than the last" to Israel's enemies.[101] Lebanon loomed at the time as Israel's next target.[102] But Hezbollah had amassed a "deterrence capacity" of its own. Israel was unwilling to risk the massive civilian casualties that would ensue in the event of an attack. At the end of the day, defenseless Gaza would continue to be Israel's preferred punching bag.

The nine passengers killed aboard the *Mavi Marmara* were the first casualties of the Goldstone Report's interment. If it had not been effectively "vetoed," Palestinian human rights lawyer Raji Sourani observed, "if the international community had fulfilled its obligation to enforce international humanitarian law, and if the rule of law were respected, it is almost certain that the unjustifiable bloodshed in the Mediterranean could have been prevented."[103] However, although Israel managed to clear the Goldstone hurdle, it now had to contend with the new international outcry after the commando raid. Not for the first time, it decided to appoint a commission of inquiry to investigate the incident. The expectation was that by blending judicial gravitas with craven subservience to the state, such an investigation would placate international opinion or, at any rate, those portions of it that counted.[104] The commission did not disappoint.

100. Yaakov Katz, "The Dahiya Doctrine: Fighting dirty or a knock-out punch?," *Jerusalem Post* (28 January 2010); Jeffrey White, *If War Comes: Israel vs. Hizballah and its allies* (Washington, DC: 2010), pp. 10, 12, 35, 40. See Chapter 2 for the Dahiya doctrine.

101. Barbara Opall-Rome, "Israel's New Hard Line on Hizbollah," *DefenseNews* (31 May 2010).

102. Finkelstein, *"This Time,"* pp. 184–97.

103. Raji Sourani, "1,000 Days," in Bayoumi, *Midnight,* p. 147.

104. The classic precedent was Israel's appointment of the Kahan Commission of Inquiry after the Sabra and Shatila massacre evoked an international outcry. For the Commission's whitewash of the massacre, see Noam Chomsky, *The Fateful Triangle: The United States, Israel and the Palestinians* (Boston: 1983), pp. 397–409; and Amnon Kapeliouk, *Sabra and Shatila: Inquiry into a massacre* (1982).

EIGHT

Whitewash I

THE TURKEL REPORT

IN JUNE 2010, ISRAEL ESTABLISHED an "independent public commission" to investigate the "maritime incident of 31 May 2010." In January 2011, the commission, chaired by former Israeli Supreme Court justice Jacob Turkel, released its findings.[1] The Turkel Report, running to nearly three hundred pages, exonerated Israel of culpability for the carnage aboard the *Mavi Marmara* and, instead, pinned blame on a cadre of passengers who had allegedly plotted and armed themselves to kill the Israeli commandos. The Report divided into two principal sections: a legal analysis of the Israeli blockade, and a factual reconstruction of the events that climaxed in the violence. It began, however, by recounting the historical context of the Israeli blockade. These passages of the Report provided instructive insight into its objectivity. The Report stated that "in October 2000 violent incidents broke out in the West Bank and the Gaza Strip, which were given the name 'the Second Intifada.' . . . In these, suicide attacks were restarted in cities in Israeli territory."[2] Its capsule description of the second intifada omitted mention that Israel had used massive, indiscriminate, and lethal firepower to quell largely nonviolent demonstrations, and that Palestinians endured five months of bloodletting before

1. Public Commission to Examine the Maritime Incident of 31 May 2010, *The Turkel Commission Report, Part One* (January 2011); hereafter: Turkel Report. (The second part of this report, *Israel's Mechanism for Examining and Investigating Complaints and Claims of Violations of the Laws of Armed Conflict,* was published in February 2013. It didn't directly address the events of 31 May 2010, and so will not be considered here, but see Chapter 13.) Shortly after publication of the Turkel Report, the Turkish government released the findings of its own investigation, Turkish National Commission of Inquiry, *Report on the Israeli Attack on the Humanitarian Aid Convoy to Gaza on 31 May 2010* (February 2011); hereafter: Turkish Report.
2. Turkel Report, para. 16.

they resorted to suicide attacks.[3] The Report began by highlighting that "since the beginning of 2001, thousands of mortars and rockets of various kinds have been fired in ever growing numbers from the Gaza Strip."[4] But this depiction ignored that Israel directed far more lethal firepower at Gaza during the same period.[5] Although the Report did concede that human rights and humanitarian organizations, as well as a leading Israeli jurist, had concluded that Gaza remained occupied after Israel's 2005 "disengagement," it nevertheless sustained the contrary position of the Israeli government.[6] The Report asserted that the June 2008 cease-fire between Israel and Hamas "collapsed in December 2008, when the rocket and mortar attacks against Israel recommenced."[7] In fact, as Amnesty International observed at the time, the lull "broke down after Israeli forces killed six Palestinian militants in air strikes and other attacks on 4 November [2008]."[8] The Report thus skewed the critical historical context wholly in Israel's favor.

The Turkel Report upheld the legality of the Israeli blockade of Gaza on dual grounds: (1) the people of Gaza didn't experience starvation and their physical survival wasn't at risk; and (2) whatever hardship Gaza's civilian population did endure was the "collateral" and "proportional" damage of a blockade targeting Hamas's military capabilities.

1. *If Gazans weren't starving and their essential needs were met, then the blockade was legal.* The Turkel Report juxtaposed the consensus opinion of human rights and humanitarian organizations that Israel's siege of Gaza had caused a humanitarian crisis[9] with Israel's denial of such a crisis.[10] It resolved these "two very different perceptions of reality"[11] by concluding, for example, that even if 60 percent of Gazans did experience "food insecurity,"[12] still Israel met its legal obligations inasmuch as the people weren't dying of starva-

---

3. See Chapter 1.

4. Turkel Report, para. 1.

5. The Turkel Report did mention Israeli strikes against Gaza further on (paras. 16, 18), but deemed them retaliatory (Israel "responded"), whereas in actuality, conflict pauses between Israel and the Palestinians were "overwhelmingly" broken by Israel. See Chapter 1 and Chapter 2.

6. Turkel Report, p. 48n143, paras. 45–47.

7. Ibid., para. 19.

8. See Chapter 2.

9. Turkel Report, para. 72.

10. Ibid., para. 73.

11. Ibid., para. 71.

12. Ibid., paras. 72, 76. The Report cited the definition of "food insecurity" used by the UN Office for the Coordination of Humanitarian Affairs: "people lack sustainable physical

tion but were merely hungry. The Report approvingly quoted Israeli officials to the effect that "no one has ever stated . . . that the population of the Gaza Strip is 'starving.'" It went on to defend the siege's legality on the grounds that "'Food insecurity' does not equate to 'starvation.'"[13] Prima facie, it would be odd if current international law, which accords so many safeguards to civilians in times of war and under occupation, sanctioned a just-shy-of-genocidal policy.[14] Indeed, seemingly cognizant that such a legal standard was too lax (not to mention cruel, coming from an esteemed former Supreme Court justice),[15] the Report simultaneously purported that even if the law kicked in not just for starvation but also for the less exigent condition of hunger, and even if the siege did induce hunger, still Israel wasn't *deliberately* inducing hunger, and if it wasn't a willful policy, Israel wasn't legally culpable: "The Commission found no evidence . . . that Israel is *trying* to deprive the population of the Gaza Strip of food."[16] But if the foreseeable and inevitable effect of barring foodstuffs from entering Gaza was to cause hunger, it is hard to make out how the punitive outcome was mere happenstance and not Israel's intention.[17] Or, put otherwise, for want of trying to induce hunger, Israel was awfully good at it.

Just as it exonerated Israel of denying Gazans food, so the Turkel Report exonerated Israel of denying Gazans other "objects essential for the survival of the civilian population." It acknowledged that Israel blocked entry of construction materials but rationalized this policy on the grounds that, according to "intelligence information," Hamas might use them for "military purposes." The Report made short shrift of the possibility that the motive behind this ban was to punish the people of Gaza: "It is clear that the restrictions were not imposed in order to prevent the use of these materials by the civilian

---

or economic access to adequate[,] safe, nutritious and socially acceptable food to maintain a healthy and productive life."

13. Ibid., paras. 76, 77.

14. See Douglas Guilfoyle, "The *Mavi Marmara* Incident and Blockade in Armed Conflict," *British Yearbook of International Law* (2011), pp. 197–204, which contends that international law doesn't prohibit only literal starvation or sustain Israel's ban on foodstuffs entering Gaza as its population suffered from hunger.

15. For murky acknowledgment that international law prohibited sieges causing not only starvation ("hunger blockade") but also "less extreme instances" of "suffering," see Turkel Report, para. 90 (see also ibid., p. 102n363).

16. Ibid., para. 76, emphasis added.

17. On this point, see also Guilfoyle, "*Mavi Marmara* Incident," p. 200.

population."[18] One searched in vain, however, for proof of this confident assertion. What's more, the Report contended both that Israel denied entry of essential objects, such as construction materials (but only on security grounds), *and* that there was "no evidence" Israel denied entry of such essential objects.[19] The Report further stated that "no evidence was presented . . . that Israel prevents the passage of medical supplies apart from those included in the list of materials whose entry into the Gaza Strip is prohibited for security reasons."[20] Yet that Israeli list included "vital medical supplies," according to the World Health Organization, such as "X-ray machines, electronic imaging scanners, laboratory equipment and basic items, such as elevators for hospitals."[21] If Israel was depriving Gazans of "vital medical supplies," then it *was* denying them "objects essential" to their "survival." The Report also inconsistently alleged both that Israel had denied entry of essential objects on security grounds, *and* that Israel allowed entry of many of these same objects—apparently without jeopardizing its security—after the flotilla attack evoked international outrage.[22] The Report, finally, never attended to the obvious question: *Why did so many respected human rights and humanitarian organizations sound the alarm of a humanitarian crisis in Gaza if none existed?*

The upshot was, the Turkel Report alleged that Israel's blockade did not breach humanitarian law on the bizarre ground that Gazans weren't literally starving to death; that if the legal threshold was causing hunger, then Israel didn't deliberately cause hunger—even if hunger was the inevitable and predictable result of its blockade; that Israel did prevent entry of essential construction materials and that it categorically did not prevent entry of essential construction materials; and that Israel did not prevent entry of vital medical supplies—even if it did prevent entry of vital medical supplies. If the Report

18. Turkel Report, para. 79.

19. Ibid., paras. 80 ("There is . . . no evidence . . . that Israel is denying objects essential for the survival of the civilian population"), 90 ("Israel has not prevented the passage of objects essential for the survival of the civilian population").

20. Ibid., para. 82.

21. Lisa Schlein, "WHO: Medical supplies blocked from entering Gaza," *Voice of America* (31 May 2010).

22. Turkel Report, paras. 19, 68, 97. The Report also repeatedly stated that breaching the blockade was unnecessary as Israel conveyed beforehand to the flotilla its willingness to deliver "humanitarian" supplies on board the vessels to Gaza. But the Report also made clear that "humanitarian" supplies did *not* include prohibited items on board the flotilla, such as cement and other construction materials (see ibid., paras. 3, 27, 110, 113, 149, 198).

managed to prove the blockade was legal, it was, alas, at the price of sacrificing logic, consistency, and fact.

2. *If the harm to Gaza's civilian population was proportional and collateral, then the blockade was legal.* The Turkel Report applied a proportionality test to the blockade.[23] It found that if Gazans did endure hardship as a result of the Israeli siege, it constituted "collateral" damage "proportional" to the security objective of degrading Hamas's military capabilities. Although it occasionally suggested that the blockade was more than just a security measure,[24] the Report was emphatic that it did not target the civilian population. In one of its various formulations, the Report depicted the siege as having "two goals: a security goal of preventing the entry of weapons, ammunition and military supplies into the Gaza Strip . . . , and a broader strategic goal of 'indirect economic warfare,' whose purpose is to restrict the Hamas's economic ability as the body in control of the Gaza Strip to take military action against Israel."[25] The Report further found that Israel was not guilty of inflicting "collective punishment" because "there is nothing in the evidence . . . that suggest[s] that Israel is *intentionally* placing restrictions on goods for the sole or primary purpose of denying them to the population of Gaza" (emphasis in original).[26] But if the intent of the Israeli siege was to degrade Hamas's military capacity, not to harm Gaza's civilian population, surely it was cause for wonder why Israel severely restricted entry of goods "not considered essential for the basic subsistence of the population," and why it allowed passage of only a "humanitarian minimum" of civilian goods.[27] It was also cause for puzzlement why Israeli officials kept repeating privately that they intended "to keep the Gazan economy on the brink of collapse without quite pushing it over the edge."[28] In other words, why was the blockade calibrated so as to keep Gaza's civilian population teetering on the precipice, if the civilian population was not being targeted? Although tediously repetitive and replete with minutiae on arcane

23. Under international humanitarian law, *proportionality in attack* is defined as a prohibition against "launching an attack which may be expected to cause incidental loss of civilian life, injury to civilians, damage to civilian objects, or a combination thereof, which would be excessive in relation to the concrete and direct military advantage anticipated." International Committee of the Red Cross, *Customary International Humanitarian Law, Volume I: Rules* (Cambridge: 2005), rule 14.

24. Turkel Report, paras. 50, 63. For a detailed analysis, see Chapter 9.

25. Turkel Report, para. 67.

26. Ibid., para. 106.

27. See Chapter 2.

28. "Cashless in Gaza?," *WikiLeaks* (3 November 2008).

points of law, the Report was notably silent on exactly what items Israel interdicted to thwart Hamas's offensive capabilities. It omitted that the seemingly endless list of *verboten* items included sage, coriander, ginger, jam, halva, vinegar, nutmeg, chocolate, fruit preserves, seeds and nuts, biscuits, potato chips, musical instruments, notebooks, writing implements, toys, chicks, and goats.[29] "The purpose of the economic warfare in the Gaza Strip," the Report asseverated, was "to undermine the Hamas's ability to attack Israel and its citizens. The non-security related restrictions on the passage of goods—such as the restrictions upon certain food products—are a part of this strategy."[30] Who could doubt the offensive potential of chocolate, chips, and chicks?[31]

Neither the facts nor the legal reasoning presented in the Turkel Report refuted the consensus opinion that Gaza was experiencing a humanitarian crisis; that the Israeli siege was causing the humanitarian crisis; that Israel was deliberately causing this humanitarian crisis; that the Israeli siege consequently constituted an illegal form of collective punishment; and that the use of force against the humanitarian flotilla, insofar as it was designed to prolong the illegal siege, was also illegal.

The second half of the Turkel Report reconstructed the events that climaxed in the killing of nine passengers aboard the *Mavi Marmara* by Israeli commandos.[32] The Report cleared Israel of legal culpability for the violence and deaths and, instead, pinned responsibility on a cadre of passengers who allegedly plotted and armed themselves in advance to kill Israelis. It also determined that the lethal use of force by the Israeli commandos constituted justifiable self-defense.

The Turkel Report's major conclusions diametrically opposed those of an eminent UN Fact-Finding Mission.[33] Without access to the evidence on

---

29. Gisha (Legal Center for Freedom of Movement), *Partial List of Items Prohibited/ Permitted in the Gaza Strip* (May 2010).

30. Turkel Report, para. 91.

31. At one point the Report seemed to concede that Israel restricted passage of foodstuffs "used solely for civilian needs," but then justified this policy (albeit with caveats) by invoking the US-UK genocidal sanctions on Iraq (ibid., paras. 91–93). For the Iraqi sanctions, see Joy Gordon, *Invisible War: The United States and the Iraq sanctions* (Cambridge: 2010).

32. See Chapter 7.

33. UN Human Rights Council, *Report of the International Fact-Finding Mission to Investigate Violations of International Law, Including International Humanitarian and Human Rights Law, Resulting from the Israeli Attacks on the Flotilla of Ships Carrying*

which each side based its conclusions, a third party would be hard-pressed to definitively decide between them. Nonetheless, on the basis of their internal coherence and judged against uncontested facts, it is possible to render a judgment on which of the findings are more persuasive. On a preliminary point, the sources on which the Turkel Report leaned prompt skepticism. The government resolution mandating the Turkel Commission excused "IDF [Israel Defense Forces] soldiers" from testifying before it.[34] The Report accordingly had to depend on "soldiers' statements [that] were only documented in writing and submitted to the Commission."[35] The Report deemed the commando testimonies "credible and trustworthy" because the soldiers "gave detailed information, used natural language, and did not appear to have coordinated their versions."[36] It puzzled what evidentiary value should be attached to the written submissions' "natural language"—did it enhance the commandos' credibility that they reflexively called everyone who crossed their paths on the *Mavi Marmara* a "terrorist"?[37] It was also unclear how the Commission could determine whether or not the commandos coordinated beforehand their written submissions. The Report stated that "the soldiers' accounts were examined meticulously, cross-referenced against each other."[38] Was it so far-fetched that the soldiers also "examined meticulously, cross-referenced" *each other's* statements before submitting them? (It was not even clear that prescribed protocol barred such prior coordination.) Indeed, the soldiers could infer prior to giving testimony that they would not suffer judicial penalties for perjury, or even undergo rigorous interrogation: "The soldiers were not put on notice that their rights were implicated when giving their statements and they did not undergo cross-examination."[39] In general, the Commission invested enormous faith in the testimony of Israeli civilian and military officials, even as respected Israeli commentators had ridiculed their record of truth telling.[40]

Humanitarian Assistance (27 September 2010); hereafter: *Report of the Fact-Finding Mission.* See Chapter 7 for the UN Report's findings.

34. Israel Ministry of Foreign Affairs, "Government Establishes Independent Public Commission" (14 June 2010).

35. Turkel Report, para. 237.

36. Ibid., para. 236.

37. The Turkel Report expressly noted the exception of one commando who called his assailants "activists" (ibid., p. 157n533).

38. Ibid., para. 236.

39. Ibid., para. 237.

40. See Chapter 3.

Except for the oral testimony of two Israeli Palestinians, sketchy and mostly unsigned statements extracted by Israeli jailers and military intelligence from the flotilla detainees before their release, and a book publication by one of the Turks on board the *Mavi Marmara*,[41] the Turkel Report did not benefit from the input of the passengers and crew. Upon their release, former captives asserted that the statements and signatures were given under extreme physical and emotional duress, while the secretly filmed footage of their interrogations had been distorted by editing.[42] The Report alleged that due to the noncooperation of other witnesses, it was "compelled to rely mainly on testimonies and reports of Israeli parties."[43] (Amnesty reported that although "the Commission invited flotilla participants to testify, it appeared to make only half-hearted attempts to secure their testimony."[44]) The Report did not explain, however, why unsworn testimonies of Israeli commandos constituted credible evidence, whereas eyewitness testimonies of numerous passengers, accessible in the public domain, did not.[45] On a cognate point, although the UN Fact-Finding Mission failed to secure the cooperation of the Israeli government, it did make extensive use of the available public testimony before the Turkel Commission, whereas the Turkel Report "made no effort to utilize the extensive eyewitness testimony collected by the International Fact-Finding Mission."[46] The juxtaposition suggested two very different judicial temperaments at play, of which only one appeared to be seeking truth. Let us now examine the major points of contention between the UN Fact-Finding Mission and the Turkel Report.

Which party initiated the violence? The UN Fact-Finding Mission concluded that as Israeli speedboats "approached" the *Mavi Marmara*, they were

41. Turkel Report, paras. 9, 237, pp. 211n736, 212n737. It cited the testimony of one Israeli Palestinian but only to discredit it by citing the testimony of another Israeli Palestinian. It also cited crucial testimony of the *Mavi Marmara*'s captain during interrogation but only to peremptorily dismiss it on the basis of contrary testimony by an Israeli aerial lookout (ibid., paras. 144, 125, 203).

42. Turkish Report, pp. 40–42, 44, 47, 108.

43. Turkel Report, paras. 9, 237.

44. Amnesty International, "Israeli Inquiry into Flotilla Deaths No More than 'Whitewash'" (28 January 2011).

45. For a sampling of these testimonies, see Moustafa Bayoumi, ed., *Midnight on the Mavi Marmara: The attack on the Gaza Freedom Flotilla and how it changed the course of the Israel/Palestine conflict* (New York: 2010), part 1. Exceptionally, the Report made passing reference at the end of a long footnote to a *Haaretz* interview with one of the passengers (Turkel Report, pp. 202–3n703).

46. Amnesty, "Israeli Inquiry."

"firing . . . non-lethal weaponry onto the ship, including smoke and stun grenades, tear gas and paintballs" and possibly "plastic bullets"; and that "minutes after" this initial Israeli assault was repelled by passengers, Israeli helicopters moved in, opening fire with "live ammunition . . . onto the top deck prior to the descent of the soldiers."[47] The Turkel Report presented an altogether different picture. It did acknowledge that the Israeli rules of engagement allowed for "use of force . . . required to fulfill the mission, i.e., stopping the vessels," albeit it "must be minimal" and might be considered only "as a last resort." It also acknowledged that operational orders allowed that "before the stage of taking control of the vessels . . . , the force commander was permitted to employ various measures to stop the vessels, including firing 'skunk bombs' . . . forcing the vessels to change their course or stop by means of . . . firing warning shots into the air and 'white lighting' (blinding [by] using a large projector)." At the very least, then, Israeli operational planning did not outright prohibit initiating force. But on the basis of "closed door testimony of the Chief of Staff," the Report concluded that "in practice, no use was made of these measures."[48] The Report found that Israeli commandos in speedboats approached the *Mavi Marmara* peacefully and resorted to paintball guns and stun grenades only after they "encountered resistance."[49] Besides Israeli testimonies, the Report cited video recordings. It is impossible sight unseen to evaluate the video evidence, although it can't but be wondered why Israel didn't make it available after release of the UN Fact-Finding Mission's conclusions. If Israel had in its possession compelling evidence that refuted the UN Mission, why would it keep this proof, the release of which couldn't pose a security threat, under wraps? The Report recorded the precise times when passengers resorted to force against the commandos in speedboats.[50] It did not, however, record the times when these commandos resorted to supposedly "retaliatory" force. In a typical non sequitur, the Report, attempting to refute "suggestions that the IHH [İnsani Yardım Vakfı] activists were acting in self-defense," stated: "In seeking to capture and board the ship, the Israeli forces had to respond to the violence offered first by the IHH. This is evident from the magnetic media that shows

---

47. *Report of the Fact-Finding Mission,* paras. 112–14. The Mission referred to the Israeli speedboats as *zodiacs,* whereas the Turkel Report called them *Morenas.*

48. Turkel Report, para. 121.

49. Ibid., para. 128.

50. Ibid., para. 130.

the extreme levels of violence used against the IDF's soldiers."[51] But footage of passengers resorting to "extreme levels of violence" does not corroborate that they *initiated* the violence. The Report also concluded that live ammunition was not fired from Israeli helicopters that subsequently moved in. It did acknowledge, however, that stun grenades were thrown down from the helicopters before the commandos hit the deck. It stated that the helicopters did not use live ammunition because "the accurate use of firearms from a helicopter requires both specific equipment and specially trained personnel, with which the helicopters were not equipped."[52] But if, on the one hand, the purpose of the firepower had been—like the stun grenades—to terrorize the passengers and clear the deck before the commandos rappelled on board, then precision marksmanship wasn't even required, while, on the other hand, it perplexes that trained marksmen were in short supply among Israel's elite fighting unit.

The decision to intercept the flotilla in the dead of night appeared to belie the Turkel Report's sequencing of what unfolded. The Report stated that if Israel launched its operation at 4:26 a.m., it was because "during such an operation, there is a great advantage to operating under the cover of darkness" (quoting the Israeli chief of staff).[53] But it isn't self-evident why a commando raid in the dead of night would be to Israel's advantage. The Report repeatedly emphasized that "throughout the planning process" Israeli authorities at all levels anticipated that "the participants in the flotilla were all peaceful civilians," and they "seem not to have believed that the use of force would be necessary." They "had expected" the commandos to meet "at most, verbal resistance, pushing or punching," "relatively minor civil disobedience," "some pushing and limited physical contact." The Report quoted the commandos themselves testifying, "we were expected to encounter activists who would try to hurt us emotionally by creating provocations on the level of curses, spitting . . . but we did not expect a difficult physical confrontation"; "we were expected to encounter peace activists and therefore the prospect that we would have to use weapons or other means was . . . nearly zero probability."[54] But if it didn't expect forceful resistance, why didn't Israel launch the operation in broad

51. Ibid., para. 200.
52. Ibid., para. 230.
53. Ibid., para. 174.
54. Ibid., paras. 132, 180, 213, 243, 244, p. 149n518. The Report states that "in the strategic discussions prior to the operation, the possibility that firearms might be present was mentioned," but it had no practical consequences (ibid., p. 247n863, para. 243).

daylight, indeed bringing along journalists who could vouch for its nonviolent intentions? An operation launched in the blackness of night *did* make sense if Israel wanted to sow panic and confusion as a prelude to, and retrospectively to justify, a violent assault, as well as to obscure from potential witnesses its violent mode of attack. In the planning of such an operation—that is, an operation predicated on the use of violent force—there clearly was "great advantage to operating under the cover of darkness." A premeditated decision to violently assault the *Mavi Marmara* would also account for the scope and nature of the planning. It would reconcile why Israel undertook intricate and ramified preparations that engaged the gamut of Israel's political, military, and intelligence apparatuses, including the "Prime Minister and the Minister of Defense," the "senior political-security echelon and persons with experience in these fields," the "Ministry of Foreign Affairs, the Ministry of the Interior, the Ministry of Public Security, the Ministry of Justice, IDF officers and public relations personnel";[55] why it "decided that the command level would be very senior, including the Commander of the Navy himself";[56] why it imposed a "communications blackout" on the flotilla;[57] and why it deployed the elite Special Forces unit Shayetet 13, which was trained for lethal combat, instead of a routine police unit trained to quell civil resistance. The Report stated that "Special Forces trained teams are often used when a boarding is anticipated to be 'opposed,' or 'non-compliant.'"[58] But, surely, apprehending passengers predisposed to "curses, spitting" didn't require deployment of Israel's elite fighting unit. It also stated that Special Forces were used because of the "specialized training" needed "for fast-roping onto the deck of a ship at night."[59] However, that still leaves unanswered the question why the assault was launched at night.

It might be wondered why Israel was at pains to emphasize that it didn't anticipate violent resistance. Couldn't it just as easily have alleged that although committed to a peaceful resolution of the crisis, it *did* expect violence, which was why the operation was launched before daybreak and so much military-like planning went into it? The reason, however, was not hard to find. If the commandos had been primed for a violent confrontation, then what ensued aboard the *Mavi Marmara* truly was, as Israeli pundits rued, a

55. Ibid., paras. 115–22.
56. Ibid., para. 121.
57. Ibid.
58. Ibid., para. 182.
59. Ibid., para. 242.

"disgraceful fiasco" and "national humiliation."[60] The only alibi Israel could fabricate to preserve the commandos' aura was that they were taken off guard by the violence; if the elite unit performed so poorly, it was because it hadn't prepared for armed resistance. Indeed, one of the Turkel Report's more comical aspects was the commandos' tales of derring-do, plainly designed to restore the IDF's heroic image and boost national morale:

- Soldier no. 1[61] recalled that "ten people jumped onto me and began brutally beating me from every direction, using clubs, metal rods and fists"; that "a number of attackers grabbed me by my legs and my torso and threw me over the side to the deck below"; that "I fractured my arm, and a mob of dozens of people attacked me and basically lynched me—including pulling off my helmet, strangling me, sticking fingers into my eyes to gouge them out of their sockets, pulling my limbs in every direction, striking me in an extremely harsh manner with clubs and metal rods, mostly on my head"; that "I took an extremely harsh blow directly to my head from a metal rod. . . . A lot of blood began streaming down my face from the wounds to my head"; that after his capture by passengers, the "only thing" the ship's medic did was to "wipe the blood from my forehead" although he had a "very deep scalp wound and a fractured skull" (it later allegedly required 14 stitches); and that—despite excruciating blows and gushing blood, fractured arm and fractured skull—he managed to break free of one of the guards: "I jabbed my elbow into his ribs and jumped into the water. . . . As soon as I reached the water, I dove underneath, so that they would not be able to hit me from the ship. I took off my shirt while diving and swimming, and I intended to swim and dive rapidly in a 'zigzag' to escape from the enemy on the ship. After my first dive, I rose to the water's surface and I saw a . . . speedboat," which rescued him after he swam "rapidly" toward it, and then "I picked up an M-16 rifle . . . and I began shooting . . . because I was concerned that the mob on the ship wanted to abduct soldier no. 4 back into the ship, and I wanted to deter them."[62]

- Soldier no. 3 recalled that "I was struck with metal poles and rocks . . . I fel[t] a very strong blow to the neck from behind"; that "people . . . hit me with full force with poles and clubs"; that "a mob of people around me are hitting me with many blows, mainly towards my head"; that "I con-

60. See Chapter 7.
61. The numerical designations are used in the Report.
62. Turkel Report, paras. 133, 135, 140.

tinue to take very strong blows to the abdomen"; that "I am fighting with all my strength until a certain stage when they manage to get me over the side of the boat. I am holding onto the side, with my hands, and hanging from the side. . . . [T]he people from above me are hitting my hands and a second group of people is pulling me from below by grabbing my legs"; that "I am lying on the deck, there are many people above me, one of the people jumps on me and I feel a sharp pain in the lower abdomen . . . and I realize that I've been stabbed . . . during this stage I'm taking many blows, including from clubs"; that after his capture by passengers, the only assistance he received from the ship's medic was a "gauze pad," although "I am bleeding massively, that is, I am losing a lot of blood, and I can tell that part of my intestines are protruding . . . I also notice a deep cut in my left arm, from which I'm also losing a great quantity of blood. I also feel blood flowing from my nose into my mouth"; that "they tied my hands and feet with rope. They station a person above me who is holding a wooden pole. . . . He beats me with the wooden pole"; that "as a result of the loss of blood, I started to become groggy"; and that—despite excruciating blows (fracturing his nose and tearing a tendon in his finger) and gushing blood, stab wounds, and protruding intestines—he managed to escape: "I run to the side of the ship, jump into the water from a height of 12 meters, and start swimming toward our boats."[63]

Is it ungenerous to wonder whether these commandos had watched a few too many *Rambo* flicks?

Did Islamic "activists" plot and arm themselves to murder Israelis? The Turkel Report found that passengers aboard the *Mavi Marmara*, the "hard-core group" of which comprised about 40 "IHH activists,"[64] had plotted before embarkation "to resist with force,"[65] even to commit murder, and had sought out martyrdom. "I have no doubt," an Israeli commander of the operation testified, "that the terrorists on the vessel planned, organized, fore-saw the events, and planned to kill a soldier."[66] "It is evident," the Report concluded, that "the IHH organized and planned for a violent confrontation with the Israeli military forces"; "the IHH had a preexisting plan to violently oppose the Israeli boarding"; and "a number of IHH activists took part in hostilities from a planning and logistical perspective well before the arrival

63. Ibid., paras. 133, 135, 140, p. 250n871.
64. Ibid., paras. 165, 192.
65. Ibid., para. 169.
66. Ibid., para. 167.

of the Israeli armed forces."[67] The Report alleged that as against the overwhelming majority of "relatively moderate"[68] passengers, IHH activists "boarded the *Mavi Marmara* separately and without any security checks" and thus were able to smuggle on an arsenal of weapons to execute their murderous plot.[69] Contrariwise, and for what it's worth, the Turkish government protested that not just once but twice "all crew members and passengers were subjected to . . . stringent x-ray checks as well as customs and passport controls. . . . All personal belongings and cargo were also thoroughly inspected and cleared. . . . [T]he cargo contained no arms, munitions or other material that would constitute a threat."[70] The Report's inventory of the "combat equipment apparently brought on board by the flotilla participants" included "150 protective ceramic vests . . . , 300 gas masks . . . , communication devices, optical devices (several night vision goggles and a few binoculars), slingshots of various kinds, 200 knives, 20 axes, thousands of ball bearings and stones, disk saws, pepper sprays, and smoke flares."[71] This cache of "combat equipment," "concentration of weaponry," "extensive equipment which was brought on board" to implement the plot[72] appeared in a somewhat less sinister light when juxtaposed with the Report's itemization that "kitchens and the cafeterias on the ship" contained "a total of about 200 knives," and the ship's "fire-extinguishing equipment" included "about 20 axes."[73] It flabbergasts that the obvious correlations escaped—or did they?—the Commission's notice. The Report "did not find that the evidence point[s] conclusively to the fact" that the IHH activists brought firearms aboard the *Mavi Marmara*.[74] But if they plotted a "violent confrontation" with one of the world's most formidable military powers, and if they could freely carry on board the weapons of their choosing, it perplexes why the most lethal

67. Ibid., paras. 196, 199, 201, 220.
68. Ibid., para. 136.
69. Ibid., paras. 165, 196.
70. Turkish Report, pp. 15–16, 56, 113.
71. Turkel Report, para. 165. The Turkel Report stated that "four bullet casings not used by the IDF were found on board," but "it cannot be said with complete certainty that these were bullets fired from a non-IDF weapon since it cannot be ruled out that these bullets somehow made their way into the IDF ammunition." The Report also cited but appeared not to credit the testimony of one IDF officer that "he saw Molotov cocktails which had been placed in orderly stacks" (ibid., p. 207n718, para. 145).
72. Ibid., p. 211nn735, 736, para. 169.
73. Ibid., para. 167.
74. Ibid., para. 221.

implements they thought to bring along were slingshots and glass marbles. Truly, these *shaheeds* were meshugge. The Report noted that just before the Israeli operation began, the Islamic extremists "improvised" weapons, such as iron rods and wooden clubs.[75] The Commission apparently never pondered the obvious question: *If they were hell-bent on committing bloody murder "well before the arrival of the Israeli armed forces," why didn't the Islamists bring on board firearms and why did they wait until the last minute before producing makeshift weapons?*

The UN Fact-Finding Mission "found no evidence that any of the passengers used firearms . . . at any stage."[76] But whereas the Turkel Report found no proof that the passengers brought along firearms, it still concluded that "members of the IHH activists used firearms against Israeli forces,"[77] which they presumably seized from the commandos before wounding two of them. The Report stated that it consulted "medical documents regarding the injuries to the soldiers."[78] But it did not cite hospital records documenting the commandos' alleged bullet wounds; instead, it cited a statement submitted by the IDF and the oral testimony of the chief of staff.[79] In the case of non-bullet wounds incurred by the commandos, the Report did cite hospital records.[80] Since the Report failed to cite hospital records attesting to the alleged bullet wounds, it is doubtful they existed, but even if they did, they could just as easily have been inflicted by other Israeli commandos. The Report itself acknowledged that "the melee on board the *Mavi Marmara,* especially during the initial stages on the roof, was a situation of considerable confusion."[81] In fact, one of the commandos allegedly hit by a bullet initially thought his wound resulted "from the Israeli forces."[82] The Report enumerated three grounds for its conclusion that passengers used firearms: "physical evidence of gunshot wounds"—which didn't speak to the point of origin of the gunshots; "statements of numerous soldiers"—which were as credible as their *Rambo* fantasies; and "the fact that IHH activists had access to

75. Ibid., para. 167.
76. *Report of the Fact-Finding Mission,* paras. 116, 165.
77. Turkel Report, para. 222.
78. Ibid., para. 236.
79. Ibid., pp. 155n529, 157n531, para. 221.
80. Ibid., p. 250nn871, 873.
81. Ibid., para. 222.
82. Ibid., para. 221. It might be recalled that almost half the Israeli combat fatalities during Operation Cast Lead were caused by "friendly fire" (see Chapter 4).

captured IDF" weapons—which proved nothing.[83] Still, why would the Report conclude on the basis of such flimsy evidence that passengers used firearms against the commandos? The Report itself provided the answer. While it contended that the commandos' resort to lethal force would have been justified even if the passengers did not shoot at them,[84] the Report went on to say that "the use of firearms by IHH activists is an important factor" because it "significantly heightened the risk posed to the soldiers and their perception of that risk," and "establishing the level of threat that the Israeli soldiers believed they were facing is a factor in the assessment as to whether their response was proportionate."[85] If the Report wanted to definitively conclude that the commandos' resort to lethal force was legally justifiable, it had to find evidence that the passengers used firearms against them. The predetermined exoneration dictated the evidentiary finding.

The Turkel Report quoted the harrowing accounts by the captured commandos of the Islamists' murderous ambitions. Soldier no. 1 testified that "the terrorist group wanted to attack me and kill me." Soldier no. 3 testified that they were "crazed" and "very eager to kill us. They tried to strangle me and soldier no. 4. The hate in their eyes was just burning"; "This attempt to strangle me was made several times."[86] The Report also highlighted that the cadre of Islamic killers were "very large and strong men, approximately ages 20–40," "very big and heavy,"[87] and that "some of those activists also expressed their wish to be 'shaheeds.'"[88] The obvious question was, Why didn't this mob of burly homicidal *shaheeds* manage to kill any of the captured commandos? Quoting the commandos, the Report's unfazed response was that the peaceniks on board—"older men and women who showed restraint," "non-violent peace activists"—came to the commandos' rescue: "The terrorist group wanted to attack me and kill me, while the moderate group tried to protect me"; "There were two groups there, the one which tried to kill us and . . . the ones who prevented the extreme group from killing us."[89] In other words, the crazed jihadists were stopped dead in their tracks by Grannies for Peace and the Birkenstock Brigade.

83. Turkel Report, para. 222.
84. Ibid., paras. 217–19.
85. Ibid., paras. 220, 223.
86. Ibid., paras. 135, 136, 140.
87. Ibid., paras. 136, 167.
88. Ibid., paras. 166, 168, 197.
89. Ibid., paras. 135, 136, 167, 190.

Did the Israeli commandos use lethal force only as a last resort? "The conduct of the Israeli military and other personnel towards the flotilla passengers was not only disproportionate to the occasion," the UN Fact-Finding Mission concluded, "but demonstrated levels of totally unnecessary and incredible violence. It betrayed an unacceptable level of brutality."[90] The Turkel Report concluded that, on the contrary, the commandos exercised maximum restraint and used lethal force only as a last resort. It stated that during Israeli preparations for the interception, "special attention" was paid "to the value of human life," and "all of the persons involved" evinced a "high level of awareness . . . of the need to carry out the operation without any injuries to the participants of the flotilla"; that either the rules of engagement or operational orders, or both of them, stipulated that "if force had to be used, it had to be exercised gradually and in proportion to the resistance met, and only after examining alternatives to prevent deterioration of the situation," "the only case in which [use of] lethal weapons was permitted was in self-defense—to remove a real and imminent danger to life, when the danger cannot be removed by less harmful means," "there should be no use of force at a person who has surrendered or has ceased to constitute a threat"; that "the training and preparation of the soldiers leading up to the operation was very thorough, with a particular emphasis on the use of less-lethal weapons," "the default position was to use less-lethal weapons until an opposing threat forced the use of the lethal options"; that it was stated at an operational briefing, "'opening fire should only take place in a life threatening situation, to neutralize the person presenting the danger,['] but nonetheless, 'where possible, the benefit of doubt should be given'"; that even after "shooting" could be heard on the *Mavi Marmara,* "the Shayetet 13 commander refused to give approval for shooting 'in order to prevent deaths among the participants of the flotilla'"; and that "the IDF soldiers made considerable use of graduated force"—that is, "firing at the legs and feet of a person"—"during the operation, with soldiers switching repeatedly between less-lethal and lethal weapons," even after passengers had allegedly used firearms against them.[91] The Israeli commandos were so solicitous of the passengers' well-being, according to the Report, that following the bloody confrontation, "some IDF wounded only received treatment after the treatment of wounded flotilla participants"; the commander of the takeover force testified that he risked "danger to my people aboard the vessel" in order to

90. *Report of the Fact-Finding Mission,* para. 264 (see also ibid., paras. 167, 169, 172).
91. Turkel Report, paras. 119, 121, 140, 206, 223, 228, 229, 245.

"evacuate the wounded [passengers] from the vessel, despite their lack of desire to be evacuated, in order to save their lives."[92] The Report concluded that "the IDF personnel acted professionally in the face of extensive and unanticipated violence" and did not "overreact."[93]

The manner of death of the nine passengers aboard the *Mavi Marmara* appeared to belie the Turkel Report's rendition. The UN Fact-Finding Mission found that "the circumstances of the killing of at least six of the passengers were in a manner consistent with an extra-legal, arbitrary and summary execution."[94] The Report itself recounted the findings of an "external examination" by Israeli doctors, according to which all of the dead passengers suffered multiple bullet wounds and five were shot in the neck or head; for example—quoting the Israeli examination—"Body no. 2" contained "bullet wounds on the right side of the head, on the right side of the back of the neck, on the right cheek, underneath the chin, on the right side of the back, on the thigh. A bullet was palpated on the left side of the chest," while "Body no. 9" contained "bullet wounds in the area of the right temple/ back of the neck, bullet wound in the left nipple, bullet wound in the area of the scalp-forehead on the left side, bullet wound on the face (nose), bullet wound on the left torso, bullet wound on the right side of the back, two bullet wounds in the left thigh, two bullet wounds as a result of the bullet passing through toes four and five on the left foot."[95] The Report did not attempt to square the gruesome facts of these passengers' deaths with its sublime finding that the commandos exercised maximum restraint. The closest it came was brief mention in another context, and not referring specifically to the dead passengers, that "in some instances, numerous rounds were fired either by one soldier or by more than one soldier to stop an IHH activist who was a threat to the lives of themselves or other soldiers."[96] What's more, the Report was curiously uncurious about the passengers' deaths, which were blandly dispatched in just two of the Report's nearly three hundred pages.[97] The Report cited the chilling testimony of Israeli commandos on every scratch they incurred, yet it expended not a single word on how it came to

92. Ibid., paras. 141, 142.
93. Ibid., paras. 239, 246.
94. *Report of the Fact-Finding Mission,* para. 170.
95. Turkel Report, para. 155.
96. Ibid., para. 230.
97. Ibid., para. 155. The Report contained two other references to the nine deaths (ibid., paras. 143, 168).

pass that, despite taking every possible precaution and exercising every conceivable restraint, the commandos ended up killing nine passengers, shooting nearly all of them multiple times.[98] Perhaps the Commission forgot—*forgot?*—to request specific information on their deaths,[99] or the commandos forgot—*forgot?*—to mention the killings in their statements. Neither possibility speaks very highly to the Report's credibility. The Report stated that "the Commission has examined each instance of the use of force reported by the IDF soldiers in their testimonies." But it didn't bother to mention whether any of these testimonies recounted the killings of the nine passengers.[100] It also stated that "the Commission examined 133 incidents in which force was used ... which were described by over 40 soldiers ... [and] also includes a few incidents that were depicted on the available relevant magnetic media and that did not correspond to the soldiers' testimonies."[101] But it didn't bother to mention whether the magnetic media captured the killings of any of the passengers. In addition, whereas the UN Fact-Finding Mission requested the Turkish autopsy reports, the Turkel Commission apparently did not.[102] The bottom line was that although the killings of the nine passengers aboard the *Mavi Marmara* sparked an international outcry, the Report contained not a single syllable on how any of them died. The nearest it came was a vague allusion buried in a footnote, quoting a commando that he "fired 2–3 rounds to the center of mass and below and one round to the head (the soldier testified that after firing the last round the IHH personal [*sic*] fell and he ceased fire)."[103] The Report was so intent on demonizing the

98. The Turkish Report stated (pp. 27–28) that two passengers were "killed by a single gunshot wound." It perhaps omitted mention of their nonlethal bullet wounds. The UN Fact-Finding Mission stated that all but one of the nine deceased suffered multiple bullet wounds.

99. In the section devoted to analyzing "the use of force by IDF soldiers during the takeover operations," the Report stated that "the Commission furnished written requests to IDF authorities seven times in order to deepen and expand the inquiries that were conducted" (Turkel Report, para. 236).

100. Ibid., para. 233. It noted that the "detailed testimonies of the soldiers as well as their analysis can be found in an annex to the report" (ibid., para. 235). This annex was apparently never released to the public.

101. Ibid., para. 239.

102. The Report stated only that the Commission "did not have access to autopsy reports ... because [of] the Turkish government's request, immediately after the event, that the Israeli government would not perform autopsies on the bodies of the deceased" (para. 237). The Turkish autopsy reports concluded that "five of the deceased were shot in the head at close range" (Turkish Report, pp. 26, 85, 114).

103. Turkel Report, p. 261n929.

dead passengers, yet so unconcerned with how they came to die, that it took no notice of an odd paradox lodged in its conclusions: the *shaheeds* plotted and armed themselves to kill Israelis, but didn't manage to kill even those in their custody, whereas the Israelis took every precaution and exercised every restraint not to kill anyone, but ended up killing nine people. Lest it be thought that Israel was wholly unmoved by the passengers' ordeal, the Report did duly record that a military court sentenced a corporal to five months in prison for stealing a laptop computer, two camera lenses, and a compass.[104]

In the preface to the Report, the members of the Turkel Commission—including a former Supreme Court justice, a former director-general of the Ministry of Foreign Affairs, a former president of a distinguished scientific institute, a respected professor of law, and a foreign observer who won the Nobel Peace Prize—stated that "we took upon ourselves jointly and as individuals the difficult and agonizing task of ascertaining the truth." The US Department of State praised the investigation that culminated in the Report as "credible and impartial and transparent," and the document itself as "independent."[105] Regrettably, neither the factual information nor the legal analysis in the Report cast light on what happened on the fateful night of 31 May 2010. The sole reflection stimulated by the Report was, How could any self-respecting individual have signed off on such rubbish? But beyond this sordid spectacle of moral degradation looms, albeit inversely, an inspiring testament to the majesty of austere Truth. "Oh, what a tangled web we weave," Walter Scott observed, "when first we practice to deceive." If the Turkel Commission tied itself in a thousand mortifying knots, that's because it set out not to find Truth, but to vindicate Israel, whatever the cost.

104. Ibid., para. 160.
105. US Department of State, "Daily Press Briefing" (24 January 2011).

NINE

Whitewash II

THE UN PANEL REPORT

ISRAEL'S DEADLY ASSAULT ON THE *MAVI MARMARA* refused to go away. Turkey wouldn't relent in its demand for accountability, and as a state of some standing in the international community, it appeared better poised than Gaza to gain satisfaction. The president of the UN Security Council issued a statement on 1 June 2010 (the day after the incident) calling for "a prompt, impartial, credible and transparent investigation, conforming to international standards."[1] It was initially a standoff, as Israel opposed an international investigation, no doubt because a truly independent inquiry would perforce reach the damning conclusions of the UN Human Rights Council Fact-Finding Mission.[2] But Ban Ki-moon, ever attuned to the signals emanating from the White House, came to Israel's rescue. He negotiated the creation of a Panel of Inquiry (hereafter: UN Panel) with an eviscerated mandate; it was tasked not to conduct an "impartial, credible and transparent investigation," but merely to "review ... reports of national investigations into the incident."[3] Leaving nothing to fortune, Ban appointed singularly corrupt and criminal Colombian ex-president Álvaro Uribe, who was also an outspoken proponent of closer military ties between Colombia and Israel, as vice-chair of the Panel.[4] (A former prime minister of New Zealand was designated the chair.) Israel

1. "Statement by the President of the Security Council" (1 June 2010), S/PRST/2010/9.
2. See Chapter 7 and Chapter 8.
3. *Report of the Secretary-General's Panel of Inquiry on the 31 May 2010 Flotilla Incident* (July 2011), para. 3; hereafter: UN Panel. The UN Panel was also empowered to "request such clarifications and information as it may require from relevant national authorities" (ibid.).
4. International Federation for Human Rights, "FIDH Deeply Concerned by the Composition of UN Panel of Inquiry into the Flotilla Events" (6 August 2010); "Álvaro Uribe, el más investigado en la Comisión de Acusaciones," *Elpais.com.co* (8 November 2013).

then reversed itself, acquiescing in the secretary-general's proposal as it proclaimed that it had "nothing to hide."[5] It was predictable—and predicted at the time—that the Panel would produce a whitewash.[6] Still, Israeli opposition leader Tzipi Livni deplored the creation of a UN panel because "international intervention in military operations carried out by Israel is unacceptable.... Israel is investigating the events of the flotilla itself, and that is enough."[7] Indeed, who could doubt that Israel's killing of foreign nationals in international waters was an internal Israeli affair? The *Report of the Secretary-General's Panel of Inquiry on the 31 May 2010 Flotilla Incident* was released in July 2011. Basing itself on Israel's Turkel Report[8] and a reciprocal national report submitted by Turkey, the UN Panel set forth "the facts, circumstances and context of the incident," and "recommended ways of avoiding similar incidents in the future."[9] Although it did find that Israel's killing of the nine passengers aboard the *Mavi Marmara* could not be justified, the Panel vindicated Israel's central contention that the naval blockade of Gaza was legal. If the people of Gaza had not suffered enough, the secretary-general now lent the UN's imprimatur to the prime instrument of their ongoing torture. The report itself was probably the most mendacious and debased document ever issued under the UN's aegis.

The UN Panel alleged that Israel had a right to impose a naval blockade on Gaza in order to defend itself against Hamas rocket and mortar attacks. The historical background sketched in by the Panel was as skewed as that presented by Israel's own inquiry.[10] "Israel has faced and continues to face a real threat to its security from militant groups in Gaza," the Panel observed. "Rockets, missiles and mortar bombs have been launched from Gaza towards Israel.... Since 2001, such attacks have caused more than 25 deaths and hundreds of injuries."[11] The Panel devoted not a single syllable to Israeli attacks on Gaza. Since 2001, or during the same period, Israeli assaults killed some

5. Israel Ministry of Foreign Affairs, "Israel to Participate in UN Panel on Flotilla Events" (2 August 2010).

6. Norman G. Finkelstein, *"This Time We Went Too Far": Truth and consequences of the Gaza invasion,* expanded paperback edition (New York: 2011), pp. 195–96.

7. Shlomo Shamir, "Livni Tells UN to Mind Its Own Business over Flotilla Probe," *Haaretz* (6 October 2010).

8. Public Commission to Examine the Maritime Incident of 31 May 2010, *The Turkel Commission Report, Part One* (January 2011); hereafter: Turkel Report. See Chapter 8.

9. UN Panel, para. 3.

10. See Chapter 8.

11. UN Panel, para. 71 (see also ibid., para. 78).

4,500 Gazans, overwhelmingly civilians.[12] According to the Panel, "the purpose of these [Hamas] acts of violence, which have been repeatedly condemned by the international community, has been to do damage to the population of Israel."[13] But a study published in the journal of the National Academy of Sciences found that Palestinian violence directed at Israel "reveals a pattern of retaliation."[14] If the Panel couldn't conceive that Palestinian violence might be reactive, that's because by its reckoning, the initial Israeli assaults didn't happen; only Gazans fired "rockets, missiles. . . ." The Panel was apparently unaware that Israel's attacks on Gaza also "have been repeatedly condemned by the international community." The Panel stated that "it seems obvious enough that stopping these violent [Hamas] acts was a necessary step for Israel to take in order to protect its people and to defend itself."[15] If the Panel had noticed Palestinian deaths, it would perhaps also have been "obvious enough" that Hamas had a right to impose a naval blockade on Israel "in order to protect its people and to defend itself." Amnesty International pointed out that it is illegal under international law to transfer weapons to a consistent violator of human rights and that, accordingly, an "immediate, comprehensive arms embargo" should be imposed on both Hamas *and Israel.*[16] If the Panel ignored this "obvious enough" fact, it's maybe because Vice-Chair Uribe, in one of his periodic rants against human rights organizations, denounced the "blindness" and "fanaticism" of Amnesty.[17]

The UN Panel found that the Israeli naval blockade of Gaza constituted a "legitimate security measure . . . and its implementation complied with the requirements of international law."[18] But the Panel also repeatedly "stressed" that it was "not asked to make determinations of the legal issues" and was

12. B'Tselem (Israeli Center for Human Rights in the Occupied Territories), *Statistics*, btselem.org/statistics.

13. UN Panel, para. 71.

14. Johannes Haushofer, Anat Biletzki, and Nancy Kanwisher, "Both Sides Retaliate in the Israeli-Palestinian Conflict," *Proceedings of the National Academy of Sciences of the United States* (4 October 2010).

15. UN Panel, para. 71.

16. See Chapter 4.

17. Amnesty International, "Colombian President Should Stop False Accusations against Human Rights Group" (28 November 2008).

18. UN Panel, para. 82.

"not asked to determine the legality or otherwise of the events."[19] If it nonetheless made such a legal determination, it could only have been to gratuitously validate Israel's throttling of Gaza. The Panel stated that it "will not add value for the United Nations . . . by arguing endlessly about the applicable law."[20] Yet, it devoted the vast preponderance of its report (including a 25-page appendix) to a legal analysis of the blockade that vindicated Israel. The Panel's exoneration of Israel was the sole legal verdict it delivered in the report. It found that Israel's land blockade of Gaza and its killing of nine passengers aboard the *Mavi Marmara* were both "unacceptable." But it did not determine that these constituted illegal, let alone criminal, acts.[21] The Panel stated that it couldn't render "definitive findings of fact or law" because it couldn't "compel witnesses to provide evidence" and couldn't "conduct criminal investigations." However, it went on to state that "it can give its view."[22] But if it could "give its view" of the legality of the naval blockade absent these judicial powers, it could surely also have rendered an opinion on the legality of the land blockade and the killings of the nine passengers. In other words, the one and only potentially consequential verdict the Panel reached was favorable to Israel, whereas its unfavorable judgments of Israel amounted to little more than rhetorical slaps on the wrist. In contrast, Amnesty deemed the Israeli blockade a "flagrant violation of international law,"[23] while the UN Human Rights Council's Fact-Finding Mission on the flotilla assault found that "the circumstances of the killing of at least six of the passengers were in a manner consistent with an extra-legal, arbitrary and summary execution."[24] The Panel also *un*did the law when it suited Israel's purposes. Thus, it referred to the "uncertain legal status of Gaza under international law," although the legal consensus was that even after Israel's 2005 "disengagement," Gaza remained "occupied" territory.[25]

19. Ibid., paras. 5, 67.
20. Ibid., para. 15.
21. Ibid., p. 4 (viii), paras. 134, 151.
22. Ibid., para. 6.
23. Amnesty International, "Suffocating Gaza: The Israeli blockade's effects on Palestinians" (1 June 2010).
24. UN Human Rights Council, *Report of the International Fact-Finding Mission to Investigate Violations of International Law, Resulting from the Israeli Attacks on the Flotilla of Ships Carrying Humanitarian Assistance* (27 September 2010), para. 170.
25. See Chapter 1.

The argument contrived by the UN Panel to justify the Israeli naval blockade comprised a sequence of interrelated propositions:

1. The Israeli naval blockade of Gaza was unrelated to the Israeli land blockade;
2. Israel confronted a novel security threat from Gaza's coastal waters when it imposed the naval blockade;
3. Israel imposed the naval blockade in response to this security threat;
4. The naval blockade was the only means Israel had at its disposal to meet this security threat; and
5. The Israeli naval blockade achieved its security objective without causing disproportionate harm to Gaza's civilian population.

To pronounce the naval blockade legal, the Panel had to sustain each and every one of these propositions. If even one were false, its defense of the blockade collapsed. The astonishing thing was, they were *all* false. Each proposition will be addressed in turn.

Spurious proposition no. 1: The Israeli naval blockade of Gaza was unrelated to the Israeli land blockade. The dual objective of Israel's blockade was to prevent weapons from reaching Gaza and to destabilize the Hamas regime by blocking passage of vital civilian goods. The land and naval prongs of the blockade constituted, in conception as well as execution, complementary halves of Israel's strategy, while the efficacy of each prong depended on the efficacy of the other. But the critical premise of the UN Panel was that the Israeli naval blockade was distinct from the land blockade. It posited that whereas the land blockade subserved the dual objective, the naval blockade was a mere security measure and therefore legal. The Panel contrived this bifurcation; it had no basis in reality. Indeed, the Israeli government itself denied such a distinction. The Panel invented it in order to avoid passing legal judgment on Israel's collective punishment of Gaza's civilian population; it set as its mandate to assess only the legality of the allegedly separate and distinct naval blockade. But the Panel simultaneously upheld Israel's right to inflict such collective punishment, by purporting that Israel was acting in self-defense against arms smuggling when it blocked the flotillas.

Since the inception of its occupation in 1967, Israel had regulated passage of goods and persons along Gaza's land and coastal borders. After Hamas consolidated its control of Gaza in 2007, Israel imposed a yet more stringent blockade on it.[26] The motive behind the blockade was twofold: a *security* objective of preventing weapons from reaching Gaza; and a *political* objective of bringing Gaza's economy to the "brink of collapse" (as Israeli officials repeatedly put it in private), in order to punish Gazans for electing Hamas and to turn them against it. The list of items Israel barred from entering Gaza—such as chocolate, chips, and chicks—pointed up the irreducibly *political* aspect of the blockade.[27] The UN Panel, citing Israel's Turkel Report, did acknowledge that the Israeli blockade was "designed to weaken the economy" of Gaza. But it then immediately qualified, "in order to undermine Hamas's ability to attack Israel."[28] One could only shiver at the potency of Hamas's military arsenal if Israel had allowed bonbons to enter Gaza. In fact, although Israel's Turkel Report vindicated Israel on all key points regarding the flotilla assault, even it had to concede (albeit circumspectly) the dual objective of the naval blockade. Consider the testimony it cited by Tzipi Livni, who was foreign minister when the naval blockade was imposed, and the document it cited by Major-General (res.) Amos Gilad, head of the Political, Military, and Policy Affairs Bureau at the Ministry of Defense, which delineated the purposes of the blockade:

> Tzipi Livni said . . . that the imposition of the naval blockade . . . was done in a wider context, as part of Israel's comprehensive strategy (which she referred to as a "dual strategy") of delegitimizing Hamas, on the one hand, and strengthening the status of the Palestinian Authority vis-à-vis the Gaza Strip, on the other. . . . According to her approach, . . . the attempts to transfer [humanitarian] goods to the Gaza Strip by sea . . . give legitimacy to the Hamas regime in the Gaza Strip. . . . Livni also stated that *it would be a mistake to examine the circumstances of imposing the naval blockade from a narrow security perspective only.* . . .
>
> The document [by Gilad] contains two considerations [behind the blockade]: one . . . is to prevent any military strengthening of the Hamas; the other . . . is to "isolate and weaken Hamas." In this context, Major-General (res.) Gilad stated that the significance of opening a maritime route to the Gaza Strip was that the Hamas's status would be strengthened significantly from economic and political viewpoints. He further stated that opening a maritime route to the Gaza Strip, particularly while it is under Hamas control, . . . would be

26. Israel's closure policy in Gaza was first imposed in 1991 and was incrementally tightened as time elapsed. See Gisha (Legal Center for Freedom of Movement), *A Guide to the Gaza Closure: In Israel's own words* (Tel Aviv: 2011).

27. See Chapter 8.

28. UN Panel, para. 153.

tantamount of [*sic*] a "very significant achievement for Hamas." ... Major-General (res.) Gilad concluded: "In summary, the need to impose a naval blockade on the Gaza Strip arises from security and military considerations ... and also *to prevent any legitimization and economic and political strengthening of Hamas and strengthening it in the internal Palestinian arena* [vis-à-vis the Palestinian Authority in the West Bank]."

"It would therefore appear," the Turkel Report concluded, "that even though the purpose of the naval blockade was fundamentally a security one in response to military needs, *its imposition was also regarded by the decision makers as legitimate within the concept of Israel's comprehensive 'dual strategy' against the Hamas in the Gaza Strip.*"[29] The Turkel Report also did not dispute that the naval blockade was *integral* to the global strategy of achieving the twin objectives. On the contrary, it was emphatic that the land and sea blockade must be treated as a seamless whole:

> Both the naval blockade and the land crossings policy were imposed and implemented because of the prolonged international armed conflict between Israel and the Hamas.... [O]n the strategic level ... the naval blockade is regarded by the Government as part of Israel's wider effort not to give legitimacy to the Hamas's rule over the Gaza Strip, to isolate it in the international arena, and to strengthen the Palestinian Authority.

The Turkel Report further pointed out that "the naval blockade is also connected to the land crossings policy on a tactical level": whenever cargo aboard vessels headed for Gaza was rerouted through the land crossings, it was subject to the land restrictions barring passage of critical goods such as "iron and cement." It continued: "In other words, as long as the land crossings are subject to Israeli control, there is prima facie a possibility that the opening of an additional route to the Gaza Strip, such as a maritime route that is not controlled by the State of Israel, will affect the humanitarian situation in the Gaza Strip."[30] Put simply, if the flotillas pried open a sea route to Gaza, essential civilian goods currently blocked by Israel at the land crossings could reach it. "Therefore," the Turkel Report concluded, "it is possible that the enforcement of the naval blockade, in addition to the implementation of the land crossings policy, has a humanitarian impact on the population, at least in principle"; "The approach of the Israeli Government ... created ... a

29. Turkel Report, para. 50, emphases added.
30. Ibid., para. 63.

connection regarding the humanitarian effect on the Gaza Strip between the naval blockade and the land crossings policy."[31] The long and short of it was that even the Turkel Report, which Israel submitted to the Panel and to which the Panel otherwise reflexively deferred, depicted the naval blockade as no less critical than the land blockade to achieving Israel's political objective of bringing Gaza's economy to the "brink of collapse."[32]

If the Turkel Report held that the land and naval blockades both "in principle" and as a "tactical" (practical) matter constituted a single, unified whole, it could defend the propriety of the Israeli naval blockade only by simultaneously defending the propriety of the land blockade and treating each "in conjunction"[33] with the other; to separate them out, to pretend that the naval blockade differed in kind from the land blockade, would have been an exercise in casuistry. "Given the [Turkel] Commission's approach that regarded the naval blockade and the land restrictions as inter-linked," a pair of Israeli scholars observed, "it could only justify the former by defending the legality of the latter."[34] In the event, the Turkel Report found, if only by tortuous reasoning and factual elision, that the unified land-naval blockade passed legal muster.[35] The UN Panel was consequently confronted with a dilemma. If it retraced the Turkel Report's line of argument, it would have to pass judgment on Israel's blockade policy as a whole. But if it passed such a comprehensive judgment, the Panel could vindicate Israel only by blatantly contradicting near-unanimous legal opinion, which declared the Israeli blockade of Gaza a form of collective punishment in flagrant violation of international law.[36] To meet the challenge of upholding the legality of the siege while not offending international opinion, the Panel resolved on an altogether singular strategy. It artificially pried the land blockade from the naval blockade, relegated the land blockade to a secondary and side issue, and proceeded to home in on the naval blockade as if it were a thing apart.[37] It cannot be over-

31. Ibid.
32. Quoted phrase from *WikiLeaks* (see Chapter 8).
33. Turkel Report, para. 107.
34. Amichai Cohen and Yuval Shany, "The Turkel Commission's Flotilla Report (Part One): Some critical remarks," *EJIL: Talk!* (28 January 2011).
35. See Chapter 8.
36. For a contemporary restatement of this consensus opinion, see "Flotillas and the Gaza Blockade," *Diakonia* (2011).
37. The UN Panel's legal strategy recalled the approach of the Israel High Court in the *Wall* case. In 2004, the International Court of Justice (ICJ) delivered an advisory opinion that found Israel's construction of a wall inside occupied Palestinian territory illegal. When

stressed just how radical a surgical procedure the Panel performed; for all its apologetics, not even the Turkel Report conceived such a divorce. In his dissenting letter appended to the Panel's final report, the Turkish representative justly took the Panel to task because it "fully associated itself" with Israel's legal analysis justifying the blockade, whereas the Turkish report's assessment that the blockade was illegal found support among the "vast majority of the international community."[38] He missed, however, the most telling point: in order to vindicate Israel, the Panel ventured on a bizarre legal terrain that was alien even to Israel's own Turkel Report. Once embarked on this path, the Panel did not even recoil at flagrant distortion. It stated that "several international organizations and institutions, including the UN High Commissioner for Human Rights and the ICRC [International Committee of the Red Cross], have declared that the land restrictions constitute collective punishments."[39] However, these organizations declared not just the "land restrictions" but the whole of Israel's border policy—the land *and* *naval* blockade—illegal. It was the Panel that cooked up the idea that the naval blockade existed apart from and independent of the "land restrictions." Indeed, the Turkel Report itself acknowledged that "various human rights and humanitarian organizations . . . conclude that the collapse of the economy of the Gaza Strip derives from the naval blockade imposed by Israel and its land crossings policy."[40] If the Gazan economy was imploding, it was not due just to "land restrictions."

The UN Panel purported that the Israeli land blockade and naval blockade constituted "two distinct concepts which require different treatment and analysis." It "therefore treat[ed] the naval blockade as separate and distinct from the controls at the land crossings," which are "not directly related to the naval blockade."[41] In order to sustain this anomalous contention, the Panel pointed to the facts that, chronologically, imposition of the land blockade (in 2007) preceded imposition of the naval blockade (in 2009); that the "inten-

---

the Israel High Court subsequently heard the case, it sought to avoid a ruling that frontally contradicted the ICJ. Instead, the High Court, taking issue with the ICJ's comprehensive finding, proposed that the legality of the wall should be assessed on a segment-by-segment basis. For a juxtaposition of the ICJ advisory opinion and Israel High Court rulings, see Norman G. Finkelstein, *Knowing Too Much: Why the American-Jewish romance with Israel is coming to an end* (New York: 2012), pp. 307–53.

38. UN Panel, p. 105.
39. Ibid., p. 43n274.
40. Turkel Report, para. 72.
41. UN Panel, paras. 70, 77.

sity" of the land blockade "fluctuated" over time whereas the naval blockade "has not been altered since its imposition"; and that the naval blockade "was imposed primarily to enable . . . Israel to exert control over ships attempting to reach Gaza with weapons and related goods."[42] This series of affirmations confused and conflated the strategic objectives of the Israeli blockade with the tactical modalities of its enforcement. Although Israel periodically adjusted its siege policies to accommodate new political contingencies, the dual security-political objective stayed constant. The premise effectively underpinning the Panel's legal analysis—that as against the security *and* political functions of the land blockade, the purpose of the coastal blockade was *exclusively* to prevent weapons from reaching Gaza—did not just contradict Israel's own testimony. It also overstepped the Panel's terms of reference. The Panel was mandated only to "review" the Israeli and Turkish national reports. But neither of these reports disputed the dual objective of the unified land-naval blockade; neither alleged that the naval blockade differed in kind from the land blockade; neither alleged that the naval blockade was designed only to interdict weapons. The Panel conjured a distinction to resolve a nonexistent controversy. The bottom line was that the Panel sought to sidestep the legality of laying economic siege to a civilian population; to avoid rendering judgment on whether Israel was legally within its right to block the passage of essential civilian goods as well as chocolate, chips, and chicks. If the Panel upheld the legality of such a siege, it risked provoking an outcry from the human rights community, but if it declared the blockade illegal, it infringed on Israel's inalienable right to torment Gaza—*that,* it couldn't do. It extricated itself from this impasse by artificially splitting the land from the naval blockade and focusing exclusively on the naval blockade, while pretending that the naval blockade did not interdict civilian goods, only weapons. To be sure, a legal assessment of, respectively, the land and naval blockades did require a differentiated analysis because the relevant bodies of law do not fully overlap.[43] But until the Panel came along, it was never suggested, not even by Israel's Turkel Report, that the broad purposes of the naval blockade fundamentally differed from those of the land blockade. Only the Panel dared to purport that the naval blockade had no political dimension; that it didn't crucially figure in Israel's strategy of destabilizing Hamas by

42. Ibid.

43. For the legality of a naval blockade, see especially the *San Remo Manual on International Law Applicable to Armed Conflicts at Sea* (1994).

punishing Gaza's civilian population. The ultimate irony was that, *sensu stricto*, the naval blockade did serve only one of the two purposes, but it was *not* the military one; its purpose was narrowly political. The Panel was thus doubly wrong: the naval blockade was not "distinct from" the land blockade, and the purpose of the naval blockade was not "primarily" security.

Spurious proposition no. 2: Israel confronted a novel security threat from Gaza's coastal waters when it imposed the naval blockade. "The fundamental principle of the freedom of navigation on the high seas," the UN Panel observed, "is subject to only certain limited exceptions under international law."[44] A state attempting to restrict this freedom accordingly bears a heavy legal burden of justification. It follows from these tenets that the greater the impediment a state places on freedom of navigation, the greater the legal onus it must bear. If a fundamental freedom is at stake, then infringements on it must be graduated: an extreme restriction would not be justified if a lesser restriction would intercept the perceived threat. In the instant case, if the "visit and search" of a vessel (where "reasonable grounds" existed for suspicion) was an effective means of preventing contraband[45] from reaching Gaza, then it couldn't be justified to impose the more stringent measure of a naval blockade that indiscriminately barred passage of all goods, military and nonmilitary, and consequently inflicted harm on the civilian population.[46] (For argument's sake, it will be set aside that not just the blockade but also Israel's visit-and-search procedure was illegal.[47])

The UN Panel purported that Israel confronted a novel security threat from Gaza's coastal waters that could be met only by a naval blockade. However, the evidence it adduced in support of this contention underwhelmed. It cited, on the basis of the Turkel Report, *three* alleged instances of attempted weapons smuggling into Gaza from the sea, the last of which, in 2003, had occurred *six years before* Israel's imposition of the naval

---

44. UN Panel, para. 82.

45. *Contraband* denotes "goods which are ultimately destined for territory under the control of the enemy and which may be susceptible for use in armed conflict." UK Ministry of Defense, *The Manual of the Law of Armed Conflict* (Oxford: 2005), p. 350.

46. The Turkel Report was at pains to argue that the visit-and-search procedure did not meet the challenge Israel confronted and was replaced by a naval blockade "only" as a last resort. Still, the Report alleged—without authoritative citation and against common sense—that "during an armed conflict, it is lawful to impose a naval blockade, *without considering alternatives*" (para. 51, emphasis added).

47. Douglas Guilfoyle, "The *Mavi Marmara* Incident and Blockade in Armed Conflict," *British Yearbook of International Law* (2011), pp. 204–7.

blockade.[48] It further alleged, citing the Turkel Report, that after its 2005 Gaza "disengagement," Israel had to establish a new legal basis if it still sought to prevent weapons from reaching Gaza. Even if this were true, it still wouldn't explain why the visit-and-search procedure proved effective from 2005 until mid-2008, when, according to the Panel (echoing the Turkel Report), its implementation abruptly posed "practical difficulties."[49] It was not as if, nor did the Turkel Report allege that, Israel was suddenly overwhelmed by a large number of weapons-smuggling operations, such that visit and search had become too cumbersome a procedure. The Panel, citing the Turkel Report, also alleged that only a naval blockade provided a legal basis for preventing Hamas from smuggling weapons out of Gaza to launch attacks on Israel from the sea.[50] However, the Panel cited no instances—none apparently existed— of Hamas attempting such a maneuver. It did cite Israeli concerns that Hamas might attempt such a maneuver in the unbounded future. But insofar as it had not been attempted in the past; and insofar as Israel apparently did not harbor any such fear before 2009 (otherwise it would have imposed the

48. UN Panel, para. 72, citing Turkel Report, para. 22. The three named attempts occurred in, respectively, 2001 (*Santorini*), 2002 (*Karine A*), and 2003 (*Abu Hassan*). (The 2002 attempt has been disputed.) The Turkel Report also alleged (para. 27) a fourth attempt in 2009 (*Tali*), but the UN Panel did not cite it, while not even the Israeli Ministry of Foreign Affairs alleged that this vessel was carrying weapons. "Cargo Boat Attempting Illegal Entry to Gaza Intercepted," *Israel Ministry of Foreign Affairs* (5 February 2009).

49. UN Panel, paras. 72, 74, citing Turkel Report, para. 49. The Turkel Report alleged that visit and search was impracticable because of the "virtual certainty that consent for search would not be granted by the Masters of the ships bent on reaching Gaza," and "it was not certain that the consent of the flag State would actually be obtained" (para. 52). However, it adduced no evidentiary basis—none existed—for its "virtual certainty." In another itera- tion, the Turkel Report alleged that "a key requirement is that such a right [of visit and search] cannot be arbitrarily exercised. The challenge that confronted the Israeli authorities was to obtain sufficient information regarding the cargo and/or personnel on board the vessels in order to find a ground for suspicion that the vessel is engaged in transporting contraband, enemy combatants" (para. 54). But the Turkel Report did not cite a single inci- dent in which visit and search was hindered by this requirement. Other countries have exer- cised the right of visit and search on the basis of reasonable suspicion in wartime; why did it work elsewhere? The Turkel Report also alleged that if Israel could not resort to the lesser measure of declaring Gaza's coastal waters an "exclusion zone," it was because "there is a lack of clarity in the law as to whether such a zone provides an authority to *only* search for contra- band" (para. 53, emphasis added). In other words, the difficulty was that declaring an "exclu- sion zone" did not explicitly allow Israel to turn back vessels *not* carrying contraband but only civilian goods.

50. UN Panel, para. 72, citing Turkel Report, para. 48 (see also Turkel Report, paras. 55, 89).

naval blockade earlier); and insofar as Israel cited no evidentiary basis for its claim that such a maneuver might be attempted by Hamas at some point in the nebulous future—insofar, then, as Israel did not materially ground this alleged fear, it was a palpably flimsy justification for so restrictive a curb on freedom of navigation. The upshot was that the Panel adduced zero evidence that Israel confronted a novel security threat from Gaza's coastal waters when it escalated its infringement on the freedom-of-navigation principle by imposing an indiscriminate naval blockade.

Spurious proposition no. 3: Israel imposed the naval blockade in response to this security threat. The UN Panel alleged, on the basis of the Turkel Report, that Israel imposed the naval blockade "in order to prevent weapons, terrorists and money from entering or exiting the Gaza Strip by sea."[51] But although Israel formally gestured to this threat, the Panel did not present a persuasive case for crediting this official Israeli testimony. In its legal analysis of the naval blockade, the Panel's point of departure was, *If Israel says so, it must be true:* "The Israeli report to the Panel makes it clear that the naval blockade . . . was adopted for the purpose of defending its territory and population, and the Panel accepts that was the case"; "[I]t is evident that Israel had a military objective. The stated primary objective of the naval blockade was for security. It was to prevent weapons, ammunition, military supplies and people from entering Gaza and to stop Hamas operatives sailing away from Gaza with vessels filled with explosives."[52]

Still, the perplexity remains, If it wasn't to prevent weapons smuggling, why *did* Israel impose the naval blockade? In fact, the explanation was right there in the Turkel Report. Beginning in mid-2008, the Turkel Report observed, "various flotillas whose stated destination was the Gaza Strip were organized. In view of the fact that the ships concerned were neutral, the IDF [Israel Defense Forces] had relatively limited options, which mainly included the power of visit and search, a power that can be used, inter alia, on condition that there are reasonable grounds for suspecting that a ship is subject to capture"—that is, that it was carrying contraband. The quandary confront-

51. UN Panel, para. 46, citing Turkel Report, paras. 48–50, 112 (see also Turkel Report, para. 89).

52. UN Panel, paras. 72, 77. The Panel also appeared to allege, copying from the Turkel Report, that a decrease in Hamas rocket and mortar attacks on Israel was somehow related to the naval blockade (para. 72, citing Turkel Report, para. 89). The basis for this claim was, to put it most charitably, thin, not least because the Panel adduced no evidence that weapons *ever* reached Gaza by sea.

ing Israel, however, was that the flotillas did *not* carry weapons; hence, it lacked a legal basis for blocking their passage into Gaza. Initially, Israel let a succession of vessels pass *without even bothering to search them,* in the hope that the flotilla phenomenon would peter out. (Between August and December 2008, Israel let six vessels pass into Gaza.[53]) When the ships kept coming, Israel responded with escalating violence, but still they kept coming. It was "in these circumstances, on January 3, 2009," the Turkel Report continued, that "the Minister of Defense ordered a naval blockade. . . . The significance of imposing a naval blockade according to the rules of international law is that it allows a party to an armed conflict to prevent entry into the prohibited area of any vessel that attempts to breach the blockade (*even without it being established that the vessel is assisting terrorist activity*)."[54] In testimony quoted by the Turkel Report, which the Panel once again prudently overlooked, Israel's military advocate-general stated that the naval blockade was imposed specifically in order to prevent the humanitarian flotillas from reaching Gaza:

> The Military Advocate-General testified before the Commission that the IDF was compelled to find a suitable operational solution for the maritime zone *in view of the increase in the phenomenon of flotillas.* . . . A naval blockade was regarded as the best operational method of dealing with the phenomenon because other solutions, such as the use of the right of visit and search, were proved to be problematic and other sources of authority were regarded as weaker.
>
> . . . [T]he Military Advocate-General apprised the Chief of Staff . . . that he had spoken with the Attorney-General, who also expressed the position that the declaration of a naval blockade on the Gaza Strip gave the "optimal legal-operational solution to preventing the entry of foreign shipping vessels into the Gaza Strip, and gave the Navy all of the tools and powers required to prevent the passage of shipping vessels. The sources of authority that allow action to be taken against shipping vessels, in the absence of a declaration of a 'naval blockade,' are weaker, and their practicability is doubtful." . . .
>
> . . . On December 30, 2008, the Military Advocate-General once again contacted the Chief of Staff and said that in the early hours of the morning the Navy forces were required to contend with the yacht *Dignity* [one of the earlier humanitarian ships] that left Cyprus for the Gaza Strip and that the incident highlighted the legal difficulty of dealing with foreign civilian shipping vessels trying to reach the coast of the Gaza Strip. He once again asked

53. Turkel Report, paras. 25, 53.
54. Ibid., para. 26, emphasis added.

the Chief of Staff to bring his recommendation of a naval blockade before the political echelon.

    ... On January 3, 2009, after the security establishment's legal advisor gave his opinion on the subject, the Minister of Defense signed an order to impose the blockade.[55]

It was evidently not the *type* of vessel—civilian-commercial versus military-naval—that posed a complication for Israel. It already possessed the legal authority under visit and search to stop a civilian vessel and prevent passage of weapons, and the procedure had proven practicable. Indeed, Israel neither bothered to search humanitarian vessels headed for Gaza (it was presumably privy to the fact that they weren't stashing weapons), nor did it suddenly have to cope with a rash of arms smuggling. Further, if weapons were to be smuggled in, they almost certainly would be secreted in a civilian-commercial vessel. The advent of the flotillas, then, did not alter the legal situation: *before* as well as after, Israel's principal legal preoccupation, officially, must have been civilian ships. The actual challenge facing Israel was that it lacked legal authority to bar humanitarian cargo unless it imposed a naval blockade. In the Panel's disingenuously opaque language, the blockade was imposed not because of weapons smuggling but "in reaction to certain incidents when vessels had reached Gaza via sea."[56] The "certain incidents" gestured to the determination of the flotilla passengers, come what may, to deliver essential humanitarian goods to Gaza's besieged population. What Israel dreaded was not arms transfers but the *political* defeat it would suffer if a maritime route were opened, allowing humanitarian vessels to reach Gaza, and that in the course of opening such a route, these flotillas would spotlight Israel's illegal, immoral, and inhuman siege. The irony was that the Panel falsely separated out the land from the naval blockade in order to justify the naval blockade on security grounds, whereas even senior Israeli officials conceded that the naval blockade was imposed to meet, not a security threat but "the increase in the phenomenon of flotillas . . . the entry of foreign civilian vessels." Indeed, it was *because* Israel did not confront a security threat that it replaced visit and search with a naval blockade: if it had stuck to the former procedure, it could legally seize only contraband but would otherwise have to let vessels pass;[57] while if it imposed a naval blockade, it

55. Ibid., para. 49, emphasis added.
56. UN Panel, para. 70.
57. *San Remo Manual,* "Section II: Visit and Search of Merchant Vessels."

could legally interdict strictly humanitarian vessels from reaching Gaza. But (it might be argued), if a succession of humanitarian flotillas opened a maritime route to Gaza, wouldn't it eventually create a security threat to Israel, as vessels smuggling weapons could pass? Even if such a contingency were real, however, it still remained that the blockade was not imposed because of an actual security threat to Israel. It would be difficult to justify so restrictive a curb on the fundamental right to freedom of navigation on the basis of a threat that might—but also might *not*—materialize in a nebulous future. The imposition of a draconian blockade on the basis of a speculative future contingency would be yet more difficult to justify in the face of the humanitarian harm it entailed in the here and now.

Spurious proposition no. 4: The naval blockade was the only means Israel had at its disposal to meet this security threat. The purpose of the naval blockade was not to meet a security threat but to preempt the political fallout if the siege of Hamas-controlled Gaza were breached. Even if, for argument's sake, the claim were credited that, as a practical matter and setting aside the law, no country at war would permit a convoy of ships—even a declared humanitarian convoy that had been vetted beforehand—to pass freely into enemy territory under its control, Israel still had at its disposal another option. The UN Panel itself alluded to it, if only in passing and in another context. "At a briefing immediately after the 31 May 2010 incident," the Panel reported, "a senior United Nations official noted that the loss of life could have been avoided if Israel had responded to repeated calls to end its closure of Gaza."[58] If Israel wanted to put a stop to the humanitarian convoys headed for Gaza, then obviously all it needed to do was lift the illegal economic blockade that was causing the humanitarian crisis in the first place. And yet so averse was the Panel to dropping the charade that the naval blockade was designed to interdict weapons—and thus exposing Israel to the charge of collective punishment—that it completely ignored this option in its analysis of the blockade's legality.

Spurious proposition no. 5: The Israeli naval blockade achieved its security objective without causing disproportionate harm to Gaza's civilian population. Whereas the Turkel Report defended the legality of the siege as a whole, the UN Panel endeavored to preempt the scandal of such a broad legal writ by redefining the naval siege as a thing apart, the legality of which rose and fell on its own merits. Thus, according to the Panel, even if the land blockade was

58. UN Panel, para. 151.

designed to prevent humanitarian goods from reaching Gaza, it did not necessarily make the naval blockade illegal. The Panel's audacious surgical procedure did not, however, salvage Israel's case. In fact, it rendered Israel's case yet more *un*tenable. The Panel contended that in the "absence of significant port facilities in Gaza," the harm caused by the naval blockade to Gaza's civilian population was "slight," and consequently not disproportionate to the military gain.[59] But if, as the evidence unambiguously showed, the Israeli naval blockade did not serve the purpose of self-defense against an armed attack but was imposed to achieve a political objective, then the proportionality test was wholly irrelevant. As the Panel itself observed, "The imposition of a blockade must have a lawful *military* objective."[60] Put otherwise, even if the humanitarian value of the maritime point of entry were minimal, the naval blockade would still cause proportionally greater harm because its military value was nil; it was not put in place to deter weapons smuggling or achieve any other legitimate military objective, while the visit-and-search procedure, which did not hinder the passage of humanitarian goods, could have neutralized the (speculative) threat of such smuggling. In addition, even if the naval blockade did subserve an actual military objective, it would still have been hasty to conclude that it did not cause disproportionate damage. The Turkel Report itself cautioned against being too dismissive of Gaza's potential for maritime traffic, not least because it undercut Israel's rationale for imposing a blockade. If goods could just barely enter Gaza by sea, then weapons too could just barely enter, but in that case a naval blockade would be redundant and any justification for it unsustainable: "The absence of a commercial port is not a decisive factor, since it is clear that it is possible to find other ways of transporting goods arriving by sea, such as by means of unloading the goods with the help of fishing boats. Moreover, the assumption that goods cannot be transported into the Gaza Strip in the absence of a commercial port inherently contradicts the main purpose of the blockade, i.e., preventing the passage of weapons to the Gaza Strip, since, according to the same logic, it would not be at all possible to transport weapons to the Gaza Strip by sea."[61] The furthest the Turkel Report would venture was that "in the absence of information and records, it is difficult to determine the effect of the naval blockade alone on the humanitarian situation in the Gaza

59. Ibid., para. 78 (see also ibid., para. 72).
60. Ibid., para. 33, emphasis added; see also International Committee of the Red Cross, *Customary International Humanitarian Law, Volume I: Rules* (Cambridge: 2005), rule 53.
61. Turkel Report, para. 62.

Strip."[62] It cannot but perplex how the Panel ascertained that the potential harm of the naval blockade was "slight," when even the egregiously apologetic Turkel Report pleaded agnosticism. In fact, if a humanitarian crisis existed in Gaza, and if the maritime passageway was the last and only remaining point of entry to Gaza's besieged population, then the collateral damage of the naval blockade would have to be reckoned severe, while the likelihood of Israel passing a proportionality test would be drastically reduced. The Panel rejected this calculation of proportionality, as it downplayed the humanitarian potential of a maritime passageway to Gaza: "Smuggling weapons by sea is one thing; delivering bulky food and other goods to supply a population of approximately 1.5 million people is another."[63] But the reverse could just as easily be said: "Smuggling bulky weapons by sea is one thing; delivering desperately needed medicines and other basic, portable goods to supply a population. . . . "[64] The upshot was that if the Panel's proportionality test vindicated Israel, that's because it was based on false premises, while the blockade almost certainly couldn't have passed a proportionality test anchored squarely in the factual situation. Lest it be forgotten, the Panel's spurious proportionality test did not just vindicate Israel; it also condemned Gaza's civilian population to a stringent blockade, not only from land but also from sea, as it suffered a humanitarian crisis. To be sure, however large a breach in the naval blockade, it could not have solved Gaza's humanitarian disaster. The overarching objective of the flotillas was, in fact, not to deliver humanitarian cargo but rather to shine a bright light on the illegality and inhumanity of the blockade. The Panel found this last objective if not legally then, still, morally culpable.

The UN Panel presented a sequence of interrelated propositions to legally justify Israel's naval blockade of Gaza. If any of these propositions proved to be false, the Panel could not have sustained its defense of the siege. It turns out that each and every one of the propositions proves on close inspection to be spurious: the Israeli naval blockade *was* related to the Israeli land blockade; Israel did *not* confront a novel security threat from Gaza's coastal waters when it imposed the naval blockade; Israel did *not* impose the naval blockade

62. Ibid.
63. UN Panel, para. 78.
64. On this point, see also Guilfoyle, "*Mavi Marmara* Incident," p. 203.

in response to a security threat; the naval blockade was *not* the only means Israel had at its disposal to meet the alleged security threat; and the Israeli naval blockade could achieve its alleged security objective only by causing *dis*proportionate harm to Gaza's civilian population.[65] It would be hard to exaggerate the sheer mendacity of the multiplex rationale contrived by the Panel to justify the naval blockade. But the Panel did not just shamelessly legitimize Israel's illegal, immoral, and inhuman siege. It also denounced the "dangerous and reckless act" of the flotilla passengers as they attempted to breach this blockade.[66] It went on to exhort states to actively intervene so as to prevent these irresponsible undertakings in the future: "It is important that such events are not repeated"; "It is important that States . . . make every effort to avoid a repetition of the incident"; "It is in the interests of the international community to actively discourage attempts to breach a lawfully imposed blockade."[67] The fate and future of the people of Gaza, the Panel suggested, would be better served by and should be the exclusive preserve of states, not ordinary citizens. Consider, however, what transpired when the international community of states *did* control Gaza's fate and future. In 2007, Israel imposed a blockade on Gaza that as a form of collective punishment constituted a flagrant violation of international law. The international community did not lift a finger. Journeying to Gaza around this time, former high commissioner for human rights Mary Robinson declared that Gaza's "whole civilization has been destroyed, I'm not exaggerating." The international community still did not lift a finger. In 2008, Israel tightened the blockade, bringing Gaza's infrastructure—in the words of an Israeli human rights organization—"to the brink of collapse." The international community still did not lift a finger. "The breakdown of an entire society is happening in front of us," Harvard political economist Sara Roy publicly anguished, "but there is little international response, beyond UN warnings which are ignored." In late 2008, Israel invaded Gaza and in the course of what Amnesty called "22 days of death and destruction" massacred the civilian population

65. Elizabeth Spelman, "The Legality of the Israeli Naval Blockade of the Gaza Strip," *European Journal of Current Legal Issues* (2013), "accepts that the naval blockade was imposed on the Gaza Strip alongside, but separate to, the land and air closures," and "accepts that the Israeli naval blockade of the Gaza Strip is part of an Israeli military 'dual strategy' against Hamas." The author provides no evidentiary basis for this acceptance; none exists.

66. UN Panel, para. 92.

67. Ibid., paras. 96, 148, 149, 159.

and laid waste the civilian infrastructure.[68] In early 2009, the UN Security Council finally reacted to global outrage at Israel's crimes by passing a resolution (1860) that expressed "grave concern . . . at the deepening humanitarian crisis in Gaza," and called for "the unimpeded provision and distribution throughout Gaza of humanitarian assistance, including of food, fuel and medical treatment."[69] But Israel persisted in its strangulating blockade, and the international community still did not lift a finger. It was only *after* the martyrdom of the *Mavi Marmara* passengers, as the Panel itself effectively conceded,[70] that the world's leaders suddenly experienced the epiphany that the Israeli blockade was "unsustainable,"[71] and some—albeit grossly insufficient—relief was granted to Gaza's desperate civilian population. But if the Panel had its way, and the Freedom Flotilla had not committed a "dangerous and reckless act" that infringed on the prerogatives of states, Israel would have been left undisturbed and the people of Gaza left to languish and expire. The achievements of the flotilla may have ultimately proved marginal,[72] but in the Kingdom of Justice it could hardly be faulted. The passengers put their lives at risk, and several were martyred, so that the people of Gaza could breathe. What did the community of states do except saturate the atmosphere with continuous emissions of hot air?

Whereas the UN Panel did deem the deaths caused by Israeli commandos aboard the *Mavi Marmara* "unacceptable," it strove hard to "balance" this criticism by also casting doubt on the passengers' motive. The Turkel Report had alleged that the organizers of the *Mavi Marmara* were jihadis hell-bent on killing Israelis. It had some difficulty sustaining this charge, however, as the most lethal weapons "smuggled" on board by these alleged jihadis, according to the Turkel Report itself, were slingshots and glass marbles, while it was hard to explain why these young, burly, fanatical men did not manage to kill anyone, not even the three commandos who were being held captive by them.[73] Just as the Panel adopted a novel strategy to prove the legality of the blockade, so it also conjured a creative proof to vindicate the Turkel Report's traducing of these alleged jihadis. The Panel gravely observed that it "seriously questions the true nature and objectives of the flotilla organizers."

68. See Chapter 2.
69. UN Security Council resolution 1860 (S/RES/1860) (8 January 2009).
70. UN Panel, paras. 151, 154.
71. See Chapter 7.
72. See Chapter 7.
73. See Chapter 8.

Why? Because it discovered that they intended not only to deliver humanitarian relief but also "to generate publicity about the situation in Gaza." To clinch its indictment, the Panel reproduced with a great flourish this document "prepared by" the organizers:

> Purpose: Purposes of this journey are to create an awareness amongst world public and international organizations on the inhuman and unjust embargo on Palestine and to contribute to end this embargo which clearly violates human rights and delivering humanitarian relief to the Palestinians.[74]

If this statement of intent weren't incriminating enough, the Panel laid out yet more evidence of the sinister and nefarious plot: "The number of journalists embarked on the ships gives further power to the conclusion that the flotilla's primary purpose was to generate publicity."[75] It must be a first, and surely marks a nadir, in the annals of the United Nations that a report bearing its imprimatur vilified the victims of a murderous assault because they sought to cast light on an ongoing crime against humanity.[76]

---

74. UN Panel, paras. 86–87.

75. Ibid., para. 89. Whereas the Turkel Report did take note that passengers sought to publicize the blockade's dire impact, not even it dared impugn their integrity on this account. It just flatly stated, "The goal of the Flotilla was obviously not just to break the blockade, but also to bring international pressure to bear in a bid to end the land based restrictions" (para. 62).

76. Compounding obscenity by imbecility, the UN Panel (paras. 88, 93) also condemned this alleged cabal of publicity-seekers for not sufficiently alerting the other passengers to the dangers that lurked in the event that they attempted to breach the blockade—as if the other dedicated activists who joined the flotilla hadn't a clue that Israel was capable of committing murder.

FIGURE 4. Gaza, August 2014. © REUTERS/Finbarr O'Reilly.

PART FOUR

Operation Protective Edge

TEN

Stalled Juggernaut

ON 14 NOVEMBER 2012, ISRAEL LAUNCHED Operation Pillar of Defense. It lasted only eight days and inflicted much less death and destruction than Operation Cast Lead (2008–9) or Operation Protective Edge (2014). Its modus operandi and outcome pointed up constraints on Israel's freedom to launch deadly military operations. The official Israeli account followed a familiar story line: it only reacted after stoically absorbing hundreds of Hamas rockets. "Israel does not want war," Defense Minister Ehud Barak declaimed. "But Hamas's... incessant rounds of artillery rockets and mortars... forced our hand into acting."[1] The facts, however, suggested otherwise. From 1 January until 11 November 2012, one Israeli had been killed as a result of attacks from Gaza, whereas 78 Gazans had been killed by Israeli strikes.[2] If Israel's objective was to restore calm on its southern border, why did it trigger the new round of violence by assassinating Hamas military chief Ahmed Jabari, who was Israel's principal interlocutor in Gaza—or, as *Haaretz*'s security analyst put it, the "subcontractor, in charge of maintaining Israel's security in Gaza"?[3] The precise timing of the assassination was yet more incriminating. Jabari was in the process of "advancing a permanent

---

1. Israel Ministry of Foreign Affairs, "Pillar of Defense—Statement of DM Ehud Barak" (14 November 2012).

2. "Gaza Abacus," *Economist* (19 November 2012).

3. Aluf Benn, "Israel Killed Its 'Subcontractor' in Gaza," *Haaretz* (14 November 2012). Benn notes that "Jabari was also Israel's partner in the negotiations for the release of Gilad Shalit; it was he who ensured the captive soldier's welfare and safety, and it was he who saw to Shalit's return home last fall."

cease-fire agreement" when Israel liquidated him.[4] Although it was alleged that Hamas had been itching for a fight when Israel launched Pillar of Defense, in fact the Islamic government had mostly avoided armed confrontations with Israel. It did, however, recoil at becoming a clone of the Palestinian Authority (PA) by engaging in "security cooperation" with Israel. Hence, it could turn a blind eye, or joined in (if only to prevent an escalation), when Israeli provocations triggered retaliatory strikes by Hamas's militarized rivals.[5]

The rationale behind Hamas's pursuit of a long-term cease-fire was straightforward. It had been on a roll prior to the outbreak of hostilities. Its ideological bedfellow, the Muslim Brotherhood, had won Egypt's first democratic election in June 2012. The emir of Qatar had journeyed to Gaza in October 2012 carrying the promise of $400 million in aid, while Turkish prime minister Recep Tayyip Erdoğan was scheduled to arrive soon.[6] In the meantime, Gaza had witnessed "an enormous building boom"; it "boasted a stunning 23 percent GDP growth rate in 2011 alone," "unemployment fell rapidly," and Saudi Arabia had promised to double its investment in Gaza.[7] On still another front, Gaza's Islamic University had pulled off a diplomatic coup of its own in October 2012, as it convened an academic conference attended by renowned linguist Noam Chomsky.[8] Hamas's star was slowly but surely on the rise, at the expense of the hapless PA. The very last thing it needed was an armed confrontation with Israel that undercut these hard-won, steadily accreting gains. A clutch of skeptical Israeli pundits speculated that Prime Minister Benjamin Netanyahu launched Pillar of Defense to boost his prospects in the upcoming election.[9] As a general rule, however,

4. Reuven Pedatzur, "Why Did Israel Kill Jabari?," *Haaretz* (4 December 2012); Gershon Baskin, "Assassinating the Chance for Calm," *Daily Beast* (15 November 2012); Nir Hasson, "Israeli Peace Activist: Hamas leader Jabari killed amid talks on long-term peace," *Haaretz* (15 November 2012); Crispian Balmer and Nidal al-Mughrabi, "Gaza Militants Signal Truce with Israel after Rockets," *Reuters* (12 November 2012).

5. Baskin, "Assassinating." See also International Crisis Group, *Fire and Ceasefire in a New Middle East* (2012), pp. 1, 4.

6. Jodi Rudoren, "Qatar's Emir Visits Gaza, Pledging $400 Million to Hamas," *New York Times* (23 October 2012); Jodi Rudoren, "Turkish Leader Says He Plans a Visit to Gaza Soon," *New York Times* (2 November 2012).

7. Sara Roy, *The Gaza Strip: The political economy of de-development*, expanded third edition (Washington, DC: 2016), pp. xxxviii–xxxix; for qualifications to this upbeat picture, see ibid., pp. xli–xlvi, lxii.

8. "Chomsky in First Visit to Gaza: End the blockade," *Haaretz* (19 October 2012).

9. Benn, "Israel Killed"; Pedatzur, "Why Did Israel?"

Israeli leaders have not undertaken major military operations or jeopardized critical state interests for the sake of partisan electoral gain.[10] It was also purported that Israel's governing coalition felt compelled to appease popular indignation at the Hamas projectiles. But they had barely registered on Israel's political radar; public opinion was focused on the Islamic Republic of Iran and sundry domestic issues. Why, then, did Israel attack?

At one level, Israel was transparent in its motive. It kept repeating that it wanted to restore its "deterrence capacity." The puzzle was the nature of the threat it hoped to quash, or exactly what it sought to deter. Israel's decision to launch Pillar of Defense emerged out of a succession of foreign policy setbacks. Netanyahu had endeavored to rally the international community around an attack on Iran. He ended up looking the fool, however, as he held up to the UN General Assembly in September 2012 a cartoonish depiction of "The Iranian Bomb."[11] A couple of weeks later, Hezbollah boasted that a drone launched by it had penetrated Israeli airspace and passed over "sensitive sites."[12] Meanwhile, its "terrorist" twin upstart in Gaza was entrenching its own credibility as regional powers thumbed their collective nose at Israel on its doorstep. The ultimate outrage was that Hamas refused to carry on like a terrorist organization and, instead, acquitted itself as a responsible *legitimate* sovereign power. A long-term cease-fire would only enhance its bona fides. It was time to remind the natives who was in charge. Put otherwise, and in Israel's preferred metaphor, it was time to "mow the lawn" again in Gaza. "At the heart of Operation Pillar of Defense," the Crisis Group shrewdly observed, "lay an effort to demonstrate that Hamas's newfound confidence was altogether premature and that, the Islamist awakening notwithstanding, changes in the Middle East would not change much at all."[13] Still, Israel needed an alibi to justify yet another murderous Gaza invasion. When Israel needed a pretext to launch Cast Lead, it broke the cease-fire (by killing six militants) in order to provoke a retaliatory attack by Hamas.[14] Four years later, it killed the cease-fire-maker to provoke Hamas.

The actual operation, however, differed in kind from its precursor. Pillar of Defense was qualitatively less destructive than Cast Lead. The pundit class

10. See Chapter 2.

11. Harriet Sherwood, "Netanyahu's Bomb Diagram Succeeds—But Not in the Way the PM Wanted," *Guardian* (27 September 2012).

12. "Hezbollah Admits Launching Drone over Israel," *BBC* (11 October 2012).

13. Crisis Group, *Fire and Ceasefire*, p. 8.

14. See Chapter 2.

postulated that Israel had mastered the art of avoiding civilian casualties: the IDF used precision weaponry during the operation, while the "lessons" of Cast Lead/the Goldstone Report had been "learned and internalized."[15] But 99 percent of its air strikes during Cast Lead had hit targets accurately, while Israel's manifest objective had been to "punish, humiliate and terrorize" Gaza's civilian population (Goldstone Report).[16] If Cast Lead had proved so murderous, it was not due to "errors" in planning or execution, and if Pillar of Defense proved less lethal, it was not because Israel was careful to avoid such "errors." Indeed, when the constellation of political forces realigned in Israel's favor in 2014 as it unleashed Protective Edge, the IDF reflexively discarded all the lessons it had supposedly learned.[17] Israel's decision to ratchet down its violent force in 2012 traced back to the unique political matrix in which Pillar of Defense unfolded. *First,* Turkey and Egypt had made abundantly clear that they would not sit idly by if Israel launched a repeat performance of Cast Lead, and they explicitly drew a red line at an Israeli ground assault.[18] In an unprecedented display of solidarity, the Egyptian prime minister and Turkish foreign minister journeyed to Gaza amid the Israeli assault. (Cairo also recalled its ambassador to Israel.) Put on notice by these regional power brokers, the White House counseled Israel not to invade. *Second,* the prospect of a "mega-Goldstone"[19] hung over Israel. After Cast Lead, Israeli officials had just barely managed to elude legal accountability. But if it committed yet another massacre, and if Cairo (where Hamas's progenitor currently held power) and Ankara (still smarting from the *Mavi Marmara* attack[20]) pressed Gaza's case in the international arena, Israel might not again be so fortunate. *Third,* Gaza was swarming with foreign journalists. Israel had sealed Gaza off from the outside world in collaboration with Hosni Mubarak's Egypt before Cast Lead. In the initial phase of that operation, Israel had enjoyed a near-total monopoly on media coverage. But this time around, journalists could freely enter Gaza via Egypt (Israel didn't bother to block entry from its side) and credibly report Israeli atrocities

15. Nathan Jeffay, "Israel Learned the Lessons of the Last Gaza War," *Forward* (26 November 2012); Ari Shavit, "End the War While You're Ahead," *Haaretz* (19 November 2012).

16. See Chapter 3 and Chapter 5.

17. See Chapter 11.

18. Crisis Group, *Fire and Ceasefire,* p. 17n117.

19. Ben Dror Yemini, "Ceasefire Now," *NRG-Ma'ariv* (18 November 2012).

20. See Chapter 7.

in real time. On account of this trio of factors, Israel mostly targeted "legitimate" sites during Pillar of Defense. At the same time, the death and destruction inflicted by Israel, although on a diminished scale, received in-depth graphic news coverage. When Israel tested the limits of the laws of war, trouble loomed. After it flattened civilian governmental structures in Gaza, the headline on the *New York Times* website read, "Israel targets civilian buildings." A few hours later, it metamorphosed into "*government* buildings" (presumably after a complaint filed by Israel's minions). But the writing was on the wall: Israeli conduct was being scrutinized abroad, so it had better tread carefully.

True, some 100 Gazan civilians were killed (including 35 children), and Israel did in fact commit multiple war crimes (126 homes were completely destroyed),[21] but in the court of public opinion they could plausibly be chalked up to "collateral damage." The precipitous escalation of attacks on civilians coincided with the start of diplomatic negotiations.[22] As the hostilities wound to a close, Israel reverted to its standard operating procedure of targeting or indiscriminately firing on civilians in order to extract the best possible terms in a final agreement. Four times as many Gazan civilians were killed in the last four days as in the first four days of the assault. Israel also targeted journalists in the last four days to block transmission of these terror attacks and, preemptively, in the event talks broke down and the IDF had after all to embark on a murderous ground invasion.[23] Hamas, too, stood accused of committing war crimes, such as "launching hundreds of rockets toward population centers in Israel." Four Israeli civilians were killed. In addition, Human Rights Watch reported damage to civilian Israeli property; for example, "a rocket tore the roof off a school."[24]

21. "One Year Following the Israeli Offensive on Gaza," *Palestinian Center for Human Rights* (14 November 2013); OCHA, "Escalation in Hostilities, Gaza and Southern Israel" (26 November 2012).

22. Julian Borger and Harriet Sherwood, "Israeli Envoy Arrives in Egypt for Gaza Ceasefire Talks," *Guardian* (18 November 2012); Ibrahim Barzak and Karin Lamb, "Israel Intensifies Attacks despite Truce Talks," *Associated Press* (20 November 2012); B'Tselem (Israeli Information Center for Human Rights in the Occupied Territories), "Human Rights Violations during Operation Pillar of Defense" (2013).

23. Human Rights Watch, "Unlawful Israeli Attacks on Palestinian Media" (20 December 2012); Reporters without Borders, "RWB Condemns Air Strikes on News Media in Gaza City" (18 November 2012); Committee to Protect Journalists, "Three Journalists Killed in Airstrikes in Gaza" (20 November 2012).

24. Human Rights Watch, "Palestinian Rockets Unlawfully Targeted Israeli Civilians" (24 December 2012).

The armed resistance Hamas put up during the eight-day Israeli assault was largely nominal. The lopsidedness of the "war" was suggested by Defense Minister Barak, as he boasted that "Hamas only succeeded in hitting Israeli targets with a single ton of explosives, while targets in Gaza were hit with a thousand tons."[25] On the other hand, although Israel celebrated its deployment of "Iron Dome,"[26] the antimissile defense system did not "save countless Israeli lives."[27] Compare civilian casualties before and after Israel's antimissile defense system became operative (see Table 3). The bottom line was, Iron Dome effectively made little difference (it saved perhaps three lives). It was unlikely that in the main and allowing for the occasional aberration, Hamas used more sophisticated projectiles during Pillar of Defense. Through its army of informers and state-of-the-art aerial surveillance, Israel would have been privy to any large quantities of technically sophisticated Hamas weapons, and would have destroyed these stashes before or at the start of the attack. Israel announced on the first day of the operation that "the IDF seriously damaged Hamas' long-range missile capabilities (40 km/25 mi range) and underground weapons storage facilities," and on the third day that "the IDF has destroyed a significant portion of the Hamas' Fajr-5 arsenal, many of them in underground launch sites."[28] It was also improbable that Netanyahu would have risked an attack just on the eve of an election if Hamas possessed weapons capable of inflicting heavy casualties. A handful of Hamas projectiles did reach deeper inside Israel than previously, but these lacked explosives; an Israeli official derisively dismissed them as "pipes, basically."[29] If Israel hailed Iron Dome, it was because it sought to salvage something redemptive from its otherwise failed operation. Shortly after Pillar of Defense ended, MIT missile-defense expert Theodore Postol voiced

25. Elie Leshem, "Israel Dealt Hamas 'A Heavy Blow' and Is Prepared to Resume Offensive If Need Be, Netanyahu Says," *Times of Israel* (22 November 2012).

26. Inbal Orpaz, "How Does the Iron Dome Work?," *Haaretz* (19 November 2012); Charles Levinson and Adam Entous, "Israel's Iron Dome Battled to Get Off the Ground," *Wall Street Journal* (26 November 2012).

27. Norman G. Finkelstein, "Iron Dome or Swiss Cheese?" (23 November 2012), normanfinkelstein.com/2012/11/23/iron-dome-or-swiss-cheese/; Israel Defense Forces, "2012 Operation Pillar of Defense" (n.d.), idfblog.com/about-the-idf/history-of-the-idf/2012-operation-pillar-of-defense/. "Countless" quoted from this source.

28. mfa.gov.il/MFA/ForeignPolicy/Terrorism/Palestinian/Pages/Operation_Pillar_of_Defense_Nov_2012-IDF_updates.aspx; idfblog.com/blog/2012/11/17/hamas-fajr-5-missiles-uav-targets-damaged/.

29. Dan Williams, "Some Gaza Rockets Stripped of Explosives to Fly Further," *Reuters* (18 November 2012).

TABLE 3 Miracle of Iron Dome?		
	"Rockets" reaching Israel	Civilian casualties
Before Iron Dome (Cast Lead)	617[a]	3
After Iron Dome (Pillar of Defense)	1,350[b]	4

[a] State of Israel, *The Operation in Gaza, 27 December 2008–18 January 2009.*
[b] Israel Defense Forces, "2012 Operation Pillar of Defense."

doubts. "Initially, I drank the Kool-Aid on Iron Dome," he admitted. "I'm skeptical [now]. I suspect it is not working as well as the Israelis are saying." A senior Israeli rocket scientist subsequently rated the claims made for Iron Dome "exaggerated," at best.[30]

The denouement of Pillar of Defense set in as Israel hit up against a tactical cul-de-sac. It had struck all preplanned military targets in Gaza and couldn't resort to sustained terror bombing, yet Hamas, adapting Hezbollah's strategy, kept up its projectile volleys into Israel. The psychological upshot was that Netanyahu wasn't able to declare victory, forcing on him the prospect of a ground invasion to stop the projectile attacks. However, he could avoid heavy combatant losses only if the IDF blasted everyone and everything in (and out of) sight as it cleared a path into Gaza. But in the novel political context of Pillar of Defense—powerful regional actors dead set against an Israeli invasion; the threat of a Goldstone redux; a foreign press corps embedded not in the Israeli troops but among the people of Gaza—Israel recoiled at launching a murderous Cast Lead–style ground assault. The Israeli prime minister was caught between the proverbial rock and a hard place. He couldn't subdue Hamas without a ground invasion, but he couldn't unleash a ground invasion without incurring either a domestically unacceptable cost, that is, too many combatant casualties on the Israeli side, or a diplomatically unacceptable cost, that is, too many civilian casualties on the Palestinian side.[31] It was possible to pinpoint the exact moment when Pillar of Defense collapsed. At a 19 November press conference, Hamas leader Khalid Mishal in effect told

30. Paul Koring, "Success of Israel's Iron Dome Effectiveness Questioned," *Globe and Mail* (29 November 2012); Reuven Pedatzur, "The Fallibility of Iron Dome Missile Defense," *Haaretz* (11 November 2013). See also Chapter 11.

31. Norman G. Finkelstein, "I Still Say, No Invasion" (19 November 2012), normanfinkelstein.com/2012/11/19/norman-finkelstein-i-still-say-no-invasion/.

Netanyahu, *Go ahead, invade!* "If you wanted to launch it," he taunted, "you would have done it."[32] The Israeli prime minister panicked; his bluff had been called. What happened next was a repeat of Israel's 2006 assault on Lebanon. Unable to stop the Hezbollah rocket attacks, yet fearful of a full-blown ground invasion entailing hand-to-hand combat, Israel had called in US secretary of state Condoleezza Rice to negotiate a cease-fire. This time around, US secretary of state Hillary Clinton was hauled in to bail Israel out. Even a 21 November bomb attack on a Tel Aviv bus, injuring 28 civilians—which normally would have triggered a negotiating freeze and massive Israeli retaliation—did not shake Netanyahu from his resolve to end Pillar of Defense posthaste, before Hamas resumed its verbal digs.[33]

The formal terms of the agreement ending Pillar of Defense[34] marked a stunning reversal for Israel. It called for a *mutual* cease-fire, not one, as Israel demanded, unilaterally imposed on Hamas. It also incorporated language implying that the siege of Gaza would be lifted, and notably omitted the precondition that Hamas must terminate its smuggling or manufacture of weapons. The reason why was not hard to find. Under international law, peoples resisting foreign occupation are not debarred from using armed force.[35] Egypt, which brokered the cease-fire, was not about to barter away Hamas's legal prerogative.[36] Israel undoubtedly anticipated that Washington would use its political muscle to extract better cease-fire terms from Cairo. Throughout the attack, the United States had lent Israel unstinting public support.[37] But President Obama, hoping to bring the "new" Egypt under the US's wing, backed away from lording it over the Muslim Brotherhood and

32. Fares Akram, Jodi Rudoren, and Alan Cowell, "Hamas Leader Dares Israel to Invade amid Gaza Airstrikes," *New York Times* (19 November 2012).

33. Harriet Sherwood, "Tel Aviv Bus Bombing Hardens Israeli Public Opinion against Gaza Ceasefire," *Guardian* (21 November 2012); Barak Ravid, "During Gaza Operation, Netanyahu and Obama Finally Learned to Work Together," *Haaretz* (26 November 2012). The bus attack was eventually traced back to a Palestinian citizen of Israel.

34. "Ceasefire Agreement between Israel and Gaza's Palestinians," *Reuters* (21 November 2012).

35. See Chapter 11.

36. In a diplomatic sidenote to Netanyahu, US president Barack Obama vaguely promised to "help Israel address its security needs, especially the issue of smuggling of weapons and explosives into Gaza." Office of the Press Secretary, The White House (21 November 2012).

37. US Department of State, "Gaza Rocket Attacks" (14 November 2012); White House, "Remarks by President Obama and Prime Minister Shinawatra in a Joint Press Conference" (18 November 2012).

"brought all his weight to bear on Israel."[38] If any doubt remained as to who won and who lost the latest round, it was quickly dispelled. Israel launched Pillar of Defense to restore Gaza's fear of it. But after the cease-fire and its terms were announced, Palestinians flooded the streets of Gaza in a celebratory mood as if at a wedding party.[39] In a CNN interview with Christiane Amanpour, Hamas's Mishal cut the figure and exuded the confidence of a world leader.[40] Meanwhile, at the Israeli press conference announcing the cease-fire, the ruling triumvirate—Netanyahu, Barak, and Foreign Minister Avigdor Lieberman—resembled grade-schoolers called down to the principal's office, counting the seconds until the humiliation was over. Loyal Israeli pundits tried to spin Pillar of Defense as a "swift military success," an "impressive success," or—more cautiously—"successful, up to a point,"[41] but only the willfully gullible would swallow it. Still, it could already be safely predicted back then that Israel wouldn't fulfill the terms of the final agreement to lift the siege of Gaza.[42] During Israeli cabinet deliberations on whether or not to accept the cease-fire, Defense Minister Barak cynically dismissed the fine print, scoffing, "A day after the cease-fire, no one will remember what is written in that draft."[43] The distance Egypt and Turkey would be willing to go in support of Gaza was also exaggerated.[44] Many

38. Matthew Kalman and Kim Sengupta, "Fragile Truce Deal Hailed as a Victory on Both Sides," *Independent* (21 November 2012).

39. Crispian Balmer, "Relief at Gaza Ceasefire Can't Mask Its Frailty," *Reuters* (21 November 2012).

40. Christiane Amanpour, "Israel-Hamas Cease-Fire; Interview with Hamas Political Leader Khaled Meshaal," *CNN* (21 November 2012).

41. Anshel Pfeffer, "Winners and Losers of Israel-Hamas Cease-Fire," *Haaretz* (22 November 2012); Ari Shavit, "Operation Rectification," *Haaretz* (22 November 2012); Amos Harel, "Bullet Points from Israel's Home Front," *Haaretz* (30 November 2012).

42. Norman G. Finkelstein, "Israel's Latest Assault on Gaza," *New Left Project* (28 November 2012).

43. Barak Ravid, "Behind the Scenes of Israel's Decision to Accept Gaza Truce," *Haaretz* (22 November 2012).

44. This writer observed back then:

Egypt will probably not pressure the US to enforce the cease-fire terms on Israel. The respective interests of the "new" Egypt and Hamas mostly diverge, not converge. Egypt desperately needs US subventions and is currently negotiating a $5 billion loan from the International Monetary Fund, where Washington's vote is decisive. The popularity of President Mohammed Morsi's Muslim Brotherhood government will ultimately hinge on what it delivers to Egyptians, not Gazans. US political elites are lauding Morsi to high heaven, stroking his ego, and speculating on the "special relationship" he has cultivated with Obama. Those familiar with the psychological manipulations of Washington when it comes to Arab leaders—in particular, mediocre ones, such as Anwar Sadat—will not be surprised

Palestinians inferred from the resounding setback Israel suffered that only armed resistance could and would end the Israeli occupation. In fact, Hamas's resistance operated for the most part only at the level of perceptions—the projectiles heading toward Tel Aviv did unsettle the city's residents. There was precious little evidence, however, that Palestinians could ever muster sufficient military might to compel a full Israeli withdrawal from the occupied territories. But Gaza's steadfastness until the final hour of Operation Pillar of Defense did demonstrate the indomitable *will* of the people of Palestine. If this potential force could be harnessed in a campaign of mass civil resistance, and supporters of Palestinian rights abroad in tandem mobilized international public opinion, then Israel might be coerced into ending the occupation, while fewer Palestinian lives would be lost than in (futile) armed resistance.

---

by the current US romancing of Morsi. It's also improbable that Turkey will exert itself on Hamas's behalf. Right now, Ankara is smarting from Obama's rebuff of designating not itself but Cairo as prime interlocutor in brokering the cease-fire. (Turkey was apparently disqualified because it labeled Israel a "terrorist state" during Pillar of Defense.) Still, aspiring to be the US's preeminent regional partner, and calculating that the road to Washington passes through Tel Aviv, Turkey has resumed negotiations with Israel to break the diplomatic logjam after Israel's lethal assault on the *Mavi Marmara* in 2010. Meanwhile, its recent operation has brought home to Israel that alienating both its historic allies in the region, Egypt and Turkey, is not prudent policy, so a face-saving reconciliation between Ankara and Tel Aviv (the Turkish government is formally demanding an apology, monetary compensation, and an end to the Gaza siege) is probably in the offing. The long and the short of it is that, even in the new era that has opened up, definite limits exist on how much regional support the Palestinians can realistically hope to garner. (Finkelstein, "Israel's Latest Assault")

ELEVEN

Israel Has the Right to Defend Itself

ON 8 JULY 2014, ISRAEL LAUNCHED Operation Protective Edge. It marked the longest and most destructive of Israel's recent attacks on Gaza; indeed, it was "the most devastating round of hostilities in Gaza since the beginning of the Israeli occupation in 1967."[1] Operation Cast Lead (2008–9) lasted 22 days, whereas Protective Edge lasted fully 51 days (it ended on 26 August). Some 350 children were killed and 6,000 homes destroyed during Cast Lead, whereas fully 550 children were killed and 18,000 homes destroyed during Protective Edge. Israel left behind 600,000 tons of rubble in Cast Lead, whereas it left behind 2.5 million tons of rubble in Protective Edge. What's more, Protective Edge "impacted an already paralyzed economy at a time when socioeconomic conditions were at their lowest since 1967. This operation therefore had a more severe impact on socioeconomic conditions compared to the previous two military operations in 2008 and 2012."[2] But in contrast to Cast Lead and the 2006 Lebanon war, Protective Edge was not preplanned long in advance; the decision to attack resulted from contingent factors.[3] Israeli officialdom also thought twice during Protective Edge before making those brazen incriminating statements that got it in legal hot water in the past. On the morrow of Cast Lead, Foreign Minister Tzipi Livni

1. United Nations Country Team in the State of Palestine, *Gaza: Two years after* (2016).

2. United Nations Conference on Trade and Development, "Report on UNCTAD Assistance to the Palestinian People: Developments in the economy of the Occupied Palestinian Territory" (July 2015), paras. 27, 42 (2.5 million tons).

3. Julia Amalia Heyer, "Ex-Israeli Security Chief Diskin: 'All the conditions are there for an explosion,'" *Spiegel Online International* (24 July 2014). On the preplanning for Cast Lead, see Chapter 2; on Lebanon in 2006, see Benjamin S. Lambeth, *Air Operations in Israel's War against Hezbollah: Learning from Lebanon and getting it right in Gaza* (Arlington, VA: 2011), p. 97.

publicly bragged about the criminal orders she issued, but she then found herself the target of criminal prosecution.[4] Sobered by this brush with the law, Livni sang a different tune as minister of justice after Protective Edge: "When the fire stops, the legal fire directed at Israel, its leaders, its soldiers, and its commanders will begin. I . . . intend to stand at the frontlines in this battle . . . and will give each soldier and each commander in the IDF [Israel Defense Forces] a legal bulletproof vest."[5] Still, many of Israel's tactics—provocations, massive force—conformed to a decades-old pattern. Protective Edge also ended on a familiar note: Israel was unable to claim decisive military victory, while Hamas was unable to extract concrete political gain.

Protective Edge traced back to yet another reckless display of Hamas pragmatism. At the end of April 2014, the Islamic movement and its secular Palestinian rival Fatah formed a "consensus government." The United States and the European Union did not suspend engagement but instead "cautiously welcomed" the Palestinian initiative, adopting a wait-and-see approach.[6] It was evidently payback time, as Israel had aborted the 2013–14 peace initiative of US secretary of state John Kerry.[7] If only through a back door, Hamas had won unprecedented legitimacy, but it also made an unprecedented concession. The United States and the European Union had long predicated diplomatic engagement with Palestinian leaders on a trio of preconditions: recognition of Israel, renunciation of violence, and recognition of past agreements.[8] Hamas did not object when Palestinian president Mahmoud Abbas, speaking on behalf of the new unity government, reiterated his support for the preconditions. As these developments unfolded, Israeli prime minister Benjamin Netanyahu erupted in a rage.[9] The prospect of "Palestinian unity" was a "red line" for Netanyahu (and Israeli leaders

---

4. See Chapter 3 and Chapter 5.

5. B'Tselem (Israeli Information Center for Human Rights in the Occupied Territories), *Whitewash Protocol: The so-called investigation of Operation Protective Edge* (2016), pp. 4–5.

6. Peter Beaumont, "Palestinian Unity Government of Fatah and Hamas Sworn In," *Guardian* (2 June 2014); "Why Hamas Fires Those Rockets," *Economist* (19 July 2014).

7. Nahum Barnea, "Inside the Talks' Failure: US officials open up," *ynetnews.com* (2 May 2014).

8. See Chapter 1.

9. Jack Khoury, "Abbas: Palestinian unity government will recognize Israel, condemn terrorism," *Haaretz* (26 April 2014); Jeffrey Heller, "Netanyahu Urges World Not to Recognize Palestinian Unity Government," *Reuters* (1 June 2014); Arab Center for Research and Policy Studies, "The US Stance on the Palestinian Unity Government" (Doha: 19 June 2014).

in general), so he reflexively sought to sabotage it.[10] In the event that the Palestinian consensus held, he could no longer invoke standard Israeli alibis—Abbas represented only one Palestinian faction; Hamas was a terrorist organization bent on Israel's destruction—to evade a settlement of the conflict.[11] The prime minister's ire was yet more aroused as the United States and the European Union had already ignored his premonition that Iran was intending to visit a "second Holocaust" on Israel. Instead, they had entered into diplomatic talks with Tehran to obtain an agreement on its nuclear weapons program.

In June 2014, a gift dropped into Netanyahu's lap. A rogue Hamas cell abducted and killed three Israeli teenagers in the West Bank. Netanyahu was aware early on that the teenagers had been killed (not captured for a future prisoner swap) and that Hamas's leadership wasn't responsible.[12] "The government had known almost from the beginning that the boys were dead," J. J. Goldberg, the former editor in chief of the (Jewish) *Forward,* observed. "There was no doubt."[13] But never one to pass up an exploitable moment, Netanyahu parlayed this macabre "boon"[14] to break up the Palestinian unity government. Feigning a rescue mission, Israel launched Operation Brother's Keeper in mid-June. At least five West Bank Palestinians were killed, homes were demolished and businesses ransacked, and seven hundred Palestinians, mostly Hamas members, were arrested, including many who had been released in a 2011 prisoner exchange.[15] The rampage was patently tailored to elicit a violent response from Hamas, so as to "prove" it was a terrorist organization. Netanyahu could then, and in fact later did, rebuke Washington to

10. The imminence of a Palestinian unity government in 2006 precipitated the identical Israeli response. Jean-Pierre Filiu, *Gaza: A history* (New York: 2014), p. 295.

11. Idan Landau, "The Unfolding Lie of Operation Protective Edge," *+972* (15 July 2014); Avi Issacharoff, "PM: Palestinian unity government would kill off the peace process," *Haaretz* (18 March 2011).

12. Amos Harel and Yaniv Kubovich, "Revealed: Behind the scenes on the hunt to find kidnapped teens," *Haaretz* (1 July 2014); Katie Zavadski, "It Turns Out Hamas May Not Have Kidnapped and Killed the 3 Israeli Teens After All," *New York* (25 July 2014); "Hamas: We wouldn't target civilians if we had better weapons," *Haaretz* (23 August 2014); Amos Harel, "Notes from an Interrogation: How the Shin Beth gets the lowdown on terror," *Haaretz* (2 September 2014).

13. J.J. Goldberg, "How Politics and Lies Triggered an Unintended War in Gaza," *Forward* (10 July 2014).

14. Landau, "Unfolding Lie."

15. Human Rights Watch, "Serious Violations in West Bank Operations" (3 July 2014).

"never second-guess me again."[16] Hamas at first resisted the Israeli provocations, although other Gaza factions did fire projectiles. But in the ensuing tit-for-tat, Hamas entered the fray and the violence spun out of control.[17]

Once hostilities broke out, Israel faced a now familiar dilemma. Short-range projectiles of the kind Hamas[18] possessed couldn't be disabled from the air; they had to be taken out at ground level. But a ground invasion would cost Netanyahu either too much domestically, if many Israeli soldiers were killed fighting Hamas street by street, or too much internationally, if Israeli soldiers immunized themselves from attack by indiscriminately targeting the civilian population and infrastructure as they advanced.[19] Unable to carve out a safe path through the thicket of political unknowns, Netanyahu initially held back from launching a ground invasion. But then two more gifts dropped into his lap. *First,* former British prime minister Tony Blair apparently contrived, while Egyptian strongman Abdel Fattah el-Sisi[20] formally presented, a cease-fire deal (on 14 July), according to which Hamas would stop firing projectiles into Israel and Israel would ease the blockade of Gaza when "the security situation stabilizes."[21] The prior cease-fire agreements Hamas had entered into with Israel did not contain such a "security" caveat.[22] Insofar as Israel designated Hamas a terrorist organization, the security situation in Gaza could stabilize only when Hamas either was defeated or disarmed itself, in the absence of which the siege would continue. It surely didn't come as a shock when Hamas rejected these cease-fire terms. Whereas el-Sisi's proposal did not bring a halt to armed hostilities, it did hand Israel a credible pretext for a brutal ground invasion. What choice did it have (Israel could protest) in the

16. "Netanyahu to US: 'Don't ever second-guess me again,'" *ynetnews.com* (2 August 2014).

17. Christa Case Bryant, "Ending Détente, Hamas Takes Responsibility for Today's Spike in Rocket Fire," *Christian Science Monitor* (7 July 2014); David C. Hendrickson, "The Thrasybulus Syndrome," *National Interest* (29 July 2014); Nathan Thrall, "Hamas's Chances," *London Review of Books* (21 August 2014); Assaf Sharon, "Failure in Gaza," *New York Review of Books* (25 September 2014).

18. Here as elsewhere, *Hamas* is used as shorthand for all Palestinian armed groups in Gaza when referring to Palestinian military actions and capabilities.

19. See Chapter 10.

20. In July 2013, el-Sisi had replaced Egypt's democratically elected government led by the Muslim Brotherhood in a bloody coup.

21. "The Full Text of the Egyptian Ceasefire Proposal," *Haaretz* (15 July 2014); Barak Ravid, "Secret Call between Netanyahu, al-Sissi Led to Abortive Cease-fire," *Haaretz* (16 July 2014).

22. "Israel and Hamas Ceasefire Begins," *BBC* (19 June 2008); "Ceasefire Agreement between Israel and Gaza's Palestinians," *Reuters* (21 November 2012).

face of Hamas's intransigence? *Second,* on 17 July, a Malaysian airliner flying over Ukraine was downed.[23] The politically charged incident instantly displaced Gaza as the headline news story. Ever the consummate and cynical politician, Netanyahu seized on this golden opportunity. Shortly after the Tiananmen Square massacre in 1989, Netanyahu reportedly declared that Israel had committed a major blunder when it didn't expel "five, 50 or 500" Palestinian "inciters" of the first intifada while the media was riveted on China.[24] The downed Malaysian airliner was Netanyahu's "Tiananmen moment." Freed up by the diversion to unleash a no-holds-barred attack, Netanyahu launched the ground invasion hours later, on the night of that very day.[25] The new regional constellation, as the Arab Spring degenerated into the Arab Winter, further emboldened him. Hamas was left out in the cold, without any states willing to go to bat for it and many rooting for its defeat. Fate had lined up Netanyahu's ducks: the perfect pretext, the perfect decoy, the perfect alignment of earthly bodies politic. He could finally settle scores with Hamas and, incidentally, exact sweet revenge for the humiliation he suffered in Operation Pillar of Defense (2012).[26]

As ground troops crossed into the Strip, Israel let loose with abandon its explosive arsenal. Gaza's civilian population and infrastructure—homes and businesses, schools and mosques, hospitals and ambulances, power stations and sewage plants, civilian shelters and civilians fleeing in panic—came under relentless, indiscriminate, disproportionate, and deliberate attack. Israel reportedly fired 20,000 high-explosive artillery shells, 14,500 tank shells, 6,000 missiles, and 3,500 naval shells into the enclave.[27] This breakdown

---

23. Sabrina Tavernise, Eric Schmitt, and Rick Gladstone, "Jetliner Explodes over Ukraine; Struck by Missile, Officials Say," *New York Times* (17 July 2014).

24. Menachem Shalev, "Netanyahu Recommends Large-Scale Expulsions," *Jerusalem Post* (19 November 1989). The first intifada began in 1987 and was still going strong in 1989.

25. In a retrospective one year after Protective Edge, *Haaretz* observed that one of the "external factors" operating in Israel's favor during Protective Edge was "the July 17 downing of Malaysian Airlines Flight 17." Chemi Shalev, "Israel's Deceptive Diplomatic Success," *Haaretz* (n.d.). For a rigorous study demonstrating that "Israeli authorities may choose the timing of their attacks strategically to minimize negative international publicity," see Ruben Durante and Ekaterina Zuravskaya, "Attack When the World Is Not Watching? International media and the Israeli-Palestinian conflict," *Becker Friedman Institute for Research in Economics* (2015).

26. See Chapter 10.

27. United Nations Office for the Coordination of Humanitarian Affairs (OCHA), *Humanitarian Bulletin—Monthly Report* (June–August 2014); "Taking Stock," *BaYabasha* (Ground Forces Journal) (October 2014), p. 47 (Hebrew).

did not yet include bomb tonnage—*over 100 one-ton bombs were dropped on the Shuja'iya neighborhood alone.* More than 1,500 Gazan civilians were killed during Protective Edge. (In Israel, six civilians were killed.)[28] In a 2014 global ranking of the number of civilian casualties resulting from explosive weapons, tiny Gaza placed third—below Iraq and Syria, but ahead of Afghanistan, Pakistan, and Ukraine.[29] Large swaths of Gaza were reduced to rubble; Gaza's economy "effectively collapsed," while recovery was "expected to take decades."[30] The overwhelming violent force Israel unleashed was designed to limit IDF combat casualties by blasting everything and everyone within sight of the invading army, and to subvert Gaza's will to resist by terrorizing the civilian population and pulverizing the civilian infrastructure. But it also indexed the sadism and brutalized indifference permeating the ranks of the IDF. The Goldstone Report had concluded that the Israeli objective in Cast Lead was to "punish, humiliate and terrorize a civilian population."[31] Protective Edge was a repeat Israeli performance but on a vastly greater scale. Peter Maurer, president of the International Committee of the Red Cross, observed after touring the ravaged Strip, "I've never seen such massive destruction ever before," while the UN special coordinator for the Middle East peace process observed, "No human being who visits can remain untouched by the terrible devastation that one sees."[32] It was a "wild war of revenge," *Haaretz* journalist Zvi Bar'el recalled, that "turned the entire Gaza population into an 'infrastructure' to be destroyed."[33] "In the 30 years that I have spent researching and writing about Gaza and her people," Sara Roy of Harvard University reflected after Protective Edge, "I can say without hesitation that I have never seen the kind of human, physical, and psychological destruction that I see there today."[34] Even UN secretary-general Ban

28. See Chapter 12 for sources.

29. Action on Armed Violence (AOAV), *Explosive States: Monitoring explosive violence in 2014* (2015). The ranking was based on Gazan casualties throughout 2014, not just during Protective Edge.

30. Sara Roy, *The Gaza Strip: The political economy of de-development,* expanded third edition (Washington, DC: 2016), p. 401 ("expected to take" quoted from United Nations special coordinator for the Middle East peace process).

31. See Chapter 5.

32. Sudarsan Raghavan, "Month-Long War in Gaza Has Left a Humanitarian and Environmental Crisis," *Washington Post* (9 August 2014); "Arriving for Talks in Gaza, New UN Envoy Urges Palestinian Unity, End to Israeli Blockade," *UN News Centre* (30 April 2015).

33. Zvi Bar'el, "Israeli Security Assessments Are Reality Built on a Lie," *Haaretz* (19 April 2016).

34. Roy, *Gaza Strip,* p. 395.

Ki-moon, who habitually took his cues from Washington, was moved (or felt compelled) to tell the UN General Assembly during the operation, "The massive death and destruction in Gaza have shocked and shamed the world," while a few months later he told a press conference after visiting Gaza, "The destruction I have seen coming here is beyond description."[35] Meanwhile, the consensus opinion inside Israel was that Protective Edge constituted a "limited military operation."[36]

To extenuate Gaza's civilian death toll, Israel, per usual, accused Hamas of using civilians as "human shields."[37] But reputable human rights organizations and journalists, per usual, found no evidence to sustain Israel's allegation.[38] In a comprehensive defense of its conduct during Protective Edge, Israel professed that the "IDF sought to achieve the goals set by the Government of Israel while adhering to the Law of Armed Conflict—and in certain respects, the IDF went beyond its legal obligations."[39] As if reading from the official Israeli script, an international High Level Military Group—sponsored and selected by the "Friends of Israel Initiative," and including perennial Israel pom-pom Colonel Richard Kemp—proclaimed, "The IDF not only met its obligations under the Law of Armed Conflict, but often exceeded them." Indeed, it purported that the "IDF showed significant restraint," and that a "life-preserving ethos . . . is propagated throughout its ranks." It even went so far as to "express strong concerns that the actions and practices of the IDF to prevent collateral damage were so extensive . . . that they would curtail the effectiveness of our own militaries, were they to become constraining norms of warfare enacted in customary law."[40] The

35. Raghavan, "Month-Long War"; Peter Beaumont and Hazem Balousha, "Ban Ki-moon: Gaza is a source of shame to the international community," *Guardian* (14 October 2014).

36. Meron Rapoport, "The Coup against Israel's Army," *Middle East Eye* (21 May 2016).

37. State of Israel, *The 2014 Gaza Conflict, 7 July–26 August 2014: Factual and legal aspects* (2015), paras. 161–65.

38. Amnesty International, *Israel/Gaza Conflict: Questions and answers* (25 July 2014); "Jeremy Bowen's Gaza Notebook: 'I saw no evidence of Hamas using Palestinians as human shields,'" *New Statesman* (25 July 2014); Kim Sengupta, "The Myth of Hamas's Human Shields," *Independent* (21 July 2014). For Hamas's alleged "human shielding" in Operation Cast Lead, see Chapter 4; for Protective Edge, see also Chapter 12 and Chapter 13.

39. State of Israel, *2014 Gaza Conflict*, para. 15.

40. High Level Military Group, *An Assessment of the 2014 Gaza Conflict* (2015), paras. 7, 59, 119, 216, 207 (see also paras. 12, 24, 30, 54, 63, 103, 113, 169, 180, 205). The group described itself as "top-level practitioners from democratic nations whose expertise covers the entire

credibility of these attestations, however, crashed up against the testimonies of Israeli soldiers who actually saw combat during Protective Edge. In contrast, the "assessment" of the High Level Military Group largely consisted of a stenographic transcription of what senior Israeli officials told it. The IDF eyewitness accounts were compiled by Breaking the Silence, an Israeli nongovernmental organization comprising former Israeli soldiers. None of the hundreds of testimonies collected by this organization over more than a decade has ever been proven false, and all of them were approved for publication by the IDF censor. The politics of Breaking the Silence were not aberrantly leftist (it did not support the Boycott, Divestment and Sanctions movement, and opposed criminal prosecution of Israeli officers), while most of the soldier-witnesses did not even appear contrite.[41] The criminal dimensions of Protective Edge could be gleaned from these IDF eyewitness accounts (see Table 4). Although Israel flinches at juxtapositions of its own conduct with that of the Nazis, one of the Breaking the Silence testimonies (no. 83) breached this taboo: "There's that famous photo that they always show on trips to Poland [in which Israeli youths visit Holocaust memorial sites] that shows Warsaw before the war and Warsaw after the Second World War. The photo shows the heart of Warsaw and it's this classy European city, and then they show it at the end of the war. They show the exact same neighborhood, only it has just one house left standing, and the rest is just ruins. That's what it looked like." To avoid mind-numbing redundancy, Table 4 omits the succession of combatants who testified that the IDF's modus operandi during the operation was *shoot to kill anything that moves,* often on explicit orders but also because it was "cool."[42] If the High Level Military Group peremptorily dismissed all these combatant testimonies, it was because "senior [Israeli] commanders as well as those leading the fight on the ground" contradicted

gamut of the conduct of warfare, its strategic, tactical, operational and legal frameworks" (paras. 1, 201). Kemp alleged that if the High Level Military Group's findings were "the diametric opposite of those of the UN Human Rights Council, human rights groups," it was because these groups "analyze the situation based on human rights law, not the laws of armed conflict." The most charitable thing one can say is that Kemp didn't read a single word in any of these critical reports, which of course based their analyses overwhelmingly on the laws of armed conflict. Richard Kemp, "We Put Our Reputations on the Line: This is why," *Jewish Chronicle* (16 December 2015). For Kemp, see Chapter 4 and Chapter 5.

41. Haggai Matar, "Why Do So Many Israelis Hate Breaking the Silence?," *+972* (14 December 2015).

42. Curious readers should consult numbered testimonies 2, 3, 16, 17, 22, 24, 28, 40, 51, 52, 55, 56, 63, 75, 81 (reference at Table 4).

TABLE 4 How Israel Fought Operation Protective Edge: A Selection of
IDF Testimonies

18[a]	When we left after the operation, it was just a barren stretch of desert.... We spoke about it a lot amongst ourselves, the guys from the company, how crazy the amount of damage we did there was. I quote: "Listen man, it's crazy what went on in there," "Listen man, we really messed them up," "Fuck, check it out, there's nothing at all left ..., it's nothing but desert now, that's crazy."
21	I remember that the level of destruction looked insane to me.
22	We entered Gaza ... with an insane amount of firepower.
25	It all looked like a science fiction movie ... serious levels of destruction everywhere.... [E]verything was really in ruins. And non-stop fire all the time.
30	Before the entrance on foot [to the Gaza Strip], a crazy amount of artillery was fired at the entire area.... Before a tank makes any movement it fires, every time. Those guys were trigger happy, totally crazy.[b]
31	The explosions' effects cause major amounts of damage, but that doesn't interest anyone. "Use it, use it, explosives can't be taken back," the platoon commander says, "I don't want to leave explosives with me."
36	Our view was of the center of the Strip. Let's say it was a real fireworks display. From a distance it looked pretty cool.... If you looked through a night vision scope you saw crazy wreckage, it was a real trip.
38	[Y]ou're shooting at anything that moves—and also at what isn't moving, crazy amounts.... [I]t also becomes a bit like a computer game, totally cool and real.
49	It was total destruction in there—the photos on line are child's play compared to what we saw there in reality.... I never saw anything like it.
70	[T]he unfathomable number of dead on one of the sides, the unimaginable level of destruction, the way militant cells and people were regarded as targets and not as living beings—that's something that troubles me.
74	[I]t's destruction on a whole other level.
94	The air force carries out an insane amount of strikes in the Gaza Strip during an operation like "Protective Edge."
96	[S]hells are being fired all the time. Even if we aren't actually going to enter: shells, shells, shells.... What happens is, for seven straight days it's non-stop bombardment, that's what happens in practice.

SOURCE: Breaking the Silence, *This Is How We Fought in Gaza: Soldiers' testimonies and photographs from Operation "Protective Edge"* (2014).

[a] Testimonies are numbered in the collection.

[b] The official Israeli postmortem on Protective Edge stated that "artillery was used in a restrained and calculated fashion, after taking various technical and doctrinal precautions intended to minimize potential civilian harm and optimize the fire's accuracy" (State of Israel, *2014 Gaza Conflict*, para. 357), while the High Level Military Group stated that "the vast majority of artillery fire during the ground operation was fired into open areas in Gaza with no civilian presence.... The IDF further employs a number of technical and operational means to ensure the accuracy of its artillery" (*Assessment*, para. 117).

them.[43] Who could quarrel with such disinterested authority? The last testimony (no. 111) in the Breaking the Silence collection provided insight into the society that nurtured "the most moral army in the world." "You leave the [Gaza Strip] and the most obvious question is, 'Did you kill anybody?,'" an IDF infantry sergeant rued. "Even if you meet the most left-wing girl in the world, eventually she'll start thinking, 'Did you ever kill somebody, or not?' And what can you do about it? Most people in our society consider that to be a badge of honor. So everyone wants to come out of there with that feeling of satisfaction."

Israel fared both better and worse than it could have predicted going into the operation. On one side of the ledger, despite the murder and mayhem that Israel was daily inflicting on Gaza, the White House signaled it the green light to proceed. Human rights organizations reported from fairly early on that Israel was probably targeting or firing indiscriminately at civilians and civilian infrastructure.[44] But notwithstanding some behind-the-scenes friction,[45] the United States did not publicly pressure Israel to desist. On the contrary, President Barack Obama or his spokespersons dutifully invoked Israel's "right to self-defense," while turning a blind eye to IDF atrocities and a deaf ear to Gaza's wails.[46] The inescapable fact was that Obama did not just facilitate this latest Israeli massacre in Gaza; he was its enabler in chief. It might be wondered why he supported the assault if he had earlier supported negotiations with the Hamas-Fatah unity government. The simple answer was that once Hamas projectiles started flying over Israel, and Israel's domestic lobby lined up wall-to-wall congressional support,[47] it would have required spine, which Obama conspicu-

43. High Level Military Group, *Assessment,* para. 115.

44. Amnesty International, "UN Must Impose Arms Embargo and Mandate an International Investigation as Civilian Death Toll Rises" (11 July 2014); Human Rights Watch, "Gaza: Airstrike deaths raise concerns on ground offensive" (22 July 2014). To be sure, Human Rights Watch (HRW) was ultracautious in its criticism of Israel at the inception of Protective Edge; see "Indiscriminate Palestinian Rocket Attacks" (9 July 2014). For HRW's equivocating record on Israel, see Norman G. Finkelstein, *Knowing Too Much: Why the American Jewish romance with Israel is coming to an end* (New York: 2012), pp. 123–54.

45. Marissa Newman, "Israeli Official Confirms US Nixed Arms Shipment," *Times of Israel* (14 August 2014).

46. Gareth Porter, "US Avoided Threat to Act on Israel's Civilian Targeting," *Inter Press Service* (12 August 2014).

47. Ramsey Cox, "Senate Passes Resolution in Support of Israel," *The Hill* (17 July 2014); Connie Bruck, "Friends of Israel," *New Yorker* (1 September 2014).

ously lacked, to defy it. Still, did realpolitik compel him to reaffirm Israel's "right to defend itself" day in and day out, even as human rights organizations documented Israeli atrocities? In addition, Israel hugely profited and Gaza hugely lost from a dramatic regional reconfiguration. Both Egypt and Saudi Arabia openly longed for Hamas's eviction from power,[48] while the Arab League—in its sole meeting on Gaza—backed el-Sisi's cynical cease-fire ultimatum.[49] Only Iran, Turkey, and Qatar among Middle Eastern powers opposed the Israeli onslaught. If Israel showed relative restraint during Operation Pillar of Defense, this was because of the red lines drawn by Egypt and Turkey in support of Hamas.[50] But after the July 2013 coup, Egypt turned on Hamas with a vengeance, while Turkey was preoccupied with and bogged down in Syria. Convulsed by its own internal conflicts and humanitarian crises, the so-called street across large swaths of the Arab world fell mute during Protective Edge. Arab despots accordingly paid no domestic price for egging on Israel. Meanwhile, the European Union also gave Israel a free pass as it dreaded "militant Islam," which was spreading like wildfire under the ISIS banner, and to which Hamas was reflexively assimilated. The redemptive global exception was the Latin American bloc. In an exemplary display of selfless solidarity with beleaguered Gaza, the governments of Argentina, Bolivia, Brazil, Chile, El Salvador, Peru, Uruguay, and Venezuela registered disgust at Israeli actions.[51] Nonetheless, amid the slaughter, Gaza was effectively on its own, alone and abandoned.

On the opposite side of the ledger, Israel was taken off guard by the robust and ramified network of tunnels that Hamas had constructed. Adopting and adapting Hezbollah's strategy during the 2006 Lebanon war, Hamas used projectiles to lure Israel into a ground invasion. It then emerged from tunnels that withstood Israeli aerial bombardment and inflicted an exceptional number of combatant casualties.[52] Only ten Israeli soldiers had been killed

48. David Hearst, "Saudi Crocodile Tears over Gaza," *Huffington Post* (28 July 2014).
49. "Arab League Urges 'All Parties' to Back Egypt's Gaza Truce Plan," *Arab News* (15 July 2014).
50. See Chapter 10.
51. Robert Kozak, "Israel Faces Latin American Backlash," *Wall Street Journal* (30 July 2014).
52. High Level Military Group, *Assessment,* para. 110; Nahum Barnea, "Tumbling into Gaza, and Climbing Out Again," *ynetnews.com* (29 July 2014); Nidal al-Mughrabi, "Hamas Fighters Show Defiance in Gaza Tunnel Tour," *Reuters* (19 August 2014); Gili Cohen, "Tunnel Vision on Gazan Border," *Haaretz* (17 July 2014); Mark Perry, "Why Israel's Bombardment of Gaza's Neighborhood Left US Officers 'Stunned,'" *Al Jazeera America* (27 August 2014); Amos Harel, "Israel and Hamas Are in an Underground Race in Gaza,"

in Cast Lead, four by "friendly fire"; many Israeli soldiers had testified to not having even seen a Hamas fighter.[53] This time around, however, fully 62 Israeli soldiers were killed by militants.[54] In the face of this surprisingly stiff resistance, the IDF marked time once having crossed into Gaza, not venturing more than two to three kilometers beyond the border.[55] As it launched the ground invasion, Israel abruptly recalibrated its mission from destroying Hamas's "rockets" to destroying Hamas's cross-border "terror tunnels." Yet, of the 32 tunnels Israel reportedly discovered and detonated, only 12–14 actually passed under the border.[56] It was cause for perplexity why Israel couldn't have sealed them from its side, just as Egypt after the July 2013 coup sealed some 1,500 commercial tunnels passing from Gaza into the Sinai. Later, when Egypt flooded the still extant tunnels (allegedly to preempt weapons smuggling), Israeli energy minister Yuval Steinitz praised it as a "good solution."[57] Why was it a "good solution" for Egypt but not a "good solution" for Israel? Perhaps Israel couldn't on technical grounds duplicate Egypt's modus operandi. Still, the question was not even posed why Israel was ravaging Gaza to eliminate "terror tunnels" if it seemingly had less destructive options at hand. Once the IDF breached Gaza's border and met fierce resistance, it sought to destroy the tunnel network *inside* Gaza, so that Hamas couldn't inflict heavy casualties when Israel next set out to "mow the lawn." If Israel asserted a "right" to destroy the tunnels—a prerogative endorsed by much of official public opinion around the world—it was declaring that Gaza had no right to defend itself against Israel's periodic massacres. Even were it true that Israel sought to destroy only the cross-border tunnels, it would still be hard to figure out why this was a legitimate preemptive goal. Inveterate Israel propagandist Colonel Richard Kemp compared these tunnels to no less than Auschwitz: "The purpose of both of those things was to kill Jews."[58]

Haaretz (31 January 2016); Shlomi Eldar, "Is Hamas on the Offensive or Defensive?," *Al-Monitor* (18 April 2016).

53. See Chapter 3 and Chapter 4.

54. Three other Israeli soldiers were killed by friendly fire and a fourth was killed in an operational accident.

55. Amos Harel, "Using Gaza Lessons to Prepare for Next Hezbollah War," *Haaretz* (7 August 2014).

56. Amos Harel, "Gaza War Taught Israel Time to Rethink Strategies," *Haaretz* (5 August 2014).

57. "Egypt Flooded Gaza's Tunnels at Israel's Request," *Agence France-Presse* (8 February 2016).

58. "Kemp: Hamas tunnels like Auschwitz," *Australian Jewish News* (16 March 2015).

Samantha Power, US representative at the United Nations, scolded the Security Council for "saying nothing of the resources diverted from helping Gaza's residents to dig tunnels into Israeli territory so that terrorists can attack Israelis in their homes."[59] But these cross-border catacombs were *only used to conduct attacks directed at IDF positions in Israel in the vicinity of the Green Line, which are legitimate military targets.*[60] Do the laws of war prescribe that planes, artillery shells, and tanks get to breach Gaza's border at Israel's will and whim, but Hamas tunnels targeting combatants must not transgress Israel's sacred space?

Israel misrepresented not only the threat posed by Hamas "terror tunnels." It also inflated the performance of its antimissile defense system and the threat posed by Hamas "rockets." Hamas reportedly fired five thousand rockets and two thousand mortar shells at Israel during the operation.[61] To reconcile the vast discrepancy between the many thousands of projectiles Hamas unleashed, on the one hand, and the minimal death and destruction they inflicted, on the other, Israel motioned to its wondrous Iron Dome antimissile defense system. A leading Israeli military correspondent posited that were it not for Iron Dome, "the Israeli casualty count would have been infinitely higher," while an Israeli diplomat purported that Iron Dome "prevented thousands of potential Israeli civilian casualties."[62] But this explanation does not persuade. Whereas Israel alleged that Iron Dome intercepted 740 rockets, the UN Department of Safety and Security put the number at closer to 240.[63] However, the most skeptical reckoning came from one of the

59. "US Ambassador to the UN Samantha Power's Full Speech at the Security Council," *Haaretz* (24 December 2016). The ever-righteous Power also condemned the Security Council for failing to "muster the will to adopt the simplest of resolutions calling for a seven-day pause in the savage bombardment of innocent civilians, hospitals, and schools in Aleppo," even as she and the Obama administration had blocked any UN action against Israel's savage bombardment of innocent civilians, hospitals, and schools in Gaza.

60. UN Human Rights Council, *Report of the Detailed Findings of the Independent Commission of Inquiry Established Pursuant to Human Rights Council Resolution S-21/1* (2015), para. 108, emphasis added.

61. UN Department of Safety and Security (UNDSS), cited in *Addendum to Report of the United Nations High Commissioner for Human Rights* (A/HRC/28/80/Add.1) (26 December 2014), p. 8.

62. Hirsh Goodman, "Israel's Narrative—An Overview," and Alan Baker, "The Limits of the Diplomatic Arena," in Hirsh Goodman and Dore Gold, eds., *The Gaza War: The war Israel did not want and the disaster it averted* (2015), pp. 12, 70.

63. UN Office for the Coordination of Humanitarian Affairs, *Humanitarian Bulletin* (June–August 2014), p. 19.

world's leading authorities on antimissile defense, Theodore Postol of MIT.[64] (Postol had previously debunked claims hyping the Patriot antimissile defense system in the 1991 Gulf War.[65]) He concluded that Iron Dome successfully intercepted 5 percent of incoming Hamas rockets, or, on the basis of Israel's raw data, an underwhelming 40 of them.[66] Even accepting, for argument's sake, the official Israeli tally of 740 successful interceptions, it still perplexed why the thousands of Hamas projectiles that Iron Dome did not intercept caused so little damage. Indeed, even before Israel first deployed Iron Dome (during Pillar of Defense in 2012), the material consequences of Hamas projectiles barely registered. Consider these figures. Whereas Hamas fired some 13,000 rockets and mortar shells at Israel between 2001 and 2012, a total of 23 Israeli civilians were killed, or one civilian killed per 500 projectiles fired.[67] In the course of Cast Lead, Israel's most violent confrontation with Gaza prior to Protective Edge and before Iron Dome was deployed, Hamas fired some 900 projectiles, yet a total of only 3 civilians were killed.[68] Even during Protective Edge, fully 2,800 Hamas projectiles, or 40 percent of the total number, landed in Israel's border region[69] where Iron Dome was not deployed, yet only one Israeli civilian was killed by a rocket.[70] (Most Israelis in the border region "remained in their home communities" during the

64. Theodore Postol, "The Evidence That Shows Iron Dome Is Not Working," *Bulletin of the Atomic Scientists* (19 July 2014); "Iron Dome or Iron Sieve?," *Democracy Now!* (31 July 2014), democracynow.org/2014/7/31/iron_dome_or_iron_sieve_evidence, democracynow .org/blog/2014/7/31/part_two_theodore_postol_asks_is.

65. Theodore A. Postol, "Lessons of the Gulf War Patriot Experience," *International Security* (Winter 1991/92).

66. Israel alleged that Iron Dome intercepted 740, or 90 percent of, incoming Hamas rockets in populated areas where it was deployed, which would put the total number of incoming rockets in these areas at 820. Yoav Zitun, "Iron Dome: IDF intercepted 90 percent of rockets," *ynetnews.com* (15 August 2014).

67. State of Israel, *2014 Gaza Conflict,* paras. 44, 51, p. 58n174; B'Tselem (Israeli Information Center for Human Rights in the Occupied Territories), *Attacks on Israeli Civilians by Palestinians,* btselem.org/topic/israeli_civilians. The first Hamas rocket attack to cause Israeli civilian casualties didn't occur until 2004, "after so many rockets that had caused only material damage or slight wounds." Filiu, *Gaza,* p. 274.

68. 617 were rockets (see Chapter 10).

69. State of Israel, *2014 Gaza Conflict,* para. 114, p. 122n361. It stated that "more than 60 percent" of Hamas projectiles landed in the border areas, but it put the total number of Hamas projectiles fired during Protective Edge at 4,000 (ibid., paras. 103, 112), whereas the more reliable UNDSS figure was 7,000.

70. The other five civilian deaths in Israel resulted from mortar shells. State of Israel, *2014 Gaza Conflict,* pp. 112–13nn328–32.

operation,[71] and most of the Hamas projectiles struck "built up areas" there.[72]) Postol ascribed the fewness of Israeli civilian casualties in Protective Edge primarily (but not exclusively) to Israel's early warning/shelter system,[73] which had been significantly upgraded in recent years.[74] But that still couldn't fully account for the fewness of civilian casualties before Israel overhauled its civil defense system. What's yet more telling, it couldn't account for the minimal Israeli property damage during Protective Edge. The Israel Ministry of Foreign Affairs website tracked on a daily basis the damage caused by Hamas rockets to civilian infrastructure.[75] Table 5 summarizes its entries. The official Israeli postmortem on Protective Edge alleged that "several residential communities on the border with the Gaza Strip ... were battered by rocket and mortar fire."[76] Yet, even allowing that a certain percentage landed in open areas, how could the thousands upon thousands of Hamas rockets have inflicted so little damage? How could only one Israeli house have been destroyed and 11 others hit or damaged by a mega barrage of rockets?[77] The obvious and most plausible answer was that the preponderance of these so-called rockets amounted to enhanced fireworks or "bottle rockets."[78]

The triad of media takeaways from Protective Edge—"Hamas rockets," "terror tunnels," and "Iron Dome"—in actuality constituted meta-props in Israel's *hasbara* (propaganda) campaign. Israel initially inflated the threat posed by Hamas's projectiles to justify its "insane" and "crazy" assault on Gaza's civilian population and infrastructure. However, the pretext backfired as the

---

71. Ibid., para. 210.

72. *Report of the Detailed Findings of the Independent Commission of Inquiry Established Pursuant to Human Rights Council Resolution S-21/1* (22 June 2015), para. 90.

73. The circumstantial evidence lent credence to Postol's contention. Although Hamas rocket attacks killed only one civilian in two of the Israeli border regions unprotected by Iron Dome, mortar shells killed four others. The differential result was perhaps due to the fact that Israel's warning system provided a lead time, to those seeking shelter, of 15 seconds in the case of a rocket but only 3–5 seconds in the case of a mortar attack. Postol also mentioned the modest size of Hamas rocket warheads as a factor.

74. State of Israel, *2014 Gaza Conflict,* para. 183, p. 111n327; Itay Hod, "The Israeli App Red Alert Saves Lives," *Daily Beast* (14 July 2014).

75. mfa.gov.il/MFA/ForeignPolicy/Terrorism/Pages/Israel-under-fire-July-2014-A-Diary.aspx.

76. State of Israel, *2014 Gaza Conflict,* p. 65 (caption).

77. This tally jibed with the established pattern: all of one Israeli home was "almost completely destroyed" during Cast Lead (see Chapter 3); for minimal property damage prior to Cast Lead, see Human Rights Watch, *Indiscriminate Fire: Palestinian rocket attacks on Israel and Israeli artillery shelling in the Gaza Strip* (2007), pp. 24–28.

78. Mark Perry, "Gaza's Bottle Rockets," *Foreign Affairs* (3 August 2014).

TABLE 5 Israeli Property Damage Resulting from Hamas Rocket Attacks
during Operation Protective Edge

Date	Description
7 July	
8	property damage
9	building near kindergarten hit
10	
11	one house completely destroyed, two others damaged
12	
13	rocket hits Israeli electrical plant supplying power to Gaza
14	
15	significant damage to cars and property; school for special needs children hit
16	house damaged
17	building damaged
18	kindergarten and synagogue damaged
19	massive damage in residential area
20	
21	house hit, building damaged
22	house damaged
23	
24	
25	
26	
27	two houses hit
28	
29	
30	
31	
1 August	
2	
3	school grounds hit
4	
5	house hit
6	
7	
8	house hit
9	
10	
11	
12	
13	

14	
15	
16	
17	
18	
19	shopping center hit
20	
21	building hit
22	house and synagogue hit
23	
24	
25	
26	house and playground hit

SOURCE: Israel Ministry of Foreign Affairs.

projectiles kept coming and Israel's tourism industry took a big hit.[79] When a Hamas projectile landed in the vicinity of Ben-Gurion Airport, prompting international airlines to suspend flights destined for Israel, former New York City mayor Michael Bloomberg obligingly flew over in order to reassure prospective travelers.[80] But if tranquility reigned in the Promised Land, then why was Israel pulverizing Gaza? Not missing a beat, Israel conjured a new rationale, quickly aped by credulous journalists: Hamas "terror tunnels" which "have the sole purpose of annihilating our citizens and killing our children" (Netanyahu).[81] This newly minted alibi also backfired, however, as Israeli evacuees recoiled at the prospect of returning to their border communities. It was then widely conceded in Israel that Hamas fighters infiltrating via tunnels targeted the IDF, not civilians.[82] In a retrospective marking the first anniversary of Protective Edge, a senior Israeli military correspondent flatly stated, "These tunnels allowed Hamas to move commando forces under the border

79. "Israel Visitor Numbers Nosedive during Gaza Offensive," *Agence France-Presse* (11 August 2014).

80. "In CNN Interview, Combative Bloomberg Says US Flight Ban a Mistake," *cnn .com* (22 July 2014).

81. Tamer el-Ghobashy and Joshua Mitnick, "Israel Says It Is Escalating Gaza Campaign," *Wall Street Journal* (29 July 2014).

82. Aaron J. Klein and Mitch Ginsburg, "Could Israeli Soldiers, Not Civilians, Be the Target of the Attack Tunnels?," *Times of Israel* (29 July 2014); Emanual Yelin, "Were Gaza Tunnels Built to Harm Israeli Civilians?," *+972* (11 August 2014); "Can Complete the Destruction of Tunnels within 24 Hours," *Galei Tzahal* (14 August 2014) (Hebrew).

and into Israel without warning, to carry out attacks *on soldiers*."[83] Israel touted the technical wizardry of Iron Dome after Pillar of Defense in order to compensate for the operation's meager returns.[84] It hyped it again during Protective Edge in order to soothe the jittery nerves of both its indoctrinated domestic population and would-be tourists. (Israel's flourishing arms trade also stood to reap rich dividends from the Iron Dome fanfare.) But in its official postmortem on Protective Edge, Israel reversed itself in order to rationalize the death and destruction it wreaked in Gaza. It downplayed Iron Dome's efficacy and instead magnified the vulnerability of Israel's home front.[85] Spewing forth one lie after another, Israel kept catching itself in the tangled web of its deceits. If its misrepresentations and contradictions went unnoticed, it was testament to the competence of Israeli *hasbara,* on the one hand, and the bias of Western media, on the other.

When Israel hit civilians who took refuge in UN schools, leaving scores dead and hundreds wounded, it crossed a red line.[86] (A UN Board of Inquiry later found that Israel had in its possession up-to-date GPS coordinates of all the UN shelters it targeted, and that it used indiscriminate weapons, such as artillery, in densely populated areas where these shelters were situated, as well as precision weapons, such as guided missiles. The board did not credit Israel's various justifications for these attacks.[87]) As the international community reacted in shock,[88] the diplomatic dominoes began to fall in Israel's direction. Feeling the heat from inside the UN bureaucracy, Ban Ki-moon denounced on 3 August one of these atrocities as a "moral outrage and criminal act."[89] Left isolated on the world stage, and unwilling to bear the onus of this latest

---

83. Amos Harel, "The Last Gaza War—and the Next," *Haaretz* (1 July 2015), emphasis added. See also Ron Ben Yishai, "Ten Years of Lessons Learned," *ynetnews.com* (19 June 2016).

84. See Chapter 10.

85. State of Israel, *2014 Gaza Conflict,* paras. 189–90 (see also paras. 4, 113, 190). The report, which was issued in 2015 to preempt the anticipated critical findings of a UN Human Rights Council inquiry (see Chapter 13), devoted just 2 of 460 paragraphs to Iron Dome, and emphasized not its brilliant performance but, instead, that it was "fallible" and couldn't prevent "extensive harm to civilian life and property."

86. Human Rights Watch, *In-Depth Look at Gaza School Attacks* (New York: 2014). HRW determined these attacks to be "war crimes."

87. *Summary by the Secretary-General of the Report of the United Nations Headquarters Board of Inquiry into Certain Incidents That Occurred in the Gaza Strip between 8 July 2014 and 26 August 2014* (2014).

88. Pierre Krähenbühl, "In the Eye of a Man-Made Storm," *Foreign Policy* (26 September 2014).

89. "Gaza: Ban condemns latest deadly attack near UN school as 'moral outrage and criminal act,'" *UN News Centre* (3 August 2014).

string of Israeli atrocities, the White House joined on 3 August in the chorus of condemnation, while Israel's cheerleaders in the US Congress fell silent. Once the United States declared that it was "appalled" by Israel's "disgraceful" lethal shelling in proximity of a UN shelter,[90] it sunk in on Israel that it was time to wind down the operation. On 2 August, Netanyahu had nipped in the bud rumors of an impending Israeli troop withdrawal: "We will take as much time as necessary, and will exert as much force as is needed."[91] But disabled by his chief enabler in the White House, Netanyahu announced on that same 3 August that Israeli troops were withdrawing.[92] To cover up for its failure to destroy Hamas's catacombs, Israel entered the discreet qualifier that it had detonated nearly all of Hamas's "known" tunnels.[93] The operation dragged on for another three weeks, however, as Israel sought to extract the best possible terms in the final diplomatic phase, and still harbored hopes of inflicting a decisive military defeat on Hamas by attrition. It resorted to indiscriminate aerial bombardments, killing and wounding many civilians, and assassinated senior Hamas military leaders.[94] After the beheading of an American journalist on 19 August,[95] media attention shifted to ISIS, and the Gaza massacre entered the ho-hum, more-of-the-same phase of the news cycle. Israel was able to resume the precision terror strikes with unprecedented abandon, flattening high-rise apartment buildings, as if playing a video game and with barely a pretense that they constituted legitimate mili-

90. Donna Chiacu, "US Slams 'Disgraceful Shelling' of UN School in Gaza," *Haaretz* (3 August 2014).

91. Griff Witte and Sudarsan Raghavan, "Netanyahu Says Israeli Military 'Will Take as Much Time as Necessary' in Gaza," *Washington Post* (2 August 2014).

92. A tactical consideration also figured in the withdrawal decision. Israel could proceed with the ground invasion only if it ventured into Gaza's built-up areas. To avoid street-by-street fighting and attendant combatant casualties, Israel would have to blast everything in sight, causing many thousands of civilian deaths, which international public opinion would not abide, and even then Israel would still suffer heavy combatant losses as Hamas fighters popped out of the tunnels. Amos Harel, "Operation Protective Edge Advances with No Exit Strategy," *Haaretz* (20 July 2014); Amos Harel, "As Bulldozers Destroy Hamas' Underground Network, IDF Sees Light at End of Tunnel," *Haaretz* (1 August 2014); Amos Harel, "IDF Wary of New Gaza Ground Op Even as Diplomacy Lags," *Haaretz* (25 August 2014).

93. Gili Cohen, "Senior Officer: Hamas still able to carry out tunnel attacks against Israel," *Haaretz* (31 July 2014); "Operation Protective Edge in Numbers," *ynetnews.com* (27 August 2014).

94. Nidal al-Mughrabi and Maayan Lubell, "Israeli Air Strike Kills Three Hamas Commanders in Gaza," *Reuters* (21 August 2014).

95. "James Foley: Islamic State militants 'behead reporter,'" *BBC* (20 August 2014).

tary objectives.[96] But the Hamas projectiles and mortar shells kept coming, causing Israeli civilian casualties to mount. On 26 August, a cease-fire agreement went into effect. Its essential terms stipulated that Israel (and Egypt) would ease the blockade of Gaza, while the Palestinian Authority (PA) would administer the border crossings, coordinate the international reconstruction effort, and prevent weapons from entering Gaza. The agreement deferred to future talks other points of contention, such as a prisoner release and construction of an airport and seaport in Gaza.[97]

At a news conference after the cease-fire was reached, Netanyahu boasted of Israel's "great military and political achievement."[98] But Israel did not attain its avowed goals. Initially, Netanyahu hoped to fracture the Palestinian unity government by provoking a violent reaction from Hamas and then redemonizing it as a terrorist organization. But the unity government held together, even as President Abbas probably longed for Israel to deliver Hamas a deathblow. If Israel hoped to show that Hamas was an unreconstructed terrorist organization, it ended up persuading many more people that Israel was an unrepentant terrorist state. If Israel hoped to convince the United States and European Union not to negotiate with a unity government that included Hamas, it ended up itself negotiating with the unity government and indirectly with Hamas. "Effectively," an influential Israeli columnist observed, "Israel has recognized Hamas."[99] If the unity government ultimately yielded no fruit, it was because of factional infighting, not Protective Edge.[100] Once hostilities escalated, Netanyahu's avowed objective was to destroy Hamas "rockets" and "terror tunnels." But both these aims proved beyond his reach. Hamas kept firing projectiles (killing two Israelis in the last hour before the cease-fire), while an unknown number of tunnels remained intact. Israel's larger goal of inflicting a comprehensive military and political defeat on Hamas also went unfulfilled. Although Israel had made

96. Alessandria Masi, "Israeli Airstrikes on Gaza Collapse Apartment Building," *International Business Times* (23 August 2014). See also Chapter 12.

97. Nidal al-Mughrabi and Luke Baker, "What's in the Gaza Peace Deal?," *Reuters* (26 August 2014); Ilene Prusher, "Israel and Palestinians Reach Open-Ended Cease-Fire Deal," *Time* (26 August 2014).

98. Barak Ravid, "Netanyahu: Gaza op was great military, political achievement," *Haaretz* (28 August 2014).

99. Zvi Bar'el, "With Truce, Israel Talks to Hamas and Islamic Jihad," *Haaretz* (27 August 2014).

100. Amira Hass, "Tensions between Hamas and Fatah Overshadow Reconciliation Government," *Haaretz* (6 September 2014).

any concessions contingent on Hamas's disarmament, the cease-fire agreement did not oblige the Islamic resistance to lay down its weapons, and only a vague promise was extracted from the PA to stem the flow of arms into Gaza. The cease-fire's terms "didn't include any statement, not even a hint, regarding Israel's security demands," an Israeli diplomatic correspondent groused. "There was nothing about the demilitarization of the strip, the rearming or the issue of the tunnels."[101] Although it was the regional powerhouse, Israel "failed to impose its will on an isolated enemy operating in a besieged territory without advanced weaponry."[102] The chief beneficiary of this latest Gaza massacre was Lebanon. After its military fiasco, Israel would think twice before attacking Hezbollah, as it possessed a formidable arsenal of real, sophisticated rockets,[103] reducing Iron Dome's potential efficacy quotient from single-digit percentages to near zero; it also possessed a tunnel network dug deep inside mountains. In a replay of the last act, last scene of Pillar of Defense, the Israeli prime minister, defense minister, and chief of staff cut sorry figures at the news conference proclaiming Israel's "victory" in Protective Edge.[104] Still, Netanyahu could exult in a pair of complementary triumphs. He satiated the bloodlust of Israeli society that he himself had whipped up. It could now savor the prospect of Gazans confronting, once the soot had settled, the massive death and destruction Israel had visited on them. "The latest military operation," a comprehensive UN report found, "has effectively eliminated what was left of the middle class, sending almost all of the population into destitution and dependence on international humanitarian aid."[105] Israel had, concomitantly, battered if not yet completely broken the spirits of the people of Gaza. The ever-escalating violence, the wreckage left in its wake, the futureless future had finally taken a toll. Nine months after Protective Edge, "not a single totally destroyed home" had

101. Barak Ravid, "Netanyahu Saw His Chance to Run Away from Gaza, and He Took It," *Haaretz* (26 August 2014).

102. Mouin Rabbani, "Israel's 'Operation Status Quo,'" Norwegian Peace-Building Resource Center (25 August 2014).

103. Jassem Al Salami, "Rockets and Iron Dome, the Case of Lebanon," *Offiziere.ch* (5 August 2014), offiziere.ch/?p=17519; "Israel Preparing for 'Very Violent' War against Hezbollah, TV Report Says," *Times of Israel* (6 September 2014).

104. Yossi Verter, "Netanyahu after the War: Less popular, but still unchallenged," *Haaretz* (29 August 2014).

105. United Nations Conference on Trade and Development, "Report on UNCTAD Assistance" (2015), para. 30.

been rebuilt.[106] Fully half of Gazans polled after Protective Edge expressed a desire to leave. In extreme but still indicative instances, they boarded rickety vessels to escape (hundreds drowned), crossed into Israel illegally in search of work or the comfort of a jail cell, and—in unprecedented numbers—committed suicide.[107] If Israel's tacit goal in its recent major operations had been to "punish, humiliate, and terrorize" Gaza's civilian population (Goldstone Report), then this time around it could take pride in a job well done. It also put the lie to the bromide that violence doesn't work. It does, and did.

Hamas also flourished the V sign for victory.[108] Indeed, its popularity among Palestinians surged after fighting Israel to a stalemate.[109] But the uptick proved ephemeral. When armed hostilities broke out, Hamas's primary goal was to end the blockade of Gaza. Whereas the original Egyptian cease-fire proposal stipulated that the siege would be lifted only after "the security situation stabilizes" in Gaza, the final cease-fire agreement omitted this precondition. However, it called only for the blockade to be eased (not lifted) and did not include an external enforcement mechanism, which Hamas had earlier demanded.[110] In effect, it reinstated the cease-fire terms ending Pillar of Defense, which Israel had back then proceeded to scrap.[111] Hamas settled for less than its bottom line because of Israel's relentless bombardment. "Our demands were just," Hamas leader Khalid Mishal told a news conference, "but in the end we had the Palestinian demands, on the one

106. United Nations Relief and Works Agency, *Gaza Situation Report No. 93* (22 May 2015).

107. Roy, *Gaza Strip,* pp. 405–6; Jack Khoury, "Thousands of Gazans Fleeing to Europe via Tunnels, Traffickers and Boats," *Haaretz* (17 September 2014); Shlomi Eldar, "Escaping Gaza, Hundreds of Palestinians Drown," *Al-Monitor* (19 September 2014); Mohammed Othman, "Suicide Rates on Rise in Gaza," *Al-Monitor* (9 February 2015); Jodi Rudoren and Majd Al Waheidi, "Desperation Drives Gazans over a Fence and into Prison," *New York Times* (17 February 2015); Mohammed Omer, "'The Smell of Death Hangs Everywhere': Blockade drives Gazans to suicide," *Middle East Eye* (11 April 2016); Sanaa Kamal and Hunter Stuart, "Palestinians Paying Thousands in Bribes to Leave Gaza," *Al Jazeera* (5 September 2016).

108. Khaled Abu Toameh, "Ismail Haniyeh Makes First Appearance since Start of Gaza Operation," *Jerusalem Post* (27 August 2014).

109. Palestinian Center for Policy and Survey Research, "Special Gaza War Poll" (2 September 2014).

110. Ehab Zahriyeh, "Citing Past Failures, Hamas Demands an Enforceable Cease-fire," *Al Jazeera America* (16 July 2014).

111. Mohammed Daraghmeh and Karin Laub, "Hamas Claims 'Victory for the Resistance' as Long-Term Truce Is Agreed with Israel," *Independent* (26 August 2014).

hand, and the pain of Gaza's civilian population, on the other." "We agreed to the cease-fire," Mishal continued, "in the knowledge that the siege will be lifted."[112] But it was already clear at the time[113] that this was wishful thinking until and unless Hamas disarmed. Two years after Protective Edge, Defense Minister Avigdor Lieberman still maintained that only "if Hamas stops digging tunnels, rearming and firing rockets, we will lift the blockade."[114] As the Islamic movement wouldn't capitulate, the siege showed no signs of abating: "the virtual ban on exports from Gaza has not been lifted," while at the volume of truck traffic Israel allowed, it would take "174 years to return Gaza to where it was in May 2014."[115] If Gazans flocked into the streets after the cease-fire was declared, it was to proclaim, firstly to themselves and then to the world, that however enormous the toll, however bottomless the sacrifice, the people of Palestine still lived. *We were, we are, we will be!*

An official consensus crystallized during Protective Edge according to which Israel had the right to defend itself, even though it had initiated the armed hostilities, and Hamas would have to disarm, even though it had acted in self-defense. In July 2014, the European Union called on "Hamas to immediately put an end to these acts and to renounce violence. All terrorist groups in Gaza must disarm." At the same time, it recognized "Israel's legitimate right to defend itself against any attacks," with the throwaway caveat that the "Israeli military operation must be proportionate and in line with international humanitarian law."[116] This allocation of rights and obligations did not just contradict the circumstantial facts of the operation; it also contradicted the overarching legal framework of the occupation. Whereas international law prohibits an occupying power from using force to suppress a struggle for self-determination, it does *not* debar a people struggling for self-determination from using force. Israel consequently has no legal mandate to use force

---

112. Jack Khoury, "Meshal: Hamas will go back to war against Israel if upcoming truce talks fail," *Haaretz* (28 August 2014); Amira Hass, "Hamas Trying to Sell 'Victory' to Gazans," *Haaretz* (27 August 2014).

113. Norman G. Finkelstein, *Method and Madness: The hidden story of Israel's assaults on Gaza* (New York: 2014), pp. 159–60.

114. Jack Khoury, "Israel Will Help Rebuild Gaza If Hamas Disarms, Lieberman Says," *Haaretz* (24 October 2016).

115. Roy, *Gaza Strip*, pp. xxxi, 406 (citing the humanitarian relief organization Oxfam).

116. Council of the European Union (22 July 2014).

against the Palestinian self-determination struggle.[117] It might be argued that insofar as this self-determination struggle has been unfolding within the framework of a belligerent occupation, Israel has the legal right, as the occupying power, to enforce the occupation so long as it endures.[118] But the International Court of Justice (ICJ) ruled in 1971 that since South Africa had refused to carry out good-faith negotiations to terminate its occupation of Namibia, the occupation had eventually become illegal. In light of the Namibia precedent, Israel's failure to carry out good-faith negotiations based on international law has delegitimized its occupation as well.[119] If Israel can lay title to any "right," it is—in the exhortation of the United States at the time of the Namibia debate—"to withdraw its administration . . . immediately and thus put an end to its occupation." Whereas it proclaims the right of self-defense against Hamas projectiles, Israel is in effect promulgating a right to use force to perpetuate the occupation. Were Israel to cease its violent repression, the occupation would end and, ideally, the projectile attacks would also stop as Palestinians went about the business of consolidating their own independent state. The right to self-defense could justly be invoked by Israel only if the attacks continued regardless. On the one hand, Israel cannot pretend to a right of self-defense if the exercise of this right traces back to the wrong of an illegal occupation/denial of self-determination (*ex injuria non oritur jus*[120]). On the other hand, Israel would not need to invoke the right if it ceased inflicting the wrong. In 2016, the European Union issued a statement calling for "all parties to . . . produce a fundamental change to the . . . situation in the Gaza Strip, including the end of the closure and a full opening of the crossing points, *while addressing Israel's legitimate security concerns.*"[121] But Israel cannot lay claim to "legitimate security concerns" vis-à-vis Gaza so long as the force it deploys there is designed to entrench an illegitimate regime. The legally correct position was enunciated by the UN Human Rights Council mission on Protective Edge, which called on Israel to "lift, immediately and unconditionally, the blockade on Gaza."[122] The

117. See Chapter 7.
118. Ibid.
119. See Appendix.
120. No legal benefit or right can be derived from an illegal act.
121. "Council Conclusions on the Middle East Peace Process" (18 January 2016), consilium.europa.eu/en/press/press-releases/2016/01/18-fac-conclusions-mepp/; emphasis added.
122. See Chapter 13.

refrain that Israel has a right to defend itself is a red herring. The real question is, *Does Israel have the right to use force to perpetuate an illegal occupation?* The answer is no.

But (it might be contended), even granting that unlike Israel, Palestinians can legally resort to force, doesn't Hamas's use of indiscriminate projectiles and its targeting of Israeli civilians still constitute war crimes? The situation is more equivocal than is often acknowledged. *First,* what constitutes an indiscriminate weapon isn't clear, while the implicit standard isn't just. A class of weapons apparently passes legal muster if its probability of hitting a target is *relatively* high. This legal threshold is keyed to and correlates with cutting-edge technology. The couplets advanced/primitive and discriminate/indiscriminate overlap; a high-tech weapon can, whereas a low-tech weapon cannot, discriminate between targets. But then, only a people sufficiently endowed to purchase high-tech weaponry can defend itself against a high-tech aerial assault. If it lacks material resources, if compelled by circumstance to use rudimentary weapons, a people engaging in a war of self-defense or a struggle for self-determination cannot prevail except by breaching the laws of war; if it obeys the laws of war, it will almost certainly suffer defeat. If this be the law, it is a most peculiar law, for it negates a raison d'être of law—the substitution of might by right—as it enshrines might, or the rich and powerful, above right. *Second,* it was asserted that even if the civilian population of one party to a conflict comes under relentless attack, it does not have the legal right to carry out "belligerent reprisals"—that is, to deliberately target civilians of the opposing party until that party desists from its initial illegal attacks. "Regardless of who started this latest round, attacks targeting civilians violate basic humanitarian norms," Human Rights Watch stated right after Protective Edge began. "All attacks, including reprisal attacks, that target or indiscriminately harm civilians are prohibited under the laws of war, period."[123] But was that true? In fact, international law does not—at any rate, not yet—prohibit belligerent reprisals.[124] The United States and United Kingdom have even defended the right to deploy *nuclear* weapons in belliger-

123. Human Rights Watch, "Indiscriminate Palestinian Rocket Attacks" (9 July 2014).

124. International Committee of the Red Cross, *Customary International Humanitarian Law, Volume I: Rules* (Cambridge: 2005), rule 146. The United Nations Human Rights Council cites this study as authoritative on the current state of customary law. *Report of the Detailed Findings of the Independent Commission of Inquiry Established Pursuant to Human Rights Council Resolution S-21/1* (22 June 2015), para. 33. See also A. P. V. Rogers, *Law on the Battlefield,* second edition (Manchester: 2004), p. 235.

ent reprisals.[125] The people of Gaza surely, then, had the right to use make-shift projectiles to end an illegal, merciless seven-year-long Israeli blockade targeting a civilian population, and to end Israel's criminal bombardment of a civilian population. Indeed, in its landmark 1996 advisory opinion on the legality of nuclear weapons, the ICJ stated that international law was not settled on the right of a state to use nuclear weapons when its "survival" was in jeopardy. But if that elusive abstraction called a state might legally use nuclear weapons when its survival is at stake, then a *people* surely has the right to use makeshift projectiles when its survival is at stake. The political prudence of Hamas's strategy could be legitimately questioned. But the law is not unambiguously against it, while the scales of morality tilt in its favor. Israel has imposed a brutal siege on Gaza that halved its already "de-developed" GDP. As a result of the blockade and recurrent military assaults, Gaza's population has been "denied a human standard of living," while some 95 percent of its water is unfit for human consumption. "Innocent human beings, most of them young," Sara Roy bewailed, "are slowly being poisoned by the water they drink." They were not only consigned but also literally confined to a slow death. "When a place becomes unlivable, people move," the United Nations Relief and Works Agency has observed. "This is the case for environmental disasters such as droughts, or for conflicts, such as in Syria.

> Yet this last resort is denied to the people in Gaza. They cannot move beyond their 365 square kilometers territory. They cannot escape, neither the devastating poverty nor the fear of another conflict. Its highly educated youth . . . do not have the option to travel, to seek education outside Gaza, or to find work, anywhere else beyond the perimeter fence and the two tightly-controlled border-checkpoints in the north and south of the Gaza Strip.
>
> With the Rafah crossing between Egypt and Gaza almost entirely closed except for a few days per year, and with Israel often denying exit even for severe humanitarian cases or staff of international organizations, the vast majority of the people have no chance of getting one of the highly sought-after "permits." They can also not leave across the sea without the risk of being

---

125. *Legality of the Threat or Use of Nuclear Weapons* (8 July 1996)—Letter dated 16 June 1995 from the Legal Adviser to the Foreign and Commonwealth Office of the United Kingdom of Great Britain and Northern Ireland, together with Written Comments of the United Kingdom; Letter dated 20 June 1995 from the Acting Legal Adviser to the Department of State, together with Written Statement of the Government of the United States of America; Oral Statement of US representative (15 November 1995); Dissenting Opinion of Vice-President Schwebel. The ICJ itself elected not to rule on the legality of belligerent reprisals (para. 46).

arrested or shot at by the Israeli or Egyptian navies, and they cannot climb over the heavily guarded perimeter fence between Israel and Gaza without the same risks.[126]

The people of Palestine embraced Hamas as it launched belligerent reprisals against Israel. In the climacteric of their martyrdom, Gazans chose to die resisting rather than to live expiring under an inhuman blockade.[127] The resistance was mostly notional, as the rudimentary projectiles caused little damage. So the ultimate question is, *Do Palestinians have the right to symbolically resist slow death punctuated by periodic massacres, or is it incumbent upon them to lie down and die?*

126. B'Tselem (Israeli Information Center for Human Rights in the Occupied Territories), "Over 90 Percent of Water in Gaza Strip Unfit for Consumption" (9 February 2014); United Nations Relief and Works Agency, "Denied a Human Standard of Living: The Gaza blockade has entered its tenth year" (21 October 2016); Roy, *Gaza Strip*, pp. lii–lvii, lxviii, 402–3.

127. Amira Hass, "Hamas's Rejection of the Cease-Fire Deal Was a Foregone Conclusion," *Haaretz* (16 July 2014).

TWELVE

Betrayal I

AMNESTY INTERNATIONAL

ALTHOUGH "OPERATION PROTECTIVE EDGE" (2014) PROVED to be the most destructive of Israel's recent assaults on Gaza, it elicited a muted response from human rights organizations. It would be only a slight exaggeration to say that they sat it out. In the aftermath of Operation Cast Lead (2008–9), as many as three hundred human rights reports were issued.[1] Human Rights Watch (HRW) alone released five substantial studies.[2] But HRW just barely issued one report on Protective Edge.[3] The outlier appeared to be Amnesty International, which published a series of reports. Yet, far from being the exception that proved the rule, Amnesty actually constituted a variant of the rule: instead of falling silent on Israeli crimes during Protective Edge, Amnesty whitewashed them. In particular, its comprehensive indictment of Hamas,[4] *Unlawful and Deadly: Rocket and mortar attacks by Palestinian armed groups during the 2014 Gaza/Israel*

Most of the Israel data in this chapter draw from State of Israel, *The 2014 Gaza Conflict, 7 July–26 August 2014: Factual and legal aspects* (2015).

　1. See Chapter 5.

　2. *Rain of Fire: Israel's unlawful use of white phosphorus in Gaza* (2009); *Precisely Wrong: Gaza civilians killed by Israeli drone-launched missiles* (2009); *Rockets from Gaza: Harm to civilians from Palestinian armed groups' rocket attacks* (2009); *White Flag Deaths: Killings of Palestinian civilians during Operation Cast Lead* (2009); *"I Lost Everything": Israel's unlawful destruction of property during Operation Cast Lead* (2009). These reports ranged in length from 25 to 115 pages.

　3. *In-Depth Look at Gaza School Attacks* (2014). It ran to only 15 pages, and inasmuch as UN secretary-general Ban Ki-moon and the Obama administration had already deplored the attacks (see Chapter 11), it was not especially notable.

　4. *Hamas* is here used to denote all armed groups in Gaza.

conflict,[5] amounted to an abdication of its professional mandate and a betrayal of the people of Gaza.

A human rights assessment of Protective Edge necessarily begins with the civilian death and destruction it entailed. Table 6 summarizes the raw data. "On both sides," Amnesty observed in *Unlawful and Deadly,* "civilians once again bore the brunt of the third full-scale war in less than six years." Although arguably true,[6] this assessment obscured the yawning gap separating the magnitude of suffering inflicted on Gazan as compared to Israeli civilians.[7] It would be hard to come up with a more palpable instance of a quantitative difference turning into a qualitative one than the single Israeli child versus the 550 Gazan children killed, and it doesn't diminish the sanctity of every human life to take note that if the death of one Israeli child was terrible, then on the same calculus the child deaths in Gaza were 550 times as terrible. An international Medical Fact-Finding Mission, assembled by the Israeli branch of Physicians for Human Rights and composed of eminent medical practitioners, concluded its report on Protective Edge with this caveat: "While not wishing to devalue in any way the traumatic effects of the war on Israeli civilians, these pale in comparison with the consequences of the massive destruction wreaked on Gaza."[8] Even UN secretary-general Ban Ki-moon, who disgraced his office with apologetics on Israel's behalf,[9] carefully discriminated between Israel's lethal attacks on UN facilities during Protective Edge, which "I deplore," and Hamas's misuse of UN facilities, about which "I am dismayed."[10] One searched *Unlawful and Deadly* in vain for comparable acknowledgment or nuance by Amnesty. In keeping with its pretense to evenhandedness, Amnesty conveyed the impression that Israel and Hamas were equally guilty

---

5. Amnesty International, *Unlawful and Deadly: Rocket and mortar attacks by Palestinian armed groups during the 2014 Gaza/Israel conflict* (2015).

6. On the other hand, only 8 percent of total Israeli fatalities were civilians.

7. However, in its report, *"Strangling Necks": Abductions, torture and summary killings of Palestinians by Hamas forces during the 2014 Gaza/Israel conflict* (2015), Amnesty did briefly mention that "The extent of the casualties and destruction in Gaza wrought by Israeli forces far exceeded those caused by Palestinian attacks on Israel, reflecting Israel's far greater firepower, among other factors."

8. Jutta Bachmann et al., *Gaza 2014: Findings of an independent medical fact-finding mission* (2015), p. 101; hereafter: Medical Fact-Finding Mission.

9. See Chapter 5 and Chapter 9.

10. Ban Ki-moon's remarks were appended to the summary of the final report of a UN Board of Inquiry he commissioned to investigate "certain incidents that occurred in the Gaza Strip between 8 July 2014 and 26 August 2014." For the UN Board of Inquiry report, see Chapter 11; hereafter: UN Board of Inquiry.

TABLE 6 Civilian Losses in Operation Protective Edge

	Total fatalities (of whom children)	Civilians (% of total fatalities)	Combatants (% of total fatalities)	Direct damage to civilian infrastructure (in dollars)	Civilian homes destroyed/ rendered uninhabitable
Israel	73 (1)	6[a] (8)	67 (92)	55,000,000[b]	1[c]
Gaza	2,200 (550)	1,560 (70)[d]	640 (30)	4,000,000,000[e]	18,000[f]

NOTE: Some figures are rounded off.

[a] One civilian was a Thai guest worker.

[b] State of Israel, *2014 Gaza Conflict*, reported that total compensation for direct damages to Israeli civilians would reach $40 million, while the state would spend an additional $15 million to repair public infrastructure that was damaged (paras. 112, 223).

[c] Eleven others suffered some damage.

[d] The casualty figures and breakdowns for Gaza are based on UN Office for the Coordination of Humanitarian Affairs (OCHA), *Fragmented Lives* (2015). The major Gaza-based human rights organizations (Al Mezan, Palestinian Center for Human Rights) put the number of civilians killed at 1,600–1,700, while Israel's major human rights organization (B'Tselem) put the number of civilians killed at 1,400. Israel's official postmortem on Protective Edge alleged that of a total of 2,125 Gazan fatalities, 936 (44 percent) were Hamas "militants," 761 (36 percent) were civilians, and 428 (20 percent) were "yet to be categorized." It also stated that "in all but a few rare instances, women, children under the age of 16, and the elderly were automatically categorized as 'uninvolved'" in its calculations. But according to OCHA, the number of Gazan women and children killed—that is, not including *any* adult males—already totaled 850. (The one slight definitional discrepancy was that OCHA reckoned a child as under 17 years of age.) The Israeli report faulted OCHA for basing its combatant/civilian breakdown on "daily fatality lists issued by the Hamas-controlled Gaza Ministry of Health," which, it continued, "do not identify whether the deceased was a militant." It's hard to figure out how OCHA could have relied on the ministry's breakdown if the ministry didn't give a breakdown. State of Israel, *2014 Gaza Conflict*, p. 56n165; annex, paras. 9, 13, 25–27.

[e] State of Palestine, *The National Early Recovery and Reconstruction Plan for Gaza* (2014), p. 9.

[f] 113,000 others suffered some damage.

of breaching the laws of war. During a crucial period when it could still inflect public policy, Amnesty issued a pair of reports documenting Israel's crimes and a pair of reports documenting Hamas's crimes (four altogether), while, amazingly, it devoted, all told, many more pages to indicting Hamas (107) than Israel (78).[11] It was not so wide of the mark in the past. In *Operation*

11. In addition to *Unlawful and Deadly* and *"Strangling Necks,"* Amnesty issued *Families under the Rubble: Israeli attacks on inhabited homes* (2014); and *"Nothing Is Immune": Israel's destruction of landmark buildings in Gaza* (2014). These four reports were released during the critical window of opportunity before the UN Human Rights Council released its own report in June 2015. The UN report cited extensively from Amnesty's quartet of publications (see Chapter 13). Amnesty issued another report on Protective Edge (more on which presently), but this was after publication of the UN report when it was too late to influence it.

"*Cast Lead,*" Israel bore the brunt of Amnesty's indictment: its space allocations (60 pages to Israeli crimes versus 13 pages to Hamas crimes) were more, if still far from fully, commensurate with the relative death and destruction inflicted by each side.[12] The introduction to each of Amnesty's four reports on Protective Edge cautiously balanced the distribution of guilt. As if that weren't problematic enough, *Unlawful and Deadly* detailed the death of the single Israeli child killed by a Hamas attack across more than two pages. Were it truly committed to effecting—as against affecting—balance, shouldn't Amnesty have devoted 1,100 pages to the 550 children in Gaza who were killed? Amnesty even intimated that Hamas was the more manifestly culpable party to the conflict. Thus, *Unlawful and Deadly*'s conclusion unequivocally deplored Hamas's "flagrant disregard for international humanitarian law," whereas one of Amnesty's reciprocal reports, *Families under the Rubble: Israeli attacks on inhabited homes,* gingerly concluded that the havoc wrought—18,000 Gazan homes were destroyed or rendered uninhabitable,[13] and 110,000 people were left homeless—"raise[s] difficult questions for the Israeli government which they have so far failed to answer."[14] It is of course conceivable that Hamas committed as many war crimes as Israel, if not more, during Protective Edge, but prima facie that would be a most anomalous conclusion. In both absolute and relative terms, the scales of guilt appeared to tilt heavily to the Israeli side: Hamas killed 73 Israelis of whom only 8 percent were civilians, whereas Israel killed 2,200 Gazans of whom fully 70 percent were civilians; the damage inflicted on Gaza's civilian infrastructure ($4 billion) exceeded by a factor of 70 the damage inflicted on Israel's infrastructure ($55 million), while the ratio of civilian dwellings destroyed by Israel versus Hamas stood at 18,000:1. The intriguing question is, how did Amnesty manage to turn this wildly imbalanced balance sheet into a "balanced" indictment of both parties to the conflict?

To justify the massive violence it unleashed on Gaza, Israel harped on the arsenal of deadly rockets Hamas had allegedly amassed. Echoing Israeli *hasbara*

12. This report was cited extensively in Part One. A precise juxtaposition cast an even darker shadow on Amnesty's space allocations in its Protective Edge reports: in absolute numbers, the scale of civilian death and destruction inflicted by Israel during Protective Edge was much more massive than during Cast Lead, whereas in the case of Hamas it was roughly the same.

13. Gisha, "Where's the Housing Boom?" (2015).

14. To be sure, *"Strangling Necks"* did categorically state, "Israeli military forces committed war crimes and other grave violations of international law during Operation Protective Edge."

(propaganda), *Unlawful and Deadly* reported that as far back as 2001, Hamas had been stockpiling short-range rockets; that it then "developed longer-range Qassam rockets"; that "in more recent years, armed groups in Gaza have produced, upgraded or smuggled in thousands of BM-21 Grad rockets of different types, with ranges varying from 20km to 48km, and acquired or produced smaller numbers of medium- and long-range rockets," including "the Iranian Fajr 5 and locally produced M-75 (both with a range of 75km), and the locally produced J-80 rockets with a range of 80km." "The majority of Israel's 8.3 million people, and all 2.8 million Palestinians in the occupied West Bank," Amnesty ominously concluded, "are now within range of at least some of the rockets held by Palestinian armed groups in the Gaza Strip. . . . [T]he circle of fear has widened." Although Amnesty didn't cite the basis for these data,[15] they almost certainly emanated from official Israeli sources, and it is hard not to be skeptical of them. Israel's official postmortem on Protective Edge alleged that on the eve of Operation Pillar of Defense (2012), Hamas "had stockpiled over 7,000 rockets and mortars," while on the eve of Protective Edge it "had acquired more than 10,000 rockets and mortars." It also provided a precise breakdown of these projectiles ("6,700 rockets with a range of up to 20km," "2,300 rockets with a range of up to 40km," etc.).[16] It is anyone's guess how Israel came by such detailed information and why, if possessing it, Israel didn't militarily preempt Hamas's use of this terrifying weaponry. If it could ascertain the quantity and quality of these projectiles, it must also have been privy to where Hamas stockpiled them, while Israel has never shied away from launching a preemptive attack to nip in the bud an "existential" threat, real or contrived. If it didn't launch such an attack, it was almost certainly because either Hamas didn't possess such an arsenal or, if it did, Israel was in the dark about it. In either case, Israel must have plucked its published data, on which Amnesty (and others) leaned, from thin air. If Hamas had indeed amassed a humungous arsenal of lethal weapons, the wonder would be that it inflicted so little death and destruction. Stealing another page from Israeli *hasbara*, Amnesty ascribed this miracle to Israel's antimissile batteries: "Israel's Iron Dome missile defense system helped limit civilian casualties in many areas," and was used "to protect civilian areas from projectiles launched from the Gaza Strip." In fact, it was per-

15. It also didn't provide a basis for its perverse inclusion of West Bank Palestinians in the "circle of fear"—did they really fear Hamas rockets?

16. State of Israel, *2014 Gaza Conflict,* paras. 51, 54.

fectly obvious from public sources that Hamas's stockpile consisted of enhanced fireworks or "bottle rockets," while Iron Dome saved few if any Israeli lives.[17] In its hyperbolic inventory of Hamas's arsenal, Amnesty also cited the Israeli allegation that it had intercepted a vessel carrying Iranian rockets "bound for Gaza." It omitted the widely reported finding of a UN expert panel that the Iranian weapons were bound not for Gaza but the Sudan.[18] By adopting Israel's story line of a lethal Hamas rocket arsenal, Amnesty became, wittingly or not, a purveyor of state propaganda. Its depiction of the Hamas catacombs was no less tendentious. Amnesty repeated the official Israeli allegation that the ground invasion was launched to "destroy the tunnel system . . . , particularly those with shafts discovered near residential areas located in Israel," and that Israeli troops repeatedly preempted Hamas infiltrators from targeting civilian communities. It ignored evidence from unimpeachable Israeli sources that Hamas fighters exiting the tunnels targeted Israeli soldiers, not civilians.[19] Even as Israel's official postmortem on Protective Edge portentously reported that Hamas tunnels exited "in or close to residential communities,"[20] its actual breakdown, too, showed that *every* instance of Hamas infiltration climaxed not in a headlong assault on civilians but instead in an armed engagement with Israeli combatants.[21]

The upshot of Amnesty's reliance on official Israeli sources was that it magnified Hamas's and diminished Israel's criminal culpability. This distortion resulted in part from another of Amnesty's strategic "balancing" acts. Israel barred Amnesty (and other human rights organizations) from entering Gaza during[22] and after Protective Edge. Consequently, except for at most a couple of its fieldworkers based in Gaza, Amnesty had to carry out its research from the outside. As a practical matter, this Israeli-imposed constraint repeatedly prevented Amnesty from assessing the veracity of official Israeli exculpations. How did Amnesty resolve this forensic challenge? It typically

17. Mark Perry, "Gaza's Bottle Rockets," *Foreign Affairs* (3 August 2014). See Chapter 11 for details.

18. Louis Charbonneau, "UN Panel: Arms ship seized by IDF came from Iran, but not bound for Gaza," *Haaretz* (28 June 2014).

19. See Chapter 11.

20. State of Israel, *2014 Gaza Conflict,* paras. 91, 109, 119 (see also paras. 56, 85, 91, 220, and p. 42n130).

21. Ibid., paras. 96, 119.

22. Amnesty International, "Israel 'Playing Games' as Human Rights Organizations Denied Access" (20 August 2014); Human Rights Watch, "Provide Rights Groups Access to Gaza" (20 August 2014).

reported the allegation of an Israeli war crime, then the Israeli denial, and then "neutrally" proceeded to call for a proper on-the-ground investigation—an investigation that as Amnesty knew full well Israel would never allow. The reader was thus left in perfect and permanent limbo as to where the truth lay. When assessing allegations that Hamas violated international law during Protective Edge, Amnesty gestured to prior Hamas misconduct as corroborative evidence of its guilt.[23] Shouldn't Amnesty also have contextualized Israeli denials of guilt with the caveat that prior Israeli denials regularly proved on inspection to be flagrant falsehoods? Indeed, the UN Board of Inquiry investigation of Israeli attacks on UN facilities during Protective Edge repeatedly put the lie to Israel's pleas of innocence.[24] In its press release deploring Israel's refusal to grant it entry, Human Rights Watch pointedly observed, "If Israel is confident in its claim that Hamas is responsible for civilian deaths in Gaza, it shouldn't be blocking human rights organizations from carrying out on-site investigations." Amnesty itself observed that "governments who wish to hide their violations of human rights from the outside world have frequently banned Amnesty International from accessing the places in which they have been committed."[25] So if Israel blocked access to Gaza after Protective Edge, shouldn't Amnesty's working assumption have been that Israel's counterclaims would not withstand an on-site investigation? If a suspect denies eminently impartial investigators access to a crime scene, then the inexorable inference is that he or she has something to hide. True, to justify its refusal Israel has repeatedly alleged that Amnesty is biased against it. But it would be odd indeed if Amnesty itself credited this accusation as compelling grounds for it to suspend judgment. The relevant principle at play is not whether Israel is innocent until proven guilty. It's whether Israel's plea of not guilty should carry probative weight even as it refuses to prove its innocence before a nonpartisan third party, in the face of credible charges based on a mass of incriminating evidence. Ultimately, Amnesty's neutrality incentivized Israeli noncooperation. For if granting human rights groups entry into Gaza would enable them to document Israeli crimes, then

---

23. "[T]he numerous specific incidents of attacks launched in close proximity to civilian buildings reported by the Israeli authorities, together with accounts of journalists in Gaza during the conflict *and the findings of Amnesty International researchers documenting previous rounds of hostilities,* indicate that attacks by armed groups in Gaza launched from within residential areas were far from isolated occurrences" (*Unlawful and Deadly;* emphasis added).

24. More on which presently; see also Chapter 11.

25. Amnesty International, *Families under the Rubble.*

prudent state policy would be to bar these organizations altogether and settle for an agnostic verdict. In the event, that's what Israel did and that's the verdict Amnesty delivered. Finally, one egregious lacuna as Amnesty pretended to balance deserves special notice. It cited in abundance the junk claims of Israeli *hasbara,* but *not once* did it report the pertinent findings of Gaza's respected human rights organizations, such as the Al Mezan Center for Human Rights and the Palestinian Center for Human Rights.[26] The *methodology* section of *Unlawful and Deadly* stated: "Amnesty International studied relevant documentation produced by UN Agencies, the Israeli military and Israeli governmental bodies, Israeli and Palestinian NGOs, Palestinian armed groups, and media reports, amongst other sources, and consulted with relevant experts and practitioners before writing the report. Amnesty International would like to thank the Israeli NGOs and other Israeli bodies that provided assistance to its researchers."[27] Whereas the report amply represented the claims of Israeli military and governmental bodies, it did not contain a single reference to any Palestinian NGO.

Amnesty's problematic evidentiary standards in *Unlawful and Deadly* subtly shifted to Hamas a portion of culpability for Israel's most egregious crimes during Protective Edge. Consider these examples:

Hospitals Israel destroyed or damaged 17 hospitals and 56 primary health-care centers during Protective Edge.[28] *Unlawful and Deadly* pointed to Hamas's alleged misuse of three of these facilities.

1. *Al-Wafa.* Israel repeatedly attacked and then reduced to rubble al-Wafa hospital, the sole rehabilitation facility in Gaza. It wasn't the first time Israel targeted the hospital. During Cast Lead, al-Wafa sustained direct hits from eight tank shells, two missiles, and thousands of bullets, even as Israel publicly avowed that it did not target "terrorists" who launched attacks "in the vicinity of a hospital."[29] This time around, Amnesty cited the Israeli allegation that al-Wafa was a "command center." It could have noted that "command center" was Israel's default alibi for targeting

---

26. The Medical Fact-Finding Mission paid tribute to the "independence and credibility of local civil society groups such as Al Mezan, PCHR" (p. 100).

27. The list of specific Israeli organizations assisting Amnesty is omitted here.

28. Al Mezan Center for Human Rights et al., *No More Impunity: Gaza's health sector under attack* (2015).

29. See Chapter 3.

civilian objects during Protective Edge,[30] and that in other contexts Amnesty itself treated this allegation as baseless.[31] Displaying an aerial photograph, the Israeli military alleged that Hamas fired a rocket from al-Wafa's immediate vicinity. Amnesty found, however, that "The image tweeted by the Israeli military does not match satellite images of the al-Wafa hospital and appears to depict a different location." This finding seemed to dispose of Israel's pretext, except that, ever-so-evenhandedly, Amnesty concluded that it "has not been able to verify Israeli assertions that the hospital was used to launch rockets," and that the Israeli claim should be "independently investigated." In other words, even if the single piece of evidence adduced by Israel was demonstrably false, it still remained an open question whether or not the alibi was true. On this evidentiary standard, Amnesty couldn't find that Israel had committed a war crime unless and until Israel acknowledged its commission. As it happened, Israel itself eventually dropped the rocket allegation.[32] Amnesty further noted that "according to media reports" an "anti-tank missile was fired from al-Wafa." The "media reports" cited by Amnesty turn out to be little more than an official Israeli press handout dutifully reprinted by the *Jerusalem Post*.[33] It's as instructive what Amnesty elected *not* to cite. If it adduced Israeli *hasbara* as credible evidence, shouldn't it also have cited al-Wafa's director, who told *Haaretz* that Israeli claims were "false and misleading," or the representative of the World Health Organization in Gaza, who forthrightly acknowledged the probable presence of a "rocket launching site in the vicinity" of al-Wafa but contended that "it was more than 200 meters away from the hospital"?[34] "Israeli forces contest having directly and intentionally

30. State of Israel, *2014 Gaza Conflict*, paras. 54, 129, 145, 151, 153, 254, 275, 277, 278, 280.

31. Amnesty International, *"Nothing Is Immune."*

32. State of Israel, *2014 Gaza Conflict*, para. 129. Incidentally, this report depicted Israel's obliteration of al-Wafa as having "returned fire in a precise and discriminate manner" (para. 285).

33. "Terrorists in Gaza fired an anti-tank missile at the IDF from the Al-Wafa hospital on Thursday, using the structure as an attack base despite Israel's air strike on the structure on Wednesday following previous gunfire and missiles fired from it by Hamas. The IDF fired back, killing two terrorists, and the air force later struck the building from which the missile was fired. The air force also struck a structure near the Al-Wafa hospital used to store weapons, and as a command and control center." Yaakov Lappin, "Terrorists Fire Anti-tank Missile from Al-Wafa Hospital in Gaza," *Jerusalem Post* (25 July 2014).

34. Gili Cohen et al., "Israel Bombs Empty Gaza Hospital, Calling It Hamas Command Center," *Haaretz* (23 July 2014); Medical Fact-Finding Mission, p. 50. In another context of *Unlawful and Deadly*, Amnesty did quote a "senior Hamas official" to the effect

targeted [al-Wafa] hospital, claiming that they sought to neutralize rocket fire originating in the vicinity of the hospital," an International Federation for Human Rights (FIDH) delegation observed after entering Gaza and sifting through the evidence. "However, various elements indicate that the hospital was in fact the target of a direct and intentional attack on the part of Israeli armed forces."[35] Opting instead to quell doubts of Israel's innocence, Amnesty reported, "An internal investigation by the Israeli military into its attacks on al-Wafa . . . found that the attacks had been carried out in accordance with international law." Shouldn't it also have mentioned that all major human rights organizations, Amnesty included, have dismissed the results of Israeli internal investigations as worthless?[36]

2. *Al-Shifa.* On the basis of "credible" evidence that Hamas fired a rocket from behind al-Shifa hospital, Amnesty called for an independent investigation. It then proceeded to call for an investigation of "other reports and claims that Hamas leaders and security forces used facilities within the hospital for military purposes and interrogations during the hostilities." Israel leveled cognate allegations during Cast Lead, but the evidence it adduced in support of them was razor thin.[37] This time around, Amnesty cited many sources of varying quality.[38] What it flagrantly did not do, however, was cite sources that disputed the allegation. It ignored the compelling and nuanced testimony of two respected Norwegian surgeons who volunteered in al-Shifa during Protective Edge: although "able to roam freely at the hospital," they came across no

---

that rockets were fired "200 or 300 meters away" from schools or hospitals, and also that "there were some mistakes made and they were quickly dealt with." The evidentiary value of a self-interested statement by a "senior Hamas official" is, of course, equal to that of an Israeli Foreign Ministry press release—i.e., zero.

35. International Federation for Human Rights (FIDH), *Trapped and Punished: The Gaza civilian population under Operation Protective Edge* (April 2015), p. 40.

36. See, e.g., B'Tselem (Israeli Information Center for Human Rights in the Occupied Territories), *Israeli Authorities Have Proven They Cannot Investigate Suspected Violations of International Humanitarian Law by Israel in the Gaza Strip* (5 September 2014), btselem .org/accountability/20140905_failure_to_investigate.

37. See Chapter 3.

38. Both Amnesty and Israeli *hasbara* leaned on the journalistic scoops of *Washington Post* foreign correspondent William Booth for the more sensational charges against Hamas. State of Israel, *2014 Gaza Conflict,* pp. 76n234, 91n269, 214n496. Booth's creative journalism had earlier caught up with him when he was suspended by the *Post* for plagiarism. Paul Farhi, "*Washington Post* to Suspend William Booth over Panama Canal Story," *Washington Post* (18 January 2013).

indication that it was a "command center for Hamas."[39] At this author's request, one of the world's leading academic specialists on Gaza, Sara Roy of Harvard University, consulted a clutch of her own Gaza-based sources, whose personal and professional integrity she attested to. The consensus among them was that although rockets had been fired in the vicinity of al-Shifa (but not from hospital grounds), it was highly improbable that Hamas made military use of the hospital building.[40] Amnesty either chose to ignore or didn't bother to solicit such contrary opinions from impeccable, easily accessible sources. It also reported the supposedly incriminating tidbit that "a Palestinian journalist . . . was interrogated by officers from Hamas' Internal Security in an abandoned section of the hospital." Al-Shifa was filled to the brim with as many as 13,000 homeless people during Protective Edge. Because it enabled access to satellite news-gathering equipment, the hospital also served as a hub for the media, political spokespeople, UN officials, human rights organizations, and other NGOs. It is cause for wonder why Amnesty would consider it sinister, or even noteworthy, if a besieged party fending off a murderous foreign invasion questioned—not physically abused or intimidated, just *questioned*—someone in a facility packed with a throng of random people, some among them presumably spies, saboteurs, and provoca- teurs.[41] Was Gaza's governing body not even allowed to carry out routine security functions? In its report, *"Strangling Necks": Abductions, torture and summary killings of Palestinians by Hamas forces during the 2014 Gaza/Israel conflict,* Amnesty flatly stated, "Hamas forces used the abandoned areas of al-Shifa hospital in Gaza City, including the outpa- tients' clinic area, to detain, interrogate, torture and otherwise ill-treat suspects." The evidence Amnesty adduced for the most incendiary of these asseverations—that is, Hamas systematically tortured suspects at al-Shifa—underwhelmed.[42] How, incidentally, did this torture chamber

39. "I have been able to roam freely at the hospital and take the pictures that I wanted and talk to whomever I wanted. I can of course not say that I have been in every corner of the hospital, but concerning what I and [Dr.] Erik Fosse have seen, then none of us have seen that it is a command center for Hamas." Norwegian surgeon Mads Gilbert, cited in en.wikipedia .org/wiki/Al-Shifa_Hospital.

40. E-mail correspondence dated 15, 17 April 2015, forwarded by Dr. Roy from three of her contacts.

41. Hamas alleged that the Palestinian Authority provided Israel with targeting infor- mation collected via its agents in Gaza. Elhanan Miller, "Hamas: PA gave Israel nearly a third of its Gaza targets," *Times of Israel* (5 February 2015).

42. Of the 17 cases documented in the report of Hamas human rights violations, the relevant ones mentioning al-Shifa were these:

escape the notice of swarms of journalists, UN officials, and NGOs ensconced at al-Shifa until Amnesty's solitary fieldworker in Gaza came along to scoop all of them? Even Israel's official postmortem on Protective Edge, although replete with the most egregious propaganda and falsehoods, didn't go beyond alleging that Hamas used al-Shifa for "security service interrogations."[43] Was Amnesty bending over backward to the point of coming out from under itself in order to demonstrate its nonpartisanship?

3. *Shuhada al-Aqsa.* Israel shelled Shuhada al-Aqsa hospital, killing at least four people and wounding dozens. Noting that Israel alleged it had targeted a cache of antitank missiles stored "in the immediate vicinity of the hospital," Amnesty stated that it "has not been able

---

The [Hamas] officers took Saleh Swelim to their Jabalia detention facility, known as the al-Sisi centre, and then to the outpatients' clinic at al-Shifa hospital in Gaza City, which Hamas forces were using to detain and interrogate suspects. M.S., a younger brother of Saleh Swelim, told Amnesty International that Internal Security officers also detained him that day and that he saw Saleh Swelim both at the al-Sisi facility and at al-Shifa hospital, and that Internal Security officers tortured both of them. [A lengthy testimony by M.S. follows describing his torture, but it ends on this note:] "We were both made to confess by being beaten. We remained in the al-Sisi camp until the following day, then were transferred to the al-Shifa hospital. We were received respectfully there in the outpatients' clinic. They did not beat us and treated us with respect, especially after they saw the burns on my body and the marks from the beatings. They applied ointment to my wounds and gave me medical treatment."

The three [Hamas] men took both Ali Da'alsa and M.D. away in a black Hyundai car but after about 10 minutes, during which they assaulted him, the three let M.D. go, dropping him near al-Quds Open University. The next day, M.D. went to the part of al-Shifa hospital used by Internal Security to inquire about Ali Da'alsa. He told Amnesty International: "I went to al-Shifa hospital outpatients' clinic where the Internal Security had a room. I knocked on the door and nobody answered. I kept on knocking on the door until they [Internal Security] finally arrived. They grabbed me and hit me and insulted me and treated me harshly, and increased their beatings of me."

A.H., 43, a member of Fatah, activist and former PA senior officer, told Amnesty International that members of Hamas's Internal Security force detained him as he left a mosque in the eastern area of Gaza City on 17 August 2014 and took him to the outpatients' clinic at al-Shifa hospital. There, he said, they tortured him for about two hours by tying his hands behind his back, blindfolding him and beating him, including with a hammer and plastic pipes, causing him to lose consciousness several times, and verbally abused him, before asking him about his links to the PA's security forces: "It was not really questioning, just a torture session."

The second of these three testimonies doesn't appear to rise to the practice of torture, at any rate as human rights organizations have defined it; otherwise, every Israeli soldier who roughed up a Palestinian in the West Bank would be guilty of torture—a charge Amnesty has, wisely, never leveled. Thus, only the third testimony would appear to be evidence of torture at al-Shifa, but it came from a "member of Fatah, activist and former PA senior officer," not necessarily the most reliable of sources.

43. State of Israel, *2014 Gaza Conflict*, para. 129.

to confirm this" incident and called for it to be "independently investigated." Insofar as it obligingly reported Israel's pretext for this atrocity, shouldn't Amnesty also have cited the eyewitness account of a nurse at her station? She testified that after four Palestinians were killed in vehicles parked outside, "the hospital was then hit 15 times in quick succession by tank strikes." Whereas in Amnesty's assessment Hamas and Israel might have been equally culpable of violating international law,[44] the Medical Fact-Finding Mission concluded: "what is important here is that [al-Aqsa] was attacked by the Israeli military while patients were admitted, health professionals were at work and civilians were seeking refuge from attacks in the surrounding area."[45]

4. *Ambulances.* Fully 45 ambulances were either damaged or destroyed as a result of direct Israeli attacks or collateral damage during Protective Edge. Amnesty reported that Israel "released video footage which it claimed showed Palestinian fighters entering an ambulance." This 24-second video clip was the one and only piece of evidence Israel adduced to justify its repeated targeting of ambulances during Protective Edge.[46] In fact, the evidentiary value of the video could be precisely calculated at zero. It captured a pair of unarmed Hamas militants on an unknown date at an unknown place entering an ambulance belonging to the emergency medical unit of Hamas's armed wing (al-Qassam Brigades). For all anyone could tell from the clip, they were participating in a routine medical rescue mission. (It merits parenthetical notice that the health ministry had instructed ambulance crews not to allow any weapons on board, not even pistols.) Since it referenced this vacuous video, why didn't Amnesty also note that Israel repeatedly targeted Palestinian ambulances in prior operations;[47] that notwithstanding its high-tech surveillance technology, Israel adduced evidence justifying such a criminal attack on an ambulance in *only one single incident* way back in 2002; and that in this sole instance Amnesty itself found the evidence dubious?[48] In fact, Amnesty, the Medical

44. "If Palestinian armed groups violated international humanitarian law by storing munitions near the hospital, and this was what Israel was targeting when it struck the hospital and killed civilians, serious concerns about the manner and execution of Israel's attack would remain."

45. Medical Fact-Finding Mission, pp. 50–51; see also FIDH, *Trapped and Punished,* p. 44.

46. State of Israel, *2014 Gaza Conflict,* para. 129.

47. See Chapter 3.

48. Norman G. Finkelstein, *Beyond Chutzpah: On the misuse of anti-Semitism and the abuse of history,* expanded paperback edition (Berkeley: 2008), pp. 128–30.

Fact-Finding Mission, and the FIDH delegation extensively documented premeditated and unprovoked attacks by Israel on Palestinian ambulances during Protective Edge.[49]

Schools Israel destroyed 22 schools and damaged 118 others during Protective Edge.[50] "The Israeli military has stated that rockets or mortars were launched from within several schools in the Gaza Strip during the hostilities," Amnesty reported, and that "at least 89 rockets and mortar shells were launched within 30m of UN schools." After professing its inability "to verify any of these specific claims," Amnesty recommended that "they should be independently investigated." But why did *Unlawful and Deadly* cite only—and ad nauseam—Israel Ministry of Foreign Affairs and Israel Defense Forces (IDF) press handouts?[51] Surely it could have cross-checked the official Israeli alibis by consulting Palestinian human rights groups, UN officials, and relevant NGOs based in Gaza. The UN Board of Inquiry investigated seven Israeli attacks, many deadly, on UN schools, all but one of which had been converted into emergency shelters. The board found no evidence to sustain, but copious evidence, including security guard and other witness testimony, to refute, boilerplate Israeli allegations that Hamas launched rockets from within or in the vicinity of those UN schools attacked by Israel.[52]

49. Amnesty International, "Evidence of Medical Workers and Facilities Being Targeted by Israeli Forces in Gaza" (7 August 2014); Medical Fact-Finding Mission, pp. 44–49; FIDH, *Trapped and Punished*, pp. 32–38.

50. An Israeli document reprinted in its official postmortem brazenly purported that up until the last two days of Protective Edge, "the IDF has refrained from causing damage to schools," while the report itself stated that Israel targeted schools in only "a very few cases." State of Israel, *2014 Gaza Conflict*, p. 176, paras. 281, 404.

51. Herewith is the totality of sources cited by Amnesty:

Israel Ministry of Foreign Affairs, *Hamas' Violations of the Law*, pp. 20, 23.

Israel Ministry of Foreign Affairs, *Hamas' Violations of the Law*, p. 25; IDF, *Declassified Report Exposes Hamas Human Shield Policy*, slide 13.

Israel Ministry of Foreign Affairs, *Hamas' Violations of the Law*, pp. 20, 22; IDF, *Declassified Report Exposes Hamas Human Shield Policy*, slide 14.

Israel Ministry of Foreign Affairs, *Hamas' Violations of the Law*, pp. 20–21.

Israel Ministry of Foreign Affairs, *Hamas' Violations of the Law*, pp. 20–26.

52. On a related note, basing itself on UN press releases, Amnesty recounted Hamas's misuse of other UN schools not targeted by Israel: "Palestinian armed groups stored rockets and other munitions in ... UN schools. UNRWA [United Nations Relief and Works

Mosques Israel destroyed 73 mosques and damaged 130 others during Protective Edge. Amnesty reported that according to Israel's Ministry of Foreign Affairs, "at least 83 rockets and mortars were launched from within 25m of mosques during the hostilities, in some cases from directly within the mosque compounds." No other source was cited by Amnesty. It was not the first time Israel targeted mosques in Gaza. It destroyed 30 mosques and damaged 15 more during Cast Lead. Back then, the UN Human Rights Council mission headed by Richard Goldstone investigated an "intentional" Israeli missile attack on a mosque that killed at least 15 people attending prayers. It found "no evidence that this mosque was used for the storage of weapons or any military activity by Palestinian armed groups."[53] If it quoted official Israeli justifications for the wholesale—indeed, Kristallnacht-like—assault on Islamic houses of worship, shouldn't Amnesty at least have noted that in the past these justifications had proven to be spurious?[54]

Power Plant Israel repeatedly attacked Gaza's only power plant during Protective Edge. The attacks exacerbated already severe electricity blackouts and devastated water, sanitation, and medical services. It was not the first time that Israel had attacked Gaza's only power plant. In 2006, Israel launched multiple missile strikes precisely targeting the plant's transformers. B'Tselem (Israeli Information Center for Human Rights in the Occupied Territories) deemed the 2006 attack a "war crime."[55] Amnesty stated that

---

Agency] discovered Palestinian munitions in three of its vacant schools in the Gaza Strip," specifically, "20 rockets in an elementary school in Gaza City"; "rockets . . . in an elementary school in Jabalia"; "another cache of rockets . . . at a school in Nuseirat." The Board of Inquiry later found, however, that the weapons stored in these empty schools (they were closed for summer recess) were not rocket caches but, rather, one mortar and twenty shells in the Gaza City elementary school, "an object, seemingly a weapon" in the Jabalia school, and one mortar and three shells on one occasion and one mortar and twenty shells on a second occasion at the Nuseirat school. (UNRWA itself acknowledged that it had overstated the case because of misreporting and a lack of technical expertise on the part of the UNRWA Gaza field office.) The official Israeli postmortem on Protective Edge falsely stated that according to the UN Board of Inquiry, "at the time the weapons were found" in one of the three schools, it "sheltered approximately 300 Gazans." State of Israel, *2014 Gaza Conflict*, p. 82 (caption), para. 280.

53. See Chapter 3.

54. The case Israel has mounted over the years to justify its targeting of Gaza's mosques lacks coherence. See Chapter 3.

55. B'Tselem (Israeli Information Center for Human Rights in the Occupied Territories), *Act of Vengeance: Israel's bombing of the Gaza power plant and its effects* (Jerusalem: 2006).

the attack on Gaza's power plant during Protective Edge "could amount to a war crime,"[56] but then hastened to enter this qualification: "An Israeli brigadier-general denied that Israel had targeted the power plant intentionally, but did not rule out the possibility that it was hit by mistake." If Amnesty quoted the brigadier-general's predictable denial, shouldn't it also have taken note that Israel had intentionally targeted the very same power plant in the past? "The power plant's location was well known," the FIDH delegation visiting Gaza after Protective Edge noted. "Repeated strikes . . . and the refusal [by Israel] to guarantee the security of the plant do not support the assertion that these strikes were accidental."[57] It is remarkable how out of step Amnesty was with human rights delegations that did manage to enter Gaza.

Amnesty's biased rules of evidence also tainted its report on Israeli aerial attacks targeting civilian residences during Protective Edge. The report, *Families under the Rubble,* did conclude that the eight attacks Amnesty investigated were on various grounds unlawful and possibly war crimes. In particular, it found that "the loss of civilian lives, injury to civilians and damage to civilian objects appear disproportionate, that is, out of proportion to the likely military advantage of carrying out the attack." Israel itself "made no statement about who or what was being targeted, or even acknowledged that it carried out these particular attacks." But although Amnesty properly asserted that "the onus is on Israel to provide information concerning the attacks and their intended targets," bizarrely, it took upon itself the burden of ferreting out pretexts that could justify them. The result hovered between satire and scandal (see Table 7). *First,* Amnesty repeatedly speculated, often on the flimsiest of grounds, that Israel targeted a home because a Hamas militant might have been hiding inside. *Second,* it didn't ask the obvious question, How would Israel even have been privy to the militant's alleged presence if most neighbors appeared to be in the dark?[58] *Third,* it detected in each and every attack a possible Gazan militant targeted by Israel. But even Israel's harshest critic would concede that one or another of the civilian homes might have been hit not intentionally but due to an operational

56. In a press release it issued during Protective Edge, Amnesty stated that the attack "very likely" amounted to a "war crime." "Gaza: Attacks on UN school and power plant are likely war crimes" (30 July 2014).

57. FIDH, *Trapped and Punished,* pp. 48–52.

58. On another incongruous note, Amnesty repeatedly faulted Israel for not issuing alerts before its attacks. But if the intended target was a Hamas militant, wouldn't it have defeated the purpose to warn him in advance?

TABLE 7 Amnesty International: Why Israel Targeted Civilian Homes in Gaza

Case 1:
18 Palestinian civilians killed, 11 from one family, 7 from another

One of the neighbors said that he had heard from others that a group of unknown people were walking around in the corridor somewhere downstairs on the night of the attack. Some neighbors speculated, without seeing them, that they might have been members of an armed group. . . . It is unclear what the intended target of this attack was. Even if a group of men had entered the building and were assumed or known to have been members of an armed group by the military, its actions of targeting two family apartments was reckless and disproportionate.

Case 2:
26 Palestinian civilians killed, 25 from one family

The apparent target of Israel's attacks was Ahmed Sahmoud, a member of the al-Qassam Brigades, Hamas' armed wing. According to Israeli sources, he was a high-ranking officer in the Khan Yunis command. Early reports of the attack said that he was inside the building visiting a member of the Abu Jame' family. Surviving family members and neighbors denied this. . . . [N]eighbors believed that Ahmed Sahmoud might have been under the balcony of his mother's apartment on the ground floor when the house was attacked. . . . If Ahmed Sahmoud was the intended target this would constitute a grossly disproportionate attack.

Case 3:
36 Palestinians killed, 16 from one family, 7 from a second family, 7 from a third family, 4 from a fourth family

By questioning many of the family members and their neighbors, an Amnesty International fieldworker found three residents who might have been the object of an attack. [Four long paragraphs follow filled with inconclusive speculations on them.] *Even if all the three men who might have been targets had been directly participating in hostilities, their presence in the house would not have deprived the other residents of their immunity, as civilians, from direct attack. . . . The effects of an attack . . . should have been . . . regarded as manifestly disproportionate.*

Case 4:
14 Palestinian civilians killed, 5 from one family, 4 from a second family

[T]wo neighbors maintained that, following the attack, they found out that at least four members of the al-Qassam Brigades, the armed wing of Hamas, including a battalion commander and a communications officer, were apparently using the empty apartment in the building for some time prior to the attack. . . . Amnesty International has been unable to verify this information. However, even if the empty flat in the . . . building was used by the al-Qassam Brigades, the loss of civilian life in this attack was clearly disproportionate.

Case 5:
5 Palestinian civilians killed, all from one family

Neighbors told Amnesty International's fieldworker that they believed that the attack was intended to target the home of the man who went by the name of "Abu Amra," who was not in his apartment at the time. . . . Amnesty International has been unable to confirm the identity of "Abu Amra" nor [sic] whether or not he did have any relationship with any armed group. Even if "Abu Amra" was a fighter or otherwise had been directly participating in hostilities, this attack was carried out in a manner that violated international humanitarian law.

Case 6: 6 Palestinian civilians killed, 5 from one family	*Although family members denied it, both Ramadan Kamal al-Bakri and Ibrahim al-Mashharawi* [two of the deceased] *were members of Islamic Jihad's al-Quds Brigades.... [If these two men] were the intended targets, ... the Israeli forces should have taken necessary precautions to minimize the risk to civilians in the house.*[a]
Case 7: 8 Palestinian civilians killed, all from one family	*All witnesses who gave statements said that none of the family members was involved with armed groups....* [The brother of the deceased head of household] *said: "Earlier Ra'fat had gone out with a torch to investigate a rocket that he thought had gone up from the olive fields east of our house.... They probably thought that Ra'fat had shot the rocket from the field and thought he was from the resistance."... Even if they believed that a fighter was present, Israeli forces should have realized that bombing the house would be a disproportionate attack.*
Case 8: 8 Palestinian civilians killed, all from one family	*The intended target of the attack appears to have been Hayel Abu Dahrouj, a member of Islamic Jihad's al-Quds Brigades, who had returned to his house shortly before the attack. "He missed his kids so he came back to the house," his brother Wael told Amnesty International's fieldworker.... If Hayel Abu Dahrouj was the intended target, it is unclear why Israeli forces did not take necessary precautions to minimize the risk to civilians in the homes.*

NOTE: The italicized text in the right-hand column is quoted directly from *Families under the Rubble*.

[a] Notwithstanding Amnesty's intrepid sleuthing, the official Israeli postmortem on Protective Edge (published after Amnesty's report) pointed to "Omar Al-Rahim, a senior commander in Palestinian Islamic Jihad" as the actual target of this attack. State of Israel, *2014 Gaza Conflict*, paras. 267, 456.

mishap. Amnesty was so determined to provide Israel with alibis that it ended up going overboard, as its apologetics preempted even the plausible excuse of human error.[59]

The thrust of Amnesty's report *Families under the Rubble* conveyed the impression that Israel overwhelmingly targeted Hamas militants in its attacks on civilian homes. It exonerated Israel of the charge that would most

59. Contrariwise and as implausibly, Israel purported that even if many civilians did die when it targeted Hamas militants in civilian dwellings, still these deaths resulted from operational errors—in particular, the IDF had been caught unawares that noncombatants were present. B'Tselem (Israeli Information Center for Human Rights in the Occupied Territories), *Whitewash Protocol: The so-called investigation of Operation Protective Edge* (2016), p. 21. But if it was real-time intelligence that alerted it to the sudden appearance of a Hamas militant in a civilian dwelling, it was almost certainly a Gazan informer who tipped off Israel. Didn't the informer mention that civilians were also present—or did Israeli minders not even bother to ask?

appall in the court of public opinion—that the IDF was deliberately target-ing civilians and civilian objects. By supplying Israel with pretexts for atroci-ties that were among the most heinous it committed during Protective Edge, Amnesty conveniently eased the burdens of Israeli *hasbara*. It is much easier to rebut the nebulous, subjective, and relative charge of a "disproportionate" attack than the charge of a deliberate attack on the civilian population. Indeed, the official Israeli postmortem on Protective Edge repeatedly invoked the numberless caveats attached to the proportionality principle, which in effect demonstrated the near-impossibility of nailing down a conviction based on it.[60] But the bigger scandal is this: the impression left by *Families under the Rubble* was flat-out false—and Amnesty must have known it. In a state of inflamed madness, but also in a sober calculation of its pedagogical value, Israel inflicted a grotesque form of collective punishment as it indis-criminately or intentionally leveled a staggering number of Gazan dwellings. It initially targeted the hearths of Hamas militants,[61] then, as the ground invasion got under way, embarked on a wild wrecking spree, and then, in Protective Edge's denouement, pulverized four multistory landmark edifices in Gaza. In its report *"Nothing Is Immune": Israel's destruction of landmark buildings in Gaza,* Amnesty acknowledged that the destruction of these landmark buildings was "a form of collective punishment." But it also brack-eted off Israel's climactic act as the exception to the rule: "[T]he attacks are of great significance because they are examples of what appears to have been deliberate destruction and targeting of civilian buildings and property on a large scale, carried out without military necessity." In fact, the vast prepon-derance of Israeli destruction throughout Protective Edge consisted of col-lective punishment on a lunatic scale and devoid of military purpose, let alone military necessity. If situated in the full scope of this systematic wreck-age, Israel's specific targeting of Hamas militants occupying or deploying

60. State of Israel, *2014 Gaza Conflict*, paras. 49, 317–33, 401–2, 452, 456; annex, paras. 6–8. See also B'Tselem, *Whitewash Protocol*, p. 23. On a related note, when Hamas fired mortar shells in a populated area, Amnesty accused it of a straightforward "indiscriminate" attack, whereas when Israel dropped a 2,000-pound bomb and fired artillery shells in a densely populated area, killing large numbers of civilians, Amnesty accused it of committing a "disproportionate" attack—an accusation that Israel was then invited to rebut ("The onus is on Israel to provide information relating to why it targeted ..."). See *Families under the Rubble*, Al-Dali Building, Al-Louh Family Home.

61. B'Tselem (Israeli Information Center for Human Rights in the Occupied Territories), *Black Flag: The legal and moral implications of the policy of attacking residential buildings in the Gaza Strip, summer 2014* (2015), pp. 37–41.

from civilian homes amounted at most to the equivalent of statistical error. Could Amnesty have possibly believed that a Hamas militant was secreted in all, or even most, of the *18,000 homes* Israel destroyed in Gaza? The ghastly truth of what unfolded in Gaza was captured not in Amnesty's effective whitewash but instead in the Breaking the Silence collection of testimonies of IDF soldiers who served in Protective Edge (see Table 8).[62]

In its introduction to *Families under the Rubble*, Amnesty exhorted Israel to "learn the lessons of this and previous conflicts and change its military doctrine and tactics for fighting in densely populated areas such as Gaza so as to ensure strict compliance with international humanitarian law." But Israel had already learned the lessons of fighting in Gaza; its military doctrine had already incorporated these lessons; and the IDF brilliantly executed them in this last operation. It required exceptional mental discipline not to notice that ensuring "strict compliance with international law" wasn't an Israeli consideration, let alone a priority. On the contrary, the whole point of Protective Edge was to leave "families under the rubble."[63]

The pretense that not just Israel but Hamas as well committed massive, egregious violations of international law underpinned Amnesty's "balanced" indictment. Its accusation that Hamas was guilty of "flagrant violations of international law"—that is, war crimes—fell under two heads: (1) Hamas's use of inherently indiscriminate weapons, and (2) its indiscriminate or deliberate targeting of Israeli civilians and civilian objects. In addition, Amnesty accused Hamas of violating the rule of international law that required it to take all feasible precautions in order to protect civilians in the combat zone. Each of these will be analyzed in turn.[64]

Indiscriminate Weapons Amnesty asserted that "all the rockets" in Hamas's arsenal constituted "unguided projectiles which cannot be accurately

---

62. Breaking the Silence, *This Is How We Fought in Gaza: Soldiers' testimonies and photographs from Operation "Protective Edge"* (2014).

63. For Israel's indiscriminate destruction of homes, which "must have entailed approval from top-level decision-makers in the Israeli military and/or government," see also Medical Fact-Finding Mission, pp. 35–37, 98.

64. In *"Strangling Necks,"* Amnesty also accused Hamas of having committed "war crimes" in its "torture" and "summary, extrajudicial executions" of "at least 23" alleged collaborators in Gaza. This subject matter will be considered in Chapter 13.

TABLE 8 Property/Home Destruction in Gaza during Operation Protective Edge: A Selection of IDF Testimonies

---

1[a]   [*Did you see any "before and after" aerial photos?*][b]

Sure. Neighborhoods erased. You know what joke was being told in the army at the time? The joke says that Palestinians only sing the chorus because they have no verses [*houses*] left. [*in Hebrew, the word for verses is the same as the word for house*]

5   During the talk [while in training] he [high-ranking armored battalion commander] showed us the urban combat facility and said, "Everything you see here—picture it as though someone came through now and destroyed everything. There are almost no buildings left standing." The inclination is to avoid risks—rather to destroy everything we come across.

14   I got the impression that every house we passed on our way got hit by a shell—and houses farther away too. It was methodical. There was no threat.

15   While we were stationed there, the armored forces would fire at the surrounding houses all the time. I don't know what exactly their order was, but it seemed like every house was considered a threat, and so every house needed to be hit by at least one shell. . . .

[*After you left, were there still any houses left standing?*]
Nearly none.

20   [*What were you shooting at?*]
At houses.
[*Randomly chosen houses?*]
Yes.
[*How much fire were you using?*]
There was constant talk about how much we fired, how much we hit, who missed. There were people who fired 20 shells per day. It's simple: Whoever feels like shooting more—shoots more. Most guys shot more. Dozens of shells [*per day*], throughout the operation. Multiply that by 11 tanks in the company.

21   I don't know how they pulled it off, the D9[c] operators didn't rest for a second. Nonstop, as if they were playing in a sandbox. Driving back and forth, back and forth, razing another house, another street. And at some point there was no trace left of that street. . . . Day and night, 24/7, they went back and forth, gathering up mounds, making embankments, flattening house after house.

29   There was no threat and it was quiet, and then suddenly there's this command on the two-way radio: "Guys, everyone form a row, facing the neighborhood of al-Bureij." . . . I remember it, all the tanks were standing in a row, and I personally asked my commander: "Where are we firing at?" He told me: "Pick wherever you feel like it." And later, during talks with the other guys—each one basically chose his own target, and the commander called it on the two-way radio, "Good morning al-Bureij." "We are carrying out, a 'Good morning al-Bureij,' guys" that was the quote. . . . And everyone fired shells wherever they wanted to, obviously. Nobody had opened fire at us—not before, not after, not during.

30   Everything "wet" [*using live fire*]. From the moment we went in, we were firing MATADOR and LAW [*portable anti-tank*] rockets on every house we entered before "opening" them up, everything "wet," grenades, the whole thing. War.

[Every room you go into you open "wet"?]

Everything. When I got to a house, it was already half destroyed. Lots and lots of bullet holes inside it, everything inside a total mess.

[The two hours of artillery fire before—what were they shooting at?]

At scattered areas near the houses. All those agricultural areas near the houses. Before a tank makes any movement it fires, every time. Those guys were trigger happy, totally crazy. Those were their orders, I'm certain of it, there's no chance anybody would just go around shooting like that. *[The brigade's]* conception was, "We'll fire without worrying about it, and then we'll see what happens."

[The fire was directed at places deemed suspicious?]

No, not necessarily. The tank fires at places that you know you will need to enter, it fires at those houses.

[Only at the houses you're going to enter?]

No, at the surrounding houses too. There are also agricultural fields there, the D9 rips them all up. And tin sheds. It takes down whatever's in its way, it topples greenhouses. Lots of houses were flattened in "Bar's Bar" *[the nickname given to a housing compound in which the forces were positioned]*. Empty houses that bothered us. Bothered us even just to look at.

33   The very day we left Gaza, all the houses we had stayed in were blown up by combat engineers.

34   We [armored corps] were given a number of targets.... It's not like any normal city, where you'll see a building next to another building and there's a space between them. It looks like one fused layer.

[And at that point were you being fired at?]

No fire was directed toward us, but these were deemed "suspicious spots"— which means a very lax policy of opening fire *[was being employed]*. That can mean anything that looks threatening to us.... Every tank commander knew, and even the simple soldiers knew, that if something turns out to be not OK, they can say they saw something suspicious.

37   One of the high ranking commanders, he really liked the D9s. He was a real proponent of flattening things. He put them to good use. Let's just say that after every time he was somewhere, all the infrastructure around the buildings was totally destroyed, almost every house had gotten a shell through it. He was very much in favor of that.

42   The forces ... destroyed everything still left there. Literally not a single house was left standing.... "We are entering the area in order to destroy the entire tunneling infrastructure that still remains there." If you think about it, that really means every house in the area.

[You said that according to the intelligence the IDF had, no tunnels were left there.]

Right. What they mean is, this is the area in which the brigade moves around, if it's still standing, it needs to be taken down.... This incursion happened the night before there was a cease-fire.... [T]hey went in just to destroy stuff. Just to purposelessly destroy stuff, to finish the job, until they were told to stop.

46   There was one afternoon that the company commander gathered us all together, and we were told that we were about to go on an offensive operation, to "provoke" the neighborhood that dominated us, which was al-Bureij.... Because up until then, we hadn't really had any real engagement with them.... [W]hen it started

(continued)

TABLE 8 *(continued)*

getting dark my tank led the way, we were in a sort of convoy, and there was this little house. And then suddenly we see an entire neighborhood opening up before us, lots of houses, it's all crowded and the moment we got to that little house, the order came to attack. Each [*tank*] aimed at whichever direction it chose.... And that's how it was, really—every tank just firing wherever it wanted to. And during the offensive, no one shot at us—not before it, not during it, and not after it. I remember that when we started withdrawing with the tanks, I looked toward the neighborhood, and I could simply see an entire neighborhood up in flames, like in the movies. Columns of smoke everywhere, the neighborhood in pieces, houses on the ground, and like, people were living there, but nobody had fired at us yet. We were firing purposelessly.

51 A week or two after we entered the Gaza Strip and we were all firing a lot when there wasn't any need for it—just for the sake of firing—a member of our company was killed.... The company commander came over to us and told us that one guy was killed due to such-and-such, and he said, "Guys, get ready, get in your tanks, and we'll fire a barrage in memory of our comrade."... [T]here was a sort of building far away near the coastline, around 4.5 kilometers from us.... It wasn't a threat to us, it had nothing to do with anybody, it wasn't part of the operation, it was out by the sea, far away from anything and from any potential threat—but that building was painted orange, and that orange drove my eyes crazy the entire time.... So I told my platoon commander: "I want to fire at that orange house," and he told me: "Cool, whatever you feel like," and we fired....

[*Did your guys discuss it later?*]

The bit about shelling purposelessly? No, because when you look at the bigger picture, that's something we were doing all the time. We were firing purposelessly all day long. Hamas was nowhere to be seen.

52 [*Is the tank's M16 being used the whole time?*]

The more the merrier. What weapons? The tank, endless ammunition, and a crazy amount of firepower. Constantly. If not via the cannon, then via the tank's heavy machine gun.

[*Where is it shooting at?*]

At everything, basically. At suspicious houses. What's a "suspicious spot?" Everything is a suspicious spot. This is Gaza, you're firing at everything.

54 Any house that infantry guys enter—a tank precedes them. That was really the formulation: any force that enters a house—first, at least one tank shell is fired at it before the force even goes in. Immediately after the engagement we set up in this orchard, we blasted shells at the surrounding houses. Even my commander, because he was hyped up to fire his personal weapon, took the entire team out just to shoot at the house, which was already obviously empty. So many shells were fired at it, and it was clearly empty. "Well, fire," he told us. It was meaningless. It was just for kicks—the sort of fun you have at a shooting range.

63 [The commander] tells you, "Listen, this is the first line—I can't take any risks on the first line of houses, use artillery on those."

[*Did he have any intelligence on those houses?*]

No, no, he has no intelligence.

67   [*Combat engineering forces*] blew up a lot of houses.... There are all kinds of
       considerations about why to blow up a house. One of them, for example, is when
       you want to defend some other house. If there's a house blocking your field of
       vision, [*and you want to*] expose the area so that it's easier to defend....
       Sometimes we blew up a house when we suspected there was an explosive device
       in it, but I think ultimately we blew up pretty much the entire neighborhood.

71   On the day the fellow from our company was killed, the commanders came up
       to us and told us what happened. Then they decided to fire an "honor barrage"
       and fire three shells....

       [*A barrage of what?*]

       A barrage of shells. They fired the way it's done in funerals, but with shellfire
       and at houses. Not into the air. They just chose [*a house*]—the tank commander
       said, "Just pick the farthest one, so it does the most damage." Revenge of sorts.
       So we fired at one of the houses.

74   I remember one time that explosives were detonated in order to clear passage
       routes. They told us, "Take cover, it's about to be used 100–150 meters away."
       Then an explosion—I've never heard anything like it. Lamps crashing, it was
       insane—a crazy mushroom of fire, really crazy. Then we went down into the
       street and the houses we were supposed to take over no longer existed. Gone.

83   There was a humanitarian cease-fire that went into effect at 6:00 AM. I
       remember they told us at 5:15 AM, "Look, we're going to put on a show." ... It
       was amazing. Fire, nonstop shelling of the "Sevivon" neighborhood [*east of Beit
       Hanoun*].... Nonstop. Just nonstop. The entire Beit Hanoun compound—in
       ruins.... Nothing. Absolutely nothing. Nothing.

110   [A] very senior officer from the army strike coordination center comes in
       running and says, "Listen up, the brigade commander was killed and a soldier
       was kidnapped, it's a mess, we need to help them." ... One of the most senior
       officials in the IDF, he just marked off houses on an aerial photo of Shuja'iyya,
       to be taken down. He simply looked at the map and saw commanding points
       and commanding houses and [*picked targets*] in a way that was in some sense
       sort of random.... It's not like in every building that was struck in Shuja'iyya
       there was some Hamas militant or somebody firing at our forces.

       [*So why was it attacked?*]

       In order to keep their heads down and allow our forces to get out of there, to use
       firepower—that's how the military works.

       [*I'm trying to understand: it was random, or as part of a target list prepared in
       advance?*]

       It wasn't prepared in advance at all. In the inquiry later on it was described as a
       mistake.

---

[a] Testimonies are numbered in the collection.
[b] Bracketed, italicized interpolations by Breaking the Silence.
[c] Armored bulldozers.

directed at specific targets." Furthermore, although acknowledging that Hamas did "appear to have aimed some mortars at military objectives," Amnesty entered the critical caveat that mortars "are still an imprecise weapon and must therefore never be used to target military objectives located amidst civilians or civilian objects." In a second iteration, the legal standard was set yet higher: "Even in the hands of a highly experienced and trained operator, a mortar round can never be accurate enough to *hit a specific point target*. Hence, when mortars are used with the intent of striking military targets located in the vicinity of civilian concentrations, but strike civilians or civilian objects, they constitute indiscriminate attacks" (emphasis added). Except for handheld weapons, such as pistols, antitank missiles, and IEDs, Amnesty effectively declared illegal the whole of Hamas's mostly archaic military arsenal. Indeed, according to Amnesty, "international humanitarian law prohibits the *use* of weapons that are by nature indiscriminate"; "*using* prohibited weapons is a war crime"; "*firing* the rocket was a war crime" (emphases added). Thus, in Amnesty's bookkeeping, each time Hamas fired a rocket or mortar shell, it committed a war crime, regardless of whether the weapon struck a civilian or civilian object. Insofar as Hamas fired seven thousand rockets and mortar shells at Israel, it would have, on Amnesty's reckoning, committed perhaps as many as seven thousand war crimes,[65] even if only six civilians in Israel were killed and only one Israeli house was destroyed. Such a calculation might appear to go some distance toward vindicating Amnesty's "balanced" indictment, but only at the price of turning international law—or at any rate Amnesty's construal and application of it—into an object deserving of derision. If Hamas's mere use of these weapons constituted war crimes, it's also cause for wonder why Amnesty took the trouble to investigate the ensuing civilian death and destruction. One might think that after a bill of indictment already tallying thousands of war crimes, supplementary documentation of war crimes would be redundant, akin to beating a dead horse. But there's another anomaly as well. Amnesty alluded in passing to the fact that Israeli "violations" of international law during Protective Edge included "attacks using munitions such as artillery, which cannot be precisely targeted, on very densely populated residential areas." In fact, had Amnesty bothered to pursue this line of inquiry, it would have discovered that Israel fired no less than *20,000* unguided high-explosive artil-

---

65. Each of the 5,000 rockets fired would automatically constitute a war crime, as would each of the 2,000 mortar shells fired in the vicinity of a civilian concentration.

lery shells into Gaza, an estimated 95 percent into or near populated civilian areas. The Israeli artillery shells were doubly indiscriminate: they couldn't be directed at, and their blast and fragmentation effects couldn't be limited to, a specific target. Thus, on the one hand, an attack with a 155mm "Doher" howitzer was technically reckoned a "hit" if the shell landed within 46 meters of the target—a far cry from Amnesty's "specific point target" threshold and, anyhow, as the Breaking the Silence testimonies confirmed, the artillery was frequently fired with abandon—while on the other hand, the expected casualty-producing radius of each 155mm artillery shell was about 300 meters.[66] The official Israeli postmortem on Protective Edge purported that "in the overwhelming majority of cases" Israel fired high-explosive artillery shells into "open areas devoid of civilian presence."[67] But it also stated that "rather than utilizing the less populated areas of the Gaza Strip where they operate during lulls in hostilities," Hamas had relocated its "assets and operations to built-up civilian areas in order to shield them from IDF attack."[68] If this authoritative Israeli publication was to be believed, Israel must have deliberately fired the overwhelming majority of 20,000 high-explosive artillery shells into empty spaces devoid of military value. Meanwhile, to go by Amnesty's bookkeeping, wherein each use of an indiscriminate weapon constitutes a war crime, Israel committed nearly three times as many war crimes as Hamas just in its use of artillery shells—although one would never know it from Amnesty's reports.[69] It was symptomatic of

66. Action on Armed Violence, *Under Fire: Israel's artillery policies scrutinized* (2014).

67. State of Israel, *2014 Gaza Conflict*, para. 347 (see also paras. 354–57).

68. Ibid., para. 123 (see also p. 152n417).

69. In *Unlawful and Deadly*'s précis of international humanitarian law, Amnesty stated that parties to the conflict

> must choose appropriate means and methods of attack when military targets are located within residential areas. This requirement rules out the use of certain types of weapons and tactics. The use of weapons that are inherently indiscriminate such as unguided rockets is prohibited. And the use in densely populated areas of imprecise weapons that cannot be directed at a military objective with sufficient precision, such as mortars, is likely to result in indiscriminate attacks and is also prohibited.

Setting aside that, unlike Israel, Hamas didn't enjoy the luxury to "choose" its means and methods of attack, it was telling that Amnesty alluded to Hamas's unguided rockets as "prohibited weapons" and its use of mortars in densely populated areas as "prohibited," but didn't allude to Israel's illegal use of artillery shells (on a far larger scale) in populated civilian areas. It might be supposed that the omission was owing to the fact that *Unlawful and Deadly* focused on Hamas war crimes. But in the respective précis of international humanitarian law complementing Amnesty's two reports on Israeli crimes, the inherent criminality of Israel's artillery barrages in populated civilian areas also went unnoticed.

Amnesty's extreme bias that whereas it meticulously inventoried Hamas's military arsenal, the reader was left utterly clueless about the quantity and quality of firepower Israel visited on Gaza. How many bombs (and how much tonnage) did Israel drop? How many missile attacks did Israel launch? How many tank and artillery shells did it expend? One searched Amnesty's reports on Protective Edge in vain for answers to these basic questions, even though these data were publicly accessible.[70] A juxtaposition of the arsenals each side deployed would have made mockery of Amnesty's pretensions to balance. If *war* connotes an armed conflict between more or less evenly matched belligerents, then what unfolded during Protective Edge did not remotely rise to this threshold: Hamas's oh-so-criminal primitive projectiles vanished to negative invisibility beside Israel's ever-so-legal high-tech killing machine.

Indiscriminate and Deliberate Targeting of Civilians and Civilian Objects Amnesty did not criminally indict Hamas just for deploying indiscriminate weapons. It also, and as a discrete line in its ledger, criminally indicted Hamas for deploying these indiscriminate weapons in order to launch "indiscriminate attacks" and "attacks targeting civilians." Put otherwise, Hamas stood charged with deploying indiscriminate weapons *and also* for deploying these weapons in order to launch intentionally indiscriminate and targeted attacks on civilians and civilian objects. Article 51 of the Additional Protocols to the Geneva Conventions prohibits "indiscriminate attacks." It defines such attacks (inter alia) as "those which are not directed at a specific military objective" *or* "those which employ a method or means of combat which cannot be directed at a specific military objective." Thus, *both* these prohibitions are subsumed under the single rubric "indiscriminate attacks": if an indiscriminate weapon is used, or if a weapon is fired indiscriminately, or if an indiscriminate weapon is fired indiscriminately, it constitutes *one and the same war crime* of an indiscriminate attack.[71] Amnesty, however, cleft it into separate and distinct crimes. It exhorted Hamas to "end the use of inherently indiscriminate weapons such as unguided rockets, denounce attacks targeting civilians and indiscriminate attacks." The "value" of each Hamas projectile in Amnesty's bill of indictment accordingly dou-

70. See Chapter 11.
71. International Committee of the Red Cross (ICRC), *Commentary on the Additional Protocols of 8 June 1977 to the Geneva Conventions of 12 August 1949* (Geneva: 1987), article 51. Amnesty correctly cited this provision in *Unlawful and Deadly*'s précis of international humanitarian law.

bled: Hamas committed a war crime each time it made "use" of an indiscriminate weapon and also each time it launched an "attack"—either indiscriminate or targeting civilians—with an indiscriminate weapon. That neat linguistic subtlety would have enabled Amnesty to boost its indictment of Hamas to as many as 14,000 war crimes (for those who were still counting), even if, still, only six civilians in Israel were killed and only one Israeli house was destroyed. Consider further Amnesty's criminal indictment of Hamas for "targeting" civilian areas. It reported that "in many cases" Hamas was, or declared it was, "directing" its projectiles "towards Israeli civilians and civilian objects," that it "directed them at specific Israeli communities." If Amnesty determined that Hamas breached the laws of war by deploying rockets that "cannot be accurately targeted at specific targets," it's hard to make out how Amnesty could also charge Hamas with "targeting" civilian communities when it fired them: how does one target an "inherently" untargetable weapon? If Hamas publicly declared its intention to target a civilian community, it might be guilty of bluster, but not of a deliberate attack; it was, on Amnesty's own evidence, incapable of launching a deliberate attack. Still (it might be contended), weren't Hamas rockets sufficiently accurate to target a large civilian community, if not a specific object within it? But then it puzzles why so many Hamas rockets landed in vacant areas away from Israeli conurbations. (Of the five thousand Hamas rockets fired at Israel, well under one thousand came within range of Iron Dome, which was deployed around Israel's major population centers.) It's not very persuasive that Hamas was targeting empty space; if so many Hamas rockets landed in empty space, it's because they couldn't be targeted. What's more, Amnesty accused Hamas of deliberately targeting an Israeli civilian community not only when that was its declared intention but also when its declared target was a military object located in or around the community: "These [Hamas] statements, most of which specified the time of each attack, the community (or in rarer cases, *the military base*) targeted, and the munition used indicate that these attacks were directed at civilians or civilian objects" (emphasis added). If, according to Amnesty, a Hamas press release served as proof of intent, it perplexes how it proved intent to target civilians even when it manifestly eschewed such an intent.[72] In one instance, Hamas verged on scoring a trifecta of war crimes as

72. According to Amnesty, Hamas also claimed that its attacks on civilian areas were "committed in reprisal for Israeli abuses or aggression." For the legal status of these belligerent reprisals, see Chapter 11.

Amnesty indicted it for firing mortar shells at a kibbutz: the mortar was an "imprecise weapon," *and* it was a "direct attack on civilians or civilian objects," *and* "even if the attack had targeted IDF troops or equipment in the vicinity of the kibbutz . . . , the attack would still have been indiscriminate." The most extravagant entry in Amnesty's charge sheet, however, zeroed in on a rocket misfire that killed 13 Gazan civilians. Hamas was saddled with a foursome of war crimes: "it was an *indiscriminate attack* using *a prohibited weapon* which *may well have been fired from a residential area* within the Gaza Strip and *may have been intended to strike civilians in Israel*" (emphases added). It would unduly tax the forbearance of the reader to parse the incongruities of this ejaculation. For one, "indiscriminate attack" *against whom?* In any case, however many multipliers Amnesty applied to Hamas's war crimes, the sum total would still pale beside the horror Israel inflicted.

Failure to Take All Feasible Precautions International humanitarian law obliges parties to a conflict to take "all feasible" precautions or precautions "to the maximum feasible extent," in order "to protect civilians and civilian objects under their control against the dangers resulting from military operations." One such precaution is to "avoid locating military objectives within or near densely populated areas." The critical caveat, of course, is "feasible." The inclusion of this adjectival qualifier in binding law "reflected the concern of small and densely populated countries which would find it difficult to separate civilians and civilian objects from military objectives"; these countries "stressed the fact" that the principle to "avoid locating military objectives within or near densely populated areas" was "difficult to apply." The provision has generally been construed to mandate "precautions which are practicable or practically possible taking into account all circumstances ruling at the time, including humanitarian and military considerations."[73] Therefore, to plausibly indict Hamas for violating the "precautions" provision, it was incumbent upon Amnesty to demonstrate at a minimum one of two things: either (1) in each *specific* combat situation, Hamas had a feasible alternative "taking into account all circumstances ruling at the time." But as Amnesty itself noted, "Israeli authorities' denial of access to the Gaza Strip . . . has made documenting and verifying specific violations" by Hamas "more difficult." Indeed, it

73. International Committee of the Red Cross, *Customary International Humanitarian Law, Volume I: Rules* (Cambridge: 2005), rules 22, 23; ICRC, *Commentary on the Additional Protocols,* article 58.

would be difficult to assess from a remote venue whether, in the "circumstances ruling at the time" of each alleged breach of the precautions principle, Hamas did have another option; or (2) even if *general* "circumstances ruling at the time" rendered it "difficult to apply" the "precautions" provision—Gaza is among the "most densely populated places on earth"[74]—Hamas still put civilians and civilian objects at gratuitous risk. How did Amnesty negotiate these evidentiary hurdles? It purported that "there is substantial evidence that some of the military operations and conduct" by Hamas "violated their obligation to take all feasible precautions to avoid and minimize harm." It did not, however, adduce such evidence. Instead, it simply discarded the critical "feasibility" caveat. It will be recalled that in one incident after another, Amnesty conscientiously searched out—often to the point of absurdity—an alibi that effectively exonerated Israel of the charge of targeting civilians and civilian dwellings. In the case of Hamas, however, it did precisely the reverse. Instead of investigating whether or not, in each alleged violation of the "precautions" principle, Hamas had a feasible alternative, Amnesty found prima facie evidence of a violation of the "precautions" principle whenever and wherever it could be shown (however tenuously) that Hamas was fighting in proximity to civilians (see Table 9).[75] But such a proof in and of itself proved nothing; fighting in proximity to civilians is not the standard of illegality set by international law. In each particular incident, one would have to determine whether other "practicable or practically possible" options for resisting existed and what were the "circumstances ruling at the time." In its previous report on Operation Cast Lead, Amnesty *did* take into account these factors and, as a result, a nuanced, genuinely balanced picture emerged.[76] But in its assessment of Hamas's military tactics during Protective Edge, Amnesty jettisoned its surgical kit in favor of a sledgehammer.

It would be the wonder of wonders if Hamas wasn't resisting much of the time during Protective Edge in proximity to the civilian population—it was

74. Human Rights Watch, *Indiscriminate Fire: Palestinian rocket attacks on Israel and Israeli artillery shelling in the Gaza Strip* (2007), p. 19.

75. In fairness to Amnesty, it did absolve Hamas (if just barely) of the widely reported charge of "human shielding." The official Israeli postmortem on Protective Edge alleged that Hamas had engaged in coercive "human shielding" on the dubious basis of "eyewitness testimony from a number of IDF officers." State of Israel, *2014 Gaza Conflict,* paras. 161–64. But just as in Cast Lead, it turned out that it was not Hamas but Israel that practiced human shielding in Protective Edge. See Chapter 4, Chapter 11, and Medical Fact-Finding Mission, pp. 91, 94.

76. See Chapter 4.

TABLE 9 A Selection of Amnesty International's Evidence That Hamas
Did Not Take "All Feasible Precautions" to Protect Civilians

The UN Office of the High Commissioner for Human Rights (OHCHR)
documented cases of the firing of rockets from in and around a cemetery in the
al-Faluja neighborhood in densely populated Jabalia, in the northern Gaza Strip.

[A] France 24 correspondent was reporting live from a civilian area in Gaza City
when a rocket was launched from very nearby. The same reporter subsequently
broadcast footage of the launcher he believed the rocket had been fired from,
located some 50m from a hotel frequented by international correspondents, 100m
away from a UN building, and very near several civilian homes; his report includes
footage of children playing next to the rocket launcher.

A rocket launched . . . just down the street from an Al Jazeera film crew reporting
from Gaza City was also captured on camera.

[A] crew from NDTV, an Indian television network, filmed members of an armed
group burying and rigging a rocket launcher under a tent in an open area next to the
al-Mashtal hotel in Gaza City. The same film crew captured the launch of the rocket
. . . ; it was one of several rockets launched around the same time. . . . Their report
noted that a rocket had been fired from the same location [earlier]. The hotel and
area from which the rockets were launched are surrounded by residential buildings.

Gaza, after all. And in fact, Amnesty was not indifferent to this dilemma,
yet the solution it proposed in *Unlawful and Deadly* cannot but bewilder: "It
should be noted that even though the overall population density in the Gaza
Strip is very high, particularly in and around Gaza City, significant areas
within the 365km² of territory are not residential, and conducting hostilities
or launching munitions from these areas presents a lower risk of endangering
Palestinian civilians." In laying out this (as it were) "feasible" alternative,
Amnesty omitted the critical factual and legal context: "open areas are relatively scarce" in Gaza;[77] "fighting in urban areas per se is not a violation of
international humanitarian law";[78] "a Party to the conflict cannot be expected
to arrange its armed forces and installations in such a way as to make them
conspicuous to the benefit of the adversary."[79] But even setting aside these
far-from-trivial considerations, Amnesty's "feasible" alternative would still
invite ridicule. On the one hand, since 2005 Israel had maintained its occupation of Gaza largely by remote control. "Modern technology now permits

77. Human Rights Watch, *Indiscriminate Fire,* p. 7.
78. Amnesty International, *Operation "Cast Lead": 22 Days of death and destruction*
(London: 2009), p. 75.
79. ICRC, *Commentary on the Additional Protocols,* article 58.

effective control from outside the occupied territory, and this is what Israel has established," distinguished international jurist John Dugard observes.

> Before Israel's physical withdrawal from Gaza in 2005, Palestinian acts of violent resistance were directed at Israeli forces within the territory. This was during the second intifada. Since then, Palestinian militants have been obliged to take their resistance to the occupation and the illegal siege of Gaza to Israel itself. The alternative is to do nothing, a course no occupied people in history has ever taken. It is unusual for an occupied people to take its resistance outside the occupied territory. But it is also unusual for an occupying power to maintain a brutal occupation from outside the territory.[80]

On the other hand, Amnesty declared nearly all projectiles in Hamas's arsenal illegal. It follows that if Israel established its control of Gaza from afar, and if Hamas's projectiles were illegal, then Hamas couldn't be "conducting hostilities or launching munitions" to end the occupation and still pass legal muster. The long and short of Amnesty's counsel was this: in order to resist Israel's inhuman and illegal occupation,[81] compounded by its illegal and inhuman blockade, and punctuated periodically by its large-scale massacres, Hamas militants should have gathered, en masse and unarmed, in an open field. Still, to facilitate and expedite matters, shouldn't they also have lined up like ducks? But there's more. Just as it applied a multiplier to "indiscriminate attacks" by Hamas, so Amnesty also verbally inflated Hamas's violations of the "precautions" provision. What began in *Unlawful and Deadly* as "some" and "certain" cases in which Hamas breached this provision, morphed into "far from isolated" and "not . . . infrequent" violations, until in the report's conclusion Hamas stood accused of "routinely" violating the "precautions" provision and a "consistent failure" to abide by it. Meanwhile, it was no less instructive what Amnesty elected to pass over in silence. "In Ashkelon, Sderot, Be'er Sheva and other cities in the south of Israel, as well as elsewhere in the country, military bases and other installations are located in or around residential areas, including kibbutzim and villages," Amnesty breezily reported. "During Operation Protective Edge, there were more Israeli military positions and activities than usual close to civilian areas in the south of Israel, and Israeli forces launched daily artillery and other attacks into Gaza

---

80. John Dugard, "Debunking Israel's Self-Defense Argument," *Al Jazeera America* (31 July 2014), america.aljazeera.com/opinions/2014/7/gaza-israel-internationalpolitics unicc.html.

81. On the illegality of the occupation, see Appendix.

from these areas along Gaza's perimeter." But according to the "precautions" provision, "governments should endeavor to find places away from densely populated areas to site" fixed military objectives, such as military bases, and "as regards mobile objectives, care should be taken in particular during the conflict to avoid placing troops, equipment or transports in densely populated areas."[82] Israel was far from lacking in empty spaces; it could also choose from a dazzling spectrum of weapons, which could be launched from virtually any terrain, altitude, and distance. Didn't Israel, then, flagrantly violate the "precautions" provision? Apparently not, according to Amnesty, which uttered not a word of criticism.

The point at issue is not whether Hamas breached international law during Protective Edge. Some fighters probably did seek out the protection of civilian objects, such as dwellings and mosques, in Gaza,[83] although by the time Israel blasted the ten thousandth civilian edifice, it must have been brought home that they provided no deterrence. On the contrary, Israel would have relished the prospect of, so to speak, targeting two birds with one stone: a Hamas fighter and a civilian object. The pertinent question, however, is whether Hamas's violations were remotely on the same scale as the violations by Israel. The subtext of Amnesty's presentation, which carefully "balanced" the death and destruction inflicted as well as the criminal culpability of both parties, conveyed that it was. But the pretense that the pitiable spree of "bottle rockets" directed at Israel compared to the hecatomb visited on Gaza is materially ludicrous and morally a travesty. The question then becomes, How did Amnesty manage to prove the unprovable? It did so by acting less as a neutral arbiter, and more as the defense counsel for Israel. It made the best case for Israel by obscuring factual evidence that incriminated it, adducing speculative evidence that exonerated it, and applying a lax legal standard that gave Israel the benefit of a doubt when it didn't deserve it. It made the worst case for Hamas by obscuring factual evidence that vindicated it, adducing speculative evidence that incriminated it, and applying an over-the-top legal standard that inflated its criminal culpability and left it no other military option, if it wanted to stay within the law, save to lie down and

82. ICRC, *Commentary on the Additional Protocols,* article 58.

83. These exceptions, it ought to go without saying, couldn't justify Israel's indiscriminate, systematic targeting of civilian, let alone religious objects. It is also possible that some mosques had an underground tunnel, not to stash weapons (Hamas stored them in open spaces away from civilians), but to serve as an escape route in the event of an Israeli attack, and that some minarets had cameras installed to monitor Israeli troop movements.

die. If Amnesty sustained its case for a "balanced" verdict, that's because the case was rigged in advance.

. . .

After the UN Human Rights Council issued its report on Operation Protective Edge,[84] Amnesty International released another report of its own, *"Black Friday": Carnage in Rafah during 2014 Israel/Gaza conflict.* Its belated publication[85] precluded it from having an impact on the critical UN report. Still, this fifth and final Amnesty installment was unusually ambitious, and on this ground alone merits close inspection. *"Black Friday"* homed in on Israel's resort to massive violence against the civilian population of Rafah between 1 and 4 August 2014. The assault occurred after an Israeli officer, Lieutenant Hadar Goldin, was reportedly captured alive by Hamas fighters. In conjunction with Forensic Architecture, a research team based at the University of London, Amnesty made use of sundry cutting-edge technologies to reconstruct with striking visual effect the sequence of events on the ground. This analysis, however, will focus only on Amnesty's written text.

The packaging of *"Black Friday"* set it off from Amnesty's prior quartet of reports on Protective Edge. (For the record, before it issued *"Black Friday,"* Amnesty had already read this author's analysis of its earlier publications. It is not known if and how this critique influenced Amnesty's presentation in its last report.[86]) Amnesty no longer pretended to an illusive "balance." In the "Background" section of this report, the death and destruction in Gaza during Protective Edge fills five times as much space as the death and destruction in Israel.[87] A pair of incendiary subtitles, *Carnage in Rafah during 2014 Israel/ Gaza conflict* (on the cover page) and *Israel's mass killing of civilians in Rafah during 2014 Gaza conflict* (on the table of contents page) likewise registered a palpable shift in tone. Moreover, *"Black Friday"* repeatedly gestured to the input of Gaza's major human rights organizations, naming in particular and conspicuously the Palestinian Center for Human Rights and Al Mezan

---

84. See Chapter 13.
85. 2015.
86. A draft had been forwarded to Philip Luther, director of Amnesty International's Middle East and North Africa division, and parts of it were serialized on www.Byline.com, "Has Amnesty International Lost Its Way?" (9, 13, 17 July 2015).
87. Amnesty International, *"Black Friday,"* pp. 16–18 (684 versus 131 words).

Center for Human Rights.[88] Nonetheless, the core of *"Black Friday,"* comprising a factual presentation and legal assessment of Israel's violations of international law, carried over the apologetic analytical framework of Amnesty's prior reports. If the offense grated more deeply this time around, it was because of the density of the crimes committed in Rafah. All the same, it should be noted straightaway that whereas Amnesty conveyed the impression—not least by the extraordinary investment it made in chronicling what happened—that the bloodbath in Rafah marked a sharp departure from Protective Edge as a whole, in fact, as the Breaking the Silence testimonies confirmed, although the wanton destruction there might have been quantitatively worse,[89] it did not differ in kind from what unfolded elsewhere in Gaza.[90]

The Israeli bombardment of Rafah commenced after a firefight in which Hamas apparently captured alive Lieutenant Hadar Goldin. Israeli political culture does not abide its combatants being held in captivity, but it also recoils at prisoner exchanges, which invariably entail the release of many Palestinians held in Israeli jails. To reconcile these conflicting impulses, Israel codified a macabre military doctrine, dubbed the Hannibal Directive, that effectively sanctioned the killing of its own combatants if they fell into enemy hands and could not be rescued, on the tacit principle that "the death of captured soldiers is preferable to them being taken alive." It could hardly be doubted that the IDF intended not to rescue Goldin but to kill him: it didn't launch a pinpoint commando raid; instead, it turned the area which it "believed to be the location of Lieutenant Goldin" into an inferno.[91] As an aside, it's hard to fathom the ethos of a nation that goes into deep mourning when one of its soldiers is held in captivity, yet prefers that he be killed rather than captured alive. In any event, when Goldin was taken prisoner by Hamas on the morning of 1 August and his whereabouts could not be tracked, Israel unleashed maximum firepower in Rafah's densely populated civilian areas in order to kill him. Even after it became clear from forensic evidence that

88. Ibid., pp. 13, 22, 39, 53, 78. Their omission in earlier Amnesty reports on Protective Edge had been noted by this author in his critique.

89. Ibid., p. 44.

90. *"Black Friday"* itself noted that even before the Israeli assault on Rafah began, the IDF was ordered at the start of a cease-fire to fire indiscriminately so as to "make a big boom" (quoting an Israeli soldier) and, as it set out to destroy a tunnel, to demolish "every house and agricultural structure in the area ... purposelessly destroy stuff" (quoting another Israeli soldier), while it was standard IDF procedure throughout Protective Edge "to fire missiles or tank shells at buildings before approaching them" (ibid., pp. 23–26).

91. Ibid., pp. 19–20, 29–31, 34.

Goldin was dead, however, the murderous assault continued, although at a somewhat diminished intensity, as an act of revenge and to administer a lesson. The assault on Rafah unfolded in the near absence of armed resistance. "Hardly any return fire was reported," Amnesty found, and the IDF suffered no casualties,[92] as "jets, drones, helicopters and artillery [were] raining fire at pedestrians and vehicles at the intersections, indiscriminately hitting cars, ambulances, motorbikes and pedestrians," while "civilians attempting to flee the inferno were hit by missiles and artillery."[93] More than two thousand bombs (including one-ton bombs), missiles, and artillery shells were fired on the first day (one thousand shells within three hours of Goldin's capture). By the end of the attack on 4 August, at least two hundred civilians had been killed and 2,600 homes completely or partially destroyed. In the lucid idiom of law, Israel committed a crime against humanity in Rafah— except that whereas the factual record just recapitulated was culled directly from *"Black Friday,"* Amnesty's legal assessment veered in an altogether different direction. It indicted Israel for (1) *indiscriminate* attacks, that is, for recklessly hitting civilians or civilian objects as it targeted military objectives;[94] (2) *disproportionate* attacks, that is, for causing excessive collateral damage to civilians or civilian objects as it targeted military objectives;[95] and (3) a *failure to take all feasible precautions* in order to minimize incidental harm to the civilian population in the course of military operations.[96] It was only in the rarest of instances that Amnesty indicted Israel (if gingerly) for targeting civilians and civilian objects, even as its own evidence attested that the murderous assault on Rafah unfolded in the near-total absence of a legitimate military objective.

But (it might be contended), whereas Hamas returned "hardly any" fire, still, in the initial phase of the Rafah assault, liquidating Goldin constituted a legitimate military objective. Couldn't that goal justify a portion, if not the full magnitude, of the firepower Israel unleashed? For an objective to qualify as legitimate, however, its achievement must confer a *concrete and direct*

92. Ibid., p. 37.
93. Ibid., p. 27.
94. ICRC, *Customary International Humanitarian Law,* rule 12; ICRC, *Commentary on the Additional Protocols,* article 51.
95. ICRC, *Customary International Humanitarian Law,* rule 14; ICRC, *Commentary on the Additional Protocols,* article 51.
96. ICRC, *Customary International Humanitarian Law,* rule 15; ICRC, *Commentary on the Additional Protocols,* article 57.

military advantage.[97] It would be a most bizarre linguistic usage to construe Israel's calculated killing of its own soldier as conferring on it a military advantage. The UN Human Rights Council report on Protective Edge dispatched the notion that "abstract political and long-term strategic considerations," such as a potential prisoner swap in the future, could legitimately be factored into the calculus of military advantage; the advantage, it underscored, must be *concrete* and *direct.*[98] It follows that the inferno Israel created in Rafah in order to kill Goldin could not be legally comprehended in the ambit of an indiscriminate attack, a disproportionate attack, or a failure to take all feasible precautions, each of which presupposes the existence of a legitimate military target. Inasmuch as Rafah's densely populated civilian neighborhoods were the object of saturation bombardment during the manhunt phase, and inasmuch as this bombardment occurred amid only scattered return fire (which wasn't even the object of the bombardment), the dispositive legal principle was the *deliberate targeting of civilians and civilian objects.* Still (it might also be contended), Israel's intention was to kill Goldin, not to inflict death and destruction on Rafah's civilian population. But in law, "the doer of an act must be taken to have *intended* its natural and foreseeable consequences."[99] The natural and foreseeable consequences of bombarding Rafah's civilian neighborhoods were massive death of civilians and massive destruction of civilian objects. Even if Israel's avowed goal was to kill Goldin, the bombardment still constituted, as a matter of law, an intentional attack on civilians and civilian objects. *Categorizing the Rafah massacre as a disproportionate attack, an indiscriminate attack, or a failure to take all feasible precautions, on account of Israel's intent to kill Goldin, amounted to legitimizing the wholly illegitimate goal of launching an armed attack on a civilian population in order to preempt a future prisoner swap.* It is true that to depict the Rafah inferno as an intentional attack on a civilian population, although correct as a matter of law, does

97. ICRC, *Customary International Humanitarian Law,* rules 8, 14; ICRC, *Commentary on the Additional Protocols,* articles 51, 52, 57.

98. *Report of the Detailed Findings of the Independent Commission of Inquiry Established Pursuant to Human Rights Council Resolution S-21/1* (22 June 2015), paras. 369–70. *"Black Friday"* (pp. 91–92) took note of this finding by the UN commission. If Lieutenant Goldin had been targeted because he was in possession of plans for an imminent attack on the enemy, it would of course pose different questions.

99. International Court of Justice, Advisory Opinion, *Legality of the Threat or Use of Nuclear Weapons* (8 July 1996), "Dissenting Opinion of Judge Weeramantry," ch. III, "Humanitarian Law," sec. 10, "Specific rules of the humanitarian law of war," (a) "The prohibition against causing unnecessary suffering"; emphasis in original.

not yet encapsulate the full reality of the manhunt phase. The correct formulation would then go something like, *an intentional, targeted attack on a civilian population in pursuit of an illegitimate military objective.* If the phrasing is ungainly, that's because the reality it endeavors to capture is so deviant: it's not every day that a state carries out a massacre in order to kill its own soldier in order to preempt a future prisoner exchange.

But what difference does it make how Amnesty categorized and depicted the Rafah massacre if it still found that Israel committed war crimes?[100] The answer is this. Distilled to its essence, Protective Edge was designed—as the Goldstone Report put it in the context of Operation Cast Lead (2008–9)—to "punish, humiliate and terrorize" a civilian population. The other major atrocities during Protective Edge—Khuza'a, Shuja'iya—manifestly lacked a military rationale.[101] The Rafah massacre appeared to be different, as it purportedly traced back to a military objective. The fact that Amnesty's most ambitious report focused on the Israeli intention to kill Goldin and its concomitant, the Hannibal Directive that triggered the bloody manhunt, conveyed the distinct impression that Protective Edge was a military operation gone awry: wrong, even criminal, but still "understandable" in military terms. But in fact, not even the initial manhunt phase of the Rafah massacre, properly understood, could be regarded as a military operation. Even as Goldin's death was confirmed (probably by the end of the third hour of the first day),[102] "the Israeli military continued its attacks" in Rafah, not in pursuit of a so-called military objective but to "show them," "settle accounts," and "extract [*sic*] a price" (Amnesty, quoting Israeli soldiers). If, as Israeli officers "maintain, there were no serious fire fights," Amnesty ultracautiously speculated, "the question arises as to whether the army's use of massive firepower was in fact intended to 'take revenge' on Rafah."[103] In other words, the Rafah assault emerged after the manhunt phase as a straight-up massacre.

The premeditated "carnage in Rafah" and "mass killing of civilians in Rafah" comprised, in its parts (including the initial manhunt phase) and as a totality, an incontrovertible war crime, as Israel *targeted* civilians and civilian objects in the absence of a legitimate military objective (apart from desultory return fire), and also a crime against humanity, as it launched "a

100. Amnesty International, *"Black Friday,"* p. 91 ("Conclusion and Recommendations").
101. See Chapter 13.
102. Amnesty International, *"Black Friday,"* p. 30. Goldin was officially declared dead on the night of 2 August.
103. Ibid., pp. 36–37, 42–43.

widespread or systematic attack directed against [a] civilian population" (Rome Statute, Article 7). But instead of stating the obvious, Amnesty chose to systematically occlude the terroristic essence of the Rafah massacre by churning out one Israeli alibi after another. It stated that after Goldin was officially pronounced dead, "the Israeli army continued the destruction of greenhouses and homes, *apparently as part of the search for Lieutenant Goldin or his remains.*"[104] It did not adduce a smidgen of evidence in support of this speculation, while the report itself documented that Israel sought via its wanton destruction to exact revenge and administer a lesson. Indeed, did it forget that these IDF tactics constituted standard operating procedure across Gaza throughout Protective Edge, independent of Goldin's fate? Amnesty then went on to observe, "The military did not manage to retrieve the remains of Lieutenant Goldin's body. Heavy bombing of tunnel areas reduced the likelihood of finding him."[105] But if "heavy bombing ... reduced the likelihood of finding" Goldin's remains, then maybe retrieving his remains wasn't the bombing's objective, while taking revenge was. What's more, Amnesty parsed the Hannibal Directive, which underpinned the four-day assault, under the subhead "SHIFT IN PROPORTIONALITY."[106] But inasmuch as killing Goldin wasn't a legitimate military objective, and neither "revenge" nor "deter future capture attempts" (Amnesty's phrases) could be construed as a legitimate military objective, of what possible relevance was the proportionality principle, which presupposes such an objective? *"Black Friday"* further noted in this "shift in proportionality" section:

> Post-conflict briefings to soldiers and public statements of Israeli officers suggest that the high death toll and massive destruction were not seen as regrettable side effects but "achievements" or "accomplishments" that would keep Gaza "quiet for five years." An Intelligence Corps soldier quoted senior army officers saying: "2,000 dead and 11,000 wounded, half a million refugees, decades' worth of destruction. Harm to lots of senior Hamas members and to their homes, to their families. These were stated as accomplishments so that no one would doubt that what we did during this period was meaningful." Another Israeli soldier told Breaking the Silence that the aim in bombings was to "deter them, scare them, wear them down psychologically."
> ... These statements indicate an intention to generate material damage as deterrent.

104. Ibid., p. 42, emphasis added.
105. Ibid.
106. Ibid., pp. 43–44.

If the professed purpose of the assault on Rafah was to achieve a "high death toll and massive destruction" in order to shatter the will of Gaza to resist, it wasn't a disproportionate attack but unambiguously a terror assault on the civilian population.

"*Black Friday*" assembled 15 case studies in which civilians were killed during the four-day assault on Rafah. These case studies, far from shedding light on Amnesty's perverse conclusions, bewilder and appall in their resort to legalistic gymnastics that evade and obscure the obvious. However tedious it might appear, in order to expose Amnesty's disingenuousness each case study must be individually examined (see Table 10).

The Israeli massacre in Rafah constituted in its parts and as a totality an intentional attack on a civilian population in order to achieve a dual objective: (1) to kill a captured Israeli soldier so as to preempt a future prisoner swap, which wasn't a legitimate military objective, and (2) "a desire for revenge, to teach a lesson to, or to punish the population of Rafah for the capture of Lieutenant Goldin" (*"Black Friday,"* conclusion), which, a fortiori, wasn't a legitimate military objective.[107] Yet, Amnesty found that Israel directly targeted civilians and civilian objects in only two of the fifteen cases it investigated.[108] In the report's comprehensive *factual* conclusion, the maximum Amnesty would allow was that "*In some cases,* there are *indications* that [Israeli military forces] directly fired at and killed civilians, including *some* who were fleeing . . . *in some cases* they warned civilians to stay in their homes which were then bombarded."[109] In the other thirteen incidents, Amnesty neither reported return fire nor adduced creditable evidence of a legitimate military target. Instead, it conjured wildly speculative scenarios that enabled it to invoke legal principles—distinction (between civilians and combatants), proportionality, precautions—presupposing a military objective, or it invoked legal principles presupposing a military objective without even bothering to speculate on the objective. It might be argued that Amnesty entertained so many of Israel's premises, or premises favorable to Israel, in order to show that even if one were to accept those premises, Israel would *still* be legally culpable. The upshot, however, of such a preemptive strategy (if

107. Ibid., p. 91.
108. Case 1 ("direct attacks on civilians") and Case 10 ("targeting of ambulances and medical personnel").
109. Amnesty International, *"Black Friday,"* p. 91, emphases added.

TABLE 10 Amnesty's Case Studies

Case Study	Amnesty's Description	Amnesty's Legal Assessment	Finkelstein's Comment
1[a]	On 1 August, a one-ton aerial bomb targeting a building killed at least 18 people in its environs. One witness recalled simultaneous targeted attacks on the civilian population ("The minute I left the house . . ., an Apache [helicopter] started shooting at us"), while others recalled indiscriminate attacks ("The shells were raining down on us") as well as targeted attacks to prevent ambulances from reaching the dead and wounded.	"Even if the house did cover an opening to a tunnel, dropping a one-ton bomb on the building . . . was clearly disproportionate. The artillery shelling of the area was indiscriminate and the reported helicopter fire at civilians and ambulances amounted to direct attacks on civilians."	Elsewhere in the report, Amnesty cited some circumstantial evidence that the attack *might* have been targeting a tunnel entrance that *might* have been beneath the building where Israel *might* have believed that Goldin *might* have been hidden.[b] But even if, for argument's sake, one credits this monument to extenuating speculation, the relevant legal principle still wouldn't be a disproportionate attack, as killing Goldin did not confer a concrete and direct military advantage; the proportionality test was therefore wholly irrelevant. The incident constituted an intentional attack on civilians and civilian objects.
2[c]	On 1 August, "amidst heavy Israeli bombardment," a drone-missile attack killed one or more members of a family fleeing the Rafah inferno, and also killed another man. One witness recalled Israeli missiles, bombs and shells "hitting the whole street."	"It is possible that one of the intended targets of the attack was a motorcycle that was passing by at the time and may have been carrying a fighter, as local groups reported. Amnesty International was unable to verify whether this was the case. Even if it were the case, the use of such massive firepower in a populated neighborhood indicates that the attack was disproportionate or otherwise indiscriminate."	On the basis of an account by unspecified "local groups," that Amnesty couldn't verify, of an alleged motorcyclist allegedly transporting a fighter, the Israeli drone-missile attack on a civilian neighborhood "amidst heavy Israeli bombardment" morphs into a "disproportionate or otherwise indiscriminate attack," while the possibility that it might have been an intentional attack on civilians isn't even contemplated.
3[d]	On 1 August, amid "heavy bombardment of a civilian area," a drone-launched missile killed a 20-year-old man. Multiple witnesses recalled relentless bombing, shelling, and missile attacks, while "people were running . . . , all raising white flags."	"The attacks . . . appeared to be indiscriminate."	But if Amnesty didn't identify *or even speculate on* a military target, wasn't it an intentional killing?

4^e	On 1 August, amid "heavy bombardment of a civilian area," an elderly woman carrying a boy was killed by a drone missile. One witness recalled "repeated Israeli air strikes on civilians and what appeared to be civilian vehicles."	"The attacks . . . appeared to be indiscriminate, with all vehicles evidently being targeted without distinction."	But if the elderly woman was killed, and vehicles were randomly targeted in the absence of a military objective, wasn't this a deliberate attack on civilians and civilian objects?
5^f	On 1 August, amid massive artillery fire on a civilian neighborhood—"50–60 shells were falling every minute," one witness recalled—a family fled their home, only then to confront a barrage of tank shells and "an incredible number of missiles." The witness's daughter was killed in the "madness."	"[I]t is likely that the attack that killed [the girl] was indiscriminate."	In the absence, however, of a military target, it was a lot more likely to have been an intentional killing of a civilian.
6^g	Two family members, who had fled their home on 1 August amid "random" missile attacks and "heavy shelling" by tanks, were killed on the evening of 2 August as they returned in a car to retrieve their belongings. One of the dead was thrown onto high voltage wire ("If it hadn't been for his shirt, I wouldn't have recognized him. . . . His face and left hand were all burnt and his fingers were cut off except for one," a relative recalled), while the other was decapitated.	"It is unclear why Israeli forces attacked the area at the time, since the attack occurred after Lieutenant Hadar Goldin's death was officially declared. The Israeli army was under an obligation to take all precautions to verify that the car was indeed a military objective, and if in doubt to assume that it was civilian. The attack on the . . . car therefore appears to have been undertaken without proper precautions."	It is unclear why Amnesty professed to be "unclear" as to Israel's motive. Didn't it cite numerous statements by Israelis that after Goldin's death they were exacting revenge and administering a lesson? It is also unclear why Amnesty inferred that Israel believed the car was "a military objective." Didn't Amnesty itself cite numerous testimonies that the IDF was targeting civilian vehicles at random in its killing spree? It is also unclear why Amnesty invoked the principle of "proper precautions" if there wasn't even a military target? What *is* clear, however, is that invoking the "precautions" principle in this context—as if Israel's worst illegality was manslaughter—is a compound scandal and disgrace.
7^h	On 1 August, a drone-missile attack killed a father and his daughter en route to a hospital. One family member recalled, "My father had lost his legs and his elbow had been cut off. . . . My sister . . . had lost her right leg and shrapnel had punctured her eye approaching her brain."	"It is unclear why Israeli forces fired the missile that killed [the father and daughter]. The circumstances of the attack suggest that it was at best indiscriminate."	If it had read its own report, Amnesty would perhaps not have suffered from a lack of lucidity: the attack was part and parcel of an inferno Israel created to kill Goldin and exact revenge. It was not "at best indiscriminate." In the absence of reasonable doubt (the case for which Amnesty didn't even attempt to make), it was a deliberate attack on civilians, full stop.

(continued)

TABLE 10 *(continued)*

Case Study	Amnesty's Description	Amnesty's Legal Assessment	Finkelstein's Comment
8[i]	On 1 August, a woman lost her baby son as they fled a civilian neighborhood "amid heavy bombardment" from the air and then tank shelling. The cause of death was a one-ton bomb dropped on a nearby residential building: "He died in my hands.... My son got hit in the head and his face split open."	"The attack on a residential building with a one-ton bomb despite the nearby presence of large numbers of civilians indicates that the Israeli military failed to take adequate, if any, precautions to avoid excessive harm to fleeing civilians. Even if there had been a military target in the building (there is some indication that the Israeli army thought there was a tunnel entrance there), the attack appears to have been grossly disproportionate."	On the evidence cited by Amnesty, the attack was not "disproportionate." The possible existence of a tunnel entrance did not in and of itself make the building subject to a proportionality test. It would have to be shown that destroying the tunnel would confer a *concrete* and *direct* military advantage. If every building in Gaza alleged to be situated atop a tunnel automatically lost its civilian immunity, it would make mockery of the Geneva Conventions and First Protocol. The incident constituted a deliberate attack on civilians and a civilian object. (See also Comment on Case 1 above, which refers to the same incident.)
9[j]	On 1 August, air strikes and artillery and tank fire targeted the premises and environs of Abu Youssef al-Najjar hospital, seriously damaging the building, injuring dozens inside, and eventually forcing the hospital's evacuation. The hospital staff was in direct telephone contact with the IDF. The assault tapered off after a first phone conversation, but intensified again an hour later, causing patients to spontaneously evacuate. The IDF alleged in a second phone conversation that Goldin was in the hospital and—according to one doctor's testimony cited by Amnesty—threatened that "we wouldn't be allowed to leave the hospital until we released the soldier." The Israeli allegation was	"The reasons for Israel's attacks around the Abu Youssef al-Najjar hospital appear to have been linked to the capture by Hamas of Lieutenant Goldin. Rumors circulating in the Abu Youssef al-Najjar hospital that a wounded soldier might be in the hospital were also reported by Israeli TV Channel 10. However, even if the Israeli military believed Lieutenant Goldin was in the hospital again [?], the attacks on the hospital and its vicinity were reckless and indiscriminate.... Even if a hospital were being misused to commit acts harmful to an attacking party—and there is no indication that this was the case with the Abu Youssef al-Najjar	It is hard to figure out why Amnesty so readily credited a causal nexus between Goldin's supposed presence in the hospital and the attack on it. It was not as if this would have been the first time Israel targeted a hospital without justification. Didn't Amnesty itself document kindred attacks on ambulances? (See Case 10.) The first IDF phone call to the hospital came many hours after the assault on the hospital began, yet made no mention of Goldin's alleged presence, while the assault subsided for a short period after this first call. This suggests that the rhythm of the assault was unrelated to securing Goldin's release. The second IDF call, like the report in Israel's compliant media, might just have been the improvisation of an official alibi. It was also cause for wonder why Amnesty speculated on the

emphatically denied by the hospital staff. A witness to the spontaneous evacuation recalled, "I looked at the hospital and will never forget what I saw. People leaving the hospital on hospital beds holding drips, being pushed on carts also holding drips. I saw doctors in hospital clothes carrying white sheets." The remaining staff and patients left in an organized evacuation several hours later.

hospital—according to the Fourth Geneva Convention, the protection enjoyed by the hospital may only cease after due warning and reasonable time for evacuation has [sic] been given."

hospital "being misused to commit acts harmful to an attacking party," if "there is no indication that this was the case." If there wasn't any indication, why conjure this sinister scenario in the first place—except as a sop to Israel?

10[k]   On 1 August, multiple drone-missile attacks wounded nine civilians, including three children, in the vicinity of a mosque. Another drone missile targeted an ambulance just as it headed back to the hospital loaded with several of the wounded, incinerating eight people, including the three children, two medics, and a volunteer. Yet another drone-missile attack targeted a second ambulance that arrived belatedly on the scene. A witness recalled, "What we saw was really horrible. The ambulance looked like a tree branch that was completely charred. The bodies had no parts—no legs, no hands—they were severely burned."

"In answer to letters written by Amnesty International . . . to Israeli embassies . . . , a spokesman of the Israeli embassy in New Zealand wrote that ambulances in Gaza were frequently used to carry military personnel. The Israeli military has not provided any explanation for why they attacked ambulances in this case. The targeting of ambulances and medical personnel is prohibited under international humanitarian law."

If Amnesty quoted Israel's stock alibi as issued by its New Zealand embassy, couldn't it also have noted that in prior operations Israel had repeatedly targeted Palestinian ambulances; that notwithstanding its high-tech surveillance technology, in *only one single incident* did Israel *ever* endeavor to adduce specific evidence justifying such a criminal attack; and that in this sole instance Amnesty itself found the evidence dubious? Also, why did Amnesty state merely that the "targeting of ambulances and medical personnel is *prohibited* under international humanitarian law," and not that it's a *war crime*—indeed, a particularly heinous one?[l]

11[m]   On 2 August, a missile attack destroyed a family home, killing nine civilians, including four children. The father of the four dead children recalled going to the hospital after the attack. "The bodies of my children were placed in a vegetable freezer. I cannot describe what it is like to see the bodies of my children in a vegetable freezer."

"It is possible that the Israeli military targeted the building where Abdel-Wahhab's wife and children were killed because, according to a family member, the owner . . . may have been involved with Palestinian armed groups. Amnesty International was unable to verify this information or to clarify whether he

On the fragile basis of a possibility that the owner of the house "may have been involved with Palestinian armed groups," and may have been (or may not have been) "involved in hostilities at the time," and even if "he was not present at the time of the attack" but "may have been expected" to return at the time of the attack—on the basis of this infinite regression of "may haves," Amnesty went on to

(continued)

TABLE 10 *(continued)*

Case Study	Amnesty's Description	Amnesty's Legal Assessment	Finkelstein's Comment
		was involved in hostilities at the time. In any case . . . , he was not present at the time of the attack . . . he had been away from his home for the majority of the war, but may have been expected to come back. . . . If the Israeli military intended to attack [the owner] and they believed he was present at the time of the attack, the strike should have been cancelled given the number of civilians present. The attack is likely to have been disproportionate."	further speculate that "if" Israel intended to target the "may have been" member of the armed group who may have been (or may not have been) "involved in hostilities at the time," because it may have believed he was there because he "may have been expected" to return, then "The attack is likely to have been disproportionate." But on the principle of Occam's razor, the better explanation would appear to be this: As it set about turning Rafah into an inferno, Israel randomly targeted this family home (along with 2,600 others), killing and injuring its occupants.
12"	On 2 August, one or more missiles were fired at a civilian home in a refugee camp, killing four family members, including three children. One relative recalled, "They brought Youssef [aged 10] out on a blanket without a head or arms, only the lower part of his body."	"Amnesty International has no information indicating that any of the men who were in the house were members of a Palestinian armed group. However, even if one or more of them was and were being targeted, the attack appears to have been disproportionate."	If Amnesty "has no information" that anyone except civilians was present in the home, then it was an intentional attack on civilians and a civilian object. To invoke, ex nihilo, the possibility ("Even if. . .") that Palestinian fighters were inside, and then, on the basis of this baseless speculation, to pronounce the attack apparently "disproportionate," is a cowardly and shameful dodge.
13°	On 1 August, a bomb was dropped on a home, killing 15 of the 19 family members present, including 10 children; "all were civilians," and all the adults except one (a 51-year-old unemployed worker) were female. One witness recalled, "It took three days to find all the bodies. The decomposing body of [one dead child] was found on the roof of the neighboring house."	"Amnesty International has been unable to identify any potential target or reason for the attack. . . . Even if there had been a military target nearby, the attack appears to have been disproportionate or otherwise indiscriminate."	If there was no known "potential target or reason for the attack," it perplexes why Amnesty speculated on the possibility ("Even if. . .") that there was one. If a legal assessment is to be based on evidence, this was a straightforward targeted attack on civilians and a civilian object.
14ᵖ	On 2 August, a bomb was dropped on four adjacent makeshift dwellings, killing eight civilians, including six children; none of those	"Amnesty International has not been able to determine what may have been the intended target of this attack. Those killed	Had Amnesty perused its own report, it might have been able to determine that in order to exact "revenge" and "deter future capture attempts," Israel

present were identified as members of armed groups. One witness recalled the prior Israeli alert. "They were saying, 'The Israel Defense Forces is warning you not to go outside your houses or move from one place to another, unless you want to put yourself in danger—you've been warned.' So they tell us not to go out and then they destroy our house on top of us." One dead child was "thrown onto the roof of a concrete house," a second was "shredded into pieces," while a third's "head was cut open and his brain was coming out."

and injured were civilians and there was no fighting in the vicinity of the attack."

intentionally targeted these civilians.

15[q] On 2 August, an air strike on a residential building killed nine people, including five children. One witness recalled that the blast blew her daughter-in-law "17 meters from the blast site, and we found parts of her scattered on the neighbors' rooftops."

"All the witnesses who spoke to Amnesty International said that no one in the building at the time of the attack was a member of an armed group. The Israeli army's intended target in this attack remains unclear. Even if there had been a military target nearby, the attack appears to have been disproportionate."

If there was no evidence of a military target, wasn't it prima facie an intentional attack on civilians and a civilian object? But Amnesty decided that "the attack appears to have been disproportionate." Leaving all else aside, in the absence of a known military target, how could Amnesty even calculate whether or not the attack was proportionate? If a legal assessment no longer requires evidence, then the home "may have been" sitting on top of a Hamas nuclear weapons program.

[a] Amnesty International, "Black Friday," pp. 45–46 (Bin Hammad Family).

[b] Ibid., pp. 31–34.

[c] Ibid., pp. 46–47 (Lafi Family).

[d] Ibid., pp. 47–49 (Qishta Family).

[e] Ibid., pp. 48–49 (al-Saba Family).

[f] Ibid., pp. 49–50 (Abu Mohsen Family).

[g] Ibid., pp. 50–52 (Abu Duba Family).

[h] Ibid., pp. 52–53 (al-Gharib Family).

[i] Ibid., pp. 53–54 (Arafat Family).

[j] Ibid., pp. 54–56 (Abu Youssef al-Najjar Hospital); see also pp. 39–41.

[k] Ibid., pp. 56–58 (ambulance in Musabbeh, Eastern Rafah).

[l] Commentary on the Additional Protocols, Article 12.

[m] Amnesty International, "Black Friday," pp. 58–59 (Abdel-Wahhab Family).

[n] Ibid., pp. 59–60 (Abu Taha Family).

[o] Ibid., pp. 60–62 (Zoroub Family).

[p] Ibid., pp. 62–64 (Neireb, Ghoul, Manyarawi, Abu Ayta Families).

[q] Ibid., pp. 64–65 (Abu Suleiman Family).

preemptive strategy it was) was that it winded up misrepresenting what happened and letting Israel off the hook on the more serious legal charges. The ghastly, heartrending stories assembled in Amnesty's case studies leave little room for doubt that far from being a military operation, the inferno Israel created in Rafah was a terror assault on a defenseless people. And yet, in its report's comprehensive *legal* conclusion, the maximum Amnesty would allow was that "To the extent that *some* of the violations committed by the Israeli army in Rafah . . . *may* have been carried out as part of a widespread or systematic attack on the civilian population . . . , in furtherance of a state policy, they *may* also constitute a crime against humanity."[110] However, the evidence collected in *"Black Friday"* points ineluctably to the conclusion that not just "some" instances "may," but the *whole* of this murderous assault *did* constitute a crime against humanity. Although it invested considerable resources in *"Black Friday,"* Amnesty ultimately, and to its eternal shame, recoiled from its own factual findings and delivered up a legal whitewash.

. . .

It cannot be seriously doubted that Amnesty International's reports on Operation Protective Edge lacked objectivity and professionalism. They betrayed a systematic bias against Hamas and in favor of Israel. They also registered a steep regression from the exacting standard Amnesty set in its reports spanning the past two decades on the Israel-Palestine conflict. Amnesty might be tempted to respond: If an acknowledged supporter of Palestinian human rights (such as this writer) criticizes its pro-Israel bias while Israel criticizes its pro-Palestinian bias, then it must be doing something right. But that's as if to say, if one gets attacked by the flat-Earthers at one extreme and the round-Earthers at the other, then it proves the oblong-Earthers must be telling the truth. The only valid criterion is what the facts themselves show; the imputed bias of the bearer of those facts is beside the point. Judging by this standard, and the mass of evidence assembled in this chapter of its dereliction of duty, Amnesty would have been hard-pressed to defend its performance after Protective Edge. When it did accept the challenge, what most impressed was the feebleness of Amnesty's reply.[111]

110. Ibid., emphases added.
111. See Addendum to this chapter.

There is a separate but still critical question: *What happened?* In the absence of a smoking gun, one can only speculate on the springs of Amnesty's abrupt change of course. It can probably better be understood if located in a broader political context. In recent years, Israel has been slowly but steadily losing the battle for public opinion in the West.[112] The proactive and principled stance of credible human rights organizations in exposing Israeli violations of Palestinian human rights has played a catalytic role in this historic shift. The high-water mark was set after Operation Cast Lead, when scores of human rights reports meticulously documented Israeli crimes during the assault, and it appeared as if, finally, Israel might be held legally accountable for its crimes. Confronted by this grave, palpable threat, Israel and its powerful international lobby set out to reverse the tide by combatting what was dubbed "lawfare"—that is, "isolating Israel through the language of human rights."[113] A furious and ruthless campaign was mounted, replete with smears, slanders, and strong-arm tactics, targeting critics of Israel's human rights record. The most notorious casualty of this juggernaut was Richard Goldstone: a Jewish-Zionist judge with impeccable professional credentials was forced to deliver a humiliating, highly public mea culpa that damaged his career and tarnished his reputation for life.[114] Goldstone's fate served as a cautionary tale for the human rights community; none of Israel's critics was beyond its reach, none was safe from its retribution. In short order, respected jurists Christian Tomuschat[115] and William Schabas[116] were devoured by the Israeli maw. If any doubts lingered after Goldstone's fall from grace, the handwriting was now on the wall: if you (or someone close to you) had skeletons in the closet, the prudent move was not to go too hard on Israel or, wiser still, to cross Israel off your agenda. Undeniably, other factors came into play. The human rights reports on Cast Lead ultimately died a slow death in the UN bureaucracy as the United States, Israel, and the Palestinian Authority colluded to kill them.[117] It appeared pointless to churn out more human rights reports if they too would be consigned to oblivion, not least by the victims themselves—or at any rate by their official representatives. By the time Israel launched

112. Norman G. Finkelstein, *Knowing Too Much: Why the American Jewish romance with Israel is coming to an end* (New York: 2012), pp. 5–95.

113. See Chapter 5.

114. See Chapter 6.

115. Ibid.

116. See Chapter 13.

117. See Chapter 5.

Protective Edge, public opinion had also grown inured to Israel's periodic massacres. Minutely documenting the carnage seemed less urgent, as fewer people any longer harbored doubt that Israel was capable of such brutality. In the meantime, as the Arab Spring metamorphosed into the Arab Winter, the ensuing regional upheaval and attendant human rights catastrophe dwarfed and marginalized the Palestine question. But the intimidation factor was almost certainly the overriding one in Amnesty's volte-face. Indeed, Israel lobby groups, such as NGO Monitor, had openly set their crosshairs on Amnesty.[118] Besides the flawed reports it issued on Protective Edge, a vote on anti-Semitism by Amnesty's UK branch registered the heat it was feeling. All the available evidence pointed to the conclusion that anti-Semitism was at most a marginal phenomenon in British life. According to survey results, well under 10 percent of the population held a negative opinion of Jews, whereas 60 percent held a negative opinion of Roma/Gypsies and 40 percent a negative opinion of Muslims.[119] The manifest purpose of the periodic campaigns bewailing a "new anti-Semitism" has been to stifle criticism of Israel's atrocious human rights record.[120] Yet Amnesty's UK board signed on to, while the membership narrowly defeated (468 to 461), a 2015 resolution calling for an Amnesty UK campaign against resurgent anti-Semitism.[121]

---

118. NGO Monitor, *Amnesty International: Failed methodology, corruption, and anti-Israel bias* (2015). For the Israel lobby targeting Human Rights Watch, see Chapter 5. For the Israel lobby targeting kindred human rights groups, such as UNRWA, see Alex Delmar-Morgan, "Pro-Israel NGO Puts Pressure on UNRWA for Aiding Palestinian Refugees," *Middle East Eye* (7 March 2016). See also Sarah Marusek and David Miller, "How Israel Attempts to Mislead the United Nations: Deconstructing Israel's campaign against the Palestinian Return Centre," *spinwatch.org* (2015).

119. Pew Research Center, *Faith in European Project Reviving* (2015); YouGov, "Roma People and Muslims Are the Least Tolerated Minorities in Europe" (2015).

120. Finkelstein, *Beyond Chutzpah,* part 1. In the United Kingdom, the anti-Semitism bogey was additionally conjured in 2016 to discredit the elected, insurgent leadership of the Labour Party. Despite the paucity of substantiating evidence, the allegations against Labour received ubiquitous and uncritical media coverage. See Jamie Stern-Weiner, "Jeremy Corbyn Hasn't Got an 'Antisemitism Problem.' His Opponents Do," *openDemocracy* (27 April 2016); Norman G. Finkelstein and Jamie Stern-Weiner, "The American Jewish Scholar behind Labour's 'Antisemitism' Scandal Breaks His Silence," *openDemocracy* (3 May 2016); Jamie Stern-Weiner, "Labour Antisemitism Witch-Hunt Turns on Leading Anti-racist Campaigner," *jamiesternweiner.wordpress.com* (9 May 2016).

121. Amnesty International, UK, Section Board Meeting, "Draft Minutes of the Meeting Held on Saturday 21 March 2015," MB 39/15, amnesty.org.uk/webfm_send/1287; Rosa Doherty, "Amnesty Rejects Call to Campaign against Anti-Semitism," *Jewish Chronicle* (21 April 2015).

If Amnesty capitulated to political blackmail, it also reflected the fact that for the first time, it was forced to fend for itself in the jungle of Israel-Palestine politics. Up until Protective Edge, Amnesty and Human Rights Watch (HRW) typically issued corroborative or complementary reports/position papers on potentially explosive issues. Each had the back of the other; each could count on the other for moral-political support. Both organizations issued reports documenting Israel's pervasive practice of torture during the first intifada; both issued statements supporting the right of Palestinian refugees to return to their homes in Israel; both documented Israeli war crimes during Operation Defensive Shield (2002); both issued damning reports on Cast Lead.[122] But HRW basically sat on the sidelines after Protective Edge. It was missing in action. If Amnesty hadn't published five reports on Protective Edge, this chapter couldn't have documented its multitudinous transgressions. If this chapter was silent on HRW, that's because HRW was effectively silent on Protective Edge.[123] It will be left to moralists to decide which was worse, Amnesty's sin of commission or HRW's sin of omission.

It would be hard to exaggerate the damage wreaked by Amnesty's reversal. Supporters of Palestinian human rights and a just and lasting peace have come to depend on Amnesty as a credible corrective to Israeli *hasbara* and pro-Israel media bias. The abdication of its professional mandate could not but dismay and dishearten. Amnesty's worst sin, however, ran much deeper: its abandonment of a forsaken people suffering under an illegal and inhuman blockade punctuated by recurrent, ever-escalating massacres; its open invitation to Israel to commit new and worse massacres, in the sure knowledge that human rights organizations have been cowed into reticence. If only for the sake of the people of Gaza, one hopes that Amnesty (as well as HRW) will yet find its way.

122. Finkelstein, *Beyond Chutzpah*, pp. 102–3, 155–56, 349–51. See also Part One.

123. By contrast, HRW was dogged and unequivocal in its condemnation of the Syrian government and Russia for having "deliberately targeted civilians and civilian institutions" in Aleppo, which was a "blatant war crime." To support this allegation, Executive Director Kenneth Roth adduced the evidence that "Assad-Putin" repeatedly attacked "hospitals or markets, and the like" using "precision weapons." When so inclined, HRW was quite able to connect the dots. "Slaughter or Liberation? A debate on Russia's role in the Syrian war and the fall of Aleppo," *democracynow.org* (14 December 2016). HRW might also want to excuse its inaction on the grounds that it couldn't gain access to Gaza during or after Protective Edge. However, it did issue one, if measly, report; the other major human rights organizations managed, despite the same onerous conditions, to issue substantial reports; and such an excuse effectively incentivizes Israel to seal off the scene of the crime. HRW always had the option of reaching provisional conclusions on the basis of available evidence or partnering with reputable local human rights organizations that did have easy access.

Once Israel successfully browbeat the international human rights community into submission, the only remaining chink in its armor was domestic human rights organizations. Of these, Breaking the Silence most aroused Israel's wrath.[124] The soldier eyewitness testimonies it had compiled after each of Israel's massacres in Gaza were as unimpeachable as they were devastating. Israel consequently set out in a very public way to destroy Breaking the Silence.[125] In the United States, the slander campaign was spearheaded by former Harvard law professor Alan Dershowitz, who accused the group of "doing tremendous damage to Israel because they are not telling the truth."[126] Should it neutralize Breaking the Silence, Israel will have cleared the last obstacle on its path to committing future massacres in Gaza. Henceforth, no one will be around to compellingly document its crimes for a Western audience. However reputable and reliable Palestinian human rights organizations might be, unfortunately and unfairly, they lack credibility among the broad public in the West. In the "operations" to come, Israel will be able to carry on as it pleases, emboldened in the knowledge that it can do so with guaranteed impunity. It's a new sequence of catastrophes waiting to happen.

It wasn't just reputable human rights organizations that failed Gaza. The statements issued by UNICEF during Protective Edge by and large disingenuously balanced the operation's impact on Gazan and Israeli children: "The escalating violence in Gaza and Israel threatens devastating harm for children on all sides"; "Children are bearing the brunt of the worsening violence in Gaza and Israel"; "[T]he violence in Gaza claims even more young lives and . . .

124. B'Tselem, the most prominent Israeli human rights organization monitoring the occupied Palestinian territories, acquitted itself without distinction in its reporting on Gaza. It had little to say, and of this little, a portion would have been better left unsaid. Its research director, Yael Stein, told the *New York Times* after Cast Lead, "I do not accept the Goldstone conclusion of a systematic attack on civilian infrastructure. It is not convincing." Ethan Bronner, "Israel Poised to Challenge a UN Report on Gaza," *New York Times* (23 January 2010). In the face of a mountain of evidence pointing to such a systematic Israeli attack, it was her denial that wasn't convincing. B'Tselem has always been careful to situate itself within the Israeli national consensus. As that consensus drifted inexorably rightward, it was no longer tenable for B'Tselem to gain a hearing among the Israeli public if it appeared to be "defending terrorists" in Gaza. It accordingly vacillated between near silence and gross apologetics. See also Chapter 3 and Chapter 4.

125. Ben Sales, "Breaking the Silence Comes under Withering Attack after Questioning Israel's Military," *Forward* (18 December 2015).

126. Paul Miller, "Controversy Erupts over Anti-Israel Group at Columbia University Hillel," *Observer* (1 April 2016).

its toll on children on both sides deepens"; "Another school in Gaza has come under fire.... [C]hildren in Israel have lived with the threat of indiscriminate attacks"; "The deaths of children on all sides constitute further tragic evidence of the terrible impact the conflict is having on children and their families on all sides."[127] Then, despite the pleas of Save the Children, War Child, and even UNICEF, as well as a dozen Palestinian human rights organizations and B'Tselem, Israel was crossed off a 2015 UN list of grave violators of children's rights after top UN officials "buckled under political pressure" from Israel.[128] One by one, a phalanx of humanitarian institutions melted like butter after Protective Edge as Israel turned up the heat. In the midst of Protective Edge, venerable British medical journal *The Lancet* had published an "open letter" signed by a score of medical professionals that decried Israel's "aggression" and "massacre" in Gaza. The letter provoked a firestorm of protest, charge, and countercharge that was played out in the journal's pages over the next four months. Although he had to endure a barrage of ad hominems, editor in chief Richard Horton initially stood his ground as the journal ran an editorial describing Gaza as a "prison," cataloging the carnage that attended Israel's assault, and defending the decision to publish the letter. But as Israel's far-flung network of apparatchiks escalated the smear campaign and threatened a boycott, Horton succumbed. What ensued was a strange echo of Paul on the road to Damascus combined with Mao's Cultural Revolution. In a Goldstone-style ritual of self-abasement, Horton embarked on a trip to Israel that was a "turning point for me," a "revelatory experience." He reached the epiphany that he had been badly misinformed—the Israeli reality as he now experienced it was an "inspiring model of partnership between Jews and Arabs ... a vision for a peaceful and productive future between peoples"—and then delivered a public self-criticism pledging inter alia that he would "never publish a letter like that again." He apparently uttered not a single word critical of Israel during his stay, or afterward. But he did additionally find time to attend a lecture by and personally converse with Israeli philosopher Asa Kasher, who

127. UNICEF, "Escalating Violence in the Gaza Strip and Israel Threatens Devastating Harm for Children" (10 July 2014); UNICEF, "Children Are Bearing the Brunt of the Worsening Violence in Gaza and Israel" (13 July 2014); UNICEF, "Basic Services for Children under Assault in Gaza" (18 July 2014); UNICEF, "'Outrage Has Become Commonplace'" (30 July 2014); "UNICEF Statement on Latest Deaths of Children in Israel and Gaza" (23 August 2014).

128. Harriet Sherwood, "UN Officials Accused of Bowing to Israeli Pressure over Children's Rights List," *Guardian* (17 March 2015).

wrote Israel's code of military ethics and had earlier been "deeply impressed with the courage" of Israeli soldiers in Cast Lead. Horton proceeded to express "immense respect" for the "point of view" that Israeli combatants "took extreme precautions to prevent civilian casualties and . . . put themselves at personal risk to this end" during Israel's latest operation. He went on to ponder: "In that situation how would I behave? It's very easy from an armchair in London to be critical, and much more difficult when you're in a combat zone to live out your ideals." Isn't that every war criminal's defense? It's hard to decide whether this cringeworthy profile in pusillanimity disgusts more in its unctuousness or its banality.[129] Shortly thereafter, Jacques de Maio, International Committee of the Red Cross (ICRC) representative in Israel and the occupied Palestinian territories, gave a speech in Jerusalem on humanitarian law. He not only didn't criticize Protective Edge but instead singled out Israel for praise: "[H]umanitarian access in Israel and the O/T [occupied territories] is, in a comparative sense, outstandingly good. In fact, I can think of no other context where the ICRC operates . . . where the access for humanitarian organizations is as good as it is here." De Maio sang this groveling paean to his host even as Israel repeatedly blocked access by humanitarian organizations, including the Red Cross, even as it mercilessly targeted first responders on rescue missions, and even as the Red Cross had itself "firmly condemn[ed] this extremely alarming series of attacks against humanitarian workers, ambulances, and hospitals," during Israel's latest operation.[130] It would not be the last time de Maio plumbed the depths of moral depravity as he whitewashed Israeli crimes.

Meanwhile, former International Criminal Court chief prosecutor Luis Moreno-Ocampo has in recent years reinvented himself as Israel's chief counsel.

129. During the Cultural Revolution, Chinese who had dissented from Mao's "correct political line" in the past were made to publicly confess the error of their ways. "An Open Letter for the People in Gaza," *Lancet* (2 August 2014); "Gaza: An urgent call to protect civilian life and health," *Lancet* (9 August 2014); Judy Siegel-Itzkovich, "The Lancet Editor Relents on Medical Journal's Unbalanced Attacks on Israel," *Jerusalem Post* (2 October 2014); Andrew Tobin, "'Lancet' Editor Sees Positive Side of Israel in Visit," *Times of Israel* (13 October 2014); Ben White, "Lobbying the Lancet: How Israel's apologists smeared 'Doctors for Terrorism,'" *Middle East Monitor* (15 October 2014); Richard Horton, "Offline: People to people," *Lancet* (11 October 2014); Richard Horton, "Geopolitical Issues and Responsibilities of Medical and Scientific Journals," *Rambam Maimonides Medical Journal* (January 2015). For Kasher, see Chapter 4.

130. Jacques de Maio, opening address, Ninth Annual Minerva/ICRC International Conference on Humanitarian Law (3–4 November 2014). *Report of the Detailed Findings*, paras. 330–32, 355, 378–79, 456–65, 521.

On his periodic trafficking to Israel, he heaped praise on its respect for the "rule of law," purported that the legal status of Israeli settlements in the occupied Palestinian territories was a "completely new" and open question (even as the 15 judges on the International Court of Justice unanimously declared them illegal more than a decade ago[131]), and alleged that as a matter of law, Protective Edge was "highly complicated."[132] It's unclear exactly where the complication lay: Was it when Israel dropped more than one hundred one-ton bombs on Shuja'iya or when it indiscriminately fired 20,000 high-explosive artillery shells in densely populated civilian areas? Was it when Israel methodically razed to the ground thousands of civilian homes or when it fired on civilians carrying white flags? Was it when Israel targeted clearly marked ambulances or when it targeted clearly marked civilian shelters even after explicitly promising not to target them? His Israeli audiences no doubt warmed up to Moreno-Ocampo's soothing words, whereas the informed reader cannot but shudder in revulsion at these wanton acts of criminal prostitution.[133]

Lancet, Red Cross, International Criminal Court . . . : the capitulation was as pervasive as it was pathetic. In yet another abject spectacle of professional dereliction, even the UN Human Rights Council betrayed Gaza after Protective Edge.

ADDENDUM

The critique of *"Black Friday"* in this chapter was submitted to Amnesty International for comment. This addendum includes a slightly edited version

131. See Chapter 2.

132. Anshel Pfeffer, "Israel Has Little to Fear from the International Criminal Court," *Haaretz* (20 May 2014); Yonah Jeremy Bob, "Former ICC Prosecutor: High Court approval could save settlements from war crime label," *Jerusalem Post* (10 December 2015).

133. Even honorable international civil servants from whom one would expect better disappointed. The distinguished diplomat Álvaro de Soto penned a scathing report documenting US and Israeli highhandedness, on the one side, and UN supineness, on the other, during his stint as UN envoy for the Middle East peace process. Still, he reserved his harshest language for Hamas, which he repeatedly accused of initiating the violence to which Israel retaliates. Indeed, de Soto himself confessed: "There is a seeming reflex, in any given situation where the UN is to take a position, to ask first how Israel or Washington will react rather than what is the right position to take. I confess that I am not entirely exempt from that reflex, and I regret it." Álvaro de Soto, *End of Mission Report* (May 2007), paras. 25, 74–76, 134. But to his credit, de Soto did make the point in telling detail that Hamas was never given a chance to govern and to evolve into a responsible political actor (see Chapter 1).

of Amnesty's response (which is reprinted with its gracious consent) and this author's rejoinder.

Response to Norman G. Finkelstein's Critique of Amnesty International's "Black Friday" Report[134]

We consider that your critique misrepresents our work on the Israel/Gaza 2014 conflict and our legal analysis, disregards our efforts to campaign for justice for the victims of crimes committed during the conflict, and fails to consider the body of evidence we made publicly available from our joint investigation with Forensic Architecture. While we welcome substantive engagement with our work, including critical engagement, we reject entirely your conclusion that our *"Black Friday"* report represents a "whitewash."

Amnesty International, together with Forensic Architecture, chose to focus on investigating Israel's assault on Rafah from 1 to 4 August 2014 for a number of reasons. These include: the ability of fieldworkers in the Gaza Strip contracted by Amnesty International to obtain eyewitness testimonies and other relevant information; the amount of photographic and video material posted on media and social media in real time, which enabled analysts to reconstruct specific attacks and locate them in time and space; the availability of high-resolution satellite images of Rafah, including from 11:39 a.m. on 1 August 2014, when some of the heaviest attacks were being launched; and the fact that the Hannibal Directive had been invoked. This combination of factors led Amnesty International and Forensic Architecture to conclude that—in spite of Israel's continued denial of access to the Gaza Strip to Amnesty International researchers during and after the 2014 war—strong evidence that Israeli forces committed crimes during the assault on Rafah could be obtained. Israel's violations of international humanitarian law (IHL) and crimes during Operation Protective Edge were certainly not confined to Rafah; Amnesty International has not implied that they were, in *"Black Friday"* or any of its other publications on the 2014 war, and the organization has documented Israeli attacks in many areas of the Gaza Strip that it believes should be investigated as possible war crimes. In particular, Israel's massive use of artillery and other firepower on residential areas such as Shuja'iya and Khuza'a bear many similarities to its assault on Rafah.

134. September 2015.

Amnesty International uses international law as its framework to push state and non-state actors around the world to uphold human rights and protect civilians, including in situations of armed conflict, and to press for justice, truth and reparation when rights are violated and crimes are committed. As part of that work, we rigorously gather evidence of violations and, based on our findings, analyze what occurred in light of the relevant international standards (primarily, but not exclusively, IHL in situations of armed conflict). We use our findings and legal analysis to campaign publicly and to make recommendations to governments, international bodies and others in an effort to stop further violations and ensure redress for those already committed. We also engage with national and international investigatory mechanisms and judicial bodies, where appropriate. However, Amnesty International is not a judicial body. Our legal analysis is therefore neither an indictment nor a final judgment; instead, it is presented in light of the information we have collected and in order to support the recommendations we are making to governments, international bodies and others. In conducting our legal analysis on specific cases, particularly those that may amount to crimes under international law, we are mindful of the standards of evidence and the burden of proof that would be necessary to make such an argument before a competent court, which are far higher than those used to make a particular argument in an academic or journalistic article.

We are also mindful of the fact that, even in cases when crimes under international law are committed, anyone prosecuted for committing or ordering such crimes has a right to fair trial proceedings, including the presumption of innocence until proven guilty on specific charges. Presuming that a particular attack was premeditated, or that an entire lengthy military operation such as Israel's Operation Protective Edge was "designed ... to 'punish, humiliate and terrorize' a civilian population," is not an option for judges or juries in courts that adhere to international standards.

Our remit is to rigorously gather, assess and publicize information documenting violations and to campaign for justice and reparation for victims and their families, all tasks that we have undertaken during and after the Israel/Gaza war in 2014. Our outputs have consistently been widely reported on by the media, keeping justice for victims firmly on the agenda, and have been noted by governments and judicial bodies, including the Office of the Prosecutor of the International Criminal Court (ICC), which is conducting a preliminary examination on Palestine. Our efforts to end impunity for those responsible for war crimes and other violations of IHL in Israel and the

Occupied Palestinian Territories (OPT), including but not limited to those committed during the 2014 Israel/Gaza war, will continue. Within our limited resources and other constraints, we do our best to conduct this work in a way that is strategic and will contribute to achieving genuine long-term human rights change. This, rather than criticism of our work on Israel and the OPT from various standpoints, is what guides us.

In situations of armed conflict where a military force possesses and uses sophisticated weaponry, part of the factual and legal analysis Amnesty International must conduct is indeed trying to understand and evaluate the premises used by the military planners and decision-makers, which is not the same as condoning them. In other words, we need to consider whether there was, or could have been, a genuine military objective for each Israeli attack analyzed, even when the attack occurred in a context like the assault on Rafah during 1–4 August 2014, where the scale and toll of the Israeli attacks cannot possibly be justified by the objective of preventing the capture of one Israeli soldier.

Military targets could include Palestinian fighters and military objectives, such as installations or structures used for military purposes, weapons and ammunition stores. Other objects which are not necessarily military in nature, including tunnels and civilian homes or other buildings, may become military objectives when they are used at the time of the attack to make an effective contribution to military action, and if their destruction or capture offers a definite military advantage in the circumstances ruling at the time. The Israeli authorities do not release sufficient information on targets and specific objectives to enable a full assessment of their legality—a fact for which we have consistently criticized them. Nevertheless, in the context of the hostilities in Rafah on 1–4 August 2014, and more generally during the Israel/Gaza 2014 war, we cannot necessarily assume that there was no legitimate military target for each specific Israeli attack just because we did not uncover information pointing to one. Since the Israeli military used targeted munitions such as drone-fired missiles during the assault on Rafah (in addition, obviously, to the use of massive amounts of artillery and other area weapons), and since Palestinian fighters and military installations were present in at least some parts of Rafah during the hostilities, we have to entertain the possibility that each Israeli attack had a legitimate military target. The most we can say is that after various types of research, we have not been able to discover a legitimate military target for a particular attack; this does not mean we necessarily believe there was one. It is even harder to determine the intent of a particular attack based on the available information, since even when targeted weaponry is used, IHL allows for the possibility that a "reasonable commander" bases a decision on the information available to him/her at the time and makes a mistake. Basically, we have to analyze each case and present our conclusions in a deliberately cautious and considered manner, which often means stating the minimum that could be concluded about the case rather than the maximum. With the cases in the *"Black Friday"* report, we believe we have indeed made a strong argument that even when they are considered from the standpoint of a "reasonable commander," the cases should be independently investigated as war crimes and individuals should be held criminally liable. In other words, the strategy is in fact similar to what you surmise when you stated, "Amnesty entertained so many of Israel's premises, or premises favorable to Israel, in order to show that, even if one were to accept those premises, Israel would *still* be legally culpable" (emphasis in original). We believe this strategy is the correct one to employ if we want to move closer to Israeli military or political personnel being prosecuted for their responsibility for war crimes.

Consequently, we reject your criticism that this strategy "winds up misrepresenting what happened and letting Israel off the hook on the more serious legal charges."

Legally, there is no hierarchy among different types of war crimes or between war crimes and crimes against humanity; all are considered "the most serious crimes of concern to the international community as a whole [which] must not go unpunished." When sufficient admissible evidence exists, all states are permitted—and, sometimes, obliged—to bring to justice any person responsible for committing or ordering these crimes, regardless of which category of war crime was committed or whether it was an act committed as part of a crime against humanity. Crimes against humanity are defined in Article 7 of the Rome Statute of the ICC, and include acts such as murder when committed "as part of a widespread or systematic attack directed against any civilian population, with knowledge of the attack."

In terms of war crimes, legally speaking, intentionally launching an attack in the knowledge that the attack will cause civilian casualties or damage to civilian objects that would clearly be excessive in relation to the concrete and direct military advantage anticipated (i.e. a disproportionate attack) is just as criminal as intentionally launching a direct attack on civilians or civilian objects, or an attack which strikes military objectives and civilians or civilian objects without distinction, or which treats as a single military objective a number of distinct military objectives located in a civilian city or town. All are prohibited by IHL and all are war crimes.

In cases where Amnesty International was unable to determine whether an attack which killed or injured civilians was aimed at a military objective, we stated, depending on the particular circumstances, that the particular attack was disproportionate or otherwise indiscriminate—if not a direct attack on civilians or civilian objects. It is simply incorrect to argue that the organization was somehow seeking to minimize Israeli crimes or ignoring the fact that the attack was committed as part of a four-day military assault seemingly motivated by a desire to extract [exact?] revenge or punish the civilian population of Rafah.

You appear to confuse our analysis of specific attacks within the Israeli assault on Rafah with our analysis of the overall Israeli assault. We are not "categorizing the Rafah massacre as a disproportionate attack, an indiscriminate attack, or a failure to take all feasible precautions on account of Israel's intent to kill Goldin"; as described above, each attack must be analyzed individually, and then conclusions can be drawn about the four-day assault in which the attacks took place. Nevertheless, we strongly disagree that our analysis "amounts to legitimizing the wholly illegitimate goal of launching an armed attack in order to preempt a future prisoner swap." Nor does using language such as "shift in proportionality" to refer to the logic of the Hannibal Directive and the logic of the Israeli military in implementing it imply that we are somehow endorsing that logic. In our report, we considered what we know about the Hannibal Directive (since the actual directive is classified) and the way it was implemented in Rafah from 1–4 August 2014; we absolutely did not endorse, in any way, either the directive or the way it was implemented. Arguing that we did so would misrepresent our report.

Rejoinder to Amnesty's Response

The crux of this chapter's argument with Amnesty International boils down to a single question: *Did Israel primarily set out to target Gaza's civilian population or legitimate military objectives during Operation Protective Edge?* Whereas Amnesty's factual evidence overwhelmingly affirmed the former, its legal analysis of this evidence consistently presumed the latter. In other words, its legal analysis repeatedly contradicted its own evidentiary findings and effectively exonerated Israel of the most explosive charge leveled against it.

Amnesty's multiple reports on Protective Edge analyzed the assault at three discrete levels: individual incidents (e.g., a single home), major attacks (e.g., Rafah), and the operation as a whole. At each of these levels, Amnesty's legal analysis reached a similar conclusion: Israel might have committed war crimes in the course of pursuing legitimate military objectives, but it almost never intentionally targeted civilians. For example, in *Families under the Rubble,* which analyzed Gazan homes targeted by Israel that resulted in large numbers of civilian deaths, Amnesty divined a possible military objective in each and every attack. In *"Black Friday,"* which investigated Israel's assault on Rafah, when its "insane" and "crazy" use of firepower peaked, Amnesty still divined a possible military objective in all but two of the fifteen separate incidents it analyzed. *"Black Friday"* accordingly concluded that Israel "may" have targeted civilians and committed crimes against humanity in at most "some" instances. But the evidence assembled by Amnesty in *"Black Friday"* pointed ineluctably to a very different conclusion. At the micro and macro levels, the assault on Rafah was a premeditated and deliberate attack on a civilian population. It constituted a crime against humanity.

Instead of engaging this chapter's specific criticisms of *"Black Friday,"* Amnesty's Response for the most part lapses into broad, and often at best tangential, generalities. It is consequently inadequate to the task at hand: the devil is in the details, and by evading the details, the Response cannot convince. This brief rejoinder will focus on the few substantive arguments Amnesty does endeavor to make. The italicized text is culled from its Response:

1. *Presuming that a particular attack was premeditated, or that an entire lengthy military operation such as Israel's Operation Protective Edge was "designed . . . to 'punish, humiliate and terrorize' a civilian population," is not an option for judges or juries in courts that adhere to international standards.*

Amnesty appears to invert the criticism leveled at it. A juxtaposition of the factual evidence Amnesty gathered in *"Black Friday"* against the legal analysis it rendered demonstrates that in incident after incident Amnesty itself kept "presuming" that the Israeli attack did *not* premeditatedly target civilians, notwithstanding its own factual evidence clearly showing that it did. Amnesty itself was "presuming"—against its own evidence and in favor of Israel. For a typical example, see Table 11 (adapted from Table 10 above).

The legal analysis Amnesty presented was premised on a hypothetical scenario, divorced from the actual facts, that shielded Israel from the politically explosive charge of targeting civilians. It is instructive to compare Amnesty's chain of deductions in another of its regional reports issued

TABLE 11 Amnesty's Case Studies: Detail

Amnesty's evidence	Amnesty's legal analysis	Finkelstein's comment
On 1 August, a bomb was dropped on a home, killing 15 of the 19 family members present, including 10 children; "all" the occupants of the home "were civilians," and all the adults except one (a 51-year-old unemployed worker) were female.	"Amnesty International has been unable to identify any potential target or reason for the attack. . . . Even if there had been a military target nearby, the attack appears to have been disproportionate or otherwise indiscriminate."	If there was no known "potential target or reason for the attack," it perplexes why Amnesty speculated on the possibility ("Even if . . .") that there was one. If a legal assessment is to be based on evidence, this was a straightforward targeted attack on civilians and a civilian object.

contemporaneously. In *"Bombs Fall from the Sky Day and Night": Civilians under fire in northern Yemen* (2015), Amnesty stated:

> The evidence from . . . attacks on military objectives, infrastructure, government buildings, moving vehicles and other targets elsewhere in Yemen indicates that coalition forces are capable of striking their chosen targets with a certain degree of accuracy. In investigations into airstrikes in other parts of the country, Amnesty International found that Huthi/Saleh-loyalist-controlled military bases or other military objectives had been repeatedly targeted by coalition airstrikes. Yet researchers found civilian objects in Sa'da governorate which had been struck more than once, suggesting that they were in fact the intended target of the attack.
>
> For example, in at least four of the airstrikes investigated by Amnesty International, houses were struck more than once, suggesting that they were the intended targets. Amnesty International also visited six markets in and around Sa'da city that were struck by airstrikes and analyzed video footage of the aftermath of airstrikes on a number of markets in other nearby towns and villages. Some markets were attacked repeatedly on separate occasions, at times of day when many civilians were present. . . . Amnesty International found no evidence indicating that the markets had been used for military purposes.

The evidentiary standard used by Amnesty in the Yemeni case was this: if a belligerent possesses weapons capable of "striking . . . chosen targets with a certain degree of accuracy"; and if civilian objects were "attacked repeatedly on separate occasions, at times of day when many civilians were present"; and if Amnesty "found no evidence indicating" that the civilian objects "had been used for military purposes"; then it suggests that the civilian population was "in fact the intended target of the attack." But then didn't Israel's saturation bombing, precision-missile attacks, and intensive artillery shelling of Rafah's densely populated civilian neighborhoods, stretching nonstop over a four-day period and in the near-total absence of a legitimate military target, suggest that the civilian population was "the intended target of the attack"? Put otherwise, why didn't Amnesty enter the weasel caveat in the case of Yemen— "Amnesty International found no evidence indicating that the markets had been used for military purposes. *Even if there had been a military target* . . ."?

The distortions that set in from Amnesty's modus operandi became yet more painfully and nauseatingly apparent in a document it issued two years after Protective Edge, which deplored the lack of accountability for atrocities committed during the operation.[135] It recalled the details of a notorious incident in which four Palestinian children, aged 10–14, were killed "while they played hide and seek on the beach": "the attack took place in full view of international journalists . . . they could see clearly that the people running across the beach were children"; an Israeli military spokesman "announced . . . that the attack was targeting a Hamas Naval Forces 'compound,' which journalists described as a small, broken-down fisherman's hut"; "none of the [journalists] reported seeing military operatives in the vicinity of the hut." What did Amnesty conclude from this accumulation of damning evidence? "At the very least, the attack failed to take required precautions to protect civilians, including to ensure that targets are of military nature before proceeding with an attack." Is it the mandate of a human rights organization to report what "at the very least" happened or, based on all the available evidence, what *probably* happened? Amnesty noted that an Israeli investigation absolving the military of responsibility for the killings "did not explain why the army had not identified" the children "as such." It couldn't even conceive, or wouldn't let itself conceive, that the IDF *had* identified four children frolicking on a beach "as such"—and then proceeded to murder them.[136]

The Response alleges that bodies bound by international law do not have the "option" of concluding that the carnage in Rafah was "designed . . . to 'punish, humiliate and terrorize' a civilian population." But the internal quote comes from the Goldstone Report on Operation Cast Lead (2008–9).[137] It is

135. Amnesty International, "Time to Address Impunity: Two years after the Gaza/Israel war" (8 July 2016).
136. See also Chapter 13 on this incident.
137. See Chapter 5.

a depressing commentary that Amnesty now distances itself from Goldstone, although it previously issued no less than 15 statements embracing the report.[138] For example, one of these Amnesty statements declared:

> All relevant UN bodies must act promptly and in coordination to implement the recommendations of the UN-mandated Goldstone report on violations of international law.... *The report's findings are consistent with those of Amnesty International's own field investigation.*... Key findings [of the Goldstone Report include]: Israeli forces committed violations of human rights and international humanitarian law amounting to war crimes and some possibly amounting to crimes against humanity. Notably, investigations into numerous instances of lethal attacks on civilians and civilian objects revealed that the attacks were intentional, that some were launched with the intention of spreading terror among the civilian population and with no justifiable military objective.[139]

The bigger point, however, is this. In its objectives and modus operandi, Protective Edge did not substantively differ from Cast Lead, except that the devastation wreaked by Protective Edge was on a vastly greater scale. On the basis of the evidence collected by it, the Goldstone Report concluded, and Amnesty's own findings corroborated, that Israel deliberately targeted Gaza's civilian population in "numerous instances." Yet although the evidence assembled by Amnesty's Protective Edge reports in general and *"Black Friday"* in particular pointed to the same conclusion, Amnesty's legal analysis inferred, hypothesized, or speculated to the contrary that Israel almost without exception targeted not the civilian population but instead legitimate military objects. It is also unclear why Amnesty did not as a matter of law have the "option" of concluding that Israel sought to "punish, humiliate and terrorize" Gaza's civilian population in Protective Edge. Indeed, *"Black Friday"* itself found that Israel committed "carnage in Gaza" in "a desire for revenge, to teach a lesson to, or to punish the population." Barely a flea's hop separates this factual description of the Rafah massacre from the phrase "punish, humiliate and terrorize" that Amnesty alleges it did not have the "option" to utilize. The real problem would appear to be that in its legal findings Amnesty took flight from its own factual findings of what happened. In

138. NGO Monitor, "Amnesty International's Goldstone Campaign, with a Review of Statements from Other NGO's" (22 October 2009), ngo-monitor.org/article/amnesty_international_goldstone_s_cheat_sheet_#amnesty.

139. Amnesty International, "UN Must Ensure Goldstone Inquiry Recommendations Are Implemented" (15 September 2009), emphasis added.

its Response, Amnesty reprimands this author, as he allegedly "fails to consider the body of evidence we made publicly available." But isn't it Amnesty that failed to consider this—that is, its own—body of evidence?

2. *[W]e cannot necessarily assume that there was no legitimate military target for each specific Israeli attack just because we did not uncover information pointing to one. Since the Israeli military used targeted munitions such as drone-fired missiles during the assault on Rafah (in addition, obviously, to the use of massive amounts of artillery and other area weapons), and since Palestinian fighters and military installations were present in at least some parts of Rafah during the hostilities, we have to entertain the possibility that each Israeli attack had a legitimate military target. The most we can say is that after various types of research, we have not been able to discover a legitimate military target for a particular attack; this does not mean we necessarily believe there was one.*

The essence of this statement is, Whenever Israel uses precision weapons, Amnesty "cannot necessarily assume that there was no legitimate military target"; indeed, it must "entertain the possibility" that there *was* one, *even if all the available evidence points to the conclusion that Israel was targeting civilians.* This acknowledgment intrigues on multiple counts. *First,* whereas it earlier argued against "presuming" that Israel targeted civilians, here Amnesty itself argues *in favor of* "presuming" that Israel targeted a military objective whenever it used precision weapons and even if all the available evidence demonstrates otherwise. *Second,* Amnesty reverses the intuitive presumption that if precision weapons are used in an attack that results in civilian deaths, and no evidence exists of a military objective, then—precisely *because* precision weapons were used—the attack on civilians must have been deliberate. Instead, Amnesty declares that if precision weapons were used, the presumption must be that Israel did not target civilians, even as all the evidence points to the conclusion that it did. Amnesty provides no basis for its poignant presumption that Israel would not use precision weapons to target civilians, although voluminous evidence exists that Israel has repeatedly and brazenly targeted civilians, including children, and civilian objects, much of it collected by Amnesty itself. *Third,* if it is incumbent upon Amnesty to "entertain the possibility" that Israel's objective was a "legitimate military target" when it used precision weapons, then Amnesty by definition *cannot* find that Israel targeted civilians when it used precision weapons unless Israel itself confesses, because the *possibility* will always exist that its objective was a "legitimate military target." In other words, if Amnesty did not find that Israel was targeting civilians, it was not for a deficit of evidence—indeed, it was despite overwhelming evidence, much of it emanating from Israelis themselves—but because it was an epistemological impossibility: on the one hand, its working presumption was that Israel did not target civilians when it used precision weapons while, on the other hand, the logic of its reasoning was such that *no amount of evidence* could persuade it otherwise.

It's worth pausing for a moment to ponder Amnesty's astonishing assertions. A typical human rights report includes a section on international law that cites the relevant provisions of international humanitarian and human rights law. For example, the legal chapter of *"Black Friday"* includes these subheadings: "Prohibition on direct attacks on civilians and civilian objects—the principle of distinction," "Prohibition on indiscriminate and disproportionate attacks," "Precautions in attack," "Precautions in defense," "Collective punishment," "Investigation," and "International human rights law." All these sections cite from standard sources, such as the 1949 Geneva Conventions and Additional Protocols I and II (adopted in 1977). But unbeknownst to its readers, Amnesty interposes between its factual findings and legal analysis a phantom special presumption for Israel—let's call it SP4I— according to which, whenever Israel deploys precision weapons, the operative presumption must be that it is targeting a military objective and, even if all the evidence demonstrates otherwise, the possibility must still be entertained that a military objective was targeted. It ought to be obvious that SP4I is not anchored in any extant provision of international law; that this extenuating dispensation is applied only to Israel (would Amnesty invoke such a presumption for the Syrian regime?); and that no basis exists for it in Israel's extant record of conducting armed hostilities. If nothing else comes of this exchange, it's surely worthwhile that SP4I, hitherto invisible in Amnesty's legal analysis, has now been dredged to the surface.

3. *Legally, there is no hierarchy among different types of war crimes or between war crimes and crimes against humanity; all are considered "the most serious crimes of concern to the international community as a whole [which] must not go unpunished."* ... *In terms of war crimes, legally speaking, intentionally launching an attack in the knowledge that the attack will cause civilian casualties or damage to civilian objects that would clearly be excessive in relation to the concrete and direct military advantage anticipated (i.e. a disproportionate attack) is just as criminal as intentionally launching a direct attack on civilians or civilian objects, or an attack which strikes military objectives and civilians or civilian objects without distinction, or which treats as a single military objective*

a number of distinct military objectives located in a civilian city or town. All are prohibited by IHL and all are war crimes.

If a hierarchy does not exist among war crimes, it is cause for wonder why Amnesty is so cautious *not* to accuse Israel of intentionally targeting civilians; and why it starts from the presumption that Israel was not targeting civilians; and why it persists in this presumption even if all the evidence it gathered showed that Israel was targeting them; and why, a contrario, in a press release for the Amnesty report deploring lack of accountability two years after Protective Edge, it chose to highlight "several attacks that *clearly targeted civilians* in violation of international humanitarian law."[140] But, of course, a hierarchy *does* exist, if not in a strictly legal sense then as a *political* matter. The public's threshold of tolerance is much higher for civilian deaths in an operation that targets legitimate military objectives than for civilian deaths in an operation calculated to "punish, humiliate and terrorize the civilian population." A 2016 International Committee of the Red Cross survey found that only half of public opinion among the five permanent members of the UN Security Council (and Switzerland) believed it was wrong to target "enemy combatants in populated areas . . . knowing that many civilians would be killed," whereas fully 80 percent believed it was wrong to target "hospitals, ambulances and health-care workers in order to weaken the enemy."[141] What's more, if civilians are killed in the absence of a military objective, it's a straightforward grave breach of international law, akin to rape or the coercive use of human shields. However, the killing of civilians in the context of a military objective, which is what indiscriminate and disproportionate attacks presuppose, diminishes the probability of a conviction, as it introduces an element of murkiness and opens up wide latitude for judgment. The International Court of Justice couldn't even reach consensus that the use of *nuclear* weapons was disproportionate or indiscriminate in all circumstances—or, put otherwise, the categories *proportionate* and *discriminate* are so elastic that they can even accommodate the use of nuclear weapons.[142] Amnesty accuses Israel of committing disproportionate and indiscriminate attacks during its assault on Rafah while it scrupulously avoids accusing

---

140. Amnesty International, "Time to Address Impunity," emphasis added.

141. International Committee of the Red Cross, *People on War: Perspectives from 16 countries* (Geneva: 2016), pp. 7, 9.

142. International Court of Justice, Advisory Opinion, *Legality of the Threat or Use of Nuclear Weapons* (8 July 1996), paras. 95–97.

Israel of premeditated attacks on the civilian population despite overwhelming evidence. This was clearly a political decision: Amnesty calibrated its legal findings so as not to incur the full force of Israel's wrath. The political decision, however, came at a heavy price. It shielded Israel from the full force of justified public outrage by whitewashing the ugliest truth about the Rafah inferno: it resulted not from the excesses of a legitimate military operation gone awry, but from an operation that ab initio *intentionally targeted* the civilian population.

The remainder of Amnesty's "Response" consists of self-congratulatory bromides or unargued counterclaims.

THIRTEEN

Betrayal II

UN HUMAN RIGHTS COUNCIL

IN AUGUST 2014, THE UN HUMAN RIGHTS COUNCIL APPOINTED a fact-finding mission "to investigate purported violations of international humanitarian and human rights law" during Operation Protective Edge (2014).[1] William Schabas, a respected international jurist, was named chair of the mission. Israel immediately jumped into high gear to oust him, as he had previously uttered sacrileges such as, "Why are we going after the president of Sudan [at the International Criminal Court] for Darfur and not the president of Israel for Gaza?" Foreign Minister Avigdor Lieberman weirdly analogized Schabas's recruitment to "appointing Cain to investigate who killed Abel." Unable to withstand the juggernaut, Schabas duly "resigned" and was replaced as chair by a US judge, Mary McGowan Davis, who hailed from New York State.[2] The outcome at this point was as predictable as when UN secretary-general Ban Ki-moon appointed Álvaro Uribe vice-chair of the Panel of Inquiry after Israel's assault on the *Mavi Marmara*.[3] The betrayal had begun.

1. "UN Rights Council Appoints Members of Commission to Investigate Purported Gaza Violations," *UN News Centre* (11 August 2014).

2. Tovah Lazaroff, "UNHRC Investigator Schabas Stays Mum on Hamas as 'Terror Group,'" *Jerusalem Post* (12 August 2014); Stuart Winer, "UN Gaza Probe Head Says He's Not Anti-Israel, Will Be Impartial," *Times of Israel* (12 August 2014); Raphael Ahren, "Watchdog Group Demands That Schabas Quit UN Gaza Inquiry over Anti-Israel Bias," *Times of Israel* (4 September 2014); "Head of UN Inquiry into Gaza Conflict to Quit," *ynetnews.com* (2 February 2015); Barak Ravid and Jack Khoury, "Netanyahu: After Gaza inquiry head quit, UN should shelve report," *Haaretz* (3 February 2015); Barak Ravid, "New Head of UN Inquiry into Gaza War Expected to Be More Balanced toward Israel," *Haaretz* (3 February 2015). The immediate impetus of Schabas's resignation was the "revelation" that he once did a routine paid consultancy for the Palestine Liberation Organization but didn't mention it in the résumé he submitted. Had Schabas reported it, he perhaps would have survived the witch hunt.

3. See Chapter 9.

In June 2015, the UN Human Rights Council (UNHRC) mission released its report.[4] It predictably accused Hamas[5] of having committed war crimes. But a close reading of the UN Report could not have pleased Israel either. In its discrete analyses of numerous incidents during the assault, the Report's factual findings repeatedly suggested that Israel might also have committed war crimes. A reader unfamiliar with the facts would perhaps be impressed at the Report's evenhanded presentation, whereas a reader familiar with them would probably recoil in outrage at this spurious balance. The odd thing about the Report was that it did chronicle, often in harrowing detail, the horrors that Israel inflicted on Gaza. However, it then proceeded to render legal analyses that methodically and, in many instances, comically buffered the gravity of Israel's crimes. In other words, it precisely replicated the apologetic modus operandi of the Amnesty International reports on Protective Edge.[6] The upshot was that the UN Report conveyed a wholly misleading, distorted picture of what happened in Gaza. Whereas it suggested that Protective Edge was a legitimate military campaign lamentably marred by sundry excesses, in fact the assault was a terror campaign designed, if not to break, then at any rate to temper Gaza's will to resist. In order to convincingly demonstrate the Report's bias, there's no alternative except to sift through its findings piecemeal fashion. It is to be hoped that by the time readers complete this chapter, they will be persuaded that if this writer has reached a harsh conclusion, it springs neither from malice nor prejudice but was arrived at only after scrupulously parsing the evidence, albeit also amid his mounting feelings of despair commingled with indignation that even at this late date, when a seemingly endless river of blood has passed under the bridge in the course of Israel's numberless "operations" targeting the martyred people of Gaza, a document bearing the imprimatur of the Human Rights Council should still so want in courage and integrity.

The UN Report on Protective Edge did not lack in redemptive features. It confirmed previous authoritative statements of law on a number of critical points. Thus, it reiterated that "the Occupied Palestinian Territory is com-

4. *Report of the Detailed Findings of the Independent Commission of Inquiry Established Pursuant to Human Rights Council Resolution S-21/1* (22 June 2015); hereafter: UN Report.

5. *Hamas* is here used to denote all armed groups in Gaza.

6. See Chapter 12.

prised of the West Bank, including East Jerusalem, and the Gaza Strip."[7] It also concluded, after painstaking analysis, that despite its ballyhooed 2005 redeployment, Israel "has maintained effective control of the Gaza Strip. . . . Gaza continues to be occupied by Israel."[8] The Report went on to state that "the blockade of Gaza by Israel" has been "strangling the economy in Gaza"; that the dire situation in Gaza since the end of Protective Edge "cannot be assessed separately from the blockade imposed by Israel"; and that current international relief efforts are "not a substitute for lifting the blockade."[9] The most resonant pronouncement in the whole of the Report called on Israel to "lift, immediately and unconditionally, the blockade on Gaza."[10] On another charged legal point, the Report rejected Israel's contention that if it could avert the capture of one of its soldiers, resort to otherwise disproportionate force would be legitimate; the proportionality test, Israel had argued, "must take into account the strategic consideration of denying the armed groups the leverage they could obtain over Israel in negotiations for the release of the captured soldier." The Report persuasively rejoined that this line of reasoning constituted "an erroneous interpretation of international humanitarian law":

> The leverage that armed groups may obtain in negotiations does not depend solely on the capture of a soldier, but on how the Government of Israel decides to react to the capture in the aftermath. The strategic military or political advantage sought is therefore not a concrete and direct military advantage as required by international humanitarian law. . . . Indeed, the proposed interpretation of the anticipated military advantage, which would allow for abstract political and long-term strategic considerations in carrying out the proportionality analysis, would have the consequence of emptying the proportionality principle of any protective element.[11]

Still, these various legal determinations contained in the Report, although to be welcomed, did not remotely vindicate its numerous problematic, and at times outrageous, findings.

7. UN Report, para. 26.
8. Ibid., paras. 26–30.
9. Ibid., paras. 54, 598, 599.
10. Ibid., para. 681(d). The Report implicitly distanced itself on this point from the UN Panel of Inquiry appointed by Secretary-General Ban Ki-moon, which determined the coastal blockade of Gaza to be legal (see Chapter 9).
11. Ibid., paras. 369–70.

The UN Report's mandate formally covered only *jus in bello* (rules governing the conduct of armed conflict), and not *jus ad bellum* (rules governing the resort to armed conflict). However, its pronouncements on the triggers of Protective Edge effectively justified the Israeli offensive. It neutrally began, "The hostilities of 2014 erupted in the context of the protracted occupation of the West Bank, including East Jerusalem, and the Gaza Strip, and of the increasing number of rocket attacks on Israel."[12] But then, crossing into the juridical terrain of *jus ad bellum,* the Report cited without caveat Israel's public rationales for launching the initial air assault and subsequent ground invasion:[13] "On 7 July 2014, the Israel Defense Forces commenced operation 'Protective Edge' in the Gaza Strip, with the stated objective of stopping the rocket attacks by Hamas and destroying its capabilities to conduct operations against Israel"; "[O]n 17 July 2014, the IDF launched a ground operation into Gaza. Official Israeli sources indicated that they did so to degrade 'terror organizations' military infrastructure, and [. . . neutralize] their network of cross-border assault tunnels.'"[14] But as a matter of law, Israel couldn't resort to armed self-defense unless it had exhausted nonviolent options and, hence, was driven by "necessity" to launch an attack.[15] In the event, Israel did have at hand an effective nonviolent remedy. Even egregious Israeli propagandists acknowledged that Hamas's objective from the inception of hostilities was to

12. Ibid., para. 53.

13. The Report also uncritically repeated Israel's rationale for launching Operation Brother's Keeper, which directly preceded Protective Edge: "On 12 June 2014, 19-year-old Eyal Yifrah and 16-year-olds Gilad Sha'er and Naftali Frenkel were abducted and brutally murdered.... In response to their kidnapping, from 12 to 30 June 2014, Israel launched Operation 'Brother's Keeper,' which the IDF stated aimed to find the three youths and simultaneously 'weaken Hamas terror'" (ibid., para. 503). However, in an apparently botched operation, their abductors immediately killed the Israeli teenagers. The Israeli government, which was almost certainly privy to this turn of events *before* launching Brother's Keeper, exploited the killings in the service of a larger political agenda. See Chapter 11.

14. UN Report, paras. 58, 246. The ground invasion, it continued, "followed what Israel described as 'a militant attack inside Israel on 17 July carried out through a tunnel from inside Gaza, the launch of an unmanned aerial vehicle (UAV) into Israeli airspace, an attempted infiltration by sea into Israel by Hamas naval commandos, continued rocket fire from Gaza and Hamas's refusal to accept a cease-fire'" (ibid., para. 246). But the more likely impetus behind Israel's decision to launch the ground invasion on 17 July was the downing of the Malaysian airliner over Ukraine on that same day. See Chapter 11.

15. Yoram Dinstein, *War, Aggression and Self-Defence,* fourth edition (Cambridge: 2005), pp. 209–10.

"reopen Gaza's borders."[16] The World Bank reported at the time that "access to Gaza remains highly controlled," while Amnesty had deemed the siege a form of "collective punishment," and the UN Report itself called on Israel to "lift, immediately and unconditionally, the blockade on Gaza."[17] It follows that if the cessation of Hamas rocket attacks was Israel's objective, then it only had to terminate its suffocating siege of Gaza—which would have put Israel on the right side of the law and preempted its "necessity" of armed self-defense, while sparing Gazans a murderous assault and allowing them, finally, to breathe. But what about Hamas's "cross-border assault tunnels"? For argument's sake, let's say that they posed a lethal threat. What prevented Israel from sealing the tunnels from *its* side of the border, as Egypt did to block cross-border tunnel traffic and raids between Gaza and the Sinai?[18] Indeed, in mid-2016, Israel declared plans to "build a concrete wall tens of meters deep underground and aboveground to counter the threat of Hamas attack tunnels."[19] Earlier in the year, the Defense Ministry announced that "a solution for the tunnels" would cost several hundred million dollars, but that "such funding has not been earmarked in the defense budget for the coming years"—which would seem to indicate that Israeli leaders didn't attach special urgency to the danger posed.[20] It speaks to the Report's deep-seated bias that it didn't even ponder Israel's options short of armed force, but instead blithely repeated Israeli *hasbara* (propaganda).

The UN Report perfectly balanced its overall verdicts on Protective Edge: "[T]he high incidence of loss of human life and injury during the 2014 hostilities is heartbreaking"; "Palestinians and Israelis were profoundly shaken by the events of the summer of 2014"; "The 2014 hostilities have had an

16. Gaza Conflict Task Force, *2014 Gaza War Assessment: The new face of conflict,* Jewish Institute for National Security Affairs (JINSA) (2015), p. 8 (see also pp. 16, 19). The task force was commissioned by JINSA.

17. Sara Roy, *The Gaza Strip: The political economy of de-development,* expanded third edition (Washington, DC: 2016), p. xxx; *Amnesty International Report 2015/16: The State of the World's Human Rights* (2016), p. 201.

18. See Chapter 11.

19. Nahum Barnea, "Israel to Build Underground Wall around Gaza Strip," *ynetnews .com* (16 June 2016).

20. Amos Harel, "Israel Doesn't Intend to Strike Gaza over Hamas Tunnels," *Haaretz* (2 February 2016). It was subsequently reported that although work on the wall had begun, "it is at risk of being defunded, as no money has been allocated to the project for fiscal years 2017–2018." (The Ministry of Finance insisted, however, that "there is in fact a budget for the project.") Matan Tzuri, "Building Starts on Underground Gaza Barrier," *ynetnews.com* (7 September 2016).

enormous impact on the lives of Palestinians and Israelis. The scale of the devastation was unprecedented and the death toll and suffering from injuries and trauma speak volumes"; "The commission was deeply moved by the immense suffering of Palestinian and Israeli victims, who have been subjected to repeated rounds of violence."[21] In general, *balance* is an admirable quality: it connotes nonpartisanship and objectivity. But balancing out a wildly imbalanced balance sheet amounts to a partisan act of misrepresentation. The findings of UN-appointed commissions in other situations do take note of grossly lopsided balance sheets.[22] To be sure, the Report's space allocations were not quite so evenly distributed. The ratio of paragraphs devoted to breaches of international law by Israel versus Hamas came to 4:1,[23] while the ratio of paragraphs in the chapter devoted to the human and material toll on Gaza versus Israel stood at 4:3.[24] Still, although "favorable" to Gaza, these ratios didn't remotely approach the relative magnitudes of death and destruction during Protective Edge. Indeed, as the Report itself documented, Israel killed as many Palestinian children in the West Bank—which wasn't even a theater of war—as the total number of Israelis killed during Protective Edge, and Israel destroyed more Palestinian homes in the West Bank than the total number of Israeli homes destroyed.[25] Whichever metric one zeroes in on, the colossal imbalance emerges in full view (see Table 12). The gross inequity registered in these ratios was barely perceptible in the Report. For example, whereas raw data, such as total casualty figures, typically occupy a salient place in human rights documents and, accordingly, the number of Israeli fatalities showed up early in the Report,[26] the figure for Palestinian casualties was buried deep inside its pages.[27] However much it played with these data, to credibly preserve its pretense to balance, the Report nevertheless had to pour substantive content into its many paragraphs devoted to Israel's "heartbreaking" loss of life, "devastation," and "immense suffering." But callous as it might sound, the fact is there just wasn't all that much to say. How many

21. UN Report, paras. 16, 555, 597, 668. The only "false" note in this litany of evenhandedness was a passing one-sided recognition that "Palestinians have demonstrated extraordinary resilience in recent years" (para. 54).

22. See, e.g., *Report of the International Commission of Inquiry on Darfur to the United Nations Secretary-General* (25 January 2005), paras. 190, 271, 285.

23. UN Report, paras. 110–465, 503–50 (Israel); paras. 59–109, 466–502 (Hamas).

24. Ibid., paras. 573–96 (Gaza); paras. 556–72 (Israel).

25. Ibid., paras. 526–46.

26. Ibid., para. 66.

27. Ibid., para. 574.

TABLE 12 Operation Protective Edge: Some critical comparisons

	Gaza	Israel	Ratio
Civilians killed	1,600	6	270:1
Children killed	550	1	550:1
Homes severely damaged or destroyed	18,000	1	18,000:1
Houses of worship damaged or destroyed	203	2	100:1
Kindergartens damaged or destroyed	285	1	285:1
Medical facilities damaged or destroyed	73	0	73:0

NOTE: See sources cited in Part Four.

lines could the Report invest in the death of one Israeli child and the destruction of one Israeli home? It resolved this dilemma by effectively upgrading into a breach of the laws of war, even a quasi war crime, Hamas's infliction of psychological/emotional distress on Israelis.

In armed conflicts, human rights investigations properly focus on violations of the laws of war; in particular, intentional, indiscriminate, and disproportionate attacks on civilians and civilian objects. Thus, the Gaza section of the UN Report's "Impact" chapter overwhelmingly chronicled the massive death and destruction inflicted by Israel on Gaza's civilian population; just three paragraphs at the tail end gestured to pervasive "trauma" and "hopelessness" in the Strip.[28] However, the "Impact" chapter's Israel section reversed these proportions. It prudently passed over in silence total Israeli civilian casualties and consigned the economic damage Hamas wreaked to three concluding paragraphs.[29] (To exemplify this damage, it spotlighted a kibbutz member whose "photography business in Beer Sheva stopped during the war as she was too afraid to take public transport, which made her run into debt together with many other members of the kibbutz.") Instead, the Report opened the Israel section with a profile of Protective Edge's "Psychological Impact," and then proceeded to describe these effects with mind-numbing repetition, piling one anecdote of "distress" upon another of "anxiety," as if even after contriving this unorthodox rubric to balance out the Gaza section, it still strained to fill space (see Table 13). International law forbids "acts or threats of violence the primary purpose of which is to spread

28. Ibid., paras. 593–95.
29. Ibid., paras. 569–71.

TABLE 13 Operation Protective Edge: Impact on Israel

"Children couldn't speak, they were shaking at night, wetting the bed. Now, a lot of the children became more violent, they say it's post-trauma."[a]

Many Israelis experienced what they describe as indelible suffering caused by the constant threat of attacks by Palestinian armed groups. The stress and trauma had serious effects on their wellbeing. . . . The commission interviewed several witnesses who indicated that the sound of rockets, the running to bomb shelters and the pervasive fear was [sic] seriously affecting their and especially their children's wellbeing.[b]

The psychological impact of the conflict on Israeli civilians is also manifest in numerous accounts of anxiety disorders that were brought to the attention of the commission. . . . For example, a resident of Ashdod wrote to the commission about the way in which her fear of indiscriminate attacks significantly reduced her sense of safety and wellbeing, making her "lose peace of mind and security of person." The psychological consequences reported in submissions from Israelis include fear, restlessness, decreased ability to focus, Post-Traumatic Stress Disorder and other stress-related symptoms. These effects were especially observed in children, for whom the summer holiday season became a daily struggle to cope with the anxiety induced by the sound of sirens. In one case, for example, a physician . . . reported that his 11-year-old girl became unable to sleep or take showers unsupervised after she was traumatized by the sound of alarms. . . . In another case, a nine-month-old baby, who was four months old during the conflict, developed a form of anxiety which made him panic at the sound of any alarm for months afterwards. A witness told the commission that her two grown stepdaughters were so traumatized by the repeated conflicts that one suffered from epileptic style seizures whenever she heard a rocket, while the other suffered from severe anxiety attacks.[c]

Children, particularly those who live in areas neighboring Gaza, suffered worse mental health effects than adults as a result of the [experience of] displacement. . . . A social worker who closely followed these children's experiences of displacement reported a number of symptoms, including restlessness, lack of sleep, inability to concentrate at school, and violent behavior. Witnesses also informed the commission that some children in their communities had to undergo specialized treatment to cope with the threat of displacement.[d]

159 people were injured or traumatized as a result of stumbling or falling on their way to shelters. Israeli authorities report that two elderly women died as a result of heart failure while trying to seek cover in Haifa and Jerusalem. . . . [O]lder persons in northern cities of Israel . . . suffered physical and mental traumas as they were making their way to shelters. . . . [A] resident of Kibbutz Be'erim in the Gaza rim told the commission that her children had to hide under the staircase and endure the stress of hearing sirens and loud explosions because 15 seconds was not enough time for them to move into an underground shelter. In one case, a victim—who refers to herself as an "old widow" living on her own—said that she was not able to leave her home in Sderot for a month out of fear. In another, the grandson of an 89-year-old holocaust survivor, who currently lives in Ashkelon, said that his grandmother had to live through an average of 5 sirens a day during the summer and find a way to a shelter within 15 seconds without falling. The son of a 92-year-old lady who resides in Bat Yam near Tel Aviv described that his mother had to stay put during attacks, cry and pray for safety as she was too frail to even reach the staircase.[e]

NOTE: Quoted statements are culled from Israeli testimonies cited by the UN Report.

[a] UN Report, para. 559.

[b] Ibid., para. 560.

[c] Ibid., para. 563.

[d] Ibid., para. 564.

[e] Ibid., para. 568.

terror among the civilian population."[30] However, the laws of war do not prohibit acts of violence that might induce "some degree of terror" among civilians, which is an unavoidable accompaniment and consequence of any substantial resort to armed force.[31] Otherwise, the laws of war would effectively outlaw major armed conflict; their purpose, however, is not to eliminate war—a utopian goal, at any rate, at this juncture in time—but rather to minimize its destructiveness. The various anxieties, stresses, fears, and traumas experienced by Israeli civilians during Protective Edge appeared to fall into this category of states of being that, unpleasant and disorienting as they might be, normally and inevitably attend armed conflict. To tacitly put civilian *stress and trauma* on a par with civilian *death and destruction* undercuts the critical legal distinction between those acts of war that humanity has resolved to abolish (or contain), and those that to date it hasn't so resolved. If an Israeli civil defense siren set off by a rocket attack from Gaza caused anxiety among Israelis, it doesn't follow that Hamas breached the laws of war. In effect, the Report overreached its legal mandate by stretching and, consequently, mangling the laws of armed conflict. Moreover, by equating conditions of suffering that these laws have endeavored to differentiate, it has homogenized situations that by common consent and as a point of law qualitatively differ. If Israelis experienced the distress of not being able to leave their homes, Palestinians experienced the distress of no longer having a home to which they could return. The Report likewise failed to distinguish between situations so radically different in degree as to make them qualitatively incomparable. If Israelis experienced fear and incurred injuries en route to a shelter, then Gazans experienced fear of having nowhere to run in the midst of an inferno and then coming under deliberate attack or, if fortunate enough to find refuge in that rare shelter, of being slaughtered by Israeli precision weapons targeting it. If Israelis had to endure the concussive effects of bottle rockets, then Gazans had to endure the concussive effects of one-ton bombs. It cannot be doubted that the drafters of the Report were cognizant of these elementary distinctions. They elected, however, to collapse them, not because of a high-minded sensitivity to the full gamut of human suffering, or an enlightened refusal to rank human suffering, but almost certainly because otherwise the Report's pretense to balance could not be sustained. If the

30. International Committee of the Red Cross (ICRC), *Commentary on the Additional Protocols of 8 June 1977 to the Geneva Conventions of 12 August 1949* (Geneva: 1987), article 51.
31. Ibid., Commentary (para. 1940).

Report had properly fulfilled its essential mandate to investigate violations of the laws of war during Protective Edge, the whole of the Israel section in the "Impact" chapter could have been reduced to one sentence: *Six civilians were killed and one house was destroyed.*

The UN Report's elevation of fear inducement into a breach of the laws of war similarly marred its treatment of the Hamas tunnel network. It did acknowledge that "the tunnels were only used to conduct attacks directed at IDF [Israel Defense Forces] positions in Israel in the vicinity of the Green Line, which are legitimate military targets."[32] But still, it harped on the "sense of insecurity" and "panic attacks," "trauma and persistent fear," "great anxiety," and so on that the tunnels engendered among Israelis.[33] It then proceeded to imply that the fear induced by these tunnels amounted to a violation of the laws of war. In its "concluding observations," the Report bracketed together these "serious concerns" regarding Hamas: "the inherently indiscriminate nature of most of the projectiles directed towards Israel . . . and . . . the targeting of Israeli civilians, which violate international humanitarian law and may amount to a war crime. The increased level of fear among Israeli civilians resulting from the use of tunnels was palpable."[34] Its final "recommendations" correlatively called upon Hamas "[t]o respect the principles of distinction, proportionality and precaution, including by ending all attacks on Israeli civilians and civilian objects, and stopping all rocket attacks *and other actions* that may spread terror among the civilian population in Israel" (emphasis added). The only "other actions" chronicled in the Report were Hamas tunnel excavations/infiltrations. But if Hamas must desist from these belowground excavations/infiltrations—which target only combatants—because they induce fear among Israelis, shouldn't Israel have to desist from aboveground attacks with bombs, missiles, and shells—which overwhelmingly target civilians—because they induce fear among Gazans? In addition, international law does not debar a people fighting for self-determination from resorting to arms, whereas it does prohibit a state suppressing such a struggle from deploying violent force.[35] Israel has deprived the people of Gaza of their right to self-determination via an externally imposed occupation.[36] Surely, then, Hamas has the right to target via tunnels Israeli

32. UN Report, para. 108.
33. Ibid., paras. 55, 74, 104, 106, 108, 558, 561.
34. Ibid., para. 673.
35. See Chapter 7 and Chapter 11.
36. See Chapter 12.

combatants enforcing this occupation from without, however much anxiety these tunnel attacks might induce among the civilian population. Or are Palestinians permitted to use armed force only if it doesn't rattle Israelis?

However ingenious the rhetorical strategies deployed by the UN Report to even out Hamas's and Israel's breaches of international law (see Table 14 for another illustration), they still couldn't bridge the chasm separating the devastation inflicted, respectively, by each party. It is of course possible that even if it caused less death and destruction, Hamas might have committed as many war crimes as Israel. But it's also true that once the proportion reached an order of magnitude of, say, 550:1 (children killed by Israel versus Hamas) or 18,000:1 (homes destroyed by Israel versus Hamas), such a claim not only lacks plausibility but also appears positively ridiculous. How, then, did the Report resolve this dilemma? It in part misrepresented the relevant facts, but—more significantly—it mangled the relevant law by repeatedly invoking *ir*relevant law. This disingenuousness permeated the Report's treatment of Hamas and Israeli war crimes.

Hamas War Crimes The UN Report set the stage for its indictment of Hamas by citing directly or indirectly official Israeli sources depicting a formidable Hamas weapons arsenal.[37] But the battlefield performance of these weapons strongly suggested that the bulk of them consisted of little more than enhanced fireworks.[38] The Report also dutifully regurgitated Israeli claims regarding the dazzling performance of the Iron Dome antimissile defense system,[39] even though recognized experts and the facts on the ground refuted them.[40] In an unusual acknowledgment, the Report did observe that according to "security experts," Hamas's "declared official policy" during Protective Edge was "to focus on military or semi-military targets and to avoid other targets, especially civilians."[41] It went on to document instances in which Hamas appeared to be targeting Israeli combatants and military objects, while Israel itself acknowledged that Hamas mortar shells killed ten IDF combatants positioned on the Israeli side of the border.[42] The Report also observed that Hamas attempted "in a few instances" to warn Israeli

37. UN Report, paras. 63–64.
38. See Chapter 11 and Chapter 12.
39. UN Report, paras. 78, 95, 556, 565, 566.
40. See Chapter 11.
41. UN Report, para. 60 (see also para. 89).
42. Ibid., paras. 78, 80, 91.

TABLE 14 "The Commission Notes..."

The UN Report was studded with exculpatory Israeli claims signaled by the deferential phrase, *The commission notes*. But why would it want to take "note" of crude propaganda?

- The UN Report quoted Israeli statements that, judging by its own findings, were patently false. For example: "The commission notes Israel's assertion that 'during the 2014 Gaza Conflict, whenever feasible, the IDF selected munitions that would minimize potential civilian casualties and injuries'"; "The commission notes that, according to official sources, 'the IDF directives applicable to the 2014 Gaza Conflict set stringent restrictions on the use of HE [high explosive] artillery shells'"; "The commission notes Israel's assertion that it will investigate 'fully any credible accusation or reasonable suspicion of a serious violation of the Law of Armed Conflict.'"[a] If the Report itself refuted these ludicrous assertions, why did it respectfully "note" them?

- The UN Report enabled Israeli *hasbara* to set the parameters of permissible criticism. For example: "The commission notes official Israeli statements indicating that artillery was used in urban areas only on an exceptional basis when neighbourhoods were known to be largely evacuated and followed stringent protocols. *Even with these strict conditions*, the use of artillery with wide-area effects in densely populated areas resulted in a large number of civilian casualties and widespread destruction of civilian objects" (emphasis added).[b] But according to an Action on Armed Violence (AOAV) study, of the 20,000 high-explosive artillery shells Israel fired into Gaza, an estimated 95 percent landed in or near populated civilian areas. Although the Report cited the AOAV study, it omitted mention of this critical finding.[c]

- The UN Report lent credibility to Israeli propaganda by repeating unsubstantiated allegations. For example: "The commission notes the IDF's general allegation that Palestinian armed groups used ambulances to transport fighters, i.e. for military purposes. As no specific information was received in this regard, the commission is unable to verify this claim." If the Report was "unable to verify" this allegation, it wasn't because Israel didn't, but because it *couldn't*, provide proof; the one and only piece of generic evidence adduced by Israel proved to be worthless.[d]

- Echoing former US secretary of defense Donald Rumsfeld's notorious apothegm, "The absence of evidence is not evidence of absence," the UN Report qualified the absence of evidence to sustain Israeli exculpations by entertaining the possibility that they might nonetheless be true. For example: "The commission also notes the [Israeli] claims concerning the apparent extensive use of Al-Wafa hospital and its surroundings to conduct military operations. All relevant witnesses interviewed by the commission, including medical staff, rejected the allegation that the hospital was being used for military purposes before its evacuation. However, the commission cannot exclude the possibility that military activity took place."[e] But the "possibility" *always* exists that contradictory evidence might eventually surface; on this evidentiary standard, how can a guilty verdict ever be reached? The Report even left open such a future possibility when not just Hamas but *Israel itself* excluded it. For example: "While the commission cannot completely exclude the possibility that misfired shells by a Palestinian armed group may have resulted in injury to civilians [in this incident], it has not received or found any information to support that version of events. Witness interviews *and statements by the MAG* [Israeli military advocate-general] appear rather to confirm that it was the two rounds of mortar shells fired by the IDF that resulted in death and injury to civilians" (emphasis added).[f]

- The UN Report cited evidence that had been manipulated by Israel. For example: "The commission notes the IDF asserts it found an Al-Qassam Brigades manual on urban warfare, which is said to explain the advantage of conducting military operations in populated areas and allegedly provides instructions on how to hide weapons in buildings. . . . The IDF only presented a few selected pages of the manual on their website. The commission was not able independently to verify the content of this manual or specific incidents."[a] If the Report "was not able independently to verify" this claim, that's because Israel *chose* to post only "a few selected pages." If, however, it corroborated the Israeli claim, why wouldn't Israel post the whole manual?[b]

In the meantime, the most compelling evidence at the Report's disposal was the collection of soldier eyewitness testimonies compiled by Breaking the Silence.[i] The soldiers plainly had nothing to gain and everything to lose by contradicting Israeli *hasbara*. But whereas it gave free airtime to official Israeli propaganda, the Report gave short shrift to these soldier eyewitness testimonies, which were breezily described as "anecdotal,"[j] and it ignored the most revelatory among them.[k]

---

[a] UN Report, paras. 225, 412, 610 (see also paras. 232, 238, 385).

[b] Ibid., para. 408 (see also para. 412).

[c] Action on Armed Violence (AOAV), *Explosive States: Monitoring explosive violence in 2014* (2015).

[d] UN Report, paras. 461, 477. See also Chapter 12.

[e] UN Report, para. 477.

[f] Ibid., para. 385 (see also para. 376). The Report also argued "hypothetically" in Israel's defense (ibid., para. 339), even as Israel itself didn't advance the posited alibi, and fabricated an argument on Israel's behalf (ibid., para. 365) that by its own admission was contradicted by the evidence.

[g] Ibid., para. 472.

[h] The snippets allegedly culled from Hamas manuals that Israel translated were riddled with tendentious interpretations and interpolations. State of Israel, *The 2014 Gaza Conflict, 7 July–26 August 2014: Factual and legal aspects* (2015), paras. 125–26.

[i] Breaking the Silence, *This Is How We Fought in Gaza: Soldiers' testimonies and photographs from Operation "Protective Edge"* (2014).

[j] UN Report, para. 418.

[k] See Chapter 11 and Chapter 12.

---

civilians of impending attacks and, in fact, these Hamas alerts were more effective than those issued by Israel "because—unlike in Gaza—residents could flee to other areas of Israel less exposed to threats."[43] However, the Report found that the "vast majority" of Hamas projectiles targeted "population centers in Israel."[44] It devoted fully 15 paragraphs to depicting in graphic detail the effects of these Hamas attacks, even though only six civilians in Israel were killed and property damage was negligible. It is often suggested (although not by the Report) that if so few civilians died it was only on

43. Ibid., paras. 92, 95.
44. Ibid., para. 90.

account of Iron Dome, and a proper calculation would reckon the probable number of civilian deaths in its absence. The argument is factually false— Iron Dome probably didn't save many and perhaps not any lives—and even were it true, irrelevant: if additional civilians would have been killed absent Israel's civil defense/shelter system and structurally sound edifices, should the casualty count then tally how many Israelis would have died if they lived in substandard, Gaza-like conditions? If a calculation were to be based on "all things being equal," it abstracts from the root injustice that Israel and Palestine are *not* equal.

The UN Report found that Hamas's projectile attacks "may" have constituted "war crimes":

- *Hamas rocket attacks*—"rockets cannot be directed at a specific military objective and therefore strikes employing these weapons constitute indiscriminate attacks"; "statements . . . indicate intent to direct those attacks against civilians";

- *Hamas mortar attacks*—"statements . . . indicate in some cases . . . intent to target civilian communities . . . if they were used to target civilians or civilian objects, this would be a violation of the principle of distinction"; "[i]n the cases in which attacks were directed at military objectives located amidst or in close vicinity to civilians or civilian objects, mortars are not the most appropriate weapons. The imprecise nature of mortars makes it difficult for an attacking party using this weapon in an area in which there is a concentration of civilians to distinguish between civilians and civilian objects and the military objective of the attack."[45]

In its defense, Hamas pleaded that "Palestinian rockets are 'primitive' and not very technologically advanced but nevertheless the factions attempted to direct their rockets at military targets in Israel."[46] The Report curtly and coldly rejoined: "The military capacity of the parties to a conflict is irrelevant

---

45. UN Report, paras. 97–102. It also noted (ibid., paras. 484–86) that "Rockets fired by Palestinian armed groups in several cases appear to have malfunctioned or were fired carelessly and fell short, in some cases in densely populated areas of Gaza, causing deaths and injuries." In one particularly tragic incident, eleven Gazan children and two adults were killed. Although it did call on Hamas to "conduct a thorough investigation of the case to determine the origin and circumstances of the attack," the Report treated this incident with decidedly less malice than Amnesty did (see Chapter 12).

46. Ibid., para. 85.

to their obligation to respect the prohibition against indiscriminate attacks." The humanitarian rationale behind prohibiting use of indiscriminate weapons is self-evident. But (in)discriminateness is a relative notion. It varies according to the most sophisticated guidance system currently available for a particular line of weaponry. So it is equally self-evident that the prohibition against indiscriminate weapons discriminates against poor states or nonstate actors that cannot afford cutting-edge technology. In the instant case, the Report effectively criminalized nearly the whole of Hamas's primitive arsenal. And thereby it denied Gaza the "inherent" right (anchored in the UN Charter) of armed self-defense, and the right (effectively sanctioned by international law) of armed resistance in its self-determination struggle. Even if it is admitted that notwithstanding its discriminatory effects, cogent reasons might be adduced to preserve intact the prohibition, still it hardly befits a human rights document to peremptorily dismiss as "irrelevant" a wholly reasonable (if debatable) objection. It also warrants attention how much more sensitive the Report was to Israeli concerns. For example, the Report "recognizes the dilemma that Israel faces in releasing information that would disclose in detail the targets of military strikes, given that such information may be classified and jeopardize intelligence sources."[47] Although it still placed "the onus ... on Israel to provide sufficient details on its targeting decisions to allow an independent assessment of the legality of the attacks," the Report not only evinced a sensitivity absent in its high-handed dismissal of Hamas, but it also credited the Israeli alibi that information was withheld out of security concerns, and not because its release might undercut official lies. The Report proceeded to infer a sinister motive lurking behind Hamas rocket attacks. If these projectiles couldn't accurately target military objectives, then the Report "cannot exclude the possibility that the indiscriminate rocket attacks may constitute acts of violence whose primary purpose is to spread terror amongst the civilian population."[48] Spreading terror might have been Hamas's motive, but other possible motives also leap to mind. The rocket attacks could have been "belligerent reprisals" (which international law does not forbid[49]) to compel Israel to cease and desist from its terroristic assault on Gazan society. The Report itself noted that Hamas "issued a statement confirming [its] intention to target Israeli civilians in response to Israel's 'target-

47. Ibid., para. 669 (see also para. 215).
48. Ibid., para. 99.
49. See Chapter 11.

ing of Palestinian civilians in their homes and shelters.'"[50] Or consider the motive professed by Hamas leader Khalid Mishal during Operation Cast Lead (2008–9): "Our modest, home-made rockets are our cry of protest to the world."[51] One wonders why the Report did not entertain these more benign possibilities.

International law requires all parties to a conflict to "take all feasible precautions in the choice of means and methods of attack with a view to avoiding . . . injury to civilians and damage to civilian objects."[52] The UN Report alleged that despite substantial impediments to its investigation, it was able to divine "patterns of behavior" by Hamas that breached this legal obligation.[53] It cited a quartet of incidents where Hamas fired rockets in close proximity to civilians.[54] As it happens, Amnesty pointed to the identical four incidents in its indictment of Hamas.[55] The duplication suggests a paucity of corroborative evidence. The Report also cited a handful of instances where Hamas conducted "military operations within or in close proximity to sites benefiting from special protection under international law"—in particular, the environs of two to three schools and a church. These incidents were also cited in earlier investigations.[56] The Report further noted that "official Israeli" sources repeatedly accused Hamas of violating the "feasible precautions" obligation, but it "was not able to independently verify" these allegations.[57] The Report acknowledged that the "feasible precautions" obligation "is not absolute"; that "even if there are areas that are not residential, Gaza's small size and its population density makes it particularly difficult for armed groups always to comply" with the obligation; and that several signatories to the relevant international instrument stipulated that "for densely populated countries, the requirement to avoid locating military objectives within densely populated areas would be difficult to apply."[58] Still, the Report concluded that in light of "the number of cases" in which Hamas "carried out military operations within or in the immediate vicinity of civilian objects and specifically protected objects, it does not appear that this behavior was

50. UN Report, para. 90.
51. See Chapter 2.
52. ICRC, *Commentary on the Additional Protocols,* article 59.
53. UN Report, paras. 466–69.
54. Ibid., para. 471.
55. See Chapter 12.
56. UN Report, para. 475.
57. Ibid., paras. 472, 476–77.
58. Ibid., para. 473.

simply a consequence of the normal course of military operations," and, "therefore," the law "was not always complied with."[59] Although this was a cautious and qualified finding, the question must nonetheless be posed, Did the Report substantiate it? It would have to show that the instances it documented gave proof of a deliberate Hamas choice not to avoid civilian and protected objects, and were not just random events consequent on "the normal course of military operations" in a densely populated civilian terrain. But the handful of incidents recycled by the Report, during a 51-day armed conflict in which Hamas fired seven thousand projectiles and engaged an invading army with unprecedented combat losses on both sides, does not appear to reach the evidentiary threshold of a "pattern."[60] The Report not only failed to substantiate its qualified assertion but also indulged in groundless speculation. For example, it stated that "*if* it is confirmed that in using . . . locations to conduct military operations, armed groups did so with the intent to use the presence of civilians or persons *hors de combat* . . . to prevent their military assets from being attacked, this *would* constitute a violation of the customary law prohibition to use human shields" and "*would* amount to a war crime."[61] But the Report didn't provide a scintilla of evidence demonstrating such "intent." What was the point of such baseless conjecture, of which this is just one example,[62] except to plant a false image in the reader's mind, or to appease Israel, which repeatedly accused Hamas of human shielding, or both? In its most audacious—or outrageous—speculation, the Report verged on criminalizing nonviolent civil resistance as it posited that Hamas might wrongly exploit it:

In one case of the bombing of a residential building examined by the commission, information gathered indicates that following a specific warning by the

59. Ibid., para. 478.

60. In a subsequent paragraph (ibid., para. 482), the Report adduced one, if underwhelming, proof. It cited "several" Hamas public declarations exhorting Gazans on the eve of Israel's threatened ground invasion to stand steadfast and "not to heed the warnings issued by the IDF instructing residents . . . to evacuate. . . . [T]he declarations are a clear indication that the authorities in Gaza did not take all the necessary precautions to protect the civilian population." If Hamas didn't physically prevent Gazans from evacuating; and if Gazans chose, as an act of their own volition and fully conscious of the impending dangers, to remain in place; and if the active agent endangering the civilian population was Israel not Hamas—then Hamas's only documented violation of the "precautions" obligation would appear to be fairly trivial.

61. Ibid., para. 479, emphases added.

62. See also ibid., para. 480.

IDF that the house was to be targeted, several people went to the roof of the house in order to "protect" the house. *Should* they have been directed to do so by members of Palestinian armed groups, this *would* amount to the use of the presence of civilians in an attempt to shield a military objective from attack, in violation of the customary law prohibition to use human shields. With regard to this incident, the commission is disturbed by the reported call by the spokesperson of Hamas to the people in Gaza to adopt the practice of shielding their homes from attack by going up on their roofs. Although the call is directed to residents of Gaza, it *can be seen and understood* as an encouragement to Palestinian armed groups to use human shields.[63]

Instead of showing compassion for Gazans as they risked life and limb to protect their, and their neighbors', family homes, the Report zeroed in on Hamas in order to deny it, on purely conjectural grounds, one of the few means of nonviolent resistance available to it in the midst of an annihilative attack—even going so far as to brand the Islamic movement's encouragement of such self-willed, heartrending acts, whose spiritual lineage traces back to Gandhi,[64] an embryonic war crime. It is also cause for sheer bewilderment why the Report designated an unambiguously civilian dwelling as a "military objective"—did it automatically lose its protected status once Israel decided to target it, or did the Report start from the premise that everyone and everything in Gaza was, if not aligned, then alloyed with terrorism?

Finally, the UN Report indicted Hamas for its "extrajudicial executions" of suspected collaborators during Protective Edge. "The fact that the majority of the victims had been arrested and detained before the conflict," it observed, "prompts concerns that they were executed in order to increase pressure on Gaza's population, with a view to preventing others from spying."[65] Most executions "occurred a day after three [Hamas] commanders were killed by the IDF." The Report also noted that because of the "stigma" attached to collaboration, these executions had "devastating" effects on family members, who had to cope with "indelible stains" on their "reputation and honor." Inasmuch as the Report expressed sympathy for an alleged Israeli quandary (on releasing classified information), it might have paused to con-

---

63. Ibid., para. 483 (see also para. 177), emphases added. In 2006, Human Rights Watch leveled a nearly identical charge but, after it came under public pressure, retracted it. Norman G. Finkelstein, *Knowing Too Much: Why the American Jewish romance with Israel is coming to an end* (New York: 2012), p. 126.

64. Norman G. Finkelstein, *What Gandhi Says: About nonviolence, resistance and courage* (New York: 2012), pp. 72–73.

65. UN Report, paras. 492–502.

template Hamas's quandary of resisting a brutal invasion while plagued by internal collaborators directly or indirectly on the payroll of the enemy. The Russian revolutionist Leon Trotsky cogently argued that in the midst of a foreign invasion, the threat of incarceration will not deter potential collaborators, because the very premise of aligning with the enemy is that its victory impends: "[T]hey cannot be terrorized by the threat of imprisonment, as [they do] not believe in its duration. It is just this simple but decisive fact that explains the widespread recourse to shooting."[66] It is in no way to extenuate Hamas executions to pose the inescapable question, *How else was Hamas supposed to deter collaborators?* The prohibition on executing collaborators would appear to fall into the same category as the prohibition on indiscriminate weapons: an insoluble dilemma. It might be recalled that a leader of the Warsaw Ghetto Uprising expressed as "our great guilt" that "immediately, from the first day, we didn't kill" the Jewish collaborators. "If a few of them had been killed, others would have been afraid to join the police. They should have been hanged on lamp poles, to threaten them. . . . I'm sure that whenever there is internal treason, war must begin by destroying it."[67] The Report determined that these Hamas executions, not "may" but unquestionably *did* "amount to a war crime," and it exhorted, "whoever is responsible for the killings . . . must be brought to justice."[68] Nowhere in its indictment of Israel did the Report use such unequivocal and emphatic language. It also called upon Hamas to "combat the stigma faced by families of alleged collaborators."[69] Although it acknowledged that Hamas had already undertaken to "support the families of persons accused of collaboration," the Report concluded that "the far-reaching effects of stigma call for a stronger response."[70] Was Hamas legally required to organize a Collaborator Pride parade?

Israeli War Crimes The UN Report divided allegations of Israeli war crimes into multiple, somewhat arbitrary and frequently overlapping categories. If it had let the evidence speak for itself, the Report would have compiled a devastating dossier on Israel's prosecution of Protective Edge. But it didn't.

66. Leon Trotsky, *Terrorism and Communism* (Ann Arbor: 1972), p. 58.
67. Yitzhak Zuckerman, *A Surplus of Memory: Chronicle of the Warsaw Ghetto Uprising* (Berkeley: 1993), pp. 192, 209.
68. UN Report, paras. 502, 673.
69. Ibid., para. 683(b).
70. Ibid., para. 499.

Instead, between its factual findings, on the one hand, and its conclusions, on the other, it interpolated contorted legal analyses. The Report asserted that "[t]he factual conclusions formed the basis for the legal analysis of the individual incidents."[71] In reality, its legal analyses watered down the ghastly reality. The upshot of its intercession as interpreter and arbiter of the law was a dossier that, although it might not have satisfied Israel (except for a full-throated apologia, what would?), failed to meet the most exiguous standards of justice. In its parts and as a totality, the Report was, simply put, a cover-up. In order to bring home this truth, there's no alternative except to juxtapose the facts presented in each incident (or group of incidents) with the Report's tendentious legal interpretation of them.

1. *Air strikes.* The UN Report observed that as a result of Israeli air strikes targeting residential and other buildings, at least "142 Palestinian families had three or more members killed in the same incident ... for a total of 742 fatalities."[72] Two survivors of such attacks recalled, respectively, these scenes:

> I found the decapitated bodies of my uncle and daughter. My cousin was alive but died on the way to [the] hospital. Another cousin's body was found sliced in two. We had ten corpses in the first ambulances. No other survivors were found. [...] After having removed the cement I identified my cousin Dina's body. What I witnessed was horrible. She was nine months pregnant and she had come from her home to her parents' house to have her baby. We could not imagine that she had passed away. Her stomach was ripped open and the unborn baby was lying there with the skull shattered. We kept searching for other corpses and found my uncle's wife. We had great difficulty removing all the pieces of cement from her body.[73]

> I had a close look at the bodies. Only the upper part of my nine-year-old daughter's body was left. My son Mohamed had his intestines coming out. My 16-year-old cousin had lost his two legs. My son Mustapha, who was five meters away from me, had received shrapnel that almost completely severed his neck. My 16-year-old nephew lost both his legs and arms. He asked for my help. I just really wanted him to die quickly. I didn't want him to go through so much suffering. There was also my one-year-old daughter who was in her mother's arms. We found her body on a tree. . . . I myself lost my left arm.[74]

71. Ibid., para. 20.
72. Ibid., para. 111.
73. Ibid., para. 134 (Case 4, Abu Jabr).
74. Ibid., para. 190 (Case 13, Al Sayam and Abu Sanimah).

The Report was unable to find a "possible military target" in six of the fifteen air assaults it investigated.[75] In one such lethal attack absent a military objective, a precision-guided 500-pound bomb targeted children on a roof, who had gone there "to feed the birds," killing three of them and injuring two others.[76] The Report's tabulation, which pointed to a possibly legitimate military target in 60 percent (9/15) of the incidents, cast the Israeli attacks in a more favorable light than the established facts warranted. Consider the evidentiary basis of its calculations. The semiofficial Israeli Intelligence and Terrorism Information Center (ITIC) posted the name, date, location, and combatant ("terrorist operative")/civilian ("noninvolved") status of Gazans killed during Protective Edge.[77] If this *hasbara* outfit listed a person killed during one of the Israeli air strikes on a residential home as a "terrorist operative," the Report automatically denoted him a "possible military target."[78] But setting aside its dubious determination of a victim's status (where and how did it get this information?), ITIC never asserted that the building was targeted *because of* the "terrorist operative's" presence or, for that matter, that Israel was even aware of his presence when it attacked the building. In addition, the Report itself observed that the presence of a Hamas member did not in itself transform the residence into a military object: "the mere fact of being a member of the political wing of Hamas or any other organization in Gaza, or working for the authorities ..., is not sufficient in and of itself to render a person a legitimate military target."[79] Taking all these factors into account, it's possible that the Israeli air strikes investigated by the Report targeted combatants or military objects in only a small minority of cases.

The UN Report documented that in many of the incidents it chronicled, Israel launched the air strike at a time of day when a large number of civilians

75. Ibid., para. 220.

76. Ibid., paras. 193–200 (Case 14, Shuheibar).

77. *Preliminary, Partial Examination of the Names of Palestinians Killed in Operation Protective Edge and Analysis of the Ratio between Terrorist Operatives and Noninvolved Civilians Killed in Error* (28 July 2014), terrorism-info.org.il/Data/articles/Art_20687/E_124_14B_472268844.pdf.

78. UN Report, para. 119 (Case 1, Al Hajj), para. 160 (Case 8, Al Batsh), para. 185 (Case 12, Dheir Family), para. 191 (Case 13, Al Sayam and Abu Sanimah). In one instance, although a militant was apparently present in the building, Israel justified its attack on altogether different grounds (ibid., paras. 178–79; Case 11, Kaware). The Report's determination of "possible military targets" also leaned on questionable data supplied by Amnesty (see Chapter 12).

79. UN Report, para. 220 (see also para. 222).

was likely to be present. For example, "the family was preparing for the *iftar* meal, the breaking of the fast at sunset"; "it was only a few minutes after they got up to have *suhhur,* the last meal of the day during Ramadan until the breaking of the fast in the evening"; "all 12 members of the family were at home, preparing to break the Ramadan fast"; "the family had just finished a long meal in honor of the second day of the Eid, and most of the family members were taking a nap"; "they were gathered for *iftar.*"[80] The Report also found that Israel did not give warnings in at least 11 of the 15 incidents, while among some of the warnings that Israel did give, "only a few minutes (between 3 and 5) elapsed" between them and the actual attack.[81] The Report additionally found that Israel used precision-guided missiles or precision-guided 500–2,000-pound bombs in all 15 incidents. Here's how weapons experts described the impact of the GBU-31, which Israel used in "several" of the air strikes investigated by the Report:

> The explosion creates a shock wave exerting thousands of pounds of pressure per square inch [psi]. By comparison, a shock wave of 12 psi will knock a person down; and the injury threshold is 15 pounds psi. The pressure from the explosion of a device such as the Mark-84 JDAM[82] can rupture lungs, burst sinus cavities and tear off limbs hundreds of feet from the blast site, according to trauma physicians. When it hits, the JDAM generates an 8,500-degree fireball, gouges a 20-foot crater as it displaces 10,000 pounds of dirt and rock and generates enough wind to knock down walls blocks away and hurl metal fragments a mile or more. There is a very great concussive effect. Damage to any human beings in the vicinity would be pretty nasty.[83]

In regard to Israel's use of, inter alia, the GBU-31/MK-84 2000-pound bomb, the Report concluded, "regardless how precise the bomb is, it remains *extremely questionable* whether a weapon with such a wide impact area allows its operators to adequately distinguish between civilians and civilian objects and the military objective of the attack, when used in densely populated areas."[84] On this last point, recall that the Report denoted Hamas's deployment of primitive rockets carrying 10–20 pounds of explosives inherently

---

80. Ibid., para. 122 (Case 2, Qassas), para. 128 (Case 3, Al-Najjar), para. 141 (Case 5, Al Hallaq and Ammar), para. 147 (Case 6, Balatah), para. 170 (Case 10, Al Salam Tower–Al Kilani and Derbass).

81. Ibid., paras. 233, 237.

82. The GBU-31 and Mark-84 JDAM belong to the same family of weapons.

83. UN Report, para. 225.

84. Ibid., para. 226, emphasis added.

indiscriminate attacks because they "cannot be directed at a specific military objective." It perplexes, then, why it's not also an inherently indiscriminate attack when Israel unloads, in a precision strike in the heart of a densely populated civilian neighborhood, a 2,000-pound bomb that "generates an 8,500-degree [Fahrenheit] fireball, gouges a 20-foot crater as it displaces 10,000 pounds of dirt and rock and generates enough wind to knock down walls blocks away and hurl metal fragments a mile or more." Instead, the Report deemed Israel's use of such a weapon in such circumstances "extremely questionable." Pray tell, *what questions remained?*[85]

The bigger point, however, is this: The UN Report failed to adduce credible evidence that Israel mostly targeted military objectives in these air strikes on civilian buildings. Even if in a handful of incidents Hamas militants were present, still, judging by the timing of the attacks (i.e., as large numbers of civilians predictably assembled), the paucity and inefficacy of the warnings issued, the use of high-explosive precision weapons in densely populated civilian areas, and the "wholesale destruction" of civilian buildings that had already been abandoned[86]—judging by the accumulation and compounding of these factors, *the Israeli air strikes constituted neither disproportionate attacks nor even indiscriminate attacks but, on the contrary, targeted attacks on Gaza's civilian population and infrastructure, in which the occasional presence of a Hamas militant was less a target than a pretext, the objective of these air strikes almost certainly being, beyond the exaction of crude revenge, to terrorize*

85. The Report's determination regarding use of high-explosive artillery shells by the IDF in densely populated areas of Gaza also perplexes. Beyond the explosive power of these shells, the Report observed that "indirect-fire systems such as 155mm artillery . . . are considered 'statistical weapons' . . . the wide area dispersal of their shells is an expected outcome, as this is how these weapons were designed to work." Nearly *20,000* of these doubly indiscriminate high-explosive artillery shells were fired with reckless abandon (as the Breaking the Silence compilation shows), 95 percent in or near densely populated civilian areas, making Israel's use of them triply indiscriminate: a *high-explosive* shell with a *wide-area* dispersal was fired *blindly* into densely populated areas. The Report bizarrely concluded that "the use of such artillery is not appropriate in densely populated areas regardless of the legality of resorting to such weapons." It's hard to figure out which appalls more—the Report's use of the Emily Post–like locution "not appropriate," or its unmistakable implication that Israel's use of this artillery in Gaza was legal. But six paragraphs later, the Report seemed to reverse itself: "the use of weapons with wide-area effects by the IDF in the densely populated, built up areas of Gaza, and the significant likelihood of lethal indiscriminate effects resulting from such weapons, are highly likely to constitute a violation of the prohibition of indiscriminate attacks," and "may . . . amount to a war crime" (ibid., paras. 408–9, 415). See also Chapter 12.

86. UN Report, para. 208.

the people of Gaza into submission by causing sufficient death and destruction as to break their will or turn them against Hamas. The Report, however, did not reach this conclusion. It did find that the six targeted Israeli air strikes where a military objective wasn't discernible, as well as "most cases" reported by nongovernmental organizations, "may...constitute a direct attack against civilian objects or civilians, a war crime," while the other nine incidents, where a possible military objective was discernible, "could be disproportionate, and therefore amount to a war crime."[87] But although it did not recoil from speculating that Hamas fired rockets to "spread terror," the Report fell silent, despite an abundance of circumstantial evidence, on the possibility that Israel's overarching purpose in these air strikes might have been to spread terror. It acknowledged that "the attacks were carried out when it could be expected that most family members would be at home (in the evening or at dawn when families gathered for *iftar* and *suhhur,* the Ramadan meals, or during the night when people were asleep),"[88] and that "large weapons apparently meant to raze buildings were used."[89] But it scrupulously avoided posing the question, *Why* did Israel choose these times of day and these types of weapons? The Report acknowledged that in the handful of instances where Israel did provide a few minutes' notice of an impending air strike, "by giving a warning, the IDF accepted that the attack did not require the element of surprise; accordingly, there appears to be no reason why more time was not granted to the residents of the house to evacuate."[90] But it did not pose the obvious next question, *Why* did Israel leave the occupants so little time to vacate their homes? The Report acknowledged that "regarding the destruction of high-rise buildings [during the last week of Protective Edge], a statement by an IDF General seems to suggest that the objective of these strikes was to exercise pressure on the 'social elite' of Gaza by destroying the high-rises."[91] But if it sought to exert political pressure on civilians via targeted air strikes on civilian objects, wasn't Israel's goal to spread terror? The Report acknowledged that an air strike using "precision weapons . . . , which indicates that specific objectives were targeted,"[92] killed children playing on a roof. It then went on to suggest that Israel "may have breached its

87. Ibid., paras. 219–21.
88. Ibid., para. 221 (see also para. 232).
89. Ibid., para. 221.
90. Ibid., para. 237.
91. Ibid., para. 222. For Israel's attacks on the high-rise buildings, see Chapter 11.
92. UN Report, paras. 227–28, 230, 241.

obligations to take all feasible measures to avoid or at least to minimize incidental harm to civilians." But wasn't the relevant point of law that Israel "took all feasible measures" to *maximize* harm to civilians, including children—that is, that it *targeted* these children with precision weapons? The Report observed that "the massive scale of destruction and the number of homes and civilian buildings attacked raise concerns that Israel's interpretation of what constitutes a 'military objective' is broader than the definition provided by international humanitarian law," and also "raises concerns that these strikes may have constituted *military tactics reflective of a broader policy* ... [that] prioritized the perceived military objective over other considerations, disregarding the obligation to minimize effects on civilians."[93] It strenuously circumvented "concerns" that massive devastation *was* Israel's "military objective," in order to *maximize* "effects on civilians" by terrorizing them; that its "military tactics" were "reflective" of *this* "broader policy"; and that its premeditated, preplanned "military tactics" and "military objective" were not merely "broader than the definition provided by" but *conceived in shocking willful breach of* "international humanitarian law."

2. *Ground operations.* The section of the UN Report devoted to Israeli ground operations focused on IDF atrocities in Shuja'iya (19–20 July), Khuza'a (20 July–1 August), Rafah (1–3 August), and Shuja'iya Market (30 July). It stated that "the combined impact of these ground operations has had a devastating impact on the population of Gaza, both in terms of human suffering as well as in terms of damage to the infrastructure." At least 150 civilians were killed and more than two thousand homes were completely destroyed.[94] The Report scrutinized these operations individually and then presented a synoptic analysis of them.

A. *Shuja'iya.* Located near the Green Line, Shuja'iya is among the most densely populated neighborhoods in Gaza. Although Israel issued warnings before the ground operation, most residents elected to stay put. On 20 July, 13 IDF soldiers in Shuja'iya were killed by Hamas militants in firefights. Israel then intensified its bombardment, ostensibly to rescue injured soldiers, at which point about half the residents fled.[95] The UN Report noted that Israel fired six hundred artillery shells into Shuja'iya in less than an hour on 20 July (the shelling continued for more than six hours), and dropped "over

93. Ibid., paras. 223, 243, emphasis in original.
94. Ibid., paras. 248, 250.
95. Ibid., paras. 257–60.

100 one-ton bombs in a short period of time." An IDF eyewitness testimony cited by the Report recalled, "The artillery corps and the air force really cleaned that place up," while another testimony recalled, "One of the most senior officials in the IDF . . . just marked off houses on an aerial photo of Shuja'iya, to be taken down." By the operation's end, Shuja'iya was a "razed area," and "likely levelled as a result of focused IDF demolitions efforts." Fully 1,300 buildings were completely destroyed or seriously damaged, and many civilians were killed or injured.[96] The Report's legal analysis found that the methods and means employed by the IDF in Shuja'iya "raise questions" and "raise serious concerns" as to its respect for the laws of war: **Distinction.** The overwhelming firepower "could not, in such a small and densely populated area, be directed at a specific military target," and also "violated the prohibition of treating several distinct individual military objectives in a densely populated area as one single military objective." Therefore, "strong indications" exist that the operation "was conducted in violation of the prohibition of indiscriminate attacks and may amount to a war crime"; **Feasible precautions.** It "is questionable whether the use of such immense firepower in such a short period would have allowed the IDF . . . to respect its obligation to do everything feasible to verify that the targets were military objectives," while the fact that the IDF persisted in this "intensive shelling" long after it must have known of the "dire impact . . . on civilians and civilian objects . . . evidences the commander's failure to comply with his obligation to do everything feasible to suspend an attack if it becomes apparent that it does not conform to the principle of proportionality"; and **Proportionality.** "The objective of the shelling and heavy bombardment appears mainly to have been force protection. . . . [G]iven the means and methods used by the IDF in Shuja'iya, it is possible to conclude that a reasonable commander would be aware of the potential for such an intense attack to result in the death of a high number of civilians. As such, it is highly likely that a reasonable commander would therefore conclude that the expected incidental loss to civilian life and damage and destruction of civilian objects would be excessive in relation to the anticipated military advantage of this attack."[97] Before assessing the Report's legal findings, it's useful to take a step back. After enduring an unusual number of IDF casualties, Israel fired probably thousands of high-explosive artillery shells and dropped scores of one-ton bombs

96. Ibid., paras. 262–78, 283–85, 292–93.
97. Ibid., paras. 293–96.

on Shuja'iya. Israel alleged that it deployed such massive firepower in order to rescue injured combatants.[98] The Report didn't even try to demonstrate a logical nexus between such massive indiscriminate force, on the one hand, and a rescue operation, on the other. Instead, it faithfully echoed Israeli *hasbara*—"the objective of the shelling and heavy bombardment appears mainly to have been force protection." *How on earth does one rescue injured soldiers by firing with abandon thousands of indiscriminate artillery shells and dropping scores of one-ton bombs in a densely populated civilian neighborhood? How does one rescue injured soldiers by methodically demolishing hundreds upon hundreds of civilian homes?* The Report noted that "Hamas accused the IDF of taking revenge on the civilian population for its military defeat in the battleground."[99] But it brushed aside this explanation although, prima facie, it's surely the more plausible one. Indeed, IDF testimonies themselves recalled the targeting of random civilian homes in revenge after a soldier's death.[100] The Report stated that the IDF "may" have committed "indiscriminate attacks." But in dropping one-ton bombs on, and firing high-explosive artillery shells into, a densely populated civilian neighborhood absent a credible military objective, didn't the IDF conduct *discriminate* attacks on civilians? Was the essence of Israel's crime that it treated "several distinct individual military objectives ... as one single military objective," or that it treated the entire civilian population and infrastructure as its military objective? The Report faulted Israel for not doing "everything feasible to verify that the targets were military objectives," and persisting in the operation long after it must have been aware of its "dire impact" on civilians. But wasn't the manifest purpose of the operation to target, not "military objectives," but civilians and civilian objects? Didn't Israel persist not despite but *because of* the operation's "dire impact" on the civilian population? The Report stated that Israel didn't properly balance "incidental" loss of civilian life and destruction of civilian objects against "military advantage." But what "military advantage" could Israel possibly have reaped by deploying such massive firepower in a densely populated civilian neighborhood? How could the devastation have been "incidental" to the operation when it was its very essence? The Report observed that "in spite of the significant destruction and credible allegations of civilian casualties" in Shuja'iya, there wasn't "any on-going investigation

98. Israel never alleged that it was attempting to prevent Hamas from capturing an injured soldier, as in Rafah when the Hannibal Directive was invoked.

99. UN Report, para. 286.

100. See, e.g., Chapter 12, Table 8, Testimony 51 and Testimony 71.

into the events" by Israel.[101] But if the operation's objective was to inflict significant civilian death and destruction, wouldn't such an investigation be superfluous? Instead of illuminating, via the idiom of law, the nature of Israel's crimes in Shuja'iya, the Report occluded them; the crux of its legal analysis—that is, that Israel was pursuing a "*military* objective" and was seeking a "*military* advantage"—was a whitewash and a sham. It also cannot but bewilder that whereas the Report expressed certainty that Hamas's executions of alleged collaborators "amount to a war crime," Israel's saturation bombing of a densely populated civilian neighborhood "*may* amount to a war crime."

B. *Khuza'a.* On 21 July, the village of Khuza'a, located near the Israeli border, came under Israeli air assault, and on 22 July the IDF physically isolated it from the outside world, fragmented it internally, cut off the electricity, and shot up the water supply. The village then came under "intense fire from the air and the ground." The Report stated that Khuza'a became "a zone of active fighting and everything in it was turned into a target." But it's unclear why the Report used the phrase "zone of active fighting"; neither it nor other sources[102] documented *any* firefights or IDF casualties. By the operation's end, some 70 Gazans, including at least 14 civilians, were dead and 740 buildings were damaged or destroyed.[103] The Report homed in on several incidents during the assault on Khuza'a, among them: "civilians holding a white flag and attempting to leave Khuza'a were confronted by a group of IDF soldiers who ... opened fire on them ... 11 people were seriously injured"; "Khuza'a's only clinic ... was struck by repeated Israeli air strikes"; an "ambulance found a 6-year-old boy ... who was critically injured. He was taken to an IDF checkpoint in order to be transferred to the closest ambulance. The ambulance was kept waiting for at least 20 minutes in spite of the evident seriousness of the victim's injuries and his being a child. The boy died"; a family "fled ... in a state of complete panic, leaving behind one of the family members ... , a woman aged about 70, in a wheelchair. ... [When a family member returned home] a few days later, he found [her] dead body. She had a bullet mark in her head and blood on her face. The doctor who later examined the body [stated] that she had been shot from close range, from a distance of about two meters. ... [S]ome days or weeks later, an Israeli soldier posted on Twitter a

101. UN Report, para. 299.
102. Human Rights Watch, "Gaza: Israeli soldiers shoot and kill fleeing civilians" (4 August 2014).
103. UN Report, paras. 308–13.

picture of another IDF soldier offering water to [her]."[104] The UN Report's legal analysis found that the "*intensity of the shelling*," which decimated Khuza'a's civilian infrastructure, and the "bulldozing of buildings throughout the ground operation, . . . raise concerns that the IDF shelling and airstrikes were not exclusively directed at military objectives"; that "it appears highly unlikely that the 740 buildings either destroyed or damaged all made 'an effective contribution to military action'"; and that "the complete razing of some areas of Khuza'a . . . indicates that the IDF may have treated several distinct individual military objectives in a densely populated area as one single military objective," and also "indicates that the IDF carried out destructions that were not required by military necessity." The Report concluded that "strong indications" exist that these "elements" of the IDF assault on Khuza'a "may qualify as direct attacks against civilians or civilian objects and may thus amount to a war crime."[105] It went on to find that by "refusing to allow civilians to flee," despite the "intense shelling and aerial bombardment" and "full knowledge of their presence," the IDF "very likely" committed "indiscriminate or disproportional" attacks, and it "also raises concern that not all feasible precautions to minimize danger to civilians were taken by the IDF in its attack against the town of Khuza'a."[106] It additionally observed, "The extent of the destruction combined with the statements made during the operation by the commander of the Brigade responsible for the Khuza'a operation to the effect that 'Palestinians have to understand that this does not pay off,' are indicative of a punitive intent . . . and may constitute collective punishment."[107] The Report's legal analysis was as revealing in what it did *not* say as in what it did say. It registered "concern" that Israel's massive shelling and air strikes, which leveled Khuza'a's civilian infrastructure, "were not exclusively directed at military objectives." But although it didn't identify a single firefight or IDF casualty, and although it didn't identify a single military objective, the Report never broached the possibility that Israel's firepower *overwhelmingly targeted civilians and civilian objects*. The Report deemed it "highly unlikely" that Israel's systematic demolition of civilian buildings made an "effective contri-

104. Ibid., paras. 329–33.
105. Ibid., paras. 337, 340, emphasis in original.
106. Ibid., para. 339.
107. Ibid., para. 341. The Report noted in this context that "Article 33 of Geneva Convention IV establishes that 'collective penalties and likewise all measures of intimidation or of terrorism are prohibited.'" But it limited the charge directed at Israel to collective punishment.

bution to military action." But even as it concluded that the devastation "may qualify as direct attacks against civilians and civilian objects," it steered clear of the possibility that if Israel was engaged in a "military action," its "military objective" was to destroy civilian buildings. It posited the scenario that by effacing parts of Khuza'a from the map, "the IDF may have treated several distinct individual military objectives in a densely populated area as one single military objective," and may have "carried out destructions that were not required by military necessity." But it didn't consider the possibility that Israel's "objective" was not military but wholly civilian, while "military necessity" didn't even figure as an element in its calculation—how could it in the absence of a military objective? The Report reckoned it "very likely" that trapping civilians in a village and then bombarding it constitutes an "indiscriminate and disproportionate" attack. It would appear to be even more likely that it constituted a *targeted attack on civilians,* especially as the Report didn't identify any fighting, military objective, IDF casualties, or military value against which to weigh the loss of civilian life. The Report did acknowledge, in a single paragraph, that the impetus behind the operation may also have included a "punitive" element and therefore constituted "collective punishment." But the death and destruction Israel visited on Khuza'a were not merely incidental to, or a subordinate component of, an otherwise "military" operation; they were the natural and foreseeable result—that is, the *intention*[108]—of an operation that primarily targeted, and was primarily designed to punish and terrorize, the civilian population.

C. *Rafah.*[109] After Hamas killed two IDF combatants in Rafah and apparently captured a third soldier alive, Israel launched a major military operation, "Black Friday," on 1 August. The Report stated that the IDF sealed off Rafah, "fired over 1000 shells against Rafah within three hours and dropped at least 40 bombs," launched "intense attacks" against inhabitants "in their homes and in the streets," fired on "ambulances and private vehicles trying to evacuate civilians," and "demolished dozens of homes." The ferocity of "Black Friday" traced back to Israel's dread of a replay of the Gilad Shalit affair,[110] in which Hamas's capture of an IDF soldier eventually led to the release of more than one thousand Palestinian detainees in a prisoner exchange. The Report focused on several egregious incidents; for example, a hospital that was struck by two

---

108. See Chapter 12.
109. For a detailed treatment of the Rafah massacre, see Chapter 12.
110. UN Report, para. 359.

missiles and "dozens of shells." It quoted "leaked audio recordings of IDF radio communications" indicating Israel's unrestrained use of firepower, and concluded that "virtually every person or building in Rafah became a potential military target."[111] The Report's legal analysis stated that information of "attacks on *all* vehicles in the area, including ambulances, as well as incidents in which groups of civilians appear to have been targeted by tank fire, raises serious concerns as to the respect by the IDF of the principle of distinction. . . . This amounts to a deliberate attack against civilians and civilian objects and may amount to a war crime." It went on to state that in light of the massive, unrestrained use of firepower "in a densely populated and built up area over the period of a few hours," the assault "appears to have violated the prohibition of indiscriminate attacks." Of the massacres profiled in the Report, Rafah was the only instance in which Israel appeared to have an identifiable quasi military objective—that is, to kill the captured Israeli soldier so as to preempt a future prisoner exchange—although as the Report made clear, this objective could not legitimize what ensued.[112] The Report stated unequivocally that Israel's "attacks on all vehicles" and its targeting of "groups of citizens . . . amount to a deliberate attack against civilians and civilian objects." But it then inserted the caveat, "and *may* amount to a war crime" (emphasis added). Even as the Report dared utter the unutterable—that Israel *targeted* civilians—it recoiled at the legal complement: How can "a deliberate attack against civilians and civilian objects" *not* be a war crime?

D. *Shuja'iya Market*. On 30 July, Israel announced a four-hour unilateral truce, but it qualified that the cease-fire would "not apply to the areas in which IDF soldiers are currently operating." The Report homed in on a bloody sequence of incidents in a Shuja'iya neighborhood. The roof of a home was hit by high-explosive mortar shells that killed eight family members, including seven children aged between three and nine, who were playing there, and their grandfather aged seventy. Israel purported that the attack was in response to an "anti-tank missile" and a "burst of mortar" fired from the neighborhood that injured one soldier. The IDF then fired "another round of shells" ten minutes later "just as three ambulances and the paramedics arrived at the scene," which also hit "many of the people who had gathered around the [family] house to try and help survivors." The Report cited a journalist eyewitness who was "stunned" by the "apparent targeting of ambulances and journalists

111. Ibid., paras. 352–57.
112. Ibid., paras. 365–66, emphasis added; see Chapter 12.

who had rushed to provide assistance to the injured and cover the incident."
It further noted that eyewitness accounts "are corroborated by two video
recordings," one of which showed a "dying cameraman continuing to film,
and the ambulances being hit by a rocket." The Report found, "As a result of
the second round of shelling, 23 persons were killed, including 3 journalists, 1
paramedic, and 2 firemen. In addition, 178 others were injured, among them
33 children, 14 women, 1 journalist, and 1 paramedic. Four are reported to have
died as a result of the injuries they sustained in this attack." Although Israel
subsequently alleged "that it did not have real-time surveillance" of the lethal
assault, the Report didn't buy this alibi: "The commission finds it hard to
believe that the IDF had no knowledge of the presence of ambulances in the
area in the aftermath of the initial strike, especially when the rescue crews, a
fire truck, and three ambulances arrived at the scene with sirens blazing
loudly."[113] The Report's legal analysis faulted Israel for using indiscriminate
mortars "in a built-up, densely populated area." It consequently found that the
attack "may" have violated the "prohibition of indiscriminate attacks," and the
obligation to "take all feasible precautions to choose means ... to spare
civilians."[114] Try as one may, it is most difficult to make sense of this legal
analysis. For argument's sake, let it be granted that the seven children playing
on the rooftop and their 70-year-old grandfather were killed in an indiscriminate attack, although as the Report itself and previous human rights reports[115]
documented, this wouldn't have been the first time that Israel targeted children playing on a roof. But what about the second attack ten minutes later?
The assault began "just as" neighbors, ambulances, rescue crews, and a fire
truck arrived at the family's home. A journalist testified to the *targeting* of
ambulances and journalists" (emphasis added), while a video recording captured "ambulances being hit by a rocket." The Report itself dismissed the
possibility that Israel was unaware of the bloodbath "especially when the rescue crews, a fire truck, and three ambulances arrived at the scene with sirens
blazing loudly." To classify this focused artillery and rocket barrage on a
civilian-medical rescue operation, absent any discernible military objective, as
an indiscriminate attack in which Israel didn't take sufficient precautions to
protect civilians, with the afterthought that it "may qualify as [a] direct attack

113. UN Report, paras. 376–85.
114. Ibid., paras. 386–88.
115. Human Rights Watch, *Precisely Wrong: Gaza civilians killed by Israeli drone-
launched missiles* (2009).

against civilians," and not as a clear-cut targeted attack directed at civilians, makes mockery of language, law, and human suffering.

The UN Report also undertook a synoptic analysis of Protective Edge's ground operations under several heads: (1) **Protection of civilians, force protection.** The Report found that Israel prioritized the safety of its combatants over humanitarian concern for Gaza's civilian population. The "protection of IDF soldiers was a major consideration for the IDF, overruling and, at times eliminating, any concern for the impact of its conduct on civilians.... [W]hen soldiers' lives were at stake or there was a risk of capture, the IDF disregarded basic principles" of the laws of war;[116] (2) **Warning and the continued protected status of civilians.** The Report found that Israeli warnings yielded equivocal results. The "IDF sought to warn the population in advance by means of leaflets, loudspeaker announcements, telephone and text messages and radio broadcasts, which led to the successful evacuation of some areas.... While these general warnings appear to have saved the lives of many people who heeded them, in other cases, inhabitants did not leave home for a number of reasons." On the last point, the Report observed that Gaza lacked secure places of refuge where civilians could flee ("44 per cent... is either a no-go area or has been the object of evacuation warnings"), that "[a]ll areas in Gaza, including those towards which the population was directed, had been or were likely to be hit by air strikes," and that "the generalized and often unspecific warnings sometimes resulted in panic and mass displacement." Indeed, the spokesperson for the major refugee relief organization in Gaza, Chris Gunness of the United Nations Relief and Works Agency (UNRWA), painfully reflected in the midst of the Israeli assault: "Gaza is a conflict with a fence around it. It is unique in the annals of contemporary warfare. There's nowhere safe to run and now there's nowhere safe to hide." The Report further observed that, on the one hand, the effective rules of engagement treated civilians who stayed put as enemy combatants, even though the IDF "should have been well aware" that civilians had remained behind, and that, on the other hand, the prior alerts "could be construed as an attempt to use warnings to justify attacks against individual civilians" who didn't flee;[117] (3) **Use of artillery and other explosive weapons in**

116. UN Report, para. 392.

117. Ibid., paras. 396–405; Charlotte Alfred, "'The Present Is Tragic But the Future Is Unthinkable' in Gaza," *Huffington Post* (31 July 2014) (Gunness); B'Tselem (Israeli Information Center for Human Rights in the Occupied Territories), *Whitewash Protocol: The so-called investigation of Operation Protective Edge* (2016), pp. 22–23.

built-up areas. The Report found that Israel made "significant use of explosive weapons with wide-area effects in densely populated areas," which "resulted in a large number of civilian casualties and widespread destruction of civilian objects." It further noted that Israel persisted in its use of such indiscriminate weapons in densely populated civilian areas even "after" they "resulted in significant civilian casualties";[118] (4) **Destruction**. The Report found that the firepower "used in Shuja'iya, Rafah and Khuza'a resulted in significant destruction . . . some areas were virtually 'razed' . . . completely obliterated." It also quoted Israeli soldiers testifying that "every house we passed on our way [into the Gaza Strip] got hit by a shell—and houses farther away too. It was methodical," and "the damage to Palestinian property was not a consideration when determining the scope and force of fire." The Report went on to say that "the vast scale of destruction may have been adopted as tactics of war," that "the IDF followed a pre-calculated pattern of wide-spread razing of neighbourhoods in certain areas," and that this "razing of entire areas . . . may not have been strictly required by military necessity";[119] and (5) **Targeting of civilians.** In a brief treatment (just one paragraph), the Report noted "a number of cases in which civilians, who were clearly not participating in the hostilities, appear to have been attacked in the street." It pointed to a couple of incidents in which "civilians, including children, allegedly carrying white flags were fired upon by soldiers," and a third incident, in which "a wounded man . . . lying on the ground was shot again two times and killed."[120] The Report found that Israel deliberately killed just *two* civilians during the whole of the ground operation.

In essence, the picture presented by the UN Report looked something like this. Israel launched Protective Edge in order to achieve a pair of unimpeachable military objectives: end Hamas's projectile attacks, dismantle Hamas's tunnel network. In the course of the assault, it resorted to indiscriminate and disproportionate force primarily because it attached a higher priority to the lives of its own combatants than to Gaza's civilian population. Still, on the one hand, Israel did issue warnings that although not always effective, "saved the lives of many people" (the Report didn't provide a basis for this calculation),[121] and, on the other hand, although many civilians were injured and killed, Israel

118. UN Report, paras. 406–15.
119. Ibid., paras. 416–19.
120. Ibid., para. 420.
121. The Report also asserted without a source that "attacks on more than 200 residential buildings by air strikes resulted in no civilian casualties" (ibid., para. 234).

intentionally targeted only a handful of them. Put simply, Protective Edge was a legitimate military operation that, alas, often went awry but only exceptionally crossed the red line of targeting Gaza's civilian infrastructure, and next to never crossed the red line of targeting its civilian population. The Report's overarching conceit could not, however, accommodate many of its own findings and conclusions. If the warnings were designed to save lives, why were so few issued, why was so little advance notice given when they were issued, and why were so many of them, such as the "roof-knock," ineffective by the Report's own account?[122] If the areas toward which Israel directed the civilian population "were likely to be hit by air strikes," then those fleeing after an alert found safe haven more as a result of serendipity than anything else. In fact, Israel almost certainly issued these warnings in order to embroider its *hasbara* campaign, and to provide itself with legal cover in the event of postwar prosecutions—or in the Report's own words, "to justify attacks against individual civilians" who didn't flee after the alerts. They also served to foment "panic and mass displacement," which the Report depicted as collateral effects, but which to judge by prior Israeli operations were a premeditated objective.[123] The denouement of Protective Edge provided the most compelling proof that, overwhelmingly, Israeli warnings were contrived, not to save lives but with these other goals in mind. Although it had been forced to terminate the ground invasion in early August after international outrage peaked, Israel still sought to gain leverage in the ongoing negotiations by launching air strikes, in late August, on four high-rise buildings occupied by Gaza's social elite.[124] However, fearful of evoking renewed condemnation, Israel was at pains not to kill civilians, particularly influential civilians, so it issued effective warnings that enabled all the buildings' residents to evacuate safely.[125] The fact that no Gazans died in these air strikes pointed up that if Israel were so inclined, it could have issued truly effective warnings. The Report praised these late August warnings as a "good practice, through which Israel attempted to . . . minimize civilian casualties."[126] Wasn't it a tad unseemly to congratulate Israel on its "good practice . . . to minimize civilian casualties" when, in this

122. Ibid., paras. 235–39; Jutta Bachmann et al., *Gaza 2014: Findings of an independent medical fact-finding mission* (2015), assembled by Physicians for Human Rights–Israel, pp. 39–44.

123. See Chapter 3.

124. See Chapter 11; UN Report, paras. 210–11, 233–34.

125. UN Report, paras. 211, 234.

126. Ibid., para. 234.

last scene of the last act of a terror assault on a defenseless civilian population that had already left more than a thousand civilians dead and tens of thousands homeless, Israel proceeded to level yet more homes, in particular as this "good practice" was proof positive that except when it was politically advantageous, Israel issued warnings only to grease its PR machine and sow panic, not to save lives, while Israel's primordial objective, made manifest by its use of one-ton bombs in densely populated civilian neighborhoods, was—so far as diplomatic constraints would allow it—to *maximize* civilian casualties? If as the Report inferred, the principal impetus behind Israel's resort to indiscriminate and disproportionate force was to protect its combatants, that might explain why it adopted a criminal shoot-to-kill-anything-that-moves policy in areas where ground troops were operating. But why did Israel indiscriminately fire from afar tens of thousands of indiscriminate high-explosive artillery shells into densely populated civilian neighborhoods, which "resulted in a large number of civilian casualties and widespread destruction of civilian objects," and why did it persist in its use of such indiscriminate, high-explosive weapons in densely populated civilian areas even "after" it was clear that they "resulted in significant civilian casualties"? Why did it drop hundreds of one-ton bombs over densely populated civilian neighborhoods? Why did it "raze" to the ground and "obliterate" entire civilian neighborhoods, in the total absence, as IDF eyewitness accounts repeatedly attested, of military activity? The Report did acknowledge that Israel perhaps inflicted this "pre-calculated" devastation as "tactics of war" that weren't "strictly required by military necessity." It was, to be sure, an odd way to describe a destruction process in which, overwhelmingly, neither "military necessity" nor for that matter military considerations of any kind figured as even a factor. The Report didn't pose, let alone answer, the question begging to be asked: *If not from "military necessity," then why did Israel, in a "pre-calculated" fashion, adopt "tactics of war" that wreaked massive death and destruction in Gaza?* In fact, if safeguarding the lives of Israeli combatants at any cost was the modus operandi of Protective Edge, then punishing and terrorizing the civilian population into submission was its overarching objective. The Report itself copiously documented that Israel fired tens of thousands of high-explosive artillery shells into, and dropped hundreds of one-ton bombs over, densely populated civilian neighborhoods, targeted hospitals, ambulances, rescue teams, civilian vehicles, and "groups of citizens," and pursued a shoot-to-kill-anything-that-moves policy in pacified areas that still contained civilians. But nonetheless it was the finding of this cynical, craven document that of the 1,600 Gazan civilians killed by Israel during the 51-day terror onslaught, only two were killed deliberately.

The UN Report included a miscellany section that analyzed Israeli attacks on (1) civilian shelters, (2) Gaza's only power plant, and (3) ambulances.

1. *Civilian shelters.* The UN Report noted that Israel attacked multiple civilian shelters, and it investigated the attacks on three of them—Beit Hanoun Coeducational A and D School (Beit Hanoun School), Jabalia Elementary Girls A and B School (Jabalia School), and Rafah Preparatory Boys A School (Rafah School)—that resulted in the deaths of some 45 persons, including 14 children:

- *Beit Hanoun School.* The Report stated that UNRWA was in "regular contact" with Israeli officials, had "given them the school's coordinates on twelve occasions," and had informed them that the school was being used as a Designated Emergency Shelter. It further stated that Beit Hanoun was witness at the time of the incident to "heavy fighting," including "daily shelling in the vicinity of the school." As the fighting intensified, the shelter's occupants were persuaded to leave, and a "time slot" for their evacuation was synchronized between the IDF and UNRWA. An IDF commander subsequently conveyed his intention to target other schools in the area, allegedly because a "Hamas arsenal" was hidden among them, but "had reconfirmed at least twice" that the Designated Emergency Shelter would not be targeted. However, as families gathered their belongings and assembled in the school courtyard on 24 July to await bus transportation, the building "was suddenly attacked" by "at least two 120 MM high explosive (HE) mortar projectiles . . . , one hitting the middle of the schoolyard and a second the steps in front of the school's entrance." Israel variously alleged that Hamas prevented the shelter's occupants from leaving at the assigned time, that "the attacks had been caused by Hamas rockets misfiring," and that "soldiers returned fire at locations from which Palestinian missiles had been fired at them." The Report found no evidence supporting these official Israeli alibis. On the contrary, it noted that witnesses consistently affirmed that there had been no rocket fire from the school, nor militants operating in its vicinity, nor any "suspicious activity." The Report concluded, "The fact that the attack occurred before implementation of an evacuation agreement indicates that the advance warning communicated to UNWRA [*sic*] by the IDF was not effective."[127]

127. Ibid., paras. 425–30.

- *Jabalia School.* The Report stated that "[p]rior to 30 July, Israeli agencies were notified 28 times in 14 days about the site's use as an UNRWA shelter," and that Israel had confirmed receipt of this information. In addition, UNRWA was in steady contact with the relevant Israeli agencies by e-mail and telephone. But on 30 July, without advance warning, "the school was hit by a barrage of four 155 MM high explosive (HE) projectiles, an artillery indirect fire weapon." Eighteen people were killed, including three children. The IDF alleged that "Hamas had fired at Israeli armed forces from the vicinity of the school." The Report, however, found no evidence corroborating the Israeli allegation.[128]

- *Rafah School.* The Report stated that on 3 August "a precision-guided missile hit the street in front of" the school, killing fifteen people, including at least seven children. Israel alleged that "the IDF had fired an aerial-launched missile at [a] motorcycle, which had been carrying three militants from Palestinian Islamic Jihad." The Report didn't adduce evidence either supporting or belying the official Israeli version of what happened.[129] (A subsequent investigation by the Al Mezan Center for Human Rights found that two, not three, Gazans were riding the motorcycle, and both were civilians.[130])

The UN Report's legal analysis of the first two incidents (Beit Hanoun and Jabalia)[131] stated that Israel "must have been aware" that by deploying relatively indiscriminate weapons, such as artillery or mortars, "to strike a target located in a densely populated area and adjacent to UNRWA schools used as a shelter," it might also hit civilian objects. It went on to express "serious concerns" that Israel's "choice of means for the attack did not take into account the requirement to avoid ... incidental loss of civilian life, ... did not take all feasible precautions to choose means with a view to avoiding ... casualties." Hence, these assaults "are highly likely to constitute an indiscriminate attack ... and may ... amount to a war crime." The explicit premise underlying the Report's legal analysis was that Israel targeted military objects in these attacks. But the Report didn't adduce a jot of evidence to sustain this premise. On the contrary, the mass of evidence assembled by it dictated the conclusion that Israel intentionally targeted civilians taking shelter. The Report's own

128. Ibid., paras. 433–38.
129. Ibid., paras. 439–43.
130. Al Mezan Center for Human Rights, "Israeli Military Refuses to Investigate Attack near UNRWA School in Rafah, Gaza That Killed 14 Civilians" (31 August 2016).
131. UN Report, paras. 445–49.

factual summary (in the Beit Hanoun incident) pinpointed that the "attack occurred" not during an exchange of fire but "before implementation of an evacuation agreement." How else is one to interpret this contextualization except that the assault was timed with, or geared to, the scheduled evacuation, and that the object of the attack was the shelter grounds? The undisputed facts that an agreement had been reached with the IDF for a peaceful, orderly exodus, and that the IDF commander twice expressly promised not to target this particular shelter, compounded the crime as an appalling act of perfidy. The Report's contention that these incidents constituted "indiscriminate" attacks flew in the face of its own factual findings, while its depiction of the ensuing civilian deaths as "incidental" begs the question—incidental *to what?* The Report didn't point to a military objective in either incident while, as it itself documented, Israel's official story kept shifting as each of its successive alibis kept unraveling. The Report reckoned it a critical finding of fact that Israel's "advance warning" was "not effective," even though the warning proved to be a most effective instrument of criminal perfidy, while the Report reckoned it a critical finding of law that Israel did not take "all feasible precautions" to protect civilians, even though it did take all feasible precautions to set them up for a bloodbath. It was as if the Report were playing a Victorian parlor game: *Who can contrive the most absurd factual or legal description of a manifestly criminal act?* In another contrived iteration, the Report stated that whereas Israel relied on its civilian agencies "to facilitate communication between international organizations and the Israeli military, and ... there seem to have been attempts to notify UNRWA about possible attacks in the case of Beit Hanoun, the incident suggests that communication between UNRWA and the IDF was not effective." But the Report itself documented that even though the IDF coordinated the evacuation with UNRWA, and even though the IDF commander made repeated, explicit promises not to target the shelter, the IDF launched an attack on the shelter grounds just before the agreed-upon "time slot" while "families started gathering their belongings in the courtyard so as to be ready when the buses arrived." The upshot was not a communications breakdown but criminal bad faith. Indeed, not even Israel in its various official justifications blamed the attack on a lapse in communications; the Report created this alibi out of whole cloth. The Report's legal analysis additionally observed, "Even though the attack against the UNRWA schools may not have been deliberate, the IDF is bound by the obligation of precautionary measures and verification of targets 'to avoid attacks directed by negligence at civilians or civilian objects.'" The choice of phraseology, "Even though the attack . . . may not have been deliberate," was twice-over peculiar. On the one hand, the Report's legal findings never even hinted that the attacks were deliberate—to the contrary, it studiously avoided this conclusion—while, on the other hand, the factual evidence assembled in the Report left little doubt that they in fact were deliberate. The Report also considered it a relevant legal point that Israel didn't take sufficient precautions "to avoid attacks directed by negligence at civilians or civilian objects," whereas it was hard not to conclude from the Report's own rehearsal of the factual record that Israel, far from being negligent, took every precaution and acted with full premeditation to target civilians and civilian objects.[132] Even ever-cautious UN secretary-general Ban Ki-moon finally blurted out after the Israeli attack on Rafah School—*the seventh civilian shelter to be targeted*—that it was a "moral outrage and criminal act."[133]

2. *Gaza's only power plant.* The UN Report noted that Israel's repeated shelling of the only power plant in Gaza at the end of July caused severe damage. The last shelling on 29 July caused one of the plant's fuel tanks to explode, which "eventually destroyed almost an entire section of the plant and damaged other parts." It also noted that "[a]s a result of that attack, and of damage to the electricity infrastructure more generally, . . . Gaza experienced power outages of 22 hours a day during the hostilities," which "forced hospitals to operate at limited capacity; led to a drastic reduction in the pumping of water to households; and affected desalination plants and sewage treatment." A year later, Israel purported that its shells had "unfortunately missed their intended target." Although the Report pleaded agnosticism ("the commission is unable to verify this account"), it also observed that Israel had already hit the power plant back in 2006 as well as during Operation Cast Lead; that at the inception of Protective Edge, a senior Israeli official had called on the government "immediately to cut off fuel and electricity supplies to the Gaza Strip," and also exhorted the government to "use all of the levers of pressure . . . at its disposal in order to coerce Hamas to accept a cease-fire"; and that "the plant had been hit three times" in the days just prior to the climactic 29 July strike. The Report's legal analysis reiterated that "[o]wing to the limited evidence available, . . . it is unable to determine whether the power plant suffered incidental damage from an attack directed elsewhere, or whether it was the object of a deliberate attack."

132. Ibid., paras. 446–48. The Report's legal analysis did not directly assess the third incident at Rafah School.

133. See Chapter 11.

Still, it went on to speculate, "If the strike against the power plant was accidental, as Israel claims, there remain nonetheless questions as to whether all appropriate precautions were taken by the IDF to avoid damage to a civilian object."[134] Noticeably, it didn't ponder the possibility that the attack was deliberate, and the attendant legal consequences if it was. But the larger point is this: The Report's avowed legal mandate was not to reach a definitive determination but instead to use a less stringent "'reasonable ground' standard in its assessment of incidents investigated and patterns found to have occurred"—that is, what a "reasonable and ordinarily prudent person would have reason to believe" happened. It appears a safe bet that a "reasonable and ordinarily prudent person" would have concluded something along these lines: *In light of the pattern of targeted Israeli attacks on the power plant in previous years[135] and multiple shellings of the plant in the days preceding the 29 July attack; and in light of the minatory statements by a senior Israeli official before the attack; and in light of the fact that the only counterevidence consisted of boilerplate Israeli denial that has rarely withstood scrutiny in the past—in light of this compelling and cumulative circumstantial evidence, the attack on Gaza's only power plant, which exacerbated its already dire shortage of electricity, was most likely deliberate and amounted to a war crime.* If the Report didn't reach this conclusion, that's because it construed the better part of prudence to be pusillanimity.

3. *Ambulances.* The UN Report noted that Protective Edge "resulted in damage to 16 ambulances [and] the death of 23 health personnel." It focused on a trio of incidents that it had already dissected, in Shuja'iya, Shuja'iya Market, and Rafah, and on a pair of cognate incidents in Al Qarara village and Beit Hanoun, in which ambulances came under Israeli attack and 35 medical personnel and other civilians were killed and many more injured. It presented a condensed version of the first three incidents and a more detailed account of the two others:

- *Shuja'iya*—"a military medical aid ambulance was directly hit twice while attempting to provide first aid to victims."
- *Shuja'iya Market*—"in a context of intense fire, a shell struck the ground close to three ambulances in the proximity of a house that had been attacked."

134. UN Report, paras. 450–55, 581–83.
135. B'Tselem (Israeli Information Center for Human Rights in the Occupied Territories) deemed the 2006 attack a "war crime" (see Chapter 12).

- *Rafah*—"eight people burned to death in an ambulance that was hit."

- *Al Qarara*—"Mohammed Hassan Al Abadla, an ambulance driver, . . . came under fire while evacuating an injured person. . . . [W]hen [Al Abadla's] ambulance arrived at the location, the IDF instructed the crew to exit the vehicle and continue on foot. Mohammed Hassan Al Abadla and one of two volunteers got out of the ambulance and approached the patient with a flashlight on, as directed. They had walked about twelve meters when they came under fire and Mohammed Hassan Al Abadla was hit in the chest and thigh. Two ambulance teams that arrived a little later to rescue their wounded colleague also came under fire, despite earlier ICRC [International Committee of the Red Cross] information that the IDF had approved their entry to the area. A third team was finally allowed to take Al Abadla to Nasser hospital in Khan Younis, where he died shortly upon arrival. The ambulances' movements were at all times coordinated with the IDF through the ICRC."

- *Beit Hanoun*—"a missile appears to have hit the back of a PRCS [Palestine Red Crescent Society] ambulance during a rescue operation in Beit Hanoun. As a result, . . . an ambulance volunteer . . . was killed and two other rescuers inside the ambulance were injured. When another ambulance team was dispatched to respond, a missile hit the rear part of this vehicle, which caught fire. The ambulance had its siren and flashing red light on and, at the time of the strike, the street was deserted."

The Report did not discover in any of the five incidents "any information, or receive any allegations indicating that the ambulances involved were used for a purpose other than their humanitarian function." It went on to observe that "reports of repeated strikes on ambulances that came to the rescue of injured staff . . . suggest that the ambulances and personnel may have been specifically targeted"; that "Many, if not most, of the reported strikes on ambulances appear to have occurred without there having been any obvious threat or military activity in the area"; and that "ambulances were marked with emblems, health workers wore uniforms, and the IDF had been notified repeatedly of their movements." The Report's legal analysis found that "Some of the incidents . . . constitute a violation by the IDF of the prohibition of attacks on medical transports and medical personnel, and may amount to war crimes, in particular, if the vehicles or personnel attacked used the distinctive emblems of the Geneva Conventions."[136] Although they appear rea-

136. UN Report, paras. 456–65.

sonable, at any rate by the dismally low standard set by the Report, one can still quarrel at points with this factual presentation and legal finding. It stated that ambulances in Shuja'iya Market came under attack "in a context of intense fire." But if none of the witnesses reported return fire by Palestinians, shouldn't it have said, "in a context of intense fire *by Israel*"? It stated that "*some* of the incidents" violated the laws of war. Which of the five shocking incidents, it might be wondered, didn't? If the Report unequivocally found that Hamas's executions of alleged collaborators "amount to a war crime," it might also be wondered why, even though the Report compiled a mass as well as a pattern of damning evidence, it could find only that Israel's repeated targeting of clearly marked ambulances in the absence of any military justification "*may* amount to a war crime." If the Report could exhort that "whoever is responsible" for the executions of alleged collaborators in Gaza "must be brought to justice," it might also be wondered why it wasn't equally emphatic that whoever was responsible for the targeting of medical personnel and rescue crews must be brought to justice. The Report's legal finding stated that Israel may have committed a war crime because it violated the prohibition against attacks on "medical transports and personnel." But wouldn't it also be a war crime if they weren't medics but simply civilians? This prompts the most perplexing and serious question of all. The Report found convincing evidence that Israel "specifically targeted" these medical personnel/civilians absent any military rationale and in the full knowledge of their noncombatant status. It tallied 35 deaths as a result of the five ambulance attacks it investigated. But why then did the Report calculate under its rubric *Targeting of civilians* that Israel had committed only two targeted killings of civilians during Protective Edge? Indeed, Israel's targeting of ambulances, medical personnel, and rescue crews absent a discernible military objective itself did not deviate from, but merely shone a brighter light on, the actual strategic goal of Protective Edge: to punish, humiliate, and terrorize Gaza's civilian population, part and parcel of which was the infliction of massive civilian casualties.

Finally, a glaring omission in the UN Report's inventory of Israeli war crimes warrants notice. Israel destroyed 70 mosques and damaged 130 more during Protective Edge. It is a war crime under international law to target "places of worship which constitute the cultural or spiritual heritage of people."[137] The Report made precisely four passing allusions to attacks on

137. ICRC, *Commentary on the Additional Protocols,* article 53.

Gaza's mosques, of which three repeat Israeli *hasbara* that Hamas hid weapons inside or fired from them, and one is a sentence fragment that a mosque had been hit.[138] The Report devoted many paragraphs to the psychic distress Israelis suffered during Protective Edge, but it had not a single word to say about the psychic impact in a deeply religious society of Israel's assault on Gaza's mosques. If Hamas had destroyed scores of Israeli synagogues, is it conceivable that the Report would have ignored it? The issue isn't whether or not Israel deliberately targeted Gaza's mosques without military justification, although the available evidence overwhelmingly suggests that it did.[139] The telling point is this: The Report didn't deem the mass destruction of mosques worthy of attention, let alone investigation.

The UN Report's penultimate chapter analyzed steps taken by each party to hold accountable violators of the laws of war during Protective Edge. The section on Palestine, consisting of nine paragraphs, essentially pleaded that "little information was available," and then concluded that "Palestinian authorities have consistently failed to ensure that perpetrators of violations" of the laws of war "are brought to justice."[140] The heart of this chapter, running to fully 45 paragraphs, parsed Israel's judicial response.[141] The sheer amount of space devoted by the Report to this undertaking conveyed the impression that Israel's system of legal accountability was a worthy object of investigation. The facts, however, reveal that this system is a farce.

The UN Report observed that Israel has in the past "failed to hold accountable those responsible for alleged grave violations" of the laws of war. For example, during Cast Lead, 1,400 Gazans were killed, up to 1,200 of them civilians, while much of Gaza's civilian infrastructure was laid waste. But only four Israelis were convicted of wrongdoing, and only three of them were sentenced to jail (the maximum sentence was seven and a half months for theft of a Palestinian's credit card).[142] The Report further noted that Israel hadn't

138. UN Report, paras. 247, 355, 474, 476.

139. See Chapter 12.

140. UN Report, paras. 652–61, 666.

141. Ibid., paras. 607–51 (see also ibid., para. 681[b]).

142. See Chapter 4; B'Tselem (Israeli Information Center for Human Rights in the Occupied Territories), "Israeli Authorities Have Proven They Cannot Investigate Suspected Violations of International Humanitarian Law by Israel in the Gaza Strip" (5 September 2014).

"launched a single criminal investigation" regarding Operation Pillar of Defense (2012). It concluded that the track record of Israel's judicial system "raise[s] serious questions regarding the effectiveness of the current mechanisms to hold to account those responsible for the most serious alleged crimes." It then went on to observe that "the picture is equally bleak when reviewing other data," whether they pertained to the many killings of Palestinians in the West Bank ("only ... two indictments and one conviction") or the many allegations of torture and ill-treatment of Palestinians ("not a single criminal investigation was opened"). Still, the Report espied a silver lining in the cloud. It purported that Israel has in recent years significantly upgraded its system of legal accountability. In 2010, Israeli commandos launched an assault on the Gaza Freedom Flotilla, killing nine passengers aboard the flagship *Mavi Marmara*.[143] The international outrage after these deaths compelled Israel to appoint an investigative commission chaired by former Supreme Court justice Jacob Turkel. The findings of the Turkel Commission comprised two volumes, published separately. The first volume (2011), which pretended to examine the circumstances surrounding the commando raid on the flotilla, although replete with scholarly footnotes and erudite references, proved on close inspection to be a whitewash.[144] The second volume (2013) was mandated to assess whether Israel's "mechanism" for prosecuting violators of the laws of war met international standards; unsurprisingly, the Turkel Commission found that the Israeli mechanism "generally" passed muster, but it also recommended several improvements. The UN Report heaped praise on the Turkel Commission's recommendations, as they lent "momentum" to the "noteworthy"/"significant"/"welcome" reforms that Israel subsequently instituted. The UN Report also delineated the remaining "procedural, structural and substantive" flaws, already adumbrated by the Turkel Commission, and kept repeating, mantra-style, that if Israel remedied them, its judicial system would come close to ensuring full legal accountability. A typical passage melding the "bleak" past with the roseate future went like this:

> The [UN Report] is concerned that impunity prevails across the board for violations of international humanitarian and human rights law allegedly committed by Israeli forces, whether it be in the context of active hostilities in Gaza or killings, torture, and ill-treatment in the West Bank. Israel must break with its recent lamentable track record in holding wrong-doers

143. See Chapter 7.
144. See Chapter 8.

accountable.... Those responsible for suspected violations of international law at all levels of the political and military establishments must be brought to justice. An important factor in enabling such a process will be the implementation of the Turkel Commission's recommendations.[145]

The UN Report's analysis zeroed in on Israel's legal "mechanism" as the critical locus in need of repair. Just a mite more tweaking, it anticipated, and everything would be hunky-dory. But the rational basis of its Pollyannaish optimism perplexes. Consider this chronology. The Report highlighted that Israel had already implemented several of the Turkel Commission's proposed reforms *before* Protective Edge, and it praised these as "noteworthy"/"significant"/"welcome" initiatives. But it also noted that after Protective Edge, and notwithstanding these touted reforms, B'Tselem (Israeli Information Center for Human Rights in the Occupied Territories) and Yesh Din—the premier guardians of Palestinian human rights in Israel—refused to cooperate with official Israeli inquiries into the operation. "The existing investigation mechanism," they jointly declared, "precluded serious investigations and is marred by severe structural flaws that render it incapable of conducting professional investigations."[146] It would appear that these Israel-based human rights organizations were rather less sanguine than the Report about the alleged Israeli reforms. Furthermore, if these indeed constituted "noteworthy"/"significant"/"welcome" improvements, how did it come to pass that the material results of Israeli investigations into Protective Edge read like a carbon copy of Operation Cast Lead? As of 2015, the Report noted, Israel had issued three indictments: "Two soldiers were accused of looting NIS 2,420 (over USD 600) from a Palestinian home in Shuja'iya, Gaza City. A third soldier was accused of assisting them." Unless the Report was of the opinion that an indictment for stealing cash instead of for stealing a credit card registered a civilizational leap, a wide chasm separated the Report's brimming enthusiasms from these measurable outcomes. A year after publication of the UN Report, B'Tselem issued a report of its own, *The Occupation's Fig Leaf: Israel's military law enforcement system as a whitewash mechanism*.[147] It announced that henceforth it would cease cooperating with Israel's military law enforcement system. Inter alia, it commented on the Turkel Commission, which so

145. UN Report, para. 664.
146. Ibid., para. 609.
147. B'Tselem (Israeli Information Center for Human Rights in the Occupied Territories), *The Occupation's Fig Leaf: Israel's military law enforcement system as a whitewash mechanism* (2016).

impressed the UN Report: "The Commission . . . recommended a number of improvements to the military law enforcement system. . . . The implementation of these recommendations, which has already begun, may improve appearances of the current system, but it will not remedy the substantive flaws." The B'Tselem report concluded:

> [T]he semblance of a functioning justice system allows Israeli officials to deny claims made both in Israel and abroad that Israel does not enforce the law on soldiers who harm Palestinians. . . . These appearances also help grant legitimacy . . . to the continuation of the occupation. It makes it easier to reject criticism about the injustices of the occupation, thanks to the military's outward pretense that even it considers some acts unacceptable, and backs up the claim by saying that it is already investigating these actions. . . . B'Tselem's cooperation with the military investigation and enforcement system has not achieved justice, instead lending legitimacy to the occupation regime and aiding to whitewash it. . . . [T]here is no longer any point in pursuing justice and defending human rights by working with a system whose real function is measured by its ability to continue to successfully cover up unlawful acts and protect perpetrators.

The purpose of Israeli pseudo-investigations undertaken after Protective Edge, B'Tselem further observed in a complementary publication, *Whitewash Protocol: The so-called investigation of Operation Protective Edge,* was "to prevent the International Criminal Court (ICC) in The Hague from addressing the issue itself."[148] If only the UN Report had summoned up such courage, candor, and principle; instead, it lent its good offices to the whitewash as it waxed the occupation's fig leaf.

The UN Report's assessment of Israel's accountability mechanism included a case study of four Palestinian children killed by Israeli missiles.[149] The children were playing hide-and-seek around a small, dilapidated fisherman's hut, "which was in plain sight of nearby hotels housing international journalists, none of whom described seeing militants in the area at the time of the attack" (British *Guardian*).[150] The Report noted that "the boys were

148. B'Tselem, *Whitewash Protocol,* p. 25. For Israel's failure to investigate violations of international law after Protective Edge, see also Al Mezan Center for Human Rights, *Gaza Two Years On: Impunity over accountability* (28 August 2016).

149. UN Report, paras. 630–33.

150. Tyler Hicks, "Through Lens, 4 Boys Dead by Gaza Shore," *New York Times* (16 July 2014); Peter Beaumont, "Israel Exonerates Itself over Gaza Beach Killings Last Year," *Guardian* (11 June 2015); Peter Beaumont, "Gaza Beach Killings: No justice in Israeli exoneration, says victim's father," *Guardian* (13 June 2015).

aged between 9 and 11 years, and were therefore small in stature in comparison to the size of an average adult," while Amnesty noted that "video footage quickly emerged in which individuals targeted were clearly visible as children."[151] But the official Israeli investigation concluded that the children had been mistaken for "militants" and that "the attack process ... accorded with Israeli domestic law and international law requirements." If the Report's legal assessment differed from Israel's, it was only on the narrowest of grounds: it "found strong indications that the IDF failed in its obligations to take all feasible measures to avoid or at least minimize incidental harm to civilians." It is unclear why the Report ruled out the possibility that the Israeli missile strikes intentionally targeted the children. It's not as if the IDF had never before targeted Palestinian children or, for that matter, tortured them[152] and used them as human shields;[153] or that Israeli settlers, many of whom at some point pass through the IDF, hadn't committed the most heinous atrocities against Palestinian children, such as burning them to death.[154] The Report just barely, and only indirectly, paused to reflect on the plausibility of the claim that the IDF confused four children "small in stature in comparison to the size of an average adult" with Hamas "militants." Thus, in keeping with its "all feasible precautions" line of analysis, the Report criticized the IDF as it "could have more exhaustively verified whether those being targeted were taking a direct part in the hostilities." What "hostilities"? The Report itself stated, "there were no IDF soldiers in the area, as the ground operations had not commenced, nor were there any other persons in imminent danger." Wasn't the Report's tacit premise, that the IDF believed the children were "taking a direct part in the hostilities ... ," a leap of *bad* faith, unargued, unsubstantiated, and—in light of a gory Israeli track record of killing and torturing Palestinian children—wholly unwarranted? The Report continued, "[T]he compound was located in the centre of a city of almost 550,000 residents, between a public beach and an area regularly used

151. Amnesty International, *"Black Friday,"* p. 77. For this report, see Chapter 12.
152. UN Committee against Torture, "Concluding Observations on the Fifth Periodic Report of Israel" (3 June 2016), para. 28; *Amnesty International Report 2015/16* (it also reported that "children ... appeared to be victims of unlawful killings"), pp. 201–2; UN Report, para. 517.
153. See Chapter 4. Israel's use of Gazan children as human shields has a long history; see Jean-Pierre Filiu, *Gaza: A history* (New York: 2014), p. 98.
154. Jodi Rudoren, "Autopsy Suggests Palestinian Teenager Was Burned to Death after Abduction," *New York Times* (5 July 2015); Jack Khoury, "Palestinian Infant Burned to Death in West Bank Arson Attack," *Haaretz* (31 July 2015).

by fishermen. . . . It could therefore not be ruled out that civilians, including children, might be present. These factual elements suggest that by assuming that the individuals were members of armed groups merely on the basis of their presence in a particular location, the IDF reversed the presumption of civilian status." This passage puzzles on several counts. *First,* the Report took for granted that the target of the Israeli missile strike was a Hamas "compound," even though journalist-eyewitnesses attested that it was a beaten shack. *Second,* it itself acknowledged that the targeted area was a densely populated civilian locale. *Third,* it was most improbable that children "small of stature" would be confused with Hamas militants. Why then did the Report infer that the IDF had been "assuming that the individuals were members of armed groups"? On the basis of the circumstantial evidence, which the Report itself assembled, it would seem much more probable that the IDF deliberately targeted innocent children; indeed, except for pro forma Israeli denials, no basis existed for inferring otherwise. By starting from the assumption that the children were militants, not civilians (instead of the reverse), the Report concluded, Israel "appears to have validated [an] incorrect application of international humanitarian law." The irony, entirely lost on this wretched document, was that by starting from the highly dubious premise that the IDF had been "assuming" the dilapidated shack was a Hamas "compound," and the diminutive children were an "armed group," the Report itself validated an incorrect application of international humanitarian law: the applicable legal principle was not "all feasible precautions" but, plainly, the deliberate targeting of civilians.[155]

The UN Report's analysis of Israeli legal accountability was embedded in, and went awry because of, a chain of false, if anodyne and convenient premises, to wit: Israel has periodically launched military operations in Gaza with legitimate, conventional military objectives and targets; in the course of these operations, the IDF has, alas, committed excesses—which army hasn't?—sometimes spilling over into war crimes; if Israel has been remiss in

155. It depresses that Israel's preeminent human rights organization B'Tselem also sustained the official fiction that Israel targeted a Hamas compound and that the child killings resulted from imperfect surveillance equipment. B'Tselem, *Whitewash Protocol,* pp. 17–21. On the latter point, were it true that Israel couldn't distinguish between ten-year-olds playing hide-and-seek in broad daylight in a civilian area, on the one hand, and Hamas militants about to launch a lethal attack, on the other, then it's hard to fathom Israel's generic claim that it was careful not to target civilians. How would it even know whether it was targeting civilians or combatants?

prosecuting these breaches of the laws of war, it's on account of a still flawed legal-administrative "mechanism." But fortunately it requires just a little tinkering—if Israel would only implement a couple more Turkel Commission recommendations—to eliminate the glitches and enable the wheels of justice to turn smoothly. The picture looks radically different, however, if Protective Edge is viewed through the optic of the Goldstone Report, issued by the UN Human Rights Council after Cast Lead.[156] The Goldstone Report found that the death and destruction Israel visited on Gaza's civilian population were not "incidental" or the result of a "failure to take all feasible precautions" but, on the contrary, calculated and deliberate, "designed to punish, humiliate and terrorize a civilian population."[157] The military doctrine driving Protective Edge was carried over from Cast Lead; it was a repeat performance, but writ larger. The factual evidence collected in the UN Report left little space for doubt that Israel was deliberately targeting Gaza's civilian population and infrastructure during Protective Edge. If the Report's legal analysis concluded otherwise, it was due not to a deficit of material evidence but to a deficit of moral integrity. The Report deployed the idiom of law, not to shed light on the criminal nature of Israel's undertaking but to sanitize it. True, the Report at multiple junctures "raises concerns" that Israel "may" have committed war crimes. But it willfully, repeatedly, and unforgivably ignored dispositive evidence that these Israeli crimes, far from being collateral to or springing from tactical excesses in the pursuit of a bona fide military objective, were integral to and inherent in a criminal strategy targeting Gaza's civilian population. Whether it traced back to careerism, cowardice, or cynicism, the bottom line was that the Report transparently and shamelessly fled from the damning conclusions that flowed, inexorably, from its own factual findings. Did it not border on the absurd, indeed, was it not squarely in absurdist terrain, when the Report indicted Israel for not taking "all feasible precautions to avoid . . . incidental harm to civilians" after Israeli missiles targeted and killed four children playing hide-and-seek in an open civilian area, absent any military activity, in broad daylight, in the presence of numerous credible eyewitnesses who contradicted Israel's pro forma denials on each and every point? In two places, the Report pondered whether Israel's "massive and destructive" force was "approved at least tacitly by

156. See Chapter 5.
157. Ibid.

decision-makers at the highest levels of the Government," and gingerly touched on "the role of senior officials who set military policy . . . individual soldiers may have been following agreed military policy." It also posed the tantalizing question, Why did "the political and military leadership . . . not revise their policies or change their course of action, despite considerable information regarding massive death and destruction in Gaza"? It further noted that the relevant Israeli bodies had not initiated judicial proceedings against the "military and civilian leadership." But still, the Report chased after the will-o'-the-wisp that if the Turkel Commission recommendations were fully implemented, Israel's judicial system would "hold to account individuals who may have played a role in wrong-doing, regardless of their position in the hierarchy."[158] In reality, if senior Israeli officials willfully persisted in a course of action causing murder and mayhem in Gaza, and if none of them was subsequently indicted, let alone convicted, it was no mystery at all as to why: the operation unfolded according to plan, and the plan enjoyed near-universal support. If the Report's authors didn't see this, that's because they didn't want to see it—and didn't want anyone who read their findings and conclusions to see it. The Report was a monument to sophistry, obfuscation, and deflection. It conjured up the absurd panacea of "comprehensive and effective accountability mechanisms,"[159] when in fact nearly the whole of (Jewish) Israeli society, from top to bottom and across the board, was united in the dual conviction—on full display in the Breaking the Silence testimonies—that Arab life was worthless and Jewish life worth its weight in gold. That, too, the Report pretended not to see, and didn't want others to see.[160] For were this sordid reality to be acknowledged, its fateful implication would have to be confronted: that the obstacle to achieving justice was not localized but systemic. Israel will not reform itself because it cannot reform itself. It is contaminated at every level, not least the judiciary, by a virulent brew of racism and arrogance freely circulating in a body politic whose immune system has collapsed. By fostering the illusion that if Israel incorporated a handful of internal administrative reforms it would heal itself, the Report conveyed and validated the utterly counterfeit image that Israel was essentially a healthy society. But a state that every couple of years launches—with over-

158. UN Report, paras. 243, 640–43, 671–72.

159. Ibid., paras. 667, 675.

160. To the contrary, it quoted wholly unrepresentative expressions of Israeli solicitude for Gazans (ibid., paras. 75, 77).

whelming popular support and without a hint of remorse—yet another high-tech blitzkrieg against a defenseless, trapped civilian population is profoundly sick. If another Protective Edge is to be avoided and the people of Gaza are to be spared another massacre, it requires pressure to be exerted from without, not meaningless, irrelevant tinkering from within.

The betrayal of Gaza by human rights organizations, chronicled in these pages, constitutes a harsh truth. Still, it must be brought to light. "The beginning of wisdom," Confucius said, "is to call things by their proper name."

FIGURE 5. *From left to right, starting at top left:* Philip Luther, Amnesty International; Kenneth Roth, Human Rights Watch; Luis Moreno-Ocampo, International Criminal Court; Mary McGowan Davis, UN Independent Commission of Inquiry; Jacques de Maio, International Committee of the Red Cross; Richard Horton, *The Lancet.*

Photo credits: Karen Hatch Photography; Harald Dettenborn; Estonian Foreign Ministry; Jean-Marc Ferré; ICRC Audiovisual Archives; Bluerasberry.

Conclusion

A 2012 UN REPORT POSED the poignant question, *Will Gaza be a "liveable place" in 2020?* Its response, based on current trends, was just barely, while it would require "herculean efforts" to reverse these trends.[1] The prognosis appeared yet bleaker a few years later. "Three Israeli military operations in the past six years, in addition to eight years of economic blockade," a 2015 United Nations Conference on Trade and Development (UNCTAD) report found, "have ravaged the already debilitated infrastructure of Gaza, shattered its productive base, left no time for meaningful reconstruction or economic recovery and impoverished the Palestinian population in Gaza." At the time of writing, some 50 percent of Gaza's population is unemployed, while 70 percent is food-insecure and dependent on humanitarian aid; 70 percent of the nearly 20,000 homes destroyed during Protective Edge have still not been rebuilt; 70 percent of Gazans have piped water supplies for only 6–8 hours every two to four days, while nearly all Gazans suffer from power outages lasting 16–18 hours each day. For the first time in a half century, a team of health researchers found, "mortality rates have increased among Palestine refugee newborns in Gaza." In answer to the question posed by the 2012 UN report, the 2015 UNCTAD report forecast that on the present trajectory, "Gaza will be unliveable" in 2020.[2] It's possible that this projection, which gave Gaza a five-year window of opportunity, was too san-

1. United Nations Country Team in the Occupied Palestinian Territory, "Gaza in 2020: A liveable place?" (2012), p. 16.
2. United Nations Conference on Trade and Development, "Report on UNCTAD Assistance to the Palestinian People: Developments in the economy of the Occupied Palestinian Territory" (July 2015), paras. 25, 60; United Nations Country Team in the State of Palestine, "Gaza: Two years after" (2016), pp. 4–5, 9; Maartje M. van den Berg et al.,

guine. Another war with Gaza was "inevitable," senior Israeli officials ominously observed in 2016. "We cannot conduct a constant war of attrition. Therefore, the next conflict has to be the last conflict."[3]

The proximate cause of Gaza's desperate plight is the siege. The 2015 UNCTAD report observed that "the complete and immediate lifting of Israel's blockade [is] more urgent than ever if Gaza is to have a chance to avoid further damage and develop into a liveable place." In a follow-up report a year later, UNCTAD again sounded the alarm: "The population of Gaza is locked in, denied access to the West Bank and the rest of the world. Even people in need of medical treatment are not allowed to travel to obtain essential health care.... Full recovery of the Gaza Strip is challenging without a lifting of the blockade, which collectively negatively affects the entire 1.8 million population of Gaza and deprives them of their economic, civil, social and cultural rights, as well as the right to development."[4] The siege, which constitutes a form of collective punishment, is a flagrant violation of international law. The UN Human Rights Council report on Operation Protective Edge, although a whitewash and a sham, nonetheless called on Israel to lift the blockade "immediately and unconditionally."[5] Israel's severe restrictions on exports from the Gaza Strip, Sara Roy of Harvard University concluded, "have little or anything to do with security.... [T]heir purpose clearly is to maintain the separation of Gaza and the West Bank."[6] Its severe travel restrictions, according to Gisha, the Israeli Legal Center for Freedom of Movement, "result more

---

"Increasing Neonatal Mortality among Palestine Refugees in the Gaza Strip," *PLOS ONE* (4 August 2015).

3. Amos Harel, "Israel's Defense Ministry Takes Harsher Tone, and IDF Better Prepare," *Haaretz* (15 June 2016); Nahum Barnea, "Israel to Build Underground Wall around Gaza Strip," *ynetnews.com* (16 June 2016).

4. United Nations Conference on Trade and Development, "Report on UNCTAD Assistance" (2015) para. 55; United Nations Conference on Trade and Development, "Report on UNCTAD Assistance to the Palestinian People: Developments in the economy of the Occupied Palestinian Territory" (September 2016), paras. 22, 28.

5. See Chapter 13.

6. Sara Roy, *The Gaza Strip: The political economy of de-development,* expanded third edition (Washington, DC: 2016), p. xxxi. A UN report concretized the impact of the export ban: "In the five-year period from 2000–2004, the average annual number of truckloads exported from Gaza stood at almost 11,500. In the first five years following the blockade, this figure dropped by 7000% to 162 truckloads per year. While there has been a recent increase (621 truckloads exported in 2015 and almost 500 truckloads so far this year), the scale of exports from Gaza is still only 5% of pre-2007 levels." United Nations Country Team, "Gaza: Two years after," p. 11.

from Israel's minimalist approach to its obligations toward the 1.8 million Palestinians living in the Gaza Strip than from its obligation to protect the security of Israeli citizens.... [The] benefits to Israeli security are hard to identify."[7] Even Israel's prestigious newspaper *Haaretz* scoffed at the notion that the blockade provided security, and called for it to be lifted: "There is no justification for the closure of Gaza. It hasn't prevented missiles from being fired at Israel. It hasn't caused the hoped-for public uprising against the Hamas government. And it constitutes an incubator for the development of despair and cycles of violence that have made the lives of residents of southern Israel intolerable.... The Israeli government must immediately end its blockade of Gaza.... This Palestinian ghetto must be opened."[8]

In all likelihood, the lethal trends prefiguring Gaza's exhaustion as a viable habitat won't be checked. The political muscle needed to reverse Israeli policy vis-à-vis Gaza is sorely lacking. In the newly emerging constellation of regional and global political alignments, Israel's star is waxing, as it has made significant diplomatic inroads among key state actors.[9] Meanwhile, Palestine's star is on the wane. Whereas it benefited from a unique salience on the world stage this past half century, the cause of Palestine has now been eclipsed by the numberless humanitarian crises wracking the Middle East. Even if and when the dust settles, it's improbable that Palestine will regain its former moral resonance. Inexorably, it will be reduced to the minuscule geopolitical weight of its demography and territory, and come more closely to resemble the self-determination struggles in East Timor and Western Sahara. If it was an uphill battle before, the path henceforth will be immeasurably steeper.

A cascade of recent developments impinging on Gaza flesh out this forbidding picture. At worst, regional players, such as Egypt, turn the screws on Gaza tighter than even Israel would counsel.[10] At best, regional players, such as Saudi Arabia, try to score points with Arab public opinion and purchase local patronage by earmarking aid packages—in the event, mostly

7. Gisha (Legal Center for Freedom of Movement), *Split Apart* (2016), p. 1. For Israel's travel restrictions on Gaza, see also Amira Hass, "Israel Clamps Down on Palestinians Seeking to Leave Gaza, Cites Security Concerns," *Haaretz* (15 July 2016).

8. "It's Been a Decade: Open Gaza, the Palestinian ghetto," *Haaretz* (17 May 2016).

9. Luke Baker, "Diplomatic Ties Help Israel Defang International Criticism," *Reuters* (5 July 2016).

10. "The Enemy of My Enemies," *Economist* (23 July 2016).

unfulfilled—for Gaza.[11] None of the regional powers, however, is about to expend political capital on Gaza's behalf. On the contrary, both Egypt and Saudi Arabia are forging a long-term strategic alliance with Israel.[12] After the *Mavi Marmara* incident, Turkey conditioned a resumption of normal relations with Israel on an end to the blockade.[13] But in 2016, President Recep Tayyip Erdoğan capitulated. He reestablished diplomatic ties after derisory Israeli concessions enabling him to save face.[14] In the meantime, the Middle East Quartet—the US, EU, UN, and Russia—issued in 2016 a long-awaited statement on the "peace process." It pinned primary culpability for the deterioration in Israeli-Gazan relations on "the illicit arms buildup and militant activity by Hamas," and it determined that "preventing the use of territory for attacks against Israel is a key commitment that is essential for long-term peace and security." Its only direct mention of the horror that unfolded during Protective Edge read, "in the course of the 2014 conflict, Israel discovered 14 tunnels penetrating its territory." The report did acknowledge in passing that the "dire humanitarian situation" in Gaza was "exacerbated by the closures of the crossings," and that "Israeli restrictions on external trade and access to fishing waters contribute to food insecurity and humanitarian aid dependency." But the Quartet called on Israel not to end but only to "accelerate the lifting of movement and access restrictions to and from Gaza," and then interpolated the escape clause that "due consideration" should be given to Israel's "need to protect its citizens from terrorist attacks."[15] Thus, so long as Israel purports that sealing off Gaza from the outside world is necessary to protect itself from Hamas terrorism—or, in other words, until and unless Gaza surrenders its fate to Israel—the siege will continue with the Quartet's

11. Association of International Development Agencies, "Charting a New Course: Overcoming the stalemate in Gaza" (2015), p. 16, table B; Annie Slemrod, "18 Months On, Gaza Donors Still Falling Way Short," *IRIN* (18 April 2016).

12. Ben Caspit, "Is Israel Forming an Alliance with Saudi Arabia and Egypt?," *Al-Monitor* (13 April 2016); Zena Tahhan, "Egypt-Israel Relations 'at Highest Level' in History," *Al Jazeera* (20 November 2016).

13. See Part Three.

14. Turkey was permitted to deliver humanitarian aid and build a hospital, power station, and desalination plant in Gaza. If Israel made these "concessions," Prime Minister Benjamin Netanyahu declared, it was because Israel would also stand to benefit from them. Barak Ravid, "Israel and Turkey Officially Announce Rapprochement Deal, Ending Diplomatic Crisis," *Haaretz* (27 June 2016). See also Raphael Ahren, "Taking Up Post, Turkish Envoy Hails New Start with 'Friend Israel,'" *Times of Israel* (12 December 2016).

15. "Report of the Middle East Quartet" (1 July 2016). The report vaguely alluded to the destruction wreaked by Protective Edge.

blessing. Of the complementary international reconstruction plans for Gaza, Roy observes, they "read more like security plans, carefully laying out Israeli concerns and the ways in which the United Nations will accommodate them.... Israel must approve all projects and their locations, and will be able to veto any aspect of the process on security grounds.... [N]ot only will the blockade of Gaza be maintained, but responsibility for maintaining it will in effect be transferred to the UN, which is tasked with monitoring the entire process of which Israel retains full control."[16] True, after a visit to Gaza in 2016, UN secretary-general Ban Ki-moon told a news conference, "The closure of Gaza suffocates its people, stifles its economy and impedes reconstruction efforts. It is a collective punishment for which there must be accountability."[17] Alas, he only reached this epiphany six months before the end of his ten-year term of office. In the instant case, late was not better than never; it *was* never.

Gaza has not yet crossed the threshold of no return. To be sure, one would have to be blinder than King Lear to believe that diplomatic negotiations in and of themselves might yet yield fruit. When the current phase of the "peace process" was inaugurated in 1993, 250,000 illegal Jewish settlers resided in the occupied Palestinian territory; by 2016, 600,000 settlers resided in the West Bank (including East Jerusalem). The bitter fruit it yielded in Gaza requires no further comment. If the essence of a phenomenon is to be grasped not in its packaging but in its content, then Palestine has borne witness not to a peace process but to an *annexation-cum-despoliation process*. The Quartet report called for the "resumption of meaningful negotiations." But it isn't possible to resume what never began. Still, it is no more likely that Hamas's strategy of armed resistance can achieve substantive results. However legally and morally defensible, firing bottle rockets at one of the world's most formidable military powers will not bring it to its knees. It merely provides Israel with a convenient alibi when it periodically decides—in pursuit of objectives wholly divorced from these rockets—to annihilate Gaza.

A strategy of mass nonviolent resistance, by contrast, might yet turn the tide. Gaza's richest resources are its people, the truth, and public opinion. Time and again, and come what may, the people of Gaza have evinced a granite will, born of a "sheer indomitable dignity" (UNRWA spokesperson Chris

16. Roy, *Gaza Strip*, pp. 407–9.

17. United Nations Relief and Works Agency (UNRWA), "Remarks by UN Secretary-General Ban Ki-moon at Press Encounter in Gaza" (28 June 2016).

Gunness), not to be held in bondage.[18] Protective Edge battered that will but, it appears, did not yet shatter it. Truth is on the side of Gaza. If this book rises to a crescendo of anger and indignation, it's because the endless lies about Gaza by those who know better cause one's innards to writhe. Gandhi called his doctrine of nonviolence *satyagraha,* which he translated as "Hold on to the Truth." If the people of Gaza, in their multitudes, hold on to the truth, it's possible—which is not to say probable, let alone certain, just possible, and not without immense personal sacrifice, up to and including death—that Israel can be forced to lift the suffocating blockade. "What Iron Dome or what tunnel detection system can stop them," an Israeli observer rhetorically asked, "if one day a few tens of thousands, or maybe a few hundreds of thousands, decide to climb the fence, or hold a hunger strike next to it?"[19] The cause of Palestine still inspires and can draw from huge reserves of international public support, including in recent years wide swaths of Jewish opinion estranged from Israel's lurch rightward and leap into the moral abyss.[20] At the core of this mass of sympathetic opinion stands an international solidarity movement ready, willing, and able, when the moment of reckoning is upon it, to give its all for Gaza. If the people of Gaza, on the one hand, and global public opinion, on the other, are mobilized, galvanized, and organized; and if a cause guided by truth, fortified by law, animated by righteousness, and bending toward justice can unleash, as history is testament, an irresistible moral power able to defeat, disarm, and diffuse brute force; then a small miracle might yet come to pass: the people of Gaza will be able, at least, at last, to breathe again and ultimately, if they—if we all—persevere, to end the occupation.

In *A Century of Dishonor,* written at the end of the 19th century, Helen Hunt Jackson chronicled the destruction of the Native American population by conscious, willful government policy. The book was largely ignored, then

18. Sara Roy, "Interview: Chris Gunness," *Middle East Policy* (Spring 2016), p. 146. UNRWA is the major refugee relief organization in Gaza.

19. Zvi Bar'el, "Israeli Security Assessments Are Reality Built on a Lie," *Haaretz* (19 April 2016).

20. Norman G. Finkelstein, *"This Time We Went Too Far": Truth and consequences of the Gaza invasion,* expanded paperback edition (New York: 2011), pp. 107–29; Norman G. Finkelstein, *Knowing Too Much: Why the American Jewish romance with Israel is coming to an end* (New York: 2012).

forgotten, and finally rediscovered by later generations ready to hear and bear the truth. Speaking to the fate of the Cherokee nation, which was expelled from one tribal homeland after another and finally stripped of its tribal holdings by the US government, Jackson wrote, "there is no record so black as the record of its perfidy to this nation."[21] The present volume was modeled after her searing requiem. The author holds out faint hope that it will find an audience among his contemporaries. Still, the truth should be preserved; it is the least that's owed the victims. Perhaps one day in the remote future, when the tenor of the times is more receptive, someone will stumble across this book collecting dust on a library shelf, blow off the cobwebs, and be stung by outrage at the lot of a people, if not forsaken by God then betrayed by the cupidity and corruption, careerism and cynicism, cravenness and cowardice of mortal man. "There will come a time," Jackson anticipated, "when, to the student of American history, it will seem well-nigh incredible" what was done to the Cherokee. Is it not certain that one day the black record of Gaza's martyrdom will in retrospect also seem well-nigh incredible?

21. Helen Hunt Jackson, *A Century of Dishonor: A sketch of the United States government's dealings with some of the Indian tribes* (Boston: 1889), p. 270.

APPENDIX

Is the Occupation Legal?

ABSTRACT

A broad consensus exists among representative and authoritative bodies that under international law, the Israeli blockade of the Gaza Strip is illegal and, even after its 2005 redeployment, Israel remains the occupying power in Gaza. But what is the legal status of the Israeli occupation itself? The essence of an occupation under international law is that it is a temporary situation. An occupation that does not *and cannot* end is de facto an irreversible annexation. Inasmuch as the acquisition of territory by war is illegal under international law, an occupation that morphs into an irreversible annexation must also be illegal. In light of the International Court of Justice's jurisprudence in the *Namibia* case, on the one hand, and Israel's persistent refusal to negotiate an end to the occupation on the basis of international law, on the other, it is submitted that the Israeli occupation of the West Bank, including East Jerusalem, and the Gaza Strip, has become illegal under international law. As such, Israel has forfeited its rights as an occupying power. The one and only "right" still accruing to it is to execute a full withdrawal from the Palestinian territories that it illegally occupies.

1.0. THE INTERNATIONAL LAW OF OCCUPATION

1.1. *Does the legal status of an occupation depend on how it originated?*

1.1.1. The broad consensus is that international law does not distinguish between a military occupation that results from a war of self-defense and a military occupation that results from a war of aggression. The same rights and obligations, codified in the Hague Regulations (1907) and the Fourth Geneva Convention (1949), accrue to the occupying power in either case.[1] It thus resembles the laws of war, which

---

1. Adam Roberts, "What Is a Military Occupation?" (1985), pp. 293–94, bybil.oxford journals.org/content/55/1/249.full.pdf.

apply equally to both parties in a conflict regardless of which side initiated it and which acted in self-defense.

1.1.2. A dissenting view, based on more recent developments in international law, holds that military occupation is intrinsically illegal, as it results from illegal use of force and violates the customary law of self-determination. The sole exception would be an occupation that both ensues from lawful use of force and is of limited duration.[2]

1.1.2.1. Even if one subscribes to the novel contention that a military occupation is inherently illegal, and even if the Israeli occupation did not qualify as an exception, it still could not circumvent the fact that UN Security Council resolution 242, which endures as the recognized basis for resolving the Israel-Palestine conflict, made Israel's withdrawal conditional on a negotiated agreement. However it originated, Israel's occupation cannot then be illegal by virtue of it *being* an occupation.

1.1.2.2. The preambular paragraph of a December 1975 General Assembly resolution, "Implementation of the Declaration on the Granting of Independence to Colonial Countries and Peoples" (3481), recited that "any military occupation, however temporary," constituted an "act of aggression," and an operative paragraph accordingly "condemn[ed] Israel's occupation of Arab territories in violation of the Charter of the United Nations, the principles of international law and repeated United Nations resolutions."[3] But this isolated resolution does not appear to have had political consequence or diplomatic resonance.

1.1.3. In the early years of the occupation, it was alleged by Israel's supporters that insofar as Israel came to administer the Arab territories while fighting a defensive war, it was a "lawful entrant [that] has a right of occupation ... pending conclusion of a peace treaty."[4] If the Israeli occupation was legal, it was allegedly because it sprang from a war of self-defense.

1.1.3.1. This contention was anchored in the two-pronged claim that Israel (believed it) faced an imminent Egyptian attack when it struck in 1967, and that Israel's resort to force was subsequently validated by the United Nations. A careful reading of the documentary record shows, however, that an Egyptian attack was not impending, Israeli leaders did not fear such an attack, and the international community did not ex post facto embrace Israel's "narrative" of the chain of events climaxing in its first strike.[5]

---

2. Antonio Cassese, *Self-Determination of Peoples: A legal reappraisal* (Cambridge: 1995), pp. 55, 90–99, 335.

3. I am grateful to Professor John Quigley for this reference.

4. Allan Gerson, *Israel, the West Bank and International Law* (London: 1978), pp. 75–76.

5. Norman G. Finkelstein, *Knowing Too Much: Why the American Jewish romance with Israel is coming to an end* (New York: 2012), pp. 170–75, 205–8. Israel's leading authority on international law, Yoram Dinstein, has consistently maintained that Israel's first strike

1.1.4. Even though the international community did not embrace Israel's "narrative" of how it came to occupy Arab lands, it did not call on Israel to unilaterally withdraw. After protracted debate, first in the General Assembly and then in the Security Council,[6] the United Nations resolved, in 242, to make an Israeli withdrawal from occupied Arab territory (in accordance with the customary rule of the "inadmissibility of the acquisition of territory by war") conditional upon the "termination of all claims or states of belligerency" by neighboring Arab countries (in accordance with the principle of international law barring "threat or use of force against the territorial integrity or political independence of any state").

1.1.5. The essential picture, then, is that the legality of Israel's occupation does not hinge on how it originated. Whether the occupation resulted from a war of self-defense or a war of aggression is beside the point. Even if Israel's claim of self-defense could be shown to be false, still Israel was not legally bound to withdraw so long as neighboring Arab countries did not recognize its reciprocal rights as a State. The Israeli occupation "had no time-limit" and "could, from the legal point of view, continue indefinitely," former Israeli chief justice Meir Shamgar inferred, "pending an alternative political or military solution."[7]

1.2. *The legal status of a recalcitrant occupier*

1.2.1. But could the Israeli occupation "from the legal point of view . . . continue indefinitely" if Israel balked at withdrawal even after Arab States expressed a readi-

---

was lawful. But he simultaneously maintains that international law permits use of force in "self-defense" only in response to an "armed attack" or—in his various formulations—"the imminence of an armed attack," "as soon as it becomes evident to the victim State (on the basis of hard intelligence evidence at the time) that the attack is in the process of being mounted," "after the other side has committed itself to an armed attack in an ostensibly irrevocable way." In order to reconcile Israel's resort to armed force in 1967 with the stringent criteria he sets forth, Dinstein asserts that "the Israeli campaign amounted to an interceptive self-defense, in response to an incipient armed attack by Egypt . . . it seemed to be crystal-clear that Egypt was bent on an armed attack, and the sole question was not whether war would materialize but when." The single piece of evidence Dinstein adduces in support of this pivotal point, however, consists of an article he published 40 years ago. He willfully ignores the voluminous record that has since become available showing that Egypt was not poised to attack, and Israeli leaders did not believe an attack was imminent when they struck. Incidentally, if except for an armed attack the only situation allowing for resort to force in self-defense is the "imminence" of a strike, wouldn't the "sole question" of "when" Egypt was planning to attack be critical? Yoram Dinstein, *War, Aggression and Self-Defence,* fourth edition (Cambridge: 2005), pp. 182–92. For misrepresentations of the 1967 war in legal scholarship, see especially John Quigley, *The Six-Day War and Israeli Self-Defense: Questioning the legal basis for preventive war* (Cambridge: 2013).

6. Finkelstein, *Knowing Too Much,* pp. 209–16.

7. Meir Shamgar, "Legal Concepts and Problems of the Israeli Military Government—The initial stage," in Meir Shamgar, ed., *Military Government in the Territories Administered by Israel 1967–1980: The legal aspects,* vol. 1 (Jerusalem: 1982), p. 43 (see also p. 46).

ness to recognize it? Shamgar entered the critical caveat, "pending an alternative political . . . solution." What if Israel were offered such a solution, but rejected it?

1.2.2. This question first arose in the context of Israel's occupation (following the 1967 war) of the Egyptian Sinai. In the course of UN-mandated mediation (the "Jarring Mission"), Egypt had agreed to a full peace treaty with Israel, but Israel still refused to withdraw from the Sinai. Once these negotiations broke down, and all avenues toward a diplomatic settlement were thwarted by Israeli intransigence, Egypt repeatedly warned that it would go to war in order to recover the occupied Sinai. It made good on this threat in 1973.[8]

1.2.2.1. Just before Egypt launched its offensive, the UN Security Council convened to deliberate on the diplomatic impasse. Israel purported that per resolution 242, it was not obliged to withdraw until and unless a mutually agreed upon resolution of the conflict was reached. The Kingdom of Jordan cogently rejoined, however, that disputing axiomatic legal principles did not constitute negotiations but, instead, was tantamount to evading a settlement:

> While agreement has a necessary and proper place in the peace-making efforts, it should not be allowed to be employed as a subversive tactic and pretext. One cannot reopen every established and fundamental principle of the [UN] Charter and its logical consequences . . . at every juncture at which a party to a dispute deems it serviceable to its illegitimate interest to veto the application of the principles. . . . We wish that complete withdrawal should occur through agreement. But if the party in occupation and in objective opposition to a just settlement insists on placing its non-agreement as a barrier to both withdrawal and peace, what are we to do?[9]

1.2.2.2. A draft resolution tabled at this Council session "strongly deplore[d] Israel's continuing occupation of the territories occupied as a result of the 1967 war."[10] In his gloss on the resolution, the Indian drafter stated, "[W]e totally reject any claim that either resolution 242 (1967) or the cease-fire agreement in any way gives tolerance, much less authority, direct or indirect, tacit or implicit or explicit, for Israeli forces to *continue* to occupy Arab territories."[11] The United States vetoed the resolution on the grounds that condemning the Israeli occupation "bears no relationship to the provisions and principles of resolution 242 (1967)."[12] But the consensus opinion minus the American delegate was that once Israel refused to

8. Norman G. Finkelstein, *Image and Reality of the Israel-Palestine Conflict,* expanded second paperback edition (New York: 2003), pp. 150–71.

9. *United Nations Security Council Official Records,* S/PV.1735 (26 July 1973), paras. 46–47; hereafter: *UNSCOR.*

10. Security Council draft res. S/10974, reproduced in M. Cherif Bassiouni, ed., *Documents of the Arab-Israeli Conflict: Emergence of conflict in Palestine and the Arab-Israeli wars and peace process,* vol. 1 (Ardsley, NY: 2005), pp. 631–32.

11. *UNSCOR,* S/PV.1735 (26 July 1973), para. 86, emphasis added.

12. Ibid., para. 129.

negotiate a peaceful settlement based on international law, it effectively forfeited its right to *be* an occupant. In keeping with this determination, after Egypt crossed the Suez Canal in October 1973 in order to eject the Israeli occupier and recover the Sinai, "not a single government accused Egypt of 'aggression,'" as Abba Eban later rued in his memoir, *not even the United States.*[13]

1.2.3. The scholarly literature on the law of occupation makes scant mention of the legal status of a recalcitrant occupier. The most comprehensive study to date, Yutaka Arai-Takahashi's *The Law of Occupation: Continuity and change of international humanitarian law, and its interaction with international human rights law,*[14] doesn't contemplate such a scenario. Yoram Dinstein's *The International Law of Belligerent Occupation* disposes of the "myth" that an occupation "becomes in time inherently illegal under international law" in one curt, unenlightening paragraph.[15]

1.2.3.1. An article by Orna Ben-Naftali, Aeyal Gross, and Keren Michaeli, "Illegal Occupation: Framing the occupied Palestinian territory,"[16] is often cited by writers who assert that Israel's occupation is illegal. It argues, albeit in occasionally opaque language, that the infrastructure Israel has entrenched in the West Bank (settlements, bypass roads, the wall, etc.) constitutes a "de facto annexation," in violation of the "basic principle of temporariness" that defines an occupation, and that Israel has also committed "gross violations of humanitarian and human rights norms" in the annexation process. The cumulative effect of these illegal Israeli actions, the authors conclude, has been to render the occupation illegal. The force of this thesis is that Israel has been pursuing policies that will *eventually* and *inexorably* make the occupation irreversible, in breach of its obligations as an occupier, on the one hand, and the Palestinian right to self-determination, on the other. But inasmuch as Israeli settlements, etc., have not *yet* made the occupation irreversible, it appears legally more nuanced, and in keeping with precedent, to discretely condemn the illegal Israeli practices without however declaring the occupation as such illegal.

1.2.3.1.1. The UN Security Council has designated Israel's settlement policy and annexation of East Jerusalem illegal,[17] and the General Assembly has referred to Israel's "de facto annexation of large areas of territory."[18]

---

13. Abba Eban, *Personal Witness: Israel through my eyes* (New York: 1992), p. 541; William B. Quandt, *Peace Process: American diplomacy and the Arab-Israeli conflict since 1967* (Berkeley: 1993), p. 152.

14. Leiden: 2009.

15. Cambridge: 2009, p. 2, para. 5.

16. *Berkeley Journal of International Law* (2005). See also Aeyal Gross, "A Temporary Place of Permanence," *Haaretz* (27 October 2015).

17. United Nations Security Council (UNSC) resolution 446 (22 March 1979); UNSC resolution 478 (20 August 1980).

18. United Nations General Assembly resolution ES 10/14 (8 December 2003).

1.2.3.1.2. In its 2004 landmark advisory opinion, *Legal Consequences of the Construction of a Wall in the Occupied Palestinian Territory,* the International Court of Justice (ICJ) more tentatively stated, "the construction of the wall and its associated régime create a 'fait accompli' on the ground that *could* well become permanent, in which case, and notwithstanding the formal characterization of the wall by Israel, it *would* be tantamount to de facto annexation."[19] In a separate opinion, however, Judge Koroma concluded without qualification that "the construction of the wall has involved the annexation of parts of the occupied territory by Israel."[20]

1.2.3.1.3. Eminent international law specialist James Crawford has observed that the Israeli settlements constitute a "de facto annexation of West Bank territory that ... has prevented the Palestinian people from exercising their right to self-determination."[21]

1.2.3.1.4. However, neither the Security Council nor the General Assembly, neither Judge Koroma nor Crawford, determined that Israel's annexation of Palestinian territory perforce rendered the occupation itself illegal. The prudent determination would appear to be that even if an occupier's recalcitrance has over time resulted in a de facto (or, in the case of East Jerusalem, de jure) annexation, it doesn't yet illegalize the occupation as such.

1.2.3.1.5. For the record, Israel's official position is that the Jewish settlements, and the wall running along the periphery of the major settlement blocs, are "inherently temporary" (Israel High Court of Justice),[22] and "do not annex territories to the State of Israel."[23] In the course of the wall's construction, however, senior Israeli government officials, including former justice minister Tzipi Livni, former prime minister Ariel Sharon, and former defense minister Ehud Barak, publicly conceded that the wall marked off Israel's future border.[24]

1.2.3.2. Israeli legal scholar Eyal Benvenisti tackles the legal challenge posed by a recalcitrant occupier from a different angle in *The International Law of Occupation.* He begins (like Shamgar) by asserting that international law neither "limits the duration of the occupation [n]or requires the occupant to restore the territories to

---

19. *Legal Consequences of the Construction of a Wall in the Occupied Palestinian Territory,* Advisory Opinion, I.C.J. Reports (2004), p. 184, para. 121, emphases added.

20. Judge Koroma, Separate Opinion, ibid., p. 204, para. 2.

21. James Crawford SC, "Third Party Obligations with Respect to Israeli Settlements in the Occupied Palestinian Territories" (July 2012); copy on file with this writer.

22. HCJ 7957/04, *Zaharan Yunis Muhammad Mara'abe v. The Prime Minister of Israel* (15 September 2005), para. 100.

23. *UNSCOR,* S/PV.4841 (14 October 2003), p. 10.

24. B'Tselem (Israeli Information Center for Human Rights in the Occupied Territories), *Arrested Development: The long term impact of Israel's separation barrier in the West Bank* (October 2012), pp. 5, 75.

the sovereign before a peace treaty is signed." However, Benvenisti then enters this caveat:

> an occupation regime that refuses to earnestly contribute to efforts to reach a peaceful solution should be considered illegal. Indeed, such a refusal should be considered outright annexation. The occupant has a duty under international law to conduct negotiations in good faith for a peaceful solution. It would seem that an occupant who proposes unreasonable conditions, or otherwise obstructs negotiations for peace for the purpose of retaining control over the occupied territory, could be considered a violator of international law.

He goes on to observe that "an occupant that in bad faith stalls efforts for a peaceful ending to its rule would be considered an aggressor and its rule be tainted with illegality."[25]

1.2.4. The determination that if an occupier negotiates in bad faith, then it has "tainted" the occupation "with illegality" was in fact already arrived at in the *Namibia* case. After protracted, fruitless negotiations, the UN General Assembly followed by the Security Council passed resolutions declaring South Africa's "occupation" of Namibia "illegal," and subsequently the ICJ upheld the validity of these UN decisions. The *Namibia* case bears strong resemblances to the Israeli occupation of Palestinian territory. Its unfolding and denouement provide a road map for the international community as it confronts another recalcitrant occupier.

2.0. THE *NAMIBIA* CASE

2.1. *Historical context*

2.1.1. Although largely forgotten today, in the mid-20th century the Namibia Mandate of South Africa "prompted more resolutions, promoted more committees and produced more judicial decisions," recalled leading authority John Dugard, "than any other matter to come before the organs of the United Nations." It was, in Dugard's words, "the international *cause célèbre*"[26] or, as one of the ICJ judges hearing the case put it, "the most explosive international issue of the post-war world."[27] In later years, it was displaced on the international agenda by the larger question of South African apartheid, of which Namibia was henceforth a subsidiary issue, and

25. Eyal Benvenisti, *The International Law of Occupation* (Princeton: 1993), pp. 145–46, 214–16.

26. John Dugard, ed., *The South West Africa/Namibia Dispute: Documents and scholarly writings on the controversy between South Africa and the United Nations* (Berkeley: 1973), p. xi.

27. Judge Nervo, Dissenting Opinion, *South West Africa Cases (Ethiopia v. South Africa; Liberia v. South Africa)*, Second Phase, Judgment, I.C.J. Reports (1966), p. 452.

by the Palestine question, which was the other gaping wound lingering from the Mandates era.

2.1.2. After seizing power in Russia, the Bolsheviks denounced World War I as imperialistic and trumpeted their support for the principle of self-determination of oppressed nations. Largely in reaction and as a result, US president Woodrow Wilson himself championed the right of self-determination and imposed on the Allied Powers the principle of nonannexation of the colonies of the defeated Central Powers.[28]

2.1.3. A Mandates System was created at war's end and codified in Article 22 of the League of Nations Covenant. Each of the former colonies of the Central Powers, allegedly "not yet able to stand by themselves under the strenuous conditions of the modern world," came under the "tutelage" of an "advanced nation" that was mandated to prepare it for the exercise of self-determination. The tutelary role of the Mandatory power, acting "on behalf of the League" to promote the ex-colony's "well-being and development," was denoted a "sacred trust of civilization."

2.1.4. The Mandate over the former German colony of Namibia (South-West Africa) was "conferred on His Britannic Majesty to be exercised on His behalf by the Government of the Union of South Africa." Under the Mandate's terms and subject to oversight by the League (and ultimately the Permanent Court of International Justice), South Africa was obliged to "promote to the utmost the material and moral well-being and the social progress of the inhabitants."

2.1.5. After the League's dissolution in 1946, it was "clearly contemplated"[29] that the Namibia Mandate would be converted into a UN Trusteeship, en route to statehood.[30] South Africa envisaged a different future, however, as it was intent on annexing Namibia (or the most desirable parts thereof).[31]

---

28. The Soviet Union was also the driving force behind decolonization and self-determination in the international arena after World War II. James Crawford, *The Creation of States in International Law*, second edition (Oxford: 2006), p. 108; Cassese, *Self-Determination*, pp. 19, 38, 44–52, 71, 321; David Raič, *Statehood and the Law of Self-Determination* (The Hague: 2002), pp. 200, 204. For the Wilson-Lenin relationship, see Erez Manela, *The Wilsonian Moment: Self-determination and the international origins of anticolonial nationalism* (Oxford: 2007), p. 41. Besides hoping to steal the Bolsheviks' thunder, Wilson pressed the principle of self-determination in order to preempt Japan's acquisition of strategic Pacific islands.

29. *Legal Consequences for States*, I.C.J. Reports (1971), p. 33, para. 56.

30. The Trusteeship System, established under Chapters XII–XIII of the UN Charter, had essentially the same goal as the Mandates System, namely of preparing territories under its aegis for self-government.

31. Solomon Slonim, *South West Africa and the United Nations: An international mandate in dispute* (Baltimore: 1973), pp. 75–109. By the early 1950s, South Africa had effectively annexed Namibia. In the late 1950s, South Africa mooted the partition, and its annexation of a part, of South-West Africa but was overwhelmingly rebuffed by the United Nations. (A

2.1.6. Thence ensued a protracted political and legal tug-of-war. The United Nations, led by a contingent of African States, demanded that South Africa recognize the General Assembly's supervisory powers and Namibia's right to independence, while in the face of Pretoria's persistent stonewalling, it simultaneously kept referring the Namibia question to the ICJ in order to clarify and certify South Africa's legal obligations.

2.1.7. A sequence of contentious and divisive proceedings unfolded at The Hague.

2.1.7.1. In a 1950 advisory opinion, *International Status of South-West Africa,* the ICJ concluded that even after dissolution of the League of Nations, South Africa was still duty-bound to promote the "material and moral well-being and the social progress of the inhabitants"; that the League's supervisory powers over South Africa's Mandate had been transferred to the General Assembly; and—controversially—that although "it was expected that the mandatory States would follow the normal course indicated by the Charter, namely, conclude Trusteeship Agreements," still South Africa was not legally obligated to convert its Mandate into a UN Trusteeship, but it also couldn't unilaterally modify South-West Africa's international status.

2.1.7.1.1. In a cluster of dissents on this last point, Judge Álvarez asserted that "The Union of South Africa . . . has the legal obligation to negotiate and conclude an agreement with the United Nations to place South-West Africa under Trusteeship"; Judge de Visscher (supported by Vice President Guerrero, Judge Zoričić, and Judge Badawi Pasha) opined that South Africa incurred a "legal obligation to be ready to take part in negotiations and to conduct them in good faith with a view to conclud-

---

handful of countries, notably the US and UK, initially supported the South African démarche.) During later General Assembly debates, the delegate from Ghana distilled the South African objective thusly:

> [T]he indigenous African population was to be uprooted in order to constitute twelve artificial territorial and ethnic groupings or "homelands." In the homelands they would develop separately, each group according to its own racial talents and resources. The bulk of the habitable land in South West Africa, together with all its diamond mines and most of its other mines, would become the exclusive reserve for the white settler-descendants of the Boers, Germans and English. By a clever gerrymandering maneuver the demarcations of the settlers' homelands are carefully drawn around mineral deposits, seaports, transportation and communication facilities and urban areas.

The US delegate represented the South African plan as "plainly designed to fragment the Territory on apartheid principles"; as allocating "over one-half the Territory, including the farms, mines, and towns of the heartland, to the 16 percent of the population who are white, with the non-white majority consigned to less desirable and fractionalized units, cut off from the sea and without hope of independent economic development"; and as "a denial of self-determination and a means of perpetuating white supremacy." *General Assembly Official Records* (hereafter: *GAOR*), A/PV.1635 (16 December 1967), para. 72; *GAOR,* A/PV.1658 (20 May 1968), para. 57; *GAOR,* A/PV.1737 (10 December 1968), para. 118.

ing a [Trusteeship] agreement"; and Judge Krylov maintained that South Africa was "under the legal obligation to negotiate with a view to concluding a Trusteeship Agreement."[32]

2.1.7.2. A 1955 advisory opinion, *South-West Africa—Voting Procedure,* hinged on a technical point regarding the substance and procedure of General Assembly oversight of South Africa's Namibia Mandate. The Court upheld the Assembly's prerogatives.[33]

2.1.7.3. In a 1956 advisory opinion, *Admissibility of Hearings of Petitioners by the Committee on South West Africa,* the Court upheld the General Assembly's right to make use of supplementary procedures (such as oral testimonies by Namibian petitioners before a UN subcommittee) to facilitate its supervisory function in the face of South African intransigence.[34]

2.1.8. The proceedings at The Hague reached a tempestuous denouement in a pair of complementary yet contradictory Court decisions in 1962 and 1966.

2.1.8.1. Ethiopia and Liberia, both formerly belonging to the League of Nations, invoked a clause of the League Mandate enabling then Member States to contest via Court adjudication a Mandatory's conduct. They requested from the ICJ not an advisory opinion but an enforceable judgment[35] on (inter alia) their contention that South Africa had breached its obligations "to promote to the utmost the material and moral well-being and social progress of the inhabitants" of Namibia, and instead "practiced *apartheid,* i.e., [it] has distinguished as to race, color, national or tribal origin, in establishing the rights and duties of the inhabitants."

2.1.8.2. The (in)famous case divided into two theoretically discrete phases, "jurisdiction" and "merits." In its 1962 judgment, the Court answered affirmatively that it had jurisdiction to render a decision.[36] But then in the 1966 judgment, when it was

---

32. *International Status of South-West Africa,* Advisory Opinion, I.C.J. Reports (1950), pp. 133–45. Judge Álvarez, Dissenting Opinion, ibid., p. 184. Judge de Visscher, Dissenting Opinion, ibid., p. 188. Judge Krylov, Dissenting Opinion, ibid., p. 191.

33. *South-West Africa—Voting Procedure,* Advisory Opinion, I.C.J. Reports (1955), pp. 67–78. This case is probably best remembered for Judge Lauterpacht's elegant (if elusive) parsing in his separate opinion of the legal status of General Assembly resolutions (ibid., pp. 118–20).

34. *Admissibility of Hearings of Petitioners by the Committee on South West Africa,* Advisory Opinion, I.C.J. Reports (1956), pp. 26–32.

35. According to Article 94 of the UN Charter, "Each Member of the United Nations undertakes to comply with the decision of the International Court of Justice in any case to which it is a party," and "If any party to a case fails to perform the obligations incumbent upon it under a judgment rendered by the Court, the other party may have recourse to the Security Council, which may, if it deems necessary, make recommendations or decide upon measures to be taken to give effect to the judgment."

36. *South West Africa Cases (Ethiopia v. South Africa; Liberia v. South Africa),* First Phase, Preliminary Objections, I.C.J. Reports (1962).

due to decide on the merits of the case against South Africa,[37] the ICJ effectively reversed itself,[38] declaring, in "the most controversial judgment in its history,"[39] that it in fact lacked jurisdiction, as the Applicant States could not demonstrate "any legal right or interest appertaining to them in the subject-matter" of their brief against South Africa.[40]

2.1.8.3. Whereas both phases of the case formally turned on technical, linguistic, and historical arcana—what Judge Forster in his dissent rightly ridiculed as "an arid scrutiny and relentless analysis"[41]—and whereas it was subsequently purported by judges in the case and by legal commentators alike that it was conflicting judicial philosophies ("teleologists" versus "positivists") that rent the Court, a disinterested observer cannot but conclude that each side was able to marshal compelling evidence,[42] that the case each side mounted at The Hague was tendentious, and

37. *South West Africa Cases*, Second Phase, Judgment, I.C.J. Reports (1966).

38. Between 1962 and 1966, the composition of the Court had changed, shifting its ideological balance to the right.

39. Dugard, *South West Africa/Namibia*, p. 292.

40. *South West Africa Cases*, Second Phase, Judgment, I.C.J. Reports (1966), p. 51. Although concurring with the Court majority's finding in its 1966 judgment, Slonim nonetheless concedes, "Despite the disclaimer of the Court, it is quite clear that the 1966 decision, in fact, if not in technical form, represents a reversal of the 1962 judgment" (*South West Africa*, p. 284). He defends the Court's volte-face on the grounds that in the course of the protracted pleadings it became apparent that South Africa's apartheid policy in Namibia— "the 'heart' of the entire proceedings" (ibid., p. 224)—was "nonjusticiable," i.e., not susceptible to judicial supervision (pp. 297–98), and that, therefore, the Court had to dismiss the Applicants' submission that South Africa had breached the Mandate's terms. This thesis falls on multiple counts: (1) the Court itself did not make such a determination in its 1966 judgment but, instead, leaned on an alleged technical distinction in the Mandate's adjudicatory (compromissory) clause; (2) although Slonim persuasively argues that Counsel for the Applicants dreadfully botched the case—in particular, the "standard" or "norm" it proposed for condemning South Africa was untenable—it would also appear, and Slonim himself implicitly acknowledges (ibid., pp. 300–301, 305–6), that a competent Counsel could have mounted a credible case, on the basis of which the Court might have found in favor of the Applicants; and (3) in its 1971 opinion, the Court did find, essentially relying on the theory mooted by Counsel for the Applicants in 1966, that South Africa's apartheid policy in Namibia constituted a "flagrant violation of the purposes and principles" of the UN Charter. *Legal Consequences for States*, I.C.J. Reports (1971), p. 57, paras. 129–31. Whether the Court decided correctly is beside the point; the fact is, it did not find the apartheid policy inherently nonjusticiable. But see also Slonim, *South West Africa*, p. 338n132.

41. Judge Forster, Dissenting Opinion, *South West Africa Cases*, Second Phase, Judgment, I.C.J. Reports (1966), p. 482.

42. It was probably true that the Mandatory powers, which were never truly committed to nonannexation, had tacitly acquiesced in South Africa's eventual incorporation of South-West Africa, but it was equally true that the letter of the Mandate barred such annexation. See Susan Pedersen, *The Guardians: The League of Nations and the crisis of empire* (Oxford: 2015).

that the schism on the Court was, at its core, and however crude and reductionist it might sound, *political:* the Old World colonial powers straining to rein in the non-Western upstarts, albeit with the curious anomaly that whereas the Old World was predictably represented by a tenacious and learned, if frankly obnoxious, Brit on the Court, Judge Fitzmaurice, his archnemesis, who was also every bit his athletic and intellectual match, happened to be an *American,* Judge Jessup.[43] In a rare departure from judicial etiquette (which sustains the illusion of law standing above the political fray), Judge de Castro, in a later separate opinion, baldly (but still accurately) depicted the ICJ proceedings on Namibia as in their essence "the struggle between the colonialists and progressives."[44]

2.2. South Africa's failure to negotiate in good faith: UN deliberations

2.2.1. Appalled by the ICJ's dismissal-by-deflection of the case against South Africa, and the attendant squandering of years of time and resources invested in legal proceedings,[45] the United Nations took a series of dramatic and drastic steps to right the Court's wrong. A 1966 General Assembly resolution (2145) "terminated"

---

43. In the preliminary phase, Judge Jessup submitted a 50-page concurring separate opinion and Judge Fitzmaurice (alongside Judge Spender, an Australian) submitted a 100-page dissenting opinion, while in the merits phase, the main opinion, apparently drafted by Fitzmaurice (he had a distinctive literary style), ran to 50 pages and Jessup's dissenting opinion came to over 100 pages.

44. Judge de Castro, Separate Opinion, *Legal Consequences for States,* I.C.J. Reports (1971), p. 211.

45. The merits phase of the proceedings lasted some three years, while both phases combined lasted five years and produced nearly seven thousand pages of printed record covering both the written and oral pleadings. From a judicial perspective, the real tragedy of the ICJ's decision not to weigh the merits of the case against South Africa was that it missed a unique opportunity to capture in the idiom of law exactly what made the system of apartheid reprehensible. The fact is, prima facie, South Africa did mount a credible defense, to wit: apartheid (in particular, its finished form of "separate development" in independent homelands) merely constituted an application of the self-determination principle to culturally distinct tribes, while the tribal conflicts plaguing the African continent attested to the folly of enclosing heterogeneous groups within one and the same border. South Africa's brief could be effectively rejoined only by patient and subtle forensic analysis, not capsule formulas, still less hortatory slogans. The ICJ's passing attempts in the Namibia case to define apartheid's evil (see especially Judge Tanaka's 1966 dissenting opinion, but see also *Legal Consequences for States*), however laudable, did not rise to the judicial challenge. In his 1971 dissenting opinion, Judge Fitzmaurice fairly chastised the Court for treating apartheid as "self-evidently detrimental to the welfare of the inhabitants of the mandated territory," without providing or even being open to argument. Still, it must be said that Fitzmaurice's reprimand of the Court verged on the outrageous, inasmuch as he himself played the pivotal role in preempting the Court's judicial parsing of apartheid in 1966. Judge Tanaka, Dissenting Opinion, *South West Africa Cases,* Second Phase, Judgment, I.C.J. Reports (1966), pp. 310–13; *Legal Consequences for States,* I.C.J. Reports (1971), p. 57, paras. 129–31; Judge Fitzmaurice, Dissenting Opinion, ibid., pp. 222–23.

South Africa's Mandate over Namibia; a 1967 resolution (2325) declared that "the continued presence of South African authorities in South West Africa is a flagrant violation of its territorial integrity"; and a 1968 resolution (2372) condemned "the action of South Africa to consolidate its illegal control over Namibia," and called upon "all States to desist from those dealings with the Government of South Africa which would have the effect of perpetuating South Africa's illegal occupation."

2.2.2. Emphasizing "the inalienable right of the Namibian people to freedom and independence and the legitimacy of their struggle against foreign occupation," the General Assembly justified its resolve (in 2145) to terminate South Africa's "illegal occupation" under three heads:

- *Breach of international obligations.* South Africa's administration in Namibia violated "the Mandate, the Charter of the United Nations and the Universal Declaration of Human Rights";
- *Imposition of apartheid.* The "policies of apartheid and racial discrimination practiced by the Government of South Africa in South West Africa" constituted "a crime against humanity"; and
- *Failure to negotiate in good faith.* The "efforts of the United Nations to induce the Government of South Africa to fulfill its obligations in respect" of Namibia "have been of no avail."

2.2.3. For the purposes of the argument presented here, the focus in this text will be on the last of these rationales.

2.2.4. The failure of South Africa to negotiate in good faith had already been mooted in the ICJ deliberations on Namibia prior to the General Assembly resolutions.

2.2.4.1. In a dissenting opinion (1950), Judge Álvarez stated, "It would not be possible to admit that . . . an agreement which is intended to fix an important international status cannot be established solely because of the opposition, the negligence or the bad faith of one of the parties"; if "it is impossible to reach such an agreement, the United Nations must then take the appropriate measures."[46] In a cognate dissenting opinion (1950), Judge de Visscher, albeit more restrainedly, stated, "the Mandatory Power, while remaining free to reject the particular terms of a proposed agreement, has the legal obligation to be ready to take part in negotiations and to conduct them in good faith with a view to concluding an agreement."[47]

2.2.4.2. In a separate opinion (1962), Judge Bustamante pointed to the "overwhelming proof not only of the fact that repeated and reiterated negotiations took place . . . , but also that all the efforts made to find a conciliatory solution resulted

---

46. Judge Álvarez, Dissenting Opinion, *International Status of South-West Africa,* Advisory Opinion, I.C.J. Reports (1950), pp. 183–85.

47. Judge de Visscher, Dissenting Opinion, ibid., p. 188.

in failure.... For fifteen consecutive years this fundamental opposition of points of view, this unyielding opposition of the Mandatory in the face of the virtual unanimity of Member States as to the limits and obligations flowing from the Mandate, have maintained a situation of permanent deadlock." He proceeded to conclude that "no negotiation is possible and that any further negotiation ... would be ineffective to settle the dispute," counseling instead "resort to judicial decision" at The Hague in order to "re-establish the harmonious functioning of the system."[48]

2.2.4.3. In a separate opinion (1962), Judge Jessup observed that although "there certainly is no absolute litmus test which would enable a Court to assert in all situations at just what moment settlement by negotiation becomes impossible ... , it seems clear on the face of the record that the condition is fulfilled in this case." "States," he pithily concluded, "are not eternally bound by the old adage: 'If at first you don't succeed, try, try again.'"[49]

2.2.5. The General Assembly debates that culminated in a cascade of resolutions terminating South Africa's Mandate and condemning its "illegal occupation" of Namibia zeroed in on South Africa's obduracy during negotiations, while also ridiculing South Africa's appeal "to guard against the shutting of doors to further dialogue which is so necessary for better understanding and co-operation."[50]

2.2.5.1. Whereas the Member States contended that the objective of negotiations was to secure Namibia's eventual independence, South Africa insisted on negotiations without set preconditions or a predetermined outcome, technically leaving open "all possibilities," but in reality excluding real independence.[51]

2.2.5.2. The Ethiopian delegate gestured to "the fact that all avenues of peaceful negotiations have already been exhausted,"[52] while the Norwegian delegate noted, "After twenty years of futile discussions about the South African administration of South West Africa, the consensus has arisen ... that South Africa has lost its right to administer the Territory and that its Mandate is terminated."[53]

2.2.5.3. "In the face of the unbelievable intransigence of the Government of South Africa," the Uruguayan delegate recollected,

> we find a whole slew of General Assembly resolutions covering a period of twenty years and urging Pretoria to fulfill its duties and assume its responsibilities before the international community.... [W]e see an accumulation of acts of insubordination,

48. Judge Bustamante, Separate Opinion, *South West Africa Cases*, First Phase, Preliminary Objections, I.C.J. Reports (1962), pp. 385–86.

49. Judge Jessup, Separate Opinion, ibid., p. 435.

50. *GAOR*, A/PV.1451 (26 October 1966), para. 21.

51. Slonim, *South West Africa*, p. 181 (see also p. 134: "Quite obviously, the essential prerequisite to the success of any negotiations—viz., agreement on the purpose of the negotiations—was totally absent").

52. *GAOR*, A/PV.1414 (23 September 1966), para. 30.

53. *GAOR*, A/PV.1453 (27 October 1966), para. 40.

violation, of disregard of authority, abuse of rights, disobedience, mockery and defiance committed by South Africa against the United Nations.... We have waited over
twenty years. Let us hope that moderation will not become the vice of weakness. We
are supported by law, by rights, by morality, by the will of the whole world.... The
time has come to put an end to this struggle between law and arrogance. The organ of
the international community must end the Mandate on the grounds of repeated and
malicious non-fulfillment of the obligations and duties inherent in it.[54]

2.2.5.4. After recalling that "[f]or over 15 years we have waited for the South
African government to comply with its clear obligations," and that "[r]epeated
attempts by the General Assembly to persuade the South African government to
adopt a policy of co-operation have been unsuccessful," the British delegate, Lord
Caradon—who would later craft UN Security Council resolution 242—declared
that South Africa has "in effect forfeited its title to administer the Mandate."[55]

2.2.5.5. The Israeli delegate, joining the majority, observed that the Assembly had
turned to the ICJ in 1966 for a binding decision only "after a deadlock had been
reached in negotiations with South Africa to secure implementation" of the 1950
ICJ advisory opinion on Namibia; that after the ICJ "shied away from deciding
the case [in 1966], the decision now falls clearly on the shoulders of the General
Assembly"; and that South Africa was "in breach of its major obligations" because it
did not "prepare [Namibia] for independence." In a passage worth quoting at length,
the Israeli delegate concluded:

> Nearly fifty years after the Mandate was conferred [on] and accepted by the Manda-
> tory Power, South West Africa seems no nearer independence than it ever was. It is
> an ironic reflection that nearly all the other African peoples live under their own
> national sovereignty ... while, in the case of South West Africa, and only in that
> case, the sacred trust of civilization ... remains not only unfulfilled, but also not even
> within sight of fulfillment. It is a fact that all efforts to reach a mutually acceptable
> and reasonable settlement have been exhausted. Since the Mandatory Power is fail-

54. *GAOR,* A/PV.1448 (19 October 1966), paras. 126, 142. In a subsequent General
Assembly meeting, the exceptionally expressive Uruguayan delegate exhorted:

> So let us then set to work; let us face the difficulties. It is regrettable that South Africa per-
> sists in its attitude of rebelliousness against the United Nations, but this cannot paralyze our
> action. The time for warnings is past. The truth is, in fact, that the torrents of eloquence uttered
> over the past twenty-two years in the United Nations have been of no avail—*vox clamantis in
> deserto.* The South Africans have been deaf to our warnings. Perhaps the character in one of
> the plays of Benavente, the great Spanish playwright, was right when he said: "I do not believe
> that sermons have any effect. They are like the road signs on dangerous curves; useless for those
> who drive carefully, and even more useless for those who are determined to crash." (*GAOR,*
> A/PV.1515 [5 May 1967], para. 96)

55. *GAOR,* A/PV.1448 (19 October 1966), paras. 41–43. In the event, Great Britain,
which had extensive investments in South Africa, ended up opposing (usually by abstention)
UN resolutions condemning it.

ing to fulfill its essential obligations under the Mandate, it follows that the United Nations is free to take appropriate action.... [W]e believe that the General Assembly is now entitled to terminate the Mandate.... The General Assembly should take decisions on the future of the Mandated Territory on the assumption that the Mandate may be lawfully and properly terminated by the General Assembly.

If the time frame is enlarged to "nearly 100 years" after the Mandate, and if the statement that South-West Africa was the "only" Mandate where independence had not been "within sight of fulfillment" is amended by interpolating that the statehood of the indigenous population under the Palestine Mandate also was, and continues to be, placed on hold,[56] then the pertinence—and unique resonance—of the Israeli ambassador's observations, both as to diagnosis ("all efforts to reach a mutually acceptable and reasonable settlement have been exhausted") and as to proposed remedy ("the General Assembly is now entitled to terminate the Mandate"), can hardly escape notice.[57]

2.2.5.5.1. A few months later, the Israeli delegate told the Assembly:

The problem of South West Africa, which has developed into an intolerable situation, has been before the United Nations since its very first meetings over twenty-one years ago. Every conceivable approach to reaching a solution, which would conform to the principles of the Charter and assure the people of that land of their fundamental rights, has been thwarted. The United Nations has shown patience and even leniency in the face of the stubborn stand persisted in by the Government of South Africa in utter disregard of the clearly expressed position of the United Nations.[58]

In an earlier address, Israeli foreign minister Abba Eban exhorted the Assembly to "insist that a mandatory Power forfeits its mandate when it flagrantly and constantly violates the central aims for which the trust was conferred."[59]

2.2.5.6. The US delegate, also standing with the Assembly majority in the deliberations, declared that "by virtue of the breach of its obligations . . . , South Africa forfeits all right to continue to administer" Namibia.[60] "Despite the walls of censorship and propaganda, with which their own Government has surrounded them," he prognosticated, "the people of South Africa must soon realize that the system they are trying to entrench in Namibia will not work—that it will neither satisfy the wants and needs of the non-white population nor, by some conjuring trick, conveniently make them disappear."[61]

---

56. Except for (arguably) Palestine, there are currently no territories under the Mandate or Trusteeship systems.

57. *GAOR*, A/PV.1439 (12 October 1966), paras. 98, 101.

58. *GAOR*, A/PV.1515 (5 May 1967).

59. *GAOR*, A/PV.1662 (24 May 1968), para. 17 (Israeli delegate quoting Eban's Assembly speech).

60. *GAOR*, A/PV.1439 (12 October 1966), para. 73; A/PV.1453 (27 October 1966), para. 5.

61. *GAOR*, A/PV.1737 (10 December 1968), para. 122.

2.2.5.6.1. The United States condemned South Africa as well for its "imposition in South West Africa of its universally condemned policy of apartheid," and for its "clear defiance of the General Assembly's wise injunction that South Africa refrain and desist from any action, constitutional, administrative, political or otherwise, which will in any manner whatsoever alter or tend to alter the present international status of South West Africa."[62]

2.2.5.6.2. What's more, the United States opined that if some Namibians living under occupation resorted to force, it was at root a reaction to South Africa's repressive tactics that bred

> desperation and in that desperation some have found no alternative to violence as an expression of the determination to be free. The United States does not condone violence. The United States does condemn the brutality of a Government whose official policies have bred violence by closing avenues of peaceful dissent in South West Africa, thereby generating the very behavior it seeks to punish.[63]

2.2.5.6.3. The actions of the United States did not, however, rise to its lofty rhetoric. "The United States of America is economically and militarily the strongest among us," a Caribbean delegate observed. "If it wished it could, I have no doubt, reduce the Government of South Africa single-handedly; and indeed, it could do this even if the rest of us were to raise our voices against it." But even as "we have heard the representative of the United States regret, abhor and condemn the behavior of South Africa in this very chamber," he went on to rue, the existence of a domestic "lobby" that is "sufficiently influential . . . may cause even the most determined Government to pause."[64] *Plus ça change, plus c'est la même chose.*

2.2.6. Although lagging behind, the Security Council eventually echoed the resolve of the General Assembly.

2.2.6.1. The Council was first seized of the Namibia question in early 1968, when a resolution (245) took note of the Assembly's termination of the Mandate and expressed grave concern over South Africa's "illegal" repression in Namibia, while another resolution (246) later that year censured "the Government of South Africa for its flagrant defiance" of the Security Council.

---

62. *GAOR*, A/PV.1632 (14 December 1967), para. 4.

63. *GAOR*, A/PV.1632 (14 December 1967), paras. 12–13.

64. *GAOR,* A/PV.1449 (19 October 1966), paras. 19, 22. In the instant case, the "lobby" to which the delegate was referring comprised American "business interests in the South African economy." In subsequent Assembly debates, the United States persisted in preaching the virtues of "dialogue" and "diplomacy," although also purporting that it did "not thereby suggest or in any way condone indefinite delay." *GAOR*, A/PV.1505 (26 April 1967), paras. 24–25.

2.2.6.2. A 1969 resolution (264) took note of "the grave consequences of South Africa's continued occupation of Namibia," affirmed that "the continued presence of South Africa in Namibia is illegal," and called upon "the Government of South Africa to immediately withdraw its administration from the territory." A follow-up resolution (269) later in the year declared that "the continued occupation of the Territory of Namibia by the South African authorities constitutes an aggressive encroachment on the authority of the United Nations," recognized "the legitimacy of the struggle of the people of Namibia against the illegal presence of the South African authorities in the Territory," and called upon South Africa to "withdraw its administration from the Territory immediately."

2.2.6.3. Faced with Pretoria's refusal to either negotiate in good faith or withdraw, the Security Council, in a 1970 resolution (276), declared that the "United Nations decided that the Mandate for South-West Africa was terminated," that "the continued presence of the South African authorities in Namibia is illegal," and that consequently "all acts taken by the Government of South Africa on behalf of or concerning Namibia after the termination of the Mandate are illegal and invalid." It also called for the creation of a subcommittee to study "ways and means" of implementing the relevant UN resolutions "in the light of the flagrant refusal of South Africa to withdraw from Namibia." A few months later, the subcommittee recommended that the United Nations seek another ICJ advisory opinion.

2.3. *South Africa's failure to negotiate in good faith: Back to The Hague*

2.3.1. Pursuant to the subcommittee's recommendation, the Security Council adopted (in 1970) a pair of complementary resolutions. The first of these (283) reaffirmed its recognition of "the decision of the General Assembly to terminate the Mandate of South Africa," noted "with great concern the continued flagrant refusal of the Government of South Africa to comply with the decisions of the Security Council demanding . . . immediate withdrawal," and called upon "all States maintaining diplomatic or consular relations with South Africa to issue a formal declaration . . . to the effect that they . . . consider South Africa's presence in Namibia illegal." The succeeding resolution (284) referred the Namibia question back to the ICJ.

2.3.1.1. Defending this course of action against skeptics still smarting from the Court's 1966 snub (see supra, 2.1.8.2), the Finnish delegate on the Security Council stressed that "an advisory opinion of the International Court of Justice could underline the fact that South Africa has forfeited its Mandate over South West Africa because . . . South Africa has acted contrary to . . . international law. It is important . . . to expose the false front of legality which South African authorities attempt to present to the world. This would help . . . mobilize public opinion . . . especially in those countries which have the power to influence events in southern Africa in a decisive way."[65]

65. *UNSCOR*, S/PV.1550 (29 July 1970), para. 41.

2.3.1.2. During the Security Council debate, the American delegate excoriated the "callous behavior of the illegitimate occupying authority." Although South Africa "has cloaked itself in a mantle of seeming legality," he declared in another Council meeting,

> the legal justifications for its actions are spurious. Not only do these actions run contrary to actions by the political organs of the United Nations, but, in addition, the International Court of Justice has also made clear the international responsibility of South Africa with respect to the Territory.... [I]ts authority was conditioned by ... the obligation to look to the welfare of the inhabitants. Surely, by applying its apartheid laws in the Territory, it did not honor but rather breached that obligation.

In still a third intervention, the United States denounced South Africa for "not only attempting to annex Namibia, but ... also extending its heinous policy of apartheid ... to that Territory." And in a fourth Council meeting, it deplored South Africa's "policy of virtual annexation. It has compounded this evil by applying to the international Territory the odious practice of apartheid, with all the miserable human consequences that that practice entails." Nonetheless, the United States opposed international sanctions allegedly because they would "likely ... prove ineffective and ... would, far from improving the lot of the Namibians, run the risk of making their situation even worse than it is today."[66]

2.3.2. The Security Council requested of the ICJ an advisory opinion on the "Legal Consequences for States of the Continued Presence of South Africa in Namibia (South West Africa) Notwithstanding Security Council Resolution 276 (1970)."

2.3.3. The Court's opinion, delivered in 1971,[67] divided (for the purposes here) into two sections: the rationale behind the General Assembly resolution terminat-

---

66. *UNSCOR,* S/PV.1391 (16 February 1968), para. 67; *UNSCOR,* S/PV.1465 (20 March 1969), paras. 10, 15; *UNSCOR,* S/PV.1496 (11 August 1969), paras. 20, 24–26.

67. The composition of the Court changed in the interim period between the 1966 and 1971 judgments, tilting it ideologically in the opposite, progressive direction. The Court was also under tremendous international pressure to redeem itself after the 1966 fiasco. Judge Fitzmaurice submitted a one-hundred-page dissenting opinion in which he blasted nearly the whole of the Court's jurisprudence from the inception of the *Namibia* case in 1950. Indeed, by this point, he had effectively shed his judicial robe and functioned as lead counsel for South Africa. Already at the time of the 1966 judgment, Judge Jessup had observed in his dissent that the Court (under Fitzmaurice's intellectual stewardship) reached its determination, that the Court lacked jurisdiction, *"on a theory not advanced"* even by South Africa itself. Judge Jessup, Dissenting Opinion, *South West Africa Cases,* Second Phase, Judgment, I.C.J. Reports (1966), p. 328, emphasis in original (but see also Slonim, *South West Africa,* pp. 219n15, 291–92). If the vocation of lawyering is to prove (or pretend) that words do not mean what they plainly *do* mean, then Fitzmaurice must be said to have been a virtuoso practitioner of his craft; he even denied in 1971 the plain meaning of his *own* words in 1966 (Dugard, *South West Africa/ Namibia,* pp. 486–87). The gist of his 1971 dissent was that none of the UN political bodies, not the General Assembly, not even the Security Council, had any legitimate

ing the Mandate, and the "competence" (power) of the Assembly to terminate the Mandate.[68]

2.3.3.1. The advisory opinion first sketched in the background to the General Assembly's decision to terminate and declare illegal South Africa's occupation. It noted that "throughout a period of twenty years, the General Assembly ... called upon the South African government to perform its obligations arising out of the Mandate"; that the Assembly passed a succession of resolutions beginning in 1946 reminding South Africa of its obligations and urging it to comply with them; that the United Nations "undoubtedly conducted the negotiations in good faith," yet even the compromise proposals mooted by it were "rejected by South Africa"; and that "further fruitless negotiations were held." The Court then concluded:

> In practice the actual length of negotiations is no test of whether the possibilities of agreement have been exhausted; it may be sufficient to show that an early deadlock was reached and that one side adamantly refused compromise. In the case of Namibia (South West Africa) this stage had patently been reached long before the United

say over South Africa's administration of Namibia, and that although South Africa could not legally annex Namibia, if it embarked on such a course, the United Nations could not revoke the Mandate "until and unless" this sanction was imposed by "lawful means." But on the last point, if Fitzmaurice contested the whole of the Court's jurisprudence in the *Namibia* case except the 1966 decision denying the Court's jurisdiction, then, de facto, he signaled in his 1971 dissent that South Africa was free to do whatever it pleased. It was a measure of his bias that Fitzmaurice chastised the General Assembly for (1) being "unsympathetic by nature" to South Africa, whereas he himself fell mute on the Assembly's disposition toward Namibia, which after all was its prime responsibility ("sacred trust") under the Mandates System; and (2) fostering a "permanent state of tension" with South Africa by promoting Namibian independence, whereas he did not even mention the "tension" fomented by South Africa's aspiration to illegally annex Namibia, and leaving aside whether the tension engendered by each of the parties was equally culpable. The upshot of Fitzmaurice's dissent was that he construed, not Namibia but *South Africa* as the "sacred trust," and protecting its sovereignty as the preeminent object of judicial notice. It is indicative of the moral universe he inhabited that in depicting the opposed jurisdictional claims of the United Nations and South Africa over Namibia's fate and future, Fitzmaurice fastened onto this cretinous metaphor: "the United Nations backed the wrong horse." Judge Fitzmaurice, Dissenting Opinion, *Legal Consequences for States,* I.C.J. Reports (1971), pp. 226, 232–33, 252. In commentaries on the Namibia litigation, Fitzmaurice proved to be a political touchstone. Thus, between the two leading scholars on the Namibia case, Dugard, who was more sympathetic to the progressives on the Court, ridiculed Fitzmaurice's "anarchic suggestion that the court overthrow all its previous decisions on South-West Africa," whereas Slonim, who was more sympathetic to the Court's conservatives, praised his "vigorous and powerful dissent" and "formidable challenge to the majority opinion." Dugard, *South West Africa/Namibia,* p. 485; Slonim, *South West Africa,* pp. 340, 342.

68. A significant section of the advisory opinion also focused on the legal obligations of UN Member States after the Security Council affirmed the Assembly action. Insofar as a Security Council resolution affirming the illegality of Israel's occupation will not now or in the foreseeable future be spared an American veto, this section of the opinion will not be analyzed here.

Nations finally abandoned its efforts to reach agreement. Even so, for so long as South Africa was the mandatory Power, the way was still open for it to seek an arrangement. But that chapter came to an end with the termination of the Mandate.[69]

2.3.3.1.1.1. In his separate opinion, Judge Dillard (of the US) pointedly observed that negotiations become a mockery if the core assumptions of the contending parties cannot be reconciled: "It is apparent that no negotiating process can be successful if the parties are at odds as to the fundamental basis on which the process rests.... Quite obviously negotiations based on ... conflicting premises qualify, at best, as an empty time-consuming pageant and, at worst, as a mere dialogue of the deaf."

2.3.3.1.1.1. In the passage preceding these remarks, Dillard rebuked South Africa for its disingenuous negotiating posture: "The dilemma is focused on the *negotiating process* consequent upon the dissolution of the League of Nations. Although South Africa was under no duty to submit to the trusteeship system or to negotiate a specific trusteeship agreement, yet, as a Member of the United Nations, she was surely under a duty to negotiate in good faith ... with the United Nations concerning a viable alternative either within the trusteeship or outside it." In the corresponding footnote, Dillard contested a fellow judge's opinion that even if a Member State of the United Nations is bound to "consider in good faith" an Assembly resolution, it does not entail a "true legal obligation": "I cannot agree with this conclusion. The use of discretion and freedom to bargain which the system may confer does not imply the right to exercise an attitude of uninhibited freedom of action which would be tantamount to operating outside the system."[70]

2.3.3.1.1.2. In his dissenting opinion, Judge Gros, although gainsaying that either the General Assembly or the Security Council had the "power of revocation" of the Mandate, nonetheless concurred that South Africa was under legal obligation to negotiate in good faith. The relevant passage merits lengthy quotation as it lends unexpected support from a dissenting judge to the majority opinion on the decisive point of good faith:

> The conflict of standpoints can be roughly summarized as follows: The aim of the United Nations was to arrive at the negotiation of a trusteeship agreement, whereas South Africa did not want to convert the Mandate into a trusteeship. It is necessary to determine which party has been misusing its legal position in this controversy on the extent of the obligation to negotiate.... If negotiations had begun in good faith and if, at a given juncture, it had been found impossible to reach agreement on certain precise, objectively debatable points, then it might be argued that the Opinion of 1950, finding as it had that there was no obligation to place the Territory under trusteeship, prevented taking the matter further, inasmuch as the Mandatory's refusal to accept a draft

69. *Legal Consequences for States,* I.C.J. Reports (1971), pp. 43–45, paras. 84–86.
70. Judge Dillard, Separate Opinion, *Legal Consequences for States,* I.C.J. Reports (1971), pp. 159–60, emphasis in original.

trusteeship agreement could in that case reasonably be deemed justified: "No party can impose its terms on the other party" [quoting the 1950 ICJ advisory opinion; see supra, 2.1.7.1]. But the facts are otherwise: negotiations for the conclusion of a trusteeship agreement never began, and for that South Africa was responsible. The rule of law infringed herein is the obligation to negotiate in good faith. To assert that the United Nations ought to have accepted the negotiation of anything other than a trusteeship agreement on bases proposed by South Africa, that, coming from the Government of South Africa, is to interpret the 1950 Advisory Opinion contrary to its meaning.... In seeking to impose on the United Nations its own conception of the object of the negotiations for the modification and transformation of the Mandate, South Africa has failed to comply with the obligation established by the 1950 Opinion to observe a certain line of conduct. The United Nations, on the other hand, was by no means misusing its legal position when it refused to negotiate with any other end in view than the conclusion of a trusteeship agreement, for such indeed was the goal acknowledged by the 1950 Opinion.... It would have been legitimate for the United Nations to have taken note of the deadlock and demanded South Africa's compliance with its obligation to negotiate. This view is reinforced by South Africa's consistent interpretation of its own powers, whether it be its pretension to the incorporation of the Territory—something essentially incompatible with the mandate régime—or its contentions with regard to its legal titles apart from the Mandate. The legal position of Mandatory formally recognized by the Court in 1950 gave South Africa the right to negotiate the conditions for the transformation of the Mandate into a trusteeship; since 1950 that position has been used to obstruct the very principle of such transformation. An analysis on these lines, if carried out by the Court and based on a judicial finding that there had been a breach of the obligation to transform the Mandate by negotiation as the 1950 Opinion prescribed, would have had legal consequences in respect of the continued presence of South Africa in the mandated territory. I consider that, in that context, the legal consequences concerned would have been founded upon solid legal reasons.[71]

However, insofar as Gros denied that the United Nations could revoke the Mandate, it is unclear what "legal consequences in respect of the continued presence of South Africa in the mandated territory" he had in mind.

2.3.3.2. After delineating the deadlock caused by South Africa's refusal to conduct good-faith negotiations, the Court next considered whether the General Assembly had the competence to terminate the Mandate, or whether it had acted *ultra vires* (beyond its legal powers). The Court decided that it was within the Assembly's province.

2.3.3.2.1. As a general rule, Assembly resolutions are only recommendations.

2.3.3.2.2. The Court found, however, that the League of Nations' relationship with the South African Mandatory included a treaty (contract) component;[72] that it is inherent in a treaty agreement that if one party materially breaches its obligations, the other party has a right to terminate it; and that, consequently, once the League's

---

71. Judge Gros, Dissenting Opinion, *Legal Consequences for States,* I.C.J. Reports (1971), pp. 344–45, paras. 43–45.

72. Slonim, *South West Africa,* pp. 192–96.

powers had been transferred to the Assembly, and South Africa had deliberately and persistently breached its obligations under the Mandate, the Assembly's competence extended beyond making a recommendation to making a binding legal decision.

2.3.3.2.3. In sum, the Court concluded that "it would not be correct to assume that because the General Assembly is in principle vested with recommendatory powers, it is debarred from adopting, in specific cases within the framework of its competence, resolutions which make determinations or have operative design."[73]

2.3.3.2.4. In his separate opinion, Judge Nervo enlarged on the Assembly's competence beyond breach of a treaty to make legally binding decisions:

> The fact that, broadly speaking, the General Assembly's activities are mainly of a recommendatory character does not mean that the General Assembly cannot act in a situation in which it is a party to a contractual relationship in its capacity as such a party; *nor does it mean that, in regard to a territory which is an international responsibility, and in regard to which no State sovereignty intervenes between the General Assembly and the territory, the General Assembly should not be able to act as it did.* . . . [T]he General Assembly is the competent organ of the United Nations to act in the name of the latter in a wide range of matters, and in these instances it is the United Nations itself which is acting. This is especially so concerning . . . trusteeship matters, non-self-governing territories.

> South Africa has in reality and to all effects annexed as its own the Territory of Namibia. . . . *This behavior . . . [is] sufficient grounds for the revocation of the Mandate. So is the racial discrimination practiced as an official policy in Namibia with the enforcement there of the system of apartheid.* Racial discrimination as a matter of official government policy is a violation of a norm or rule or standard of the international community.[74]

2.3.3.3. In an editorial the morning after the ICJ handed down *Legal Consequences for States,* the *New York Times* hailed the "historic thirteen-to-two verdict" that "has cleared away the legal and political fog that for years obscured the status" of Namibia.[75]

2.3.4. Later that same year, the Security Council accepted the key findings of the Court.[76] The US delegate at the Council meeting registered Washington's backing

---

73. *Legal Consequences for States,* I.C.J. Reports (1971), pp. 45–50, paras. 87–105, quote at para. 105. It bears passing notice that the Court was less than lucid (or consistent) on this point. According to Judge Nervo, the General Assembly resolution did not become "fully effective" until after Security Council resolutions affirmed it, and as a result of the "combined effect of the resolutions of these two principal organs of the United Nations," while according to Judge Dillard, the Assembly had the power in this "sui generis" case to revoke the Mandate but also could do so as a general principle in conjunction with the Security Council. Judge Nervo, Separate Opinion, *Legal Consequences for States,* I.C.J. Reports (1971), p. 114; Judge Dillard, Separate Opinion, ibid., pp. 163–65.

74. Judge Nervo, Separate Opinion, *Legal Consequences for States,* I.C.J. Reports (1971), pp. 113, 123, emphases added.

75. "Clear Verdict on Namibia," *New York Times* (22 June 1971).

76. UNSC resolution 301 (1971).

for the "conclusions, which declare ... that South Africa is under obligation to withdraw its administration from Namibia immediately and thus put an end to its occupation," and it also observed that the US "position was consistent with our support of practical and peaceful means to achieve self-determination and end racial discrimination."[77]

2.4. It remains to consider if the *Namibia* precedent can dispel the "legal and political fog" that has for years shrouded Israel's occupation of Palestinian territory and, in particular, shed light on the "means to achieve self-determination and end racial discrimination" there.

3.0. NAMIBIA AND PALESTINE JUXTAPOSED

3.1. In 2002, UN secretary-general Kofi Annan conveyed to the Security Council that Israel must end its "illegal occupation" of the West Bank and Gaza.[78] His characterization triggered a swift response from Israel's defenders, who asserted that the occupation was legal until Israel was "able to negotiate a successful peace treaty."[79]

3.1.1. In a palpable retreat, the spokesman for the secretary-general issued a clarification stating that Annan had indicted not the Israeli occupation as such but rather Israel's breach of its various obligations as an occupying power.[80]

3.2. Bearing in mind the sage counsel of Judge Dillard that analogies are "always to be indulged with caution,"[81] it is nonetheless submitted that in light of the Namibia precedent, Israel's occupation of Palestinian territory is now illegal, as it has persistently refused to negotiate in good faith on the basis of international law an end to the occupation.

3.3. *Overlapping historical-political context*

3.3.1. A common matrix molded the Namibia and Palestine questions. Both originated in the postwar Mandates System, and together they constituted the salient vestiges of that era as the only mandated territories that survived dissolution of the League of Nations without being converted into UN Trusteeships.

3.3.2. The UN General Assembly asserted its authority over both lingering Mandates. It passed the Partition Resolution (181) in 1947, paving the way to Israel's creation, and it set out after the 1967 war to complete the unfinished business of

---

77. *UNSCOR*, S/PV.1598 (20 October 1971), paras. 17–18.

78. "Secretary-General Tells Security Council Middle East Crisis 'Worst in Ten Years'; Calls on Palestinians, Israelis to 'Lead Your People away from Disaster,'" un.org/press /en/2002/sgsm8159.doc.htm (12 March 2002).

79. George P. Fletcher, "Annan's Careless Language," *New York Times* (21 March 2002).

80. Frederic Eckhard, "A Delicate Word in the Mideast," *New York Times* (23 March 2002).

81. Judge Dillard, Separate Opinion, *Legal Consequences for States*, I.C.J. Reports (1971), p. 158.

creating a reciprocal Palestinian State. In the case of Namibia, the General Assembly early on rejected South Africa's bid to annex it, then claimed title to supervise South Africa's administration of it, then terminated South Africa's Mandate and declared its occupation illegal, and finally shepherded Namibia to independence.

3.4. *Overlapping legal context*

3.4.1. The Namibia and Palestine questions are juridically homologous.

3.4.1.1. If Palestine is perceived through the optic of the Mandates System, then its rights carry over as a lingering Mandate. In its 2004 *Wall* opinion, the ICJ recalled the genesis of the Palestine question in the Mandates System, and the "permanent responsibility" (quoting a General Assembly resolution) that consequently falls on the international community.[82]

3.4.1.2. If the Palestine question is perceived as it *re*emerged after 1967, then Palestine's rights derive from its status as a territory under occupation. The ICJ's 2004 opinion, which deliberated on the legal consequences of building a wall in "occupied Palestinian territory," is shot through with references to the *Namibia* precedent.[83]

3.4.2. Whether the Mandates System or the status of a territory under occupation served as the point of reference, the selfsame principles of "sacred trust" and "non-annexation" governed the Namibia and Palestine situations.

3.4.2.1. The ICJ underscored on multiple occasions that the twin principles of "sacred trust"—that is, the paramount importance of the well-being and development of the Mandate population—and "non-annexation"—that is, the Mandatory does not acquire any rights of sovereignty over a Mandate—constituted the essence of the Mandates System.[84]

3.4.2.1.1. Judges Koroma, al-Khasawneh, and Elaraby, in their respective opinions in the *Wall* case, located the obligations of "sacred trust" and "non-annexation" in Palestine's former status as a Mandate.[85]

---

82. *Legal Consequences of the Construction of a Wall*, I.C.J. Reports (2004), pp. 158–59, para. 49; p. 165, para. 70. The danger lurking behind invocation of the Mandate is that Israel's apologists can then seize on it to justify all manner of things, such as its settlements policy. See Eugene Rostow, "Correspondence," *American Journal of International Law* (1990), pp. 718–20.

83. *Legal Consequences of the Construction of a Wall*, I.C.J. Reports (2004), p. 165, para. 70, pp. 171–72, para. 88; Judge Elaraby, Separate Opinion, ibid., pp. 250–52, paras. 2.2–2.3; Judge Owada, Separate Opinion, ibid., pp. 263–64, para. 10. To be sure, in a couple of the separate opinions, the inaptness of the analogy was asserted. See Judge Kooijmans, Separate Opinion, ibid., p. 219, para. I.1, p. 226, paras. IV.23, IV.25, p. 229, para. V.33, p. 231, para. VI.39; Judge Higgins, Separate Opinion, ibid., pp. 207–8, paras. 2, 3, 5.

84. *International Status of South-West Africa*, I.C.J. Reports (1950), p. 131; *Legal Consequences for States*, I.C.J. Reports (1971), pp. 28, 43; *Legal Consequences of the Construction of a Wall*, I.C.J. Reports (2004), p. 165, para. 70.

85. Judge Koroma, Separate Opinion, *Legal Consequences of the Construction of a Wall*, I.C.J. Reports (2004), p. 205, para. 7; Judge al-Khasawneh, Separate Opinion, ibid., p. 237, para. 9; Judge Elaraby, Separate Opinion, ibid., pp. 250–51, para. 2.2.

3.4.2.2. The principles of "sacred trust" and "non-annexation" also figure as legal hallmarks of a territory under occupation.

3.4.2.2.1. Under international law, a classic text notes, "enemy territories in the occupation of armed forces of another country constitute ... a sacred trust, which must be administered ... in the interests ... of the inhabitants."[86] In the *Namibia* case, the Court recalled that in the UN Charter "the concept of the 'sacred trust' was confirmed and expanded to all 'territories whose peoples have not yet attained a full measure of self-government' (Article 73)," and that a "further important stage in this development was the 1960 Declaration on the Granting of Independence to Colonial Countries and Peoples (General Assembly resolution 1514), which embraces all peoples and territories which 'have not yet attained independence.'"[87] These precedents, although invoked in the *Namibia* jurisprudence, apply with comparable force to the occupied Palestinian territory, as it is subject to "alien subjugation" (in the language of 1514) and therefore qualifies as a quasicolonial situation.

3.4.2.2.2. It has also been observed by commentators that "The foundation upon which the entire law of occupation is based is the principle of inalienability of sovereignty through the actual or threatened use of force. ... Effective control by foreign military force can never bring about by itself a valid transfer of sovereignty."[88] Judge Koroma, in his separate opinion in the *Wall* case, pinpointed the "essence of occupation" as (inter alia) its being "only of a temporary nature."[89]

3.4.3. Beyond the principles of "sacred trust" and "non-annexation," the nonderogable right to self-determination also inhered in the legal standing of Namibia and, later, the occupied Palestinian territory.

3.4.3.1. This right derives from the former status of each as a Mandate, as well as from the rules governing decolonization after World War II, which ratified the prerogative of colonial peoples and peoples subject to foreign occupation to be independent.

3.4.3.1.1. A prominent commentator observed already decades ago that "the Security Council has begun to deal with the Israeli occupied territories as if they were colonies," while a prominent contemporary commentator places both Namibia and Palestine under the same rubric of "illegal [military] occupation."[90]

86. Arnold Wilson, "The Laws of War in Occupied Territory," *Transactions of the Grotius Society* (1932), p. 38 (see also p. 29).

87. *Legal Consequences for States,* I.C.J. Reports (1971), p. 31, para. 52.

88. Benvenisti, *International Law,* p. 5. See also Ben-Naftali et al., "Illegal Occupation," pp. 592–97.

89. Judge Koroma, Separate Opinion, *Legal Consequences of the Construction of a Wall,* I.C.J. Reports (2004), p. 204, para. 2.

90. A. Rigo Sureda, *The Evolution of the Right of Self-Determination: A study of United Nations practice* (Leiden: 1973), pp. 260–61; Cassese, *Self-Determination,* pp. 90, 94–95, 230, 240. See also Judge Higgins, Separate Opinion, *Legal Consequences of the Construction of a Wall,* I.C.J. Reports (2004), p. 214, para. 29.

3.4.3.2. The ICJ observed in the *Namibia* case that the decolonization process after World War II left "little doubt that the ultimate objective of the sacred trust [in Article 22 of the League Covenant] was the self-determination and independence of the peoples concerned," while in the *Wall* case, the Court observed after contextualizing its findings in the *Namibia* precedent that "the existence of a 'Palestinian people' is no longer in issue," and that the "legitimate rights" of the Palestinian people "include the right to self-determination."[91]

3.5. *If South Africa's occupation of Namibia was illegal, then is Israel's occupation of Palestinian territory also illegal?*

3.5.1. Whereas, per Dillard, analogies must be approached with caution, from the standpoints of history, law, and politics it would be hard to conceive a closer fit than Namibia and Palestine:

- Both situations emerged historically from the Mandates System;
- Both situations are governed by the foundational legal principles of "sacred trust" and "non-annexation"; and
- Both situations fall within the integral political and legal paradigms of decolonization and self-determination.[92]

3.5.2. But does the Israeli occupation of Palestine reach the Namibian threshold of illegality?

91. *Legal Consequences for States,* I.C.J. Reports (1971), p. 31, para. 53; *Legal Consequences of the Construction of a Wall,* I.C.J. Reports (2004), pp. 171–72, para. 88, pp. 182–83, para. 118.

92. Noted jurist Antonio Cassese disputes the parallel. He maintains that whereas the legal issues pertaining to a South African withdrawal from Namibia had early on been resolved, the parameters of an Israeli withdrawal remain in dispute, such as "legal uncertainty about who is the holder of sovereign rights over the territories." Even granting, for argument's sake, that Cassese's opinion contained some measure of truth at the time of his writing (1995), it plainly is no longer tenable in light of the numerous General Assembly resolutions passed by overwhelming majorities, and the ICJ's 2004 advisory opinion, which designated the whole of the West Bank, including East Jerusalem, and Gaza as "occupied Palestinian territory." In her separate opinion in the *Wall* case, Judge Higgins also disputes the analogy. In the *Namibia* case, she contends, all legal obligations as adjudicated by the ICJ fell on South Africa, whereas in the Israel-Palestine conflict, "the larger intractable problem ... cannot be regarded as one in which one party alone has been already classified by a court as the legal wrongdoer; where it is for it alone to act to restore a situation of legality; and where from the perspective of legal obligation there is nothing remaining for the other 'party' to do." But insofar as Palestinian interlocutors have long expressed willingness to make peace on terms prescribed by international law and endorsed by the overwhelming majority of the General Assembly, there is "nothing remaining" for Palestinians to do and the full onus of legal obligations *does* fall on Israel. Cassese, *Self-Determination,* pp. 130–31, 147–50, 240–42; Judge Higgins, Separate Opinion, *Legal Consequences of the Construction of a Wall,* I.C.J. Reports (2004), pp. 207–8, paras. 2–3 (see also p. 211, para. 18; pp. 214–15, paras. 30, 31).

3.5.3. The General Assembly terminated South Africa's Mandate over Namibia and declared its occupation illegal on three counts: breach of international obligations, imposition of apartheid, and failure to negotiate in good faith. An equally compelling charge sheet can be drawn up against Israel's occupation of Palestinian territory.

3.5.3.1. *Breach of international obligations*

3.5.3.1.1. The political organs of the United Nations, leading human rights organizations, and respected legal commentators have repeatedly deplored Israel's violations of international law in the occupied Palestinian territory, including excessive and disproportionate use of force, deliberate targeting of civilians and civilian infrastructure, torture, settlement construction, and collective punishment.[93] Many of these breaches amount to war crimes and crimes against humanity.

3.5.3.1.2. These condemnations culminated in the *Wall* opinion, wherein the ICJ found that "Israeli settlements in the Occupied Palestinian Territory (including East Jerusalem) have been established in breach of international law." The Rome Statute of the International Criminal Court defines "[t]he transfer, directly or indirectly, by the Occupying Power of parts of its own civilian population into the territory it occupies" as a war crime. The ICJ also observed in its opinion that "the route chosen for the wall ... severely impedes the exercise by the Palestinian people of its right to self-determination, and is therefore a breach of Israel's obligation to respect that right."[94] The right to self-determination is widely regarded as a "peremptory norm" of international law, from which no derogation is permissible.[95]

3.5.3.2. *Imposition of apartheid*

3.5.3.2.1. A growing consensus has emerged, embracing authoritative legal, political, and moral personalities—among them many Israelis—that Israel has established an apartheid regime in the occupied Palestinian territory. The lengthy roster of those making the apartheid analogy in the context of Israel's occupation includes former US president and Nobel Peace Prize laureate Jimmy Carter; South African archbishop and Nobel Peace Prize laureate Desmond Tutu, and distinguished South African jurist John Dugard; former Israeli deputy prime minister Dan Meridor (Likud), former Israeli attorney general Michael Ben-Yair, former Israeli ministers of education Shulamit Aloni and Yossi Sarid, former deputy mayor of Jerusalem Meron Benvenisti, former Israeli ambassador to South Africa Alon Liel, veteran Israeli journalist Danny Rubinstein, the Israeli Information Center for Human Rights in the Occupied Territories (B'Tselem), the Association for Civil Rights

93. See the main body of this book for references.

94. *Legal Consequences of the Construction of a Wall,* I.C.J. Reports (2004), pp. 183–84, paras. 120–22.

95. Dugard, *Recognition,* pp. 158–61.

in Israel, and the *Haaretz* editorial board.[96] A monograph by South African international law experts found that "Israel has introduced a system of apartheid in the OPT [occupied Palestinian territory], in violation of a peremptory norm of international law," while an article published in the prestigious *European Journal of International Law* concluded that "a system of apartheid has developed in the occupied Palestinian territory" that is "not only reminiscent of," but also "in some cases worse than ... apartheid as it existed in South Africa."[97]

3.5.3.2.2. The reference point of the apartheid analogy is most often the dual system of law that Israel has established *within* the occupied Palestinian territory that privileges Jewish settlers. But even in the absence of Jewish settlements, the occupation itself would by now constitute an apartheid regime vis-à-vis Israel proper. Some three decades ago, noted international law expert Adam Roberts speculated, "Israel may see some advantage in the continuation of the status of the occupied territory, because this arrangement provides a legal basis for treating the Arab inhabitants of the territories entirely separately from the citizens of Israel." If a prolonged occupation, in which Israel "refuse[d] to negotiate a peace treaty," came to pass, he continued, it would "pave the way for a kind of apartheid."[98]

96. Jimmy Carter, *Palestine Peace Not Apartheid* (New York: 2006); Chris McGreal, "Worlds Apart: Israel, Palestine and apartheid" and "Brothers in Arms: Israel's secret pact with Pretoria," *Guardian* (6 February 2006, 7 February 2006) (Tutu); John Dugard, "Apartheid and Occupation under International Law," Hisham B. Sharabi Memorial Lecture (30 March 2009); Michael Ben-Yair, "The War's Seventh Day," *Haaretz* (2 March 2002); Shulamit Aloni, "Indeed, There Is Apartheid in Israel," *ynet.co.il* (5 January 2006); Roee Nahmias, "'Israeli Terror Is Worse,'" *Yediot Ahronot* (29 July 2005) (Aloni); Yossi Sarid, "Yes, It Is Apartheid," *Haaretz* (24 April 2008); Meron Benvenisti, "Founding a Binational State," *Haaretz* (22 April 2004); Dinah A. Spritzer, "British Zionists Drop Haaretz Columnist," *Jewish Telegraphic Agency* (8 August 2007) (Rubinstein); Ezra HaLevi, "Haaretz Editor Refuses to Retract Israel Apartheid Statements," *israelnationalnews.com* (30 July 2008) (Rubinstein); B'Tselem (Israeli Information Center for Human Rights in the Occupied Territories), *Forbidden Roads: Israel's discriminatory road regime in the West Bank* (August 2004), p. 3; Association for Civil Rights in Israel, *The State of Human Rights in Israel and the Occupied Territories, 2008 Report,* p. 17; "The Problem That Disappeared," *Haaretz* (11 September 2006); "Where Is the Occupation?," *Haaretz* (7 October 2007); "Our Debt to Jimmy Carter," *Haaretz* (15 April 2008); Amos Schocken, "Citizenship Law Makes Israel an Apartheid State," *Haaretz* (28 June 2008); "The Price of Deception and Apartheid," *Haaretz* (27 November 2013); "Meridor Compares Likud Policies to Apartheid," *Times of Israel* (19 November 2013).

97. Virginia Tilley, ed., *Beyond Occupation: Apartheid, colonialism and international law in the occupied Palestinian territories* (London: 2012), p. 215; John Dugard and John Reynolds, "Apartheid, International Law, and the Occupied Palestinian Territory," *European Journal of International Law* 24 (2013), p. 912.

98. Roberts, *What Is?*, pp. 272–73.

3.5.3.2.3. After his notorious recantation and fall from grace,[99] jurist Richard Goldstone reinvented himself as Israel's agitprop impresario. In this capacity, he deplored the apartheid analogy on the grounds that "there is no intent" by Israel to "maintain" this regime.[100] But if Israel has persistently refused to terminate the occupation in accordance with international law; and if it has sustained the occupation for a half century, which also comprises the largest part of its total existence as a State;[101] and if it has entrenched an infrastructure designed to make the occupation irreversible—then Israel has, on the contrary, made manifest that it *is* intent on maintaining the occupation, while sufficient time has elapsed such that Roberts's premonition of an apartheid-in-the-making has become a full-blown reality.[102]

3.5.3.3. *Failure to negotiate in good faith*

3.5.3.3.1. An overwhelming consensus exists on anchoring a solution to the Israel-Palestine conflict in international law; on the applicable general legal principles and rules of law, such as the right of both peoples to self-determination; on how to apply these general principles and rules so as to concretely adjudicate the "permanent status" issues of borders, East Jerusalem, settlements, and (albeit with less precision) refugees.[103]

3.5.3.3.2. In the course of the Middle East "peace process," Palestinian negotiators have consistently embraced international law as the framework for resolving the conflict, while submitting concrete proposals that protect Palestinian rights under the law but also make allowance for political expediency,[104] such as a land swap that

99. See Chapter 6.

100. Richard J. Goldstone, "Israel and the Apartheid Slander," *New York Times* (31 October 2011).

101. This bald fact alone points up the obtuseness of Israel's boast that it is the "only democracy in the Middle East." However one assesses the situation inside the Green Line, Israel has, for the largest part of its existence, presided in the occupied Palestinian territory over a helot population, comprising nearly 40 percent of the total population on both sides of the Green Line, that lacks any rights of citizenship.

102. It might also be noted that when the United Nations condemned the apartheid regime installed in Namibia, it was regardless of the South African offer to annex "only" the parts of Namibia populated by white settlers. On this point, see also Dugard and Reynolds, "Apartheid," p. 910.

103. See Chapter 2.

104. In his 1966 dissenting opinion, Judge Tanaka usefully elucidated the distinction between law and politics:

> The essential difference between law and politics or administration lies in the fact that law distinguishes in a categorical way what is right and just from what is wrong and unjust, while politics and administration, being the means to attain specific purposes, and dominated by considerations of expediency, make a distinction between the practical and the unpractical, the efficient and the inefficient. Consequently, in the judgment of law there is no possibility apart from what is just or unjust (*tertium non datur*), in the case of politics and administration there are many possibilities or choices from the viewpoint of expediency and efficiency. Politics are susceptible of gradation, in contrast to law, which is categorical and absolute. (Judge

would enable the bulk of Israeli settlers to remain in place.[105] Contrariwise, Israel has rejected not only the consensus interpretation of international law for resolving the conflict,[106] but also international law itself as a baseline for negotiations. "I was the Minister of Justice. I am a lawyer," Foreign Minister Tzipi Livni told her Palestinian interlocutors during a critical round of the peace process in 2007, "but I am against law—international law in particular."[107]

3.5.3.3.3. In the *Namibia* case, the United Nations declared the occupation illegal on (inter alia) two intertwined grounds: (1) South Africa refused to negotiate Namibia's eventual independence in "good faith"—that is, on the basis of international law as delineated by UN resolutions and the International Court of Justice; and (2) The premises of South Africa's negotiating posture radically diverged from consensus opinion on how to resolve the conflict—that is, Pretoria was determined to annex the whole of Namibia or the prime real estate therein occupied by white settlers. Negotiations had thus become, in Judge Dillard's words, "at best ... an empty time-consuming pageant and, at worst, ... a mere dialogue of the deaf" (see supra, 2.3.3.1.1).[108] One would be hard-pressed to find a closer parallel to and precursor of Israel's recalcitrance in the "peace process," or to improve upon Dillard's phraseology to describe the resulting diplomatic impasse.

3.5.3.3.4. In other cases adjudicated by it, the ICJ also emphasized the critical role of good-faith negotiations.

3.5.3.3.4.1. In *North Sea Continental Shelf,* the Court spoke in its judgment of "an obligation to enter into negotiations with a view to arriving at an agreement, and not merely to go through a formal process of negotiation ... the parties are under an obligation to act in such a way that, in the particular case, and taking all the circumstances into account, equitable principles are applied."[109]

Tanaka, Dissenting Opinion, *South West Africa Cases,* Second Phase, Judgment, I.C.J. Reports [1966], p. 282)

105. See, e.g., the verbatim record of the Annapolis negotiations collected in the *Palestine Papers,* http://transparency.aljazeera.net/Services/Search/default.aspx, esp. "Preliminary Assessment of the Israeli Proposal on Territory" (15 August 2008); "Meeting Minutes on Borders" (4 May 2008).

106. See Finkelstein, *Knowing Too Much,* pp. 203–48.

107. *Palestine Papers,* "Minutes from 8th Negotiation Team Meeting" (13 November 2007).

108. In his approving depiction of the Oslo Accord, Cassese observes that Palestinian self-determination "will be the subject of negotiations between the democratically elected Palestinians and the Israeli authorities.... *Everything* is left to the agreement of these two Parties." Cassese, *Self-Determination,* pp. 244–45, emphasis added. But as Dillard perceptively noted in the *Namibia* case, if everything is subject to negotiations, including "the fundamental basis on which the process rests" (see supra, 2.3.3.1.1), the negotiations are predestined to fail.

109. Majority Judgment, *North Sea Continental Shelf,* I.C.J. Reports (1969), pp. 45–47.

3.5.3.3.4.2. In *Case Concerning Delimitation of the Maritime Boundary in the Gulf of Maine Area,* the Court pointed up in its judgment the "duty to negotiate with a view to reaching agreement, and to do so in good faith, with a genuine intention to achieve a positive result."[110]

3.5.3.3.4.3. In its advisory opinion, *Legality of the Threat or Use of Nuclear Weapons,* the Court underscored that "good faith" comprised not only the "conduct" (process) of negotiations but also "an obligation to achieve a precise result."[111]

3.5.3.3.5. It follows from this sampling of the Court's jurisprudence that Israel's intermittent participation in the "peace process" does not in and of itself demonstrate it is carrying out "good faith" negotiations. To pass legal muster, it must also not thwart discernible progress toward achieving its legally mandated obligation to withdraw. The premises, however, of Israel's negotiating posture—which reject not only the consensus application of international law but even international law itself—have blocked, and preempt any future prospect of, real movement toward an end to the occupation.

3.5.3.3.6. The principle of "good faith" is objective in nature, as it is registered in palpable acts or failures to act: "The principle of good faith is essentially *objective* in application ... good faith looks to the *effects* of State actions, rather than to the (subjective) intent or motivation, if any, of the State itself"; "its violation may be demonstrated by acts and failures to act which, taken together, render the fulfillment of specific treaty obligations remote or impossible or which defeat the object and purpose of the treaty." Moreover, "the principle of good faith ... cannot but apply also to customary norms having equal status with treaty norms.... Thus, states are under an obligation to refrain both from acts defeating the object and purpose of a rule and from any other acts preventing its implementation."[112]

3.5.3.3.6.1. Israel's ongoing settlement enterprise constitutes a case study of bad faith in negotiations, as these ever-multiplying "objective" facts on the ground are

---

110. Majority Opinion, *Case Concerning Delimitation of the Maritime Boundary in the Gulf of Maine Area,* I.C.J. Reports (1984), p. 299.

111. Main Opinion, *Legality of the Threat or Use of Nuclear Weapons,* I.C.J. Reports (1996), pp. 263–64. See also Judge al-Khasawneh's separate opinion in the *Wall* case:

> Whilst there is nothing wrong in calling on protagonists to negotiate in good faith with the aim of implementing Security Council resolutions, no one should be oblivious that *negotiations are a means to an end and cannot in themselves replace that end....* [I]t is of the utmost importance if these negotiations are not to produce non-principled solutions, that they be grounded in law and that *the requirement of good faith be translated into concrete steps* by abstaining from creating faits accomplis on the ground ... which cannot but prejudice the outcome of these negotiations. (Judge al-Khasawneh, Separate Opinion, *Legal Consequences of the Construction of a Wall,* I.C.J. Reports [2004], pp. 238–39, para. 13, emphases added)

112. Guy S. Goodwin-Gill, "State Responsibility and the 'Good Faith' Obligation in International Law," in Malgosia Fitzmaurice and Dan Sarooshi, eds., *Issues of State Responsibility before International Judicial Institutions* (Oxford: 2004), pp. 84, 89, 95, emphases in original.

"defeating the object and purpose" of negotiations, which under treaties,[113] norms,[114] and principles[115] of international law requires Israel's withdrawal from the occupied Palestinian territory. "The Israeli Prime Minister [Benjamin Netanyahu] publicly supports a two-state solution, but his current coalition is the most right-wing in Israeli history, with an agenda driven by its most extreme elements," US secretary of state John Kerry observed in his last major address on the Israel-Palestine conflict. "The result is that policies of this government—which the Prime Minister himself just described as 'more committed to settlements than any in Israel's history'—are leading in the opposite direction, towards one state."[116]

3.6. *Is the UN General Assembly competent to declare the Israeli occupation illegal?*

3.6.1. Israel has violated its international obligations in the occupied Palestinian territory, imposed an apartheid regime there, and failed to negotiate in good faith an end to the occupation. It has consequently breached its primordial responsibilities, as an occupying power vis-à-vis Palestine, of "sacred trust" and "non-annexation," and denied the Palestinian people its nonderogable right to self-determination.

3.6.2. If viewed through the lens of the *Namibia* precedent, the Israeli occupation has become illegal. But does the UN General Assembly have the competence to make such a determination in the case of the Israeli occupation?

3.6.3. The General Assembly has the authority to debate and pass resolutions on the Israeli occupation of Palestinian territory, as well as on the status and contours of the Palestinian right to self-determination. This competence derives from a trio of both general and particular sources:

- Article 10 of the UN Charter stipulates that the Assembly "may discuss any questions or any matters" falling within the purview of the United Nations and "may make recommendations to the Members of the United Nations or to the Security Council or to both on any such questions or matters."
- The Assembly is the inheritor of the supervisory powers exercised by the League of Nations over the Mandates System, of which the Palestine question constitutes unfinished business. In its *Wall* opinion, the ICJ grounded the Palestinian people's right of self-determination in the League Covenant ("the ultimate objective of the 'sacred trust' referred to in Article 22, paragraph 1, of the Covenant of the League of Nations 'was the self-determination . . . of the

---

113. For instance, the Fourth Geneva Convention prohibiting the transfer of an occupier's population to occupied territory.

114. For instance, the inadmissibility of acquiring territory by war.

115. For instance, the right of peoples to self-determination.

116. US Department of State, "Remarks on Middle East Peace" (28 December 2016).

peoples concerned'").[117] It is therefore within the province of the Assembly to supervise Palestine's quest for independence.

- The Assembly presided over, fleshed out the principles and rules of, and played the clinching administrative role in the decolonization/self-determination process that unfolded after World War II, which included ending "the subjection of peoples to alien subjugation."[118] In its *Wall* opinion, the Court recalled in particular the UN's "responsibility" vis-à-vis the Palestine question, which "has been manifested by the adoption of many Security Council and General Assembly resolutions, and by the creation of several subsidiary bodies specifically established to assist in the realization of the inalienable rights of the Palestinian people."[119]

3.6.4. It remains to inquire whether a General Assembly resolution, which is ordinarily a recommendation (the Assembly is not a legislature),[120] would in these circumstances also be legally binding on all Member States.

3.6.4.1. In the *Namibia* case, it was principally argued that the supervisory powers of the League of Nations over South Africa's Mandate had a *treaty* aspect; that a right of revocation inheres in a treaty; and that consequently the Assembly, which inherited the League's supervisory role, could make a binding legal decision to terminate the Mandate after South Africa's breach of its terms.

3.6.4.2. This tortuous reasoning already at the time tested the limits of plausibility,[121] while writers seeking in retrospect to defend the Assembly's competence in the *Namibia* case have developed other lines of argumentation.[122]

117. *Legal Consequences of the Construction of a Wall*, I.C.J. Reports (2004), pp. 171–72, para. 88 (the second internal quote is from *Legal Consequences for States*).

118. The original General Assembly resolution setting the process in motion for "Trust and Non-Self-Governing Territories," and "all other territories which have not yet attained independence," was 1514, "Declaration on the Granting of Independence to Colonial Countries and Peoples" (1960). It stated that "the subjection of peoples to alien subjugation, domination and exploitation constitutes a denial of fundamental rights, is contrary to the Charter of the United Nations and is an impediment to the promotion of world peace and co-operation."

119. *Legal Consequences of the Construction of a Wall*, I.C.J. Reports (2004), pp. 158–59, para. 49.

120. The principal exception pertains to matters of internal management, such as budget assessments, where General Assembly resolutions are binding. But the Assembly also admits new Members, thereby binding existing Members to treat the newly admitted entity as a State, while in the course of the decolonization/self-determination process, it was the Assembly that determined which territories qualified as non-self-governing, thereby deciding which ones had a right to self-determination. See Rosalyn Higgins, *The Development of International Law through the Political Organs of the United Nations* (New York: 1963), pp. 112–13; Sureda, *Evolution*, pp. 65–66; Crawford, *Creation*, pp. 607–8.

121. Judge Fitzmaurice, Dissenting Opinion, *Legal Consequences for States*, I.C.J. Reports (1971), p. 267, para. 69.

122. Crawford purports that the General Assembly revoked South Africa's Mandate not in the capacity of a political organ possessing such competence, but rather in a

3.6.4.3. In the Palestine instance, such a rationale would constitute an even less persuasive legal contrivance, not least because Israel never entered into a treaty obligation with the General Assembly comparable to South Africa's going back to the League.[123]

3.6.5. The legally binding nature of a General Assembly resolution terminating and declaring illegal Israel's occupation can, however, be firmly established on different foundations.

3.6.6. Judge Nervo, in a separate opinion in the *Namibia* case, contended that the Assembly's legally binding competence obtained not only "in a situation in which it is a party to a contractual relationship in its capacity as such a party," but also and more generally "in regard to a territory which is an international responsibility, and in regard to which no State sovereignty intervenes between the General Assembly and the territory." He went on to observe that South Africa's annexation, "in reality and to all effects," of Namibia and its policy there of "racial discrimination" enforced by "the system of apartheid" constituted "sufficient grounds for the revocation of the Mandate" (see supra, 2.3.3.2.4). On all these bases, separately and a fortiori combined, the Assembly would also be competent to terminate Israel's occupation of Palestinian territory.

3.6.7. The legally binding competence of the Assembly to terminate Israel's occupation is also implied and inherent in the supervisory function performed by it in the decolonization/self-determination process, of which Palestine, as a territory under "alien subjugation," forms a constituent part. If the Assembly lacked such legal competence, it could not effectively fulfill its assigned role of safeguarding the rights of peoples entitled to but not yet exercising self-determination. Isn't a supervisory function bereft of sanctioning powers a contradiction in terms?

3.6.7.1. The cumulative effect of the serial ICJ opinions in the *Namibia* case supports these contentions:

"declaratory mode" of simply spelling out or confirming the juridical consequences of South Africa's illegal conduct. Judge Nervo, in a separate opinion in the *Namibia* case, likewise contended that the Assembly's termination of the Mandate was of a "declaratory nature," whereby it "declare[d] what in fact and in law was manifest." Crawford, *Creation*, pp. 441, 588, 593–95; Judge Nervo, Separate Opinion, *Legal Consequences for States*, I.C.J. Reports (1971), p. 113.

123. Judge Elaraby, in his separate opinion in the *Wall* case, dubiously invokes the Palestine Mandate to ground the existence of what he alleges to be a "legal nexus" that makes General Assembly resolutions pertaining to a Palestinian state "binding on all Member States as having legal force and legal consequences," and endows the Assembly with "special legal responsibility … until the achievement of this objective." Judge Elaraby, Separate Opinion, *Legal Consequences of the Construction of a Wall*, I.C.J. Reports (2004), pp. 251–52, para. 2.3.

- In *International Status of South-West Africa,* the Court found that safeguarding the rights of peoples under Mandates had "required" a supervisory organ, and that the General Assembly was henceforth the appropriate organ to fulfill this "necessity for supervision" originally performed by the League Council.[124]
- In *Admissibility of Hearings of Petitioners,* the Court stated that the "paramount purpose" of the General Assembly's supervisory function was "to safeguard the sacred trust of civilization."[125]
- In *South West Africa Cases* (first phase, preliminary objections), the Court found that "international supervision" constituted "the very essence of the Mandate."[126]
- In *Legal Consequences for States,* the Court found that the Assembly's competence to terminate the Mandate inhered in its supervisory powers; otherwise, the Assembly would be impotent in the face of egregious violations by South Africa of its responsibilities: "To deny to a political organ of the United Nations which is a successor of the League in this respect [i.e., its supervisory role] the right to act, on the argument that it lacks competence to render what is described as a judicial decision, would not only be inconsistent but would amount to a complete denial of the remedies available against fundamental breaches of an international undertaking."[127]

3.6.7.2. The upshot of these Court opinions is (1) Protection of the rights of peoples not yet self-governing required a supervisory organ; (2) The General Assembly was the competent organ to safeguard this "sacred trust"; (3) Absent the power of revocation, the Assembly could not effectively perform its critical supervisory role; ergo (4) The Assembly's power of revocation necessarily inheres in the supervisory function delegated to it.

3.6.7.3. Judge de Castro, in a separate opinion in the *Namibia* case, forcefully laid out the internal logic linking this chain of arguments. He elucidated that insofar as "legal concepts" such as a "trust"

> essentially contemplate the protection of persons (in this case, peoples) who cannot govern themselves, the necessary consequence is the exercise of supervision over the person entrusted with guardianship, "supervision of the guardian," and in case of serious breaches of his duties (*fides fracta*) the loss or forfeiture of guardianship.
> ... [T]here was no need to mention revocation [in the mandate]. ... The essential nature of this concept [of trust] implies, clearly and evidently, the possibility of putting an end to the mandate. ... A mandate which could not be revoked in such a case would not be a mandate, but a cession of territory or a disguised annexation.

124. *International Status of South-West Africa,* I.C.J. Reports (1950), pp. 136–37. See also *Voting Procedure,* I.C.J. Reports (1955), p. 76.

125. *Admissibility of Hearings of Petitioners,* I.C.J. Reports (1956), p. 28.

126. *South West Africa Cases,* First Phase, Preliminary Objections, I.C.J. Reports (1962), p. 334.

127. *Legal Consequences for States,* I.C.J. Reports (1971), p. 49, para. 102.

It is difficult to believe that, on the one hand, the working of the mandates system was organized to include a Permanent Commission to control the mandatory's administration and that, on the other hand, the mandatory was left free to do what he thought fit, even if it were to run counter to the very nature of the mandate, that one should put him in possession of the territory without any obligation on his part.... Any interpretation which denied the possibility of putting an end to the mandate in the case of flagrant violation by a mandatory of its obligations would reduce Article 22 to a *flatus vocis* [empty words], or rather to a "damnable mockery," by giving some color of legality to the annexation of mandated territories.[128]

3.6.7.3.1. Judge Nervo, in a separate opinion in the *Namibia* case, also derived the Assembly's competence from the functions delegated to it:

The General Assembly has had, under the relevant international instruments, several distinct roles in regard to Namibia, and the action which it took in this instance [i.e., termination of the Mandate] finds its bases in all these roles taken either individually or together. The General Assembly acted: in its capacity as the supervisory authority for the Mandate for South West Africa; as the sole organ of the international community responsible for ensuring the fulfillment of the obligations and sacred trust assumed in respect of the people and Territory of Namibia; and as the organ primarily concerned with non-self-governing and trust territories.[129]

3.6.8. The General Assembly's competence to terminate and declare illegal the Israeli occupation springs from, on the one hand, its locus as the institution designated by the United Nations to perform the supervisory function and, on the other hand, the prerogative to sanction that inheres in this function. In the absence of a revocatory power, the Assembly could not substantively monitor the decolonization/self-determination process, of which Palestine is an integral component both as a former Mandate and as a self-determination unit under "alien subjugation."[130]

3.6.9. It cannot be credibly rejoined that the necessary power to terminate a Mandate does exist but resides in the Security Council and not the General Assembly. On the one hand, such a division of labor of the supervisory function was nowhere envisaged, while on the other, if the Assembly lacks such competence, then so does the Council.[131] It also cannot be contended that unless the UN Charter explicitly allocated a power of termination to it, the Assembly would be acting *ultra vires*. In *Case Concerning the Northern Cameroons,* the ICJ found that the Assembly

128. Judge de Castro, Separate Opinion, *Legal Consequences for States,* I.C.J. Reports (1971), pp. 214–15.

129. Judge Nervo, Separate Opinion, *Legal Consequences for States,* I.C.J. Reports (1971), p. 112.

130. For this principle of "effectiveness" in the context of the ICJ's *Namibia* jurisprudence, see Slonim, *South West Africa,* pp. 162, 210.

131. Judge Fitzmaurice, Dissenting Opinion, *Legal Consequences for States,* I.C.J. Reports (1971), pp. 291–94.

had the competence to terminate Trusteeships, but it did not ground this competence in an explicit allocation of such power in the Trusteeship chapters of the UN Charter. Instead, the Court grounded it in the *general supervisory functions* of the General Assembly in the decolonization/self-determination process.[132]

3.6.10. In light of its past pronouncements, Israel would be poorly placed to contest the binding legal power of the General Assembly to terminate the occupation. When the Assembly debated the Partition Resolution (181) in 1947, the political body representing the nascent Jewish State posited that in regard to the future of a territory that did not "touch the national sovereignty of the Members of the United Nations," but instead was "subject to an international trust," only the Assembly "was competent to determine the future of the territory and its decision, therefore, had a binding force." After its creation, Israel described the Partition Resolution as "the only internationally valid adjudication on the question of the future government of Palestine." In a Security Council debate, Israeli representative Abba Eban, gesturing to the Partition Resolution, boasted that Israel "possesses the only international birth certificate in a world of unproven virtue," and that this "*juridical status . . . arises out of the action of the General Assembly.*"[133]

3.6.11. On the same juridical basis that it issued Israel's "birth certificate," the Assembly is empowered to issue simultaneously a death certificate for Israel's occupation and a birth certificate for Palestine. Judge Dillard, in a separate opinion in the *Namibia* case, noted that "precedents exist for the exercise of such power" of termination by the Assembly, and pointed in particular to the "General Assembly action with respect to the Palestine Mandate."[134]

132. In finding that General Assembly resolution 1608 terminating the Trusteeship Agreement over the British Cameroons had "definitive legal effect," the Court specified that "the termination . . . was a legal effect of the conclusions in paragraphs 2 and 3" of 1608, the text of which endorsed the results of a UN-supervised plebiscite and called for its immediate implementation. *Case Concerning the Northern Cameroons (Cameroon v. the United Kingdom)*, First Phase, Preliminary Objections, I.C.J. Reports (1963), p. 32. But see Crawford, *Creation*, p. 614, for a caveat.

133. Sureda, *Evolution*, pp. 39–40, 45, 47–48; *GAOR*, A/648 (part 1), p. 46, para. 4.1 ("Letter, dated 5 July 1948, addressed to the United Nations Mediator by the Minister for Foreign Affairs of the Provisional Government of Israel"); *UNSCOR*, 3rd Meeting, 27 July 1948, pp. 27–33, emphasis added. The context of Eban's pronouncement was a proposal by the Syrian government to refer the Palestine question to The Hague for an advisory opinion. Rebuffing this initiative, Eban asserted that Israel's existence as a State "is not a legal question, but a question of fact, a matter to be established not by judgment but by observation." But, he went on to observe, "if legitimate origin were relevant—which it is not—in determining statehood," then Israel was in the unique position of having had its "legitimacy certified" by the General Assembly.

134. Judge Dillard, Separate Opinion, *Legal Consequences for States*, I.C.J. Reports (1971), p. 163.

3.7. The potency of a resolution declaring the Israeli occupation illegal could be fortified if the General Assembly requested (in accordance with Article 96 of the UN Charter) an ICJ advisory opinion responding to the question, *What are the legal consequences of an occupying power's failure to negotiate in good faith on the basis of international law an end to the occupation?*

3.7.1. The proposed question has been crafted in generic language, along the lines of the question posed to the Court in 1996, "Is the threat or use of nuclear weapons in any circumstances permitted under international law?" If the Assembly requested from the Court an opinion specifically on the legal consequences of *Israel's* failure to negotiate in good faith on the basis of international law an end to the occupation, it could touch on the issue of "judicial propriety"—that is, an advisory opinion by the Court should not be given if it has the effect of "circumventing the principle that a State is not obliged to allow its disputes to be submitted to judicial settlement without its consent."[135] The prudent course would be to avoid such a risk, even though the Court has only once declined to adjudicate a case due to an implicated party's lack of consent,[136] and even though a compelling brief could be filed supporting a Court opinion on a question explicitly naming Israel.[137]

3.7.2. Should the Court entertain the proposed question and Israel recycle its preliminary objection in the *Wall* case—to wit, that a Court opinion "could impede a political, negotiated solution to the Israeli-Palestinian conflict"[138]—this objection would almost certainly gain little traction, not least because the proposed question's very premise is the *absence* of real negotiations.

3.8. It might still be wondered, *What useful purpose would be served by a General Assembly resolution declaring Israel's occupation illegal, even coupled with a complementary ICJ opinion, if an action by the Assembly can be enforced only by a Security Council resolution that, now and for the foreseeable future, will almost certainly not be spared a US veto, while an ICJ advisory opinion is altogether unenforceable?*[139]

3.8.1. An Assembly resolution compounded by a Court opinion would constitute a pair of formidable weapons in the battle to win over public opinion. They would

135. *Western Sahara,* Advisory Opinion, I.C.J. Reports (1975), p. 12.

136. *Eastern Carelia* Opinion, 1923.

137. For relevant Court precedent, see also *Legal Consequences for States,* I.C.J. Reports (1971), pp. 23–24, para. 31; *Legal Consequences of the Construction of a Wall,* I.C.J. Reports (2004), pp. 157–59, paras. 46–50; Judge Owada, Separate Opinion, ibid., p. 265, paras. 13–14; Judge Koroma, Separate Opinion, ibid., pp. 204–5, para. 3; Judge Kooijmans, Separate Opinion, ibid., p. 227, para. IV.27; Judge Higgins, Separate Opinion, ibid., pp. 209–10, paras. 10–11.

138. *Legal Consequences of the Construction of a Wall,* I.C.J. Reports (2004), pp. 159–60, para. 51.

139. The Security Council can enforce, under Article 94 of the Charter, the judgment of the Court only in a contentious decision.

perform the same role, but with potentially greater persuasive power, as the Partition Resolution (181) played in the Zionist struggle for legitimacy and statehood.[140]

3.8.2. "Military and political disputes, especially in the world today," Michla Pomerance observed in the context of the *Namibia* debate, "are never devoid of the dimension of legitimacy as an important component of the conflict."[141] An Assembly resolution combined with an ICJ advisory opinion would constitute an important step toward *de*legitimizing Israel's occupation.

3.8.3. The Finnish delegate exhorted a jaded United Nations to obtain in support of its *Namibia* resolutions an ICJ advisory opinion. He persuasively argued that it would "expose the false front of legality which South African authorities attempt to present to the world," and would thereby help "mobilize public opinion . . . especially in those countries which have the power to influence events in southern Africa in a decisive way" (see supra, 2.3.1.1).

3.8.4. To highlight the salutary effects of an advisory opinion, Judge Weeramantry, in his magisterial separate opinion in *Legality of the Threat or Use of Nuclear Weapons,* harkened back to the *Namibia* case: "The Court's decision on the illegality of the apartheid regime had little prospect of compliance by the offending government, but helped create the climate of opinion which dismantled the structure of apartheid. . . . When the law is clear, there is greater chance of compliance than when it is shrouded in obscurity."[142] Indeed, the joint action by the UN's political and judicial organs in the early 1970s had little direct impact on Namibia's self-determination struggle. It did not attain statehood until some two decades later, and only after a massive loss of Namibian life and protracted negotiations. But wouldn't it be perverse to then conclude that the combined efforts of the Assembly and the Court were irrelevant?[143]

140. Norman G. Finkelstein and Mouin Rabbani, with the assistance of Jamie Stern-Weiner, *How to Solve the Israel-Palestine Conflict* (forthcoming).

141. Michla Pomerance, "The ICJ and South West Africa (Namibia): A retrospective legal/political assessment," *Leiden Journal of International Law* (1999), p. 432.

142. Judge Weeramantry, Dissenting Opinion, *Legality of the Threat or Use of Nuclear Weapons,* I.C.J. Reports (1996), p. 550.

143. See also South African jurist John Dugard's judicious weighing of the factors that led to the demise of apartheid in South Africa:

> It is not idealism and altruism that have brought the National Party to the negotiating table, but rather a combination of international pressure and internal unrest. While economic sanctions have been the most important of the international weapons employed against apartheid, the others should not be discounted. Political and moral isolation have also played their part. . . . The non-recognition of the Bantustan states has destroyed the viability of the territorial fragmentation of South Africa into a collection of ethnic "states" as an acceptable political solution. And the repeated denunciation of apartheid as morally unacceptable to the international community has undermined the moral basis for apartheid that its early ideological architects fought so hard to establish. (John Dugard, "The Role of International Law in the Struggle for Liberation in South Africa," *Social Justice* [1991], p. 91)

3.8.5. Jurist James Crawford, representing in *Legality of the Threat or Use of Nuclear Weapons* several South Pacific States devastated by nuclear testing, likewise pointed to the contribution international law could play in achieving a humane outcome:

> No-one is naive enough . . . to suggest that international law is a sovereign antidote to the risks and dangers presented by the threat or use of nuclear weapons. But neither is international law merely a charlady, a *femme de ménage* called in to clean up after the event is over and all the participants have gone home. It can be part of the solution to the problem. But it can only be part of the solution if it is brought to bear on the problem while it, and we, are still around. For the Court to declare that the use or threat of use of nuclear weapons is unlawful in all conceivable circumstances would contribute to a solution to one of our greatest modern problems.[144]

Couldn't international law also be part of the solution to another one of our greatest modern problems and, if it is to be brought to bear on this problem, isn't now the time for the international community to act, while Palestine is still around and before it is effaced from the world's map?

4.0. CONCLUDING REMARKS

4.1. Deeming it premature to recognize a State of Palestine, the selfsame James Crawford observed a while back, "The essential point is that a process of negotiation towards identified and acceptable ends is still, however precariously, in place." He then posed as the central challenge, "to change the status quo in favor of a comprehensive settlement accepted by all parties concerned—a situation that seems as remote as ever."[145]

4.2. But what if the "process of negotiation" is just a façade, if there's no agreement on "ends," if a "comprehensive settlement accepted by all parties" is not just "remote" but unattainable because—in Judge Dillard's words—"the parties are at odds as to the fundamental basis on which the process rests," and if this protracted impasse springs *entirely* from the occupying power's comprehensive repudiation of international law?

For other relevant commentary, see K. Srimad Bhagavad Geeta, "Role of the United Nations in Namibian Independence," *International Studies* (1993), pp. 33–34; and Julio Faundez, "Namibia: The relevance of international law," *Third World Quarterly* (1986), pp. 540–41, 557.

144. James Crawford, representing Samoa, the Marshall Islands, and Solomon Islands, public sitting held on Tuesday 14 November 1995, in *Legality of the Use by a State of Nuclear Weapons in Armed Conflict.*

145. Crawford, *Creation,* pp. 446, 447.

4.3. As it happens, Crawford does address, albeit obliquely, such a contingency. "A State," he opined, "cannot rely on its own wrongful conduct to avoid the consequences of its international obligations."[146] Isn't this a precise description of the "peace process"? By refusing to negotiate in good faith on the basis of international law an end to the occupation, Israel has evaded its dual obligations to withdraw from occupied Palestinian territory, and—from a legal and moral standpoint, what's most critical—to allow the Palestinian people to exercise, at long last and after so much agony, its right to self-determination.[147]

4.4. It is high time to put an end to a so-called peace process that in reality is an avoidance-cum-annexation process. "States," Judge Jessup said in the *Namibia* case, "are not eternally bound by the old adage: 'If at first you don't succeed, try, try again'" (see supra, 2.2.4.3). The moment of truth is once again upon the United Nations—in the Uruguayan delegate's words—"to put an end to this struggle between law and arrogance" (see supra, 2.2.5.3).

4.5. The UN General Assembly can and must declare, finally and conclusively, that the Israeli occupation, not just this or that constituent of it but in its essence and totality, is illegal and that a full Israeli withdrawal will no longer be held hostage to an interminable negotiating process, the manifest purpose of which, after decades of trying and trying again, can no longer be in doubt (except to those willfully blind)—that purpose being to make the occupation irreversible, and to consign to oblivion the people of Palestine.

146. Ibid., p. 448.

147. For the staggering economic costs to the Palestinian people of Israel's occupation, see United Nations Conference on Trade and Development, "Report on UNCTAD Assistance to the Palestinian People: Developments in the economy of the Occupied Palestinian Territory" (1 September 2016), paras. 29–53.

INDEX

Page numbers in italics refer to figures, boxes, and tables.

apartheid *(continued)*
  relations with South Africa during, 108;
  and *Namibia* case, 373–379, 383, 385,
  389, 394, 396n102, 401, 406; and sanc-
  tions, 12n31
Arab League, 28–29, 34, 115, 221. *See also*
  Dugard Report
Arab Spring, 215, 286
Arab world, 5n3, 19, 24–25, 33, 116, 153, 155,
  202, 209–210n44, 221, 361–362,
  368–371
Arafat, Yasser, 7, 11, 34, 35n65
Arai-Takahashi, Yutaka, 371
Ashkenazi, Gabi, 40, 94
Assad, Bashar al-, 153, 287n123
Association for Civil Rights in Israel
  (ACRI), 7, 17, 80, 113, 154n88, 394–395
asymmetry of conflict, 26–27, 40, 63–67,
  73–74, *76,* 90–91, 98, 141, 235–237,
  262–264, *311,* 314–315, 319, 363
Auschwitz, 97, 222
Avineri, Shlomo, 77
Avnery, Uri, 96, 144
Ayalon, Danny, 94, 138, 152

Ban Ki-moon: on blockade, 363; and Cast
  Lead, 49, 50n53, 100–101, 115; and
  flotilla, 177, 305, 307n10; and Protective
  Edge, 216–217, 228–229, 238n3, 239, 344
Barak, Ehud, 7–8, 23, 48, 81, 93, 107, 115,
  117, 143, 151–152, 201, 206, 209, 372
Bar'el, Zvi, 216
Begin, Menachem, 17n3, 35n65
Ben-Ami, Shlomo, 7–8, 10
Ben-Gurion, David, 5n3
Ben-Naftali, Orna, 371
Benvenisti, Eyal, 372–373
Benziman, Uzi, 40
Bernstein, Robert, 77, 114
Biden, Joseph, 147
Blair, Tony, 214
blockade: easing of, 32n57, 149, 150n65, 214,
  230, 232, 362; efforts to end, 32n57, 37,
  92, 137–138, 139n10, 141–156, 195–197,
  232–237, 269, 307, 309, 360–361, 363–
  364; and exit permits, 16, 50–51, 236;
  and export ban, 49, 149, 150n65, 233,
  360; impact of, 15–16, 37, 48–49, 137–

138, 149–150, 195–196, 236–237, 287,
  307, 359–361; import restrictions of,
  32–33n57, 49, 149, 158–162; imposition/
  tightening of, 11–13, 32–33n57, 37, 49,
  181–182, 195; Israeli justifications for,
  xi, 138, 157–162, 178–195, 233; items
  banned/restricted, 37, 48–49, 55n78,
  150n65, 160, 162, 183, 196; legal assessment of, 15, 88, 139, 149–150, 157–162,
  178–195, 197, 307n10, 309, 360, 363;
  objective of, xi, 88, 137, 139n10, 360–361;
  perpetuation of, 234, 362–363; psychological toll of, 15–16, 49, 232
Bloomberg, Michael, 227
Bolton, John, 96
Boot, Max, 96
Booth, William, 247n38
Breaking the Silence: under attack, 78–79,
  288; on Cast Lead, 45n32, 46n36, 57n88,
  57n92, 58n93, 61n111, 65n130, 67n140,
  71n7, 73n15, 74n17, 78–79, 80n46;
  politics of, 218; on Protective Edge,
  218–220, 257, *258–261,* 263, 272, 276, *317,*
  327n85, 355
Britain, xi, 72, 110, 146, 151, 154, 162n31, 214,
  289, 351, 404n132; anti-Semitism debate
  in, 286; arrest warrant for Livni in, 107;
  and *Namibia* case, 374, 375n31, 378, 381;
  and nuclear weapons, 235; Palestine
  Mandate of, 3; and Sinai invasion, 4, 5n3
Bronner, Ethan, 18, 81
B'Tselem (Israeli Information Center for
  Human Rights in the Occupied Territories): access to Gaza denied to, 78;
  on ambulances, 51, 53; on apartheid,
  394; apologetics of, 60n104, 71n7, 113,
  288n124, 353n155; under attack, 113;
  casualty figures compiled by, 15, 68n1,
  179n12, 224n67, *240;* on child killings,
  353n155; and children's rights, 289; on
  Goldstone Report, 60n104, 113,
  288n124; on human shields, 71n7; on
  Israel's justice system, 126, 350–351; on
  killings, 41–42, 126, 353n155; on
  mosques, 60n104; on Palestinian prisoners, 15; on Palestinian vs. Israeli
  violations, 113; on perpetuation of
  occupation, 350–351; on power plant,

252; on Shalit, 113; on torture, 111–112; on Turkel Report, 350–351

Buergenthal, Thomas, 30

Burston, Bradley, 77

Bush, George W. (administration of), 12, 13n40, 14

Bustamante y Rivero, José Luis (judge), 379

Cameron, David, xi

Caradon, Lord, 381

Carter, Jimmy, 10, 11, 31, 394; Carter Center, 36n72

Cassese, Antonio, 393n92, 397n108

Cast Lead, Operation (2008–9), 142, 146, 152, 156, 238, 252, 285, 299–300, 350, 354; death toll of, 23, 68–69, 125–126, 129, 204, *207*, 211, 222, 224; destructiveness of, 13, 22, 27, 45–63, 65–67, 119, 129, 137, 148–149, 204, 211; Israeli justification for launching, xi, 14–16, 41, 88; Israeli spin on, 39–83, 204; lead-up to, 13–16, 203, 211; legal accountability for, 348; objectives of, 17–38, 62–63, 65–67, 79–80, 88–89, 118–119, 128, 137, 144, 151, 212, 216. *See also* Dugard Report; Goldstone Report. *See also under* Amnesty International; B'Tselem; Human Rights Watch

Castro, Federico de (judge), 378, 402

casualty ratios, 8, 15, 35n68, 68–69, 73, 90, 128, 201, 216, 224, 239–241, 310, *311*, 315

cease-fires: and Cast Lead, 13–16, 21, 32–38, 49, 60, 66, 137; and Pillar of Defense, 201–203, 208–209, 232; and Protective Edge, 214–215, 221, 230–233, 259, 308n14, 344

Chait, Jonathan, 108

Cherokee Nation, 365

children, xii, 8n16, 34, 79, 289; attacked while feeding birds, 325; attacked while playing/studying, 72, 328, 335–336, 351–354; babies, *280*, 324, 359; and blockade, 49, 162, 359; and Cast Lead, 23, 41, 44, 49–50, 68, 71–73, 75, 82, 91n20, 96–97, *120–121*, 127, 129; imprisoned, 15, 91n20; and Pillar of Defense, 205; and Protective Edge, 211, 239, *240*, 241, *268*, *279–283*, 288–289, *298*, 299,

301, 310–311, 315, 318n45, 324–325, 328–329, 332, 338, 341–342. *See also under* Israelis

Chinkin, Christine, 130

Chomsky, Noam, 202

churches, 42, 320

Clinton, Bill, 7

Clinton, Hillary, 11, 99, 148, 208

collaborators, 5, 6–7, 10–11, 51, 202, 257n64, 322–323, 332, 347

Cordesman, Anthony, 39–42, 46, 48, 51–52, 55, 59–60, 63–66, 77

Crawford, James, 372, 400n122, 407–408

crimes against humanity: blockade as, 197; during Cast Lead, 14, 89, 107, 109, 118, 132, 300; definition of, 295; during occupation, 394; political impact of charge, 302–304; during Protective Edge, 273, 275, 284, 297; and South Africa, 379

Crisis Group, 14, 23, 26, 59, 64, 66, 148, 203

Davis, Dennis, 130

Dayan, Moshe, 5n3

demographics, 3

Dershowitz, Alan, 30, 61, 77, 79, 96–97, 108, 111, 114, 130, 288

Dillard, Hardy Cross (judge), 387, 389n73, 390, 393, 397, 404, 407

Dinstein, Yoram, 9, 119, 368–369n5, 371

"disengagement" (2005), 3, 9, 11n28, 21–22, 35–36n68, 158, 180, 188, 268–269, 307, 367

Diskin, Yuval, 36

drones: cameras mounted on missiles and, 42, 75; Hezbollah and, 203; Israeli export of, 153n83; strikes, 23, 42, 72, 75, 273, *278–279*, *281*, 294, 301; and surveillance, *120–121*, 122, 124

Dugard, John, 12n31, 47, 131–132, 269, 373, 386n67, 394, 406n143

Dugard Report (on Cast Lead), 15n50, 47, 58, 61, 89n11, 89–90n13, 105n103, 131–132

Eban, Abba, 18, 371, 382, 404

economy, xii; blockade's impact on, 11–12, 15, 36–37, 92, 137–139, 148–149, 161–162,

human shields: children used as, 44, 71, 82; Hamas accused of using, 41, 53–54, 69–72, 104, 114–115, 217, 251n51, 263, 267n75, 321–322; Hezbollah accused of using, 24–25; Israel's use of, 44, 71, 82, 89, 103, 352

humiliation, 5, 44, 88, 91n20, 102, 119, 204, 216, 232, 275, 293, 297, 299–300, 303, 347, 354

Indyk, Martin, 35n65

infrastructure, civilian: airport, 230; flour mill, 55, 124–125, 137; industries, 22, 49, 55, 58–59, 65, 123, 127, 137, 149, 215; seaport, 193–194, 230; water/sanitation systems, 37, 49, 54–55, 127, 149, 215, 252, 332, 344, 359. *See also* agriculture/fishing; education; electricity; medical facilities/services

İnsani Yardım Vakfı (IHH), 142, 153, 165, 169–172, 174–175

Intelligence and Terrorism Information Center, 32, 36, 103–104, 123, 145–146, 325

International Court of Justice (ICJ), 376n35; on good-faith negotiations, 397–399, 405–406; *Namibia* case, 234, 367, 373, 375–379, 381, 384–389, 391–393, 397, 401–402, 406; on nuclear weapons, 236, 303, 398, 405–407; and reprisals, 236n125; and UN Charter, 376n35, 405n139; on UN General Assembly powers, 403–404; *Wall* case, 12, 29–31, 140, 184–185n37, 291, 372, 391, 393–394, 399, 400, 405

International Criminal Court (ICC), 92, 99n67, 103, 107, 109, 116, 290–291, 293, 295, 305, 351, *358*, 394

International Federation for Human Rights (FIDH), 247, 251, 253

intifadas: first, 6–7, 11, 111, 126, 215, 287; second, 8, 126, 157, 269. *See also* resistance

Iran, 20–21, 28, 29n44, 33, 63, 65–66, 94, 152–153, 203, 213, 221, 242–243

Iraq, 17n3, 216; sanctions on, 162n31

Iron Dome, 206–207, 223–225, 228, 231, 242–243, 265, 315, 318, 364

ISIS, 221, 229

Islam, 61, 221, 252, 286, 347–348; Ramadan, 326–328. *See also* mosques

Islamic Jihad, *255*, 342

Israel: civil defense system of, 43n23, 69n3, 225, *312*, 313, 318; credibility of state authorities in, 40–42, 95, 163; deterrence strategy of, 18–27, 56, 65–67, 79, 144, 151, 155–156, 203, 276; and Goldstone Report, 87–132; *hasbara* (PR efforts) of, 39–83, 146, 154, 222–228, 256, 287, *317;* houses, civilian infrastructure damaged/destroyed by Hamas, 56, 60, 128, 205, 225–227, 262, 265, *240*, 310–311, 314–315, 348; image of, 5n3, 17, 77–78, 117, 147, 154–156, 167–169, 197, 209, 231; intelligence services of, 14, 19, 32, 38n79, 40–42, 46, 51, 53, 56, 62, 103, 128, 159, 164, 167, 255n59, *259–260*, 276, 319; intransigence, 3–38, 363–364, 367–373, 390–408; Knesset, 40, 93, 112; "lawfare" against, 113, 285; legal accountability of, 57, 81–82, 87–92, 100–103, 107, 109–132, 147, 156–157, 176–177, 180, 197, 204, 211–212, 243–245, 255–257, 277, 284–285, 296–306, 323–356, 363; lobby of, 98, 101, 107n117, 113, 115, 129, 220, 285–286; Magen David Adom, 53; media clampdown by, 78, 146, 204; military installations in, 269–270; on *Namibia* case, 381–382; and Palestinian "subcontractors," 6–7, 10–11, 201; right to self-defense invoked by, xi, 14–16, 38, 88, 142–144, 181, 189, 193, 234–235, 308–309, 368; rightward drift of, 288n124, 364, 399; state of democracy in, 23n27, 78–79, 112–113, 396n101; and strategic timing of attacks, 35, 215; suicide attacks against, 8, 44n26, 72, 157–158; Supreme/High Court, 7, 176, 184–185n37, 372

Israel Defense Forces (IDF): and bulldozers, 6, 46, 57, 59, *258–259*, 333; casualties among, 15, 68–69, 171n82, 221–222, *240*, 272, 315, 334; commandos, 141–157, 162–176, 196, 272, 349; "Dahiya doctrine," 21–22, 156; Entebbe raid, 151; esteem of, 95; executions by, 4, 145, 174,

Mishal, Khalid, 31, 37, 38n79, 207–209, 232–233, 320

Moreno-Ocampo, Luis, 290–291, *358*

Morris, Benny, 4–6, 18, 20, 21n17, 23, 27, 54

mosques, 42, 57, 60–61, 65, 125, 127, 215, 249n42, 252, 270, *281, 311,* 347–348

Mubarak, Hosni, 153, 204

Namibia, 234, 367–408

Nasrallah, Sayyed Hassan, 24–26, 33, 153

Nasser, Gamal Abdel, 4, 5n3, 18–19

Nervo, Luis Padilla (judge), 389, 401, 403

Netanyahu, Benjamin: on blockade, 138; brother of, 151; and flotilla, 145, 151–153, 362n14; and Goldstone, 93, 106–107, 117; and Hamas, 38n79, 69n1, 227, 230; and Iran, 153, 203; and Israeli society, 231; and Palestinian unity, 212–213, 230; and Pillar of Defense, 202–203, 206–209, 215; and Protective Edge, 212–215, 227, 229–231; and Tiananmen Square massacre, 215; and Turkey, 153, 362n14; and two-state settlement, 399

New Israel Fund, 112

NGO Monitor, 286

nuclear weapons, 17n3, 20–21, 152, 213, 235–236, 303, 405–407

Obama administration, 50n53, 98–99, 117, 147, 223n59, 238n3

Obama, Barack, 14, 35, 83n56, 147, 208, 209–210n44, 220–221

occupation: Goldstone Report on, 87, 90–92; legal status of, 234–235, 367–408; ongoing, 9, 180, 306–308, 351; by remote control, 268–269, 314–315; strategy to end, xiii, 363–364; streamlining of, 6–7. *See also* resistance

Olmert, Ehud, 81

operations, Israeli, xi, 8, 59n100, 61, 93, 109, 178, 288, 306, 353–356, 360; psychological toll of, 231–232. *See also* Cast Lead; Pillar of Defense; Protective Edge. *See also under* Lebanon; West Bank

Oren, Michael, 94

Organization of the Islamic Conference (OIC), 28–29

Oxfam, 137

Oz, Amos, 96, 154

Palestine Liberation Organization (PLO), 6–7, 31, 34–35, 305n2

Palestinian Authority (PA), 11, 13n37, 31, 43n23, 100, 115–116, 182–183, 202, 230–231, 248n41, 249n42, 285

Palestinian Center for Human Rights, *240,* 245, 271

Palestinian Medical Relief Society, 52

Pastor, Robert, 36–37n72

"peace offensives," 18, 34, 38

peace process, 8, 11–13, 27–38, 111, 362–363, 396–398, 408; Annapolis, 397n105; Arab League initiative, 28–29, 34; Camp David, 7; Kerry initiative, 212; Middle East Quartet, 12n33, 362–363; Oslo Accord, 6–7, 9–12, 397n108; *Road Map,* 12; Taba, 7

Peres, Shimon, 8, 50, 93, 108, 142, 152

Phillips, Melanie, 111

Physicians for Human Rights–Israel, 51–53, 239

Pillar of Defense, Operation (2012), 215, 228, 232, 242; death toll of, 205, 224; denouement of, 207–208, 231; destructiveness of, 203–205, 221, 224; Israeli justification for, 201; Israeli spin on, 206–207, 209; lead-up to, 201–203; legal accountability for, 349; objective of, 203

Polakow-Suransky, Sasha, 108

Pomerance, Michla, 406

Posner, Michael, 98

Postol, Theodore, 206–207, 224–225

Power, Samantha, 223

precision weapons, 62, 128, 166, 204, 229, 287n123; destroying vital civilian infrastructure, 55, 137, 252; killing civilians, 23, 42, 70–72, 75, 228, 299, 301–302, 313, 325–329, 342; touted by Israel, 42, 44, 246n32. *See also* drones

prisoners/detainees, 6, 10, 15, 32n57, 44, 54, 62, 91n20, 92, 111, 213, 230, 248, 272, 322, 334

Protective Edge, Operation (2014): access to Gaza denied to human rights organi-

www.ingramcontent.com/pod-product-compliance
Ingram Content Group UK Ltd.
Pitfield, Milton Keynes, MK11 3LW, UK
UKHW030146291224
452936UK00005B/21